The Court of the Caliphate of al-Andalus

Edinburgh Studies in Classical Islamic History and Culture

Series Editor: Carole Hillenbrand

A particular feature of medieval Islamic civilisation was its wide horizons. The Muslims fell heir not only to the Graeco-Roman world of the Mediterranean, but also to that of the ancient Near East, to the empires of Assyria, Babylon and the Persians; and beyond that, they were in frequent contact with India and China to the east and with black Africa to the south. This intellectual openness can be sensed in many inter-related fields of Muslim thought, and it impacted powerfully on trade and on the networks that made it possible. Books in this series reflect this openness and cover a wide range of topics, periods and geographical areas.

Titles in the series include:

The Body in Arabic Love Poetry: The 'Udhri Tradition Jokha Alharthi

Owning Books and Preserving Documents in Medieval Jerusalem: The Library of Burhan al-Din Said Aljoumani and Konrad Hirschler

Arabian Drugs in Early Medieval Mediterranean Medicine Zohar Amar and Efraim Lev

Towards a History of Libraries in Yemen Hassan Ansari and Sabine Schmidtke

The Abbasid Caliphate of Cairo, 1261–1517: Out of the Shadows Mustafa Banister

The Medieval Western Maghrib: Cities, Patronage and Power Amira K. Bennison

Christian Monastic Life in Early Islam Bradley Bowman

Keeping the Peace in Premodern Islam: Diplomacy under the Mamluk Sultanate, 1250–1517 Malika Dekkiche

Queens, Concubines and Eunuchs in Medieval Islam Taef El-Azhari

Islamic Political Thought in the Mamluk Period Mohamad El Merheb

The Kharijites in Early Islamic Historical Tradition: Heroes and Villains Hannah-Lena Hagemann

Classical Islam: Collected Essay Carole Hillenbrand

Islam and the Crusades: Collected Essays Carole Hillenbrand

The Medieval Turks: Collected Essays Carole Hillenbrand

Medieval Damascus: Plurality and Diversity in an Arabic Library – The Ashrafiya Library Catalogue Konrad Hirschler

A Monument to Medieval Syrian Book Culture: The Library of Ibn 'Abd al-Hādī Konrad Hirschler

The Popularisation of Sufism in Ayyubid and Mamluk Egypt: State and Society, 1173–1325 Nathan Hofer

Defining Anthropomorphism: The Challenge of Islamic Traditionalism Livnat Holtzman

Making Mongol History: Rashid al-Din and the Jami' al-Tawarikh Stefan Kamola

Lyrics of Life: Sa'di on Love, Cosmopolitanism and Care of the Self Fatemeh Keshavarz

Art, Allegory and The Rise of Shiism In Iran, 1487–1565 Chad Kia

The Administration of Justice in Medieval Egypt: From the 7th to the 12th Century Yaacov Lev

Zoroastrians in Early Islamic History: Accommodation and Memory Andrew D. Magnusson

A History of Herat: From Chingiz Khan to Tamerlane Shivan Mahendrarajah

The Queen of Sheba's Gift: A History of the True Balsam of Matarea Marcus Milwright

Ruling from a Red Canopy: Political Authority in the Medieval Islamic World, From Anatolia to South Asia Colin P. Mitchell

Islam, Christianity and the Realms of the Miraculous: A Comparative Exploration Ian Richard Netton

The Poetics of Spiritual Instruction: Farid al-Din 'Attar and Persian Sufi Didacticism Austin O'Malley

Sacred Place and Sacred Time in the Medieval Islamic Middle East: An Historical Perspective Daniella Talmon-Heller

Conquered Populations in Early Islam: Non-Arabs, Slaves and the Sons of Slave Mothers Elizabeth Urban

Medieval Syria and the Onset of the Crusades: The Political World of Bilad al-Sham, 1050–1128 James Wilson

edinburghuniversitypress.com/series/escihc

The Court of the Caliphate of al-Andalus

Four years in Umayyad Córdoba

Eduardo Manzano Moreno

Translation Jeremy Roe

EDINBURGH
University Press

For Berta, for Silvia and for Adrián

Edinburgh University Press is one of the leading university presses in the UK. We publish academic books and journals in our selected subject areas across the humanities and social sciences, combining cutting-edge scholarship with high editorial and production values to produce academic works of lasting importance. For more information visit our website: edinburghuniversitypress.com

Primera edición: enero de 2019
La corte del califa. Cuatro años en la Córdoba de los omeyas Eduardo Manzano Moreno

Av. Diagonal, 662–664, 08034 Barcelona (España)
Crítica es un sello editorial de Editorial Planeta, S. A

Edinburgh University Press Ltd
13 Infirmary Street
Edinburgh EH1 1LT

First published in hardback by Edinburgh University Press 2023

Typeset in 11/15 Adobe Garamond by Cheshire
Typesetting Ltd, Cuddington, Cheshire

A CIP record for this book is available from the British Library

ISBN 978 1 3995 1612 9 (hardback)
ISBN 978 1 3995 1613 6 (paperback)
ISBN 978 1 3995 1614 3 (webready PDF)
ISBN 978 1 3995 1615 0 (epub)

Contents

List of Illustrations vi
Foreword to the English Edition viii

Introduction 1

1 The Caliphate and the Natural and Human Cycles 31

2 The Caliphate's Resources and Wealth 59

3 The Caliph and the *Sulṭān* 104

4 The Armies of the Caliph 147

5 The Struggle against the Fāṭimid Caliphate: (I) The Background 182

6 The Struggle against the Fāṭimid Caliphate: (II) The Conflict 206

7 Defending the Muslims 243

8 The Authority of the Caliph 286

9 The Representation of Power 331

10 Córdoba and Madīnat al-Zahrā': Topography of Power and Urban Space 367

Sources and Bibliography 420
Index of Persons 450
Index of Places 457

Illustrations

Images

1 Andalusi textile from San Pedro de Montes (León) 75
2 Madīnat al-Zahrā' was built to the west of Córdoba, taking advantage of the difference in altitude between the mountains and the Guadalquivir valley 83
3 Silver dirham minted in 361 AH (971–2) 86
4 Golden dinar minted in 362 AH (972–3) in Madīnat al-Zahrā' 86
5 The 'Zamora' pixys dedicated to the caliph's concubine, Subḥ 88
6 Plan and view of the *Munyat al-Rummāniyya* 98–9
7 Mosque of Córdoba's *miḥrāb*, completed in 354 AH/965 124
8 Bible of León (960). The death of Saul and his sons at the battle of Mount Gelboe 173
9 Bible of León (960). Elijah sleeping beside his mounts 174
10 Morgan Beatus (c. 940). A military expedition with infantrymen and knights 176
11 Detail of Leyre ivory casket (1004). Horsemen fighting 178
12 Castle of Gormaz (Soria) 276
13 Madīnat al-Zahrā'. Parietal decoration in the reception *majlis* or Salón Rico 300
14 Dome of the *miḥrāb* in the Mosque of Córdoba 308
15 Funerary inscription of a manumitted slave girl of Caliph al-Ḥakam 322
16 Al-Mugīra's pixys 330
17 The central courtyard of the bath next to the reception hall of Madīnat al-Zahrā' 341

18 Madīnat al-Zahrā'. Bāb al-Sudda 358
19 The archaeology of the western suburbs of Córdoba 400

Figures

1 Map of al-Andalus xvi
2 Genealogy of the Muslim caliphates 184
3 North Africa at the time of the conflicts between Umayyads and Fāṭimids 197
4 The Muslim–Christian frontier at the upper courses of the Rivers Ebro and Duero 253
5 The palatine complex at Madīnat al-Zahrā' 343
6 Córdoba, suburbs and *munyas* 388
7 Córdoba: street plan 394

Foreword to the English Edition

The last forty years have represented a kind of golden age for historical research on al-Andalus. The scholarship devoted to this western region of the medieval *dār al-Islām* has been impressive both in terms of quantity and quality. Arab manuscripts on a wide variety of subjects – from historical chronicles to legal works, from poetry to scientific treatises on disciplines like astronomy, botany or medicine – have been edited and, in some cases, translated. Evidence hitherto considered as intractable, like the thousands of profiles of Muslim scholars included in biographical dictionaries, has been systematised and analysed by long-term projects like the *Historia de los Autores y Transmisores Andalusíes* (HATA), the *Biblioteca de al-Andalus* or the *Prosopografía de los ulemas de al-Andalus*, all of them easily accessible online. New research has also entailed the publication of a good amount of new Arab inscriptions, including those carved on stone or plaster, and also those embroidered in textiles, or engraved on metalwork or even rings. Numismatists have produced coin catalogues, as well as accurate descriptions of hoards and stray finds that have fostered detailed studies on minting and coinage circulation. On top of that, archaeology has made significant breakthroughs during these years, as regular campaigns have been undertaken at certain sites, rescue excavations, despite all their downsides, have managed to provide significant data, and analyses of materials have unveiled unexpected patterns of production, distribution and use of pottery, glass and other items.

All this activity has resulted in an exponential growth in our knowledge and understanding of the political, social and cultural processes that unfolded in Islamic Iberia. However, this exciting and novel scholarship has not always had the impact it deserves on the field of Islamic medieval history. This is partly for an objective reason: al-Andalus was a peripheral area, very distant from the main centres where classical Islam took shape. Arab geographers described it as an island (*jazīra*) detached from the rest of the *dār al-Islām* by the sea and by the frontier or *thagr* that demarcated the Christian lands. In this distant and distinctive 'island', Muslim religion and Arab culture came to flourish, but Andalusi intellectual feats were not always highly regarded in the East: 'This is our own merchandise being sent back to us', famously declared the Būyid vizier Ibn 'Abbād, after having read the *'Iqd al-Farīd*, the monumental *adab* work by the Andalusian Ibn 'Abd Rabbihi (d. 940/328 AH).

Ibn 'Abbād's words dealt a severe blow to the westerners' pride, but were also an accurate verdict. Until well into the eleventh century (fifth AH), al-Andalus was a net importer of concepts and ideas from the main intellectual centres of the *dār al-Islām*, and notwithstanding how brilliantly such scholarly 'merchandise' was assimilated and elaborated, Andalusi scholarship continued to be tainted with a blend of provincialism that exposed it as dependent on a major process of imitation. If one wants to understand how the religious, legal or cultural traits of classical Islam emerged in the first place, al-Andalus is certainly not the right place to look. In contrast, this land is an excellent ground via which to assess how processes of Arabisation and Islamisation evolved in a social milieu lacking any previous contact with the peoples who made them possible, a major issue that explains the configuration of the whole *dār al-Islām* during the Middle Ages.

There is another reason that accounts for the absence of al-Andalus in mainstream interpretations of the medieval Islamic period. Most of the scholarly work on Islamic Iberia has been published in European Union languages (Spanish, French, Catalan, Portuguese and German) whose status as languages of scholarly exchange has steadily and sadly decreased, while over recent decades English has come to predominate in the academic sphere. In many cases, these contributions have been printed in periodicals, conference proceedings or books, published by a myriad local and regional institutions lacking a well-established reputation as academic outlets, and, more often than not, good distribution networks. Although this state of affairs has been rapidly changing over recent years, particularly among university publishers, it is still understandably difficult, for those who are not familiar with its intricacies, to navigate a scholarly ocean of publications of very uneven quality and accessibility.

The English translation of this book seeks, among other aims, to address this issue, at least in an indirect manner. Its contents owe more than can be duly acknowledged in this brief foreword to the work of present and past colleagues. Their data and interpretations have helped me to make sense of an extraordinarily difficult source, the so-called *Annals* by ʿĪsā al-Rāzī, which is full of references and allusions to the persons, ideas and places that made up not only the fabric of the Umayyad caliphate of Córdoba but also many current historiographical concerns. Through my underscoring of how crucial this historiography has been for the understanding of such disparate issues, I hope that the wider audience to which this translation is addressed will get a glimpse of the exceptional achievements of recent scholarship on al-Andalus.

This book describes the structure and functioning of the Umayyad caliphate of Córdoba in its heyday. It is based on the extraordinary account written by the courtly historian ʿĪsā al-Rāzī, who registered in precise detail the day-to-day events that were considered worthy of record for a variety of reasons, so that they could subsequently be consulted if required. ʿĪsā al-Rāzī kept a written account of all the performative aspects that shaped the caliphate, and in so doing he transmitted a description of how this early medieval state worked and the issues it faced on a daily basis.

It has been a fortunate coincidence that, in 2020, following the original publication of this book, Marina Rustow's *The Lost Archive: Traces of a Caliphate in a Cairo Synagogue* was published by Princeton University Press, a major contribution to the history of this period. This scholar has managed to gather a number of documents preserved in the Cairo Geniza that were originally Fāṭimid writs, petitions or fiscal receipts and were re-used as scrap paper by Jewish communities. Rustow's thorough analysis of this precious evidence has enabled her to analyse the micro level of bureaucracy under the Fāṭimid caliphs, the Umayyads' major rivals.

Elegantly written and displaying breathtaking scholarship, this is a book whose reading instils so much joy and imparts such a wealth of historical knowledge that nothing short of a declaration of my sheer admiration can really sum up my view on Rustow's work. I am convinced that had Rustow's volume been published before the present book, my own research would have benefited enormously. It has been very rewarding, though, to confirm that a number of issues addressed by Rustow's analysis of the Fāṭimid documents concur with those I have dealt with by examining 'Īsà al-Rāzī's text, which provides us with the closest approximation we can get to the micro-level workings of the Umayyad polity in the absence of archival documents. I have mentioned these coincidences in the footnotes of the English translation wherever they are relevant, but it is also apposite to outline here a general appraisal of this scholar's main conclusions in relation to what both books have in common.

Rustow's belief that 'to call the Fatimid caliphate anything other than a state is grossly to misunderstand either the caliphate or the way states work' (p. 103) is wholly confirmed by what can be discerned concerning the Cordoban caliphate, as I have mentioned before and as will become apparent in the following pages. Neither of these states can be considered 'despotic', as Rustow rightly claims, because their rulers displayed a genuine concern for the welfare and prosperity of their subjects, and this was a key element of the legitimacy laid claim to by both dynasties. The analysis of petitions preserved in Fāṭimid documents matches al-Ḥakam II's concerns about the behaviour of his provincial governors, and frequent mentions of prosperity (*'imāra*) and welfare (*maṣlaḥa*) in the latter's decrees and official letters neatly match the 'explicit linking of prosperity and justice' (p. 225) proposed by the Fāṭimids.

There is no doubt, either, that the workings of both caliphates were based on written documents that were regularly issued by their central and provincial administrations, and then carefully conserved in archives. The evidence gathered for this by Marina Rustow is indisputable. This trait is again corroborated by 'Īsà al-Rāzī's inclusion of Umayyad caliphal decrees and letters, and also by incidental references, such as missives the caliph issued to a provincial governor granting a tax exemption, which I discuss in Chapter 2, and clearly hint at the existence of local fiscal records, which may have not been very different from those Rustow describes. The prevalence of written documents in al-Andalus is also confirmed by an extraordinary source: the *Kitāb al-wathā'iq wa l-sijillāt* by Ibn al-'Aṭṭār (d. 1009/399 AH), a meticulous and grumpy notary from the late Umayyad period, who gathered almost 250 different models of contracts on sales, donations, testaments, manumissions or *waqf* endowments.

Yet it is difficult to assess whether paper was as widely used by the Umayyads in al-Andalus, as Rustow describes having been the case for the Fāṭimid administration in Egypt. Although two or three Iberian paper manuscripts have been hesitantly dated to the late tenth century, the use of paper does not seem to have been very widespread during the period covered by the present book. Muḥammad b. 'Īsà al-Jawlānī, known as Ibn al-Qallās, was an Andalusi scholar, who had spent much of his life travelling in the Near East. Upon his return to Córdoba, he was asked to produce the works that he claimed he had collected after meeting the most reputed oriental *'ulamā'*: he only managed to produce Andalusi copies of their works on parchment. When he was required to produce the originals on paper (*uṣūl al-kāghid*), he claimed that he had lost them during a shipwreck. This explanation did not convince his colleagues, who regarded him as a liar (Ibn al-Faraḍī, *Ta'rīkh*, n. 1,243). Lack of paper, though, did not impede a widescale production of documents: the *rabaḍ al-Raqqāqīn*, an urban district in the vicinity of the Umayyad palace in Córdoba and adjacent to the butchers' shops in the souk, was, as its name suggests, inhabited by parchment makers.

A central tenet in Marina Rustow's book concerns the crucial question of what documents can tell us about the institutions that issued them, particularly if we compare these institutions with those from medieval Europe. In this regard, the fact that documents were issued and archived in great numbers is of the utmost relevance, because, as she rightly argues, it undermines the case certain scholars have made for Islamic societies having had a 'weak' institutional configuration vis-à-vis Western medieval institutions, whose 'stability and strength' were based on 'the preservation and reproduction of legal and social privileges'. Although Rustow seems to suggest I have espoused this view (p. 3 n. 10), this is far for being the case: its main advocates have been scholars of the so-called school of New Institutional Economics (NIE), who argue that institutions were key actors in the West's economic development, because, among other things, they preserved long-term written accounts, which served to cement fundamental elements of rational economic activity, such as property rights and contractual obligations. I have strongly criticised this view and argued against its teleological perspective, its lack of a sound empirical basis and its methodological bias. Therefore, I totally agree with Marina Rustow – and indeed I made this point in my 2015 article 'Why did Islamic Medieval Institutions *become* so different from Western Medieval Institutions?' – that it is misleading to describe medieval Islamic institutions as 'weak', and fundamentally wrong to qualify them as socio-political failures.

Nevertheless, Islamic and Western institutions developed major differences in the Middle Ages and it is legitimate to ask ourselves why. Comparative analysis is an excellent tool with which to identify social regularities that were at the base of institutional configuration, and, in addition, it also encourages the incorporation of Islamic history into mainstream medieval studies by challenging misconceptions that consider the history of Islamic societies as a mere succession of despotic dynasties with no rational or efficient systems of government, a perspective Marina Rustow abhors as much as I do.

A broad comparison of institutions can also allow us to avoid a problem that stems from Rustow's interpretation of the Fāṭimid state in light of Max Weber's conclusions on modern state bureaucracies (pp. 103–6.) Weber considered these bureaucracies as tokens of a process of 'rationalization', a view that is not that different from the principles upon which the NIE scholars base their claims. In fact, the German sociologist singled out the Islamic legal system as not having been based on rational law, but rather on the arbitrary and ad hoc elements that shaped the subjective rulings of those in charge of administering justice. Weber epitomised this view in the concept of 'qāḍī justice', in which he imagined Muslim judges resorting to common sense and expediency instead of conforming either to the letter of the codified law or to rational procedures of seeking evidence. Obviously, Weber's ideas can be selected à la carte; however, the interpretations that result somehow tend to lack coherence due to their being only partially based on his premises.

It is for this reason that I have pursued an alternative approach and sought an explanation for the differences between medieval Islamic and Western institutions through a consideration of the fundamental disparity between their respective tax and land-based polities, and of how this 'tributary mode of production', which John Haldon has convincingly defined as a useful epistemological tool for historical interpretation, gave rise to wholly different social formations. As a matter of fact, most of the documents that Marina Rustow compiled to reconstruct the lost archive of the Fāṭimids are related to tax matters in one way or another; in contrast, none of them includes a land property grant. Perhaps this is only a matter of chance – it is important to bear in mind that Rustow has reconstructed a disappeared and disparate archive – but from what we know of the functioning of their respective caliphates, neither the Fāṭimids nor the Umayyads made land concessions to their subjects, contrary to what rulers in Western Europe were doing at that time. The only warrants involving land that, at least in al-Andalus, Muslim sovereigns occasionally granted were the so-called *iqṭāʿat*, which were basically revocable tax assignments on a certain territory. All the evidence seems to suggest, therefore, that these Islamic states were very much concerned with the management of taxes; in contrast, they abstained from meddling in land property rights.

Fiscal documents issued by tax-based polities are ephemeral almost by definition. They are critical for tax collecting purposes and in the case of fiscal arrears or claims, but once accounts are settled, and after some reasonable time has lapsed, most fiscal documents become useless. New censuses abrogate previous estimates, taxpayers are born, die, marry or divorce, further plots of land are cultivated, and urban workshops open, close or change hands. Fiscal administration is always concerned with an ever-changing reality, in which the written memory of the past has only a limited value for all the parties involved in present tax collection. Even fiscal exemptions granted by a ruler, the Holy Grail for taxpayers, can be revoked by his successors and rendered ineffective. This explains why Fāṭimid archives would be 'pruned' regularly and their documents re-used, as Marina Rustow masterfully shows, just as nowadays we have to dispose of our old tax records.

In contrast, land-based polities, like those that emerged in feudal Europe, were based on what Marc Bloch summarised as the combination of the 'right to the revenues from the land with the right to exercise authority'. Unlike taxes, land was not ephemeral, and, once it was granted, its exploitation required social forms of extra-economic coercion that merged power with authority. The Church spearheaded this institutional articulation. In 633, the Visigothic bishops, who had gathered at the IV Council of Toledo, solemnly declared that neither freedmen nor their descendants could ever escape ecclesiastic patronage, because the Church 'is a patron who never dies'. This self-awareness of an everlasting capacity to exercise power, in this case by bishops also vested with religious authority, laid the foundations of an institutional configuration that extended to other social sectors throughout the rest of the Middle Ages.

In contrast, an increasing divergence emerged between Islamic medieval institutions that depended on power and those which adhered to principles of authority. As this book aims to explain, the Umayyads managed to merge both aspects for a short period of time, but caliphal power, which entailed heavy taxation and political coercion, was still prone to be challenged by the forceful authority of the *'ulamā'*, scholars who based their social standing on their monopoly of religious knowledge. Institutions which were attached and filled by these *'ulamā'*, like legal courts, market inspectorates or notarial offices, produced great quantities of documents, as witnessed, for instance, by the archives that both Fāṭimid and Umayyad *qāḍī*s left to their successors. The contents of these documents referred to rulings or contracts on a large range of disputes and agreements among particulars so that their preservation must have been extremely uneven. Individuals may well have kept whatever documents were relevant for them and their descendants, but medieval family archives are difficult to detect by historians, for obvious reasons. In the case of institutional archives, like those of the *qāḍī*s, the preservation of large amounts of documents that recorded infinite numbers of individual cases made little sense in the long run, for practical reasons. But this does not mean that the written testimonies were erased. Far from it. The *'ulamā'* followed a strategy that consisted of compiling treatises and compendia on legal matters, such as the collections of *fatwa*s, works on *ḥiṣba* or notarial formularies. In the well-organised chapters of these compilations, principles and practices were easier to locate than in the oceans of documents that were stored in archives, because at the end of the day it was the *'ulamā'*, and not the archivists, who were the transmitters and interpreters of religious and legal knowledge. This long-term strategy for the preservation of authority was the social practice that led to a peculiar institutionalisation of knowledge, one that was based more on libraries and chains of learning transmission than on archives. To label this institutional Islamic knowledge as 'weak' or 'irrational' is to ignore its wide circulation, its impressive coherence, the sophisticated intellectual principles that ruled its elaboration and, last but not least, the social support it enjoyed. Hopefully, contributions like Marina Rustow's or that of the present book will help to defeat such a long-lasting misconception.

I have always sympathised with authors who declare that, once they have produced a particular work, they try not to go back to it. A thorough revision of a book that has already been published always entails a certain degree of dissatisfaction with its contents: arguments should have been better laid out, the structure could have been improved, and here and there unforgivable mistakes emerge that resulted from the haste and saturation that always mark the final

Figure 1 Map of Al-Andalus

stages of a long-term endeavour. Working on this translation has forced me to confront these issues. Whenever it has been possible, I have tried to correct and improve the relevant passages. As a result, I have rectified a number of errors that came up in the Spanish version of the book and I have duly acknowledged them in the footnotes.

I owe the possible improvements of this translation to the comments of the anonymous reviewers, who rightly suggested, among other things, that I should add recent contributions that have been published since this book came out. I have followed their advice and other comments they made, for which I am extremely grateful. I would also like to thank my colleague at the University of St Andrews, Andrew Peacock, who suggested to me the possibility of proposing this translation project to Edinburgh University Press, whose editors I would also like to thank for all their hard work and understanding.

Introduction

The Umayyad sovereigns of al-Andalus resided at the very centre of Córdoba in a palace called *Alcázar*, just in front of the city's celebrated main mosque. The events that took place in this palace, and especially matters of a private nature, were rarely divulged to the subjects living outside its high walls and closely-guarded gates, as the Umayyad rulers zealously protected their intimacy. Luckily, however, there were always gossips on hand to recount intriguing stories to whoever wanted to listen to them, and likewise, even more fortunately, on rare occasions some of these stories were heard by someone who chose to write them down, and thus allowed them to survive the oblivion wrought by the passage of time.

One of the most interesting stories of the Umayyad *alcázar* was told by a certain Ṭalāl, a palace eunuch, who was in charge of the harem and was famed for his intelligence and trustworthiness. According to Ṭalāl, following a pleasant afternoon in the *alcázar* gardens in the company of his female slaves, the Emir ʿAbd al-Raḥmān III decided that he would spend that night with his wife, Fāṭima, the highest-ranking woman in his harem, as she was his paternal cousin and therefore also belonged to the Umayyad lineage. When a servant informed Fāṭima that she should make the necessary preparations to go to the emir's chambers and spend the night with him, the rest of the women of the harem congratulated and complimented her in every way. The most effusive display of good will was made by one of the emir's concubines, Marjān, a slave of Christian origin and a fierce rival of Fāṭima. Her many felicitations for having obtained the privilege of spending the night with the emir began to vex the caliph's wife, who sought to play down the event's significance by revealing that their encounters were no longer as passionate as before, whereby the matter did not merit such a fuss. Marjān nonetheless persisted. She even went so far as to say that, in exchange for the privilege of spending the night with ʿAbd al-Raḥmān, she would give away all she had, apart from the dress she was wearing. The haughty Fāṭima swallowed the bait: was Marjān really prepared to pay any price for the opportunity of spending the night with the emir? The concubine did not hesitate for an instant and asked her rival to set a price. Fāṭima said the highest sum that came into her head: 10,000 dinars, which was the equivalent of 80,000 silver coins (dirhams). To everyone's surprise, Marjān accepted without batting an eyelid and swiftly gathered together twenty bags containing the astronomical sum. Fāṭima thought she could make the deal of a lifetime and that she and her husband would amuse themselves at the expense of the unwary concubine, whereby she accepted the offer. As proof of the deal, Marjān asked for a written contract of sale to be drawn up, in which the sum to be paid in exchange for spending a night with the emir was noted down. The document was signed by Fāṭima and Marjān, with the other women of the harem acting as witnesses.

ʿAbd al-Raḥmān was greatly surprised when it was the concubine Marjān who appeared in his chambers that night instead of his wife Fāṭima. When she explained what had happened and showed him the document to prove it, the Umayyad emir was furious with his wife for being able to sell a night with him for money, while, on the other hand, he was pleased with the generosity and love shown by Marjān, who was willing to pay such an enormous sum of money when she could have patiently awaited her turn to spend the night with him. The night the emir and his concubine spent together was followed by many others, one after another, and very soon Marjān came to oust Fāṭima from the sovereign's affections, becoming his favourite. The emir compensated her lavishly for the money she had spent, and allowed her to outshine all the other women in the harem.[1]

I have often thought that this, if it actually happened, was one of the decisive events in the history of the Umayyad dynasty. Marjān not only became the principal concubine of ʿAbd al-Raḥmān III, but also the mother of his first-born son and future heir, al-Ḥakam, who was born in January 915, albeit two months premature. The lofty Fāṭima also conceived a son for her husband, but

[1] Ibn Ḥayyān, *Muqtabis V*, ed. and trans. pp. 1–6. The story was told by Ṭalāl to the legal expert (*faqīh*) al-Ḥasan b. Muḥammad b. Mufarrij al-Qubbashī.

his destiny proved to be as obscure as his mother's and scarcely merited even a passing mention by the chroniclers of the court. In contrast, Marjān went on to become the 'Grand Lady' of the court, and patron of impressive mosques and charitable foundations for the needy; meanwhile her son secured his position as successor to the throne. From an early age, al-Ḥakam was granted special distinctions, such as remaining in charge of the *alcázar* when his father was absent during military campaigns, and later on he was officially designated crown prince. It is tempting to think, therefore, that none of this, nor the rest of what is recounted over the course of this book, would have occurred if Marjān had not undertaken her cunning ploy.

Al-Ḥakam's destiny was also sealed by another important decision taken by his father. In early 929, shortly after his son's fourteenth birthday, 'Abd al-Raḥmān III decided to adopt the title of caliph. Although the Umayyad dynasty had been governing in Córdoba for more than a hundred and seventy years, none of its rulers had dared to take such an important step, one that converted the sovereign of al-Andalus into the Commander of the Faithful (*amīr al-mu'minīn*), who was endowed with both temporal power and religious authority over the whole Muslim community. From that moment on, 'Abd al-Raḥmān III's name was invoked in all the mosques of his domains, and the caliphal epithet that he adopted, *al-Nāṣir li dīn Allāh*, 'he who brings victory to the religion of God', was used on coins and inscriptions.

'Abd al-Raḥmān *al-Nāṣir* was all too well aware that he was not the only ruler with aspirations to the title of caliph over the whole Muslim community, but he argued that his rivals used the title as a mere 'metaphor'. As a descendant of the first Islamic caliphal dynasty that arose a few decades after the death of the prophet Muḥammad in 632, 'Abd al-Raḥmān III could argue that it had been the judicious policies of his ancestors, the Umayyad caliphs of Damascus, that had led to the expansion and consolidation of the Muslim community, as was evident to all three centuries later. However, and as everybody also knew very well, this first Umayyad caliphate had been short-lived: following the succession of thirteen Umayyad caliphs in Damascus between 661 and 750, a rebellion led by a member of the rival 'Abbāsid family had resulted in their dynasty being dethroned and annihilated, following which the 'Abbāsids had flaunted the title of Commander of the Faithful in their new capital, Baghdad. The Umayyads, despite having been stripped of power and all but destroyed by their enemies, miraculously survived thanks to one of their members, who escaped the massacre of his family and fled to the shores of the Iberian Peninsula. The extraordinary adventure that saved ʿAbd al-Raḥmān b. Muʿāwiya, known as 'the Immigrant', from certain death in Syria, to his rise to power in Córdoba, where he established an independent emirate, was always considered by his descendants as a sign that God had never abandoned them.

Following the proclamation of ʿAbd al-Raḥmān I 'the Immigrant' as emir in the year 755 (138 in the Islamic calendar), power was transmitted down a direct line of his descendants, almost always from father to son and, although there were occasional internal quarrels, the dynasty was relatively stable. During this period, and while the ʿAbbāsid caliphs were considered by the majority of Muslims to be the legitimate representatives of God on earth, the Umayyads of al-Andalus maintained an ambiguous position: on the one hand, they did not acknowledge the political authority of the caliphs in Baghdad, but, on the other, they upheld the same Muslim orthodoxy, yet without making any declarations on the religious authority held by the family that had been responsible for the annihilation of their ancestors. Reference to the ʿAbbāsid caliphs was carefully avoided both in mosques and on coins, while the Umayyad sovereigns in al-Andalus conferred upon themselves the modest official title of 'emir'.

Aside from their awkward legitimacy within the framework of the Islamic polity, the Umayyads faced some specific problems in the new territory they governed. By the middle of the eighth century, al-Andalus was a markedly heterogeneous society, as the recent conquest in 711 had led Arabs and Berbers to settle among an outnumbering indigenous population. As a matter of fact, early al-Andalus consisted of a range of different ethnic groups with distinctive origins and diverse social structures. Forms of feudal domination predominated among the indigenous groups, as the defeated Visigothic lay and ecclesiastical aristocracy had been exercising power by imposing bonds of personal dependence on the subjugated classes prior to the Arab conquest. In contrast, the Berber communities, who had arrived in considerable numbers from North Africa, were tribal groups in which kinship ties played a key role and were subject to powerful leaders. The Arabs, in turn, formed a warrior oligarchy structured by family lineages based on a rigorous genealogical history, and above all, on their ingrained awareness of being both the conquerors of a great empire and recipients of the divine message of salvation, which was destined to be the seal of all known religions.

During the era of the Umayyad emirate – from the mid-eighth century up until the beginning of the tenth – all these groups underwent marked, and often conflictive, processes of social change and exchange. This was the case with the Berbers, who were assimilated into the society of the Arab conquerors through Arabisation and Islamisation, which not only meant that North Africans adopted both the Arabic language and Arabic culture, as well as the Muslim religion, but also entailed their adaptation to an urban society dominated by powerful hierarchies under a centralised power, which led them to abandon their tribal structures. These transformations did not occur at the same rhythm everywhere: the Berbers who had settled between the Guadiana and the Tagus rivers maintained tribal structures until a later date than those settled in other parts of southern al-Andalus, as witnessed by the considerable number of revolts those groups led against the Umayyad emirs, which were sometimes inspired by heterodox religious ideas stirred up by the difficult process of their Islamisation. Nevertheless, the assimilation of Berber groups into Andalusi Arab society and the abandonment of their original tribalism was an irreversible process, which started very early on after their settlement and was complete by the middle of the tenth century.

The most virulent reactions to the processes of social change that were taking place in al-Andalus during the eighth and ninth centuries arose among the descendants of the old Visigothic aristocracy. After having come to terms with the Arab conquerors, many of them had also converted to Islam and had been Arabised, while maintaining their hold over the territorial possessions ruled over by their ancestors. However, over time, as an increasingly urban and politically centralised social formation took shape, one in which the Umayyads demanded ever higher quantities of tributes, this group began to feel threatened. Known as *muwalladūn*, perhaps in a pejorative sense, many descendants of the indigenous aristocracy chose to oppose Umayyad sovereignty. They built fortresses (*ḥuṣūn*) in their domains and recruited personal armies from the population under their control, while rejecting the growing fiscal demands made by tax collectors sent from Córdoba.

The *muwalladūn* rebellions against the Umayyad emirs reached their peak between the last quarter of the ninth century and the opening decades of the tenth. This period coincided with the deeds of the most renowned *muwallad* of all, 'Umar b. Ḥafṣūn (d. 918), a descendant of indigenous ancestors who had converted to Islam. He led his rebellion from his formidable fortress of Bobastro, in the midst of the mountains of Málaga. The revolt grew to such a proportion that many other regional leaders, not only from among the *muwalladūn*, but also Arabs and Berbers, decided to cut their ties with the Umayyads, the result being that al-Andalus was plunged into complete political chaos. During some periods of his rule, the Umayyad emir, 'Abd Allāh (888–912), scarcely controlled Córdoba and its environs, while the rest of the territory was left in the hands of warlords who exerted powerful social control within their territories.

The fact that the Umayyad dynasty did not disappear at that time was due to a range of factors. The proclamation of the new emir, 'Abd al-Raḥmān III, in 912 (300 AH) brought to power a young and energetic sovereign, who swiftly made the submission of the rebels the political foundation of his reign. Having declared himself a champion of religious orthodoxy, he found that the strong sectarian divisions that had just emerged in the Islamic world as a result of the proclamation of the Fāṭimid caliphate in Ifrīqiya in 909 served to his advantage. Likewise, the new social conditions that had emerged within al-Andalus favoured his rise to power. During the previous centuries, the warlike society of the early conquerors had undergone a process of military demobilisation in which their descendants had become an influential urban and educated class, which had nothing to gain from the world represented by the *muwalladūn* rebels and the local aristocracies: in contrast to a fragmented and scattered political model based on the collection of rents in rural areas, the Umayyad dynasty came to represent the political aspirations of these new social classes, who were willing to consent to a centralised taxation system in exchange for a more efficient, shared form of access to the huge resources offered by a centralised fiscal system. These emerging urban classes, consisting of merchants, artisans and scholars from Arab, Berber or indigenous origins, had been extending their social influence, as they benefited from the existence of a ruling class whose vast resources encouraged a high demand for both material goods and immaterial productions.

As a result, the final victory that 'Abd al-Raḥmān III won over each and every one of those who had rebelled against Umayyad authority was not a mere military triumph, but the enshrining of a distinctive social system relative to that represented by the rebels. The centralisation of power and resources likewise permitted their redistribution among a ruling class that had at last become unified and was ready to take advantage of the new social and cultural homogeneity of al-Andalus, as the majority of its population had become Arabised and Islamised by that time. It was in this new political and social context that ʿAbd al-Raḥmān III adopted the title of caliph in the year 929 and was acknowledged as such almost unanimously. The Umayyad Caliphate emerged thanks to its understanding of how to embody the values and aspirations of the social structure which had evolved in al-Andalus during the emirate period, and which in the long term would also survive the caliphate.[2] From a more mundane perspective, it is also intriguing to think that Caliph al-Ḥakam II came to power thanks to his mother's canny sense of the advantage to be gained from buying a night of pleasure.

The Caliphate Era

The history of the Caliphate of Córdoba can be divided into three periods. The first (929–76) comprises the government of ʿAbd al-Raḥmān III himself, who was succeeded in 961 by his son, al-Ḥakam II, also known by the honorific surname he adopted: *al-Mustanṣir bi-Allāh*, 'he who seeks the victorious aid of God'. This period marked the peak of the Andalusi Umayyads' sovereignty, as both caliphs established an unprecedented degree of power and authority and exerted tight control over all the resources of their administration.

The second period (976–1009) began with the death of al-Ḥakam II in October 976, when the irregular succession of his son, Hishām II, aged only eleven, greatly weakened an institution that Muslim law stipulated had to be exercised by an adult. The minority of Hishām II enabled power to effectively be exercised by the principal figures of the military and civil administration of the caliphate. From the ensuing internal disputes a man called Muḥammad b. Abī ʿĀmir emerged victorious. His name recurs throughout the pages of this book as a trustworthy official at the court of al-Ḥakam II, before he managed

[2] This brief overview summarises part of the conclusions drawn by M. Acién, *Entre el feudalismo y el islam. ʿUmar b. Ḥafsūn en los historiadores, en las fuentes y en la historia*, Jaén, 1994, and E. Manzano Moreno, *Conquistadores, emires y califas. Los omeyas y la formación de al-Andalus*, Barcelona, 2006.

to take control of the reins of power after the caliph's death. He became best known by the surname he adopted once in full command: al-Manṣūr (Sp. *Almanzor*). With all the state's resources under his thumb, al-Manṣūr relegated caliph Hishām to a mere testimonial role, and subsequently handed the power he had won on to his son al-Muẓaffar, who governed after his father's death in 1002 up until his own demise in late 1008.

It was from this date onwards that the third period of the Umayyad Caliphate in al-Andalus began, an era marked by civil war (1009–31). The conflict was ignited by al-Manṣūr's second son and al-Muẓaffar's successor, ʿAbd al-Raḥmān, also known as *Sanjūl* due to the fact that his mother was the daughter of King Sancho II of Pamplona. In an unprecedented move, Sanjūl convinced Hishām II to name him heir to the caliphate. This provoked a forthright response from the remaining members of the Umayyad family in Córdoba, a violent reaction that brought to the fore the social and political contradictions that the Caliphate had been founded upon. The result was more than two decades of civil war, or *fitna*, which was marked by the disappearance of both al-Manṣūr's family and Hishām II, as well as a succession of caliphs, some of whom made only a fleeting appearance and were all opposed to one another. The rule of the Umayyads in al-Andalus came to an end in late 1031 with the expulsion of the last caliph of this once-powerful dynasty from Córdoba.

Thus, having lasted little more than a hundred years (929–1031), the Caliphate of Córdoba was marked by almost fifty years of strong rule by Umayyad sovereigns, just over thirty years of power exerted by the ʿĀmirids – that is, al-Manṣūr and his sons – and two long decades of civil war or *fitna*, which brought about the demise of the Umayyad dynasty and the emergence of a mosaic of *taifa* kingdoms across the main cities and territories of al-Andalus. Significant political changes took place throughout this period, which reflect the impressive dynamism of Andalusi society. Indeed, although the political structure established by the Umayyad Caliphs foundered, the same did not occur with the social system that had sustained it: during the era of the *taifa* kingdoms, the Umayyad's successors reproduced on a smaller scale the same centralised political system, based on the redistribution of tributes, which is clear proof of the social homogenisation of al-Andalus.

Therefore, the apogee of the Umayyad dynasty coincided with the rule of ʿAbd al-Raḥmān III and al-Ḥakam II. And if one had to choose a period of splendour, this would probably be the reign of al-Ḥakam II, between 961 and 976 (which corresponds to 350 and 366 in the Islamic calendar), a period of fifteen years marked by internal peace and widespread prosperity in al-Andalus, which was reflected in the major building projects commissioned by the Umayyad Caliphs. Undoubtedly, the most spectacular of these was the city palace of Madīnat al-Zahrā', which was built five kilometres to the west of the capital. Another grand project was the extension of Córdoba's main mosque, which was finished in 971 and was completed by a spectacular *miḥrāb*, whose mosaics and inscriptions exalting al-Ḥakam II as caliph are one of the major highlights of medieval Islamic art.

It is paradoxical to note that the rule of al-Ḥakam II and the spectacular period it encompasses are relatively poorly documented in textual sources, despite the fact that scholars close to the caliphal court wrote a great deal and did so very well. The celebrated comment of G. W. F. Hegel, that eras of happiness are the blank pages of history books, might well apply to this period. One can count on the fingers of one hand the historical chronicles that provide relevant information about the years of al-Ḥakam II, and in any case most of these sources are later compilations. As a matter of fact, there are many enclaves and territories of al-Andalus about which we know no more than what is revealed by archaeologists working at those sites where excavations are possible. Despite the fact that this was an era of abundant textual production, the writings that have come down to us are usually literary works, medical or religious treatises that are just as important as regards the concerns of history, which in any case was never a branch of knowledge that was highly valued by Andalusis.[3]

Nonetheless, this general rule is broken by one exception: an extraordinary text, which has been preserved thanks to a fortunate string of events. The text in question contains the 'annals' written by a chronicler of the court of al-Ḥakam II, and is preserved in a manuscript of 130 folios, which record the events that took place in the caliph's court during a period lasting just over four years: between June 971 and July 975, corresponding to the month of *Sha'bān* in the year 360 and that of *Dhū l-qa'da* in 364 according to the Islamic calendar. As an eye-witness account, these 'annals' are like a burst of

[3] E. Manzano Moreno, '¿El fin de la historia?', pp. 407–19.

light revealing day-to-day life during the caliphate and the people who thrived at that time, all told with an extraordinary official attention to detail, which reveals infinite facts about the court of the Umayyad Caliph at its time of greatest splendour.

This book is based on these 'annals', which until now have never been the object of a comprehensive study. In the pages that follow, my intention is to provide a detailed picture of the Caliphate of Córdoba in order to address two main questions: how was this power structure capable of functioning in such an efficient manner? And, secondly, what led it to collapse so spectacularly and so soon? In order to answer these questions, it is necessary to obtain a highly detailed account of the reign of the Umayyad Caliphs, and these 'annals' provide a remarkable tool with which to achieve this. They contain a great deal of information about some extremely interesting issues, rarely mentioned in other contemporary sources: the structure and functioning of the caliphal political structure, the individuals it was formed of and the events that affected them, and the representations and rituals they adhered to, as well as the problems they tackled on a daily basis. With an omnipresent caliph presiding over receptions, issuing orders, sending letters, sacking civil servants or spending, at long last, a spring afternoon in his *almunia* or rural estate, these 'annals' provide an account of the court of al-Ḥakam II that bears no comparison to any other source of the period. The Spanish Arabist Emilio García Gómez described this text as 'un pico perforador en el murallón de la China que nos separa del califato de Córdoba [a pickaxe taken to the Great Wall of China separating us from the Caliphate of Córdoba]', and my goal has been to open up the resulting chink as much as is possible by incorporating information from other textual sources and the range of textual and archaeological research undertaken in recent decades. However, none of this would have been possible if the manuscript containing these 'annals' had disappeared without trace. And this is something that very nearly happened, and would have done had it not been for a series of fortuitous events.

The Finding of a Forgotten Manuscript

During the final decades of the nineteenth century, the scarce, yet active group of Spanish Arabists realised that there were works composed by Arab authors which contained valuable information on the history of the Iberian

Peninsula during the Middle Ages, but which remained to be studied. One of these Arabists was Francisco Codera (1836–1917), a university professor and member of the Real Academia de la Historia in Madrid. This distinguished scholar was convinced that the libraries of the Maghreb preserved manuscripts containing data of particular relevance to the history of al-Andalus that had remained unknown until then.[4] His skills of persuasion convinced the then director of the Real Academia and prominent Spanish conservative politician, Antonio Cánovas del Castillo, that the government should cover his expenses for a research trip to Algeria and Tunisia in search of such manuscripts. The aim of the mission was to inspect these countries' principal libraries and obtain copies of, or at least references to, unpublished Arab works that dealt with medieval Spain.[5]

Cordera left from the port of Cartagena in September 1887 accompanied by a young student called Francisco Pons Bohigues (1861–99).[6] Their tour led them first to Oran and Algiers, where they undertook an inspection of library catalogues in search of Arab chronicles of al-Andalus, which met almost always with negative results. The next stage of their journey was Tunisia, where they hoped to find interesting manuscripts in the large library of the mosque of al-Zaytūna. However, the scholars' zeal soon gave way to frustration. The mosque's loan system for 'unbelievers' exasperated Codera, who even considered disguising himself as a Muslim in order to enter the mosque and be able to examine its library at his leisure. The Tunisian booksellers likewise

4 M. J. Viguera, 'Voyager et chercher en Afrique du Nord: les livres comme objectif', pp. 698–700.

5 It is worth recalling that these countries, and in particular Algeria, had splendid libraries, as prior to the colonial era a very high number of the population knew how to read and write. However, matters changed in the wake of colonisation. In places such as Constantine, which was captured in 1837 by the French, the latter themselves acknowledged 'having burnt the Arab manuscripts they found there like authentic barbarians', A. Abdelhamid, *Manuscrits et bibliotèques musulmanes en Algérie*, p. 16.

6 There are three testimonies to this journey. Firstly, the memorandum that F. Codera wrote for the Academy entitled *Misión histórica en la Argelia y Túnez*, Madrid, 1892. His companion wrote a very personal and less 'official' account, in which he gave free rein to his racial and religious prejudices, thereby offering a good portrayal of the conservative ideology of Spanish Arabism at that time. The account was published in various issues of the *Revista Contemporánea*, and some decades later as part of a book containing other works by him, F. Pons Bohigues, *Estudios breves*, pp. 67–157. Finally, Codera himself kept a journal with a detailed diary of the journey, and he used this to write his memorandum, but it also contains a range of personal reflections: it is preserved in caja 81/doc 005 of the Asín Palacios–Jaime Oliver Asín collection in the library of the Universidad Nacional de Educación a Distancia (UNED) in Madrid.

tested his patience, as they assured him they had unpublished manuscripts, but then returned empty-handed or with texts that were of no interest. Cordera could not contain his anxiety, as he was never sure whether the works that they offered him really existed, or were just invented by people trying to be helpful. A linguistic barrier was added to the cultural one; despite being an excellent Arabist, Codera had never spoken Arabic, which for him was like a dead language, and so he had to hire an interpreter.

Codera, who was most probably very disillusioned by his lack of progress, then received a letter from the French Arabist Edmond Fagnan (1846–1931), who wrote to send him a piece of information that he had forgotten to mention in their previous correspondence: in the library of the heirs of a prominent figure of the city of Constantine, in Algeria, Fagnan remembered having seen a manuscript with the title '*al-Muqtabis*', which might perhaps be of interest.

The library referred to by the French Arabist was one of the most important in Algeria and belonged to Sidi Ben Hammouda, a member of a family of distinguished jurists known as the Awlād al-Fakkūn (or Ouled el-Feggoun). In this library, more than four thousand books and manuscripts were stacked on the shelves 'like wheat in a granary'. When Codera discovered that a manuscript with the title *Muqtabis* was actually held there, he quickly wrote to the Spanish vice-consul in Constantine, José Perals, and asked him to arrange for him to be allowed to examine it. Thanks to the efforts of the vice-consul, the heirs of Sidi Ben Hammouda agreed to loan the manuscript so that it could be examined over a period of fifteen days, which was fairly exceptional, as the owners of Algerian libraries were well-accustomed to Europeans who requested manuscripts and then, convinced that their colonial domination conferred a superior social status upon them, never returned them.

Codera reached Constantine on 23 January 1888 and over the course of the following week was able to confirm that the manuscript's 130 folios contained an annalistic account of various years from the caliphate of al-Ḥakam II recounted with an attention to detail not found in any other source.[7] Aware of the importance of this find, but having to return to Spain, the Arabist commissioned a copy of the manuscript. In the months that followed, a transcription

[7] Among the pages of the journal Codera wrote and deposited in the UNED is the bill from the Grand Hotel Paris in Constantine, where the Arabist and his student were lodged during this time.

of notable quality was made by al-Makkī b. ʿAlī b. Aḥmad al-Fakkūn, a member of the family who owned the library. In accordance with Codera's instructions the copy was sent to the library of the Real Academia de la Historia, where it has since remained.

Generations of Arabists, historians and archaeologists have thanked Codera for taking the wise decision to make that copy and to al-Makkī b. ʿAlī b. Aḥmad al-Fakkūn for undertaking this transcription. Without that copy, the valuable information that the manuscript contained would have been lost for ever: the splendid library of the heirs of Sidi Ben Hammouda was shortly afterwards broken up and in 1892 its last remaining holdings were sold off cheap by the pound, whereby the manuscript that Codera had had in his hands disappeared without a trace.[8] The copy held in the Real Academia de la Historia thereby became the *unicum* of the volume of the *Muqtabis* which corresponds to the Caliphate of al-Ḥakam II. Had that copy not been made, this book would not have been possible.

The Eventful History of the Manuscript's Publication and Translation

Francisco Codera used the copy of the *Muqtabis* that he had managed to obtain for the library of the Real Academia de la Historia to write a number of studies on the caliphate of al-Ḥakam II, but he never undertook a specific study of it, nor a critical edition. Another Arabist, Julián Ribera, deemed the manuscript 'inaccurate in places' and 'difficult to work with', while Évariste Lévi-Provençal branded it as 'of little use' and he barely used it when he wrote his monumental *Histoire de l'Espagne musulmane*. Despite these discouraging opinions, at the end of the 1940s the Spanish Arabist Emilio García Gómez (1905–95) announced he was undertaking the critical edition of this important manuscript. Since 1942 this Arabist had been a member of the Real Academia and was, undoubtedly, the ideal person for this venture, both for his splendid knowledge of Arabic and for his familiarity with the period.[9]

[8] A. Abdelhamid, *Manuscrits et bibliotèques musulmanes*, pp. 83–4.

[9] In 1947 García Gómez announced that 'we are at work' on a critical edition and translation of the book, 'Algunas precisiones de la ruina de la Córdoba omeya', p. 278, n. 1. The following year he stated that the edition and the translation were 'nearly complete', 'Al-Ḥakam II y los bereberes según un texto de Ibn Ḥayyān', p. 210, n. 2. Codera's studies based on the manuscript and Ribera and Lévi-Provençal's views are cited by García Gómez in the prologue to his translation.

However, the years went by, and the critical edition of the *Muqtabis* never came to fruition. Other projects, especially those related to Arab medieval poetry, and García Gómez's intense political activity (for more than a decade, between 1957 and 1968, he served as Spanish ambassador in Baghdad, Beirut and Ankara), may well have distracted him from a task that demanded a great deal of time and bibliographical resources.[10] It was at this juncture that in October 1964 a letter signed by one 'Abderrahman A. Muhammad' [*sic*] was received by the Real Academia de la Historia. It requested permission to publish, 'in accordance with the conditions agreed by the institution', the manuscript of the *Muqtabis*, which had spent almost eight decades on its library's shelves. At the meeting of the academicians held on 16 October that year, the institution's then librarian, José López de Toro, reported on the request, and pointed out that 'the only impediment to the applicant's publication of the aforementioned manuscript was the intention of the member of our academy, Emilio García Gómez, to publish it, but he had informed the Academy of his having relinquished the task as other activities prevented him from completing it'. Taking this into account, permission was granted for the edition of the manuscript; most likely, the task was facilitated by sending a microfilm copy.[11]

José López de Toro (1897–1972) was a priest from Granada and a consummate Latinist, who had joined the Real Academia de Historia in 1958.[12] Despite his having published translations of Latin texts and occasional historical studies, his true vocation was that of librarian, a post he had filled at the Universidad de Granada and the Biblioteca Nacional, of which he became vice-director. When he joined the Real Academia de la Historia it was only natural that this priest, preceded by his 'fame for being competent and obliging', went on to become the institution's permanent librarian. His duties included the review of the continual stream of requests sent by researchers seeking to use the academy's abundant holdings of manuscripts. Such requests were discussed at the academicians' weekly meetings and would

[10] R. Villanueva Etcheverría, 'Perfil y andanzas diplomáticas del embajador Emilio García Gómez', pp. 135–58; M. D. Algora Weber, 'Emilio García Gómez: de catedrático a embajador', pp. 47–58.

[11] This information is taken from the proceedings of this institution, the *Actas de la Real Academia de la Historia*, which are conserved in its archive, tomo LXIII, fol. 81.

[12] 'Catálogo de sus individuos. Noticias sacadas de su archivo', *Boletín de la Real Academia de la Historia*, pp. 62–3.

usually be given a favourable response so long as the proposal was presented with guarantees of seriousness and rigour.

However, the decision taken in October 1964 to permit the publication of the manuscript of *Muqtabis* would unleash a storm. In 1965 the manuscript was published in Beirut, edited by ʿAbd al-Raḥmān ʿAlī al-Ḥajjī, an Iraqi researcher who had completed his doctorate at the University of Cambridge on the diplomatic relationships of al-Andalus in the Mediterranean region. He had become interested in this text due to the wealth of information it provided on foreign embassies in Córdoba.[13] The publication of the *Muqtabis* included a brief prologue by Iḥsān ʿAbbās (1920–2003), one of the great Arab scholars of the day, a professor at the American University of Beirut and author of a great many studies and universally respected editions of renowned Arab texts. In his prologue, the Palestinian professor stated that the folios of the manuscript he had been sent were not in order, but that he had done all he could to sort out their disarray. In a somewhat unusual manner, and despite not being cited as editor, ʿAbbās also pointed out that he had introduced a considerable number of notes of his own in addition to those included by al-Ḥajjī, and that these were distinguished by the Arabic letter *ṣīn* written in brackets.[14] The introduction to the supplementary notes made by ʿAbbās indicate that he did not hold the work undertaken by the book's editor in very high regard.

Months after the publication of the Beirut edition of the *Muqtabis*, on 11 March 1966, at the weekly meeting of the Real Academia de la Historia in Madrid it was announced that Emilio García Gómez had renounced 'his member's medal', which was the equivalent of him submitting his resignation as a member of this institution. At a 'secret meeting' the academicians present agreed not to accept the resignation of their colleague 'and to notify him of their admiration and good will in every possible way, and express their regret for any seeming unwariness'. At this meeting, they also agreed to offer García Gómez the opportunity to publish the *Muqtabis* 'in facsimile, along with his

[13] His thesis, initially supervised by D. M. Dunlop and published in Arabic and English, was entitled *Andalusian Diplomatic Relations with Western Europe during the Umayyad period (AH. 138–366/755–976)*, Beirut, 1970.

[14] Ibn Ḥayyān, *al-Muqtabis fī akhbār balad al-Andalus*, ed. ʿAbd al-Raḥmān ʿAlī al-Ḥajjī, Beirut, 1965. pp. 9–10. From here on I cite this work as Ibn Ḥayyān, *Muqtabis VII*, ed. cit. for the reasons given below.

transcription, translation and study, with the full confidence that the learned world of Arabism would greatly value his edition and much more so than that of the Iraqi, Abdurrahman Ali El Hajji [*sic*]'. However, the dispute did not end there: at a further meeting held on 30 March, from which the librarian, José López de Toro was absent, they acknowledged receipt of a document from García Gómez, 'that remained on the table'.[15]

At present, one can only speculate on what may have happened in the months that followed. From then on, the proceedings of the academicians' meetings reveal a far greater degree of reticence when it came to approving new researchers' requests to publish or work on the library's holdings, and the work of López de Toro seems to have been called into question to an increasing degree. On 17 March 1967 the latter tendered his resignation as permanent librarian and for some time ceased to attend the institution's weekly meetings.[16] Months later, at the session held on 12 January 1968, it was agreed to not accept 'the resignation of the fellowship of our corporation, which had been presented by our colleague, Sr. García Gómez, and was pending a response' (as it had been for more than a year and a half). Two weeks later, a response was received by García Gómez, sent from Ankara, where he was then serving as ambassador, 'accepting the Academy's decision to not accept the resignation he had tendered'.[17] At the meeting held on 31 May that same year, an announcement was made about the forthcoming publication of the Spanish translation of the *Muqtabis* by García Gómez entitled *Anales Palatinos del Califato de Córdoba*, which 'the Academy had received with great satisfaction'.

However, the Academy did not have many reasons to be satisfied. The translation signed by García Gómez opened with an 'Advertencia Útil [Some useful advice]', in which the Arabist launched an invective against everything and everyone.[18] He began his diatribe by pointing out that the rise of Arab

[15] *Actas de las sesiones de la Real Academia de la Historia*, tomo LXIII, fol. 327. The academicians present at that meeting were, among others, besides the director Ignacio Sánchez Cantón, Luis Redonet, Diego Angulo, Antonio García y Bellido, Ciríaco Pérez Bustamante, Ángel Ferrari, Luis García de Valdeavellano, Julio Caro Baroja and the librarian himself, José López de Toro.

[16] *Actas de las sesiones de la Real Academia de la Historia*, tomo LXIII, Sesión del 15 de marzo de 1967, fol. 515. Months later, José López de Toro began to attend the academy's meetings once more. He died in December 1972 and his post was filled, curiously, by Elías Terés Sádaba, a student of Emilio García Gómez.

[17] *Actas de las sesiones de la Real Academia de la Historia*, tomo LXIV, fol. 41 and 48–9.

[18] The translation appeared with the following title: *El califato de Córdoba en el Muqtabis de*

nationalism had greatly affected the field of Arabism, due to the disdain and animosity that many Arabs displayed towards European oriental studies, which they identified with colonialism and imperialism. According to García Gómez, this state of affairs had given rise to the 'poaching' of manuscripts, which were published as a re-affirmation of Arab identity, especially when the Arab manuscript in question was found in Europe or being used by a European. The 'frequency of research trips', the 'provision of greater library access' and the use of microfilms had added to this new climate, and sown what the Spanish Arabist considered 'anarchy within scholarly planning'.

According to García Gómez, these circumstances had together fostered the episode of the edition of the *Muqtabis* manuscript, which had been undertaken without his knowledge and had led to his 'temporary' distance from the Real Academia de la Historia. Without naming him openly, the Arabist held Iḥsān 'Abbās responsible for what had happened, and considered him to be the 'the leader and soul of the organization, and even the mastermind of the whole operation'. Evidently 'Abbās and García Gómez knew one another – it will be recalled he had served as ambassador in Beirut – and there can be little doubt that they did not see eye to eye, their animosity being perhaps fostered by García Gómez's view that the majority of Lebanese universities had been founded 'for propagandistic reasons'. The insinuations of the Spanish Arabist also indicate that he was convinced that the Palestinian scholar had orchestrated the edition of the manuscript of the *Muqtabis*, while knowing full well that it was a project that he had long cherished.

For García Gómez, the outcome of the whole 'operation' was flawed, and he pointed out in his 'advertencia' the many errors contained in al-Ḥajjī's edition. In addition to the incorrect order of some of the pages, which had not been completely resolved, there were misread toponyms, distorted proper names, confused words, misinterpreted titles and a range of grammatical

Ibn Ḥayyān. Anales Palatinos del califa de Córdoba al-Ḥakam II por 'Īsā ibn Aḥmad al-Rāzī (360–364 = 971–975 J.C.*), traducción del ms. árabe de la Real Academia de la Historia* by Emilio García Gómez de la Real Academia Española and the Academia Nacionale dei Lincei, Madrid, 1967. García Gómez presented himself as a member of the Real Academia Española (RAE) – and indeed, he was also a member of this academy devoted to the Spanish language, and the Italian academy of the Lincei, but not the Real Academia de la Historia, which confirms that at that time he was still considering himself as having resigned. The 'Advertencia Útil', with which the book begins, runs from page 11 to page 20. From here on I cite this translation as Ibn Ḥayyān, *Muqtabis VII*, trans. cit.

errors. The Arabist offered a number of examples of all these failings, which, in his opinion, demonstrated the 'hopeless academic iniquity' of an edition produced with 'scandalous haste'.

García Gómez ended his 'advertencia' by explaining that all these circumstances had obliged him to publish his translation of the text, because 'people of my generation still have the bourgeois sense of property in their bones'. Yet, it was a translation that he acknowledged was not free of problems. It lacked notes and indexes, and with no other critical apparatus than a brief study in the form of a prologue, his translation of this text could also be classed as rushed. The Spanish Arabist said he was perfectly aware of this, but insisted that 'there are certain affairs of my own at stake in this matter, which at present have been left in the middle of the street, as if rescued from a fire. I must act to protect them from the elements, even though they later get a soaking from the hoses of the critics.' With ironic resignation, García Gómez said that events such as this increasingly distanced him from his discipline, while also announcing that he would publish partial studies based on information provided by the *Muqtabis*, and advised future readers to consult the proceedings of the Real Academia to stay abreast of new 'events' and 'even outbreaks of theatre' (probably alluding to his strange acceptance of the Academy's decision to not accept his resignation).[19]

The result of this troubled chain of events was that the manuscript Codera had found never received the treatment its value merited. Just as E. García Gómez rightly pointed out, the edition of the Arabic text is manifestly in need of improvement and beleaguered by a great deal of errors and confusions.[20] The translation signed by the Spanish Arabist, in contrast, is, as a rule, splendid: it adheres closely to the text, and is restrained without flourishes; besides, it has the added virtue that it corrects many errors of the edited version with regard

[19] E. García Gómez published three studies using information from the *Muqtabis*: 'Notas sobre la topografía cordobesa en los 'Anales de al-Ḥakam II' por 'Īsā al-Rāzī', *al-Andalus*, XXX, 2, 1965, pp. 319–79; 'Armas, banderas, tiendas de campaña, monturas y correos en los 'Anales de al-Ḥakam II' por 'Īsā al-Rāzī', *al-Andalus*, XXXII, 1, 1967, pp. 163–80; and 'Tejidos, ropas y tapicería en los 'Anales de al-Ḥakam II' por 'Īsā al-Rāzī', *Boletín de la Real Academia de la Historia*, CLXVI, 1970, pp. 43–53.

[20] A more recent edition may be added to that by al-Ḥajjī, one produced by Salāḥ al-Dīn al-Hawwārī, which has not corrected these errors and merely re-orders some parts of the text, *al-Muqtabis fī ajbār balad al-Andalus*, Beirut, 2006.

to the order of the pages, the interpretation of toponyms and the identification of names. In this sense, the reading undertaken by the translator functions as a form of critical edition, as on many occasions he not only interprets the content of the original manuscript in a more satisfactory manner than the editor, but also orders its folios in what is undoubtedly the correct order. However, the major shortcoming of this translation is that it is not easy to use, due to its lack of notes and critical apparatus, which would have helped explain the text's torrent of information.[21]

It seems likely that this chain of events led subsequent historians to approach this volume of the *Muqtabis* with a degree of caution. Devoid of context and framed by a narrative packed with diverse events and scenarios, this volume of the *Muqtabis* has been identified as a rich repository of information on a range of specific aspects of the Caliphate of Córdoba, yet no overarching interpretation of the information it provides has ever been attempted. This is the task undertaken in this book. Yet, prior to embarking on this endeavour it must be first asked who is the author of this singular text. As will be seen, this is by no means a simple question.

The *Muqtabis* and the Work of ʿĪsā al-Rāzī

The manuscript that Codera discovered in Algeria, and that was edited by al-Ḥajjī and translated by García Gómez, is part of a major historical work entitled the *Muqtabis*, which is the main chronicle and basis of our knowledge for the first three centuries of the presence of Islam in the Iberian Peninsula.[22] Its author was a historian known as Ibn Ḥayyān, who belonged to a family of clients (*mawālī*) of the Umayyad caliphs. His father, Khalaf, had distinguished himself as an excellent reader of the Qur'an since he was a child, and later he went on to undertake various roles as secretary and official at the heart of

[21] The original translation also lacked indexes, which were written years later by P. Balaña Abadía, 'Índices de los Anales palatinos de al-Ḥakam II', pp. 227–48.

[22] The discussion that follows draws on the principal works devoted to Ibn Ḥayyān: E. García Gómez, 'A propósito de Ibn Ḥayyān', pp. 395–424; P. Chameta, 'Deux précisions d'historiographie hispano-arabe', pp. 330–5; M. J. Viguera, 'Referencia a una fecha en que escribe Ibn Ḥayyān', pp. 429–32; M. L. Ávila, 'La fecha de redacción del *Muqtabis*', pp. 93–108; B. Soravia, 'Ibn Ḥayyān, historien du siècle des taifas'; L. Molina, 'Técnicas de *amplificatio* en el *Muqtabis* de Ibn Ḥayyān', pp. 55–79; J. Mohedano Barceló, *Biblioteca de al-Andalus*, vol III, s.v. Ibn Ḥayyān (nn. 584 and 585).

the caliphal administration. His son, Ḥayyān b. Khalaf, usually known as Ibn Ḥayyān, was born in Córdoba in 987 or 988 (377 AH), when al-Manṣūr was at the height of his power. During his youth, he was taught by reputed teachers, which may have set him on the path to a promising future at the heart of the Caliphal administration. However, these hopes were shattered by the start of the civil war of the caliphate in early 1009, when he was just twenty-one: during the next two decades, his life was marked by that war, which led to the traumatic demise of the Umayyad caliphate. For people like Ibn Ḥayyān, whose fortune was closely tied to the dynasty's fate, its extinction was a loss they would never recover from. In his old age – Ibn Ḥayyān died in Córdoba in 1076 (469 AH) aged almost ninety – the historian recalled the years of the *fitna*, and reflected on the profound anguish that it had caused him and the great lengths he had gone to overcome its impact.

During those troubled years, Ibn Ḥayyān came up with the idea of writing 'The Grand History' (*al-Ta'rīkh al-Kabīr*), which was to be divided into two parts: one, *al-Matīn* – 'What Is Solid' – described the events which he had himself witnessed and about which he wrote in a very personal tone that described the confusion and uncertainty of the period that the taifa kingdoms had given rise to; the other part was what we would today call a 'prequel', and contained the history of al-Andalus from its origins up until the beginning of *al-Matīn*. Ibn Ḥayyān named this part *al-Muqtabis fī ta'rīkh rijāl al-Andalus* ('What another's candle brings to the history of the men of al-Andalus'), a title justified because he based his account on the works of the Arab chroniclers who had preceded him: he copied fragments of their works, reordered them, highlighted parts that seemed important to him, and occasionally compiled various versions of the same event. He thereby took the 'lit candle of others' to narrate al-Andalus history, especially that of the Umayyad dynasty, as he usually quoted the sources he took his information from.

Ibn Ḥayyān's *Muqtabis* was composed of a number of volumes, perhaps ten, of which only three have survived in their complete form (volumes II, III and V), to which may be added the lengthy fragment contained in the manuscript rescued by Francisco Codera in Constantina.[23] Currently there

[23] They are the following: volume II, whose published text covers the years 796–881 and the rule of the emirs al-Ḥakam I (796–822) and 'Abd al-Raḥmān II (822–52) and part of the rule of the emir Muḥammad (852–86); volume III, whose published text covers the years of the emir 'Abd

is a scholarly consensus that this fragment corresponds to volume VII. It is possible that this view may change following future discoveries, but at present this is the prevailing opinion and it is adhered to here, whereby this source will be referred to as *Muqtabis VII* in this book. A reference contained in the text indicates that Ibn Ḥayyān was composing this volume at the outbreak of the disturbances that would result in the civil war, around 1010.[24] This contrasts with the internal evidence provided by the other remaining volumes, which reveal that Ibn Ḥayyān wrote them between 1039 and 1058, by which time the Umayyad caliphate of Córdoba was a thing of the past. Therefore, it would seem that the *Muqtabis* was not written following a chronological order, and that volume VII was composed by Ibn Ḥayyān while still a young man, perhaps as a scholarly exercise, whereby he would have concluded the preceding volumes at a much later date.

As has been mentioned, in the *Muqtabis* Ibn Ḥayyān compiled the work of various Umayyad authors from the caliphal period. The two authors whose work he cited with most frequency are Aḥmad al-Rāzī and his son ʻĪsā: both wrote historical texts that are today lost.[25] Aḥmad was the son of a trader originally from Persia (from Rayy, south of what is today Tehran, hence his name al-Rāzī), who travelled across northern Africa and the Near East selling both merchandise and information, and had frequent dealings with the Umayyad emir. He died suddenly in 890 while visiting al-Andalus, leaving the three-year-old Aḥmad. Somehow, this orphan made his way to the court of ʻAbd al-Raḥmān III, where he worked as a secretary, chronicler and occasional court poet. Prior to his death in 955, Ahmad wrote an ambitious work entitled *History of the Kings of al-Andalus* (*Ta'rīkh fī akhbār mulūk al-Andalus*), which began with a long geographical description of the peninsula and an account of the land's history from the pre-Islamic period to the times of the Umayyad caliphate in Córdoba.

Allāh (888–912); and volume V, which covers part of the rule of ʻAbd al-Raḥmān III from 912 up to 942. From that year and up until this caliph's death in 961 there would, therefore, exist a sixth volume with the rest of this caliph's reign. The caliphate of al-Ḥakam II would be contained in volume VII.

[24] On the period during which Ibn Ḥayyān was composing this volume see p. 164.

[25] The foregoing discussion draws on L. Molina, *Biblioteca de al-Andalus*, vol. 7, s.v. al-Rāzī (nn. 1,652, 1,653 and 1,654).

Aḥmad's son, 'Īsā, also served the caliph as a historian. He must have been born in the early tenth century. Little is known of his life, or of his character, aside from the fact that he served as a secretary in the caliphal court and had an inquisitive mind. He died in late 989 (379 AH). His most important work, written on the orders of the Caliph al-Ḥakam II, was entitled *The Complete Book* (*Kitāb al-Mū'ib*). This work, possibly written in an annalistic form, included the events that 'Īsā was witnessing at the court of al-Ḥakam II. These 'annals', which exude an official courtly style, were subsequently used by Ibn Ḥayyān to compose his volume VII of his *Muqtabis*, where he reproduced them in full, as he basically copied what had been written by 'Īsā al-Rāzī.

The fragment of Ibn Ḥayyān's manuscript, which this book is based on, comprises the years between 971 and 975 (361 to 364 AH). It is, therefore, a fragment of volume VII of the *Muqtabis*, in which Ibn Ḥayyān works as if he were the 'editor' of 'Īsā al-Rāzī's text. Given that Ibn Ḥayyān's contribution is minimal, García Gómez decided to give his translation the title *Anales Palatinos del califa de Córdoba al-Ḥakam II por 'Īsā ibn Aḥmad al-Rāzī* (*Court Annals of the Caliph of Córdoba al-Ḥakam II by Īsā ibn Aḥmad al-Rāzī*). However, this title is misleading and it is more accurate to read the text as a fragment of the volume of the *Muqtabis* written by Ibn Ḥayyān using 'Īsā al-Rāzī's annals. It is true that he reproduces *in extenso* the earlier text, and on two occasions even notes how the manuscript he is copying contains lacunas.[26] However, Ibn Ḥayyān also includes short comments of his own in parts of the text, whereby in a sense he is also editing the manuscript that he is copying.[27]

The manuscript of the *Muqtabis* found by Francisco Codera in Constantine had no title page – generations of moths may well have consumed it – whereby, with no prior explanation, it presents readers with events that

[26] Ibn Ḥayyān records one lacuna in the text of the manuscript that he was using at the end of 361 AH, between the month of *Dhū l-ḥijja* that year and the end of *Rabī' I* in 362, which corresponds to September 972 and the end of December that same year. Another lacuna is identified between the months of *Sha'bān* and *Ramaḍān* for the year 363, which corresponds with the end of April and May 974, Ibn Ḥayyān, *Muqtabis VII*, ed. cit. pp. 95–6 and 155; trans. cit. pp. 123 and 196.

[27] He specifically does so on three occasions: he comments on the events that led a number of Berber tribal leaders to seek refuge in al-Andalus; he also includes a lengthy comment very critical of the north African policy of caliph al-Ḥakam II and its consequences; and finally, he demonstrates his historical erudition quoting an Eastern precedent for a title bestowed by the caliph al-Ḥakam II, Ibn Ḥayyān *Muqtabis VII*, ed. cit. 33–8, 189–94 and 221–2; trans. cit. pp. 54–8, 228–33 and 261–2.

had taken place in Córdoba during the summer of 971 (360 in the Muslim calendar). Following several verses of a laudatory poem, the text begins as follows:

> On Friday 25 of Shaʿbān of this year [360 AH] after prayer, the public defamation of Ibn ʿUmar, the swindler known as Wāhib al-Ḥājib, was held. He was placed in the upper gallery of the Dār al-Ṣadaqa, to the west of the Friday mosque, and once he was visible to the crowds, the muezzin called out alongside the gallery: 'Oh peoples (God have mercy on us). This subject is Aḥmad b. ʿUmar, dubbed Wāhib, criminal and thief, who devours the money of Muslims with his swindlery.'

We have not the least idea who this Ahmad b. ʿUmar was, nor what his crime was. However, these brief lines land us slap-bang in caliphal Córdoba, where the crowds making their way out from the Friday prayers held in its celebrated main mosque were addressed by a muezzin announcing the offender's public humiliation. He did so from a building called the Alms House (*Dār al-Ṣadaqa*), which on its top floor had a gallery that opened onto the street. It was located in front of the west façade of the Cordoban mosque, which is today the site of various souvenir shops and a hotel. Suddenly, we can cast a glance through the thick wall of time that separates us from the caliphate of Córdoba and contemplate a crowd which gathers to hear an important announcement outside the mosque, at a recognisable location for us today. Information such as this recurs throughout *Muqtabis VII*, and in the chapters that follow this will be recounted with all the perspicuity that the data permit.

To sum up: at the court of al-Ḥakam II a secretary, called ʿĪsā al-Rāzī, following in the footsteps of his father, composed a series of official annals that described the events of the caliphal reign taking place around him. Years later, Ibn Ḥayyān, distraught at the crisis faced by the Umayyad caliphate, used these annals to compose what probably ended up being the seventh volume of his *Muqtabis*, a historical work in which he set out the grand narrative of that dynasty. As the colophon of the manuscript found by Codera informs us, centuries later, in 1249, somebody in Ceuta copied this volume of the *Muqtabis*. This manuscript was subsequently used to make another copy, one that ended up on the shelves of the library of the Awlād al-Fakkūn family in Constantine. In January 1888, Francisco Codera, the Spanish Arabist, was searching for manuscripts related to Iberian medieval history in North Africa. He was told of this manuscript and obtained a copy of it from al-Makkī b. ʿAlī b. Aḥmad al-Fakkūn – who probably did so out of altruism. This copy was deposited in the library of the Real Academia de la Historia in Madrid and became a *unicum* due to the disappearance of the Algerian library. Various decades later, in the late 1940s, another Spanish Arabist, Emilio García Gómez, planned to publish this manuscript, but he spent various decades working on this project, whereby in 1965 an Iraqi scholar, ʿAbd al-Raḥmān ʿAlī al-Ḥajjī, published his own edition first; one that can at best be said to have been rushed. Following a considerable polemic, García Gómez published his translation of the text, and while its content was excellent, it lacked the necessary critical apparatus. The history of this text, written by ʿĪsā al-Rāzī, presumably within the walls of Madīnat al-Zahrāʾ and Córdoba's *alcázar*, and later copied by Ibn Ḥayyān at the time of the outbreak of the disturbances that would bring an end to the Umayyad caliphate, dates back over more than a millennium, and has been anything but boring.

About this Book

The 'Palace Annals', as E. García Gómez termed them, or *Muqtabis VII* as the book is more appropriately referred to today, is not a mere historical chronicle, but rather a register of the many activities that took place at the court of al-Ḥakam II. It is thereby possible to imagine ʿĪsā al-Rāzī carrying out the task of taking notes about who the caliph granted receptions to, the arrangements that were made and how military expeditions were organised, as well as a lengthy 'et cetera' of occurrences and events that took place on a daily basis in the caliphate and had to be recorded. His record, therefore, forms a written register of the caliphal institution, which would have been frequently consulted whenever it had to be ascertained what had happened on a specific date, what precedence had been given to individuals at a particular reception, the circumstances in which a certain letter had been sent, or the occasion on which a particular North African tribal chieftain had pledged his obedience to the caliph. It is thus advisable to bear in mind that ʿĪsā al-Rāzī was not working for twenty-first-century historians, but for his master, the caliph, who had ordered him to draft this chronological inventory of all that was taking place during the course of his reign.

Analysed from this perspective, the historical register undertaken by ʿĪsā al-Rāzī is a solid representation of the Caliphate of Córdoba. For the reasons given in Chapter 3, this political formation should be considered as a 'state': it had a stable centralised structure that survived the individuals who ruled it; it owned resources that may be distinguished from any form of personal wealth; and, finally, it displayed rituals and symbols that articulated specific narratives. No other polity in Western Europe at that time possessed such an impressive political and institutional apparatus. Neither the Christian kingdoms and counties in the Iberian north, nor the remnants of the Carolingian empire, came close, and not even the empire the Ottonian sovereigns achieved the levels of political and organisational complexity that the people of al-Andalus were accustomed to.

My aim in this book is to offer an accurate and comprehensive account of this state. Drawing on the data provided by ʿĪsā al-Rāzī, I seek to explain how its mechanisms enabled it to operate. However, elucidating the information contained in the *Muqtabis* has proved to be a more complex task than I had initially envisioned. The people and functions that made up the caliphal state were many and varied, and the task of ordering them, making them intelligible and relating them to one another has proved to be arduous: it has been necessary to identify dozens of people; decipher the meaning of the numerous court posts and roles they undertook; understand the political and social circumstances that surrounded them; explain their motives; and locate the places they frequented. None of this is an easy task, because ʿĪsā al-Rāzī takes for granted that his readers are familiar with the references he is making, and therefore he rarely bothers to give specific explanations, which he would have deemed superfluous. An additional problem is that many references made in the text are not always evident. They include fragments of poetry by court poets, interwoven religious allusions, sayings and malicious word-plays that all in all offer a range of insights into the court and the particular culture it had evolved, yet its codes are not always easy to make sense of.

Another issue I have had to tackle is that, when using such a detailed source, its descriptions of events tend to be overly meticulous, whereby my own account risked being flooded with an infinite number of details that are not always relevant and make it hard to see the wood for the trees. I have, therefore, endeavoured to prevent my source's wealth of detail from overwhelming this book. In the chapters that follow, I have concentrated on the specific elements that guide my historical interpretation, while the numerous identifications, clarifications and explanations that ʿĪsā al-Rāzī's text requires are set out in the footnotes. On occasions these notes are somewhat lengthier than I would have liked, but I hope they will be of use to specialists on this period.

The clarification of the data provided by ʿĪsā al-Rāzī would not be of much interest were it not accompanied by an interpretation of both how and why the Umayyad caliphate could exist in the mid-tenth century yet end in failure. The interpretative dimension of this book requires a theoretical framework that permits the historical data to be interpreted in a coherent manner. As in all my work, this framework is founded on historical materialism, which in my view provides the best means via which to understand social processes of the past. In particular, and as I explain in detail in Chapter 2, the development of historical materialism in recent decades has provided an increasingly clearer understanding of tax-based social formations, among which Andalusí society was undoubtedly included. An understanding of the mechanisms that enabled the ruling classes to extract economic surplus from society provides the fundamental explanation for the main historical factors at work at the court of al-Ḥakam II.

Over the course of this book, I frequently employ the concepts *power* and *authority*, and my use of them also requires a brief explanation. When I speak of *power* I do so using Max Weber's broad definition, which refers to the capacity of social actors to impose their will irrespective of the resistance encountered or the social base that sustains it.[28] On the other hand, *authority* expresses the same concept of social actors imposing their will, but in this case resistance is vanquished through arguments of legitimacy and persuasion, which results in this relationship of domination incorporating a degree of consent among the exploited. As will be seen, the Umayyad caliphs of al-Andalus exercised their *power* through bureaucratic and military means, while their *authority* was based on their perception of themselves as legitimate heirs to a dynasty, whose ancestors had managed to preserve Muslim orthodoxy for the benefit of their subjects.

[28] N. Uphoff, 'Distinguishing Power, Authority and Legitimacy', pp. 295–322.

The Umayyad caliphs' need to clothe their *power* in a powerful narrative of *authority* based on religious orthodoxy, or in other words, the need for their power to have a generalised consent, contributed to granting the Muslim community, or *umma*, far greater political relevance than has generally been accepted. Western historiography has often applied to Islamic political formations the sweeping term of 'despotic' and has constructed a rhetorical image in which power was exercised without the least consideration for the subjects' welfare or concerns. As will be argued in this book, there are numerous reasons to dispute the validity of this idea. The Muslim community was a very active element in early medieval Islamic polities, and rulers were always wholly conscious that their policies might encounter staunch resistance from the *umma*, which upheld solid moral and doctrinal principles that were underpinned by Muslim tradition. At the height of the tenth (fourth AH) century, Islamic tradition had coalesced into a highly coherent *corpus* of beliefs and practices that could be invoked to pass judgement on any social or political question that arose, which would prompt an equally articulate response in favour or against.[29] As a result, three premises – the form adopted for the exercise of power, the way in which authority was imposed, and the modes of subjects' resistance and consent – are consistently foregrounded throughout this work, and they constitute a core focus that articulates its discussion.

Addressing the difficulties of such a detailed source, in conjunction with the need to offer an interpretation of the Umayyad caliphate, has required a much greater effort than was anticipated at the outset of this project. At times it seemed that the text's multifaceted complexity might undermine my nerve and render it yet another vain attempt to address a wholly problematic text. It has been necessary to read and reread this source many times, to think and rethink how one should interpret its content, and to check and recheck the huge amount of data and details that arise on each and every line. One result of this is the realisation that, very often, the data provided by ʿĪsā al-Rāzī are susceptible to analysis from diverse perspectives: a gift presented to a tribal chieftain by caliphal emissaries demonstrates the operation of Umayyad diplomacy, but the textiles, and other luxury objects the gift consisted of, which are

[29] E. Manzano Moreno, 'Why Did Islamic Medieval Institutions Become So Different from Western Medieval Institutions?', pp. 118–37.

duly listed by the chronicler, provide extremely valuable information about the material culture of the period. Therefore, over the course of the pages that follow, the reader may often encounter the same event studied from distinct perspectives.

The writing of this book has taken longer than had originally been expected, due in part to the aforementioned difficulties. My colleagues at St John's College Oxford, where I was a visiting researcher, and those at the University of Chicago, where I was appointed Tinker Visiting Professor in 2014, heard me make such optimistic calculations for this project's completion during talks and seminars I gave that it is very possible that its existence has slipped their minds. Yet this does not stop me from expressing my gratitude for the remarkable support they provided, as well as for the invaluable opportunity they gave me, which allowed me to refine the ideas presented in the pages that follow.

During the lengthy process of writing this book, I have likewise received a wealth of excellent insights from research projects which I have collaborated in and which have enabled me to work with some of the best medievalists, Arabists, Byzantinists, anthropologists and archaeologists of my generation. Taking part in the research project *Power and Institutions in Medieval Islam and Christendom*, which was financed by European research funding, gave me the opportunity to compare Muslim and Christian institutions, and this led to the surprising conclusion that the former had a much more accentuated community component than the latter.[30] This book has likewise benefited from a number of research projects undertaken on the palace-city of Madīnat al-Zahrā' and, in particular, the most recent of these, which undertook a comparison between the Umayyad and Fāṭimid caliphates.[31] This project has pursued a line of enquiry that has combined both an analysis of archaeological remains and the study of texts, and in particular, *Muqtabis VII*.

I would also like to express my thanks, as ever, to the staff of the Biblioteca Tomás Navarro Tomás at the Centro de Ciencias Humanas y Sociales of the CSIC (Consejo Superior de Investigaciones Científicas), without whose

[30] International Training Network Grant, *Power and Institutions in Medieval Islam and Christendom* (PIMIC), ITN no. 31672.

[31] Ministerio de Economía y Competitividad: *Fatimíes y Omeyas: la pugna de los califatos en el Magreb y sus efectos en al-Andalus*, HAR2013-40745-P.

efficiency and splendid work my efforts as a researcher in this institution would be impossible. Likewise, I must also thank the management team at the Conjunto Arqueológico de Madīnat al-Zahrā', who provided me with all the necessary facilities to study this striking architectural complex, which has recently been classified as a World Heritage site by UNESCO. In the same vein, I want to express my gratitude to the Oficina de Arqueología (Archaeology Department) at the Gerencia Municipal de Urbanismo (Municipal Town Planning Department) in Córdoba, whose staff not only allowed me to visit some of the fascinating excavations being undertaken in the city, but also supplied me with excellent reproductions with which to illustrate the final chapter of this book. Naturally, many people form part of these institutions, projects and publications; however, the reader will very likely be grateful that I pause here, and express my gratitude to them in person.

I

The Caliphate and the Natural and Human Cycles

Floods and Droughts: the Medieval Climatic Anomaly

On 19 February 974 (363 AH), after many days of heavy rain, the River Guadalquivir burst its banks and flooded Córdoba's riverside market, with the floodwater rising above the butchers' counters. A few weeks later, at the start of April, another rise in the river's level once more inundated these shops. Neither of these episodes resulted in any victims, but a few decades later, in 1010 (401 AH), another flooding of the Guadalquivir is said to have caused hundreds of deaths. When in spate, the river could wreak destruction, as it could rise seven and as much as ten metres above its normal level. Even today, and despite the Guadalquivir being carefully controlled by reservoirs and dams, the city of Córdoba floods when the river's discharge rises above 1,500 cubic metres per second; when it reaches 5,400 cubic metres it causes disaster, as occurred in 1963. Obviously, during the Umayyad caliphate much lower volumes could quite conceivably cause major catastrophes.[1]

Floods, just like droughts, had a considerable impact on the natural order of things in the caliphate of Córdoba: harvests, tax collecting, military campaigns and trading activity were all affected by torrential rain and oppressive

[1] Ibn Ḥayyān, *Muqtabis VII*, ed. al-Hajjī, pp. 209–10; trans. García Gómez, pp. 249–50. Ibn ʻIdhārī, *al-Bayān al-Mughrib*, III, ed. Lévi-Provençal, p. 105; trans. F. Maíllo p. 97. Another catastrophic flood of the Guadalquivir took place in 235 AH and affected Seville and Écija, Ibn Ḥayyān, *Muqtabis II*, 2, ed. p. 5. On modern floods in Córdoba, see M. Moya, 'Córdoba bajo las lluvias y la riada de 1963', *Cordópolis*, 17 February 2017, http://www.cordopolis.es (last accessed 12 November 2022).

droughts. As a result, at the court of al-Ḥakam II the climate, far from being considered a trivial matter, was subject to meticulous study: the weather was recorded on a regular basis, its effects on the harvests were carefully assessed, and, when conditions became severe and struck the people with unexplainable force, the caliph and the religious Muslim leaders prayed to God beseeching him to alleviate the suffering these disasters were causing. Thereby, to counter the unforeseeable nature of the elements, a powerful courtly narrative was fashioned of the Umayyad caliphate as encompassing a predictive capacity that sought to mitigate the consequences of the trials God unleashed on the peoples of al-Andalus.

From the second half of the ninth century (third AH) these trials tended to become more frequent, as extreme climatic conditions increased. This was caused by the beginning of what has been termed the 'Medieval Climatic Anomaly', which caused temperatures and rainfall in the Western hemisphere to undergo significant changes. In the North Atlantic, average temperatures rose, which caused the thaw that enabled Viking expeditions to reach North America and even the establishment of human settlements in Greenland. Confirmation of this as a period of climate warming is also found in other regions such as the Alps, where larch tree rings, whose size reflects temperature and humidity levels, record two decades of high temperatures between 960 and 980. In Morocco, the analysis of stalactites and stalagmites formed by the filtration of water in caves demonstrates that in general terms the tenth century was dry. Data from the Iberian Peninsula corroborates the same trend. The sediment of lakes such as Estanya (Huesca), Montcortés (Lérida) and Zoñar (Córdoba) reveals that more arid conditions prevailed during this period in the Iberian Peninsula.[2]

[2] General overview in U. Büntgen et al., '2500 years of European Climate Variability', *Science*, 331, pp. 578–82. A useful summary in G. Sánchez Lopez et al. 'Climate Reconstruction for the Last Two Millennia in Central Iberia' pp. 135–50. On the Alps, U. Büntgen et al., 'Summer Temperature Variations in the European Alps, A.D. 755–2004', p. 5,613. On Morocco, J. A. Wassenburg et al., 'Moroccan Speleothem and Tree Ring Records'. On Lake Estanya, M. Morelló et al., 'Climate Changes and Human Activities Recorded in the Sediments of Lake Estanya (NE Spain)', pp. 423–52. On Montcortés, J. P. Corella et al., 'Climate and Human Impact on a Meromictic Lake during the Last 6000 years (Montcortès Lake, Central Pyrenees, Spain)', pp. 351–67. On Zoñar, C. Martín Puertas et al., 'Arid and Humid Phases in Southern Spain during the Last 4000 Years', pp. 907–21. An overview in A. Moreno et al., 'The Medieval Climate Anomaly in the Iberian Peninsula', pp. 16–32.

Palaeo-climatologists attribute this period of warming to the behaviour of a phenomenon called the North Atlantic Oscillation (NAO). In very simple terms, this oscillation is explained by changes at sea level caused by high pressure in the Azores, and the shift in wind direction, which were determined by the predominant low pressure in Iceland. When this oscillation is negative west winds dominate, bringing rain and low temperatures; when the values are positive the wind direction changes, which brings warmer and drier weather. Simulations of the NAO during the 'Medieval Climatic Anomaly' confirm that in this period the prevailing conditions caused a trend towards warming. However, the reasons for this are not entirely clear, and possible causes for the environment having grown warmer during the Early Middle Ages include an increase in solar radiation or a decline in volcanic activity.[3]

Evidence for the climate in al-Andalus during this period is ambivalent. As will be seen below, the years covered by the annals of 'Īsā al-Rāzī, 971 to 975 (360–4 AH), were marked by heavy rain and even snow, which would no doubt have prompted outbursts from any climate change deniers of the day. However, a broader vision confirms that, from a century earlier, dry periods had been occurring very frequently in Iberia.[4] In 867 (253 AH) there was a decimating drought, which lasted four years. Another in 874 (260 AH) was so terrible that it was recalled in proverbial terms. The drought in 898 (285 AH) was known as the 'year of misery', and the famine of 907–8 (297 AH) led to many people emigrating to North Africa. Shortly afterwards, between 915 and 916 (302–3 AH), another drought, 'comparable' to that of 874, gripped al-Andalus with such force that 'the dead numbered so many ... they could neither be counted, nor comprehended'. There were other droughts in 887 (274 AH), 926–7 (314 AH), 929–30 (317 AH) and 936 (323 AH). The last of these did not

[3] V. Trouet, V et al., 'Persistent Positive North Atlantic Oscillation', pp. 78–80. The increase in solar activity could perhaps be confirmed by a curious report that records a cloud-like spot appearing on the sun's surface in October 939 (*Muḥarram* 328 AH), which could be seen by the naked eye and caused a partial eclipse of the sun's light for a week, J. Vernet, 'Algunos fenómenos astronómicos', pp. 25–6. It is also possible that an increase in solar activity may be related to the observation of an aurora borealis in Córdoba on 27 April 942 (7 *Sha'bān* 330 AH), as sources describe how 'a glowing light rose in the sky, while a bright luminescence lit up the branches of palm trees and the pinnacles of the *Alcázar*' and 'two arches that rose on the horizon', Ibn Ḥayyān, *Muqtabis V*, ed. and trans. p. 322. Other auroras were observed in low latitudes during these decades, J. M. Vaquero and M. C. Gallego, 'Two Early Observations of Aurora at Low Latitudes', pp. 809–11.

[4] J. C. de Miguel Rodríguez, 'Precipitaciones y sequías en el valle del Guadalquivir', pp. 55–76.

prove to be so devastating, because the caliphal administration had arranged for provisions to be brought from all around, whereby 'in general, there was prosperity, without poverty'. In 941–2 (330 AH) there was another episode of drought, which was alleviated by the arrival of rain and snow in early February, which the chroniclers attribute to the success of the caliph's order that supplications be made to God. There was a further drought in 946–7 (335 AH) and another during the rule of al-Ḥakam II, in 964 (353 AH), to which the caliph responded by providing food for the people living in Córdoba's outlying suburbs. Four years later, in 968 (358 AH), drought struck again with such severity that the caliph had to distribute 12,000 loaves of bread daily to the people of Córdoba until conditions improved.[5]

Such droughts had major repercussions, and, although it seems that things returned to normal fairly swiftly, they had a significant impact on the caliphal administration. Market prices rose considerably, to the extent that an *almudí* of wheat – just under 340 kilos – could cost as much as thirty dinars (around 240 silver dirhams), five times its usual price.[6] Food shortages also led to the suspension of military campaigns, as the uncertainty surrounding the normal supply of troops made them hazardous endeavours. The tax revenue would

[5] Ibn 'Idhārī, *al-Bayān al-Mughrib*, II, ed. Colin and Lévi-Provençal, p. 100; trans. Fagnan p. 163 on the drought of 253 AH; ed. p. 102; trans. p. 167 on that of 260 AH; ed. p. 119; trans. pp. 195–6 on that of 274 AH; ed. p. 236; trans. p. 389 on that of 353 AH; Ibn Ḥayyān, *Muqtabis, II, 2*, ed. Makki, p. 321; for 253 AH; p. 343 on that of 260 AH; Ibn Ḥayyān, *Muqtabis, III, 2*, ed. al-'Arabī, pp. 150 and 168; trans. G. Turienzo, pp. 240 and 273; Ibn Ḥayyān, *Muqtabis V* ed. and trans. F. Corriente and M. J. Viguera, pp. 67, 71–2, 83, 134, 165–6, 260 and 321 (the page numbers refer to the numbering in bold found in both the ed. and the trans.) on the droughts pp. 302–3, 314, 317, 323 and 330 AH; on the drought of 358 AH, *Dhikr bilād al-Andalus*, ed. and trans. L. Molina, pp. 173 and 183.

[6] Cancellation of the expeditions and charitable acts to be made by the caliph and his courtiers, Ibn Ḥayyān, *Muqtabis V*, ed. and trans. p. 71; difficulties in tax gathering and the brutality of tax collectors in Ibn al-Qūṭiya, *Ta'rīkh iftitāḥ*, ed. P. de Gayangos et al., pp. 87–8; trans. James, 118. The figure of thirty dinars for one *almudí* is given in Ibn Ḥayyān, *Muqtabis II*, 1, ed. Makki, p. 412; trans. F. Corriente, pp. 275–6. The exchange rate of one *almudí* of wheat for six dinars is mentioned in a letter written by the *taifa* sovereign 'Alī b. Ḥammūd to his governor of Jaén, compiled in Ibn Bassām, *al-Dhakhīra*, ed. I. 'Abbās, I, p. 120; one *almudí* of wheat and two of barley were more than sufficient provisions for a family for a period of nine months, al-Khushanī, *Quḍāt Qurṭuba*, ed. and trans. J. Ribera, pp. 110–11 and 133–6; rise in crime in ibid., pp. 178 and 220. A graphic description of a prayer for rain towards the end of the caliphate of 'Abd al-Raḥmān III, in al-Nubāhī, *al-Marqaba al-'ulyā*, ed. and trans. pp. 102–3; trans. pp. 237–8. My calculation of an *almudí* is based on information provided by E. López Martínez de Marigorta, who is currently working on a study of this subject. This unit of measurement should not be confused with the so-called 'almud of the Prophet', which I refer to below on occasions.

also fall below that of a normal year, unless tax collectors resorted to extreme violence. More crimes were committed, which in turn resulted in widespread complaints. Finally, when faced by catastrophe, there were always those who began to spread rumours and declare that the deeds of men and, above all, those of their rulers were not to God's liking, something that stirred up popular unrest in proportion to the rising prices of wheat and barley.[7]

One of the consequences of droughts was that the prices stipulated in agricultural contracts could not be paid. For farmers bound by sharecropping contracts, this was a dramatic situation, as they were unable to pay their rents due to their diminished harvest. However, the extraordinary development of Islamic law in al-Andalus during the caliphal period anticipated this type of scenario, which jurists referred to by the Arabic term *jā'iḥa*, which may be translated as 'in the event of disaster'. Drought (*qaḥṭ*) or floods were such disasters – as were frosts, hailstorms, fires and plagues – and legal texts make it clear that their occurrence permitted sharecroppers to negotiate a reduction in their payments to landlords.[8] In times of drought, a state of emergency would be officially declared following the inspection by a series of expert witnesses, who examined 'the shoots of that year's harvest' in the fields, and assessed whether 'the drought had damaged what had been sown'. Experts went on to make a record of the losses for both the harvest and the seed that had to be reserved for the next sowing season. They then drafted a document, which had a testimonial status in case of complaints by the landlord. Another way of assessing a state of disaster, and thereby protecting sharecroppers, was to ask experts (*ahl al-baṣar*) to report on the average yield of the soil. If the yield was, for example, 1:6 in a normal year, the damage was estimated on the basis of this calculation, and it would be deducted from rent payments. If the enquiry affected market garden crops, such as squash, aubergine, henna or other crops, the garden well would also be inspected: a few turns of the water-wheel by the

[7] al-Nubāhī, *al-Marqaba al-'ulyā*, ed. and trans. A. Cuellas Marqués, pp. 113–14 and 250–1.

[8] I. Camarero Castellano, 'Acerca de las calamidades agrícolas', pp. 63–78, who uses, among others, the works of 'Abd al-Malik b. Ḥabīb (d. 854/239 AH), Ibn Abī Zayd al-Qayrawānī (d. 996/386 AH), Ibn Abī Zamanīn (d. 1009/399 AH) and Ibn al-'Aṭṭār (d. 1009/399 AH), who all lived prior to the end of the Umayyad caliphate. See also I. Camarero Castellano, *Sobre el 'Estado de Ŷā'iḥa'*, pp. 65–8. In addition to these calamities, there were others such as theft and the ravages wrought by armies en route to their campaigns.

animal that powered it sufficed to reveal whether the water supply had been depleted by the drought.[9]

Therefore, many things in al-Andalus depended on the high pressure in the Azores and low pressure in Iceland remaining stable, which explains why in the caliph's court a detailed register was kept of weather changes. The official chronicler, ʿĪsā al-Rāzī, was responsible for this, and he meticulously wrote down atmospheric phenomena with the same detail as he recorded the mundane facts of courtly life. His observations reveal that at the end of 971 there were heavy rains, winds and even snow in Córdoba and its outlying districts, which continued into the spring of 972. The start of 973 was also very rainy, but at the beginning of April a dry spell was accompanied by frosts, which prompted serious concerns about the upcoming harvest. Fortunately, rains returned shortly afterwards. The autumn and winter of that year were marked by showers, with occasional hailstorms in late December. The year 974 also began with heavy rain and the spring brought strong winds that even uprooted olive trees, suggesting speeds of around 100 km/h. They were later followed by heavy rainstorms, which caused picturesque scenes, such as that which took place on Friday, 10 April (14 *Rajab*), when a heavy shower surprised people – most probably including ʿĪsā al-Rāzī himself – on their way to prayers in the main mosque in Córdoba. Crowds of soaked people pushed and shoved into the naves and galleries of the oratory seeking refuge from the torrential rain. The rainy weather continued throughout the late summer and early autumn. Finally, 975 began with snow in January, which gave way to heavy rain in March. Far away from Córdoba, in the middle of Lower Saxony, one of the authors of the *Annals of Hildesheim* described the winter of 975 as long and harsh, with snow falling even in May.[10] Thus, with the 'Medieval Climatic Anomaly' fully under way, the period from 971 to 975 proved to

[9] The testimony is based on a model listed in a notarial formula by the Cordoban Ibn al-ʿAṭṭār, *K. al-wathāʾiq wa l-sijillāt*, ed. P. Chalmeta, pp. 379–80, 383 and 391–2; trans. P. Chalmeta and M. Marugán, *Formulario notarial y judicial andalusí*, pp. 605, 613–14.

[10] Ibn Ḥayyān, *Muqtabis VII*, ed. Hajjī, pp. 66–7, 72–3, 100–1, 107, 144–5, 154, 187, 209–10; trans. E. García Gómez, pp. 88–9, 95, 129, 137–8, 183, 195, 226, 249–50. *Annales Hildesheimenses*, ed. G. Weitz, *Scriptores Rerum Germanicarum in usum scholarum ex Monumenta Germaniae Historicis recusi*, p. 23. An interpretation of these phenomena in accordance with modern study parameters in F. Domínguez Castro et al., 'Climatic Potential of Islamic Chronicles in Iberia', pp. 370–4.

be considerably rainy, as well as cold. This contrasts with the serious drought that had afflicted al-Andalus a few years before, in 968, and the one that struck afterwards in 989, yet all together these descriptions suggest a trend towards extreme climatic episodes.

As has been discussed, heavy rainfall could cause the Guadalquivir River to flood Córdoba, which was a recurrent phenomenon given the city's location along a pronounced meander of the river in its alluvial plain.[11] The Umayyad sovereigns were equally concerned about such floods. The Emir ʿAbd al-Raḥmān II (d. 852/238 AH) had ordered the construction of a stone and mortar road or pavement (*al-raṣīf*) in front of the *alcázar*'s walls that at this point merged with the walls of the medina. This road functioned as a form of defence flooding, but also as a thoroughfare running in parallel to the bank of the Guadalquivir and the southern walls of the city and of the *alcázar*: this provided an extra-mural route from one side of the city to the other without one having to wind one's way through the medina. The market stalls affected by the floods in February and April 974 formed the 'Butchers' lane' or *raṣīf al-Qaṣṣābīn*, which was to be found along the western section of this extra-mural road, a good location away from the city walls, from where unwanted scraps of butchered animals could be discarded into the river.[12]

In the following year, 975 (364 AH), the Guadalquivir flooded once more due to the March rains. This time, the flood affected the eastern section of the road built by ʿAbd al-Raḥmān II, the one running upstream from the ancient Roman bridge. On this occasion a tragic episode occurred. A woman and a eunuch wanted to return to their homes in the Shabulār suburb, on the river's right bank, from the village (*qarya*) of Secunda, on the left bank. Normally this journey would have been made by crossing the old Roman bridge and,

[11] Other floods occurred, for example, in January 850 (235 AH), *Muqtabis II, 2*, p. 5. In the winter of 1008 (399 AH) the floods rose very close to the dyers' shops in the souk and again two years later in – in 401 AH – when it is said that more than a thousand houses were destroyed and five thousand people died, figures that were perhaps exaggerated, but nonetheless confirm how destructive these floods could be, Ibn ʿIdhārī, *al-Bayān*, III, ed. Lévi-Provençal, pp. 48, 105; trans. F. Maíllo, pp. 53, 97. D. Uribelarrea and G. Benito, 'Fluvial Changes of the Guadalquivir River during the Holocene', pp. 14–31.

[12] E. García Gómez, 'Notas sobre la topografía cordobesa', pp. 343–5, 352, 370–2 and 374–5. Also *infra*, Ch. 10. For the building of the road, Ibn Ḥayyān, *Muqtabis, II, 1*, ed. and trans. pp. 280 and 172. Archaeological excavations have located its remains, J. F. Murillo et al. 'Investigaciones arqueológicas en la muralla de la Huerta del Alcázar', pp. 183–230.

without entering the city, taking a right turn along the aforementioned mortar road, which would lead to the extra-mural suburb of Shabulār. However, as this road was flooded, the pair had no other option but to enter the city by the Bridge Gateway (*bāb al-Qanṭara*), wind their way through the medina's streets and leave the city on the other side via the New Gate (*bāb al-Jadīd*) in order to enter the eastern suburb where they lived. Unfortunately, it was already night, and having crossed the Roman bridge they found the city gates to be closed, as at nightfall Córdoba's medina was sealed off. They then decided to engage the services of a boatman, who had moored alongside the bridge and was willing to take them upstream to the Shabulār suburb. However, bad luck befell them. The turbulent waters of the Guadalquivir overturned the boat. The woman and the eunuch drowned, while the boatman managed to swim to safety.[13]

The dramatic consequences of both an absence or excess of rainfall heightened concerns of finding methods of forecasting severe weather. The court astrologers offered assurances they could achieve this, as in their view the positions of the planets influenced droughts and abundant rain. In the early ninth century, ʻAbd al-Wāḥid b. Isḥāq al-Ḍabbī, an astrologer in the service of the Umayyad emirs, wrote a celebrated poem 'on predicting atmospheric events and the vicissitudes of monarchs'. A number of its verses, which describe the astrological events governing the driest and rainiest years, have survived: the presence of Saturn and Jupiter in the zodiacal fire signs (Aries, Leo and Sagittarius) announce that 'there will be drought on the plains and in the mountains, and people will die coughing. All this will be accompanied by migrations [of peoples], following a rise in prices, as well as illness afflicting the stomach and chest'. Astro-meteorology is also prominent in the work of another astrologist from this period, the Cordoban Qāsim b. Muṭarrif al-Qaṭṭān (born c. 915/302 AH), who linked the winds and the seasons to the position of the stars.[14]

[13] Ibn Ḥayyān, *Muqtabis VII*, ed. pp. 209–10; trans. pp. 249–50.

[14] J. Samsó, 'La primitiva versión árabe del *Libro de las Cruces*', pp. 149–61. Al-Ḍabbī's work underwent a re-elaboration in the mid-eleventh century; two hundred years later it was translated on the instructions of Alfonso X the Wise. J. Samsó, 'Sobre el astrólogo ʻAbd al-Wāḥid b. Isḥāq al-Ḍabbī (ca. 788–ca. 852)', pp. 657–69. J. Casulleras, 'The Contents of Qāsim b. Muṭarrif al-Qaṭṭān's *Kitāb al-Hay'a*', pp. 350–1. Another practical contribution made by this astrologer concerned the calculation of the equivalences between the Islamic and solar calendars, a matter which, as will be addressed below, was of great importance.

Weather forecasts are also found in one of the most interesting texts of this period, the so-called *Calendar of Córdoba*, written in 972 (361 AH) by a secretary of the Umayyad administration, 'Arīb b. Sa'īd, and Rabī' b. Zayd, who was the bishop of the city of Elvira (located near Atarfe, in what is today's province of Granada). It was an official document intended to be used as an almanac for administrative purposes related to the Christian community. Aside from including information on the agricultural tasks corresponding to each month and the Christian festivities celebrated around the year, this calendar also listed the dates on which taxes had to be sent to Córdoba, as we will see below. The *Calendar* likewise addressed the field of climatology, drawing on what was known as the 'traditions of the Arabs', according to which the cyclical movements of the stars (*anwā'*) indicate when rain would fall; as a specific star enters each phase of its cycle, 'it must necessarily be accompanied by rain, cold, wind and heat'.[15]

The influence of astrology upon the climate was not given any esoteric significance, but rather a practical, and to a certain extent scientific, one. In a world in which inexplicable things, such as the 'Medieval Climatic Anomaly', were occurring, writers of the caliphal period sought to amass the greatest possible number of weather and astronomical observations in the hope that they could identify relationships between them. This explains why, along with the profusion of meteorological data, the Umayyad chroniclers in general, and 'Īsā al-Rāzī in particular, likewise included astronomical observations in their writings. For example, 'Īsā al-Rāzī described a total eclipse of the moon, which took place on 15 September 973 (14 *Dhū l-Ḥijja* de 362 AH) and 'ended before dawn', an observation confirmed by modern calculations of past eclipses. However, it is harder to identify the large star that the chronicler said appeared on the southern side of the sky over Córdoba at three in the morning on 25 July that same year (21 *Ramaḍān*). It moved northwards before disappearing, and its brightness suggests it to have been a meteorite.[16]

[15] *Le Calendrier de Cordoue*, ed. and trans. pp. 4–5.

[16] Ibn Ḥayyān, *Muqtabis VII*, ed. pp. 118, 138; trans. pp. 155, 172. *Five Millennium Canon of Lunar Eclipses: -1999 to +3000 (NASA/TP-2009-214172)*, plate 358. A compilation of these phenomena in J. Vernet, 'Algunos fenómenos astronómicos observados bajo los omeyas españoles', pp. 23–30. In other regions of the Muslim world during the same period the observation of astronomical phenomena likewise permits the compilation of exact data, S. S. Said and F. R. Stephenson, 'Solar and Lunar Eclipse Measurements by Medieval Muslim Astronomers'.

ʿĪsā al-Rāzī also lists the exact date and hour of three earthquakes that were felt in Córdoba around that time. None of them was especially serious, but their frequency is striking. The most powerful one took place on Monday, 9 November 974 (21 *Ṣafar* 364) just after midday prayers, and although its effects were also noted in Coria (350 km north of Córdoba), it did not have any consequences.[17] However, the historical records compiled by ʿĪsā al-Rāzī's father, Aḥmad al-Rāzī, had also registered other earthquakes some decades earlier. A particularly violent one had shaken Córdoba in 881 (267 AH), just as evening prayers were being held, and it was also felt in the Christian territories of northern Iberia. Various tremors also affected the capital late on Sunday night and in the early hours of 8 July 944 (9 *Dhū l-qaʿda* 332 AH): they began after the final prayers of the day and after-shocks were felt throughout the night, which caused panic among the population, who sought shelter in the mosques. Another earthquake took place in August 955 (*Jumāda* I, 344 AH) and the after-shocks continued for a number of days. In cases such as these, it is often mentioned that tremors were followed by strong winds and rains.[18]

When neither planetary and astral observation nor telluric phenomena could predict the erratic behaviour of the rainclouds or drought that struck so mercilessly, there was always the option of prayer, the Islamic supplications for rain known as *istisqāʾ*. In Córdoba these supplications were often made by the city's *qāḍī* from the open-air oratory or *muṣallā* located close to the historic Secunda suburb. Another oratory of this type, which had been a former *muṣāra*, was to be found on the other side of the river and was used for holding

[17] The other two earthquakes took place on 19 December 971 (26 *Ṣafar* 361 AH) and 20 May 973 (14 *Shaʿbān* 362 AH), Ibn Ḥayyān, *Muqtabis VII*, ed. pp. 67, 107, 202; trans. pp. 89, 138, 243.

[18] Ibn ʿIdhārī, *al-Bayān al-Mughrib*, II, ed. pp. 104–5, 211 and 220; trans. pp. 171, 349–50 and 365. Earthquakes of an average intensity affected Córdoba before and after this period. Archaeologists have identified one in the final quarter of the third century CE that would have caused stairways to collapse, large blocks of stone to fall and paving to be upturned. In later periods earthquakes of middle or middle to high intensity are recorded for various years (1807, 1836 and, above all, 1900). J. M. Martínez Solares and J. Mezcua Rodríguez, *Catálogo Sísmico de la Península Ibérica (880 a.C.–1900)*; J. P. Morín et al., 'Evidencias arqueosismológicas en la Colonia Patricia Romana de Córdoba (Valle del Guadalquivir, España)', pp. 158–62. A critical overview in M. D. Ruiz Bueno, 'Actividad sísmica en el mediodía ibérico durante el siglo III d.C. La incidencia arqueológica en *Corduba* (Córdoba)', pp. 29–51; Instituto Geográfico Nacional, 'Terremotos más significativos por provincias en España', http://www.ign.es/web/ign/portal/terremotos-importantes (last accessed 12 November 2022).

special supplications from the mid-ninth century onwards. The governors of the provinces (*kūra*s) also received letters to ensure that in their districts the same measures were followed.[19]

The caliphal administration did whatever it could to predict, avoid, prepare for and mitigate the catastrophic effects of natural phenomena. At stake was not only the resources this administration depended on, but also the crucial issue of caliphal legitimacy. A caliph who shared no concerns for the needs of his subjects would have been a caliph with less right to govern, and therefore a rightful recipient of the divine punishment with which catastrophes such as droughts were associated. In periods of extreme need, the caliph by no means neglected his subjects and with noteworthy ostentation undertook the distribution of food to the poor, thereby demonstrating that his authority was not exercised in ignorance of the needs of the community of believers. This is why al-Ḥakam II distributed 12,000 loaves of bread daily to the people of Córdoba in the difficult times of the 968 (358 AH) drought. Twenty years later, in 989–90 (379 AH), a new devastating famine spread across al-Andalus and North Africa for three years. By then, al-Ḥakam II had died and his power had passed into the hands of a former civil servant from his administration, Muḥammad b. Abī ʿĀmir, who will frequently be mentioned in this book; he adopted the honorific surname al-Manṣūr ('the Victorious') around that time. Given the gravity of the situation, and in order to demonstrate his concern for the well-being of his needy subjects, al-Manṣūr ordered 22,000 loaves to be distributed daily to the people of Córdoba.[20] Furthermore, 'he helped the Muslims to feed the weak, and he pardoned the tithes, placed shrouds on the dead and aided the living'. It was this mixture of popular politics, such as the remission of taxes and pious actions that allowed the new ruler of al-Andalus to present himself as the defender of the welfare of the common people, who had been particularly afflicted by the shortages. It is evident that this was an attempt to bolster his rather weak legitimacy as the substitute of the caliph. Over the course of

[19] Ibn Ḥayyān, *Muqtabis V*, pp. 134 and 165–6. The supplications were moved to the *Muṣāra* after ʿAbd al-Malik b. Ḥabīb convinced the emir ʿAbd al-Raḥmān II that the suburb's oratory was not suitable due to the large crowds of people who blocked the bridge over the Guadalquivir, which had even caused deaths and injuries on occasions, J. Safran, *Defining Boundaries*, pp. 87–9.

[20] *Dhikr bilād al-Andalus*, ed. and trans. pp. 181–2 and 193. A. M. Carballeira, 'The Use of Charity' pp. 250–1.

this book, it will be seen how this relationship between the exercise of power and the concerns of the population is one of a number of striking factors that explain the political development of the caliphate of Córdoba.

The 'Works and Days' of the Caliph's Subjects

The chronicler 'Īsā al-Rāzī dates the events he narrates according to various calendars. First and foremost, he uses the Islamic calendar, based on the computation of the lunar years since the Hijra, or, in other words, the flight of the Prophet Muhammad from Mecca to Medina in 622 CE. This calendar consists of twelve lunar months, twenty-nine or thirty days long, whose annual cycle is shorter than a solar year, which is why years of the Muslim calendar often overlap two years of our era. The Islamic calendar was the one most commonly used in al-Andalus and it was printed on coins and used in documents and epigraphic inscriptions.

However, 'Īsā al-Rāzī also makes recourse to the solar calendar. In one case, at the beginning of the Islamic year, he notes its equivalence with the solar date: 'The 1 of Muḥarram, the start of this year (361 AH) began on Tuesday, 24 October in the solar calendar'.[21] But it is above all when including meteorological observations that 'Īsā makes recourse to the solar date in order to refer to the yearly seasons, as this is impossible with the ever-changing lunar calendar: 'At the start of the second decade of Muharram [363 AH], coinciding with the same date of the solar month of October [974], the date for the start of the sowing season, it began to rain on Córdoba and its outlying districts and did so copiously ... The people began to tend the barley (*al-qaṣīl*) and the prices, which had become very high, ceased to rise.'

Our chronicler, in fact, always records rainfall, or the lack of it, at two critical moments: in October, at the start of the sowing season in the Iberian

[21] It is striking that 'Īsā al-Rāzī also notes on two occasions the equivalence of the Islamic date with the Jewish calendar: in one case, he comments that the new moon rose in the month of *Shawwāl* in 360, corresponding to 28 *Tammūs* of the latter calendar; also, with regard to the supplications for rain referred to above, he mentions its equivalence with 29 *Nissan*, Ibn Ḥayyān, *Muqtabis VII*, ed. pp. 28 and 100–1; trans. pp. 51 and 129. I will refer below to how the Persian calendar was also used by al-Rāzī. Different dating systems were used at the Umayyad court, as is confirmed in Ibn Ḥayyān, *Muqtabis V*. ed. and trans. p. 56, in which the start of a campaign is dated with recourse to the Christian era, the so-called 'Hispanic era' and the 'era of Alexander', which began in 312 BCE. According to *Calendario de Córdoba*, ed. and trans. p. 21, the latter system was used by the Syrians.

Peninsula, and in April, when harvests are ripe. Concerns over the autumn and spring rains reflect what we know about peasants' seasonal tasks thanks to the *Calendar of Córdoba*, which accurately lists the work to be undertaken for each month of the solar year. Thus, in regions of al-Andalus, like the Llano de los Pedroches, Trujillo and the mountain districts near Córdoba, the *Calendar* states that the sowing season begins on 2 October, while in the lowland Cordoban countryside and other regions it starts later, around the twentieth of the same month. In the rest of al-Andalus, November is the month for sowing the main crops, which require a well-drenched soil after the summer heat. With regard to the harvest, for barley this begins on 5 May in places such as Córdoba, Málaga and Sidonia. Then, on 20 June the wheat starts to be harvested, whereby in July – presumably early on – the harvest of the winter cereal crops has been completed everywhere.[22]

There was, therefore, a very precise natural and administrative cycle, which was defined by a need for rain at critical moments of the year, as its absence augured drought, and, as a result, bad harvests and low fiscal revenues. What happened in April 973 is highly revealing: suddenly, at the start of this month, it stopped raining and, 'as people began to fear for their harvests', prayers were offered at the Friday mosques of Córdoba and Madīnat al-Zahrā'.[23] It sufficed for the rains not to arrive in early April for urgent invocations be made to God. The situation was not yet serious, which is why the supplications were made at the mosques, yet not at the 'suburban oratory' (*muṣallā al-rabaḍ*), as would happen at times of severe drought. However, when conditions worsened due to hailstorms on 13 April (7 *Rajab*), the supplications had to be repeated on Friday, 18 April (12 *Rajab*). Three days later the rains arrived, indicating that God had listened to prayers, so normality could be restored.[24] The year's crops, which began to be harvested in early May, had been saved.

The foregoing evidence reflects the cycle of winter cereal crops (wheat and barley mainly), which were planted between October and November and

[22] *Calendario de Córdoba*, ed. and trans. pp. 74–5, 82–3, 98–9, 148–9, 152–3, 172–3.
[23] Ibn Ḥayyān, *Muqtabis VII*, ed. pp. 100–1 and 144–5; trans. pp. 129 and 183.
[24] Ibn Ḥayyān, *Muqtabis VII*, ed. pp. 100–1; trans. p. 129. The final dating of the translation is not correct, and I have revised it in accordance with the critical edition of the manuscript. I have already underscored how striking it is that ʿĪsā al-Rāzī dates the second supplications according to the Jewish calendar. Likewise, the conversion of the Jewish date is incorrect in the translation, as 29 *Nissan* that year corresponds to 5 and not 7 April.

harvested in the spring or early summer. They were the main crops that were cultivated in al-Andalus and, as will be seen, those that determined the fiscal calendar. They were not, however, the only ones produced in al-Andalus. The *Calendar of Córdoba* lists a large number of other crops, along with the farm work undertaken for each of them during each month of the year. Summer legumes, for instance, were sown in February, and vegetables were planted in September–October, as well as other crops with short growing cycles, whose sowing had been completed by 27 April across al-Andalus. Agricultural output no longer depended solely on cereal crops, and this diversification was one of the key aspects that helped allay the effects of eventual droughts.

The *Calendar of Córdoba* also refers to the growing of sugar cane and rice, which provides the first reference to their production in the West. Sugar cane in particular was cultivated in Almuñécar, Salobreña, Seville and the Iberian Levant. The production of sugar involved a long and difficult manufacturing process in order to obtain an asset that was in as high demand by the ruling classes as it was superfluous: sugar, no less, along with precious metals, perfumes and luxury textiles, was one of the rarities included in a celebrated gift presented by the vizier Aḥmad b. Shuhayd to the Caliph ʿAbd al-Raḥmān III in 939 (327 AH). With regard to rice, sown in April and harvested in the autumn, its use had seemingly not become widespread; the earliest Andalusi agronomists only mention its production in market gardens, and still in the mid-thirteenth century a culinary treatise confines its production to the regions of Murcia and Valencia, while elsewhere 'rice is scarcely cultivated in al-Andalus'.[25]

The extension of these crops during the caliphal period has prompted considerable speculation about the rural Andalusi landscapes, which have been imagined as an extensive 'orchard', the product of a 'green revolution', whose genesis dated back to the conquest of 711, when the Arabs and Berbers had reached the peninsula with new seeds in their saddlebags and a knowledge of innovative agricultural methods, mainly related to irrigation. Today a more

[25] The classic work on the history of sugar and its links to the dominant classes continues to be S. W. Mintz, *Sweetness and Power: The Place of Sugar in Modern History*. M. Ouerfelli, *Le sucre*. pp. 24–7. E. García Sánchez 'El azúcar en la alimentación de los andalusíes', pp. 212–13. On the gift sent by the vizier, al-Maqqarī, *Nafḥ al-Ṭīb*, ed. ʿAbbās, pp. 356–60. J. E. Hernández Bermejo and E. García Sánchez, 'Las gramíneas en al-Andalus', p. 247.

rigorous and nuanced assessment may be offered.[26] Al-Andalus did not witness a 'green revolution' in the eighth century, but instead underwent a long and complex agricultural development that enabled the adaptation of new crops, the diversification of existing species and the introduction of novel irrigation techniques brought from the East.[27] The pace of growth in al-Andalus is not, therefore, to be explained by a dissemination of techniques and crops associated with ethnic groups. Instead, social developments, and in particular an increasing demand from the ruling classes and the proactive role of the central government combined to spur production of agricultural products and goods. By the mid-tenth century, rising demand and government needs were sufficiently developed to give rise to a considerable agricultural growth. From the ninth century onwards, the spread of crops linked to seasonal cycles distinct from the traditional ones, or the widespread taking up of inventions such as the Persian wheel that enabled the extraction of a continual flow of groundwater, had mitigated the region's dependence on winter cereal crops and the seasonal rains.[28] This, in turn, explains why the abundant episodes of drought during this period would only give rise to occasional shortages, whose effects were reduced by the lesser dependence on cereal crops and by the caliphate's capacity to move provisions from one place to another.

Nonetheless, Andalusi agricultural output continued to be based on winter cereal crops, which heavily depended on autumn and spring rains, whose absence was a cause of great anxiety. Soil analyses undertaken at archaeological sites have revealed a predominant presence of wheat and barley seeds, which confirm the prevalence of cereal crops in rural areas. They also reveal a significant spread of fruit species, which is corroborated by textual sources, such as the aforementioned *Calendar of Córdoba* and the agronomical treatises that began to be written during this period.[29]

[26] I have discussed this matter in E. Manzano Moreno, 'Entre faits et artefacts: interprétations historiques et données archéologiques en al-Andalus'.

[27] E. García Sánchez, 'La producción frutícola de al-Andalus', p. 53.

[28] L. García Blánquez, 'Las aceñas de acequia (islámicas) del sistema hidráulico andalusí de Murcia (Senda de Granada)', pp. 23–61.

[29] N. Alonso, F. Antolín and H. Kirchner, 'Novelties and Legacies in Crops in the Islamic Period in the North-east Iberian Peninsula', pp. 149–61; L. Peña Chocarro et al., 'Roman and Medieval Crops in the Iberian Peninsula'. The earliest Andalusi agronomical treatise to have survived was written around this time – late tenth century or early eleventh – and records the agricultural tasks associated with each month of the year. It uses both the Julian and Syrian calendars, as well as

The dominance of cereal crops in Andalusi fields is also reflected in the fiscal calendar imposed by the Umayyad administration, which was adapted to its grain-growing cycles. Tithes constituted a key element of the caliphate's tax-collecting administration. Their introduction in the early ninth century had met with major resistance, but during the caliphal period collection of tithes had become widely accepted. Land sale contracts, for instance, duly stated whether or not a specific property for sale was subject to their payment. Tithes were paid in coin (*ʿushūr darāhim*) or in kind (*ʿushūr ṭaʿām*), which seems to have been more frequent. In this case, payment involved a stipulated amount of wheat or barley, and there was a unit called *qafiz* for barley and wheat that was adapted to the 'granary measure' (*kayl al-hurī*).[30]

In order to calculate the amount to be paid in tithes, a pre-evaluation of the year's harvests was made in the spring. Then, in mid-June, just after the harvest had been completed, its yield was calculated after threshing. Then the 'guardians of the granaries' (*al-harrāʾiyyūn*), to whom the tithe was to be paid, were appointed. The tithe-paying subjects had to transport their contributions to the state granaries (*ahrāʾ*).[31] It is most likely, therefore, that the Umayyad administration possessed a preliminary estimate of the land yields. This was certainly the case for the lands of the contemporary ʿAbbāsid caliphate, where the estimate (*al-ḥazr*) was produced using complex measurements that established the equivalence (*taṣrīf*) between field sizes and the type of crops grown. The forecast of the harvests' outcome appears, for example, in

the solar one, which reveals the adaptation of geoponic knowledge from the East. For example, it states that 'the planting season for the fig tree is (the Syrian month) of *Nishrīn al-akhīr*, which is November', *K. fī tartīb awqāt al-ghirāsa wa l-maghrūsāt*, ed. A. C. López López, p. 137.

30 The revolt that broke out in the suburbs of Córdoba against the emir al-Ḥakam I in 817 (202 AH) was caused by the 'the levying of tithes on cereal crops (*ʿushūr al-aṭiʿmāt*), which they were obliged to pay as an annual tribute, without taking into account the harvest, nor its foundation in legal regulations'. The defeat of this rebellion permitted the levying of 'tithe payments on everybody in their capital and the *kūra*-s (provinces) of his kingdom, in accordance with his wishes, against their liking, and the people complied without anyone daring to say a word from then on, a custom that has continued until today; meanwhile the *sulṭān* spends this money excessively, in whatever way it wishes', Ibn Ḥayyān, *Muqtabis II, 1*, ed. Makki, pp. 161–2 and 165; trans. Corriente, pp. 72 and 75. For the translation of the final part of the first I follow P. Chalmeta, 'Derecho y práctica fiscal musulmana: el primer siglo y medio', pp. 13–14, which adheres more closely to the original. Fiscal exemptions for a property in Ibn al-ʿAṭṭār *K. al-wathāʾiq*, ed. pp. 605–6; trans. p. 886.

31 *Calendario de Córdoba*, ed. and trans. pp. 102–3. The Latin translation terms them '*custodes horreorum*'. Ibn al-ʿAṭṭār, *K. al-wathāʾiq*, ed. pp. 219–20; trans. pp. 412–13. For the measure of the *qafiz* according to the granary measure, Ibn Ḥayyān, *Muqtabis, VII*, ed. p. 148; trans. p. 187.

an Andalusi notarial formulary, in which it is described how a field of barley affected by drought was examined by various witnesses: their inspection was made in spring and the witnesses concluded that 'no part [of the loss] could be recovered and there was no solution'.[32] The same fiscal assessment was also used for vines, when the grapes were ripening in mid-July, and for olive trees in October, prior to the olive harvest.[33]

In the region around Córdoba responsibility for collecting tithes was the duty of the *ṣāḥib al-madīna*, while in the provinces it fell to the governors. Granaries were the responsibility of the aforementioned guardians (*al-harrā'iyyūn*), whose work consisted of collecting the tithes and distributing their revenue.[34] These guardians were, in turn, supervised by the officials of the granaries (*umanāt al-ahrā'*): in March 972 (*Jumādā* 361 AH) one Muḥammad b. Abī Qādim along with Aḥmad b. Qulzum was appointed to this post, which had on previous occasions been filled by a family known as the Banū Bassām, and also by the descendants of a certain Rabīʿ b. Muḥammad. The importance of these officials is underscored by the fact that they were present at official receptions and were invited to pay their compliments to the caliph. In addition, it is probable that the grain collected as tithes in Córdoba would have been milled at the water mills which had been built along the River Guadalquivir downstream from the city's Roman bridge, just in front of the caliphal *alcázar*. They were known as the 'Mills of Kulayb' (*Arḥā Kulayb*), the name of one of the sons of the first Umayyad emir, ʿAbd al-Raḥmān I (d. 788/172 AH), and they were repaired in the second half of 971 (late 360 and early 361 AH). Despite having been totally transformed and reconstructed during the modern period, these mills have survived and today form part of Córdoba's cityscape.[35]

[32] Ibn al-ʿAṭṭār *K. al-watā'iq*, ed. pp. 387–8; trans. p. 611.

[33] *Calendario de Córdoba*, ed. and trans. pp. 118–19; 158–9. C. E. Bosworth, "Abdallāh al-Khwārazmī on the Technical Terms of the Secretary's Art', pp. 113–64; A. Ehrenkreutz, 'The taṣrīf and tas'īr Calculations', pp. 46–56.

[34] Among the beneficiaries of the grain distribution were the soldiers of the sovereign's army, as is revealed in Ibn al-Qūṭiya, *Ta'rīkh*, ed. p. 93; trans. p. 78; trans. James, pp. 120–1. A passage in the same source seems to indicate that the central granaries were located on the road between Córdoba and Seville, ed. p. 113; trans. p. 97; trans. James, p. 137.

[35] Ibn Ḥayyān, *Muqtabis, VII*, ed. pp. 72 and 198; trans. pp. 94 and 239. On the mills, see ibid., pp. 64–5; trans. p. 77. The link to Kulayb b. ʿAbd al-Raḥmān in Ibn Ḥazm, *Jamharat*, ed. A. S. M. Harun, p. 94; trans. Terés, I, p. 70. This Kulayb was later imprisoned on the orders of his brother,

There was a network of granaries, and possibly also mills, that collected and ground the fiscal tithes paid in kind. It is possible that this network can also be identified with some of the numerous silos that have been found in excavations, although, regrettably, this is not a hypothesis being explored by archaeologists.[36] However, it is evident that each year the caliphal administration collected immense quantities of wheat and barley as tithes, and that this revenue was managed through a network of fiscal granaries. Part of this grain was used, as will be seen, to pay the salaries of courtiers and other officials connected to the administration. Likewise, grain received as tithes could be sold, whereby this fiscal revenue was converted into cash, which also provided a way of regulating prices. Finally, and as has already been seen, during periods of drought the existing reserves in the caliphal granaries were distributed among the population in order to alleviate shortages.

Another seasonal tax in the caliphate's fiscal system was exemption from military recruitment (*maghārim al-ḥashd*), which subjects paid at the start of the solar year, in January. This tax was levied on all adult men who would not take part in the annual military campaign. This exemption from military duties became ever more commonplace during this period, as the task of fighting was increasingly undertaken by professional soldiers: participation in military campaigns was becoming more dangerous, due to the growing resistance that the Andalusi armies encountered on the northern Christian frontier. Having male family members absent, while serving on a military campaign, meant land went untended, which is why many landowners paid the tax to ensure that their fields were not affected by a lack of workforce. Thereby the

the emir Hishām, and remained in the cells of the *alcázar* of Córdoba for twenty-seven years until he was assassinated on the orders of his nephew, the emir al-Ḥakam, Ibn Ḥayyān, *Muqtabis II, 1*, ed. cit. p. 122; trans. cit. p. 41. Furthermore, ownership of these mills was subject to judicial disputes until the emir al-Ḥakam I decided to buy them, ibid., pp. 205–6; trans. p. 109. The mills that are visible today are modern, but they are still referred to by the name 'Azuda de Culeb [Culeb's mill]'. They form a series of four mills parallel to the Roman bridge, R. Córdoba de la Llave et al., *Los molinos hidráulicos del Guadalquivir*. On the Banū Bassām family as responsible for the granaries, Ibn Ḥayyān, *Muqtabis*, 2.1, ed. p. 157; trans. pp. 68–9, based on the testimony of Ibn al-Qūṭiyya. The family of Rabiʿ b. Muḥammad, who were of Anṣārí origin, lived in Córdoba by the cemetery of the Banū 'Abbās, in the eastern part of the city, Ibn Ḥazm, *Jamhara*, ed. p. 333; trans. II, p. 337.

[36] A predominant idea is that the silos were 'collective granaries'. This is based on comparisons with contemporary North African practices that are too varied and unspecific to provide a solid point of reference, A. Bazzana, 'Subsistances et réserves de securité au village', pp. 575–608.

fiscal assessment of their property included this military service exemption tax. Notarial sale contracts for agricultural lands would always specify that the seller ceased to be responsible for the fiscal charges levied on the property, and that these included 'tithes paid in kind, exemption from military service (*ḥashd*) and legal alms (*ṣadaqa*)'.

Unlike with tithe collection, the payment for recruitment exemption was paid in coin to the agents of the *ṣāḥib al-madīna*, when in the region of Córdoba, and to the provincial governors elsewhere in al-Andalus. Very considerable sums were gained from this tax. In the mid-ninth century in the region of Córdoba alone up to 23,000 dinars were collected annually, and just one village paid as much as 72 dinars to ensure that its menfolk were free from the summer military campaigns (*al-ṣawā'if*). It is wholly possible that these figures could, at the very least, be doubled for the second half of the tenth century, due to both the increased population and the growing influence of the professional army at that time.[37]

When al-Ḥakam II decided to increase his popularity among his subjects, for reasons addressed in detail below, he decided to lower the sum to be paid for this tax by a sixth. In mid-January 975, just before it began to be collected, he sent a letter to all the provinces (*kūra*s) announcing this tax reduction. The letter was to be read in all mosques after the Friday prayer to ensure that everyone heard the news and that tax collectors did not deploy their renowned cunning by feigning ignorance of this cut, which was explicitly stated in the letter. The caliph's haste was justified, because one month later, in February, letters had to be sent to the provincial governors instructing them to proceed with the recruitment of the troops for the summer campaigns (*ḥushūd li l-ṣawā'if*). By then the lists of those who were exempt for having paid the tax should have been drawn up, and a few months later the annual summer campaign departed.[38]

The annual cycle of the caliphate was not only defined by the yearly recruitment of the troops, but also by the arrival of new horses. One source

[37] Ibn al-'Aṭṭār *K. al-wathā'iq*, ed. p. 167; trans. p. 323. Other examples on pp. 26 and 610; 93 and 889. The amount of this tax in Córdoba in al-'Udhrī, *Tarṣī' al-akhbār*, ed. al-Ahwānī, pp. 124–7; E. Manzano, *Conquistadores, emires y califas*, pp. 303 and 465.

[38] *Calendario de Córdoba*, ed. and trans. pp. 48–9; confirmed by *Muqtabis VII*, ed. p. 207; trans. p. 247.

claims that the number of horses available to the caliph both in Córdoba and along the frontiers came to 20,000. This is perhaps an exaggerated figure, but nonetheless signals the importance of horses for the smooth functioning of the administration; they meant people and supplies could be transported from one place to another with the utmost speed. The 'stables of the caliphate' (*makārib al-khilāfa*) undertook the complex administration of the state's livestock. They also provided the especially valuable horses that were sent as gifts to certain figures with whom political ties were sought, or else as remuneration for a specific service.[39]

The provisioning of these horses also took place at specific times of the year. An especially renowned area for horse breeding was the wetlands known as the Guadalquivir Marshes (*Marismas del Guadalquivir*), in places such as *Jazīrat Qabṭīl* (Isla Menor in the modern-day province of Seville). Having pastured during the January sowing season, in February the horses were fed on green barley grass from troughs. Following the eleven-month gestation period, foals were born between mid-March and mid-April. This was also the month in which the requisition of horses for the summer campaigns was undertaken. 'Īsā al-Rāzī states that in March 975 (*Rajab* 364), looking ahead to the summer military campaign that was being prepared in the wake of military unrest on the frontier with the Christians, the caliph ordered senior members of the administration to travel to the provinces and carry out the requisition of the horses that the inhabitants 'were obliged to supply'. The requisition and the delivery of new horses could go on up until the summer. The arrival of new colts from the wetlands of Seville and Niebla at Madīnat al-Zahrā' in mid-July 973 became a special occasion as Caliph al-Ḥakam and his son went to examine the new acquisitions, which were put on display by two senior officials: the official responsible for the postal services and the head of the stables.[40]

The caliphal administration also regularly ordered the requisition of other supplies at specific times of the year. Aside from such unusual materials as goat and gazelle hides for making parchment, which were delivered in May, or deer antlers for making ornamental arches, the more interesting products that

[39] Ibn Ḥayyān, *Muqtabis VII*, ed. p. 132; trans. p. 166; *Dhikr bilād al-Andalus*, ed. and trans. p. 144.

[40] *Calendario de Córdoba*, ed. and trans. pp. 36–7, 44–5, 56–7. Ibn Ḥayyān, *Muqtabis VII*, ed. pp. 117 and 216; trans. pp. 149 and 256. On Isla Menor, Ibn Ḥayyān, *Muqtabis, II, 1*, ed. pp. 452–3; trans. p. 314.

arrived on a regular basis were the supplies for the caliphal textile workshop (*dār al-ṭirāz*), above all silks and dyes. Ibn Ḥawqal, the oriental traveller – who may well have served as a spy for the Fāṭimid caliphs – visited al-Andalus circa 948 (336 AH), and extolled the high quality of the Andalusi textiles, particularly lauding the excellence of their dyes. The *Calendar of Córdoba* reaffirms this, noting that in May each year letters were sent to the officials for the acquisition of kermes (*qirmiz*), silk (*ḥarīr*) and *aizoon hispanicum* (*ghāsūl*), a species of ice plant. *Kermes vermilio* or kermes was a pigment, also known as *grana*, which provided a red dye for textiles and was obtained from the dried body of an insect that lived in the *carrasca*, a shrub of the holm-oak family that was widespread across the Mediterranean region and that was especially abundant in the area near to Senés (Almería), where mulberry trees were also common. Although less valuable, another dye sought from the provinces in the month of September was one made from rose madder roots (*fuwwat al-ṣabgh*).[41]

Finally, another material that was also delivered to Córdoba regularly was wood. In the province or *kūra* of Jaén there was a district or *iqlīm* called *Nashka*, located in the Sierra de Segura mountains, which is said to have supplied large quantities of wood for ʻAbd al-Raḥmān III's building projects. The wood was shipped down to Córdoba along the River Guadalimar, which was a tributary of the Guadalquivir and provided a fast and efficient means of river transport. By the time of al-Ḥakam II, the same region supplied wood, tar and pitch, which were also sent to Seville, presumably via the same river route, in order to be transported to the coastal city of Algeciras, where these materials were used for shipbuilding. In 973 (362 AH) the people of this *kūra* protested against the excessive zeal with which caliphal officials (*ʻummāl*) obtained these supplies, which led to the caliph's decision to exempt them from this fiscal obligation. He returned to them what his officials had illegally taken, and covered the costs of these materials from his own funds.[42]

[41] Another dye that was widely used in the caliph's textile workshops was the colour sky blue (*al-ṣabāgh al-samāwī*). Unfortunately, we do not know how it was made, but it was ordered from the provinces along with silk in mid-August. *Calendario de Córdoba*, ed. and trans. pp. 90–1, 104–5 and 132–3; al-Maqqarī, *Nafḥ al-Ṭīb*, I, p. 164. On the use of rose madder, Abū l-Khayr al-Ishbīlī, *K. ʻumdati ṭṭabīb*, ed. and trans. n. 3.818. Also Ibn Ḥawqal, *Ṣūraṭ al-arḍ*, ed. J.-H. Kramers, p. 113.

[42] Ibn Ḥayyān, *Muqtabis V*, ed. and trans. p. 115; Ibn Ḥayyān, *Muqtabis VII*, ed. p. 101; trans. pp. 129–30. In the case of *Muqtabis VII* the reference to the transport of wood by river is not as

Wheat, barley, money, recruits, horses, dye, deer horns, parchment, wood and silk arrived in Córdoba with annual regularity from across al-Andalus. The fiscal cycles described by the sources confirm that the fiscal punction exerted by the administration operated a very selective, but also highly varied and intricate procurement process. Thus, it may be inferred that the management of the state granaries required the evaluation, collection, transportation and redistribution of huge quantities of wheat and barley each year. There was also the time-consuming task of drafting lists of annual recruits, which had to be systematically updated to account for those who had paid for exemption. A further insight into what was involved in these regular administrative practices is provided by the arrival of the new colts in Madīnat al-Zahrā'. The caliph insisted on seeing them and he ordered the heads of the postal service and stables to organise a display, which involved the high-ranking civil servants who oversaw the pairing of the horses, their breeding in the Guadalquivir wetlands, their selection and their transportation to the caliph's palace. Multiple examples could be provided for the other cases cited above – such as the collection of the deer horns – and all of them offer the same image of an administration capable of mobilising immense resources at regular intervals. To ensure that this mobilisation was a success, it was necessary for the caliph's power to be deployed with razor-sharp precision: a precision that was celebrated by the caliph in each and every one of his actions.

The Muslim Religious Cycle

The Muslim year and an important part of official caliphal life revolved around festivities and religious commemorations. Notwithstanding the fact that Islam has fewer annual festivals than Christianity, its religious cycles are very clearly marked. The most prominent is the month of *Ramaḍān*, the ninth month of the Islamic year, when the first revelation of the Qur'an to the Prophet Muḥammad took place. This is a fasting period, which is practised throughout the month by all healthy Muslim adults from sunrise to sunset. It is considered

evident in the translation: 'they had received orders to provide ... the said products and transport them to Seville and Algeciras', while the text itself states 'and to transport them to Seville and from there to Algeciras'. On the district of *Nashka* and the River Guadalimar, E. Terés Sádaba, *Materiales para el estudio de la toponimia hispanoarabe*, pp. 180–2. F. Aguirre Sadaba and C. Jiménez Mata, *Introducción al Jaén islámico*, pp. 43–68.

one of the pillars of Islam, and during this month the good Muslim abstains from eating, drinking or having sexual intercourse in daylight hours, in order to instil both pious conduct and a sense of belonging to the Muslim community.

Despite the fact that fasting was obligatory during the month of *Ramaḍān*, in the caliphal administration certain activities went uninterrupted. There are reports, for example, of military campaigns undertaken during this month, for which undoubtedly the troops must have been granted dispensation from their pious obligations. Other reports indicate buildings being completed, the caliph receiving ambassadors and the holding of public executions. However, breaking the fast was unacceptable in normal conditions even for the caliph. A story that circulated among Muslim scholars, or *'ulamā'*, recounted how during *Ramaḍān*, al-Ḥakam II had succumbed to the temptation of a beautiful woman and lain with her during the day. Repentant, the caliph had confessed his failing to the legal scholars of his inner circle, who overwhelmingly agreed to proscribe almsgiving as his penitence. However, one of them, Abū Ibrāhīm Isḥāq al-Tujībī, reproached his colleagues for spending so much time fawning before the caliph, instead of studying the principles of the Māliki school of Islamic law, which was practised in al-Andalus; had they done so, they would have realised that this type of expiation could only be imposed on wealthy people, but was not appropriate for the caliph, who entirely lacked his own financial resources, as he only administered the wealth of the Muslims. The argument, which, as will be seen, has considerable substance, ended up being accepted and the caliph was given a supplementary fast as his penitence.[43]

Whether with his own money or the wealth of Muslims, al-Ḥakam II also gave out alms (*ṣadaqāt*) on a regular basis during the month of *Ramaḍān*, doing so sometimes publicly and on other occasions incognito. When he did so, he delegated the task to the *ḥukkām* and *umanā'*, who made their way through the suburbs of Córdoba and Madīnat al-Zahrā' handing out money to the needy and to secluded women (*ahl al-siṭr*). The *ḥukkām*, or arbiters, were independent people assigned to resolve judicial disputes, and their

[43] Military campaigns in Ibn Ḥayyān, *Muqtabis, V*, pp. 36–8, 84–5, 257, among many others. Completion of buildings in É. Lévi-Provençal, *Inscriptions arabes de l'Espagne*, pp. 134–5; reception of ambassadors in Ibn Ḥayyān, *Muqtabis VII*, ed. p. 21; trans. pp. 45–6. An execution in *Muqtabis, V*, pp. 84–5. The story about the caliph in M. I. Fierro, 'Caliphal Legitimacy and Expiation in al-Andalus', pp. 55–62.

appearance as distributors of alms seems to express the wish to demonstrate that the almsgiving was undertaken in accordance with strict criteria of equity. In contrast, the *umanā'* were trustworthy servants of the caliph, who undertook a range of tasks: from obtaining the oath of loyalty from the people when a new caliph was proclaimed, to managing the provisioning of the fortresses and cities on the frontier, as well as investigating accusations made against a provincial governor.[44] In making recourse to these two types of civil servants as supervisors for almsgiving – a potentially divisive matter – the caliph combined the religious dimension of his authority with the secular nature of his power.

The caliph also made donations to the people of Córdoba at other times. Perhaps the most popular occasion was the caliph's accession, on October 961, when he dedicated the astronomical sum of 100,000 dinars to almsgiving and the redemption of Muslim captives captured by the Christians. A precedent for this charitable display had been established by the emir 'Abd al-Raḥmān II, who on coming to power in May 822 (206 AH) distributed 5,000 dinars of his own money among the poor, a figure that also reveals the major difference in resources available to the sovereigns.[45]

On other occasions, almsgiving could be more spontaneous. This was the case in June 972, when al-Ḥakam II decided to present gifts to mark the day that his son and future heir Hishām began attending classes with his tutor: exultant on seeing the seemingly extraordinary aptitudes of his heir – aptitudes that the passage of time would not re-affirm – the proud father gave out a considerable sum to the poor and needy, as well as travellers. This was *Ramaḍān* in 361 AH, and just a few days beforehand the caliph had given out the alms that he traditionally gave out in that month. Now, beaming with pride at discovering how clever his son was, he ordered for Aḥmad b. Naṣr, who undertook the offices of *ṣāḥib al-shurṭa* and *ṣāḥib al-sūq*, to distribute the money to the poor 'as proof of [the Caliph's] gratitude to the Highness of God for the favour that He has dispensed in that apple of his eyes and comely youth of his glory'. Almost two years later, in April 974 (*Rajab* 363 AH), Hishām himself undertook the distribution of alms and the celebration of a reception to give

[44] Alms: Ibn Ḥayyān, *Muqtabis VII*, ed. pp. 23, 76, 110, 226; trans. pp. 47, 98, 140, 268; delegation to the *umanā'*, Ibn Ḥayyān, *Muqtabis* V, ed. and trans. p. 309; *Muqt VII*, ed. pp. 104–5, 106; trans. pp. 133, 136.

[45] A. Carballeira, 'Caridad y poder político en época omeya', pp. 98–9.

thanks to God for his recovery from smallpox, which had left him bedridden for a month and a half.[46]

Ramaḍān ended with *'Īd al-Fiṭr*, or the Feast of Breaking Fast, which took place on 1 *Shawwāl*. The other major celebration was, and is, the Feast of the Sacrifice (*'Īd al-aḍḥā*) held on 10 *Dhū l-ḥijja*. This commemoration is the great feast day of the Muslim year. It celebrates the story of Abraham, who was ordered by God to sacrifice his own son Isaac to Him. Having been duly obeyed, God halted the sacrifice at the last moment and substituted a sheep for Isaac: the celebration of this event highlights the need for men to adhere to divine plans, however strange they may seem, and also to be aware of the rewards such obedience might bring. This feast, which coincides with the month of the pilgrimage to Mecca, was widely celebrated in Córdoba. It was customary to hold a military parade the day before, which was attended by large crowds, and for which the tradespeople organised a fair (*mawsim al-'īd*) where they sold their produce. Likewise, on the morning of the Feast of Breaking of Fast the preachers of the Friday mosques of Córdoba and Madīnat al-Zahrā' said prayers in the open-air oratories or *muṣallā*s to be found in each city. Possibly, and as happens today in any Muslim society, the people also celebrated this festival on the streets and in their houses.[47]

The celebration of both these feasts in Umayyad Córdoba also included large receptions presided over by the caliph. They were held within the walls of Madīnat al-Zahrā', or else in the *alcázar* of Córdoba, the old residence of the Umayyad sovereigns. Such receptions always followed an identical pattern: the caliph took his seat and accepted the greetings from family members, dignitaries and other principal subjects, who made their entrance and were all placed according to a meticulous and hierarchical protocol. Later in this book, I will examine these receptions in more detail. Without fail, they ended with speeches and poems by orators and poets, who took advantage of the event to declaim the most impassioned panegyrics in honour of the caliph and his son.

[46] Ibn Ḥayyān, *Muqtabis VII*, ed. pp. 77, 152–3; trans. pp. 99, 193–4. On Aḥmad b. Naṣr see *infra* p. 116 and 123.

[47] Ibn Ḥayyān, *Muqtabis V*, ed. and trans. pp. 302–3. Ibn Ḥayyān, *Muqtabis VII*, ed. p. 93; trans. p. 117. The *muṣallā* was usually located alongside one of the entrances to the city. That of Madīnat al-Zahrā' has not been located; on that of Córdoba see Ch. 10. In contrast to what would take place with the 'Abbāsíd caliphs in the East, no mention is made of the Umayyads undertaking any ritual connected to the pilgrimage to the holy sites of Mecca or Medina.

Whereas at court *ʿĪd al-Fiṭr* and *ʿĪd al-Aḍḥā* gave rise to elaborate receptions that underscored the caliphate's splendour, in rural areas both dates had a different significance. Some sharecropper contracts stated that 'a live four-year-old calf, with white hide and black eyes, well-formed and adult' had to be delivered to the landowner in good time at these two feasts, and in the event of the calf not being an adult it was to be 'castrated and plump'. Other payments of rents were made according to the solar calendar, such as the remittances of milled grain that sharecroppers were required to bring on 1 August. Some contracts stated that a certain number of chickens and 'two, plump, well-reared suckling lambs, a month and a half or two months old' had to be handed over to the landowner on 1 January. What is of particular interest, and clearly reveals how social domination in al-Andalus was exerted, is that the landowners could reclaim these payments in legal procedures, in which event they would have 'to be believed ... without their being obliged to swear an oath'.[48]

There is no doubt that in caliphal Córdoba there were other key occasions during the year, but even the most generic description of them cannot be expected from a source of such an official nature as that written by ʿĪsā al-Rāzī. However, occasional chinks in the official discourse reveal that festivities other than Muslim ones were also observed in al-Andalus. For example, on referring to the meteorological phenomena that took place in early 975, ʿĪsā al-Rāzī notes that they coincided with the *Nayrūz* (or *Nawrūz*) of the Christians. The *Nayrūz* was New Year's Day in the Persian calendar and in al-Andalus it corresponded with 1 January, also known as *Yannayr*, which was celebrated by the Christians. As we have just seen, this date in the solar calendar could also serve as a point of reference for payments made not only by peasants, but also by the administration: an example of the latter are the subsidies decreed by the Emir ʿAbd al-Raṃān II to be paid to the Baghdadi musician Ziryāb when he arrived in al-Andalus in 822. He was assigned, among other things, 500 dinars payable each *Nayrūz* and *Mahrajān*. The latter was a festival in the Persian calendar, which in al-Andalus had gone on to be identified with St John's Day, 24 June, or the day of the *ʿAnṣara*, the

[48] Ibn al-ʿAṭṭār *K. al-wathāʾiq*, ed. p. 61; trans. p. 158.

summer solstice, which was associated with the tradition of marking the birth of the prophet John the Baptist (in Arabic Yaḥyā b. Zakariyyā).[49]

The celebration of both the first day of the solar year and of St John's Day in al-Andalus is confirmed in poetry and other texts. The night prior to the *Nayrūz*, 31 December, was considered one of the most propitious for consummating matrimony. Also, on that day it was customary for the wealthy to exchange gifts or a cake made in the form of a city: one poet deliciously described one of these cakes as 'made of flour, dyed with saffron' and needing no 'other keys than one's ten fingers'.[50] For *Mahrajān*, in mid-June, a special type of cake was again eaten, women doused the houses with water, put their dresses out at night to receive the dew, or kept cabbage leaves in them as a form of amulet, practices that clearly reflect fertility rituals. Some went so far as to celebrate this day by stopping work or taking a ritual bath that seemed to have had a purifying purpose. Another engrained custom on that day was the holding of horse races, and the Caliph 'Abd al-Raḥmān III himself ordered his courtiers to attend them. Among the wealthy classes, the arrival of summer was also marked by a change in clothing; white was worn until October, when they once more dressed in coloured garments.

The presence of Muslims at these non-Islamic festivals and the rites they practised on such occasions were the object of severe prohibitions by the *fuqahā'*, who considered these customs reprehensible. Already from the ninth century (third AH) respected *'ulamā'* such as Yaḥyā b. Yaḥyā (d. 848/234 AH) or Muḥammad b. Waḍḍāḥ (d. 900/289 AH) multiplied their condemnations of anyone who celebrated or took part in Christian or Jewish festivals, deeming such conduct an innovation that paved the way for Muslims converting 'themselves into Jews or Christians without realising'. Such condemnations sought to define the limits of Muslim identity vis-à-vis Christian and Jewish communities, and to limit in so far as possible any relations with them.[51]

49 Ibn Ḥayyān, *Muqtabis II, 1*, ed. pp. 309–10; trans. p. 199; *Calendario de Córdoba*, ed. and trans. pp. 26–7 and 100–1.

50 H. Peres, *Esplendor de al-Andalus*, p. 307.

51 F. de la Granja, 'Fiestas cristianas en al-Andalus (Materiales para su estudio) I', pp. 1–53; 'Fiestas cristianas en al-Andalus (Materiales para su estudio) II', *al-Andalus*, 35, 1 (1970), pp. 119–42. On the changes of colour in clothing according to the seasons introduced in accordance with the renowned Ziryāb, Ibn Ḥayyān, *Muqtabis II 1*, ed. pp. 323–4; trans. pp. 206–7.

As has been shown over the course of this chapter, in contrast to the annual, regular and unceasing natural cycles, droughts, floods and other catastrophes were unexplainable setbacks. By the mid-tenth century, the Umayyad caliphate was endeavouring to systematise these unpredictable events by recording and classifying their seemingly unforeseeable occurrences, and identifying connections between them. Attempts were even made to explain these diverse phenomena of the natural world, and recourse was only made to God when matters became definitively unknowable. The result was a 'system', a rigid and planned organisation, that offered the security of the foreseeable, in contrast to the chaos of the elements. Thereby the calendar, which was adapted from natural, fiscal and religious cycles, framed the diversity of the world in its dates and ephemera; and it did so with considerable success.

The same concern for order was also applied to daily routines. In the city palace of Madīnat al-Zahrā' fragments of two solar quadrants have been found, which permitted time to be measured within the palace precinct, where the caliph resided, governed and prayed. A solar quadrant has likewise been found in the *alcázar* of Córdoba, which reinforces the idea that daily life inside the seat of power was marked by the strict regulation of time. For the nocturnal hours or overcast days, authors such as the Cordoban astronomer Qāsim b. Muṭarrif al-Qaṭṭān (born c. 915/302 AH) suggested inventions such as a candle clock that consisted of a metal tray on which twelve glass lamps were placed with a quantity of oil proportional to an hour.[52] The same regulation of time governed the call to prayer announced by the muezzin, five times a day and at well-established intervals. In cities such as Córdoba, populated by tens of mosques, the calculation of daily time imposed a generalised regularity, yet this was not only restricted to marking ritual practices: it also implied a sense of social discipline overtly encouraged by those in power.

[52] C. Barceló and A. Labarta, 'Ocho relojes de sol hispanomusulmanes', pp. 243–6; 'Acerca de dos cuadrantes solares de Medina Azahara', pp. 281–3; A. Labarta and C. Barceló, 'Un nuevo fragmento de reloj de sol andalusí', pp. 147–50; J. Casulleras, 'The Contents of Qāsim b. Muṭarrif al-Qaṭṭān's *Kitāb al-Hay'a*', pp. 347–8.

2

The Caliphate's Resources and Wealth

Coercion and Surplus

The use of force pervaded medieval societies, including Islamic ones. Sometimes, this force was exerted physically, which could result in acts of great cruelty, but in the majority of cases the mere allusion to it in everyday life, or its reference in rules and customs, sufficed to ensure that the majority of society accepted the dominance of the minority capable of exercising it. This *extra-economic coercion* permitted a social minority to control the *surplus* produced by the majority of the population, or in other words, what was left over once the population had guaranteed both its subsistence and the repetition of the cycles of production and exchange. This *coercion* was always justified in one way or another by legal or ideological arguments, or simply on the basis of tradition.[1]

The institutional form in which the dominant classes acquired their resources could vary greatly. In many medieval European societies, this often took the form of *rent*, which included the various forms of payment that peasants, artisans and merchants had to give to feudal lords in recognition of their authority. In contrast, in societies such as al-Andalus, its centralised states

[1] The discussion that follows is based on the arguments and conclusions set out in the theoretical studies made by some of the best materialist historians of my generation, to which I have added my own ideas and reflections. My principal sources are: J. Haldon, *The State and the Tributary Mode of Production*, London, 1993; C. Wickham, *Framing the Early Middle Ages. Europe and the Mediterranean* 400–800; M. Acién, 'On the Role of Ideology in the Characterization of Social Formations. The Islamic Social Formation', in *Obras Escogidas*, vol. I, pp. 171–222; E. Manzano Moreno, 'Relaciones sociales en sociedades precapitalistas: una crítica al concepto de modo de producción tributario', *Hispania*, 58, 200 (1999), pp. 915–68 and 881–914; J. Haldon, 'Mode of Production, Social Action, and Historical Change: Some Questions and Issues', in L. da Graca and A. Zingarelli, eds, *Studies in Precapitalist Modes of Production*, Leiden–Boston, 2015, pp. 204–36.

captured the surplus in the form of *tributes*, a combination of taxes levied under different forms and periodically by the state's representatives, which were redistributed in numerous ways among the dominant classes.

The difference between *rent* and *tribute* was not qualitative, as the social conditions of those paying feudal dues were not necessarily very different from the conditions of those who paid taxes. In both cases, the surplus was obtained by way of *extra-economic coercion*, and in both cases the beneficiaries accumulated resources on a scale that was unimaginable to those who provided the surplus. Although it is true that, by demanding tributes from *all* subjects, tax-based formations differed in principle from those based on *rent*, in practice this was not always the case, as the dominant classes obtained a range of fiscal exemptions that underscored their social superiority. Furthermore, the mobility of a population subject to paying tribute could be as limited as that of those paying rent, as systems of fiscal co-responsibility required rural communities to pay pre-determined sums as a group, so that all members of the community had to make a contribution; as a result, it was the community that sought to prevent anyone leaving, as in the event of that happening it was those that remained who had to pay a larger share of the community's fiscal burden.

Where a major difference between *rent* and *tribute* arose was in the outcome of their accumulation and redistribution. In contrast to the fragmentary social model that inevitably derived from numerous lords living off their vassals' rents, a centralised tributary system meant that infinitely greater resources became available to the central elites. As a result, these elites took on a more homogeneous character, as their members shared or competed for the same resources and instruments of *power*. This in turn meant that the redistribution of resources occurred with great facility on a variety of scales, which as a result gave rise to an increase in demand and its subsequent effects. It is for this reason that tributary societies greatly incentivised exchange, as they could gave rise to multiple and varied centres of demand on distinctive scales, which in turn stimulated agrarian and commercial growth.

The tributary social model which the Umayyad caliphate of al-Andalus encompassed all the aforementioned features: *extra-economic coercion* that allowed for resources to be gathered in a centralised manner and on a grand scale; a highly homogeneous ruling class that was identified with the caliphal state; and a proliferating of demand, with the caliph, the state apparatus and the dominant class as its most active instigators. Yet this was also replicated further down the social scale, whereby other elements of society profited from the redistribution of the enormous sums gathered in the form of tributes. Furthermore, a widely embraced ideology, the result of the Islamisation of the majority of the population, bestowed a striking degree of social cohesion that sustained the state of the Umayyad caliphs and allowed them to maintain control seemingly in the absence of any opposition.

Income: Taxes and Camels

At the time of al-Ḥakam II the caliphate of Córdoba was a major centre for gathering resources obtained through the many and varied taxes that were collected on a regular basis across al-Andalus. Through this major centralisation of resources, the caliphal state was able to concentrate and redistribute enormous quantities of wealth. The available figures for monetary production, the sumptuary objects produced in state workshops, the caliph's ostentatious building projects, or even the verses recited by poets, for which they were duly paid, demonstrate that the Umayyad state was capable of transforming the resources it gathered and redistributing them from a circle of power centred around the caliph and his milieu. It is possible that this surplus was also gathered at other nexus in the social order (the territorial elites which later emerged in the *taifa* kingdoms following the fall of the Umayyad caliphate, the urban classes who accumulated wealth through artisanal and merchant activities, and even religious institutions that collected pious donations or legacies), but in these cases we lack information comparable to that provided by the Umayyad state apparatus. Given the quantity of resources that it centralised and redistributed, as well as its evident visibility, by the middle of the tenth century the state machinery of the Umayyad caliphate was the dominant element in al-Andalus.

The key to this impressive accumulation and subsequent distribution of resources was a highly developed fiscal administration that reached every last corner of al-Andalus with unheard-of efficiency. While it is true that from the time of the Arab conquest a centralised tax-collecting system had been in operation, it was only during the caliphal period that this system became fully developed and achieved an effectiveness and intensity that had never been witnessed until then. This may be demonstrated in many ways. For example, in the summer of 971 (360 AH) the caliph, al-Ḥakam, was informed about a boy from the village of Maryah, in the *iqlīm*, or district, of Cártama in the *kūra*, or province, of Rayyuh (Málaga), who was affected by giantism, whereby at the age of four he looked like a young man. The boy was ordered to come to Córdoba accompanied by his grandfather to be shown to the caliph and his son Hishām. Having been examined by both (and also by our chronicler, ʿĪsā al-Rāzī, who declared himself to be fascinated by the case), the boy and his grandfather were granted permission to return to their home laden with gifts, but not without the boy's grandfather first asking the caliph to lower the tax (*magram*) he had to pay in his village. Al-Ḥakam granted him a total exemption from the tribute and wrote to the provincial governor (*ṣāḥib al-kūra*) of the *kūra* of Rayyuh. The boy's grandfather was perfectly identified: he was called Khalaf b. Yaḥyā b. Arāqī b. Khalaf b. Muntaqim b. ʿAbd Allāh b. Badr b. Nāṣiḥ al-Farrash, and his great-grandfather had been *mawlā* to the Emir ʿAbd al-Raḥmān I.[2] The caliphal administration was capable of identifying a person from a distant village, as well as his ancestors, who had most likely also been identified for fiscal purposes over the course of generations. In addition, the administration maintained effective internal communications, as is demonstrated by the fact that the fiscal exemption was communicated to the governor.

The foregoing example explains how, by the time of ʿAbd al-Raḥmān III (d. 961/350 AH), the caliphate's fiscal revenue reached 5,480,000 dinars. This exorbitant figure does not include the income generated by the caliph's private properties (*mustakhlaṣ*), nor the markets, which amassed a further 765,000 dinars in rental payments. The importance of this revenue is underscored by the pious legacy (*ḥabus*) that the Caliph al-Ḥakam established in early 975 (*Jumāda* I, 364 AH) using the rents from the saddlers' shops in Córdoba's souk: this endowment was used to pay the salaries of the Qu'ran teachers, who educated the sons of the city's poor. An idea of how much money was involved is indicated by the fact that during the rule of the emirs the monthly rent for two shops in Córdoba's Shabulār suburb was two dinars.[3]

[2] Ibn Ḥayyān, *Muqtabis VII*, ed. pp. 62–3; trans. pp. 79–80. This anecdote seems to suggest that there was a provincial management of tax registers. M. Rustow, *The Lost Archive*, pp. 354–62 provides the best description I know of how a tax system worked at the micro level. It deals with Fāṭimid Egypt, but in general its organisation may have not been very different from that of al-Andalus.

[3] Ibn Ḥayyān, *Muqtabis VII*, ed. p. 207; trans. p. 247; Ibn Ḥayyān, *Muqtabis* II, I ed. p. 338 and trans. p. 218. A. García Sanjuán, *Till God Inherits the Earth*, p. 224.

A century before the caliphal period, at the time of the Emir 'Abd al-Raḥmān II (d. 852/238 AH), the total fiscal revenue was between five and six times lower (at around one million dinars), which demonstrates an extraordinary economic growth, which evolved in conjunction with the Umayyad fiscal system's avid concern to take advantage of this growth. Following al-Ḥakam II's death in 976 (366 AH), during al-Manṣūr's rule, in the final decade of the tenth century, the general contribution descended to 4 million dinars, a fall that was perhaps motivated by a series of fiscal cuts that are discussed below.[4] At the start of the eleventh century, the monthly fiscal revenue from Valencia alone reached the astronomical sum of 120,000 dinars.[5]

Thus, in general terms the average annual income of the caliphate of Córdoba may be established at around 4 or 5 million dinars. These figures concur with evidence stating that in the mid-tenth (fourth AH) century the caliphal coffers contained reserves of around 20 million dinars. This figure was not based solely on monetary resources, but also, and most likely, on an assessment of the stocks in the caliphal granaries Although very high, these are reliable figures: at the critical time of the civil war that marked the end of the Umayyad dynasty in the early eleventh century, one of the contenders for power was still able to find five and a half million dinars in silver, one and a half million dinars in gold, and 200 dinars in ingots in the caliph's treasury.[6]

The Umayyad caliphate's revenue was obtained from a variety of sources. As was discussed in the previous chapter, two of the principal tributes that it relied on, and that were gathered at very precise dates in the year, were the tithes and payments for exemption from military service. Both were widely collected, but they were not the only fiscal measures. Sources use three generic words – *waẓā'if*, *maghārim* and *nawā'ib* – to refer to the contributions, tributes and charges that were levied on property, individuals and professional

[4] Ibn 'Idhārī, *al-Bayān al-Mughrib*, II, ed. cit. pp. 231–2; the same report in al-Maqqarī, *Nafḥ*, I, pp. 379, 569. For 'Abd al-Raḥmān II, Ibn Ḥayyān, *Muqtabis, II, 1*, ed. and trans. pp. 280 and 172, based on Mu'āwiya b. Hishām al-Shabīnisī, who gives the figure in *dinār darāhim*, each of which, as is explained below, was equivalent to eight dirhams. On al-Manṣūr, al-'Udhrī, *Tarṣī al-akhbār*, ed. cit. p. 121.

[5] A. L. Premare and P. Guichard, 'Croisssance urbaine et societé rural á Valence', p. 23.

[6] The figure of 20 million is based on an analysis of the data provided by Ibn Ḥawqal, which included the reserves kept by the caliph, *Ṣūrat al-arḍ*, ed. cit. p. 112. Ibn 'Idhārī, *al-Bayān al-Mughrib*, III, ed. cit. pp. 61–2; trans. Maíllo, p. 65.

activities. Each of these generic terms encompassed a range of taxes. Thereby, the 'contributions' (*maghārim*) included the aforementioned exemption from military service, and the tax levied on land known as *ṭabl*. The payment of this 'census' – as it is translated in medieval dictionaries – could be paid on a monthly basis – in accordance with the lunar calendar – to the *ṣāḥib al-madīna* in Córdoba, and it affected any property irrespective of the religion its owner might profess.[7] The generic term *waẓā'if* very possibly included the tithes and tributes which, referred to as *ṣadaqa*, were levied specifically on livestock and non-cereal farm produce, as well as olive oil (*ḍarībat al-zaytūn*).[8] Finally, the 'charges' (*nawā'ib*) comprised a range of taxes, such as that levied on accommodation (*ma'arrat inzāl fī l-dūr*), which was intended to cover the provisioning of both the army and members of the caliphal administration when undertaking official missions. Another charge was the *al-qabalāt*, which was levied on commercial activity in a form we do not exactly know, although it is clear that merchant ships paid taxes on entry to and departure from ports, and a form of sales tax was also levied in the souks.[9]

This combination of fiscal payments had little or nothing to do with the strict rules established by Islam regarding taxes. Everybody knew this, and it was a serious Achilles heel for any caliph who wanted to exercise power based on a legitimate Islamic authority. In this regard, both the Qur'an and Islamic tradition established very clear precepts on the fiscal treatment of the community, precepts that did not include most taxes regularly collected by the fiscal administration of the caliphate of Córdoba. If the authority of al-Ḥakam II was based on his claim to be the Commander of the Believers, why did his own administration violate the fiscal regulations stipulated by the revelation of God?

[7] P. Chalmeta, 'Fiscalité musulmane: au sujet du ṭabl', p. 220. Ibn al-'Aṭṭār, *K. al-wathā'iq*, ed. P. Chalmeta, pp. 125, 169; trans. M. Marugán, pp. 256, 325. The list *waẓā'if*, *maghārim* and *nawā'ib* clearly reflects a formulaic expression, ibid., pp. 877 and 879; 597 and 599. The qualification for exemption from military service as *magram* in Ibn Ḥayyān, *Muqtabis VII*, ed. p. 207.

[8] Ibn al-'Aṭṭār, *K. al-wathā'iq*, ed. pp. 167, 605, 610; trans. pp. 323, 886, 889. The tax on olive oil pressing was suppressed in Córdoba on the accession of Hishām II, Ibn 'Idhārī, *al-Bayān al-Mughrib*, II, ed. cit. p. 259.

[9] The taxes on accommodation and the *alcabalas* are cited among the exemptions that the citizens of Toledo obtained following their submission to 'Abd al-Raḥmān III, Ibn Ḥayyān, *Muqtabis V*, ed. and trans. p. 217. Ibn Ḥawqal, *Ṣūrat al-arḍ*, p. 108.

'Īsā al-Rāzī compiles a text that unwittingly gets to the heart of this thorny issue. It is a copy of a diploma sent in June 973 (*Ramaḍān* 362 AH) by the Caliph al-Ḥakam to Abū l-'Aysh b. Ayyūb, a leader of the Kutāma tribe, which had settled in the Rif region in what is now Morocco.[10] At that time, al-Ḥakam was seeking to extend his influence in the area using all possible military and diplomatic means. Following the costly and difficult deployment of the Umayyad army in the region, Berber tribal leaders, such as Abū l-'Aysh b. Ayyūb, were beginning to submit to the caliph of Córdoba, albeit not without having first been appeased with generous gifts and through the incessant activity of the caliph's armies and agents. As al-Ḥakam considered that acceptance of his sovereignty involved the adoption of the rules of orthodox Islam, he sent the tribal chief a diploma stipulating a set of government rules for the Berber chief to implement within his tribal group.

One part of this official text, faithfully copied by 'Īsā al-Rāzī, is devoted to a careful description of the fiscal policy that Abū l-'Aysh b. Ayyūb should follow, and how this needed to abide by the established mālikite legal tradition. The diploma states that the basic tax is the Qur'anic *zakāt*, which is conceived as alms intended for the poor, and is referred to as *ṣadaqa* in fiscal terms. The *zakāt* is only collected from Muslims, as Christians and Jews (*dhimmis*) are subject to the payment of the poll tax (*jizyā*). Nevertheless, *zakāt* is to be paid only by those who possess a certain amount of gold, silver, livestock or crops. With regard to gold and silver, the tax is only charged if this capital is kept out of circulation, meaning that it is not being used for any commercial or money-lending activity. Nor is anyone who owns less than twenty *mithqals*' (or dinars')-worth of gold, or less than 200 dirhams'-worth of silver, obliged to pay. The tax is paid once a year and is calculated as a quarter of the tenth part (*rub' al-'ushr*) of the gold or silver owned.

The diploma also includes the complex calculation of the *zakāt* levied on livestock. This is based on the handing over of a certain quantity of livestock and depends on the size of the herd and type of animal involved. Therefore, the owner of fewer than five camels does not pay this tax, while the owner of a herd of five camels has to pay it, but with a single head of a lesser class of livestock; an owner of ten camels has to pay two head of a lesser beast, and the owner of

[10] Ibn Ḥayyān, *Muqtabis VII*, ed. pp. 112–14; trans. 143–4.

fifteen camels pays three head. For herds of more than twenty-four camels, one camel is paid per year. The bigger the herd, the greater the number of camels to be paid, and the age these are to be is also specified. Therefore, for example, the proud owner of a herd of 120 camels has to pay two two-year-old camels as *zakāt*. In the case of lesser livestock – sheep and goats – no payment is required for herds of fewer than forty head, but above this number and up to 120 head, just one animal has to be paid. From then on, the figure also increases according to the size of the herd. The same occurs with cattle: owners of fewer than thirty head are exempt: above that number they have to pay a two-year-old bullock, and the amount increases according to the size of the herd.

In addition, the diploma stated how the Qur'anic *zakāt* was levied on grain. A rule – compiled in this document and in many other legal commentators – established the minimum on which the tribute could be levied in five loads (sing. *wasq*), which were equivalent to 1,200 Madinese *mudd*. The *zakāt* was only collected on ownership above that quantity. In the case of land irrigated by rain and spring, it consisted of one tenth of the grain harvested, whereas farmers in dry regions, whose lands were irrigated by Persian wheels, were given a fiscal discount, as they only had to pay a fifth of the harvest. The *zakāt* was also levied on dates and grapes, but figs, walnuts, almonds and other fruits were exempt. Neither was it levied on olives, although olive oil was taxable.

Aside from the meticulous detail used to present this tax (the foregoing discussion is a succinct summary of a text full of lists of camels, sheep and other forms of property), what is most striking about this fiscal system is the importance of the *niṣāb*, or in other words, the minimum 'base' above which the tax can be levied. The application of the *niṣāb* ensured an extremely high number of exemptions: shepherds with fewer than forty sheep, or thirty cows or oxen – a very high figure for a peasant economy – did not have to worry in the slightest about the tax collector. The same occurred with a peasant with 1,200 Madinese *mudd* of grain in his silo (the equivalent of around six hundred kilos), a quantity that was more than sufficient to maintain a family of three members for a whole year, as a later Mālikite commentator observed.[11] If one adds to all this the restriction on customs taxes, tolls on people or travellers, and that 'neither by land, nor by sea, [could] tributes, *al-qabālat*, contributions

[11] A. Zysow, *Encyclopaedia of Islam*, 2nd ed. (hereafter EI, 2), s.v. *zakāt*.

[or] food taxes be levied, nor extortion or expenditure be demanded that imposes on their [people's] property', it is clear that what the Caliph al-Ḥakam recommended to the Berber tribal leader Abū l-'Aysh b. Ayyūb was a form of Islamic fiscal administration that went beyond being benign.

Now, if the content of this document is compared with the contemporaneous fiscal rules applied in al-Andalus – tithes, services, censuses, *al-qabālat*, charges, etc. – the contradiction was scandalous. Confronted with the paradox of a caliph who prescribed that a Berber tribal leader in the Rif implement a benign canonical tax system, while in his own domains he applied a degree of fiscal pressure that was as high as it was, scarcely backed up by Islamic tradition itself, any inhabitant of al-Andalus would have been indignant. In response to this hypothetical indignation the most likely answer would have been that requisitioning two-year-old camels would have made it impossible to collect the millions of dinars needed annually to build mosques, maintain *'ulamā'* and ensure peace across the caliph's domains. It is evident that this line of reasoning was used to ease the consciences of those *'ulamā'* who, on the one hand, endeavoured to instil the precepts of Muslim tradition, and, on the other, had no choice but to accept the fact that the complex apparatus of the Umayyad caliphate could not be sustained without the resources obtained from non-canonical taxes, which each year channelled immense resources directly into the state's coffers and indirectly into their pockets.[12] The collection of sheep and camels might have been adequate in rural and isolated tribal contexts, but it made no sense in a social and political environment as complex as that of al-Andalus.

Nonetheless, the contradiction was always a latent one. An awareness of this contradiction is fundamental to gaining an understanding of various other elements of the Andalusi caliphate, as well as medieval Muslim political structures more generally. It defines the tension between a form of power that seeks to legitimise itself through the religious inspiration of the message it was founded upon, but that finds that its authority slips due to its resounding failure to fulfil the moral programme it embodies. In times of prosperity it was easy to prioritise the pragmatism, protection and general welfare offered by

[12] A sound lesson taught to a Muslim scholar by a *ṣāḥib al-madīna* of Córdoba in response to his being criticised for collecting taxes in Ibn al-Qūṭiyya, *Ta'rīkh*, ed. pp. 94–5; trans. James p. 122.

power above any other consideration, but in times of economic, social or political crisis it was easy for the *'ulamā'*, religious preachers or common people to question the legitimacy of a power that demonstrated such little commitment to defending the principles of the Islamic orthodoxy upon which it claimed to be based.

In addition, it is highly significant that the recipient of the caliph's diploma was Abū l-ʿAysh b. Ayyūb, a Berber tribal leader from the rural Rif region, in the Maghreb, located on the margins of the geographical, social and political space that defined the Umayyad caliphate. Yet he was nonetheless charged to put into practice a rigorous programme of Islamic government. The very same precepts that the caliph himself could not, or would not, introduce to al-Andalus were to be implemented in the distant territories where this Kutāma chieftain lived. This was an implicit recognition of the impossibility of adopting the moral and religious programme that the caliph's authority embodied in the urban and highly developed social environment that flourished in al-Andalus. However, by prescribing that a peripheral group observe the strictest forms of Islamic orthodoxy, the caliph was paving the way for tribes such as the one led by Abū l-ʿAysh b. Ayyūb to claim to be guardians of religious authority in contrast to the moral decrepitude that prevailed in the centre of power. In this particular case, it does not seem that Abū l-ʿAysh carried this protest out, but the history of medieval Muslim societies is inundated with examples of other communities that did do so, thereby giving rise to movements of religious renewal that found in peripheral and tribal zones the social (and military) support they could not muster in urban environments. In later periods, following the fall of the caliphate of Córdoba, the rise of the Almoravid empire and subsequently that of the Almohads in the inland regions of Morocco, and their subsequent expansion to al-Andalus, demonstrates the effects that could result from conferring strict Islamic orthodoxy on groups that had nothing to lose by putting it into practice.

Manufacture under the Caliphs: Money, Ivory, Textiles and Ceramics

The caliph's palace or *alcázar* not only channelled an immense quantity of resources, it also transformed many of them before redistributing them. One evident case is the mint (*dār al-sikka*), which was based both in Córdoba and Madīnat al-Zahrāʾ. Precious metals were sent there for the production of dinars and dirhams in the caliph's name, thereby constituting one of the principal displays of his opulence. It was run by the head of the mint (*ṣāḥib al-sikka*), who was responsible for the quality of the coins issued, and on occasions he would engrave his own name on them. Huge quantities of wealth passed through the hands of these officials and some of them committed serious acts of embezzlement.[13] The head of the mint for much of the caliphate of al-Ḥakam II was an individual called Muḥammad b. Abī ʿĀmir, who was destined to play a key role in the events of the Umayyad caliphate.[14]

The annual coin production during this period reached an enormous scale. With regard to the silver coin, the dirham, estimates based on analysis of dies indicate hundreds of thousands of coins minted every year, and it is possible that occasionally as many as a million coins were minted. The silver supply came from a range of mining zones in al-Andalus, and there is evidence of them having functioned during this period.[15] Gold coins, or dinars, were minted thanks to the major trade routes opened up during this period between al-Andalus and the Maghreb, on the one hand, and mining centres such as Bambuk and Buré in Ghana, on the other. Gold was transported via trading cities such as Tadhmakka, in the north of what is today Mali, and, above all, Awdaghost, in today's Mauritania. The indefatigable traveller Ibn Ḥawqal visited the latter city in the mid-tenth century and what he saw there left a vivid impression on him: there was a flourishing trade linking Awdaghost with Sijilmāsa – in modern Morocco – and what was even more extraordinary was that merchants used a form of cheque as payment, whereby a trader from the latter city could record a debt of 42,000 dinars owed to a trader from Awdaghost, something Ibn Ḥawqal had never seen elsewhere. Furthermore, the sovereign of Awdaghost had ties to the king of Ghana, who was the richest man in the region thanks to the huge quantity of gold he owned.[16]

[13] Ibn Ḥayyān, *Muqtabis V*, ed. and trans. p. 327 on the case of Saʿīd b. Yassās, dismissed in 941 (330 AH) for fraud.

[14] A. Canto García, 'Las monedas del período 361–362 de la ceca de Madinat al-Zaḥra', pp. 205–10.

[15] See studies devoted to the supply of silver and other metals in A. Canto García and P. Cressier, eds, *Minas y metalurgia en al-Andalus y Magreb occidental*.

[16] Tādhmakka is cited in mid-tenth century Arabic sources as a commercial emporium, which has been confirmed by archaeological excavations undertaken in Essouk, in the north of modern Mali, S. Nixon, T. Rehren and M. F. Guerra, 'New Light on the Early Islamic West African Gold Trade', p. 1,357. N. Levtzion, 'Ibn Hawqal, the Cheque, and Awdaghost', pp. 225–7.

However, despite this route being open, the gold supply arrived in al-Andalus on an infrequent basis, due to the unstable political situation in North Africa during this period. Given the distance and lack of stable supply, Umayyad dinars were minted relatively scarcely in comparison to the silver coinage, although occasionally production figures could reach 100,000 dinars in one single year, which means that there were around four hundred kilos of gold ingots available in Córdoba.[17]

The silver dirham minted under al-Ḥakam II tended to weigh between 2.6 and 2.8 grams, and it was 70–80 per cent pure silver, which means that it was devalued by around 40 per cent with regard to the standard measure that established the coin's exact weight and purity. The Eastern traveller Ibn Ḥawqal confirms this when he states that seventeen Andalusi dirhams were needed to obtain one gold dinar, not the twelve dirhams per dinar that were the established exchange rate, which is exactly the rate to be expected from a silver coin devalued by that percentage.[18] Notarial documents used the abbreviated expression *dirham arbaʿīní*, which means 'dirham of the forty', in order to refer to this devalued dirham issued during the Umayyad caliphate. Legal contracts always had to make clear when they referred to this type of dirham, on the pretext that some wily individual might complain and argue that in reality a payment should be made in pure, and therefore more valuable, dirhams.[19]

Despite the fact that the dirham was the coin that was circulated throughout al-Andalus, the accounting system used by the Umayyad administration had always been expressed in terms of dinars, even though these gold coins were not minted before the caliphal period. This account currency was known as 'dinar of the arbaʿīn dirhams' (*dinār darāhīm bi-dakhl arbaʿīn*), or else, in its abbreviated form, *dinār darāhīm*. The equivalence between this account currency and the real dirhams minted by the Umayyads was 1:8, which means that the value of this currency of account was also devalued. However, after a long hiatus of almost two hundred years, during which no gold coins were

[17] E. Manzano Moreno and A. Canto García, 'The Value of Wealth: Coins and Coinage in Iberian Early Medieval Documents (9th–11th Centuries)'.

[18] Ibn Ḥawqal, *Ṣūrat al-arḍ*, pp. 109–10. Around this time, the exchange rate applied to dirhams issued by the Fāṭimid caliphs was 15.5 for one dinar. In other words, these were also devalued, although less so than the Andalusi dirhams, Balog, 'History of the Dirhem in Egypt', pp. 114–15.

[19] Ibn al-ʿAṭṭār *K. al-wathāʾiq*, ed. P. Chalmeta, p. 9; trans. M. Marugán, p. 45. A. Canto, 'De contenidos metálicos', pp. 133–4.

minted in al-Andalus, in 929 (317 AH) the trans-Saharan trade routes were re-established and gold brought from the mines in the Niger Basin allowed the Umayyad caliphs to resume the minting of dinars.[20] Despite the fact that the production of these coins was not as continuous or abundant as the caliphs would have wished, this did not detract from the coins' quality: the Umayyad caliphs' gold dinars were always excellent in terms of quality and weight.[21]

The exchange rate for high-quality dinars being issued at the caliphal mint was obviously superior to that for the dinar used as currency of account, which is why it was impossible to obtain one of these superior dinars for less than seventeen silver dirhams. On this issue, texts tend to be very explicit, and to avoid any confusion they refer to these real dinars with names such as '*mithqals*', 'weighed dinars' or '*ja'farid dinars*', in order to distinguish them from the lesser-value dinar used as currency of account, the *dinar of dirhams*.[22] This distinction was fundamental, as a good part of the Umayyad state structure depended upon the use of coins to pay stipends with, and to give as gifts.

Luxury textiles were also manufactured at caliphal workshops. For someone living in the tenth (fourth AH) century, these textiles were as valuable as gold and silver. Once more, the Umayyad caliphate centralised their production in the *dār al-ṭirāz*, the official workshop for textile production, whose importance is demonstrated by the inspections undertaken by the caliph himself, who was the principal 'customer' for the items made there. This workshop was located to the north-east of Córdoba's medina, and was run by a senior member of the administration. It was a relatively complex entity with both workshop staff (*al-quwwām bi l-'amāl*) and officials who undertook administrative roles (*al-quwwām min al-wukalā'*), along with a trustworthy official (*amīn*) and a secretary, who were in charge of the complex administration required to run the workshop. There was also a supervisor of

[20] Political control over these mines, possibly located on the frontier between contemporary Mali and Guinea, was held by the kingdoms that had formed in the Niger delta, S. Keech Macintosh, 'A Reconsideration of Wangara/Palolus Island of Gold', pp. 145–58.

[21] A. Canto, 'El dinar en al-Andalus', p. 333.

[22] E. Manzano Moreno, 'Moneda y articulación social en al-Andalus en época omeya', pp. 133–56. References in sources: Ibn al-'Aṭṭār, *K. al-wathā'iq*, ed. pp. 9, 92, 435; trans. pp. 45, 209, 666. The expression *dinār ṣiḥāḥ dakhl arba'īn* also appears in our source and is equivalent to that used by Ibn al-'Aṭṭār: Ibn Ḥayyān, *Muqtabis VII*, ed. p. 148; trans. p. 187. The translation of this passage ought to be corrected.

the tailors (*'arīf al-khayāṭīn*), who oversaw the weavers and was responsible for supervising production.[23]

It is possible that the *dār al-ṭirāz* supplied clothes to the employees of the administration in Córdoba, as was the case for the Fāṭimid caliphate, where every civil servant was given a ceremonial set of clothes that comprised everything 'from a turban to underpants'.[24] It is reported that the Berber troops that came to Córdoba to join the Umayyad army came dressed in rags, which they exchanged for clothes from the *ṭirāz*.[25] Also manufactured at the *dār al-ṭirāz* were the honorific garments (*khil'a*) that the caliph bestowed upon allies whom he wanted to forge diplomatic ties with, as well as members of the administration in Córdoba, who had provided outstanding service. The wearing of such textiles was a clear demonstration of status, as they displayed the wearer's special tie to the Umayyad caliph, while the garments themselves had a very high value in their own right.

As was the case with silver and gold coins, textiles were a class of wealth that was appreciated throughout the Mediterranean during the tenth (fourth AH) century. Only the most powerful sovereigns, such as the Byzantine emperors and the caliphs, could permit themselves the luxury of acquiring costly raw materials, such as silk, as well as funding the laborious and specialised processes required to treat them and manufacture the sought-after textiles. A clear indication of the value given to these textiles is provided by an incident involving Liutprand of Cremona, the Germanic Emperor Otto I's envoy to the court of Constantinople in 968. Just prior to his return, the ambassador had five pieces of purple cloth confiscated from his baggage. The officials explained to him that the export of these items was forbidden, as they were classed as an imperial monopoly. An infuriated Liutprand replied that in his country prostitutes and libertines (*obolariae mulieres et mandrogerontes*) used these supposedly so-exclusive cloths, which they obtained from merchants from the Italian cities of Venice and Amalfi. This reply surprised the Byzantines, who declared that

23 Ibn Ḥayyān, *Muqtabis VII*, ed. p. 92; trans. p. 115; on the "*arīf al-khayāṭīn*', ibid., pp. 25–6 and 48–50; also, *Muqtabis II, 2*, ed. pp. 61–2.

24 Y. K. Stillman, *Arab Dress*, p. 53.

25 Ibn 'Idhārī, *al-Bayān*, II, ed. p. 279; trans. p. 464. The soldiers' clothes were made of *khazz*, an inferior-grade silk.

they would be more vigilant in order to ensure that the textiles controlled by the emperor were not used as contraband.

Liutprand would probably have been even angrier had he known that a few years earlier merchants from Amalfi had sold batches and pieces of the precious purple to no less than the Muslim caliph of Córdoba himself, 'Abd al-Raḥmān III.[26] The ease in transporting textiles, the rarity of the materials used, the exclusivity of their colours and the originality of their designs made them highly appreciated luxury commodities, which were used not only as clothing but also for lining coffers, decorating walls and wrapping precious objects (as was done with relics in the Christian world). The thousands of fragments of textiles from the Islamic world nowadays preserved in museums around the world testify to their widespread circulation throughout the Mediterranean region from the mid-tenth century onwards, as a result of trade, but also the pillage that was a part of warfare.

Silk was the paramount luxury textile. In al-Andalus, it was produced in abundance in the provinces (*kūra*s) of Elvira and Pechina, especially in the Sierra Nevada region, from where it was sent to the *ṭirāz* in Córdoba. One of the most valuable varieties of silk was brocade (*dibāj*), a silk 'with marbled or decorated tendril motifs, woven frequently with gold or silver thread', for which it was forbidden to use dyes to enhance its effect. It was produced as individual pieces (*shuqāq*), which measured exactly three and a third palms, which the caliph made gifts of, so that their recipients would have them cut and tailored to suit their chosen purposes. On other occasions, this brocade was used to make the luxurious jubbas, long garments with wide sleeves. The same material may also have been used to make the *maṭārif* (sing. *miṭraf*), a form of waistcoat that was worn over the jubba and was produced in specific colours. Finally, *dibāj* was also used to cover the dais that the court's most senior civil servant sat upon.[27]

[26] Liutprand of Cremona, *Legatio*, ed. Becker, pp. 204–5. Ibn Ḥayyān, *Muqtabis V*, ed. and trans. p. 322. E. Manzano, 'Circulation des biens', p. 176. On the dyes used, D. Jacoby, 'Silk Economics', pp. 211–12.

[27] E. Mesa Fernández, *El lenguaje de la indumentaria*, pp. 121 and 207; E. García Gómez, 'Tejidos, ropas y tapicería', p. 49. The *dibāj* was one of the cloths used as the curtain (*kiswa*) concealing the Kaaba, R. B. Serjeant, *Islamic Textiles*, p. 135. The ban on using dyes for this cloth in Ibn 'Abd al-Ra'ūf, *Risāla fī adāb al-ḥisba wa l-muḥtasib*, ed. É. Lévi-Provençal, p. 86; trans. R. Arié, pp. 35–6. The same author records the measurements used for the individual pieces (*shuqāq*), as

The gifts sent by Caliph al-Ḥakam II to his allies in North Africa frequently included the presence of coloured *khazz* textiles from the *ṭirāz* (*al-khazz al-ṭirāzī al-mulawwan*). Although at times *khazz* is translated as 'silk', this is inaccurate, as the specific word used in the sources to designate the latter textile was *ḥarīr*. *Khazz*, an inferior-grade silk – *alchaz* or *alhaz* in contemporaneous Christian documents – was in reality a textile woven with a silk warp and a wool weft.[28] During the emirate era, a satirical poet mocked the renowned Baghdadi singer Ziryāb, who had settled in al-Andalus and had become the prescriber of good taste in Córdoba, by alluding to the sweat that stained the dresses made of *khazz* that he wore:[29]

she suffers from being alone and weeps, just as weeps
the khazz at the underarms of 'Alī b. Nafi'

In some cases, linen was used as the weft instead of wool, as was the case with a cloth from the monastery of San Pedro de Montes, most likely used for a turban, in which the warp was linen and the weft a variety of colours of silk thread.[30] Turbans (*'amā'im*) were considered a sign of identity of the Berbers, while in al-Andalus during this period people of a high social standing, as well as those knowledgeable in Islamic law, would usually wear a form

well as other measurements used for textiles, ibid., p. 114; trans. pp. 363–4. On the provenance of silk, E. López Martínez de Marigorta, *Mercaderes, artesanos y ulemas. Las ciudades del sudeste de al-Andalus en época omeya*, 60–5. On the dais covered with *dibāj* that was offered to Ja'far al-Muṣḥafi when he was appointed *ḥājib* according to an 'ancient custom', M. Marín, 'Signos visuales de la identidad andalusí', p. 155, based on Ibn Bassām.

[28] With regard to this interpretation I follow that of E. Kühnel, 'Abbasid Silks of the Ninth Century', p. 370, n. 16 as opposed to that of other authors such as Serjeant. An altar cloth *uermiculum de alhaz* is cited as early as 927 in a document from León; *casullas xiii v de alchaz* is given in another dated to 942 from the Monastery of Celanova, R. Lapesa, *Léxico hispánico primitivo*, pp. 34–5.

[29] The author of these verses was the poet Mu'min b. Sa'īd, Ibn Ḥayyān, *Muqtabis II, 1*, ed. cit. p. 334; trans. cit. p. 215.

[30] C. Bernis, 'Tapicería hispano-musulmana (siglos IX–XI)', pp. 197–8. C. Partearroyo, 'Almaizar de San Pedro de Montes', p. 264. See also 'Tejidos andalusíes', *Artigrama*, 22, 2007, pp. 371–419, for this and other textiles from this period. In the Spanish edition of this book, I stated that a textile found in the Monastery of San Salvador de Oña was dated to the Umayyad period, for which I drew on M. Casamar and J. Zozaya, 'Apuntes sobre la ŷuba funeraria de la colegiata de Oña (Burgos)', p. 40. This date should be corrected: M. A. Martínez Núñez has convincingly argued that its epigraphic style corresponds to the end of the eleventh century, see 'Al-Andalus durante el período almorávide a través de la documentación epigráfica', p. 68 and n. 14. Nevertheless, the analysis of the dyes confirms that the red used in this textile was made from kermes, the pigment for which Andalusi textiles were widely renowned, M. Barrera, C. Gómez and M. Burón, 'Estudios previos y metodologia aplicada a la conservación de ajuares funerarios textiles en Castilla y León', p. 93.

Image 1 Andalusi textile from San Pedro de Montes (León). This is a silk weave with a linen warp and silk weft. The use of red, characteristic of Andalusian textiles, stands out. As in many other cases, this precious caliphal textile ended up in the Leonese monastery of San Pedro de Montes, where it was used to wrap relics.

of high conical cap, known as a *qalansuwa*, which was on occasions made from brocade (*washī*). These were also commonly worn in the East by high-ranking individuals.[31] It is for this reason that turbans often formed part of the

[31] M. Marín, 'Signos visuales de la identidad andalusí', pp. 149–50. The brocade *qalansuwa* was also used by the heads of the standing army (*jund*), Ibn Ḥayyān, *Muqtabis VII*, ed. p. 199; trans. p. 240. It is said that al-Ḥakam II ordered that whoever knew the *Mudawwana*, a key legal text from the Mālikite tradition, by heart 'could not wear a turban', and as a result more than three hundred men were asked to do so, al-Zuhrī, *K. al-Ja'rāfiyya*, based on Ibn Ḥayyān, ed. M. Hadj Sadok, p. 219; trans. D. Bramon, pp. 153–4: as this author rightly points out, n. 750, this passage only makes sense if we think that the caliph authorised these people to wear the *qalansuwa*, worn by the *fuqahā'*. In the East the 'abbāsíd caliphs used a *qalansuwa ṭawīla*, a tall silk biretta. N. M. El Cheikh, 'The Institutionalisation of 'Abbāsid Ceremonial', p. 363.

gifts that the caliph gave to North African tribes. They were produced both in *khazz* and a form of linen (*sharb*), which was akin to gauze in its fineness. This type of linen is also cited in Egyptian documents, and was used for the production of turbans, women's underwear and even festive garments. A wide variety of colours and tonalities was used for turbans, which included sky blue, red, dark green, turquoise and apple green. In some cases, fabrics made for turbans included inscriptions.[32]

A well-known passage by the geographer Ibn Ḥawqal notes that Andalusi *ṭirāz* reached as far as Egypt and even Khurāsān. The same author praised the quality of Cordoban linen and silk, the latter in its two forms, *khazz* and *qazz*. The second of these referred to the thread obtained from the exterior of the silkworm's cocoon, which was cruder in texture. In his praise, Ibn Ḥawqal went so far as to declare that the fine *khazz* or *al-khazz al-sharb* produced in al-Andalus was better than that made for the *sulṭān* in Iraq. This was noteworthy praise, given that during the same period another Eastern author, al-Muqaddasī, declared that the turbans made from the fine silk (*sharb*) of Kūfa were one of Iraq's specialities and that not even those made in Sūs could rival them. The term *sharb* alludes to the extreme fineness of this textile, which gave it an appearance akin to flowing water.[33]

Another textile that seems to have earned al-Andalus considerable renown, again according to Ibn Ḥawqal, was felt (*labd*) made with wool. Its quality was particularly appreciated due to the exceptional Andalusi dyes. Felt items, which at times were made exclusively for the caliph, could cost as much as 50 or 60 dinars. A century before, in the East, al-Jāhiz (d. 868/255 AH) likewise referred to the quality of the Maghreb felts – with which he undoubtedly included the Andalusi ones – and praised them in comparison with those made in Khurāsān and China, deeming them superior to those made in Armenia, another region renowned for this material.[34] Although 'Īsā al-Rāzī does not

[32] X. Ballestín Navarro, 'Jil'a y monedas', pp. 399, 400, 402, 405, 407–9. E. Mesa, *El lenguaje de la indumentaria*, pp. 75 and 121. On the symbolic value of the turban, Stillman, *Arab Dress*, pp. 16–17. E. García Gómez, 'Tejidos, ropas y tapicería', p. 45, points out that the *lāsa* – name of a cloth used as a turban in our text – was still being used in Egypt during the twentieth century, but I have not been able to find any reference to it.

[33] Ibn Ḥawqal, *Ṣūrat al-arḍ*, p. 113. R. B. Serjeant, *Islamic Textiles*, p. 45. On the meaning of the *al-sharb*, Lane Pool, *Arab Dictionary*, s.v.

[34] Serjeant, *Islamic Textiles*, p. 64.

mention them, we know that they were made in the *ṭirāz* in Córdoba, as there is a reference from the time of ʿAbd al-Raḥmān III to 'purple felt from the *ṭirāz*' (*al-lubūd al-ṭirāziyya al-urjuwāniyya*) as part of a gift sent by the caliph to a North African tribal leader.[35]

The most highly esteemed silk in al-Andalus was a foreign one called *ʿubaydī*. The Caliph ʿAbd al-Raḥmān III used it as part of his attire, as he made clear to one North African tribal leader when he sent him ten pieces of this cloth. *ʿUbaydī* clothes are also listed among the gifts that the Caliph al-Ḥakam reserved for the highest-ranking North African tribal leaders and the most powerful members of his court. Sometimes pieces of coloured *ʿubayd* textiles (*shiqāq ʿubaydiyya al-mulawwana*) were given, while on other occasions these were 'lined textiles' (*mubaṭṭanāt ʿubaydiyya*) or jubbas made with dyed *khazz ʿubaydī* (*al-khazz al-ʿubaydī al-mulawwan*), clearly different from the simple *khazz* that also came from the *ṭirāz*. Although we do not know the exact place where this mysterious textile came from, nor what it looked like, *ʿubaydī* would undoubtedly have been imported from Iraq.[36]

Silk required a laborious production process that involved the use of dyes such as red or purple, which at times were extraordinarily difficult to obtain. As was discussed in the previous chapter, the pigment called *grana* was sent every spring to Córdoba and was obtained from the dried body of an insect that lived in a shrub of the holm-oak family. Al-Jāhiz stated that it was only to be found in three places in the world: al-Andalus, the Maghreb and a district of the Iranian region of Fars. In the early modern period, six to fourteen pounds of this dye were needed to colour a single pound of silk. Another highly esteemed dye in the Umayyad court was purple. This was an influence from Byzantium, where this dye was manufactured from *murex*, a relatively abundant Mediterranean mollusc: around twelve thousand of them were needed to produce just under one and half grams of purple. Such laborious production could only be justified by the close association of this dye with imperial power.

[35] Ibn Ḥayyān, *Muqtabis V*, ed. and trans. p. 208.

[36] E. García Gómez, 'Tejidos, ropas y tapicería', pp. 44–5. X. Ballestín Navarro, 'Jilʿa y monedas', p. 399, n. 19 correctly asserts that García Gómez's claim for an Iraqi provenance based on Ibn Ḥawqal is not conclusive, but the testimony provided by Ibn Ḥayyān, *Muqtabis V*, ed. and trans. p. 238 is in my view indubitable, although doubts may be raised about the passage's punctuation. For the references made in *Muqtabis VII*, see the footnotes below on the gifts sent by the caliph. Pieces of *ʿubaydí* textile in a gift described in *Muqtabis V*, ed. and trans. p. 238.

It was used as an indelible dye to stamp textiles that were then considered an imperial monopoly. Indeed, a room in the emperor's palace in Constantinople was tiled with porphyry, and was where the empresses gave birth to the royal heirs, who were referred to as *porphyrogenetos*, literally 'born to purple'. In al-Andalus, the Umayyad caliphs sought to obtain this colour by purchasing purple from merchants from Amalfi; it is also possible that the aforementioned 'purple felt from the *ṭirāz*' (*al-lubūd al-ṭirāziyya al-urjuwāniyya*), which the caliph sent to the North African leaders, was an attempt to imitate Byzantine textile production.[37]

Other caliphal productions were centralised in the 'house of manufacture' (*dār al-ṣināʿa*), which was located within the *alcázar* in Córdoba, very possibly next to an entrance on the northern perimeter of the palace complex, which was named *Bāb al-Ṣināʿa*. A great variety of items were made there under the close supervision of the caliph's trusted staff. It was in the *dār al-ṣināʿa*, for example, that a large basin, brought from Constantinople to decorate the rooms of Madīnat al-Zahrā', was adorned with twelve statues made in red gold and encrusted with pearls.[38]

Among the luxury items made in these caliphal workshops were ivory pyxides, caskets and boxes, of which just over twenty magnificent examples have survived today. They were exquisitely made objects that were often given as gifts by the Umayyad caliph, both to members of his court and to individuals with whom he wanted to establish closer ties. A gift sent by ʿAbd al-Raḥmān III to a Berber tribal chief contained, among other things, three ivory pyxides (*ḥuqqa*). The first was made in a white ivory and contained incense and amber, the second, also made of ivory, had silver hinges and inside a container from Iraq filled with civet, while the third had a flat top and silver hinges and contained royal perfumes (*bajūr al-mulūk*). The function of these ivory pyxides

[37] The account given by al-Jāhiz in Serjeant, *Islamic Textiles*, p. 65. For the calculations of the quantity of *grana* needed for silk production see D. Jacoby, 'Silk Economics', p. 211. On the *murex*, Pliny, *Historia Natural*, pp. 9, 60–3. On the purchase of purple, E. Manzano Moreno, 'Circulation de biens et richesses', pp. 31–2. It was perhaps not by chance that a form of violet limestone, emulating purple, was used in considerable quantities for the paving of Madīnat al-Zahrā', A. Vallejo Triano, *La ciudad califal de Madīnat al-Zahrā'*, pp. 353–5. Later examples, made with indigo, are discussed in L. Rodríguez Peinado, 'Púrpura. Materialidad y simbolismo en la Edad Media', p. 482.

[38] Ibn ʿIdhārī, *al-Bayān*, II, ed. p. 231; trans. p. 382.

as containers of exquisite materials or highly-esteemed perfumes is confirmed by a pyxis preserved at the Hispanic Society in New York, whose inscription includes a brief poem:

> The sight I offer is the fairest, the firm breast of a delicate girl.
> Beauty has invested me with splendid raiment, which makes a display of jewels.
> I am a recipient of musk, camphor and ambergris.

The image of the girl's firm breast in reference to the rounded lid crowned with a button, the jewels that the silver hinges were made of and the luxury perfumes and unguents it contained confirm the refinement associated with the possession of these objects.[39]

What is most striking about the caliphal ivory workshop is the extraordinary technical skills displayed through its output, despite the fact that this manufacture was unprecedented.[40] The ivory pyxides, as well as coffers, were always made as a single piece, which means a single elephant tusk was used. Elsewhere, such as in the Byzantine Empire, ivory was carved in panels, which were later joined or attached to a wooden core. In contrast, the Umayyad artisans worked directly on the elephant tusk, which must have meant a significant outlay of raw material. It also suggests there was a considerable number of tusks available, as any error or breakage meant that the piece would have to be discarded.

The ivory used in al-Andalus was most certainly African. The Eastern author al-Mas'ūdī referred to a flourishing trade in elephant tusks from East Africa, which were exported to India, as well as to China via Oman and Basra in Iraq. It is possible that a branch of this trade diverged towards North Africa, although it is more plausible to think that the ivory arrived in Córdoba via the same western route that brought the gold from the upper course of the River Niger, which was used to mint dinars. Just as was noted with regard to gold, there does not seem to have been a continual flow of ivory, and all the evidence

[39] Ibn Ḥayyān, *Muqtabis V*, ed. and trans. p. 238. E. Kühnel, *Die islamischen Elfenbeiskulpturen*, pp. 36–7; tafel XIII–XIV. M. Rosser-Owen, 'A Cordoban Ivory Pixis', p. 19; M. Rosser Owen, 'The Metal Mounts of Andalusi Ivories: Initial Observations', pp. 301–16; J. Beckwith, *Caskets from Cordoba*, p. 14.

[40] On this issue, A. Cutler, 'Ivory Working in Umayyad Cordoba', pp. 37–47.

suggests that this was a periodic trade, which greatly depended upon the diverse factors that affected such a costly commerce involving such long distances. In fact, recent analysis has shown that the ivories might be considerably older than the craftsmanship that decorated them (up to a century or two in the oldest cases), which suggests the existence of stocks of ivory that had been stored and circulated over long periods prior to their eventual carving. The discovery in Gao (Mali) of a treasury of fifty hippopotamus tusks dating from the mid-ninth century seems to indicate that these materials could be accumulated during long periods of time until finally export channels to the north were established and there was sufficient demand to justify moving them.[41]

In the case of the ivory objects produced for the Umayyad caliphate, the dates of the extant examples would seem to confirm that rather than there having been a constant flow of ivory to the Cordoban court, there were occasional deliveries of tusks, which were rapidly carved under the supervision of senior officials of the administration. This would explain the decorative and technical similitude of the examples known today, as essentially what we are dealing with are the same artisans, who undertook very similar forms of work over the course of these decades as part of the state workshops' highly centralised production process.[42]

The same homogeneity is noted in another product that can also be linked to state power: although ceramics do not seem to have formed part of the caliph's major gifts, they filled the halls of power, and there is no doubt that their production was likewise centralised. A rich variety of tableware was displayed in the residences that hosted ambassadors and visitors, and these included bowls, basins, jugs, flasks and drinking vessels. There is a wide range of archaeological evidence that testifies to a broad formal repertoire of luxury

[41] S. M. Guerin, 'Forgotten Routes? Italy, Ifrīqiya and the Trans-Saharan Ivory Trade', *al-Masaq*, 25, 1, 2013, pp. 70–91. M. Roser Owen, 'Questions of Authenticity: The Imitation Ivories of D. Francisco Pallás y Puig (1859–1926)', *Journal of the David Collection*, 2, 2, 2005, pp. 259–60. A. Shalem, 'Trade in and the Availability of Ivory', p. 29, cites a text by al-Maqqarī translated by P. de Gayangos, which refers to the gift that the North African tribal leader Zīrī b. 'Aṭiyya sent to al-Manṣūr and which included 8,000 pounds of ivory along with horses, exotic animals and clothes made of fine wool. However, this passage does not appear in the published edition of this work, and while other sources refer to this gift, Ibn Khaldūn, Ibn Abī Zar' and the anonymous *K. Mafākhir al-barbar*, they make no mention of any ivories having been included. These texts have been meticulously analysed by X. Ballestí, *Al-Mansur y la dawla 'amiriyya*, pp. 185–91.

[42] M. A. Martínez, 'Recientes hallazgos epigráficos en Madīnat al-Zahrā'', pp. 48–50 and 71–2.

Umayyad ceramics, which are referred to as green and manganese ware, and which have been found in abundance at excavations in Madīnat al-Zahrā', Córdoba and other locations. Two oxide glazes were used to make these ceramics: copper, which produced a characteristic green colour, and manganese, which contributed blackish and even purple tones that were inscribed on the white background. It is very common that the inscription *'al-mulk'* ('the power') was included on these ceramics, which reinforces the idea of their being fired in kilns located just outside Córdoba's city walls and then distributed in a centralised manner. A fairly exceptional aspect of the caliphal ceramic production was the representation of human figures, such as musicians and warriors, which were included as decoration. In contrast, the so-called 'common ware', which was also used in Madīnat al-Zahrā', had different forms – above all, large receptacles for liquids, such as pitchers and pots – but there are no examples of it being used for large plates or bowls, as is the case with the green and manganese ware. This seems to indicate that the latter tended to confer a clearly demarcated status on whoever used it.[43]

Expenditure: Building Projects, Salaries and Gifts

The corresponding entry to the fiscal revenue that filled the caliphate's coffers was the expenditure that flowed out of them, part of which was employed in maintaining the caliph and his domestic and family household. An estimate of the expenses recorded for the 'Abbāsid caliphate in 918 (306 AH) included, aside from the soldiers' and bureaucrats' salaries, payments to the caliph's mother, the princes and other family members, and the overseers of the stables and the ferrymen, as well as payments for the acquisition of animals along with their feed, for celebrations (including the ice used), for the caliph's garments, and for repairs and maintenance to the palace buildings. The total annual expenditure was over two and half million dinars, which flowed from the caliph's palace in all directions.[44]

[43] C. Cano Piedra, *La cerámica verde-manganeso de Madínat al-Zahrā*; A. Vallejo Triano and J. Escudero Aranda, 'Aportaciones para una tipología de la cerámica común califal de Madinat al-Zahra', p. 146; L. Aparicio Sánchez and E. Cano Montoro, 'Fragmento cerámico con decoración antropomorfa', pp. 194–5.

[44] al-Ṣābi', *Rusūm dār al-khilāfa. The Rules and Regulations of the 'Abbāsid Court*, trans. E. A. Salem, Beirut, 1977, pp. 23–5.

Something similar must have happened in al-Andalus. In the caliphal period, it is said that the fiscal revenue was divided into three categories: one was used to pay the army (*jund*), another for undertaking large building projects, and the third for increasing the treasury's reserves. There is no doubt that the accounting system used by the caliphate of Córdoba was far more complex and included other entries, yet there is an element of truth in this observation: the caliphs were inclined to accumulate reserves in their treasury – see the figures given above – while the army, which I refer to below, and building projects were always prominent areas of expenditure, something that helped to enhance the social impact of the exercise of the caliphs' power.

Construction projects are a particularly a good example of the multiplier effect that resulted from the demand created by the caliphate. The building of Madīnat al-Zahrā' involved very considerable expenses, and this had a multiplier effect on economic activity. The sources mention 350 to 500 deliveries of limestone and similar quantities of plaster on a daily basis. Each day, 6,000 stone blocks of varying sizes were delivered from the neighbouring quarries of Santa María de Albaida on the backs of 1,400 mules, a thousand of which had to be hired at a price of three dinars of good quality per month, which is the same as 51 dirhams. Along with these and many other expenses, the cost of building the city rose to 300,000 dinars annually over the course of the decades it took to complete, an astronomical quantity that transferred the tributes paid each year by the Andalusi population to the pockets of the thousands of people involved directly or indirectly in the project.[45]

Al-Ḥakam II spent equally high sums of money on the extension of the Mosque of Córdoba. This resulted in an addition of around 2,820 square metres, crowned by the marvellous *miḥrāb* that is still to be seen today. Begun in 962 (351 AH), it is said that this extension, according to a document in the caliph's own hand, cost just over 260,000 dinars. To set the concerns of the pious to rest, an assurance was given that this was funded with money received from the fifth part of the spoils of the military campaigns against the Christians. Additional to these expenses was the cost of the pulpit, or *minbar*, that the caliph also commissioned for the remodelled mosque: the price rose

[45] Ibn Ghālib, *K. farḥat al-anfus*, ed. L. ʿAbd al-Badīʿ, pp. 31–2; al-Maqqarī, *Nafḥ*, I, 524–6. On the provenance of the materials used A. Vallejo, *La ciudad califal*, pp. 103–15.

Image 2 Madīnat al-Zahrā' was built to the west of Córdoba, taking advantage of the difference in altitude between the mountains and the Guadalquivir valley. The city had a terraced layout, a reflection of the social and political hierarchy of the caliphate. The image shows a general view of the palace.

to over 35,705 dinars. Made out of a total of 36,000 pieces consisting of fragments of red sandalwood, ebony, aloe and ivory, the pulpit had ten steps.[46]

Apart from these major construction projects, the caliphal administration undertook many others in a variety of locations. One of them, for example, was the repair of the ancient Roman bridge of Córdoba, which began in August 971 (*dhū l-qaʿda*, 360 AH) and was completed in November the same year. A temporary dam (*sudd*) had to be built upstream, using branches of shrubs brought from the mountains, stones, sand and clay to divert the river and leave the bridge's piers fully exposed. While undertaking the work, they also

[46] Ibn ʿIdhārī, *al-Bayān*, II, ed. p. 241; trans. p. 398. M. I. Fierro, 'The Mobile Minbar in Cordoba', pp. 152–4; F. Hernández Jiménez 'El almimbar móvil del siglo X en la mezquita de Córdoba', p. 393.

renovated the foundations and pillars of the 'mills of Kulayb' (*arḥā Kulayb*), which were located downstream below the bridge, whereby their use for milling grain was interrupted during this period. This repair work was overseen by the caliph's representatives (*khulafā'*), servants and secretaries, but al-Ḥakam II did not deny himself the opportunity to spend moments of his leisure time contemplating the progress of the repairs from the balconies of the *alcázar*, as well as giving instructions to the long-suffering workers on how to do their work (thus pre-empting an activity that has a legion of adepts today).[47]

Just as the caliphate paid for the materials and workforce required for the building projects, significant expenses were also incurred when ordering luxury products from the merchants who imported raw materials or sumptuary objects from afar, or when the caliphs' patronage extended to the intellectual activity of the writers and *'ulamā'*, who lived comfortable lives thanks to the sovereign's munificence. Receiving a payment of two dinars per week for the woodwork of the pulpit (*minbar*) in the Mosque of Córdoba, selling marble for the city palace of Madīnat al-Zahrā' at three dinars a piece, or obtaining a stipend and a horse as tutor to the son of al-Ḥakam II, are examples that show how specialists could flourish and live thanks to the redistributive capacity of the caliphate of Córdoba.[48]

However, the main beneficiaries of the caliphate's capacity for redistributing wealth were the high-ranking figures along with the administration's employees, both civil and military, who formed a dominant class referred to as the *khaṣṣa*, so that all those who belonged to it had a clear sense of their status. In contrast to what was frequently encountered in Western medieval society, the Umayyad caliphs rarely gave land to members of this social class for the services they rendered; instead they were usually paid in money or kind. The holders of senior posts in the administration of al-Ḥakam II were paid stipulated salaries, as was done for the standing army, whose professional

[47] Ibn Ḥayyān, *Muqtabis VII*, ed. pp. 58 and 64–5; trans. pp. 77–8. At this point the editor has committed an error in dividing the information given in the manuscript into two parts when it ought to be a single part.

[48] The two weekly dinars for the mosque's *minbar* in al-Maqqarī, *Nafḥ*, I, p. 551; the cost of pieces of marble in Ibn 'Idhārī, *al-Bayān al-Mughrib*, ed. cit. p. 231; when Aḥmad b. Muḥammad al-Qasṭalī was named tutor to Hishām, the caliph ordered that he be assigned a stipend (*rizq*) consistent with a salary (*rātib*), a horse (*ḥumlān*) and horse fodder (*'alūfa*), Ibn Ḥayyān, *Muqtabis VII*, ed. p. 77; trans. pp. 99–100.

soldiers were paid regularly so as to be at the caliph's disposal throughout the year. Furthermore, the bags of money given to these people in turn served to encourage the agricultural and commercial activity of the lower strata of society.

This system depended on monetary circulation, which in al-Andalus was socially determined. For wide sectors of society, the only option available in order to benefit from this circulation was to cut the silver dirhams the caliph minted into pieces that were then used for the purchase of low-value items. The presence of these fragments in hoards from this period and the evident regularity with which the coins were cut – quarters and thirds of the coin – indicate that this practice was widely extended. For example, the largest ever Umayyad treasury of silver coins, which was found at Haza del Carmen (Córdoba), weighed a total of 42.28 kilos: it contained 8,000 complete coins, the most recent one minted in 386 AH (996–7), while the remainder consisted of fragments, whose total weight was 22.68 kilos.[49]

In the upper social circles, transactions were made predominantly in complete dirhams: the purchase of land, slaves, steeds, weapons and other items could only be paid for with a specific number of these silver coins. This was a much more restricted social circle, one whose members were paid for their service in the army or administration, or else as traders in luxury goods or items that were not simple everyday products. In these cases, the sums involved were stated in terms of the currency of account, the *dinār darāhīm*, which was the equivalent to eight real silver coins.

Finally, there was the gold coin, the dinar minted by the caliphs, whose circulation was restricted to the ruling class of the Umayyad state: the caliph paid the senior army generals with these dinars, used them to make gifts to powerful people with whom he wanted to establish political alliances, gave them as an ostentatious recompense for a singular service rendered, or else used them to buy luxury items brought from distant places. Therefore, in this upper echelon of society the circulation of money and wealth in general had a marked political dimension. The giving of gifts or the provision of stipends forged bonds with the powerful people the caliph depended on and thereby played a key role in articulating the dynamics of the caliphal state itself.

[49] A. Canto, *Maskukat*, pp. 25–46.

Image 3 Silver dirham minted in 361 AH (971–2). Left: 'Al imām al-Ḥakam, amīr al-mu'minīn, al-Mustanṣir bi-llāh; margin: In the name of God. This dirham was coined at *Madīnat al-Zahrā'* in 361. Right: 'There is no god but God only. No associated'; margin: Muḥammad is the Messenger of God. It is He who sent His Messenger with guidance and the religion of Truth, to prevail over all religions

Image 4 Golden dinar minted in 362 AH (972–3) in Madīnat al-Zahrā'. Left: 'Al imām al-Ḥakam, amīr al-mu'minīn, al-Mustanṣir bi-llāh; margin: In the name of God. This dinār was coined at *Madīnat al-Zahrā'* in 362. Right: 'There is no god but God only. No associated'; margin: Muḥammad is the Messenger of God. It is He who sent His Messenger with guidance and the religion of Truth, to prevail over all religions

A poet from the court of al-Ḥakam II, Muḥammad b. Shujayṣ, expressed the sense of this political and social exchange with great veracity:[50]

Islam knows very well what you spend,
whom you help with a pledge, and whom you defend.
With what you spill, you unite us all,
by scattering treasure, you bring us together.

Al-Ḥakam's redistribution of wealth effectively managed to gather around him the state's ruling class, which profited not only from abundant stipends, but also from the gifts intended for the benefit of singular individuals, whom the caliphs wished to extol above their peers. A good example is provided by the ivories that were produced in the caliphal workshops with exquisite workmanship, and that were highly esteemed possessions. The examples that have been preserved bear inscriptions that reveal that they were generally used as gifts for members of the caliph's family circle. The only (and very notable) exception is an ivory pyxis dated 359 AH (969–70), which was dedicated to Ziyād b. Aflaḥ, an official who served as vizier and *ṣāḥib al-shurṭa al-ʿulyā*. In the case of all the other ivories whose recipients have been identified, their recipients were family members of al-Ḥakam II. Of special importance among them was Subḥ, the mother of his two sons, ʿAbd al-Raḥmān, who died prematurely aged eight in 970 (359 AH), and Hishām, who would succeed his father as caliph. An ivory was made especially for her on al-Ḥakam's orders, upon which he is named as Commander of the Faithful (*amīr al-muʾminīn*). Known as the 'Pyxis of Zamora', due to it having been preserved in this city's cathedral, this ivory was made under the supervision (*ʿalā yaday*) of Durrī al-Ṣaghīr in 353 AH (964).[51] The pyxis is a celebration of Subh's fertility. It is the first known example of figurative representation being used in an Andalusi ivory – those dated to the period of ʿAbd al-Raḥmān III have only decorative plant motifs – and it depicts peacocks, birds and antelopes.

[50] Ibn Ḥayyān, *Muqtabis VII*, ed. p. 137; trans. p. 172. Little is known about this poet, except that he died before 400 AH (1009–10), *Biblioteca de al-Andalus*, s.v. Ibn Shujayṣ, Muḥammad.

[51] 'Blessing of God for the imām, the slave of God, al-Ḥakam al-Mustanṣir billâh, the emir of the faithful, who ordered this to be made for the Lady (*al-Sayyida*), mother of the prince ʿAbd al-Raḥmān, under the direction of Durrī al-Saghīr, in the year 353 (964)', É. Lévi-Provençal, *Inscriptions arabes de l'Espagne*, pp. 186–7. E. Kühnel, *Die islamischen Elfenbeiskulpturen*, p. 33, tafel XII, XIII.

Image 5 The 'Zamora' pixys is dedicated to the caliph's concubine, Subḥ, and celebrates her fertility in a lush vegetal decoration from which birds and antelopes emerge.

Two years after this pyxis was made, in 355 AH (966–7) another two ivory pyxides decorated only with plant motifs were made in Madīnat al-Zahrā' and given to Wallada, a sister of al-Ḥakam II.[52] Another two years later, in

[52] One of these boxes, preserved in the church of Fitero (Navarra), was made by a person called Khalaf, and its inscription wishes happiness, good fortune, joy and congratulation to Wallada. The other – conserved in the Instituto de Valencia de Don Juan (Madrid) – was made in Madīnat al-Zahrā' in the same year and also offers all sorts of good wishes to the caliph's sister, E. Kühnel, *Die islamischen Elfenbeiskulpturen*, pp. 34–5, tafel X, XI. É. Lévi-Provençal, *Inscriptions arabes de l'Espagne*, p. 187, provided a rather forced reading of the text to make it refer to Subḥ, the concubine of the caliph al-Ḥakam. However, the reading of the French Arabist is mistaken, as was demonstrated by R. Ocaña, *El cúfico hispánico y su evolución*, p. 37. However, historiography has continued this error. S. Blair, 'What the Inscriptions Tell Us: Texts and Message on the Ivories from al-Andalus' p. 79. I am grateful to María Antonia Martínez for her help in solving this problem.

357 AH (968–9), another ivory pyxis was made that is today preserved in the Musée du Louvre. This pyxis was made to be given to al-Mughīra, one of the caliph's half-brothers and the youngest son of 'Abd al-Raḥmān III; in his old age, the latter caliph had shown a predilection for him. Apart from the fact that al-Mughīra lived in Córdoba and rigorously attended the receptions held by his brother, the caliph, not much else is known about him. The inscription that crowns this ivory pyxis simply wishes prosperity and happiness to al- Mughīra 'son of the Emir of the Faithful'. No mention is made of al-Ḥakam having ordered the making of this pyxis, which has a singular complex iconographic design: four medallions with eight lobes framing a variety of figurative scenes ranging from a depiction of two gentlemen eating dates from a palm tree while two dogs bite their feet to one of two men stealing eggs from an eagle's nest, as well as a scene in which a slave plays the laud to two figures who carry a range of objects, while in another one two lions are depicted biting two bulls. Considerable speculation has been devoted to the meaning of these scenes, especially bearing in mind the sorry fate that awaited al-Mughīra: as will be discussed below, he was killed in cold blood just hours after his brother al-Ḥakam II died in October 976 (366 AH). However, the evidence for any political meaning of the iconography of this pyxis is very vague.[53]

Beyond his closest family circle, when the caliph received a senior member of his administration for the purposes of instructing him to undertake a mission, he would offer him a sumptuous gift at the end of the audience, a custom that was also commonplace at the court of the 'Abbāsíd caliphs. This was the case for the *qā'id*, or general, Muḥammad b. Qāsim b. Ṭumlus. In June 972 (*Ramaḍān*, 361 AH), having been received by the caliph and given orders to cross the Strait of Gibraltar and wage war against a number of North African tribal leaders, he was given a selection of honorific garments (*khil'a*) along with cloths made of *'ubaydī* silk and turbans made of the linen called *sharb* that was so fine it was similar to gauze. He was also presented with a richly engraved

[53] A complete description of the programme in E. Kühnel, *Die islamischen Elfenbeiskulpturen*, pp. 38–9. On the possibility that these scenes contain a warning for al-Mughīra and were intended to dissuade him from showing aspirations to succeed al-Ḥakam II, F. Prado Villar, 'Circular Visions of Fertility and Punishment', pp. 19–41. The idea is not based on any conclusive evidence: aside from the fact that we do not know who commissioned the ivory, at the time it was made the succession was not an issue for debate: the caliph was healthy and had two sons as candidates to succeed him, N. Silva Santa Cruz, 'Dádivas preciosas en marfil', pp. 534–6.

sword and 500 dinars, or the equivalent of 4,000 pieces of silver. A similar display of generosity was bestowed upon a merchant who captured a deserter from the Umayyad army near the coast of Ifrīqiya in the summer of 972 (361 AH): on the caliph's orders he was given the extraordinary sum of 1,000 gold dinars paid in cash. On another occasion, the grateful recipient was Qand, a palace servant (*fatā*), who had brought back from the Maghreb the head of an enemy defeated in combat: he was given 100 dinars (the equivalent of 800 dirhams), a set of clothes 'fitting for his rank', an engraved sword and a thoroughbred horse with a saddle and harness. Another example is provided by two messengers (*furāniqayn*) who were bearers of good news and were given a gift consisting of 100 dirhams each and silk cloths from the caliphal silk factory (*ṭirāz*).[54]

In all these cases, the value of the gift and the way in which it was made were directly proportional to the rank of the beneficiary. Prior to being sent on a campaign against the Christians in April 975 (*Shaʿbān* 364), the *qāʾid* Ghālib b. ʿAbd al-Raḥmān, who had just returned victorious from the Maghreb, had an audience with the caliph to prepare his next military campaign. At the end of the meeting, Ghālib was given one of the most honourable and sumptuous gifts he could have hoped for: two gilded swords from the caliph's treasury with richly adorned scabbards, which were hung upon him. The swords were used to identify those of the uppermost rank (*khaṣṣa*), whereby to be given two by the caliph himself was a sign of exceptional distinction. The gift was also accompanied by the honorific title (*laqab*) of *Dhū l-Sayfayn*, 'he of the two swords', which Ghālib was entitled to use as part of his name from then on. The caliph's generosity to his *qāʾid* did not stop there: he also gave him a dappled horse from his stable with an ornate harness, as well as the most sumptuous honorific garments (*khilʿa*) that could be given: these included a red Iraqi cloth (*thawb aḥmar ʿirāqī*) of an exceptional quality and various very expensive high conical caps (*qalansuwa*s) made of brocade (*washī*). The description of the scene records how Ghālib later met with the viziers, one of

[54] Ibn Ḥayyān, *Muqtabis VII*, ed. pp. 79, 87, 90, 143; trans. pp. 104, 111, 113 and 181. Another case on pp. 224 and 265. For the translation of 'turban [made of a] line similar to gauze' (*al-ʿamāʾim al-shurūb*) I draw on E. Mesa, *El lenguaje de la indumentaria*, p. 75. With regard to the merchant, the text uses the expression one thousand *jaʿfarid mithqal*s, which I interpret as referring to 1,000 dinars paid in cash. For the customs of the ʿAbbāsid court, D. Sourdel, 'Robes of Honour in ʿAbbasid Baghdad', pp. 137–8, in which it is stated that apart from textiles and swords, the caliph would also often give bracelets and crowns, which never appear in the Umayyad court.

whom began looking into the bag to examine the garments he had been given, while praising the caliph's generosity. This gives an idea of the value that was conferred by these gifts upon members of the caliphate's ruling class.[55]

'With what you spill, you unite us all.' The caliph's deployment of these 'necessary liberalities' allowed him to gather around him the most powerful people of his state. Likewise, this policy was also used to bolster alliances and to win over those whom the caliph sought to have as allies. This is demonstrated by the gifts sent to the Berber tribal leaders in North Africa. The dates of these gifts coincided with the military campaigns undertaken by al-Ḥakam II in that region, which were intended to counter the influence his principal enemies, the Fāṭimid caliphs, exerted there. The strategy of the Umayyad caliph consisted of combining military operations with forging ties with tribal leaders through a policy of appeasement, which involved sending gifts and subsidies in exchange for recognition of the caliph's sovereignty.[56]

Al-Ḥakam II spent astronomical sums on this policy. The most notorious case is that of Ja'far b. al-Andalusī and his brother Yaḥyā, members of a family that was highly esteemed by the Fāṭimid caliphs in Ifrīqiya. Following a bizarre incident, they deserted the Fāṭimid ranks and ended up disembarking in al-Andalus in the summer of 971 (360 AH). Al-Ḥakam II considered this desertion to be a major triumph for his cause, and apart from offering both brothers a welcome reception such as never had been witnessed in Córdoba, he decided they should reside in grand style with their costs paid for by the Andalusi treasury. In addition to a residence in Córdoba's medina, each of them was paid a monthly pension (*jirāya*) of 1,000 dinars in dirhams, which came to the incredible total of 192,000 silver coins received by each of them annually. To this were added payments in kind worth seventy *almudí*s of wheat paid monthly every year; an *almudí* was equivalent to 339.5 kilograms.

[55] Ibn Ḥayyān, *Muqtabis VII*, ed. p. 220; trans. p. 260. On these swords as elements signalling the identity of the Cordoban ruling class (*suyūf al-khāṣṣa*), ibid., pp. 29 and 30 and pp. 52 and 53, where it is translated as 'swords of the people loyal to the caliph'. Another case of a commission for a military mission that included a gift made in advance in ed. pp. 128–9 and trans. p. 162. Reference to the brocade, *al-washī*, is found in Christian documentation from the period as part of the dowry given by wealthy people such as Ilduara, the mother of Bishop Rosendo, founder of the Monastery of Celanova: in 938 she gave him an alb made of *alvexí*, A. Rodríguez, 'À propos des objets nécessaires', p. 64.

[56] X. Ballestí, 'Jil'a y monedas. El poder de los Banū Marwān en el Magrib al-Aqsā', pp. 391–415.

To form an idea of the extraordinary magnitude of these figures, it suffices to recall that a century and a half earlier the Baghdad-born musician Ziryāb had been given huge sums of money and 100 *almudis* of wheat per year when he had moved to Córdoba, and at the time these quantities had seemed an extravagance caused by the Emir ʿAbd al-Raḥmān II's passion for music.[57] Given that it is not very likely that Ziryāb or the Banū al-Andalusī brothers would eat all that grain, it may be inferred that these prominent social figures served as redistributors of their stipends among their extensive households, which consisted of family members, people in their service and supporters. Nonetheless, these incredible sums still seemed insufficient in the caliph's eyes. A few months later, in February 972 (*Jumāda* 361), Jaʿfar b. al-Andalusī's monthly stipend was increased from the 1,000 dinars in dirhams which he was receiving to 800 dinars paid in cash: apparently, this was a lesser sum of money, but with a much higher value, because, as we have been seen, this 'weighted dinar' (*wazīna*) was real and worth much more than the currency of account dinar. Jaʿfar's son, Ibrāhīm, likewise went on to receive a pension in late 973 (363 AH), which consisted of 200 dinars in dirhams – 1,600 dirhams per month – to which were added ten *almudí*s of wheat, according to the souk measurements, and two *qafīz*s of barley per night for his horses.[58]

What did other members of the Umayyad entourage think of such extravagance? We do not know. However, what can be documented is the evident disproportion of these elevated stipends in relation to other salaries paid in the caliphal administration. Around that time, a certain Muḥammad b. ʿAlī, who was appointed judge or *qāḍī* of the frontier in addition to the post of *ṣaḥib al-shurṭa al-ṣughrā* that he already held, managed to increase his income to around thirty dinars. The *fatā* Durrī, who worked for the treasury, but fell into disgrace around this time, had his stipend cut to ten dinars *wazīna* per month, still a respectable quantity, but light years away from what was received by the Banū al-Andalusī. For his first position at the court, an obscure figure from the Algeciras region, Muḥammad b. Abī ʿĀmir, was paid fifteen dinars per month for administering the properties of the caliph's heir. In all these cases, these were people of relative low rank. However, according to some sources,

[57] E. Manzano Moreno, *Conquistadores, emires y califas*, pp. 397–408.
[58] Ibn Ḥayyān, *Muqtabis VII*, ed., pp. 53, 70, 148; trans. pp. 71, 93, 187.

the salary paid to a *hājib* at this time was eighty dinars per month, which came to 960 dinars per annum, not much more than what Ja'far b. al-Andalusī was paid in a single month.[59]

On the basis of these comparisons, it is clear that there were some individuals who were especially favoured by the caliph, and who received gifts and stipends amounting to fabulous sums. The case of Ja'far b. al-Andalusī and his family was not unique. In the spring of 973 (362 AH), a certain Aḥmad b. Muḥammad, who had a formidable genealogy and a story to tell, arrived in Córdoba. He was a descendant of Abū Bakr, the first Muslim caliph, and came from a village in Syria, which had been captured by the Byzantines following the offensive undertaken in the region by the Emperor Nikephoros II Phokas (963–9). Displaced from his home, Aḥmad b. Muḥammad had made the pilgrimage to Mecca, and then had made his way through Yemen, Egypt and the Maghreb, without anyone paying him much attention. In contrast, al-Ḥakam considered that the arrival of a descendant of the first Muslim caliph in Córdoba provided him with a major propagandistic opportunity. According to the Shī'ī ideology of the Fāṭimid caliphs, the choice of Abū Bakr following the Prophet's death had been a major error, but Sunnis had always considered it as a providential event: Abū Bakr and his successors had preserved the legacy of the Envoy of God and had fostered the major expansion of the early Muslim community. Willing to play the propagandistic card of the defence of Sunni Islam, al-Ḥakam decided to welcome Aḥmad b. Muḥammad, and ordered his viziers that in addition to a monthly pension they had to provide him with garments of honour (*khil'a*) and 200 dinars per annum. The fortunate Aḥmad b. Muḥammad, who had until then not even had a house to call his own, broke down showering blessings on the caliph, although our chronicler, 'Īsā al-Rāzī, adds that he did so 'concealing his inner feelings'.[60]

[59] Ibn 'Idhārī, *al-Bayān*, II, ed. pp. 267–8; Ibn Ḥayyān, *Muqtabis VII*, ed. pp. 81, 103; trans. pp. 105, 132. Nonetheless, the figure of eighty dinars per month for the post of *ḥājib* seems to me to be too low, as in the emirate period a vizier of 'Abd al-Raḥmān II earned 350 dinars per month. This may either be due to an error, or else in this period the salaries of posts in the administration underwent severe cuts. P. Chalmeta states that the monthly salary of a vizier was 333 dinars per month, *Historia socioeconómica*, p. 505.

[60] Ibn Ḥayyān, *Muqtabis VII*, ed. pp. 105 and 111; trans. pp. 134 and 141, where it states that he arrived in Córdoba from the region of Fez accompanied by two Berbers. The Fāṭimids' dislike of caliph Abū Bakr is expressed in some verses by the poet Ibn Hānī in which he reproaches how 'these people proposed a Taymī [member of the Banū Taym] as heir to the Prophet, when no

Therefore, it is very possible that however much they formed part of the caliph's grand political designs, these displays of generosity were not always to the taste of everyone. The abundance of wealth that was centralised in the Umayyad caliphate would have given rise to a fierce struggle to win control over it, and in this sense the allocation of extensive resources to specific people would have prompted a range of opinions, and even tense quarrels within the caliphal court. Someone such as Ja'far b. al-Andalusī may have been considered a foreigner, who had betrayed his previous lord and had presented himself in Córdoba with all his family and with nowhere else to go. His career at the court in Córdoba, which began with such brilliance, ended up gaining him many enemies and, as will be seen, he came to the worst fate possible. Many people at the court seem to have thought that the political designs of the Caliph al-Ḥakam, apart from being very costly, were not always infallible.

Forms of Property: Land and Slaves

The major resources collected and redistributed by the caliphate meant that those surrounding al-Ḥakam II, including his closest family members, senior civil servants, army chiefs, and even the senior *'ulamā'* and *fuqahā'*, who made up what was known as the *khaṣṣa*, consisted of very wealthy individuals. What did they own? We can answer this question using a notarial record written down by Ibn al-'Aṭṭār (d. 1009/399 AH), which includes a document listing a man's inheritance that was to be shared out between his widow and sons. The inheritance consisted of real estate (*'aqār*) in the capital, houses (*dūr*) in the neighbourhood of a specific mosque in a suburb, estates (*amlāk*) in a village (*qarya*) of a certain rural circumscription (*iqlīm*), gold, silver, saddles, jewels, garments (*malbas*), tapestries and textile covers (*wiṭā' wa ghiṭā'*), slaves (*raqīq*), wheat (*ṭa'ām*) and merchandise (*matā'*).[61]

Thus, land, houses, slaves, money, saddles, provisions and sumptuary objects constituted the wealth that a person of high standing could accumulate during the caliphate of al-Ḥakam II. This wealth replicated on a lesser scale that of the caliph himself. This was not a rural class established in the countryside,

Taymī had ever had any family ties with Him', M. Yalaoui, 'Les relations entre Fatimides d'Ifriqiya et Omeyyades d'Espagne a travers le dīwān d'Ibn Hānī', p. 28.

[61] Ibn al-'Aṭṭār *K. al-wathā'iq*, ed. p. 422; trans. p. 656. Basically, the same items are found in another model document, 419/653.

and still less so in castles or fortifications, but an elite (*khaṣṣa*) that resided in Córdoba, had houses in the city's suburbs – filled with sumptuous objects that ranged from textiles and tapestries to magnificent tableware – and oversaw agricultural land on both peri-urban and rural estates. This class acquired its land through inheritance, as well as by purchasing it, just as is demonstrated by the large number of examples of notarial documents compiled by Ibn al-ʿAṭṭār. In these contracts for land purchases, details such as the area to be sold, its price in dirhams, and the existence or not of fiscal exemptions ascribed to the land in question, were all agreed on among other issues.[62]

Furthermore, it is evident that the members of these ruling classes did not cultivate the land they possessed by themselves. Notarial documents also suggest a predominance of forms of indirect exploitation, based on various modes of sharecropping, and with highly variable conditions. When these conditions were stipulated in writing (and perhaps this was not always the case) the landowner and the sharecropper could divide the harvest fifty–fifty, but in many other cases conditions were harsher for the sharecropper, who only received a third, a quarter, a fifth, or even just a sixth of the land's produce. The positive part of these contracts is that, as has been seen, Islamic legal practice guaranteed rights for sharecroppers such as acknowledging the existence of natural catastrophes in order to reduce the sum to be paid on any year in which these occurred. On the other hand, the contracts could also include very onerous conditions, such as the requirement that sharecroppers undertake the transport of the harvest to the landowner's house, the delivery of calves, chickens or lambs on specific days of the year, and even the obligation to grind the grain in specific mills.[63]

The agricultural properties that we know most about are those possessed by the caliphate's ruling class in the environs of Córdoba and Madīnat al-Zahrāʾ, which played a fundamental role in the configuration of the capital's urban topography. Known as *almunias* (Ar. *munya*), these estates were enclosed by a fence, and had a section for crops, pasture and gardens, and a residential area, with buildings that served as living and recreational spaces.

[62] Ibn al-ʿAṭṭār *K. al-wathāʾiq*, ed. cit. pp. 20–30; trans. cit. pp. 86–99.
[63] Ibn al-ʿAṭṭār *K. al-wathāʾiq*, ed. pp. 58–72; trans. pp. 155–69. On this issue, E. Manzano, *Conquistadores*, pp. 396ff.

One of these *almunias* was owned by a senior official from the court of al-Ḥakam II, the above-mentioned treasurer, Durrī al-Ṣaghīr, who among his many other responsibilities was also in charge of overseeing the manufacture of the ivory pyxis given to Subḥ, as mentioned above. Durrī was a former caliph's slave who had been manumitted. He had acquired this *almunia* and converted it into a 'place of retreat' and into 'the investment of all his wealth'. However, in April 973 (*jumāda* 362 AH), he fell into disgrace due to a 'negligence' committed with regard to his role as treasurer. It is not known what this 'negligence' might have been, but it was a serious misdemeanour. He was obliged to abandon the *alcázar* of Madīnat al-Zahrā' and was removed from his position, while his sizeable salary was reduced to ten dinars. Although this did not convert him into a pauper, he no longer had the wealth that he was used to having at his fingertips. In a desperate attempt to obtain his sovereign's good will (or perhaps because there was some link between the gift and the 'negligence'), weeks after his sacking Durrī offered his marvellous *almunia* to the caliph. Al-Ḥakam willingly accepted the gift, although various months went by before Durrī obtained a pardon and returned to the positions that he had previously filled.[64]

Durrī's *almunia* was known as 'al-Rummāniyya'. It was located in a very pleasant location, which the caliph had a special fondness for and where he had even spent time as a guest. It was for this reason that he was delighted to accept the gift with all that was contained in the *alumnia*, which included 'well-irrigated gardens, farming land, male and female slaves, oxen and beasts of burden'. Magnanimously, the caliph decided to maintain Durrī as its administrator (*wakīl*); the grateful and disgraced official invited the caliph to spend a Sunday of the month of May in the year 973 at his new property in the company of the crown prince, Hishām, and his entourage (*'iyāl*). In view of the possibility that the caliph's party would decide to spend the night at the *almunia*, bedrooms were prepared in the residential area, while outside tents and marquees were put up for the caliph's servants (*khuddām*) and pages (*ghilmān*). However, these measures were not needed. After a day sampling extraordinary delicacies and delicious fruits, 'enjoying innocent pleasure, free

[64] O. Herrero Soto, *El perdón del gobernante al-Andalus*, pp. 324–5.

from anything illicit', as well as Durrī's courtesy, the caliph and his entourage decided to return to Madīnat al-Zahrā', from where they had come.[65]

The 'al-Rummāniyya' *almunia*, where the caliph, his son and entourage spent that innocent spring Sunday, has been identified with some ruins ten kilometres west of Córdoba and two kilometres from Madīnat al-Zahrā'. The Guadarromán stream (*Wādī al-Rummān*), which gives it its name, is just over a kilometre from these ruins, which confirms that it was a large property, comprising not only farm land, but also woodland and quarries, which were used for constructing the *almunia*'s buildings. These buildings included a residential complex, very similar in its layout and construction to some of the rooms at Madīnat al-Zahrā', as well as a large pavilion for recreation, which overlooked three south-facing stepped terraces, upon which were arranged the tents of the caliph's servants on that spring Sunday.[66] On its north side, the pavilion looked onto an immense pool of over 1,400 square metres and four deep, made with blocks of stone covered with red-ochre-coloured plaster, which was also identical to that used to decorate many of the rooms at Madīnat al-Zahrā'. The sumptuousness of the *almunia* is also revealed by two marble basins found there that are decorated with images of lions. An inscription dated 355 AH (965–6) confirms that the *almunia* existed at least eight years prior to it being given to the caliph.[67] If someone like Durrī, a high-ranking figure in the caliphate but whose ancestry and position were not comparable to those of other still more powerful people, was able to afford an *almunia* such as al-Rummāniyya, it is evident that the class that had emerged in the caliph's shadow had an extraordinary capacity to accumulate resources and endeavoured to emulate the caliph's own magnificence.

At his *almunia*, Durrī had male and female slaves who worked his fields and attended to his residences. The use of a slave workforce for agricultural

[65] Ibn Ḥayyān, *Muqtabis VII*, ed. pp. 106–7; trans. pp. 136–7. I have corrected the translation giving *'iyāl* the meaning of 'entourage' instead of 'women', following the sense given by Lane Pool: 'a man's 'iyāl are the persons whom he feeds, nourishes or sustains; or the persons who dwell with him, and whose expenses are incumbent on him, as his young man or slave, his wife and his young child'. The meaning of 'women', offered in the translation, is, in my view, too specific and I am not sure that the caliph would arrive at a celebration held by a subordinate with his women, given the strict Arabic codes of honour in this regard.

[66] A. Vallejo, *La ciudad califal de Madīnat al-Zahrā'*, p. 69.

[67] R. Ocaña, 'Las ruinas de Alamiria', pp. 380–1. F. Arnold, A. Canto and A. Vallejo, 'La almunia de al-Rummaniyya', pp. 185–7.

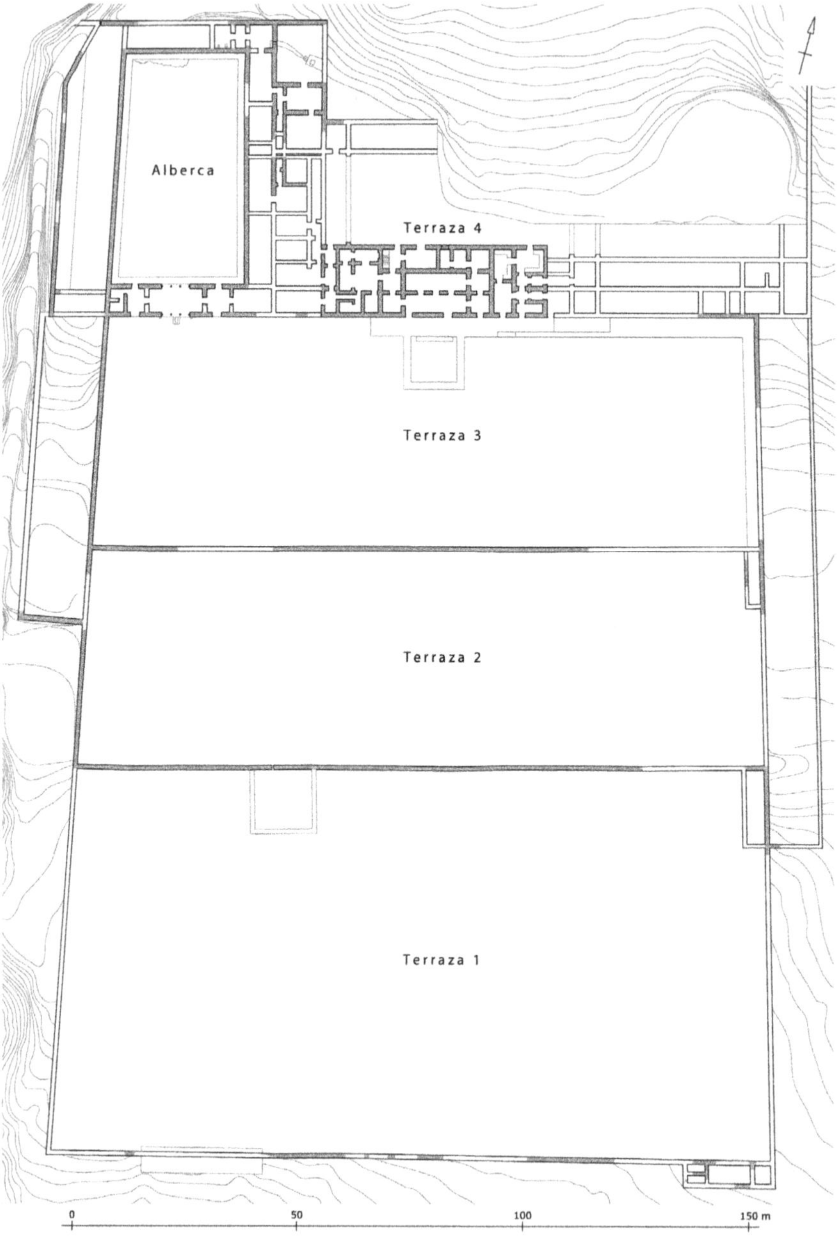

Image 6 Plan (above) and view (opposite) of the pool of the *Munyat al-Rummāniyya*, which was owned by the treasurer, Durrī, and given by him to the caliph, according to Arnold, Canto and Vallejo, La almunia de al-Rummaniyya.

work is also testified to in the case of another *almunia*. This one was located to the south of Córdoba and known as the '*almunia* of 'Ajab', which was the name of a concubine of the Emir al-Ḥakam I (d. 822/206 AH), who had founded it. This 'Ajab had established a pious legacy (*waqf*) there, whereby the income it generated was used to care for the sick.[68] The use of slaves for the farming undertaken at this and other *almunias* or the fact that, as we have seen above, ownership of them could be transmitted in inheritance demonstrates that they were also elements of the wealth owned by the Umayyad ruling classes. Although al-Andalus was not a slave society – the forms of surplus production and exploitation did not depend on their work – slaves were a form of merchandise that was widely appreciated, and therefore in demand.

Given that the enslavement of Muslims was unthinkable, the supply of slaves depended on military campaigns or long-distance trade. In the Near East, this trade reached gigantic proportions along the routes that linked

[68] A. M. Carballeira, *Legados píos y fundaciones familiares en al-Andalus (siglos IV/X-VI-XII)*, Madrid, 2002, pp. 166–7, based on the testimony of Ibn Sahl.

the ʿAbbāsid caliphate with the Nordic countries along the courses of the Russian rivers. This trade was vividly described by authors such as Ibn Faḍlān (c. 922/310 AH) and has left a significant material trace in the form of hundreds of thousands of ʿAbbāsíd dirhams found at innumerable sites across Russia and Scandinavia. The most conservative estimates state that 400,000 coins have been found in these countries, but everything suggests that this was just a small part of the overall sum of money that must have circulated as a result of this trade.[69]

In the West, this trade never reached such proportions, but there is evidence for the arrival en masse of slaves under specific circumstances. These circumstances did not always arise, but when they did, these slaves met the huge demand for this type of workforce in al-Andalus. During a number of decades of the tenth century (fourth AH) these circumstances most certainly did occur. The annual military campaigns to the north of the Peninsula, the so-called *aceifas*, had always been an efficient source of supply. However, during this period, the slave trade grew to hitherto unknown proportions, such as would not occur again in the West. This was the moment when slaves were imported from the land of the *Ṣaqāliba*, an uncertain territory that Western Arabic authors identified with zones of central and northern Europe. Places such as Prague thrived thanks to the trade in slaves, furs and tin, and were described around 961 by the Jewish trader from Tortosa, Ibrāhīm b. Yaʿqūb al-Turtūshī. This was also the period of Verdun's growth, an emporium from which slaves were transferred south, possibly along the Saône and Rhône, to the mouth of the latter river in the area near Arles. From there, the transportation of slaves to al-Andalus was undertaken by sea, with Barcelona possibly having been an important port for this trade, which would preferably have been undertaken by boat, which reduced the risk of the human cargo being harmed by long marches on foot, or succumbing to temptations to escape.

Once these slaves had arrived in al-Andalus, their destinations varied greatly. The youngest men might be converted into eunuchs by Jewish merchants in the vicinity of the Andalusi town of Pechina, and from there be sent

[69] M. Jankowiak, 'What Does the Slave Trade in the Saqaliba Tell Us About Early Islamic Slavery?', pp. 169–72.

on to more distant places, where they could reach a value of 1,000 dinars, thus attesting to an Arabic geographer's statement that 'all the eunuch slaves in the world come from al-Andalus'. In other cases, the captives were intended for the Umayyad civil service or army, while in the case of women their likely fate was, for the price of between fifty and a hundred dinars, to become slave singers or serve as concubines.[70]

Legal writings of the caliphal period confirm the importance of slaves in al-Andalus at this particular juncture. We have many notarial models of documents for the sale of slaves, for the register of complaints related to defects that went undetected at the time of purchase, for permitting marriages between slaves, and for the procedures to be followed in the event of the capture of fugitive slaves. The reading of these texts is by no means edifying: cases such as a slave being returned following the discovery of an injury or an illness that went unnoticed in the market, or the endless enquiries into the responsibility for the pregnancy of a recently purchased slave, reveal in all crudeness the details of the complex casuistry entailed in the trade in human beings.[71]

Setting aside other considerations, the abundant presence of slaves in Córdoba at the time of al-Ḥakam II is remarkable.[72] The fact that, well into the tenth century (fourth AH) and over the course of a few decades, there was a major flow of slaves into al-Andalus reveals once more the effects of the accumulation of resources by the ruling class of the caliphate: after having become a powerful source of demand, this class was capable of stimulating a trade

[70] All this discussion draws on E. Manzano *Conquistadores*, p. 406 and E. Manzano, 'Circulation des biens', p. 166. Ibn al-'Aṭṭār *K. al-wathā'iq*, ed. p. 36; trans. p. 108.

[71] Ibn al-'Aṭṭār *K. al-wathā'iq*, ed. pp. 33–4; 39–40; trans. pp. 105; 114–15.

[72] It is more difficult to talk of a slave trade in the Middle Ages as opposed to discussing this issue in relation to Antiquity. It is a known fact that the high demand for slaves in medieval Muslim societies has been used by Islamophobic historians to denigrate this religion and culture. Likewise, the presence of Jewish merchants involved in this trade has also prompted arguments supporting anti-Semitic views. Obviously, such fallacies overlook the fact that many wholly Christian agents also took part in this trade, and that the very Christian and very Western early-modern and modern societies also used slaves as a workforce (to just scratch the surface, in 1866 the Pope of Rome continued to justify slavery). I do not believe that our task as historians is to make moral judgements on the past, but rather to give interpretations that can explain its processes. Slavery in the Early Middle Ages was the consequence of the coercion and violence that impregnated the social formations of the era and affected all social groups and communities without any ethnic or religious distinction. It is morally unacceptable to single out any one of these communities in order to vilify it in the present, but it is also incorrect to endeavour to minimise a phenomenon with major implications by trying to paint over, in each case *pro domo sua*, the many cracks that appear in humanity's past.

in human beings imported from distant places. Obviously, this was not an easy trade. The presence of Muslim merchants seeking slaves in any Christian country was ruled out, which meant the role of intermediaries, possibly Jews, was indispensable. These intermediaries dealt with the captors, transported the captives, and sold the slaves at their destination. This trade flourished for a few decades and became one of the leading activities that served to re-activate long-distance commerce, which had been dormant for a long time, due to the absence of both a significant demand of Western wealth or goods whose value could justify exchanges over long distances.[73]

Therefore, to be wealthy in caliphal Córdoba meant owning a large quantity of money and products in kind, and having access to urban property or land, as well as possessing sharecroppers and slaves. To be rich in caliphal Córdoba was a status that was publicly displayed, by wearing specific textiles, possessing certain sumptuary objects or being able to carry weapons. Many of these people were linked in one way or another to the Umayyad state, and either worked for the caliph or were beneficiaries of his actions. Their ties to the caliph were reinforced by the public display of their connections through a series of highly visible gestures and marks that served to identify them as members of a ruling class that had a highly developed sense of its own status.

A survey of the resources and wealth of the caliphate at the time of al-Ḥakam II, in the mid-tenth century (fourth AH), reveals exorbitant quantities, both in terms of the sums recorded in the texts and the material evidence that has survived until today. Gold, silver, textiles, ivories, slaves, land and the *almunias* owned by the caliphate's ruling class reached proportions that reflect the extraordinary capacity to collect and redistribute the resources of the caliphate. However, it is not only the quantity that is striking in this profusion of resources and riches. What is also significant is their 'global' character. By minting gold, carving ivory objects, importing slaves, or making textiles with silk and prized dyes, the caliph of al-Andalus was on an equal standing to that of other sovereigns, who were also able to gather and elaborate such riches. It was only the Byzantine emperors, with whom al-Ḥakam maintained

[73] M. McCormick, 'New Light on the 'Dark Ages': How the Slave Trade Fuelled the Carolingian Economy', pp. 17–54; E. Manzano Moreno, 'Byzantium, al-Andalus and the Shaping of the Mediterranean in the Early Middle Ages', in L. Brubaker, ed., *Global Byzantium*, in press.

a constant flow of embassies, the Fāṭimid caliphs, with whom he maintained a sustained conflict, or the 'Abbāsíd caliphs, whose memory exerted considerable influence over him, that could likewise sustain the complex processes entailed in the collection, production and distribution of such wealth. The middle of the tenth century marks the first time in the Middle Ages that elites, albeit separated by cultural and religious barriers, made recourse to a similar set of cultural resources, and although, respectively, they were used to articulate very different political languages, in each case there was a shared concern that they should serve as a medium for the expression of power.

3

The Caliph and the *Sulṭān*

The State and its Problems

In English, the word 'sultan' means 'a prince or king's son, a high officer'. According to Arabic dictionaries, the word derives from a root meaning to possess or exercise power through the use of 'coercion'.[1] The title 'sulṭān' was in fact one that many medieval governors began to adopt from the eleventh century (fifth AH) onwards to distinguish their temporal power from the exclusively religious authority exercised by the caliphs in the Near East, albeit increasingly in name only. Around that time, Islamic political theory had assimilated the idea that the caliphate was not the only possible form of government and that other sovereigns, using titles such as that of 'sulṭān', were also capable of protecting the interests of the Islamic community.[2]

However, prior to the eleventh century, Arabic authors in general, and Andalusi ones in particular, were already using the term *sulṭān* on a frequent basis. During the caliphal era reference is made, for example, to the sulṭān's army (*'askar al-sulṭān*), the appointment of a governor of the sulṭān (*'āmil al-sulṭān*), or someone serving as the sulṭān's emissary (*rasūl al-sulṭān*).[3] In all these cases, *sulṭān* was not a title, as the word was still not used in that sense, but it referred to the power incarnated in the caliph, and that flowed from

[1] The concept of 'state' discussed here is very similar to M. Rustow's analysis of the Fāṭimid caliphate. It is also noteworthy that the problems the Fāṭimids faced with regard to those they appointed to serve them were very similar to those I address below, see M. Rustow, *The Lost Archive*, pp. 235/239. On the early meaning of the word *sulṭān*, M. Meouak, 'Las instituciones políticas del islam temprano', p. 44.

[2] A. K. S. Lambton, 'Justice in the Medieval Persian Theory of Kingship', p. 99.

[3] Ibn Ḥayyān, *Muqtabis V*, ed. and trans. pp. 86, 131, 319; other similar cases in ibid., pp. 137 (*rijāl al-sulṭān*), 141 (*'ummāl al-sulṭān*) and 257 (*jund al-sulṭān*).

him. So, for example, when al-Ḥakam II fell mortally ill in 976 (366 AH), we are told that the vizier Ja'far b. 'Uthmān al-Muṣḥafī took care of his *sulṭān* (*yudabbiru sulṭāna-hu*).[4] Many other examples confirm this: at the end of the ninth century (third AH) during the era of the *fitna* of the emirate, one group of rebels wanted to restore obedience to the centralised power of Córdoba and claimed they did so 'to uphold the old bonds that they and their ancestors had had with the *sulṭān* in times of rectitude'; at one of the receptions held at Madīnat al-Zahrā', the road to this city palace was filled with people from the suburbs of Córdoba, to whom the *sulṭān* had granted arms; and finally, the Idrīsids, who ruled over enclaves in North Africa, were concerned about the extension of Andalusi power (*sulṭān al-Andalus*).[5] In these and many other cases the word *sulṭān* did not refer to a title, which the Umayyads never adopted, but evoked the idea of the centralised power they exercised.[6]

Hugh Kennedy, drawing on an analysis of texts from the Near East written prior to the eleventh century, has proposed the stimulating idea that *sulṭān* can be translated as 'state', this being understood as the incarnation of central power.[7] The idea is highly convincing and in the context of al-Andalus it indicates that during this period the word *sulṭān* alluded to the administrative and military structure that had the Umayyad caliph as its visible head, depended on him, and at times was even identified with him. Yet it also implies the existence of an entity that functioned according to its own logic. This explains why the supervisor of the textile workshop (*dār al-ṭirāz*) was paid a 'state stipend'

[4] Ibn 'Idhārī, *al-Bayān*, II, ed. p. 253; trans. p. 418.

[5] Ibn Ḥayyān, *Muqtabis V*, ed. and trans. pp. 74 and 193. Ibn Ḥayyān, *Muqtabis VII*, ed. p. 48; trans. p. 67, where it is translated as 'armed by the government'. In our sources there are numerous cases of the word *sulṭān* used in the sense of 'state', ed. pp. 35, 52; trans. pp. 56, 71. In some cases, the state is identified with the figure of the caliph, ed. p. 38; trans. p. 58.

[6] A similar use is documented in North Africa: when the Kutāma Berbers, who supported the Fāṭimid agents in Ifrīqiya, were asked if they obeyed a power (*sulṭān*), they answered that their obedience was limited to the acknowledgement of its existence, and that this 'power' (*sulṭān*) was to be found a ten-day march from their region, making reference to the seat of the Aghlabids in Qayrawān, H. Halm, *The Empire of the Mahdi*, pp. 40–1.

[7] H. Kennedy has addressed this idea in a number of lectures, and in particular in one given at Princeton entitled 'What Does *sulṭān* Mean in the 10th Century?'. I would like to thank him for sending me a copy of his lecture, which has shaped my ideas on this matter. P. Guichard, *al-Andalus frente a la conquista cristiana*, pp. 383–7, refers to *sulṭān* as embodying a 'certain idea of the State' and cites other cases taken from sources from this period which support his interpretation.

(*rizq sulṭānī*), or why the city of Pechina (Almería) is referred to as the place in that region where the 'state' was concentrated (*mujtama' al-sulṭān*).[8]

At the height of the tenth century (fourth AH), in al-Andalus there was a clear awareness of the existence of a political and institutional fabric independent of the individuals that filled positions of power: this can be identified with what we understand as the 'state'. Despite the reticence that the use of this concept in such an early period prompts from many medievalists, Chris Wickham has argued in favour of its use for the comparison of distinctive political entities, and, above all, for the purpose of identifying the organisational elements present in or absent from the entities under study. Such comparisons permit the demonstration of the existence of strong states, such as the Roman Empire and the Arabic and Byzantine empires that succeeded it, in which the 'ruler who is in charge of a fully effective tax-raising system can finance his own army and salaried officials, and has a secure independent basis of authority'. Such states may be contrasted with other weaker political entities, in which such elements were either absent or played a less prominent role. The Umayyad caliphate of al-Andalus undoubtedly belonged to the group of 'strong states', and its chroniclers' use of the concept *sulṭān* confirms that they were well aware of the existence of 'a ruling system ideologically separable from the ruled population and from the individual rulers themselves; independent and stable resources for rulers; and a class-based system of surplus extraction and stratification'.[9]

In this sense, 'Īsā al-Rāzī's work may be considered as a chronological register of the events of the *sulṭān*. In fact, al-Rāzī uses the word with great frequency, always with the sense of 'central power' or 'state'.[10] The almost three hundred individuals mentioned in the pages of his 'annals', performing a range of activities and assigned to different posts or duties, formed the nucleus

[8] Ibn Ḥayyān, *Muqtabis II, 1*, ed. pp. 290–1; trans. pp. 179–80; al-'Udhrī, *Tarṣī*, p. 86.

[9] C. Wickham, *Framing the Early Middle Ages: Europe and the Mediterranean 400–800*, p. 57.

[10] The sending of *aṣḥāb al-sulṭān* to form part of an official procession; arrangements for the parade of infantry men 'armed by the state' (*al-musalaḥīn min 'inda l-sulṭān*); weakness of the 'Abbāsíds in the Eastern state (*fī sulṭān al-mashrīq*); mention of the diploma, presented to a Berber tribal chief, stipulating his obligations to undertake the holy war (*jihād*) against those who rebel against the caliph's *sulṭān*; the wish of the ruler of Fez to submit to the *sulṭān* of the *amīr al-mū'minīn* and the caliph's reflection on how he should behave within his state (*sulṭān*); the sending of money belonging to the *sulṭān* out to North Africa, Ibn Ḥayyān, *Muqtabis VII*, ed. pp. 45, 48, 78, 117, 168; trans. pp. 65, 67, 110, 145, 150, 206–7.

of this state (*sulṭān*), through which the caliph's power (*mulk*) was exercised. That power was in the hands of the Umayyad dynasty (*dawla*), whose authority was underpinned by a form of legitimacy, whose foundations I will analyse below. This state fabric, this *sulṭān*, extended throughout Córdoba and the other cities and regions of al-Andalus, and it was sustained by an army and a fiscal system, without which it could not exist.

The functioning of the Umayyad state/*sulṭān* created a highly complex and dynamic structure. From the most powerful vizier to the most junior soldier, all those who provided some kind of administrative or military service to the state received some form of stipend, paid either in money or kind out of the caliphate's fiscal revenue. Appointments to a post or job, recruitment for the army, the undertaking of a mission, or even honorific distinctions were forms of access to the major annual revenue collection undertaken by the state in the form of the taxes levied on surpluses. As was seen in the previous chapter, the 4 or 5 million dinars collected annually were redistributed by the *sulṭān* itself.

Nonetheless, the caliphal state always faced a serious problem: the resources that it centralised were so extensive, its staff so numerous and its territory so large that it was very difficult to control, even for its visible head, the caliph. The problem seems to have obsessed al-Ḥakam II, who was keenly aware of the shortcomings that hindered the state's effective functioning even before his accession to the caliphate. In 941 (330 AH), following the discovery of a major case of fraud committed by the supervisor of the mint, Saʿīd b. Jassās, who ended up in prison for his misdeeds, the twenty-six-year-old crown prince al-Ḥakam was commissioned by his father, ʿAbd al-Raḥmān III, to temporarily oversee the collecting of tributes, as well as the management of both the treasury and the mint. Shortly after, the *kūras* of Elvira (Granada) and Pechina (Almería) were placed under his control. These were two of the richest regions in al-Andalus, and al-Ḥakam was responsible for the appointment of their governors and judges. To undertake these and other tasks, his father provided him with a special building, the so called *Dār al-mulk*, where his servants and scribes worked, and where the heir to the caliphate kept his personal belongings.[11]

[11] Ibn Ḥayyān, *Muqtabis V*, pp. 9–10, 96, 135, 328–9; *Muqtabis VII*, p. 184; Ibn ʿIdhārī, *al-Bayān*, II, p. 231.

Once he became caliph, al-Ḥakam II continued to display a remarkable concern for the functioning of his administration. In 966 (355 AH), having only just come to power, he ordered for a commission of trusted men to visit the provinces and review his subjects' living conditions. The commission's findings were devastating. A letter sent by the caliph to his governors bitterly declared that while he zealously sought to ensure that the Muslims were 'under the care of pious and devout men, you have transformed that zeal into despotism and harshness'. Some officials were imprisoned, but the problems persisted. Four years later, at a reception held in September 971 (*Dhū l-qaʿda* 361 AH), members of the *jund* criticised the governors' behaviour to the caliph in person.[12]

To tackle the problem, al-Ḥakam endeavoured to apply corrective measures. When, in June 972 (361 AH), he appointed Aṣbagh b. Muḥammad b. Fuṭays governor of half of the province (*kūra*) of Rayyuh (Málaga), he sent him an exceptional letter, in which he ordered him to use his authority (*amr*) with clemency and not to make distinctions between subjects. The caliph also issued a veiled threat to his official by assuring him that he would find out if things were not being done as he had requested.[13] However, controlling the behaviour of the numerous civil servants who ran the provincial administration was an almost impossible task. In January 975 (364 AH), the caliph decreed that the contribution paid for exemption from military service (*naḍḍ li l-ḥashd*) was to be reduced by one sixth. He announced this by issuing a document setting out his instructions. The caliph's orders were to be read out in the mosques after the Friday prayers to ensure that the people were informed and to counter 'the ruses of the fiscal officials' (*iḥtiyāl al-ʿummāl*). This extraordinary remark in a caliphal rescript shows that these officials were deemed capable of concealing the tax cut from the people in order to pocket the difference.[14]

[12] *Dhikr bilād al-Andalus*, ed. p. 172; trans. pp. 182–3. The members of the commission of trusted men consisted, on the one hand, of the *qāḍīs* of Elvira and Murcia, and, on the other, of ʿAbda b. Muḥammad b. Abī ʿAbda, who belonged to an influential family of the caliphal administration, and Muḥammad b. Nuʿmān, who may have been a Muslim scholar listed in *Prosopografía de los ulemas de al-Andalus*; http://www.eea.csic/pua/ id. 8.649 (last accessed 12 November 2022). On the ruses used by agents, Ibn Ḥayyān, *Muqtabis VII*, ed. p. 57; trans. p. 75.

[13] Ibn Ḥayyān, *Muqtabis VII*, ed. pp. 77–8; trans. pp. 100–1. The father of Aṣbagh, Muḥammad b. Fuṭays was vizier and many of his family had served as secretaries and officials.

[14] Ibn Ḥayyān, *Muqtabis VII*, ed. pp. 207–10; trans. pp. 247–9.

In addition to the problems faced by the provincial administration, the very centre of the state was also beset by grave concerns regarding those in senior administrative posts, as shown by occasional reports on officials being imprisoned or falling from grace following accusations of embezzlement or other such misdemeanours. According to the Eastern traveller Ibn Ḥawqal, shortly after al-Ḥakam II's accession to the caliphate he confiscated the property of his father's courtiers, which added 20 million dinars to the treasury. This event might have related also to a quality review of the dirhams minted at this time, as it has been shown that during the final five years of the rule of ʿAbd al-Raḥmān III (956–61/345–50 AH) there was a significant reduction in their quality and weight. In contrast, at the start of the caliphate of al-Ḥakam II a marked improvement in the quality of these coins has been noted. Therefore, it is very possible that the reinstatement of this coin's quality was linked to the purge of the civil servants recorded by Ibn Ḥawqal.[15]

There is little doubt that al-Ḥakam II maintained tense relationships with the most prominent families of the Umayyad central administration, who for generations had been chosen for many of the senior posts. One source refers to 'the Abī ʿAbda family, the Shuhayd family, the Jahwar family and the Fuṭays family' as people who 'were accustomed to receive posts and were associated with dignities, as they were imbued with honour and self-respect'. Families such as these had effectively monopolised appointments in the Umayyad administration for generations, and they shared a pronounced oligarchic self-consciousness, which was based on their 'state lineage' (*salafiyya ṣulṭāniyya*), their sustained presence within the *sulṭān*, which was justified 'by the deeds of their ancestors'. Senior positions were shared out among them in accordance with 'the custom of granting them to those deemed most excellent and those closest to them'.[16] Lists of viziers and senior officials confirm how the families of Umayyad clients were assigned the main positions in the administration, forming an oligarchy embedded within the machinery of the *sulṭān* that ended up controlling its mechanisms.

[15] I have analysed this issue in E. Manzano Moreno, *Conquistadores*, p. 478.

[16] Ibn ʿIdhārī, *al-Bayān*, II, pp. 290–1; Ibn Khaqan, *Matmaḥ al-anfus*, ed. Constantina 1884 (1302), p. 7; al-Maqqarī, *Nafḥ*, I, p. 420, who draws on Ibn Khaqan. X. Ballestín Navarro, *al-Manṣūr*, pp. 118–19.

Contemporary texts confirm how 'the deeds of their ancestors' (i.e. the historical memory of their loyal service to the dynasty) was the fundamental argument these families used to justify their dominance. Thus, an anonymous author writing at this time recorded how the 'aristocrats' (*al-aḥrār*) were irritated by the promotion of 'the low-born' (*al-andhāl*) to positions of responsibility by 'Abd al-Raḥmān III: ignoring the merits that distinguished powerful families such as the Banū Ḥudayr, Banū Basīl, Banū Jahwar or Banū Fuṭays, this caliph had appointed his favourite, Najda, head of the army, despite him being a nonentity who was held responsible for the defeat the caliph suffered at the battle of Alhándega against the Christians (939).[17]

Another revealing text from this period is the chronicle by Ibn al-Qūṭiyya (d. 977), who lived in Córdoba and was descended from an Arab conqueror, who had married the granddaughter of the Visigothic King Witiza. For Ibn al-Qūṭiyya, the history of the Umayyads of al-Andalus was a succession of deeds that demonstrated how the families with close ties to the dynasty had served it effectively and counselled their sovereigns wisely. For instance, he recounts the origins of one of these families, the Banū Ḥudayr. In the wake of the famous revolt that broke out in Córdoba's suburb of Shaqunda in 818, which had nearly put an end to both the rule and the life of al-Ḥakam I, this Umayyad emir wanted to crucify those who were responsible for the uprising. He ordered Ḥudayr, a gatekeeper (*bawwāb*) of his *alcázar*, to arrest those who had promoted the rebellion, but he refused. When asked why he would not carry out the emir's orders, Ḥudayr declared that he would not like to encounter the emir in the afterlife reproaching him for having committed such a crime. Al-Ḥakam then ordered for him to be removed from his post and named one Ibn Nādir to replace him. However, and according to Ibn al-Qūṭiyya, from that day on the fortune of the Banū Ḥudayr never ceased to prosper, while that of the Banū Nādir declined to extinction.[18]

[17] *Akhbār Majmūʿa*, ed. and trans. pp. 155–6; trans. James, 135–6.

[18] Ibn al-Qūṭiyya, *Taʾrīkh*, ed. p. 56. trans. James p. 91. The same anecdote in Ibn Ḥayyān, *Muqtabis II, 1*, ed. p. 158; trans. p. 69, in which it is more clearly stated that Ḥudayr had the power to control access (*ḥijāba*) to the emir. Ḥudayr was a slave (*mamluk*) who had formed part of the booty won in the campaign against Narbonne led by the emir Hishām. He had been bequeathed to his successor al-Ḥakam I, who manumitted his slaves following the revolt of the *arrabal*, Ibn Ḥayyān, *Muqtabis II, 1*, ed. cit. pp. 152 and 154; trans. cit. pp. 64 and 66–7. E. Manzano Moreno, 'El medio cordobés y la elaboración cronística en al-Andalus bajo la dinastía de los Omeyas' p. 69.

Within the caliphal court, this edifying anecdote had a self-evident moral: the loyal gatekeeper had maintained upright conduct in a difficult situation, and for that reason the Banū Ḥudayr family went on to scale their position at the Umayyad court and become a seed-bed of chamberlains, viziers, provincial governors, *ṣāḥib al-madīna*s or supervisors of the mint during the caliphal period. The vindication of the deeds of the ancestors probably provided arguments for countless debates that may have taken place at the caliphal court on the merits of one family or another, the reasons why the caliph ought to choose this or that candidate for a post, or how Umayyad rulers had benefited or been hindered by decisions made in the past under the influence of this or that official. At stake were the stipends and influence associated with the positions in the caliphal administration of the families that belonged to this *salafiyya ṣulṭāniyya*. Members of these senior families considered that 'the deeds of their ancestors' demonstrated their own merits: if there were any lessons to be learnt from history, it was that the Umayyad dynasty owed everything to them. However, for their critics, if any lessons were to be learnt from the present, it was that these families were not always living up to the standards of the caliphate.

The Role of the *'Ulamā'*

In Córdoba, during the second half of the tenth century (fourth AH), there were at least five hundred *'ulamā'*, men specialised in disciplines such as Islamic law, the interpretation of the Qur'an, theology, and other religious disciplines.[19] All these men dedicated their lives to the study of these disciplines and, in some cases, they even undertook long journeys to Ifrīqiya, Egypt or Arabia, where in places such as Qayrawān, Alexandria or Medina they studied under prestigious scholars. On their return to al-Andalus, they passed on their learning and, occasionally, applied it in a range of official positions and jobs, particularly in the case of legal scholars. In the generation active around the time of al-Ḥakam II, the number of Andalusi *'ulamā'* who had travelled to North Africa or the Near East was well over a hundred. For those who did not venture beyond al-Andalus there was a community of scholars in cities such as

[19] L. Molina, 'El estudio de las familias de ulemas como fuente para la historia social del islam', pp. 160–73.

Córdoba, Seville and Zaragoza, who were also quite capable of providing them with a sound training.[20]

The *'ulamā'*'s increase in number and social presence is one of the biggest changes that occurred over the course of the tenth century (fourth AH). Their knowledge of religious disciplines enabled them to perform roles such as that of local judge or *qāḍī*, a mosque's prayer leader, or preacher. The *'ulamā'* also undertook the distribution of *bona vacantia* and in the absence of any heirs they administered them for the benefit of the community. They were also responsible for drafting notarial documents and supervising the city markets, as well as performing roles such as legal advisers and secretaries. Furthermore, all legal arbitrations were undertaken by them. Over time, these positions and duties became widespread in an increasing number of places in al-Andalus, as a result of the growing needs of an ever more complex and Islamised society. In turn, this gave rise to an exponential increase in the *'ulamā'*'s influence and prestige; for much of the Andalusi population the decisions and practices of *qāḍī*s, souk inspectors or those responsible for administering wills addressed questions of key importance, such as marriage, inheritance, commercial regulations, rents, sales, and the numerous daily affairs regulated by the normative practice of Islamic law, of whose orthodox interpretation, transmission and practice the *'ulamā'* were the guarantors. Furthermore, as many of them also had their own professions and lived among the common people, to whose complaints they would give voice, they gained status as social leaders, which always posed a potential threat to the established order.

In fact, and although there were exceptions (and in this period, as will be seen, one very important exception was made), it was rare for *'ulamā'* to perform roles in the caliphate's civil and military administration. While their presence multiplied in the aforementioned roles, the *'ulamā'* were not usually appointed as viziers, provincial governors or *qā'id*s in the army (despite the fact that some took part in military expeditions as a display of their zeal for the practice of holy war).[21] This separation of roles was rooted in the image the

[20] L. Molina, 'Lugares de destino de los viajeros andalusíes en el Ta'rīkh de Ibn al-Faraḍī', pp. 585–610. The data indicates that there were 85 ulemas who travelled abroad and died after 375 AH (985), while 93 of those who died between 351 AH (962) and 375 AH (385) had travelled abroad.

[21] Naturally, there were exceptions, such as Muḥammad b. Abī 'Īsā, who was *qāḍī* of Córdoba, but was also employed by the caliph 'Abd al-Raḥmān III to undertake duties related to the organisation

ʿulamāʾ sought to construct for themselves; it was underpinned by the idea of them acting as the guardians of a religious legacy that was continually under threat from the world's temporal corruption. Thereby, they became the moral antagonists of the caliph's power, as, in theory at least, they only paid heed to the needs of the Islamic community and did not answer to any other mandate than that which emanated from the principles established by God.

Numerous anecdotes demonstrate how the *ʿulamāʾ* boasted of their incorruptible moral authority, for example refusing to be appointed to any position by the caliphs and making a show of their rejection of earthly pomp. Although this attitude, defined as 'distance from the state' (*inqibāḍ ʿan al-sulṭān*), was by no means a predominant phenomenon (the majority of *ʿulamāʾ* undertook posts and roles within the state, and even competed with each other for appointments), this message articulated an ideal of this group's collective identity. This is shown by many anecdotes that recount how *ʿulamāʾ* blamed the powerful for the excessive luxury they relished, censured the caliph and his subordinates for failing to properly fulfil religious duties, or invoked their dignity to navigate an ocean of corruption. The rare individuals who initially followed the way of the *ʿulamāʾ* only to later join the service (*khidma*) of the caliphal administration were, as a result, treated with disdain by the peers they had associated with at first, and were criticised for yielding to mundane concerns.[22]

The *ʿulamāʾ* were evidently concerned to sustain this image, as they considered themselves to be a social group guided by the strict moral principles which ideally embodied the quintessence of the Muslim community. This bestowed upon them a strong sense of *authority* that was by definition opposed to the power of the *sulṭān*. In the best case scenario, the *sulṭān* was incapable of fulfilling the high demands set by the community's moral code; in the worst-case scenario, worldly power was perceived as mercilessly exploiting the members of the community and showing no concern for religious rules.

of the army, M. Fierro, 'El alfaquí bereber Yaḥyà b. Yaḥyà al-Laythī (m. 234 H.–848)', p. 278. His brother served as governor of Madrid on two occasions and died during a military raid, H. de Felipe, *Identidad y onomástica de los bereberes de al-Andalus*, p. 156.

22 M. Marín, 'Inqibāḍ ʿan al-sulṭān: ʿulamāʾ and Political Power in al-Andalus', in *Saber religioso y poder político en el islam*, Madrid, 1994, p. 129. E. Manzano, 'Why Did Islamic Institutions Become So Different from Western Medieval Institutions', *Medieval Worlds*, I, 2015, pp. 118–37.

One of the most renowned *'ulamā'* from the time of al-Ḥakam II was Abū Ibrāhīm Isḥāq al-Tujībī, a legal expert who was originally from Toledo. He lived a strict ascetic life, but also had close ties to the caliph, whom he served as one of his legal advisers. Various anecdotes about him are recorded. For example, al-Ḥakam would visit him at his house, yet the sage would not even stand to greet him, or else he would make a point of not deigning to reply immediately when the caliph sent for him. Mention has already been made of his ruling that the caliph could not give alms as a way of expiating his breaking of *Ramaḍān*, on the basis that al-Ḥakam did not actually own property, but merely administered the wealth of the Muslims. His concept of caliphal power reduced the role of the sovereign to a mere administrator of the community's affairs, a view al-Ḥakam would most probably not have agreed with. However, sources claim that through these critical attitudes Abū Ibrāhīm Isḥāq al-Tujībī won the obedience of the people (*al-'āmma*), while the caliph ended up fearing him: when he died in 963 (352 AH), in the midst of a victorious military campaign, al-Ḥakam II declared that he did not know what brought him greater joy, the success of the campaign or his legal adviser's death, and he gave thanks to God for freeing him from his malevolent ways.[23]

The unremitting commitment to the Muslim community's moral values demonstrated by *'ulamā'* such as Abū Ibrāhīm Isḥāq al-Tujībī earned them considerable popularity, which in turn constituted a serious threat to the caliph's power due to their unrelenting criticism of his actions. Al-Ḥakam, while still crown prince, became aware of the *'ulamā'*'s social influence and their potentially destabilising effects. To counter this, he took care to gather a select number of these religious scholars around him, whereby he created a client network of sages who were his beneficiaries and, therefore, obliged to him.[24] This is the reason why, when confronted by the evidence that many

[23] On this faqih, M. Marín, 'Altos funcionarios para el califa: jueces y otros cargos de la administración de 'Abd al-Raḥmān III', p. 97, based on the information provided by the *qāḍī* 'Iyāḍ, *Tartīb al-madhārik*, vol. 6, pp. 126–34. This information is complemented by the valuable insights provided by al-Maqqarī, *Nafḥ*, I, pp. 376–9. In these texts, it is stated that this scholar kept his *majlis* in the mosque of Abū 'Uthmān, which was near his house in the medina, to the north of the *alcázar* in Córdoba. His legal views have been addressed by M. I. Fierro, 'Los mālikíes de al-Andalus y los dos árbitros (*al-ḥakāman*)', pp. 89–95. With regard to his position on the expiation of the caliph, see above p. 53. See also J. M. Vizcaíno in *Biblioteca de al-Andalus*, IV, n. 791.

[24] M. Marín, 'Altos funcionarios', p. 96, cites Ibn al-Abbār, who states that al-Ḥakam *iṣṭinā' ahli-hi*, which indicates the establishment of a patronage relationship with these *'ulamā'*. The strength

aspects of the running of the state administration were slipping through his fingers, al-Ḥakam decided to use these *'ulamā'* as one form of support for exercising tighter control over the caliphal state apparatus and underscoring its legitimacy.

This policy is demonstrated by the evolution of one of the most interesting institutions within the Umayyad government; one that permitted subjects to denounce injustices (*maẓālim*) they had suffered from government officials. Umayyad emirs began holding sessions, on occasions in the mosque of Córdoba, in which subjects who had undergone abuses by government employees could state their complaints. However, it was Caliph 'Abd al-Raḥmān III who created a special post to oversee this task, the *ṣāḥib al-maẓālim*, who was responsible for receiving complaints from the people and was paid a salary for carrying out this role. The first appointees to this post were senior dignitaries, some of whom were viziers, and they belonged to the leading families who held other posts in the caliphal administration.[25]

At the start of the caliphate of al-Ḥakam II, this trend was maintained. The post was filled by the vizier 'Abd al-Raḥmān b. Mūsā b. Ḥudayr, who belonged to a well-known family of Umayyad officials that traced their origin back to the aforementioned Ḥudayr, the gatekeeper of the *alcázar* who had boldly stood his ground against the emir al-Ḥakam I when he had wanted to crucify the rebels of the uprising of the suburbs of Córdoba, as mentioned above. In July 972, acting as *ṣāḥib al-maẓālim*, 'Abd al-Raḥmān had to examine the complaint made by the people of Seville against their governor for unjust treatment. This complaint, which was also made by the governor's servants and entourage, led to this governor being removed from his post.[26]

'Abd al-Raḥmān b. Mūsā b. Ḥudayr went on to play a less edifying role in another event that same year, which involved the omnipresent Muḥammad

of these ties was demonstrated during the dynastic crisis that took place during the time of 'Abd al-Raḥmān III, when one of his sons, called 'Abd Allāh, plotted to kill his father and brother with the support of rival *'ulamā'*. The conspiracy was discovered and those responsible were executed.

25 On this I follow C. Müller, 'Redressing Injustice', pp. 93–104. The position was first undertaken by Muḥammad b. Ṭumlus, a member of a family of viziers and secretaries; he was succeeded by Aḥmad b. Shuhayd, one of the most powerful viziers of the time and likewise member of a prominent family.

26 Ibn Ḥayyān, *Muqtabis VII*, ed. p. 86; trans. p. 109. The governor in question was Ibn al-Khāl Sa'īd, or, in other words, a son of Sa'īd b. Abī l-Qāsim, who was a maternal uncle of the caliph 'Abd al-Raḥmān III. Below, information concerning either him or his brother is examined.

b. Abī 'Āmīr, the future al-Manṣūr. At that time, the latter was in charge of the mint, but the caliph had got wind of rumours suggesting he was committing fraud. To check the truth of the stories that were circulating, al-Ḥakam ordered his subordinate to present the accounts for the mint and give a statement of the financial records and available assets. Terrified, Muḥammad b. Abī 'Āmīr came up with no better way out of this tight corner than by asking 'Abd al-Raḥmān b. Mūsā b. Ḥudayr to loan him a sizeable sum with which to cover up his misdeeds. And this is exactly what 'Abd al-Raḥmān did. Muhammad then managed to return the money, and a lasting friendship was forged between them.[27]

It is possible that this episode is one of a series of tales that were intended to enhance the legend of the future al-Manṣūr. In any case, it shows that in caliphal Córdoba people considered it feasible that the vizier in charge of preventing injustice (*ṣāḥib al-maẓālim*) would help cover up a flagrant case of embezzlement committed in the caliph's entourage, thus suggesting that the Umayyad administration faced a serious issue of credibility. In fact, 'Abd al-Raḥmān b. Mūsā b. Ḥudayr is not mentioned again as holding the post of *ṣāḥib al-maẓālim* after this episode. This was not due to a decline in the number of complaints made by the people against their governors' behaviour: these continued, but from then on it was always *'ulamā'* who were appointed to address them. Thus, in March 973 (*Jumāda* II, 362 AH) the complaint made by the inhabitants of the *kūra* of Jaén against their governor was investigated by Aḥmad b. Naṣr, an elderly man, who among other positions had held that of *qāḍī* of the same province. The findings proved the people of Jaén to be in the right and the caliph exempted them from the payment of wood, fish and tar which they had been unjustly demanded to supply to the navy, very possibly as a fiscal payment; the caliph covered these naval expenses with his own money and the inhabitants of the *kūra* were returned what they had already paid.[28]

Around that time, another Muslim scholar, 'Abd al-Malik b. Mundhīr b. Sa'īd, held the post of *ṣāḥib al-radd*, a form of appeal judge. He was

[27] Ibn 'Idhārī, *al-Bayān*, II, p. 352; trans. p. 417.

[28] Ibn Ḥayyān, *Muqtabis VII*, ed. pp. 100–1; trans. pp. 128–30. Aḥmad b. Naṣr was born in 901 (288 AH) and undertook many roles in the caliphal administration, Ibn al-Faraḍī, *Ta'rīkh 'ulāmā' al-Andalus*, no. 165. More on him below.

commissioned to travel through the provinces of Seville, Carmona, Morón, Écija and Niebla to gain first-hand knowledge of the governors' conduct (*'ummāl*). 'Abd al-Malik was the *qāḍī* of the region of Llano de los Pedroches (*Faḥṣ al-Ballūṭ*) and belonged to an influential family of *'ulamā'*; his father Mundhīr b. Sa'īd al-Ballūṭī had been a renowned *qāḍī* of Córdoba, while two of his brothers served as prayer leaders in mosques of the capital.[29] We do not know what was the result of his enquiry, but a month later, when the people of Guadalajara presented a complaint against their governor, one of the judges appointed to the case was once again 'Abd al-Malik b. Mundhir b. Sa'īd, who very possibly went on to make powerful enemies.[30]

[29] H. de Felipe, *Identidad y onomástica*, pp. 210–20.

[30] Ibn Ḥayyān, *Muqtabis VII*, ed. pp. 104–5; trans. p. 133. The inspection undertaken in Guadalajara seems to have arisen from political factors and personal connections that are not made clear in Ibn Ḥayyān's text. The governor of Guadalajara targeted by the complaint investigated by 'Abd al-Malik b. Mundhīr b. Sa'īd was Rashīq b. 'Abd al-Raḥmān al-Barghawāṭī, one of the *qā'id*s of the Umayyad army, which was at that time campaigning in North Africa. The complaint was made in spring 973, after Rashīq had fallen into disgrace along with other soldiers 'for having abandoned the army'. In May, on the caliph's orders, a commission was sent to Arcila (Morocco) to investigate the facts. The commission was formed by the omnipresent Muḥammad b. Abī 'Āmir, the future al-Manṣūr, Aḥmad b. Muḥammad al-Kalbī, a treasury official who had accompanied 'Abd al-Malik b. Mundhīr b. Sa'īd in his investigation in Guadalajara (he had been born in Seville and, like other civil servants with the *nisba* 'al-Kalbī', was related to the treasury official Qāsim b. Walīd al-Kalbī, and his son Qāsim, who served as provincial governor, Ibn Ḥayyān, *Muqtabis V*, ed. and trans. pp. 43, 51, 53, 55, 59, 167, 189, 304). Another member of the commission was Muḥammad b. 'Alī b. al-Ḥasan b. Abī l-Ḥusayn (d. 982/372 AH), a scholar who, having travelled through Egypt and Palestine, had been appointed along with his brother as *qāḍī* of the Upper Frontier and had been also commissioned to compare the extant copies held in al-Andalus of the oldest known dictionary of Arabic, the *K. al-'Ayn* by Ḥalīl b. Aḥmad, which was composed in the eighth century (second century AH); this task was undertaken at the *Dār al-Mulk*, in the *alcázar* of Córdoba, and the commission's verdict identified the worst copy as having been made by Mundhīr b. Sa'īd al-Ballūṭī, the father of 'Abd al-Malik b. Mundhir b. Sa'īd, which is perhaps not a coincidence, *Prosopografía de los ulemas de al-Andalus*, http://www.eea.csic/pua/ (last accessed 12 November 2022), id. 9.955. Following a month in Morocco, the commission returned to Córdoba and reported its conclusions to the caliph. Shortly afterwards, Rashīq was received by the caliph along with the other disgraced soldiers, and he was ordered to return to Morocco. After the North African campaign, Rashīq was appointed *qā'id* of Lérida, which confirms that he had regained the caliph's confidence, Ibn Ḥayyān, *Muqtabis VII*, ed. pp. 81, 102, 106, 118, 129, 194 and 225; trans. pp. 104, 131, 136, 151, 163, 236, 264–66. Is it possible that the commission sent to northern Morocco undermined the accusation made against Rashīq under the auspices of 'Abd al-Malik b. Mundhir b. Sa'īd? Following the death of the caliph al-Ḥakam, this 'Abd al-Malik was accused by al-Manṣūr of conspiring with others against the heir Hishām, and he ended up being crucified in 978 (368 AH), H. de Felipe, *Identidad y onomástica*, pp. 218–19. Was all this just a coincidence?

Although there is no evidence that ʿAbd al-Malik b. Mundhir b. Saʿīd exercised the role of *ṣāḥib al-maẓālim*, his assignments seem to have paved the way for the change implemented in the final quarter of the tenth century (fourth AH) when this post would be held exclusively by *ʿulamāʾ*. Their employment to channel the subjects' discontent was intended, on the one hand, to reinforce the authority of the *sulṭān*, and on the other, to deactivate any possible leadership that these religious men could exercise within the Muslim community. By appointing *ʿulamāʾ* to these positions, al-Ḥakam looked for trustworthy men who backed his actions, helped him to control the corruption that was ingrained in the administration, and used their moral superiority to serve the dynasty.

All these virtues were considered as being possessed by the man Caliph al-Ḥakam named *qāḍī* of Córdoba in 966 (355 AH), who undertook this role throughout the remainder of his rule. Muḥammad b. Isḥāq b. al-Salīm belonged to a family of clients (*mawālī*) of the Umayyad dynasty that hailed from Sidonia. During his early life, he had followed the typical path of a good Muslim scholar: he had travelled to the East to further his studies, and on his return had dedicated himself to a life of learning and piety, living humbly off what he fished from the River Guadalquivir, and disdaining any effort from those in power, as well as the caliph himself, to seduce him with positions or wealth. All this changed when al-Ḥakam proposed that he revise the books he had in his large library. Won over by his thirst for knowledge, from then on Muḥammad b. Isḥāq b. al-Salīm not only joined the circle of beneficiaries of al-Ḥakam, but also began to accept other positions he was offered, such as *ṣāḥib al-maẓālim*, and finally, *qāḍī* of Córdoba.[31]

The transition made by this pious scholar from the most absolute disdain for mundane affairs to offering twenty dinars to a friend's slave for having eloquently recited a passage from the Qur'an and some poetry is much the same as that made by many other *ʿulamāʾ* during this period. Once he had

[31] His ancestor, Abū Ikrima Jaʿfar b. Yazīd, was a descendant of a *mawlā* of the caliph Sulaymān and took part in the battle of al-Muṣāra, which permitted the accession of the first Umayyad in al-Andalus, Ibn al-Qūṭiyya, *Taʾrīkh*, ed. p. 26; trans. James p. 70. Another ancestor of his was a vizier and governor of Toledo, Ibn Ḥayyān, *Muqtabis 2, II*, p. 1 and *ṣāḥib al-madīna*, al-Khushanī, *Quḍāt Qurṭuba*, ed. and trans. pp. 104 and 127. For his biography, M. L. Ávila and M. Penelas, *Biblioteca de al-Andalus*, V, s.v. Ibn al-Salīm (1094).

tasted the mundane delights of the court, Muḥammad b. Isḥāq b. al-Salīm ended up docilely accepting the caliph's instructions on certain aspects of legal practice.[32] His obedience proved to be fundamental for the issue that obsessed al-Ḥakam during the latter part of his life: the naming of his son, Hishām, as heir to the caliphate, despite the fact that his being a minor meant this decision contravened the principles of Islamic law. Although some texts endeavour to present Muḥammad b. Isḥāq b. al-Salīm as maintaining a deaf ear and dignified resistance to the caliph's pretensions, it is clear that the succession would never have taken place without his collaboration. When al-Ḥakam died in 976, and the caliphate was illegally transferred to Hishām, who had just turned eleven, as recompense for his support it was confirmed that Muḥammad b. Isḥāq b. al-Salīm would continue as *qāḍī* of Córdoba, a post he had held for nearly ten years. However, the proclamation of Hishām gave rise to a surge of social discontent in Córdoba, and one channel of expression for the popular indignation was the circulation of an anonymous poem. It made mention of Caliph Hishām being a minor, a rather unpleasant allusion to his mother, Subḥ, and a scabrous insult aimed at Muḥammad b. Isḥāq b. al-Salīm himself, all framed with apocalyptic allusions that reveal how tense the mood was:

> The true promise draws near [Qur'an 21:97], destruction approaches
> The most abominable things have occurred:
> A caliph plays at school,
> His mother is pregnant and a qāḍī lets others sodomize him.[33]

The Caliph's Men

Al-Ḥakam II's mistrust of the leading families that had until then dominated the Umayyad administration is clearly reflected in the names of his senior

[32] P. Chalmeta, 'Acerca del 'amal en al-Andalus. Algunos casos concretos', pp. 353–4. The legal issues concerned the proceedings for the declaration of the absence of a certain person and the rights of female descendants to pious legacies. At least in the first case, the *qāḍī* followed the caliph's instructions.

[33] Ibn 'Idhārī, *al-Bayān*, II, ed. p. 280, trans. p. 466. The translation is based on that included by M. L. Ávila and M. Penelas in *Biblioteca de al-Andalus*. The Qur'anic passage states: 'when the True Promise draws near, the disbelievers' eyes will stare in terror, and they will say, "Woe to us! We were not aware of this at all. We were wrong"' (Qur'an, 21:97). All references to the Qur'an refer to the English translation by M. A. S. Abdel Haleem, Oxford, 2016.

officials. During his father's time, most viziers had belonged to the Banū Shuhayd, Banū Abī 'Abda, Banū Ḥudayr, Banū l-Zajjālī and Banū Fuṭays families. Under al-Ḥakam's rule the members of these families appointed to this same post can be counted on the fingers of one hand. Apart from the aforementioned and untrustworthy 'Abd al-Raḥmān b. Mūsā b. Ḥudayr, the only vizier from one of these families appointed by al-Ḥakam was Muḥammad b. Fuṭays, whose son was also governor of Rayyuh (Málaga). The *qā'id* and vizier, Muḥammad b. Qāsim b. Ṭumlus, could also lay claim to a distinguished lineage, whose members had served as senior military officers and provincial governors for generations.[34] Yaḥyā b. Muḥammad al-Tujībī and his cousin al-'Āṣī b. Ḥakam al-Tujībī also served as viziers under al-Ḥakam II, and likewise belonged to a distinguished family, yet their case was different; their family dominated the frontier cities of Zaragoza, Calatayud and Daroca, where they maintained a special agreement with the caliphate: in exchange for control over their territories as well as being appointed to the vizierate, they ensured that taxes were paid in that region, and that frontier troops were supplied for caliphal military campaigns.[35]

[34] One of his ancestors had fought in the Umayyad emirate army against the Banū Qasī and was executed by them. His second uncle, Muḥammad b. Qāsim b. Ṭumlus, aside from leading various summer campaigns, was the first to be appointed to the recently created post of *ṣāḥib al-maẓālim* by 'Abd al-Raḥmān III, C. Muller, 'Redressing Injustice', p. 96. Ibn Ḥayyān, *Muqtabis V*, ed. and trans. pp. 49, 87, 93, 213. Naturally, and despite the homonyms, it is impossible that this person is the same as was named to lead the North African campaign, as is claimed by M. Meouak, *Pouvoir souverain, administration centrale et élites politiques dans l'Espagne Umayyade*, pp. 155–6. On the father of our *qā'id*, *Muqtabis V*, pp. 220, 256, 301; al-'Udhrī, *Tarṣī*, p. 82; Ibn 'Idhārī, *al-Bayān*, ed. cit. pp. 211–12; on another uncle, called Aḥmad, *Muqtabis V*, p. 256; with regard to his second cousins, one was also called Qāsim and another Aḥmad, *Muqtabis VII*, pp. 106, 119, 170, 185, 196, 228 and *al-Bayān*, pp. 260–1. At the time of al-Ḥakam I, a rebel called Ṭumlus had led an uprising in the region of Lisbon, but he had died and his head was sent to Córdoba, whereby it is impossible to know if he had anything to do with this family, Ibn Ḥayyān, *Muqtabis, 2.1*, ed. cit. p. 132; trans. cit. pp. 48–9. On Muḥammad b. Fuṭays, Ibn Ḥayyān, *Muqtabis VII*, ed. p. 150; trans. p. 190.

[35] M. J. Viguera, *Aragón Musulmán*, pp. 156–62. E. Manzano Moreno, *La frontera de al-Andalus en época de los Omeyas*, Madrid, 1991, pp. 351–61. Al-'Udhrī, *Tarṣī*, pp. 42, 46–7; Ibn Ḥayyān, *Muqtabis VII*, ed. pp. 29, 59, 82, 94, 128; trans. pp. 52–3, 81, 105, 117. After the disaster of Faḥṣ Mahrān the Tujībid family were summoned to reinforce the army in Morocco, and in fact, following Ghālib's victory and his return to the peninsula, Yaḥyā remained in charge of the troops that remained there, Ibn Ḥayyān, *Muqtabis VII*, ed. pp. 128–9, 140, 142, 177, 210; trans. pp. 162–4, 174, 179, 215, 216, 222, 251.

Other appointments show that, in contrast to his wavering trust in the senior families of the Umayyad administration, al-Ḥakam II sought to surround himself with people from humble origins, who were loyal to him and would form a 'solid core' he could trust. The idea was to dispense with those who were immersed in the web of interests, reciprocal favours and complicity that the most prominent families of the administration had been weaving on the loom of the Umayyad administration. Instead, al-Ḥakam seems to have attempted to create his own network that would depend solely and exclusively on him. The origins of these people were diverse: some were *ṣaqāliba* (slaves), others were *mawālī*, recently manumitted slaves who had become the caliph's clients, while the last social group consisted of free men, who lacked the distinguished ancestry boasted about by the senior families who had converted the *sulṭān* into their own backyard.

The most characteristic group were the *ṣaqāliba* (sing. *ṣiqlab*). Their slave origins meant they were blindly loyal to the figure of the caliph, as in principle they lacked any other family or political ties. Although in the emirate period there had been cases of eunuchs being appointed to senior posts in the administration, it was now that their number and influence grew exponentially. It is possible that some of these *ṣaqāliba* were captives taken in pillaging raids during campaigns fought in the north of the Iberian Peninsula, but their origin was above all Slavic, the people described by Arabic authors as having settled to the north and east of the lands of the Franks.[36] In the mid-tenth century (fourth AH) the trade in these *ṣaqāliba*, which operated along the routes discussed in the previous chapter, had increased dramatically. On arrival in al-Andalus, a select number of these slaves were chosen to undertake tasks in the caliphal administration. We have no idea how this was done or how those chosen were trained for their role. It seems likely that they were selected at an early age and underwent a form of education similar to that of the slave singers, who could, for example, be of Basque origin and, having undergone a long and meticulous training, eventually became consummate masters in Arabic music and poetry.[37]

[36] M. Meouak, *Ṣaqāliba: eunuques et esclaves à la conquête du pouvoir*, Helsinki, 2004.
[37] Ibn Ḥayyān, *Muqtabis II, 1*, ed. cit. p. 307; trans. cit. p. 193.

One of the most impressive careers of one of these *ṣaqāliba* in the administration of the Umayyad caliphate was that of Ja'far al-Ṣiqlabī (who should not be confused with the vizier Ja'far b. 'Uthmān al-Muṣḥafī). He was of Slavic origin and seems to have had excellent gifts of organisation and leadership. During the time of 'Abd al-Raḥmān III, he had been the head of the stables (*ṣāḥib al-khayl*) and overseer of the caliphal textiles workshop (*dār al-ṭirāz*), which, as has been seen, was of comparable importance to the mint. He had a very close relationship with the crown prince al-Ḥakam: the day after he became caliph, al-Ḥakam appointed him *ḥājib*, a position that Ja'far held until his death in 971 (360 AH). This post is usually translated as 'chamberlain', and originally referred to the person who regulated access to the caliphs, and served as a form of chief of staff. He controlled who, when and how people could gain access to the caliph. In Umayyad Córdoba, the *ḥājib* was also the sovereign's trusted adviser, and he was given a great variety of tasks, ranging from the administration of the pious legacies established by the caliph, to ensuring that his soldiers were not equipped in any way that would displease him. The lack of any clear definition of the *ḥājib*'s duties reflected the personal nature of his dependence on the sovereign, which meant he could be assigned any task without any issue arising regarding his status.[38]

Like other *saqāliba*, Ja'far al-Ṣiqlabī was a eunuch. Thus, he did not form part of any prior patronage networks within the administrative infrastructure, nor could he engender any offspring with aspirations to gain positions in the administration through the influence of his relatives. One renowned anecdote records how on a very hot day Ja'far was swimming in a pool while Caliph al-Ḥakam and the *qāḍī* of Córdoba, Mundhir b. Sa'īd al-Ballūṭī (d. 966/355 AH), sat beside it. As the *qāḍī* was complaining about the heat, the caliph recommended he bathed like Ja'far, who was placidly swimming to and fro across the pool. It is possible that Mundhir b. Sa'īd could not swim, and so refused to take the advice of the caliph, who still encouraged him to take a cooling dip. As al-Ḥakam made a point of insisting,

[38] M. Ocaña, 'Ya'far el eslavo', *Cuadernos de la Alhambra*, 12, 1976, pp. 217–23. The caliph's reprimand to Ja'far with regard to his soldiers' use of Berber saddles in Ibn Ḥayyān, *Muqtabis VII*, ed. p. 190; trans. p. 229.

the embarrassed *qāḍī* could think of no better way out than to say that the problem was that he had an anchor, whose weight pulled his body down to the bottom, while Ja'far did not.[39] The anecdote, which became famous, demonstrated that however powerful and highly esteemed the *ḥājib* might be, it did not prevent continual and frequent allusions being made about him being a eunuch.

Lacking any anchorage among the ruling class of the Cordoban administration, the *ḥājib*'s loyalty was exclusively concentrated in the figure of the caliph. Ja'far had his living quarters in Madīnat al-Zahrā', in the residential section of the *alcázar*, which underscored his proximity to al-Ḥakam, with whom he would also ride alongside, when the caliph made public appearances.[40] One of the principal tasks he was assigned by the caliph, who was passionate about building projects, was to oversee construction works being undertaken at the time. A number of inscriptions refer to him as being in charge of architectural projects at the city palace of Madīnat al-Zahrā' from at least as early as 956–7 (345 AH), during the rule of 'Abd al-Raḥmān III.[41] Years later, al-Ḥakam commissioned him to undertake one of the most important projects of his caliphate: the extension of Córdoba's mosque, a task that was extensively acknowledged in the inscriptions that adorned it. The eunuch's name is written in no fewer than four places in the impressive *miḥrāb* that was built in the Cordoban oratory, an almost extravagant insistence that is affirmed above all in the gilded letters that decorate the central arched doorway or *alfiz*, whose inscription reads as follows:

> The imām, al-Mustanṣir bi-llāh, the servant of God, al-Ḥakam, Prince of the Believers – may Allāh help him – ordered his freedman (*mawlā*) and ḥājib, Jā'far b. 'Abd al-Raḥmān – may God have mercy on him – to raise this building. And it was finished with the aid of God, under the supervision Muḥammad b. Tamlīkh, Aḥmad b. Naṣr and Khald b. Hāshim,

[39] al-Maqqarī, *Nafḥ*, II, pp. 18–19.

[40] This residence has been identified in the eastern area of the *alcázar*, A. Vallejo, 'La vivienda servicios y la llamada casa de Ya'far', pp. 129–45.

[41] M. A. Martínez, 'Epigrafía monumental y élites sociales en al-Andalus' p. 35, n. 55. Also M. A. Martínez, 'Epígrafes a nombre de al-Ḥakam en Madīnat al-Zahrā'', pp. 84–5.

Image 7 Mosque of Córdoba's *miḥrāb*, completed in 354 AH/965. The Arab inscriptions which decorate it include Qur'anic verses, and mentions of the caliph al-Ḥakam and of those who had been in charge of the works, among them the powerful eunuch and *ḥājib* Ja'far al-Ṣiqlabī.

commanders of the *shurṭa*, and Muṭarrif b. ʻAbd al-Raḥmān, the kātib, his servants.[42]

In this inscription, which crowned one of the highlights of al-Ḥakam's caliphate, homage is paid to Jāʻfar's role in this project, despite the eunuch having died shortly before, as is revealed by the expression, 'may God have mercy on him'. The other names cited are a number of *ʻulamā'*, who were also very close to the caliph, albeit not particularly prestigious among their ranks, in addition to a secretary of the administration. Only the caliph, his eunuch and the servants who had helped to complete the work were listed in this highly privileged and sacred location.[43]

[42] M. Ocaña Jiménez, 'Inscripciones árabes fundacionales de la mezquita-catedral de Córdoba', p. 17. The other three places in which Jāʻfar is mentioned are the inscriptions on the left impost of the entrance arch, the plinth of the *miḥrāb* itself, and the gilded lettering in the inner strip of the alfiz of the door leading to the corridor.

[43] Abū ʻAbd Allāh Muḥammad b. Tamlīkh al-Tamīmī (d. June–July 972/Ramaḍan 361 AH) was a legal scholar whose knowledge was not always reliable, but was worthy of confidence for his

The acquisition and practice of activities linked to the administration of the state began very early on in life, which explains why many of its employees were called *fatā* (pl. *fityān*), or youth. The Slavic *fatā*s were a highly distinctive group in the caliphal court. Those called 'grand *fatās*', whom the caliph unquestionably trusted, would serve as his 'representatives' (*khulafā'*) and perform a range of duties, just as Ja'far did. When in August 971 al-Ḥakam decided to undertake the repairs of the bridge of Córdoba, he commissioned his grand representatives (*al-khulafā'al-akābir*), assisted by secretaries, to oversee the building work. The *fatā*s' supervisory role is also recorded in inscriptions commemorating building projects, as well as exemplary pieces of goldsmithing, ivory pyxides or carved marble capitals, which, as was seen in the previous chapter, were all made in the caliphal workshops. Names such as Jawdhar, Ṣādiq or Fā'iq are listed in these inscriptions as directors of specific projects, which testifies to the strict centralisation imposed on the construction work

honesty in the distribution of alms. He was named appeals judge (*ṣāḥib al-radd*) and *qāḍī* of Sidonia by 'Abd al-Raḥmān III, and later al-Ḥakam commissioned him to undertake an inspection of the mint and also appointed him as one of the chiefs of the *shurṭa*. However, his principal speciality was medicine, on which he wrote a well-known work, Ibn al-Faraḍī, *Ta'rīkh 'ulāmā' al-Andalus*, n. 1,299 (with a malicious history about his lack of knowledge on the transmission of *Muwaṭṭa*); J. Vernet, 'Los médicos andaluces', p. 460. One of the caliph's most trusted *'ulāmā'* was another of those cited in the *miḥrāb*'s inscription: the Toledo-born Abū 'Umar Aḥmad b. Naṣr b. Khālid (901–81/288–370 AH), who had served as *qāḍī* in Jaén, the region in which he oversaw an inspection made in the wake of complaints made by its inhabitants. Later, he was appointed to oversee the souk in Córdoba, and to the *shurṭa*. He also undertook a range of assignments for the caliph and regularly attended his receptions, Ibn al-Faraḍī, *Ta'rīkh*, n. 167; Ibn Ḥayyān, *Muqtabis VII* ed. pp. 66, 70, 77, 100–1, 153, 198 and 212; trans. pp. 87, 93, 99, 128–30, 193, 239, 253. With regard to 'Khald b. Hāshim', he is most certainly Abū Zayd Khālid b. Hāshim b. 'Umar (d. 979/369 AH), who is cited in *Muqtabis VII* and in *Dhikr bilād al-Andalus* as Khālid b. Hishām. He was *qāḍī* of the *kūra* of Rayyuh until being removed from his post in the summer of 972 (361 AH), but he continued taking part in the caliph's official receptions as a serving member of the *shurṭa*. Muḥammad b. Abī 'Āmir, the future al-Manṣūr, was his son-in-law (*ṣihr*) and he commissioned him to undertake the 'inspection of public works, a role he accepted, and in carrying it out he showed his resolution and diligence as the work carried out was perfect'. Some time later he was appointed vizier by Hishām II, Ibn al-Faraḍī, *Ta'rīkh*, n. 398; Ibn Hayyān, *Muqtabis VII*, ed. pp. 86 and 198; trans. pp. 109 and 239; *Dhikr bilād al-Andalus*, ed. p. 176; trans. pp. 186–7. This source indicates that he was vizier under al-Ḥakam (ed. p. 169; trans. p. 179), but I think it is preferable to follow the testimony of Ibn al-Faraḍī. The three individuals can be identified in *Prosopografía de los ulemas de al-Andalus*, id. 8,737, 2,026 and 3,043. I have not been able to identify the secretary (*kātib*) Muṭarrif b. 'Abd al-Raḥmān, also mentioned in the inscription.

and artistic production that was undertaken by the caliphate.[44] Some of them were even invited to attend the receptions held by the caliph.[45]

One of the court's most important *fatās*, although according to his enemies one of the least intelligent, was Durrī al-Saghīr, who was also of Slavic origin and a former slave. He was referred to in the previous chapter with regard to his name being included in the inscription adorning the so-called Zamora Pyxis, which offers testimony to how it was made under his supervision (*'alā yaday*). Durrī likewise oversaw the building of a minaret for a mosque, as is recorded in an inscription, and was in charge of the carving of capitals for Madīnat al-Zahrā', as his name is engraved into the volute of one of them. Durrī also served as a treasury official, which possibly indicates that he was responsible for the stocks of materials, such as ivory and marble, that were needed for these architectural and artistic projects.[46]

I have already commented on the way in which Durrī had created his own personal landholding, the *almunia* of al-Rummāniyya, and his resounding

[44] Jawdhar is listed in an inscription found in the mosque of Córdoba that has regrettably been broken. A gold-plated casket, which is preserved in the cathedral of Girona, was made on the caliph's orders for the crown prince Hishām, and 'it was completed under the supervision of Jawdhar'. He was present in a highly privileged place alongside the caliph at the reception held for the 'Īd al-Fiṭr in 973 (362 AH) in Madīnat al-Zahrā', where he is listed as the director of the jewellers and falconers (*ṣāḥib al-ṣāga wa-l-bayāzira*); he is also recorded as accompanying the caliph when he moved from the palace city to Córdoba following his serious illness in the spring of 975 (364 AH). Lévi-Provençal, *Inscriptions*, pp. 22–4, 191; Ibn Ḥayyān, *Muqtabis VII*, ed. pp. 119 and 212; trans. pp. 152, 252; A. Labarta, 'La arqueta de Hišām: su epigrafía', pp. 1–24. Ṣādiq appears on a capital ordered by the caliph himself 'that was made with the help of God (under the supervision) of Ṣādiq al-fatā al-kātib', *Al-Andalus. Las artes islámicas en España*, p. 247, no. 39 (I have some reservations about the reading of *kātib*). Fā'iq, a grand *fatā*, was director of the postal service and the *ṭirāz*. He also took part, in a very prominent position, in the reception held for the 'Īd al-Fiṭr in 973 (362 AH), and was graced with the assignment of the house that had been occupied by the chamberlain Ja'far al-Ṣiqlabī in Madīnat al-Zahrā', after his death; it is also possible that his name appears in two inscriptions, Ibn Ḥayyān, *Muqtabis VII*, ed. pp. 64, 66, 117, 119, 173, 210; trans. pp. 79, 88, 100, 149, 152, 211, 252; M. A. Martínez, 'Recientes hallazgos epigráficos en Madīnat al-Zahrā'', p. 28.

[45] Three of these *fatās*, Ma'qil, Sukkar and Murtāḥ, attended one of the receptions held in Madīnat al-Zahrā' and were referred to as *al-fityān al-akābir al-khulafā'*. Ibn Ḥayyān, *Muqtabis VII*, p. 185; trans. p. 224. Sukkar is mentioned in inscriptions on capitals in Madīnat al-Zahrā' dated 361 and 362 AH (972–3); the latter bears 'the latest date conserved on the whole site', M. A. Martínez, 'Recientes hallazgos epigráficos en Madīnat al-Zahrā'', p. 68.

[46] Lévi-Provençal, *Inscriptions*, pp. 186–8. On his stupidity, Ibn 'Idhārī, *al-Bayān*, II, p. 263; Ibn Ḥayyān, *Muqtabis VII*, ed. pp. 24–6; trans. pp. 48–9; A. Labarta, 'Las lápidas árabes de la provincia de Jaén', *Homenaje a Manuel Ocaña Jiménez*, Seville, 1990, p. 128; M. Antonia Martínez, 'Recientes hallazgos', p. 48.

fall from grace in April 973 (*Jumāda* 362 AH) due to a 'negligence' committed while working in the treasury. The accusation made against the *fatā* was communicated to him by the vizier and *ṣāḥib al-madīna*, Muḥammad b. Aflaḥ, at a meeting held in his office in Madīnat al-Zahrā', at which Durrī was informed of the charges that had been made against him. He was required to leave the residence he had in the city palace, reside at the *alcázar* in Córdoba and be stripped of his posts. He also underwent a significant reduction in his monthly stipend. However, months later, after having made a gift of his *almunia* to the caliph, as well as inviting him to a picnic there, Durrī presented himself before al-Ḥakam in early August bearing a letter from Hishām, in which the prince interceded for him and other *fatā*s who had also fallen into disgrace. The caliph decided to pardon them all. At that time Hishām was aged eight, and it is unlikely he had a clear idea of the complex machinations that dominated the workings of the caliphal administration. However, at the court of al-Ḥakam II any opportunity to underscore the heir's presence seems to have been taken advantage of.[47]

Durrī's fall from favour demonstrated the icy disdain shown to any eunuch who lost the caliph's favour and how he would be demoted far from the public eye within the depths of the administration. However, not everything depended on the caliph. Among the senior *fatā*s there soon emerged a group with a growing sense of their own worth. Little is known about this group of courtiers, but it must have become increasingly prominent at the heart of the caliphal court. They worked in similar posts, appeared together at official receptions and had a cohort of people serving under them, whose work they supervised. Furthermore, these Slavic eunuch *fatā*s gained still greater renown from the unquestionable grandeur of buildings or artworks that bore their names, despite their inescapable status placing them firmly on the margins of society. One literary work from this period, written by one Ḥabīb al-Ṣiqlabī, was entitled 'The Advantage and Victory Over Those That Deny the Virtues of the ṣaqāliba' and sought to demonstrate the merits of these Slavs, who were always identified as liminal figures with barely a foothold in society.[48] The outcome of this growing sense of self-awareness was that the Slavic courtiers

[47] Ibn Ḥayyān, *Muqtabis VII*, ed. pp. 103, 106–7; trans. pp. 132, 136–7.
[48] M. García Novo, s.v. al-Ṣiqlabī en *Biblioteca de al-Andalus*, vol. VII.

began to create their own faction at the very heart of the caliph's court by taking advantage of the influence and power they acquired from their posts.

One clear demonstration of the *ṣaqāliba*'s marginal status is that, despite accumulating power within the palace, they were never appointed to the position of vizier, while this post was granted to clients (*mawālī*) who were manumitted slaves. This was the case with Sa'd b. al-Ḥakam al-Ja'farī, who was of Frankish origin and belonged to a group of military slaves who had been manumitted by al-Ḥakam and about whom more will be said below.[49] The brothers Muḥammad and Ziyād b. Aflaḥ both served as viziers and were sons of a client (*mawlā*) of 'Abd al-Raḥmān III, who had been this caliph's head of stables. Muḥammad b. Aflaḥ was appointed both vizier and *ṣāḥib al-madīna* of Madīnat al-Zahrā', while Ziyād, who it will be recalled had a beautiful ivory pyxis dedicated to him, also undertook the role of head of stables, just as his father had done. When his brother died in 975 (364 AH), Ziyād took his place as *ṣāḥib al-madīna* of Madīnat al-Zahrā' and used the status it gave him to ensure that the caliph appointed the sons of his deceased brother as officials within the administration.[50]

The most renowned of the clients who served as vizier was Ghālib b. 'Abd al-Raḥmān, who was also supreme commander of the army (*al-qiyāda al-'ulyā*),

[49] Sa'd (or Sa'āda or Sa'īd) al-Ja'farī belonged to the so-called group of ja'farid slaves, whose origin I address in Ch. 4. He was appointed *qā'id* of a frontier region called al-Jawf in 964 (353 AH), and two years later he was *qā'id* of Guadalajara and Toledo. In 968 (357 AH) he fortified Calahorra alongside Ghālib. He must have been appointed vizier shortly after the death of Ja'far al-Ṣiqlabī in 971 (360 AH). In 973 (362 AH), he was responsible for the recruitment of 1,700 men along the Toledo frontier for the North African campaign. Ibn 'Idhārī, *al-Bayān*, II, pp. 236, 238 and 241; Ibn Ḥayyān, *Muqtabis VII*, ed. p. 117; trans. p. 150. His son may well have been one Aḥmad, who lived in Madīnat al-Zahrā', although he had to relinquish his residence to provide accommodation for al-Zubaydī when he was named preceptor to Prince Hishām. He is recorded as serving as a bodyguard and undertaking ceremonial duties on solemn occasions. As *ṣāḥib al-shurṭa al-'ulya* he was ordered to undertake the rounding up of the horses for the campaign of 975 (364 AH). Shortly afterwards he was removed from the post due to complaints being made against him: Ibn Ḥayyān, *Muqtabis VII*, ed. pp. 44–5, 133, 183, 216, 228; trans. pp. 64–6, 168, 223, 270.

[50] On Aflaḥ b. 'Abd al-Raḥmān, Ibn Ḥayyān, *Muqtabis V*, pp. 112, 120, 132; Ibn 'Idhārī, *al-Bayān*, II, ed. cit. pp. 183, 199. On his sons, Ibn Ḥayyān, *Muqtabis VII*, ed. cit. pp. 21, 24, 26, 30, 47, 49, 50, 73, 78–9, 87, 92, 94, 103–4, 117, 119, 156, 172, 173, 184–5, 197–8, 210, 212, 230; trans. pp. 45, 49, 52, 66, 68, 69, 96–7, 101, 110–11, 116–18, 132–3, 149, 152, 171, 185, 197, 209–11, 221, 223, 224, 227, 237, 238–9, 250, 252–3, 272. The ivory pyxis preserved in the Victoria and Albert Museum in London, which was made in 969–70 (359 AH), has an inscription which wishes 'fortune and prosperity on *Ziyād b. Aflaḥ, ṣāḥib al-shurṭa al-'ulyā*', É. Lévi-Provençal, *Inscriptions arabes d'Espagne*, pp. 188–9.

a position that granted him direct access to the caliph, with whom he often had private audiences. Following his successful campaign in North Africa, Ghālib was appointed highest-ranking vizier, and was granted a preferential seat in the 'House of the Viziers' (*Bayt al-Wuzarā'*) in Madīnat al-Zahrā'. In the spring of 975 (364 AH) al-Ḥakam appointed him to command the campaign to liberate the fortress of Gormaz, which was under siege from the Christians. On this occasion, Ghālib was awarded an unprecedented honour: he received two swords and was granted a title that was until then unheard of in al-Andalus: *Dhū l-sayfayn*, 'he of the two swords'.[51]

The gallery of the caliph's men with low-born origins, who accumulated considerable power during this period, is completed with a free man, called Ja'far b. 'Uthmān al-Muṣḥafī. He was of Berber origin and born from a 'family tree lacking renown or glory', but he managed to establish a highly successful career at the heart of the administration, thanks to both his extraordinary intellectual capacity and his close ties to al-Ḥakam, which dated back to the period when he was still crown prince. As a fine poet and excellent writer of prose, Ja'far b. 'Uthmān al-Muṣḥafī began his career as a secretary, although he soon began to undertake more important roles. In 939 (328 AH), he was named governor of Elvira and Pechina, provinces that were then administered directly by al-Ḥakam. From there he went on to serve as governor of the Balearic Islands in 941 (329 AH). Three days after having been proclaimed caliph, al-Ḥakam II appointed him vizier, a position he added to that of *ṣāḥib al-madīna* of Córdoba, one of the most important positions in the Umayyad administration. Ja'far b. 'Uthmān al-Muṣḥafī also drafted many of the diplomas and official letters, whose contents reveal a bombastic florid style along with an excellent knowledge of the Qur'an and Arab culture (*adab*).

Despite his extraordinary merits, the promotion of Ja'far b. 'Uthmān al-Muṣḥafī prompted fierce resentment among the families who had traditionally dominated the caliphal administration. They 'envied him, and found him full of vices and defects, and in particular attributed to him an obsession for extreme officiousness and greed'. Ja'far's sense of isolation was underscored in February 972 (*Jumāda* de 361 AH), when he contracted a serious illness

[51] Ibn Ḥayyān, *Muqtabis VII*, ed. pp. 219–20; trans. pp. 259–60.

and thought he was at death's door. He decided to write to the caliph asking him 'not to withdraw the caliphate's favour from his sons and family'. This extraordinary petition was motivated by the evident dislike for him at the caliphal court and the fact that his son and his nephew, and perhaps also other relatives, held senior posts in the administration. The vizier clearly feared that in his absence a rival faction would exert their influence on the caliph to have the members of his family removed from their posts.[52]

However, as it turned out, there was nothing to worry about. Ja'far b. 'Uthmān al-Muṣḥafī recovered from his serious illness – a demonstration of the excellence of the court's physicians – and soon took up his duties once more. Over the course of the final years of al-Ḥakam's life, his power within the court continued to grow even greater. He became the caliph's principal ally when it came to removing any obstacles hindering his son Hishām being acknowledged as heir to the caliphate, despite not having attained his majority. During the illness that eventually led to the caliph's death in October 976, Ja'far undertook control of the state (*sulṭān*) and thereby ensured he was in the best position to control the succession. In fact, one of the first measures taken by the new caliph, Hishām, was to appoint him as his *ḥājib*. It was possibly at that moment that Ja'far thought he had achieved the peak of his power and that the members of his family and supporters would be safe in their senior positions and continue to wield enormous power. Little would he have imagined that he was on the brink of a thunderous demise. Barely a year and a half had passed since al-Ḥakam II had died when, in March 978 (*Sha'bān* 367 AH), Ja'far was removed from his posts and imprisoned along with his sons and nephew. He died in prison a few months later. The person responsible for his disgrace and eventual death was no less than Muḥammad b. Abī 'Āmir, al-Manṣūr.[53]

[52] Ibn Ḥayyān, *Muqtabis VII*, ed. and trans. pp. 69 and 92–3. Muḥammad, the son of Ja'far, was his assistant for his role as *ṣāḥib al-madīna*, see *Muqtabis VII*, ed. cit. pp. 46, 78, 143, 196, 225; trans. cit. pp. 66, 101, 180, 236, 266. His nephew, Hishām, was *qā'id* of Tortosa and *kūra* of Valencia, see *Muqtabis VII*, ed. cit. pp. 20, 21, 46, 47, 49, 50, 52, 78–9, 92, 153; trans. cit. pp. 44, 45, 65, 67–9, 71, 101, 116, 194. On the disdain shown by the senior families of the caliphate, X. Ballestín Navarro, *al-Mansur*, pp. 118–25.

[53] Ibn 'Idhārī, *al-Bayān*, II, p. 268.

The Structure of the *Sulṭān*

The complex composition of the Umayyad state had at its core a strict hierarchy, and the posts this consisted of reveal the state's structure with considerable clarity. In this section, I will present an 'X-ray image' of the caliphal *sulṭān* in the mid-tenth century (fourth AH). The discussion of this 'X-ray' is out of necessity very descriptive, but it permits a clear identification of the mechanisms of power the caliphal employed to exert its control.

As was noted above, the *ḥājib* was a post bestowed upon someone with the caliph's full confidence, which is why it was frequently given to a palace eunuch. However, following Jaʿfar al-Ṣiqlabī's death in 971 (360 AH), al-Ḥakam did not renew the post.[54] Thereby, it was the viziers who became the senior rank in the administration. Their number varied. At the time of ʿAbd al-Raḥmān III, there were between six and eleven viziers, although in some years the caliph appointed as many as sixteen. Yet this was considered unusual.[55] Al-Ḥakam's appointments of around twenty viziers throughout all his caliphate reveals a tendency to limit the number of people assigned to this post at any one time. Viziers regularly appeared before their sovereign, received summons and missives with his orders, and held periodic meetings at what was referred to as the 'the advisory council' (*majlis al-rāʾy*), which was attended by the caliph.[56] The *alcázar* in Córdoba had a room for these meetings and in Madīnat al-Zahrā' a 'House of the Viziers' (*Dār al-Wuzarāʾ*) was created and specially equipped for them.[57]

At the court of al-Ḥakam II, the viziers would often undertake a second role, either of an administrative or a military nature. As we have already seen,

[54] In contrast, during the period of Hishām II the post of *ḥājib* was filled once more. As has been already mentioned, one of the first deeds of the new caliph was to name his father's principal vizier, Jaʿfar b. ʿUthmān al-Muṣḥāfī, as *ḥājib*. Ibn ʿIdhārī, *al-Bayān*, II, p. 254. Following Jaʿfar al-Muṣḥāfī's fall from grace, caliph Hishām named al-Manṣūr *ḥājib*, and from then on this post was identified with the real exercise of power. Ibn Khaldūn confuses Jaʿfar the Slav with Jaʿfar al-Muṣḥāfī, who he states was appointed *ḥājib* by al-Ḥakam as soon as he ascended the throne. This has given rise to a considerable number of errors in the historiography, *K. al-ʿIbār*, vol. IV, p. 185. P. Chalmeta, *Historia socioeconómica de al-Andalus*, p. 114.

[55] Ibn Ḥayyān, *Muqtabis V*, ed. and trans. p. 328.

[56] Ibn Ḥayyān, *Muqtabis VII*, ed. p. 70; trans. pp. 92–3. Ja'far b. ʿUthmān al-Muṣḥāfī attended this council once he had recovered from his illness.

[57] Ibn Ḥayyān, *Muqtabis II, 1*, ed. p. 295; trans. pp. 183–4.

Ja'far al-Muṣḥafī combined the post of vizier with that of *ṣāḥib al-madīna* of Córdoba, while Ghālib served as both vizier and supreme commander of the army. Other posts such as admiral of the fleet or head of the stables were also granted to viziers. Therefore, the translation of the term 'vizier' as 'minister' is by no means imprecise, at least during this period, given that each vizier was commissioned with a specific duty.[58]

The post of *ṣāḥib al-madīna* was usually given to a vizier. It was effectively one of the most relevant posts in the Umayyad administration, and at the time of the emirs it paid a salary of over 100 dinars a month.[59] The *ṣāḥib al-madīna* was the governor of the capital and many of his duties were similar to those of a provincial governor, but as he was responsible for the caliph's place of residence he also had a number of specific duties. The most important was collecting taxes, which meant he was one of the most hated officials in the city, and the first target of popular anger in the event of a riot.[60] Just like the provincial governors, the *ṣāḥib al-madīna* had to ensure that taxes were paid on time and in full, although he also had it in his power to grant fiscal exemptions. This issue gave rise to considerable bureaucracy, but also significant resistance from rural communities, which rejected fiscal exemptions on the grounds that they meant that the fixed amounts to be paid by each village, or *qarya*, would be levied on a smaller number of contributors.[61]

Another responsibility undertaken by the *ṣāḥib al-madīna* was ensuring public order within the city, such as quelling unrest or decreeing the incarceration of anyone deemed to be a potential insurgent. It thus comes as no surprise to read of the *ṣāḥib al-madīna* pursuing possible rebels, slanderous poets and those accused of blasphemy, as well as acting as a judge in criminal trials. A case

[58] Ibn Khaldūn explicitly indicates that each vizier was given a specific duty, *Muqqāḍīma*, ed. Damascus, I, pp. 422–3; trans. p. 449.

[59] We know the complete sequence of those appointed *ṣāḥib al-madīna* of Córdoba from the beginning of the rule of 'Abd al-Raḥmān III up until the onset of the *fitna*. A total of seventeen individuals filled this post, eleven of whom, we are told, also served as viziers. J. Vallvé, 'El zalmedina de Córdoba', proposed an impossible connection with the *comes civitatis* of Roman times.

[60] Ibn Ḥayyān, *Muqtabis II*, 1, ed. cit. pp. 288–9; trans. cit. p. 178. The *ṣāḥib al-madīna* was the first victim of the suburb revolts in 818 and also the unrest that began the *fitna* of the caliphate almost two hundred years later, E. Manzano Moreno, *Conquistadores, emires y califas*, pp. 332 and 495.

[61] Apart from the references made in the chronicles, the *ṣāḥib al-madīna*'s fiscal duties are attested to in notarial documents, Ibn al-'Aṭṭār, *K. al-wathā'iq wa l-sijillāt*, ed. pp. 126, 167, 169, 220, 599–600; trans. pp. 256, 323, 325, 412–13, 879.

that took place in the mid-ninth century (third AH), at the time of the Emir ʻAbd al-Raḥmān II, reveals the *ṣāḥib al-madīna* of Córdoba investigating a murder case in which the corpse was found in a basket in the butchers' market. Having convened all of Córdoba's basket makers and traders, the wily *ṣāḥib al-madīna* discovered who had made the basket and who had sold it. Both clues led him to the murderer, who turned out to be a member of the emir's guard.[62]

Córdoba's *ṣāḥib al-madīna* was very close to the caliph. One of his duties was to oversee the oath of loyalty sworn by the people of the city following his proclamation. Likewise, when the sovereign was absent from the capital, it was the *ṣāḥib al-madīna* who remained in the *alcázar* as his representative. When al-Ḥakam II contracted a fatal illness that led to his death, as has been noted, the representation of caliphal power passed into the hands of the vizier and *ṣāḥib al-madīna*, Jaʻfar al-Muṣḥafī.[63]

Under al-Ḥakam II there were two *ṣāḥib al-madīna*: one served in Córdoba and the other in Madīnat al-Zahrā'. The former was the aforementioned Jaʻfar al-Muṣḥafī, who was assisted by his own son, while in the city palace the *ṣāḥib al-madīna* was Muḥammad b. Aflaḥ, one of the caliph's clients, who also served as vizier.[64] The headquarters of the *ṣāḥib al-madīna* were situated at a similar location in both cities: next to the main entrance or Bāb al-Sudda in the *alcázar* in Córdoba, and by the main gate, which had the same name, in the city palace. The same building (*majlis kursī al-shurṭa bi qaṣr al-Zahrā*) also lodged the *shurṭa* (military police force, discussed below). This was where disgraced officials like Durrī were taken, as well as anyone sentenced to imprisonment. The close connection between the building assigned to the *ṣāḥib al-madīna* and to the *shurṭa* is highly significant and I will return to it below.[65]

Some of the viziers were also senior commanders of the Umayyad army, as was the case with Ghālib, who was supreme *qā'id* and vizier. Another highly relevant military post was that of chief of the stipendiary troops

[62] Ibn al-Qūṭiya, *Ta'rīkh*, ed. pp. 69–70; trans. James p. 103.
[63] Ibn ʻIdhārī, *al-Bayān*, II, p. 253.
[64] Ibn Ḥayyān, *Muqtabis VII*, ed. pp. 46, 78, 196; trans. pp. 66, 101, 180, 236.
[65] Ibn al-Qūṭiya, *Ta'rīkh*, ed. pp. 94 and 95; trans. James p. 122; Ibn Ḥayyān, *Muqtabis* V, p. 128; Ibn ʻIdhārī, *al-Bayān*, III, p. 55; Ibn Ḥayyān, *Muqtabis VII*, ed. pp. 75, 103; trans. pp. 96–7, 132.

(*ṣāḥib al-ḥasham*), and this person also served as vizier, due to the growing importance of this professional corps within the army.[66] The same occurred with the admiral of the fleet (*qā'id al-baḥr*), who was based in Almería and in addition held the rank of vizier.[67] The holders of important provincial posts, such as the *qā'ids* of Zaragoza or Toledo, who were responsible for defence and troop recruitment in these frontier areas, likewise went on to become viziers.[68]

Another post held by a vizier was that of head of the stables (*ṣāḥib al-khayl*), which again reflects the growing importance of the supply of horses needed to ensure the caliphate's military and administrative machinery. The vizier and head of the stables during this period, Ziyād b. Aflaḥ, was in charge of exhibiting the horses when they arrived from Seville and Niebla, along with another official with an equally important role in the caliphate's logistics, the head of the postal service (*ṣāḥib al-burud*). The latter was responsible for all forms of communication, which is why on occasions the same person was appointed to both posts.[69] The maintenance and management of the caliphal

[66] Both Ziyād b. Aflaḥ and Muḥammad b. Qāsim b. Ṭumlus were viziers and heads of the stipendiary troops. The latter's son, Qāsim, was also appointed to the same post, which he seems to have inherited following his father's death at the disaster of Faḥṣ Mahrān. However, he was not appointed vizier, Ibn Ḥayyān, *Muqtabis VII*, ed. pp. 24, 36, 136 and 106; trans. pp. 45, 49, 135, among others.

[67] The *qā'id* of the fleet at this time was 'Abd al-Raḥmān b. Muḥammad b. Rumāḥis, who oversaw the naval operations against the Norman threat and took part in the North African campaign, which will be discussed below, Ibn Ḥayyān, *Muqtabis VII*, ed. pp. 27–8, 58, 80, 87–8; trans. pp. 48, 51, 76, 104. His father had been governor of Pechina and Almería, and had also led naval expeditions at the time of 'Abd al-Raḥmān III, al-'Udhrī, *Tarṣī*, pp. 81–2; Ibn Ḥayyān, *Muqtabis V*, ed. and trans. pp. 211 and 313.

[68] The connection between the duties undertaken by the vizier and the administration of Zaragoza and Calatayud was part of an agreement signed between 'Abd al-Raḥmān III and the Tujībid family, as has already been mentioned. However, there are other cases in which a similar connection between both positions can be established: Aḥmad b. Ya'lā was *qā'id* in Zaragoza – possibly due to a temporary rift between the caliph and the Tujībid family – in 972 (361 AH) and also served as vizier. Sa'd b. al-Ḥakam al-Ja'farī served as *qā'id* of Toledo and also as a vizier, Ibn Ḥayyān, *Muqtabis VII*, ed. p. 68; trans. pp. 90–1. There were precedents from the era of 'Abd al-Raḥmān III: Yaḥyā b. Isḥāq served as *qā'id* of the western frontier regions and vizier; Muhammad b. 'Abd Allāh b. Ḥudayr was appointed vizier and *qā'id* of Toledo; Jahwar b. 'Ubayd Allāh b. Abī 'Abda was made vizier and *qā'id* of the Upper Frontier, Ibn Ḥayyān, *Muqtabis V*, ed. and trans. pp. 306 and 313; 316 and 318; 291 and 307.

[69] At the time of 'Abd al-Raḥmān III, Sa'īd b. Abī l-Qāsim, the caliph's maternal uncle, held both posts: E. Manzano Moreno, 'El círculo de poder de los califas omeyas', pp. 16–17. Badr, the *ḥājib* of 'Abd al-Raḥmān III, held this post along with the head of the postal service, Ibn Ḥayyān, *Muqtabis V*, ed. and trans.s pp. 313 and 318; Ibn 'Idhārī, *al-Bayān*, II, p. 158. In contrast, in other cases the *ṣāḥib al-khayl* did not attain the rank of vizier: for example, Ziyād's father, Aflaḥ,

steeds were undertaken from a specific office, known as the *Dār al-Khayl*, which was probably located in Madīnat al-Zahrā'. The duties assigned to its officials (*wukalā'*) included supplying horses whenever they were needed. Thus, in the summer of 971 (360 AH), when Yaḥyā b. al-Andalusī and members of his family arrived in Pechina from North Africa, officers from the *Dār al-Khayl* were commissioned to bring 68 horses and 150 mules for the transport of the large party to Córdoba. In other cases, horses had to be supplied to the army, and once more in this case it was the stables official who was in charge of delivering them to their destination.[70] The complexity of this department of the administration is also demonstrated by the fact that crown prince Hishām had his personal stables with their own overseer.[71]

There were other departments of the administration which were not under the authority of viziers, and which, thus, seem to have taken orders directly from the caliph. What seems most likely is that, as *ḥājib*, Ja'far al-Ṣiqlabī undertook the supervision of them, but following his death, al-Ḥakam decided to take responsibility for this himself and he made all the necessary appointments, which in many cases were given to *ṣaqāliba*. This was the case with the treasury (*khizānat al-māl*), a department that had been established by the emir, 'Abd al-Raḥmān II, who had ordered for it to be located 'at the doors of his alcázar, but on the outside'. He introduced four treasury officials, who were paid a monthly stipend of twenty dinars each.[72] A century and a half later, at the time of al-Ḥakam II, there continued to be only a small number of officials responsible for the treasury, but in contrast to what had happened in other periods, none of them was a vizier, which meant that there was direct supervision from the caliph. In addition to the officials who worked for the treasury in Córdoba, there were two further treasury officials in Madınat al-Zahrā'.[73]

or Najda's father, Ibn Ḥayyān, *Muqtabis V*, ed. and trans. pp. 120, 133, 223, 313. Also see above p. 52.

70 The person commissioned to deliver the horses was an agent of the *Dār al-Khayl* called Durrī b. al-Ḥakam al-Hammāz, who should not be confused with Durrī, the aforementioned treasury official, Ibn Ḥayyān, *Muqtabis VII*, ed. p. 151; trans. 191. Also ibid., p. 40; trans. pp. 60–1.

71 This post was undertaken by one of the aforementioned manumitted Ja'farids: Shāṭir al-Ja'farī, Ibn Ḥayyān, *Muqtabis VII*, ed. pp. 136, 151, 177.

72 Ibn Ḥayyān, *Muqtabis II, 1*, ed. p. 292; trans. cit. pp. 181–2.

73 These were Aḥmad b. Ibrāhīm and Zakarīyā' b. Yaḥyā al-Shabulārī, who are listed as 'treasurers' in an account of an official reception, Ibn Ḥayyān, *Muqtabis VII*, ed. cit. p. 60; trans. p. 46.

The treasury must have been a very complex department. Aside from centralising the caliphate's tax revenue – which involved some form of supervision over the provincial administration – it managed and organised the state's resources, which included a diverse range of goods and commodities such as money, grain, raw materials and numerous manufactured items. I have already discussed how the textiles workshop (*dār al-ṭirāz*) and the mint (*sikka*) maintained close ties with the treasury, due to both the value of the raw materials used and the fact that the distribution of these products was controlled by this department. The same could be said of the officials who worked in the caliphate's granaries and those responsible for all the other forms of manufacture undertaken in the caliphal workshops.[74]

Those in charge of the storehouses (*aṣḥāb al-makhzūn*) were also linked to the treasury, and their principal role was to control the complex administration of the state's supplies; their importance is indicated by the fact that they attended the receptions held by the caliph. The weapons arsenal (*khizānat al-ṣilāḥ*) was overseen by various individuals, and their role was to provide the army with munitions. The treasury officials and those in charge of the caliph's storehouses were also responsible for delivering the money required to issue the monthly payments to the army when it was on campaign, as well as the presentation of gifts to the caliph's allies and supporters.[75] Another mission that a warehouse official might be given was to supply the items needed for journeys made by the caliph's guests, and this included objects such as coverlets, tapestries, furniture, tableware, etc.[76] The coverlets and tapestries would

[74] The promotion of Muḥammad b. Abī ʿĀmir to the position of head of the mint in autumn 967 (356 AH) was one of the key factors that allowed him to ensure his ascent within the administration: one of the treasury officials at that time was Aḥmad b. Muḥammad b. Ḥafṣ b. Saʿīd b. Jābir, who was the son of a vizier who later proved to be one his strongest supporters, Ibn Ḥayyān, *Muqtabis VII*, ed. cit. p. 177; trans. p. 222; Ibn ʿIdhārī, *al-Bayān*, II, pp. 268–9. His grandfather had been in charge of the arsenal and had also served as *ṣāḥib al-sūq* of Córdoba, Ibn Ḥayyān, *Muqtabis V*, ed. and trans. pp. 291 and 304; Ibn ʿIdhārī, *al-Bayān*, II, p. 203.

[75] Ibn Ḥayyān, *Muqtabis VII*, ed. cit. pp. 129, 131, 135–6, 149, 168, 183, 228; trans. pp. 163, 166, 170–1, 189, 206, 222, 270.

[76] Ibn Ḥayyān, *Muqtabis VII*, ed. cit. pp. 139, 151; trans. cit. pp. 174, 191–2. The *aṣḥāb al-makhzūn* combined the caliph's freed slaves and members of the administration's senior families: thus, for example, Rāʾiq b. al-Ḥakam, Subḥ's brother, was appointed to this position, which was also filled by Salama b. al-Ḥakam al-Jaʿfarī, one of the manumitted Jaʿfarids. However, another appointee to this post was Aḥmad b. ʿAbd al-Malik, who belonged to the Banū Shuhayd family; one of his sons, Marwān, also served as a treasury official, Ibn Ḥayyān, *Muqtabis VII*, ed. cit. pp. 40, 77, 104; trans. pp. 63, 100, 133.

most certainly have been manufactured in the *dār al-ṭirāz*, and their inscriptions and workmanship celebrated the magnificence of the caliph; the tableware probably consisted of the characteristic and well-known pieces of green and manganese ware that was provided for guests by the *aṣḥāb al-makhzūn*.

While, in general terms, the distinctive departments of the central administration have been clearly identified, there is not as much information about how it worked in the provinces, and above all, how the administration of these areas was integrated with the central administration. During this period, the governors of the *kūra*s tended to use the title '*qā'id*', which invoked the military dimension of their role. Mention is made of *qā'id*s who served, for example, in Guadalajara, Lérida, Tortosa, Valencia, Badajoz, Llano de los Pedroches, Jaén and Rayyuh (Málaga). This indicates that in this period the provincial governors (*'ummāl*) were increasingly appointed as *qā'id*s. In addition to this, the fact that many of these *qā'id*s were freed slaves (*mawālī*) suggests that there was a growing militarisation and centralisation of the role performed by provincial governors.[77]

Some of the *qā'id*s who are cited as serving as provincial governors are also referred to as *ṣāḥib al-shurṭa* or commander of the military police, a title also used by individuals from the central administration, some of whom had the rank of vizier. The *ṣāḥib al-shurṭa* is one of the most problematic posts in the Umayyad caliphate, as all the evidence suggests that in al-Andalus the *shurṭa* was an institution whose evolution was marked by some particularities, which led to a certain amount of confusion among medieval Arab writers.[78]

77 Hishām b. Muḥammad b. 'Uthmān al-Muṣḥafī (the vizier's nephew) served as *qā'id* of Tortosa and *kūra* of Valencia; 'Abd al-Ḥamīd b. Aḥmad b. Basīl and his brother Basīl are both listed as *'ummāl* and *qā'id*s of the *kūra* of Rayyuh; Aḥmad b. Muḥammad b. 'Abbās was appointed *qā'id* of Lérida; Yaḥyā b. 'Ubayd Allāh b. Yaḥyā b. Idrīs was made *qā'id* of Jaén; and Rā'iq b. al-Ḥakam (Subḥ's brother) served as *qā'id* of Badajoz: Ibn Ḥayyān, *Muqtabis VII*, ed. pp. 20–1, 43 and 45, 68, 72, 149; trans. pp. 44–5, 63 and 65, 94, 189. Both terms (*quwwād wa 'ummāl*) are used in Ibn Ḥayyān, *Muqtabis VII*, ed. p. 41; trans. p. 61, and in notarial documents with the expression 'qā'id of the *kūra*', Ibn al-'Aṭṭār, *K. al-wathā'iq wa l-sijillāt*, ed. p. 607; trans. p. 887.

78 The principal source of confusion may be traced to Ibn Khaldūn, who asserts that the divisions of the *shurṭa* in al-Andalus reflected social divisions: the so-called *shurṭa 'ulyā* would address matters related to the upper class, while those of the *al-shurṭa al-ṣughrā* attended to the matters of the common people, *Muqaddima*, ed. Darwish, I, p. 436; trans. p. 459. Evidently, Ibn Khaldūn, who wrote three centuries later, had no idea what he was talking about, but his testimony was compiled by Lévi-Provençal, *España musulmana. Instituciones y vida social*, pp. 88–9, and as a result this misunderstanding has been repeated by other authors. M. Marín, EI, 2, s.v. *shurṭa*.

The word *shurṭa* originally meant a 'select troop'. In the period following the Arab conquests, it referred to the soldiers who formed the caliph's guard (*ḥaras*), who were responsible for maintaining public order in the capital. On this basis, the term is very often translated as 'police', and this meaning has been preserved in modern Arabic. The soldiers enlisted in the *shurṭa* were used by the first caliphs to arrest potential rebels in the capital, to impose curfews, to keep in check possible riots and to oversee the prisons. The commander in charge of these troops was known as *ṣāḥib al-shurṭa*.[79]

Slowly but surely, the duties of the *shurṭa* also came to include the defence of the Muslim judges or *qāḍī*s so as to ensure that respect was shown to them and that their sentences were carried out. Thus, it was not unusual to see the first Muslim judges accompanied by two men behind them armed with whips. Although there was no lack of pious men of religion who grumbled and raised questions about whether it was necessary to make such a worldly display of force, once appointed the *qāḍī*s soon realised that to exercise their authority effectively they required a certain degree of coercion in order to extract witness statements, reprimand improper behaviour – including the consumption of alcohol – and carry out the punishments stipulated in the court sentences. As is discussed below, the need for a coercive force under the orders of the *qāḍī*, and not in the hands of the military, gave rise to a 'judicial' *shurṭa*, whose chief, or *ṣāḥib al-shurṭa al-ṣughrā*, tended to be overseen by the *qāḍī* himself, or else someone he trusted.[80]

The *shurṭa* was initially introduced into al-Andalus in the same form as it had existed in at the time of the Umayyad caliphate in Damascus. There was an army unit that was responsible for police duties in Córdoba, which was commanded by a senior officer appointed by the emir. This *ṣāḥib al-shurṭa* undertook the same duties as his counterparts in the East. However, a major change was introduced in the time of Emir al-Ḥakam I. This emir decided to create a *shurṭa ṣughrā*, or lower *shurṭa*, which depended on the *qāḍī* and whose mission was to chase drunks, undertake investigations for the cases of the *qāḍī*'s court, and implement judicial sentences. This lower *shurṭa* was run

[79] H. Kennedy, *The Armies of the Caliphs*, pp. 13–14.
[80] A. Mussa Rashid, 'The Role of the Shurṭa in Early Islam', unpub. Ph.D. dissertation, University of Edinburgh, 1983, pp. 96–101.

by a legal scholar, the *ṣāḥib al-shurṭa al-ṣughrā*, who was assigned premises in the gallery of the mosque of Córdoba, whereby he could undertake his duties in consultation with the *qāḍī*.[81] It is reasonable to think that the idea of Emir al-Ḥakam I in making this separation was to make a concession to the Cordoban *'ulamā'*, with whom relations had been very tense during his rule; they were provided with their own police force, *shurṭa*, distinct from that run by the senior officer or senior official, who acted as the 'commander of the upper police force' (*ṣāḥib al-shurṭa al-'ulyā*). Nonetheless, as a general rule, the Umayyads did not let this lower *shurṭa* get out of their control: they always ensured that the member of the *'ulamā'* class who was appointed to run it was either a *mawlā* or a low-profile scholar without a high intellectual reputation or following.

Just as the 'chief of the upper police force' had to collaborate with the *ṣāḥib al-madīna*, who was responsible for public order in the city, the *ṣāḥib al-shurṭa al-ṣughrā* had to do the same with the *qāḍī*. Both heads of the *shurṭa* were in charge of their respective armed forces, which were required to undertake the duties that both institutions held. In fact, the *ṣāḥib al-madīna*, the *qāḍī*, and the market inspector (*ṣāḥib al-sūq*), formed what the Andalusis understood as the government of the city (*wilayāt al-madīna*).[82] That is why the head of the lower *shurṭa* was on some occasions also the inspector of the souk.

A specific example of how the 'upper police' operated is shown by events that took place in spring 974 (363 AH), when al-Ḥakam II ordered the arrest of a distant relative, who had infuriated him for some unknown reason. The *ṣāḥib al-shurṭa al-'ulyā* at that time was Hishām b. Muḥammad al-Muṣḥafī, nephew of the vizier and *ṣāḥib al-madīna* of Córdoba, Ja'far al-Muṣḥafī, and he fulfilled the order by leading an imposing troop of officers of the guard (*'urafā' al-muḥāris*), horsemen (*fursān*), policemen (*shuraṭ*) and messengers

[81] Marín, EI, 2, s.v. 'shurṭa'. Having been proclaimed emir, 'Abd al-Raḥmān I surrounded himself with a guard formed by clients, and he appointed 'Abd al-Raḥmān b. Nu'aym (and not al-Ḥusayn b. al-Dajn as Marín states) to the *shurṭa*, *Akhbār Majmū'a*, ed. and trans. pp. 91, trans. James, 95. The first *ṣāḥib al-shurṭa al-ṣughrā* was Ḥarīth b. Abī Sa'd, al-Khushanī, *Akhbār al-fuqahā'wa l muḥaddithīn*, ed. cit. no. 87. Complete references in *Prosopografía de los ulemas de al-Andalus*, id. 2.833.

[82] Ibn Ḥayyān, *Muqtabis II, 1*, ed. cit. pp. 288–9; trans. cit., p. 178.

(*furānikin*).[83] As was always the case with certain orders issued by the caliph, the scale of the forces deployed was somewhat over the top, but there was no question about its effectiveness.

Years earlier, in 929 (317 AH) under 'Abd al-Raḥmān III, the institution of the *ṣāḥib al-shurṭa* had undergone another change when the caliph decided to split the 'upper police' by forming a new corps referred to as the 'middle police' (*al-shurṭa al-wusṭā*). The reasons for this are not clear. It is possible that 'Abd al-Raḥmān III wanted to make a clearer distinction between the functions performed by both forces. Yet it is more likely that this was merely a hierarchical distinction: on the one hand, the stipends assigned to the new middle rank were lower than those of the chief of the 'upper police', while on the other, the caliph could reward a military chief by promoting him from the 'middle police' to the 'upper'. Indeed, this is what al-Ḥakam II did when he promoted a member of the Tujībid family, whom he also granted the privilege of mounting his horse from the stone.[84]

A survey of the appointees to these posts over the course of these decades demonstrates that this interpretation of the divisions of the *shurṭa* is correct. During the caliphates of 'Abd al-Raḥmān III and al-Ḥakam II, those who served as *ṣāḥib al-shurṭa al-'ulyā* all had the experience and status to be expected for carrying out the duties performed by this corps: military commanders, members of families such as the Abū 'Abda or the Shuhayd, in addition to freed slaves of the caliph and even a member of the Umayyad family.[85]

[83] Ibn Ḥayyān, *Muqtabis VII*, ed. cit. p. 153; trans. p. 194. The prisoner was a son of Sa'īd b. al-Qāsim, a maternal uncle of 'Abd al-Raḥmān III and, therefore, the caliph's cousin. This major operation successfully arrested him at a property he owned on the outskirts of Córdoba, but three weeks later he was freed.

[84] Ibn Ḥayyān, *Muqtabis V*, ed. and trans. p. 166; Ibn 'Idhārī, *al-Bayān*, II, p. 201. The first appointee to this new post was Sa'īd b. Sa'īd b. Ḥudayr, who was a member of the omnipresent Banū Ḥudayr family. The beneficiary of the promotion granted by al-Ḥakam was 'Abd al-'Azīz b. Ḥakam al-Tujībī, nephew of the governor of Calatayud, who was cited above as serving as vizier, Ibn Ḥayyān, *Muqtabis VII*, ed. pp. 225–6; trans. cit., pp. 266–7. The privilege of mounting a horse from the stone must have been highly valued. The *qā'id* Ghālib was also granted it: on leaving an audience with the caliph during which they discussed the relief expedition to be sent to Gormaz he received a number of gifts, including a horse that 'he mounted from the stone', *Muqtabis VII*, ed. p. 220; trans. p. 260.

[85] Among those who served in this post at the time of 'Abd al-Raḥmān III were members of the Banū Abī 'Abda family, one member of the Banū Shuhayd family, another of the Tujībī family, the caliph's maternal uncle and three freed slaves. I have only been able to identify one scholar,

The same trend is noted in the heads of the 'middle police', although in this case their status was somewhat inferior.[86] In contrast, those who served as *ṣāḥib al-shurṭa al-ṣughrā* were *'ulamā'* of low rank, who were in close contact with the *qāḍīs*, although they were most certainly not chosen by them, but instead by the sovereign.[87]

Finally, in the time of al-Ḥakam II, the post of *ṣāḥib al-shurṭa* underwent a further change. While at the time of his father there only seems to have been the 'chiefs of the upper police' in Córdoba or Madīnat al-Zahrā' who collaborated with the *ṣāḥib al-madīna* in each city, under al-Hakam the *qā'ids* who served in the provinces are also listed with the title of *ṣāḥib al-shurṭa al-'ulyā*.[88] In other words, as provincial governors they combined their civil administration duties with the exercise of coercive means to enforce their role. All those *qā'ids* who were provincial governors and 'heads of the upper police' thus had troops under their control, which enabled them to make arrests, guard prisons and remind debtors of the need to fulfil their fiscal obligations. The combination of these appointments is a clear indication of how during this period a decisive change was under way in the civil administration, which was entwined with a growing trend towards militarisation and greater centralisation.

Muḥammad b. Muḥmmad b. Abī Zayd, although this is likely an error. Ibn Ḥayyān, *Muqtabis V*, pp. 65, 71, 72, 95, 130, 304, 313, 328; Ibn 'Idhārī, *al-Bayān*, II, p. 159; al-'Udhrī, *Tarṣī*, p. 47.

86 During the caliphate of 'Abd al-Raḥmān III the appointees to this post were members of the Banū Ḥudayr family, a vizier, a court poet and also a future vizier, Ja'far b. 'Uthmān al-Muṣḥafī, Ibn Ḥayyān, *Muqtabis V*, pp. 166, 318; Ibn 'Idhārī, *al-Bayān*, II, p. 254. Under al-Ḥakam, the 'heads of the middle police' were three members of the Tujībī family, Subḥ's brother, and the future al-Manṣūr at the start of his career, Ibn Ḥayyān, *Muqtabis VII*, ed. cit., pp. 72, 119, 184, 200, 225, 228; trans. pp. 81, 94, 223, 266, 252 and 270.

87 Among those appointed to this post was a member of the Banū Ḥudayr family, the aforementioned Muḥammad b. Muḥammad b. Abī Zayd, Yaḥyā b. Yūnus al-Qabrī, Muḥammad b. 'Alī b. Abī l-Ḥusayn and his brother Ḥasan: all of whom were *'ulamā'*, *Crónica Anónima, de 'Abd al-Raḥmān III al-Nāṣir* p. 30, Ibn 'Idhārī, *al-Bayān*, II, pp. 159, 167, 185, Ibn Ḥayyān, *Muqtabis VII*, ed. cit. p. 81; trans. p. 105.

88 All the following *qā'ids* are listed as holders of the post of *ṣāḥib al-shurṭa al-'ulyā*: Hishām b. Muḥammad b. 'Uthmān al-Muṣḥafī, *qā'id* of Tortosa; 'Abd al-Raḥmān b. Muḥammad b. Rumāḥis, admiral of the fleet; 'Abd al-Raḥmān b. Yaḥyā al-Tujībī, *qā'id*; Ya'lā b. Aḥmad b. Ya'lā, *qā'id* of al-Jawf; Aḥmad b. Muḥammad b. 'Abbās, *qā'id* of Zaragoza; Yaḥyā b. 'Ubayd Allāh, *qā'id* of Jaén; Rā'iq b. al-Ḥakam, *qā'id* of Badajoz; Muḥammad b. Rizq b. al-Ḥakam al-Ja'farī, *qā'id* of Lérida; Aḥmad b. 'Abd al-Ḥamīd b. Basīl, *qā'id* of Toledo; Ibn Ḥayyān, *Muqtabis VII*, ed. cit. pp. 20–1, 58, 222, 202, 68, 72 and 119, 149 and 200, 151; trans. cit. pp. 44–5, 76, 263, 243, 90, 94 and 171, 152 and 252, 207.

An Unstoppable Rise

The Umayyad *sulṭān* not only offered a regular salary to those to whom it gave posts or employment, but also a range of magnificent opportunities to exercise power and influence. I have already discussed the case of how senior officials such as Ja'far b. 'Uthmān al-Muṣḥafī and Muḥammad b. Aflaḥ used their high rank to ensure that their sons were granted posts in the caliphal administration. Another example is the son of one of the caliph's astrologers, who was a renowned blockhead, devoid of any learning and only interested in horses; however, his father did not relent until al-Ḥakam gave the order for him to be enrolled as one of his servants (*ghilmān*).[89] Even for the most inept, getting a foot inside the caliphal administration could ensure access to some of the sources of abundant resources that flowed within it.

Furthermore, there were careers within the apparatus of the Umayyad state that could lead to a provincial governorship, appointment as an official of the mint, and even vizier; in the case of an *'ulamā'*, to begin as prayer leader in a mosque and end up as *qāḍī* of a city was by no means unusual. Such posts provided a foothold from which the aspiring could ascend to higher positions and rise through the ranks, thereby enjoying increasing influence. There are many cases of people who climbed the caliphal administration's hierarchy of posts, but for the majority of them we only know their names. However, during the rule of al-Ḥakam II one individual launched a meteoric career. His remarkable ascent was destined to completely change the physiognomy of the Umayyad caliphate.

Muḥammad b. Abī 'Āmir belonged to an Arab family who had arrived at the time of the conquest and had settled in the village of Torrox, alongside the River Guadiaro to the north-east of present-day Algeciras.[90] His ancestors and relatives were by no means little-known individuals. Some had been appointed to posts such as provincial governor or *qāḍī*, while their extended family formed an influential network including jurists, courtiers and senior members of the administration. Muḥammad was still a boy when he moved

[89] The astrologer was Aḥmad b. Fāris, who wrote a fascinating treatise on folk astronomy, M. Forcada, 'Astrology and Folk Astronomy: The *Mukhtaṣar min al-Anwā'* of Aḥmad b. Fāris', pp. 107–205.

[90] E. Manzano Moreno, *Conquistadores, emires y califas*, pp. 482–6; P. Sénac, *al-Mansūr*, pp. 16–26.

to Córdoba with the intention of following in the footsteps of other young men from the provinces, who headed to the caliphate's capital to study with its reputed scholars. It is very possible that his initial idea was to study the various branches of Islamic learning in order to seek employment in one of the professions or posts held by the *'ulamā'*.

In 967 (356 AH), the young Muḥammad b. Abī 'Āmir became assistant to the *qāḍī* of Córdoba, Muḥammad b. Isḥāq b. al-Salīm, which seemed to augur a typical career in the judiciary. However, everything changed for the young man when the *qāḍī* received a message from the palace requesting him to send someone to manage the properties of Hishām, the son Caliph al-Ḥakam II had conceived with his concubine Subḥ. The person chosen for the task was Muḥammad b. Abī 'Āmir. According to some, he was selected for his impressive gifts of management, while others suggested his relationship with the *qāḍī* was so bad that the latter could not find a better way to be rid of him.

Thereby, Muḥammad b. Abī 'Āmir began a stunning career. After having been commissioned with the task of administering the properties of the caliph's son in February 967 (356 AH), a few months later, in September (*Shāwwāl* 356 AH), he was made responsible for the mint, one of the most important posts in the administration. It was rare for someone who had been trained as a Muslim scholar to be assigned to this post, which was chosen directly by the caliph, but throughout Muḥammad b. Abī 'Āmir's career extraordinary things never ceased to occur. In fact, what is most striking is that from that moment onwards, Muḥammad began to accumulate posts that had little or nothing to do with each other. In December 968 (*Muḥarram* 358 AH), he was also appointed as the official responsible for the *bona vacantia* estates (*ṣāḥib al-mawārīth*), which was more closely related to his training as a Muslim scholar, as it involved administering the estates of those who either died intestate or without any known relatives, for the benefit of the Muslim community. Shortly afterwards, in October 969 (*Dhū l-ḥijja* 358 AH), Muḥammad added a further appointment to his professional portfolio: he was made *qāḍī* of Seville. Then, in March 972 (*Jumāda* 361 AH), he was appointed *ṣāḥib al-shurṭa al-wusṭā*, although at that time he ceased to be in charge of the mint, and a few months later, in September, he also relinquished his post as *qāḍī* of Seville.

Setting aside the barbed comments that were prompted by this startling accumulation of posts, to which I will refer below, what is particularly striking is the diversity of roles Muḥammad b. Abī ʿĀmir was assigned. Indeed, it would be interesting to know what an ordinary day in his life was like in 970, when he combined the duties of judge of Seville with supervising the issue of coins from the mint of Córdoba, while also overseeing the administration of *bona vacantia* estates. However, what is especially striking is that he also undertook other duties that had nothing to do with the specific posts to which he had been appointed. For example, in September 971, Muḥammad b. Abī ʿĀmir – who was then an official of the mint, responsible for *bona vacantia* estates, and *qāḍī* of Seville – was ordered to go to Bezmiliana, in the *kūra* of Rayyuh, to receive Jaʿfar b. ʿAlī al-Andalusī along with all his family, who had deserted the Fāṭimid ranks and chosen to take up residence in Córdoba. One gets the impression that by that time he had won the caliph's trust and performed any task that was asked of him.

By May 973, the frenetic professional life of Muḥammad b. Abī ʿĀmir had abated somewhat, as his sole role was commander of the middle police – *ṣāḥib al-shurṭa al-wusṭā*. However, at that time he was sent to Aṣīla, in what is today Morocco, to inspect the activity of the Umayyad army which had been deployed in the region. This first mission in the Maghreb lasted scarcely two months and it resulted in a report on the state of the army, which was forwarded to the caliph. Shortly afterwards, in July that same year, Muḥammad b. Abī ʿĀmir added to his collection of appointments that of grand *qāḍī* of the region beyond the Straits (*qāḍi al-quḍāt bi l-ʿidwa*), that is, northern Morocco, and was given missions to deliver money and gifts to the Berber chieftains in the area, who had joined the Umayyad ranks. He continued to carry out this role until he fell sick and returned from Morocco in September 974.

Although he was not the only senior member of the Umayyad administration to be appointed to various posts, the example of Muḥammad b. Abī ʿĀmir is exceptional given the speed of his promotion. There are explanations which, as will be seen, attribute his singular fortune to a very close relationship with the caliph's concubine and mother of the heir to the caliphate, Subḥ, but in the complex world of the caliphal court he clearly would have needed support from other quarters. The text that I cited above describing the role of the senior families within the caliphal state and Caliph al-Ḥakam's scant regard for them concludes its series of reflections with a sensational revelation: these families '*honoured* Muḥammad b. Abī ʿĀmir with their exclusive favour and came to be his supporters ... and helpers. And so it was that they raised the building [of Ibn Abī 'Āmir] and they guided his aim to obtain grandeur, until he came to achieve the hopes and gifts that corresponded with his aspirations.'[91]

The striking revelation provided by this text, along with other evidence, offers a key insight into the broader context of the workings of the caliphate. The Umayyad *sulṭān* was a highly efficient mechanism for gathering and redistributing resources. Its remarkable organisation and efficient territorial extension, underpinned by its powerful authority, provided its beneficiaries with immense wealth. Al-Ḥakam II, as the one responsible for this mechanism, was wholly conscious of the moral character of his authority, whereby he was set on limiting the coercive use of power to what could be deemed strictly legitimate; there is even evidence that demonstrates that he was genuinely interested in the welfare of his subjects. However, the size of the state itself made it practically impossible to control the whole central and the provincial administration. The abuses of the governors, the ploys of his tax collectors and the scandalous cases of embezzlement committed by those responsible for minting coinage demonstrate that, despite all his good intentions, al-Ḥakam II could not always exercise exhaustive supervision over the complex state mechanism. To this was added the fact that in this period an oligarchy of families had taken root; despite having initially being clients of the Umayyads, over the course of the previous two centuries they had entrenched themselves in the administrative apparatus, and built a complex social network of reciprocal interests and obligations that prioritised their own benefit over any other consideration.

Al-Ḥakam II sought to tackle this problem, on the one hand, by reinforcing his political authority through the employment of loyal *'ulamā'*, who served as supervisors of the members of the administration, and on the other, by increasing the number of *ṣaqāliba* and people of lowly origins, who were responsible for key posts within the state. This policy created a great deal of discontent among the traditional families, who had up until then monopolised the senior positions in the administration and who considered themselves to be the legitimate managers of the *sulṭān*. The result must have been an

[91] X. Ballestín Navarro, *al-Manṣūr*, p. 119.

impassive and implacable struggle, in which the senior families refused to give in, and then finally made a resounding response: they orchestrated the accession of a person who, at the very heart of the administration, would oppose the power of the *ṣaqāliba* and other newcomers. Furthermore, he would once more demonstrate that, if the Umayyads had got to where they were, this was only thanks to all the efforts these senior families had made. It turned out that Muḥammad b. Abī ʻĀmir was to be their chosen person, and, as we will be finding out, in the years that followed everything conspired in his favour.

4

The Armies of the Caliph

The Professional Soldiers

Between June 971 and July 975 four military expeditions were dispatched from Córdoba. Two of them were deployed in June 971 and June 972 in response to sightings of Viking boats off the Atlantic coast, which stirred up fears the invaders would attack further inland. As it turned out, there was no real threat and, in both cases, the troops returned without having seen action. A very different fate awaited the third of these four military campaigns. In the summer of 972, al-Ḥakam decided to send the greater part of his army across the Straits of Gibraltar to wage war on the North African chieftains who refused to recognise his authority, and whose allegiance was shifting towards support for the Fāṭimid caliphs in what is today northern Morocco. The caliph's decision was the start of a long, costly campaign marred by disasters. Three years later, Andalusi troops were still stationed in the region. Then, in the summer of 975, with part of the army still serving in this challenging Moroccan campaign, another military expedition had to be deployed, this time to the north of the Iberian Peninsula, where a coalition of Christian kings and counts had besieged the fortress of Gormaz, on the upper course of the Duero River.

Four campaigns in four years – one of them essentially a full-blown war – are a lot. They require a well-supplied and organised army, as well as a considerable capacity for recruitment. The Umayyad caliphate of Córdoba had such a capacity, and even improved it throughout this period. Furthermore, this army was not only mobilised on campaigns. It undertook escort missions, the fortification or defence of strategic enclaves, and it also took part in the parades held to mark the caliphate's grand celebrations. Likewise, when someone incurred the caliph's wrath and had to be arrested and imprisoned, soldiers were ordered to make the arrest. In Córdoba, along the frontier, or across the provinces ruled by the *qā'ids*, the army was a constant presence, albeit not always a welcome one: it provided a clear reminder of the caliphate's coercive capacity, which was exercised openly against foreign enemies, and implicitly against its own subjects.

To sustain this capacity for coercion, a highly professionalised army was needed. The somewhat romantic idea that has fostered an image of medieval armies being made up of cohorts of men with professions other than warfare – peasants, artisans or common folk – tends to overlook the high level of physical and tactical skill that was required for the use of swords, bows and arrows, and spears, and still more so for troop deployment, long marches and man-to-man combat, not to mention the preparation, knowledge and logistics required for fighting on horseback. Only a well-trained army could guarantee the military effectiveness needed for a state as complex as the Umayyad caliphate. The Byzantine empire provides a comparable example, and its tenth-century manuals on military strategy recommend that during the winter and periods of peace soldiers should undergo continual training in handling weapons, military manoeuvres, riding skills and the correct form of sending orders. Also around this time, in Fāṭimid Egypt, facilities were created exclusively for training slave soldiers.[1]

In al-Andalus, something very similar to a professional army had existed during a good part of the Umayyad period. The conquest of 711 (92 AH) was achieved with an army that was not particularly large and consisted predominantly of Berber soldiers, who had been incorporated into Arab rule following the difficult conquest of North Africa. Despite being the majority, these North African soldiers were subject to a form of Arabic domination that became highly oppressive, just as it did for their fellow tribesmen in their homeland. The great Berber revolt that broke out on both sides of the Straits of Gibraltar in 740 (122 AH) very nearly put paid to the conquests made by

[1] *The Taktika of Leo VI*, ed. and trans. G. T. Dennis, pp. 105–43. This text is a strategy manual that was written on the instructions of the Emperor Leo VI (886–912), and was widely disseminated over the years that followed. Y. Lev, 'Regime, Army and Society in Medieval Egypt, 9th–12th Centuries', p. 143.

the Arabs in the previous years. The Umayyad caliph of Damascus had to send his best troops to stamp out the rebellion, the so-called *jund* or Syrian army that consisted of soldiers from various military districts: Damascus, Palestine, Jordan, Qinnasrīn and Ḥimṣ. In addition, they were accompanied by soldiers stationed in Egypt. All these soldiers received regular wages and, in addition, were paid in silver dirhams for each campaign they undertook. However, their performance in North Africa was calamitous: they were defeated by the Berber rebels, and ended up besieged in Ceuta in a desperate situation. Their salvation came from the then governor of al-Andalus, who proposed they be evacuated to the Peninsula in order to help quell the Berber rebellion that had broken out there as well. They had more success in the Iberian Peninsula and managed to overcome the rebels, but a problem arose when the Syrian soldiers wanted to return to their bases. The Berber revolt was still active in North Africa and maritime communications were presumably cut off, whereby these troops were left with no alternative but to remain in al-Andalus, despite staunch resistance to this decision from the early conquerors.

After a great deal of dispute, an agreement was finally reached that regulated their settlement across the Peninsula along the same lines as the model previously used in Syria. Each of the *jund*'s units was assigned a province or *kūra* to settle in; it was stipulated that the so-called *jund* of Damascus was assigned the *kūra* of Elvira; that of Ḥimṣ the *kūra* of Seville; that of Qinnasrīn the *kūra* of Jaén; the *jund* of Palestine was to be located in Sidonia; and, finally, that of Jordan was assigned to the *kūra* of *Rayyuh* (Málaga). With regard to the troops from Egypt, they were divided between the territory of *Tudmīr*, in the south-east of the peninsula, and Beja, in southern Portugal. The soldiers were not billeted in regiments, but were dispersed, as they settled in villages where they managed the collection of the taxes paid by the subjugated Christian population.

Living under these conditions, the Syrian *jund* gradually gained extensive fiscal and military control across al-Andalus. When the founder of the Umayyad dynasty, ʿAbd al-Raḥmān b. Muʿāwiya, arrived in 755 (137 AH), he had to ensure he had the support of the *jund*'s leaders, who had become powerful lords in the regions they governed. Following many long-drawn-out struggles, ʿAbd al-Raḥmān I managed to obtain an agreement that guaranteed the Syrian *jund*'s support for his dynasty. On the basis of this agreement, the *jund* was obliged to provide half a year's military service, with their troops being deployed on three-month tours of duty.[2] The *jund*'s troops, who were mobilised for active service and dispatched on campaign, were paid a stipend that was calculated according to rank: the commander of each *jund* was paid 200 dinars – in other words 1,600 dirhams – while each of his brothers, sons and nephews was paid ten dinars – in other words eighty dirhams. The rank and file were paid five dinars, which equates to forty dirhams per campaign. Needless to say, another appealing aspect of serving on these expeditions was that the soldiers were entitled to a share of any booty captured. Furthermore, the Syrian troops maintained their fiscal duties, which permitted them to keep a percentage of the revenue collected in the circumscriptions they lived in. They were also exempt from paying tithes and their sole fiscal obligation was the payment of a fixed sum that was calculated on the basis of their earnings.[3]

For almost a century, this system seems to have functioned fairly well. The *jund* became identified with the Umayyad state apparatus through the tributes they sent to Córdoba and their participation in the summer campaigns, or *aceifas*, and in the military expeditions that the emirs decreed were to be waged against rebels. As a result, they played a key role in the emirate's political and military supremacy within the peninsula. Córdoba's mint issued ever greater quantities of silver dirhams, which were needed to ensure the fiscal machinery functioned smoothly, as well as to pay the stipends of these troops and their commanders. Having settled in a permanent manner in their villages (*qurā*), many of the descendants of the initial *jund* soldiers maintained military service as a family tradition, while others gave up army life and embraced a wider range of activities, becoming traders, artisans, or else *'ulamā'*, who often went to serve as *qāḍī*s or prayer leaders, among other roles, in their local communities or provinces.[4]

[2] In some cases, when they had to crush persistent enemies, these call-up periods seem to have been extended to six months, *Akhbār Majmū'a*, ed. and trans. p. 104; trans. James, 103.

[3] E. Manzano Moreno, 'El asentamiento y la organización de los ŷunds sirios en al-Andalus', pp. 327–59.

[4] This issue has been addressed by E. López Martínez de Marigorta in his book *Artesanos, mercaderes y ulemas*.

During the final quarter of the ninth century, the Umayyad emirate's military and fiscal machinery, which for almost a century had functioned with great precision, was shattered due to the revolts led by 'Umar b. Ḥafṣūn alongside other *muwalladūn* rebels. The *muwalladūn* were descendants of the Christian aristocracy, who had converted to Islam at the time of the conquest and had negotiated an agreement granting them the right to maintain control over their rural territories.[5] Throughout the following period, they became increasingly resentful of the fiscal burden exacted by the Umayyad emirs, and of the social changes prompted by the extension of urban growth that tended to undermine their power. As a result, they ruptured the emirate's territorial cohesion, by rebelling against the Umayyad state during the last decades of the ninth century. As rebellions snowballed, the fiscal and military apparatus underwent a profound crisis, and the system of the *jund* collapsed as their leaders deserted the losing ranks of Umayyad supporters. As a consequence, silver dirhams ceased to be issued during this period, and the emirs' power scarcely extended beyond the city of Córdoba.

'Abd al-Raḥmān III made a forthright response to this crisis from the moment of his proclamation as emir in 912 (300 AH). In the following decades, his declared aim was to subjugate one by one each rebel who had taken control of an inland region of al-Andalus. A crucial aspect of the emir's strategy was to obtain the support of the Damascus *jund*, which was settled in the *kūra* of Elvira, following which the other military districts joined forces with them.[6] The reconstruction of what had been the spinal column of the Umayyad state apparatus allowed 'Abd al-Raḥmān III to reinstate his sovereignty across al-Andalus and to eventually proclaim himself caliph in 929 (316 AH). Cordóba's mint re-commenced issuing dirhams on a greater scale than ever, the *aceifas* against the Christians began to be deployed again on a regular basis, and the caliphate's fiscal revenue reached stratospheric new levels. Thus, it seemed that everything was going to be like the good old days. However, the Umayyad caliphate's revived vigour instead gave rise to new challenges, and these had a decisive effect on the army, which in turn led to unexpected consequences.

[5] M. Acién, *Entre el feudalismo y el islam*.

[6] Ibn Ḥayyān, *Muqtabis V*, ed. and trans. p. 35; Ibn 'Idhārī, *al-Bayān*, II, ed. cit. p. 159.

Freedmen, Clients and Slaves

Despite its importance, the *jund* was not the only military corps to serve the Umayyad rulers. As the *jund* was only available for limited active service and permanent military garrisons had to be maintained in cities and fortresses, the emirs and caliphs had to recruit other types of soldiers. Some of these were stipendiary freedmen (*ḥashām*) who were paid a regular wage, which meant they were constantly available. One of these units was the 'Tangerines' (*Ṭanjiyyūn*), which was formed of North African Berbers who were possibly recruited in Tangier, in the Maghreb. Although they were horsemen, they were the army's lowest-ranking soldiers. The *Ṭanjiyyūn* were needed to fulfil the duties that the regular troops could not undertake, such as when a town required the deployment of a permanent military garrison, or else when the regular troops who were serving on campaign and patrols had to be maintained in a particular region.[7]

The *Ṭanjiyyūn* were paid low wages and were not well-integrated into al-Andalus society. They were often the target of considerable animosity, and the slightest spark could ignite the population's latent dislike of them. In 958 (347 AH), during the final years of 'Abd al-Raḥmān III's reign, an expeditionary force, which included *Ṭanjiyyūn* troops, made its departure from Córdoba. The parade was attended by large crowds, but it turned into a pitched battle when those present began to throw stones and the *Ṭanjiyyūn* responded by 'giving free rein to their vile instincts', brutally attacking the women there, stripping them and raping a great many of them.[8] Some years later, in the summer of 972 (361 AH), something similar happened. There were rumours of a Viking attack in western al-Andalus and the *Ṭanjiyyūn* were deployed once more. On 26 June (11 *Ramaḍān*) a group of *Ṭanjiyyūn* met at

[7] Defence of the fortress of Esparraguera with 'cavalry, Berber Tangerines and infantrymen' and a garrison in the recently conquered city of Mérida, which included, among other troops, 1,000 *Ṭanjiyyūn* troops, Ibn Ḥayyān, *Muqtabis V*, ed. and trans. pp. 59 and 159. Rumours that the Vikings might attack western al-Andalus while the *Ṭanjiyyūn* were on campaign in June 972 (361 AH), and Ibn Ḥayyān's opinion of these troops and discussion of how they received the lowest wages and undertook the most menial duties, Ibn Ḥayyān, *Muqtabis VII*, ed. pp. 78, 190; trans. pp. 101, 228. On the tents used by the 'Tangerines', ibid., ed. p. 40 and trans. cit. p. 61.

[8] Ibn 'Idhārī, *al-Bayān*, II, p. 222. Our source concludes by saying that it would be very time-consuming to recount the whole event.

the Azuda gate of the *alcázar* of Códoba, where they also encountered soldiers from the *jund*, who were gathering prior to being sent to North Africa on the major expedition that had been decreed by Caliph al-Ḥakam II. For some reason a dispute broke out between the two groups of soldiers. Matters took a serious turn when civilians from Córdoba also got involved in the quarrel and took advantage of the situation to attack the *Ṭanjiyyūn* with stones so that a number of them was injured. Although things did not get further out of hand, the confrontation took place at the main entrance to the *alcázar*, where the caliph was residing at that moment, and it must have been sufficiently serious as the troop commanders and the deputy to the *ṣāḥib al-madīna* of Córdoba had to intervene.[9]

Such incidents demonstrate the antipathy that these troops prompted among the local population. Likewise, it should be noted that thousands of kilometres away, in ʿAbbāsid Baghdad, there were also frequent fights between the population and the stipendiary Turkish troops recruited by the caliph. The motive for these scuffles was in part due to these soldiers not understanding the language and customs of Baghdad, while, on the other hand, their ranks and salaries were considered an offence to other members of the caliphal army.[10] In Córdoba, the uneasy acceptance of these stipendiary troops would eventually set off the serious events that took place in 1009 (399 AH) and subsequently gave rise to the crisis of the Umayyad caliphate.

The Umayyad sovereigns also sought to avoid their dependence on the *jund* by recruiting slaves, known as *ʿabīd* and *mamālik*, who were used to bolster the army's strength.[11] Subject to their owner's orders, these slaves dedicated their whole life to armed service. As early as the eighth century,

[9] The commanders of the *ḥashām*, Ziyād b. Aflaḥ and Muḥammad b. Qāsim b. Ṭumlus, who also served as vizier, had to intervene to calm the tumult. The deputy (*mukhallif*) to the *ṣāḥib al-madīna* of Córdoba, Muḥammad b. Jaʿfar b. ʿUthmān, also helped reinstate order, Ibn Ḥayyān, *Muqtabis VII*, ed. p. 78; trans. p. 101.

[10] H. Kennedy, *The Armies of the Caliphs*, p. 122.

[11] The terms *ʿabīd* and *mamālīk* seem to be synonyms, as shown by the expression *al-ʿabīd al-mamālik* in Ibn Ḥayyān, *Muqtabis II*, 1, ed. p. 165. One of the slave units was the *khumsiyyūn*, which I interpret as being formed of captives corresponding to the fifth part (*khums*) of the war booty, which according to Islamic law corresponded to the caliph. The *khumsiyyūn* undertook guard duties, although they were also deployed on the expedition launched against Gormaz, Ibn Ḥayyān, *Muqtabis VII*, ed. pp. 40, 47, 48, 156, 173, 223; trans. pp. 61, 67, 197, 212, 263. In the translation of this work *ʿabīd* is always given as 'black slaves', but this choice cannot be justified.

Emir ʿAbd al-Raḥmān I (d. 788/172 AH) ordered the purchase of slaves (*mamālīk*) to reinforce his troops in the fight against the Arab leaders of the *jund*, and he also decreed that manumission would be granted for exemplary service.[12] His successors continued the same policy. It is said that his grandson, al-Ḥakam I (d. 822/206 AH), formed an army of 5,000 slaves – perhaps an exaggerated figure – consisting of 3,000 horsemen, with the remainder being infantry. Their mission was to guard the gates of the *alcázar*, but as foreigners with little command of Arabic they stood out as a military unit, and like the *Ṭanjiyyūn* were not fully integrated into society. Furthermore, they only took orders from the emir. As a result, they prompted animosity and fear among the population, and this grew when they were used to suppress the revolt against the emir by the people of the suburb of Córdoba in 818 (212 AH). Despite the hatred and fear they caused among the population, al-Ḥakam's opinion of these troops was very different: he would often say that 'there is no better equipment for kings (*mulūk*) than men, nor does anybody protect him better than his slaves (*ʿabīd*), nor is there anybody he can make recourse to so swiftly at times of need'.[13]

Despite guaranteeing blind obedience, military slaves posed complex legal questions. As will be seen below, military slaves owned by a caliph's subject could be claimed by the sovereign for himself. An equally delicate issue was raised by the Islamic legal rulings on inheritance. Slaves had to be shared out among the sovereign's sons at his death, which had the unexpected result that all his heirs might be provided with their personal own troops. This is what happened with the slaves al-Ḥakam I bought; on the emir's death, his successor, ʿAbd al-Raḥmān II, realised that his brothers owned several units of slave soldiers that could undermine the stability of his rule. As a result, he had to buy these slaves from his brothers. This must have been a very costly operation, one that underscored how the possession of military slaves was by no means the best option for dynastic stability.[14]

During the caliphal period, with the renewal of the *aceifas* along the northern frontier and the opening up of trade routes, military slaves once more filled

[12] M. Fierro, 'Bazīʿ, mawlā de ʿAbd al-Raḥmān I y sus descendientes', *al-Qanṭara*, VIII, 1987, pp. 102–4.
[13] Ibn Ḥayyān *Muqtabis II, 1*, ed. cit. pp. 154–5; trans. cit. p. 67.
[14] Ibn Ḥayyān *Muqtabis II, 1*, ed. cit. p. 297; trans. cit. p. 185.

the ranks of the Umayyad army, whereby the prickly legal issues surrounding them arose once more. In the previous chapter, I discussed Ja'far al-Ṣiqlabī, the powerful eunuch who at the time of Caliph 'Abd al-Raḥmān III had held high-ranking posts, such as head of the cavalry (*ṣāḥib al-khayl*) and overseer of the caliphal textile workshop (*dār al-ṭirāz*). He went on to be very close to al-Ḥakam II, who appointed him to the position of chamberlain (*ḥājib*) on the same day he was proclaimed caliph on 15 October 961 (3 *Ramāḍan* 350 AH). Ja'far returned the gesture with a gift that same day, which consisted of 100 Frankish military slaves which he had bought with his own money. They were all infantry soldiers and had been provided with spectacular equipment: more than three hundred and twenty breastplates of different types, 100 Indian helmets (*bayḍa hindiyya*) and fifty wooden ones, fifty Frankish helmets, known as the *tishṭāna*, 100 Frankish lances, 100 'sulṭānī' shields, ten gilded silver cuirasses and twenty-five gilded buffalo horns.[15] Known from then on as the *Ja'farids*, these slaves always stood out at military parades, when they would appear clad in their breastplates, gilded helmets and iron Frankish lances adorned with silver tubes.[16]

Given that it is unlikely that Ja'far al-Ṣiqlabī would have bought 100 military slaves without Caliph 'Abd al-Raḥmān III's authorisation, everything indicates that the gift of these *Ja'farids*, as they came to be known, was a ploy that permitted them to be transferred to al-Ḥakam following the caliph's death without him having to leave them in his will to his other sons. Once al-Ḥakam became the owner of these slaves he decided to grant them manumission. As was usual for the caliph's clients or *mawālī*, the *Ja'farids* became dependent

15 al-Maqqarī, *Nafḥ*, I, p. 382. The same account in Ibn Khaldūn, *K. al-'Ibar*, vol. IV, p. 185, although he confuses Ja'far the Slav with Ja'far al-Muṣḥāfī. The presence of armour from India is also recorded in a poem that mentions Indian swords, Ibn Ḥayyān, *Muqtabis VII*, ed. p. 127; trans. p. 206.

16 See among others Ibn Ḥayyān, *Muqtabis VII*, ed. p. 199; trans. p. 240, where the translation 'black slaves of *ḥājib* Ja'far' (*'abīd al-ḥājib Ja'far*) must be corrected, given that these men were of Frankish origin. On this occasion, the equipment these soldiers were armed with included Frankish iron javelins (*ḥirāb*) with decorative handles (*muzayyana*). This text may be linked with the content of a disc with three holes preserved in the Tonegawa Collection, which has an inscription that reads: 'Number four of the *Ja'farid ṣaqlabid* decorated (*muzayyana*). Weight 36 pounds.' A. Labarta, 'Parada militar en la Córdoba omeya y restos arqueológicos', pp. 271–4, connects this piece to the *Ja'farid* troops. If this interpretation is correct, it may be proposed that this disc was a form of label that was used when storing the weapon in question, and that the spear's weight was listed to avoid any possible frauds being committed by cutting down its size.

upon him as their lord, for whom they had to provide specified services, and whose consent was needed in order for them to travel, marry or bequeath their wealth.[17] As *mawālī*, they forged a close tie with the caliph, which ensured he could trust them to undertake important roles and govern provinces.[18]

As has been shown so far, Al-Ḥakam II's army consisted of soldiers whose social status and background varied greatly: aside from the troops that the *jund* continued to supply, other units, which above all provided support services, were formed of freemen (*aḥrār*), who were recruited in North Africa and were paid regular wages. The soldiers from territories beyond the frontiers of Islam were slaves, who possibly were captured at a very young age. Over time, many of them would end up being manumitted and converted into the caliph's clients (*mawālī*), which likewise ensured their loyalty and availability. Another type of client were the descendants of those who had rebelled against Umayyad authority and then been transferred to Córdoba and enlisted in the army.[19]

17 E. Manzano Moreno, *Conquistadores, emires y califas*, pp. 412–15, based on the evidence of contemporaneous notarial documents.

18 The most important of the Ja'farids' was Sa'd b. al-Ḥakam al-Ja'farī, who became vizier. On him see above, p. 128. The other *mawālī* or freed *Ja'farids* that I have been able to located are: Shāṭir al-Ja'farī, head of the cavalry (*ṣāḥib al-khayl*), who undertook escort duties and the reception of the Idrīsid princes: Ibn Ḥayyān, *Muqtabis VII*, ed. pp. 136, 151, 177; trans. pp. 180, 192, 205. Muḥammad b. Rizq b. al-Ḥakam al-Ja'farī served as governor of Lérida in 974 (363 AH). His sons attended the reception of prince Hishām that was held for the Feast of the Sacrifice that same year, Ibn Ḥayyān, *Muqtabis VII*, ed. pp. 151, 168, 185; trans. pp. 192, 207, 224 (although in the first reference he appears as Rizq, the coincidence of the posts suggests that this is the same person). Maysūr al-Ja'farī, who served as one of the senior *fatās* and as secretary, was deposed in the summer of 973, arrested, and reinstated along with the other *fatās* a month later. A Maysūr al-Rūmī is recorded as taking part in the celebration of the triumph in Morocco as one of the *qā'ids* who had fought alongside Ghālib. He could be the same '*al-fatā al-kabīr al-ja'farī*' who in May 975 (364 AH) was sent to join Ghālib in Gormaz along with regular soldiers (*ajnād*), slaves ('*abīd*), archers (*rūmā*) and horsemen who served in the capital (*wufūd*). Years later, in 976, along with Muḥammad b. Abī 'Āmir he was ordered to swear the oath of fidelity to prince Hishām. An inscription found in Talavera commemorating the building of a tower (*burj*) in August 968 (*Ramāḍan* 357 AH) refers to Maysūr b. al-Ḥakam, *mawlā*: Ibn Ḥayyān, *Muqtabis VII*, ed. pp. 103–4, 117, 194–5, 228; trans. pp. 132, 150, 236, 269; Ibn 'Idhārī, *al-Bayān*, II, p. 249; M. A. Martínez Núñez, *Epigrafía árabe*, pp. 220–1; Salama b. al-Ḥakam al-Ja'farī was overseer of the treasury (*ṣāḥib al-makhzūn*) and was commissioned to deliver the soldiers' wages to Morocco. Having attended the reception held for the Idrīsids in Córdoba, he was removed from his post and arrested in November 974 (*Ṣafar* 364 AH): two months later he was freed and reinstated, Ibn Ḥayyān, *Muqtabis VII*, ed. pp. 104, 106, 195, 202; trans. pp. 133, 135, 236, 242–3. Finally, Mubārak and Mubashshir were commissioned with the organisation of the *Ja'farids*' logistics in 971 (360 AH), and are referred to as *Ja'farid fityān*, Ibn Ḥayyān, *Muqtabis VII*, ed. pp. 27–8; trans. p. 51.

19 Muḥammad b. Furtūn provides a characteristic example. He is referred to as member of the *mawālī al-jund*, and of the Banū al-Ṭawīl family, who had ruled the city of Huesca during the

So, in broad terms, the caliphal army consisted of various classes of soldiers. However, there were no foreign units of Christian soldiers, as occurred later during the period of the internal struggles in the early eleventh century and of the Taifa kingdoms.

The *qā'id*s, whose background could also be highly varied, served as the commanders of these troops. The most important *qā'id* of the Umayyad army during this period was a client (*mawlā*) called Ghālib b. 'Abd al-Raḥmān, who, as will be recalled, was also appointed vizier, and played a key role in the events that took place during this period. He was originally from Medinaceli and had possibly been captured during a campaign fought in the frontier zone. Ghālib was made a slave of Caliph 'Abd al-Raḥmān III, although he was subsequently manumitted. Despite being renowned for being both mean and brutal to his soldiers, Ghālib gained fame as a victorious commander, after successful campaigns fought against Christian territories, especially in the zone of Castile. He undertook the strategic fortification of settlements along the frontier, such as Calahorra and Medinaceli, which were rebuilt under his supervision. In early 972 (361 AH), he was promoted to the rank of supreme commander (*al-qiyāda al-'ulyā*) after having submitted a series of proposals for troop mobilisation to the caliph, which al-Ḥakam considered to be wholly appropriate.[20] The high-point of his career came when the caliph appointed him to lead the war being fought in northern Morocco, where the *qā'id*s who served under him included freemen, some of whom were even descendants of prestigious Arabic families, such as the Tujībids from the Ebro River frontier region, who were also deployed in that region at that moment.

There is no documented case of a slave serving as military commander in the armies of the Umayyad caliphate: prior to being promoted to a senior rank, slaves were always manumitted. Likewise, in the caliphal period, members of the Umayyad family – the caliph's brothers, nephews or cousins – were also excluded from military positions, which contrasts with earlier periods, when

emirate; he was sent to Morocco in spring 973 (362 AH) with a group of his companions (*fī ṭā'ifa min aṣḥābi-hi*), Ibn Ḥayyān, *Muqtabis VII*, ed. p. 106; trans. p. 136. I believe that Ibn Ḥayyān refers to this class of persons later on when he comments on 'dependants who benefited from their ancestors' (*ṣanā'i' salafi-him*).

20 *Dhikr bilād al-Andalus*, ed. and trans. p. 151; Ibn 'Idhārī, *al-Bayān*, II, pp. 214, 218, 219–21, 240 and 241. Ibn Ḥayyān, *Muqtabis VII*, ed. p. 69; trans. pp. 91–2.

it was more common to see a close relation of the sovereign serving as *qā'id* and in command of a military campaign. Provided with substantial pensions and relegated to a protocolar role, the caliph's family were kept apart from any form of military command or contact with troops. A loyal army was the foundation of caliphal power, and there was no question of putting it to the test by allowing other members of the dynasty to become involved in it.

The military system in crisis

The availability of stipendiary soldiers, clients or slaves allowed the caliph to have a sort of permanent army at his disposal. This became increasingly necessary as the presence of the caliphal state expanded across al-Andalus and this required a constant deployment of troops. Furthermore, in this period, the geopolitical configuration of the Iberian Peninsula was undergoing profound changes. During the last quarter of the ninth century, the Umayyad emirate's internal struggles had undermined the strength of the Andalusi state, and the Christian forces took advantage of this to make major advances all the way along the Duero valley. As a result of this expansion, the frontier was pushed forward, and it became easier for Christian expeditions to launch surprise attacks on Andalusi enclaves and swiftly capture captives and booty before returning to their bases. Caliphal armies were constantly required to provide support to these Muslim settlements along the frontier, which became increasingly impotent against the ever more frequent Christian aggressions. One of these requests was made by the people from the town of Guadalajara in the summer of 939 (327 AH), and they managed to convince Caliph ʿAbd al-Raḥmān III to divert the major expedition he was commanding against the Christians into their region. They complained of Christians, who were launching incursions against them from the neighbouring Riaza valley. The caliph agreed to lead his army to the region, only to be ambushed by Christian bands at Alhándega, a battle in which he suffered a heavy defeat. The caliph only just escaped alive from this surprise attack, which left hundreds of soldiers dead.[21]

The disaster at Alhándega had many consequences. One of them was that the caliph decided to abandon the custom of personally leading the big military campaigns against the north. These were highly costly military endeavours that

[21] Ibn Ḥayyān, *Muqtabis V*, ed. and trans. p. 300.

involved major dangers and did not always provide the sought-after results. Faced by the powerful caliphal army, the Christians tended to abandon the lowlands and flee to the mountains, from where they sought to reduce their losses, either by attacking small groups of the enemy on foraging missions or by waiting to ambush the enemy when the opportunity arose.[22] The caliph usually returned to Córdoba in triumph displaying captives and booty, but after Alhándega many people seem to have asked themselves whether it was really worth the effort of deploying so many troops and exposing the caliph to the hardships and dangers of campaigns whose impacts were always going to be limited.

The result was a change of strategy. Instead of deploying the army each year, and endeavouring to wage war on an enemy who in the best-case scenarios vanished into thin air and in the worst-case might ambush them as had happened at Alhándega, the caliph opted for handing over the defence of the frontiers to the families who ruled over these regions and could provide a rapid response to the attacks of the Christians. As a consequence of this change, the caliph did not lead any more military campaigns, and the spectacular military expeditions became a thing of the past. When al-Ḥakam II came to power he adhered to this same policy, which he may have contributed to formulating. Thereby, when in the summer of 975 (364 AH) a band of 500 Christian raiders from Sos entered the region of Estercuel (present-day Ribafora, Navarra) stealing livestock and captives, it was the frontier leader, ʿAbd al-Raḥmān b. Yaḥyā al-Tujībī, who repelled the attack. The Tujībids were an aristocratic family who dominated a considerable section of the Ebro Valley, and with operations such as this they demonstrated that their military forces could repel Christian incursions without having to await the arrival of troops from Córdoba. Thus, it comes as no surprise that some of their members went on to be appointed viziers.[23]

The end of the regular expeditions led against the north resulted in a reduction of the *jund*'s role. Its troops were restricted to garrison and escort duties, or as reinforcements for the campaigns which still were launched sporadically, but which had nothing in common with the major expeditions of the past, in

22 A. Isla, *Ejército, sociedad y política*, p. 158.
23 Ibn Ḥayyān, *Muqtabis VII*, ed. pp. 237–9; trans. pp. 279–81.

which these troops had always played a leading role. The effects of the new policy were already visible nine years after Alhándega, when the Eastern traveller Ibn Ḥawqal visited al-Andalus in 948 (337 AH). Ibn Ḥawqal, who probably acted as a spy for the Fāṭimid caliphs, was informed that the Umayyad sovereign had ceased to lead the *aceifas* and had ordered that his frontiers be guarded by the populations that lived there. This arrangement – his informants told him – sufficed. According to them, al-Andalus did not need fear any major external threats. Border skirmishes could be resolved by frontier chieftains, and apart from occasional pillaging expeditions led by foreign peoples, such as the Vikings or the peoples of the steppes (a band of Magyar troops had surprisingly enough reached the north of the Iberian Peninsula in 942 (330 AH)), there was nothing to worry about: nobody was going to invade al-Andalus. Perhaps this is why Ibn Ḥawqal's opinion on the capacity of the Umayyad army was not overly positive: according to this traveller, its soldiers lacked fighting spirit, they were no match for a well-prepared army, and they only knew how to conduct guerilla warfare. His comments on the cavalry were especially harsh: the Andalusis were poor riders and Caliph ʻAbd al-Raḥmān III could not deploy more than five thousand professional cavalrymen.[24]

Despite all these shortcomings, in the summer of 972 (361 AH) al-Ḥakam II took the unprecedented and risky decision of deploying his troops to the other side of the Straits of Gibraltar, to the northern region of what is today Morocco. There he intended to launch an attack against the local chieftains, who refused to acknowledge his authority. I address this war and the causes that led to it in more detail in the next chapter, but for the present I am concerned with highlighting how this expedition once more revealed the weaknesses of the caliphal army. In northern Morocco, and in contrast to the army's cumbersome troop manoeuvres and immense logistical difficulties, its Berber enemies countered their attack by deploying swift groups of horsemen, who operated

[24] Ibn Ḥawqal, *Ṣūrat al-arḍ*, ed. cit. pp. 108–9 and 113; trans. cit. pp. 107 and 112–13. The caliph's change of policy in Ibn Ḥayyān, *Muqtabis V*, ed. cits pp. 296–7; the Magyar incursion, ibid., pp. 324–5. The figure of 5,000 cavalry is very low in comparison with the list drawn up in the mid-ninth century, which records 22,000 riders serving in the *kūras* of the *jund*. Ibn Ḥayyān, *Muqtabis* II, 2, ed. pp. 271–2. However, the figure refers to the total number of cavalry listed in the census, only half of whom would be deployed on a campaign. In contrast, Ibn Ḥawqal discusses the troops that the caliph was capable of deploying, which, perhaps, suggests that the *jund*'s troops had been reduced by half.

with great ease across a territory they knew well. In fact, the Umayyad army seems to have faced the same problems as before in the north of the Iberian Peninsula. And just as had occurred against its Christian enemy, matters ended badly here too. In December 972 (*Rabīʿ* I 362 AH), the Umayyad expedition suffered a defeat at Faḥṣ Mahrān (located in the region to the south of Ceuta), which led to the deaths of 500 horsemen and 1,000 infantrymen, a disaster on a similar scale to what had happened twenty-five years before at Alhándega, the last time the caliphal army had been mobilised for a specific campaign.[25]

Despite being faced with a new military catastrophe, al-Ḥakam II did not withdraw. He decided to deploy as many troops as possible, and to do this he had recourse to the soldiers and chieftains who served along the frontiers of al-Andalus.[26] They were the ones who bore the brunt of the skirmishes against the Christians, and it was surmised they had far greater military skill. At the peak of the Morocco campaign, the number of troops deployed must have reached a figure of around seven thousand soldiers. The victory that the Umayyad army finally won in northern Morocco in the spring of 974 (363 AH) was celebrated in the Umayyad court as a major military feat, but essentially it had been a mass deployment of strength that had stifled the resistance of the North African tribal leaders who had opposed the caliphate.

As a matter of fact, this victory came at too high a price, or at least that was the view of the chronicler Ibn Ḥayyān. While he was copying ʿĪsā al-Rāzī's text, which provides a detailed account of the military operations in northern Morocco, the chronicler could not contain himself and added a lengthy commentary in his own handwriting about the far-reaching consequences of this war. In this commentary, Ibn Ḥayyān blamed al-Ḥakam II's North African policy for the serious crisis, which was besetting Córdoba at that moment – the summer of 1009 (end of 399 AH) – and which the historian was witnessing. Ibn Ḥayyān's text is an invaluable source, as it records a contemporary interpretation of a chain of events that had begun at the time of the caliphate's maximum splendour and had spurred the events which would lead to the collapse of the Umayyad state. Therefore, it is worth pausing to analyse this

[25] Ibn Ḥayyān, *Muqtabis VII*, ed. p. 96; trans. pp. 123–4.
[26] Ibn Ḥayyān, *Muqtabis VII*, ed. pp. 117–18; trans. p. 150.

exceptional text, written by Ibn Ḥayyān under exceptional circumstances, which were in turn the outcome of exceptional decisions.

The Recruitment of Berber Cavalry and its Consequences

According to Ibn Ḥayyān, the origins of the troubles he was witnessing in the summer of 1009 went back to the decision taken by the Umayyad caliphs to turn their attention towards North Africa and the threat posed by the Fāṭimid caliphate.[27] In 931 (319 AH), ʻAbd al-Raḥmān III gave orders to occupy the city of Ceuta, on the other side of the Strait of Gibraltar, something none of his predecessors had done before. Nonetheless, the caliph was prudent, and given his mistrust of the North African tribal leaders, whom he treated with great caution due to 'their probable deceit', he took special care not to become too involved in the region's complex politics. Throughout his caliphate, ʻAbd al-Raḥmān III always preferred 'the men of his al-Andalus' (*rijāl Andalusi-hi*)[28] and those 'who had received benefits from his ancestors' (*ṣanāʼiʻ salafi-hi*); these were soldiers of the army, some of whom were descended from former rebels, who had fulfilled military roles in exchange for stipends.[29] In fact, the caliph only recruited from Berber tribes some 'lowborn serfs, from amongst the youngest and poorest, who were given the name of *Ṭanjiyyūn* (Tangerines)'.

Also according to Ibn Ḥayyān, during the early years of his rule, al-Ḥakam II followed the same wise policy. He also displayed a deep disdain towards everything related to North African soldiers, to such an extent that he would not allow his servants (*ghilmān*) or stipendiary (*aḥshām*) and regular (*ajnād*)

[27] Ibn Ḥayyān, *Muqtabis VII*, ed. pp. 189–94; trans. pp. 228–32.

[28] The expression 'his al-Andalus' is very interesting, as it demonstrates that the name 'al-Andalus' had a definite article, which disproves H. Halm's thesis that the toponym was derived from the Germanic term *landahlauts* which referred to how the territory among was distributed among the various Germanic peoples, H. Halm, 'al-Andalus und Gothica sors', pp. 252–63.

[29] The word *ṣanāʼiʻ* (sing. *ṣanīʻa*) is difficult to translate: basically it refers to somebody who has been rewarded in some way and has been educated by his benefactor, and how this patronage relationship also forges a bond of dependence and loyalty. The ʻAbbāsíd caliphs had used this institution to rebuild their army, R. Mottahedeh, *Loyalty and Leadership in an Early Islamic Society*, pp. 82–3. In the present context, this expression refers to the rebels who had once risen against the Umayyad government and, having been subjugated by ʻAbd al-Raḥmān III, had settled in Córdoba, where they were incorporated into the army. See, for example, Ibn Ḥayyān, *Muqtabis II, 2*, p. 4, for a clear example of this process. An insightful discussion on ṣanāʼiʻ and iṣṭināʻ in al-Andalus in P. Chalmeta, *Historia socioeconómica*, pp. 130–5.

soldiers to wear Berber garments, nor could they use Berber saddles.[30] Once having noticed a servant (*ghulām*) riding a horse saddled in the Berber manner, the caliph became furious and ordered that the saddle and bridle were to be burnt and the slave punished, and that those responsible for permitting this error be reprimanded.

The North African campaign, launched in the summer of 972, changed everything. In the wake of the defeats suffered by the Andalusi army, the caliph was obliged to mobilise a huge quantity of resources, which eventually resulted in the submission of his enemies. However, in the aftermath of his triumph, al-Ḥakam II followed the same policy his father had employed with regard to the rebels from the inland regions of al-Andalus; he decreed that the defeated North African tribal leaders were to take up residence in Córdoba, where he granted them pensions and residences. The demobilisation of the North African rebels meant that they brought their military retinues with them, consisting of horsemen, who included men beholden to the leader (*ṣanāʾiʿ*), slaves and servants (*ʿabīd* and *ghilmān*). Naturally, as a consequence of the new status of their leaders, who were now subjects of the caliph, these horsemen could not continue to serve as members of their retinues. Thereby, the decision was taken to incorporate them into the Umayyad army, although in the case of the slaves the negotiations for their transfer were protracted.[31] However, Ibn Ḥayyān stresses that nothing was to stop the caliph. One of the Berber groups that joined the Umayyad army at that time was the Banū Birzāl. These were Zanāta Berbers, who had taken refuge in al-Andalus having fled from their enemies in North Africa. The recruitment of the Banū Birzāl into the caliphal army took place despite everyone knowing that they were Khārijites, Muslims who did not recognise Umayyad authority, as they believed that any pious believer could be chosen caliph irrespective of his genealogy.[32]

[30] Ibn Ḥayyān uses the word *ghilmān*, which the translator renders as 'pages', but which refers to the military 'servants' or 'slaves', whom the text distinguishes from the stipendiary and regular troops.

[31] Ibn Ḥayyān probably refers here to the 'slaves' who had been brought by Jaʿfar and Yaḥyā b. al-Andalusī, and had been the cause of a serious confrontation with the caliph over a disagreement regarding the price that had been offered for them. The conflict was only resolved when their cession was made compulsory (*ifrāj*). In Chapter 6, I address these events in more detail.

[32] These Khārijites belonged to the Nukkārid sect, whose members were renowned for having refused to recognise the authority of the *imāms* of Tāhert. The Banū Birzāl eventually settled in Carmona, where after the fall of the caliphate of Córdoba they established a *taifa* kingdom that

The Berbers who were resettled in al-Andalus after the African campaign amounted to 700 horsemen. Ibn Ḥayyān goes on to say that from then on al-Ḥakam completely changed his opinion about the Berbers: he put behind him his previous aversion and went on to become an obsequious admirer of their skills, especially their mastery as horsemen. Highly protected at the very heart of the administration, these soldiers became irreplaceable, while their leaders took over the principal command posts. Following al-Ḥakam's death, and during the caliphate of his son Hishām II, these Berber troops became Muḥammad b. Abī 'Āmir, al-Manṣūr's, primary allies for 'seizing the power' (*al-mulk*), and he converted them into a personal force, whereby 'while he lived he sank with them into darkness'.

As mentioned above, Ibn Ḥayyān was writing these words in the summer of 1009 (399 AH). During the last few months, and since February of that year, the people of Córdoba had been witnessing a chain of alarming events. The unprecedented decision of al-Ḥakam's son and successor, caliph Hishām, to name al-Manṣūr's son heir to the caliphate had led to a forthright response from other members of the Umayyad family who opposed any such plan. From then on, events were spinning out of control: a great-grandson of Caliph 'Abd al-Raḥmān III, called Muḥammad, had managed to stir up the people of Córdoba to oppose this decision, and had obliged Hishām to abdicate. As self-proclaimed caliph, Muḥammad al-Mahdī channelled the population's hostility against the Berber troops of the caliphate, who had already been suffering attacks and killings in the capital. All the tensions that had been building up against these soldiers, seen as symbolising the state's coercive capacity, exploded during the spring of 1009. Soon it was no longer isolated incidents that were taking place, but open war. In his commentary, Ibn Ḥayyān blames al-Ḥakam II for having begun recruiting these Berber troops, who at that very moment 'are about to destroy the caliphate, shatter the unity of the state, prepare the way for civil war and lead the peninsula to the brink of death, unless God ... at the end of the century that is about to close, wishes to save Islam'.

Thus, according to Ibn Ḥayyān, the origin of all the disaster he was witnessing, while copying 'Īsā al-Rāzī's text, was to be traced back to the event the

was conquered by the 'Abbādis of Seville, H. R. Idris, 'Les Birzalides de Carmona', *al-Andalus*, pp. 49–62. On the Nukkārid sect, T. Lewicki, *Encyclopaedia of Islam*, 2nd ed., s.v. al-Nukkār.

latter mentioned in the summer of 972 (361 AH): the North African war that al-Ḥakam II had begun on that date. Embarking on this campaign required the caliphate to flex its military muscle, but it also demonstrated the serious limitations of al-Hakam II's army. There is no doubt that the situation in northern Morocco was the subject of endless discussions at the heart of the Umayyad administration. One of the reasons that led al-Ḥakam II to appoint Ghālib to the post of supreme *qā'id* (*al-qiyāda al-'ulyā*) was that he had submitted a report on the army's recruitment, which he had written following a discussion with the caliph.[33] Another individual who helped to design the North African policy was Muḥammad b. Abī 'Āmir himself, the future al-Manṣūr, who had been sent to the other side of the Straits of Gibraltar by al-Ḥakam II to gain first-hand knowledge of what was taking place there: it is very possible that he had also highlighted the need for far-reaching reform of the caliphal army.

While al-Ḥakam II lived, and despite the recruitment of the Berber troops, the regular army, the *jund*, continued to exist. Their commanders were granted special audiences with the caliph, who seems to have taken special care to meet them in private audiences, thereby making clear the powerful presence they still exerted within the state apparatus.[34] However, following the caliph's death, and once al-Manṣūr had gained control of the state, he decided to dismantle the old system of the *jund*. Some sources state that he did so because his greatest fear was that their military leaders would come to an agreement to depose him; another explanation, which perhaps complements the previous one, was that the people of al-Andalus would prefer to pay the military service exemption tax, rather than risk their lives serving in exhausting and distant campaigns. Either way, al-Manṣūr put an end to the *jund* system, which meant the caliphate's military potential depended on the Berber troops who were being recruited in large numbers.[35]

The Berber soldiers thus became the backbone of the army, despite their immense unpopularity among the population. A chronicler pointed out that they arrived famished and covered in rags, and before long they were to be seen dressed in clothes made of *khazz*, riding magnificent horses and living in

[33] The appointment was written in the caliph's own hand on the document containing the report presented by Ghālib, Ibn Hayyān, *Muqtabis VII*, ed. p. 69; trans. pp. 91–2.

[34] Ibn Hayyān, *Muqtabis VII*, ed. pp. 56–7 and 201–2; trans. pp. 74–5 and 242.

[35] E. Manzano Moreno, *Conquistadores, emires y califas*, pp. 492–3.

palaces that they could not have imagined or even dreamed of. Another author, Ibn Mas'ūd, accused them of being ignorant and of envying the prosperity of the people of al-Andalus.[36] However, they were loyal troops, who were always available, and al-Manṣūr was able to make a radical break from what had been the caliphate's military policy since the battle of Alhándega. Once more, major campaigns were launched against the Christian territories commanded by him in person, and once more the Umayyad armies made triumphal entries into Córdoba laden with captives and booty. This aggressive policy, which at times meant two campaigns being launched per year, would have been impossible with the old, slow military system of *junds*; in contrast, the availability of the Berber horsemen and their swift movements permitted a wide range of targets to be attacked, and they wreaked terror on the Christian lands through widespread sackings. Although Ibn Ḥayyān thought that al-Manṣūr had sunk into darkness along with his troops, it must be acknowledged that his strategy functioned very well for nearly over a decade and it contained the Christian attacks that had increased prior to his rule. At the time of al-Manṣūr's death in 1002 (392 AH), nobody would have imagined that his aggressive strategy would be shot apart in barely seven years.

Yet, deep down, the reforms implemented by al-Manṣūr, as was the case with the caliphs' previous recruitment of slave soldiers, responded to structural conflicts concerning the military structures of medieval Islamic states. Al-Andalus was in this sense not a unique case. A century and a half earlier, the 'Abbāsíd caliphs had also been obliged to recruit Turkish troops to overcome the weakness of their armies. The Fāṭimid caliphs had to do the same when, after having occupied Egypt, they had to do without the Kutāma Berbers, who until then had been the backbone of their army: instead these caliphs had recourse to Turkish and Daylamid troops.[37] In all these cases a similar pattern

[36] Ibn 'Idhārī, *al-Bayān*, II, ed. p. 279; trans. p. 464. Ibn Ḥayyān, *Muqtabis V*, ed. and trans. pp. 200–1. It is difficult to know for certain who Ibn Mas'ūd was, but his work entitled *K. al-'anīq* is extensively cited by Ibn Ḥayyān. It has been proposed that he might be identified as Abū 'Abd Allāh Muḥammad b. Mas'ūd al-Ghassānī, who was from Pechina and died c. 1009–10 (400 AH); he spent part of his life in prison on a charge of heresy, which would explain the critical tone that is often noted in various passages, but this identification remains to be confirmed, J. Lirola, *Biblioteca de al-Andalus*, t. IV, pp. 167–8, s.v.

[37] Y. Lev, *State and Society in Fatimid Egypt*, pp. 84–6. H. Kennedy, *The Armies of the Caliphs*, pp. 122–4.

occurred, whereby military power tended to become alienated from the social base that sustained the state, due to the recruitment of foreign professional troops who provided their services in exchange for stipends.

But why did this happen? One reason relates to the predominantly urban character of the societies governed by Umayyads, 'Abbāsíds and Fāṭimids. It was in the cities, and not the rural zones, that the dominant classes resided, and their acceptance of and submission to the state's power impeded them from having their own armed retinues, as was commonplace in feudal Western Europe. Nor was it easy to recruit soldiers on a regular basis in this urban milieu, which was dominated by bureaucrats, artisans and traders. Meanwhile, in rural areas, the heavy fiscal burden meant farmers could not afford to relinquish their workforce, as they were badly needed to extract the maximum yield from the land. What is more, they were barely accustomed to the exercise of arms. On this basis it made sense to replace conscription with a tax that levied the exemption of military service, and whose revenue permitted the recruitment of stipendiary troops and the acquisition of slave soldiers.

As a result, the military demobilisation of the social fabric was in part converted into an implicit pact underpinning the political organisation of medieval Muslim societies. In virtue of this 'pact', and in exchange for the power exercised through the state's fiscal coercion, military service was ruled out as one of the contributions its subjects were expected to provide. In principle it was a satisfactory arrangement for everyone. The state's power ensured its effective capacity for coercion through a military force that was constantly available, and in exchange it obtained the population's consent to high taxation.

However, the flip-side of this model of organisation was a socio-political situation in which the legitimacy of caliphal power haemorrhaged. Stipendiary soldiers, lacking any social roots and garrisoned in hostile urban environments, constituted a continual reminder of the coercive capacity of the state, which was becoming progressively distant from its subjects, and whose logic did not always coincide with the principles that maintained social order. This, for example, led to Ibn Ḥayyān being scandalised by the fact that al-Ḥakam II would consider recruiting the Berber Khārijites, who were opposed to the legitimacy of the Umayyad caliphs. As a result, while the use of force as the principal mode of domination became established within the state's logic of power, at the heart of

Muslim society a very distinctive notion took shape, one that was based on a set of moral ideals, which served to define the Muslim community, or *umma*, and provided it with a raison d'être. As a consequence of this contradiction, power lost its authority, which instead became enshrined in people such as the *'ulamā'*, men of religion, who took on the role of guardians of Muslim orthodoxy. In many cases, these *'ulamā'* were conscripted within the caliphs' networks, but at times of crisis they were capable of upholding values and forms of conduct that were framed by a moral outlook that was opposed to the excesses of power, and they thus identified themselves in ideal terms as its effective antithesis. It should be borne in mind that in al-Andalus many *'ulamā'* were descendants of past members of the *jund*: people who had replaced the power of the sword with the authority of the pen, and whose deeply-rooted social status stood in contrast with the social alienation that afflicted political power.

Ibn Ḥayyān belonged to a family who had prospered under the shadow of the Umayyad caliphate and whose good fortune was doomed to be mired in the crisis that beset the dynasty. Faced by the caliphate's collapse, his interpretation gave free rein to his anti-Berber feelings, which were based on the idea that the crisis would not have happened if al-Ḥakam II had continued to trust the people of 'his Andalus'. However, these Berber troops were not the cause of the problems, but rather the symptom. The caliph, and with him the caliphate's ruling elite, had become convinced that it was impossible to maintain such a huge government apparatus while relying on people who lacked a bond of loyalty with the sovereign. While some loyalty might be obtained through the recognition of the religious authority embodied in the caliph himself, experience had demonstrated that this did not suffice. Another means of ensuring loyalty was by plainly and simply buying it, whether through stipends or the acquisition of slaves. This was what was done with the army, and also, as has been seen, with the administration, which became peopled with numerous *ṣaqāliba*. The problem raised by this option was that it required astronomical quantities of resources that could only be obtained by exerting considerable fiscal pressure, which in turn delegitimised the sovereign. It was a vicious circle that was impossible to square in the terms of the virtuous dynamic sought by al-Ḥakam II.

In the summer of 1009, when Ibn Ḥayyān was writing as well as transcribing 'Īsā al-Rāzī's text, he was unaware that worse was yet to come. The backdrop to the dynastic conflict unleashed by the various pretenders to the Umayyad caliphate was, on the one hand, the Cordoban population's hatred of the Berber soldiers and the political order they served, and on the other the Berber soldiers' reaction to the crisis; they responded by placing their weight behind a member of the Umayyad family who, once converted into caliph, became their supporter. The conflict grew worse, and during the months that followed the rival claims to power led to the Berber troops' besieging Córdoba, and when it fell in spring 1013 (403 AH) they sacked the city. Thereby, the soldiers whom al-Ḥakam II had theoretically recruited to defend his community ended up turning against it.

The Dominance of the Cavalry

One of the consequences of the transformation undergone by the Umayyad army during the last quarter of the tenth century was that the cavalry played an increasingly important role relative to that of the infantry. Throughout this period, in which the army became increasingly professionalised and its social differentiation more evident, the cavalry gained importance for its rapid effectiveness in pillaging raids, displays of force, and sieges. Cavalrymen also enabled swifter communications, which in turn meant tighter administrative control and better access to the caliphate's territories, however far away they were. All this led to the state exerting a more active presence, and an ability to move across the length and breadth of al-Andalus with great ease. It was not, as is sometimes assumed, horses in their own right that established new forms of dominion; it was rather the increased power of the caliphate's privileged groups, which provided the incentive for a diversification of the instruments and symbols of their power, which thus became more effective. In addition, this development arose in parallel to events in the Christian north, where along the frontiers the cavalry also 'seem to have played a leading role, and, even, monopolized military activity'.[38]

It has already been discussed how in al-Andalus new horses were requisitioned on a regular basis, and the excitement generated by the arrival of the new colts for the caliphal stables every spring. It was not by chance that, very often, the head of the cavalry (*ṣāḥib al-khayl*) held the rank of vizier. The variety of horses

[38] A. Isla, *Ejército, sociedad y política*, p. 186.

available in these stables is also a good indicator of the growing demand: Arab and North African breeds and many other types and colours are mentioned in the sources, along with pack mules. For the former, the caliphal administration had its own stables (*dār al-khayl*), while for the latter there were 'the state pack mules houses' (*dūr duwwāb al-sulṭān*), which were used to transport the army's supplies, as well as material needed for the caliph's building projects.[39] Ibn Ḥawqal records the mules (*bighāl*) brought from Mallorca, where the absence of predators, excellent pasture and lack of epidemics permitted the breeding of these animals, whose price oscillated between 100 and 200 dinars per animal, and there were even cases of 500 dinars being paid for a pack mule. Such prices justified the Umayyad sovereigns having them brought over by boat.[40]

Despite it being very expensive, moving people or things on the back of animals meant journeys could be made far more quickly. News of events that took place in Tangier was relayed to Córdoba in three to six days thanks to an efficient postal service whose messengers (*furanik*) delivered letters and oral messages by sea and land.[41] This same speed is noted in other cases. In the spring of 975 (364 AH), the expedition sent to help the garrison besieged in the castle of Gormaz under the command of the *qā'id* Ghālib took two weeks to cover 500 kilometres between Córdoba and Barahona, today in the province of Soria, an average of thirty-five kilometres a day. Muḥammad b. Abī 'Āmir was somewhat faster when he went to collect Ja'far b. al-Andalusī and his family members, who had disembarked in Málaga in the summer of 971 (360 AH): his entourage, formed only of horsemen, covered the 160 kilometres between Córdoba and this city in southern Andalusia in just four days.[42] Years later, once he had become al-Manṣūr, he became known for undertaking lightning campaigns as part of his policy of harassment against the Christian territories, which would have been impossible without extensive cavalry resources as the core element of his army.

The variety and quality of the caliphate's stock of horses were complemented by the introduction of better equipment. One of these was the use of the stirrup, an element of equine equipment whose introduction has prompted

[39] E. García Gómez, 'Armas, banderas, tiendas de campaña, monturas y correos', pp. 170–4.
[40] Ibn Ḥawqal, *Ṣūrat al-arḍ*, ed. cit. pp. 114–15; trans. cit. p. 114.
[41] E. García Gómez, 'Armas, banderas, tiendas de campaña, monturas y correos', p. 179.
[42] Ibn Ḥayyān, *Muqtabis VII*, ed. cit. pp. 41–2, 220–1 and 226; trans. cit. pp. 62–3 and 261 and 267.

many controversies.[43] The Romans did not use them, although this did not stop their horsemen from controlling their horses and using their weapons with great efficiency.[44] It was during the Early Middle Ages that stirrups were gradually introduced, possibly due to the influx of pastoral nomads from Central Asia. With the support they provided, riders increased their control both over the horse and over their own body when brandishing swords or preparing to fire arrows, as it also increased their capacity for impact due to their kinetic strength. The first stirrups were made of wood and leather, but later on metal ones were made, although the technique of making thin yet resistant models would only have been mastered by the most skilful blacksmiths. In broad terms, it seems that the use of the stirrup became widespread in Byzantium between the seventh and eighth centuries, during which time it was also adopted by the Sasanians and the Arabs, as is demonstrated by texts and visual representations. In the Carolingian empire, although there is iconography of riders without stirrups from the early ninth century, as shown by the *Folchard Psalter*, other representations reveal that their use had become widespread by the end of the same century.[45]

With regard to al-Andalus, and despite there being an early reference to the use of the stirrup in the mid-eighth century, it is striking that in the mid-tenth century Ibn Ḥawqal stated that neither he nor anybody else had ever seen an Andalusi riding a horse with stirrups, due to their fear of getting their feet trapped in the event of a fall.[46] This statement might be read as merely the contemptuous and sneering view of an Eastern traveller, were it not for the

[43] The origin of this controversy is found in L. White's book *Medieval Technology and Social Change* (1962), which proposed that the introduction of the stirrup in France in the eighth century led to the cavalry playing an increasing military role, and with it the need to introduce fiefs to maintain horsemen. While criticised at the time, this thesis has since been discredited for its simplistic concept of feudalism and the errors in the evidence provided by White.

[44] F. Quesada, 'El gobierno del caballo montado', p. 141.

[45] S. Lazaris, 'Considérations sur l'apparition de l'etrier', pp. 275–88; H. Kennedy, *The Armies of the Caliphs*, pp. 171–2. A beautiful representation of a rider with a bow and using stirrups from the eighth century at the Umayyad palace of Qaṣr al-Ḥayr al-Gharbī in D. Schlumberger, *Qasr el-Heir el-Gharbi*, Paris, 1986, XIV, plate 34. K. Devries and R. D. Smith, *Weapons and Warfare. An Illustrated History of Their Impact*, p. 241, with reference to fol. 140r and 140v of the *Golden Psalter*. Digital ed. published at http://www.e-codices.unifr.ch (last accessed 12 November 2022). Compare its illustrations with those of the *Stuttgart Psalter* (c. 820), fol. 3v, 14v or 19r, among others. Digital ed. published by the Würtembergische Landesbibliothek at http://www.wlb-stuttg art.de (last accessed 12 November 2022).

[46] Ibn Ḥawqal, *Ṣūrat al-arḍ*, ed. cit. pp. 108–9 and 113; trans. cit. pp. 107 and 112–13. An early reference to a stirrup in *Akhbār Majmūʿa*, ed. and trans. p. 94; trans. James, 97.

fact that contemporary illustrations found in manuscripts from the Christian north provide a highly varied range of evidence on the use of the stirrup. The León Bible, produced in 960, includes a representation of the death of King Saul and his sons at the hands of the Philistines, which shows a battle scene in which a rider is depicted attacking with a bow and arrow, but without using stirrups; likewise, another horseman is depicted without them in the illustration of the death of Jezabel. In contrast, an image of the prophet Elijah besides some horses clearly depicts triangular-shaped stirrups. A similar degree of uncertainty is found in the *Gerona Beatus*, which was finished in 975: it contains representations of riders brandishing bows and arrows and lances, but without stirrups, while a knight depicted killing a serpent uses round stirrups.[47] In somewhat later Andalusi images, riders are depicted with stirrups: this is the case with the knights portrayed in the Leyre ivory casket, which was made in the caliphal workshops in 1004–5 (395 AH) and is dedicated to al-Manṣūr's son, ʻAbd al-Malik.[48]

Therefore, it may be argued that the stirrup was adopted gradually in al-Andalus during the second half of the tenth century (fourth AH), which may have been hastened by the greater role played by the cavalry, and in particular the Berber horsemen. Indeed, the changes made to the saddles used by the Andalusis, which up until then had been characterised by their high bolstered pommel and cantle, may most certainly be attributed also to the Berbers. The traditional type of al-Andalus saddle is depicted on a green and manganese ware plate found in Elvira, which includes a representation of a saddled horse. The same type of saddle is also depicted in representations of riders in a

[47] However, these representations may merely demonstrate that the artisans followed iconographic models. The archer-horsemen seen on fol. 126r of the Gerona Beatus may be compared with representations on textiles from the tomb of Saint Cunibertin in the Church of Saint Calais in Sarthe (France) and other locations, whose origin is Byzantine or Syrian, and which were made later than the eighth century. This has been confirmed by the discovery in Pskov, in north-eastern Russia, of a burial chamber dated to the very late tenth or early eleventh century, which contains a textile containing the same motif, E. Zubkova et al., 'Studies of the Textiles from the 2006 Excavation in Pskov', pp. 291–8.

[48] *Codex Biblicus Legionensis*, *Biblia Visigótico mozárabe*, fol. 124v with representation of 1 Samuel 31:1–5; fol. 144v and fol. 150v with representation of 1 Kings 21:17. *Beatus of Liébana*, *Commentary on the Apocalypse*, *Gerona Codex*, fol. 15v. a representation of the Massacre of the Innocents; fol. 126r. a representation of the Opening of the Four Seals (Revelation, 6:1–8); fol. 134v. a representation of a rider killing a serpent; fol. 159v. a representation of the Horses of Fire, Hyacinth and Brimstone (Revelation 9:17). In the Beatus preserved in the Morgan Library in New York, which was made in the Monastery of Tábara in c. 940–5, there is a beautiful illustration that shows infantrymen and riders with a sword, bow and flag, who are depicted without stirrups.

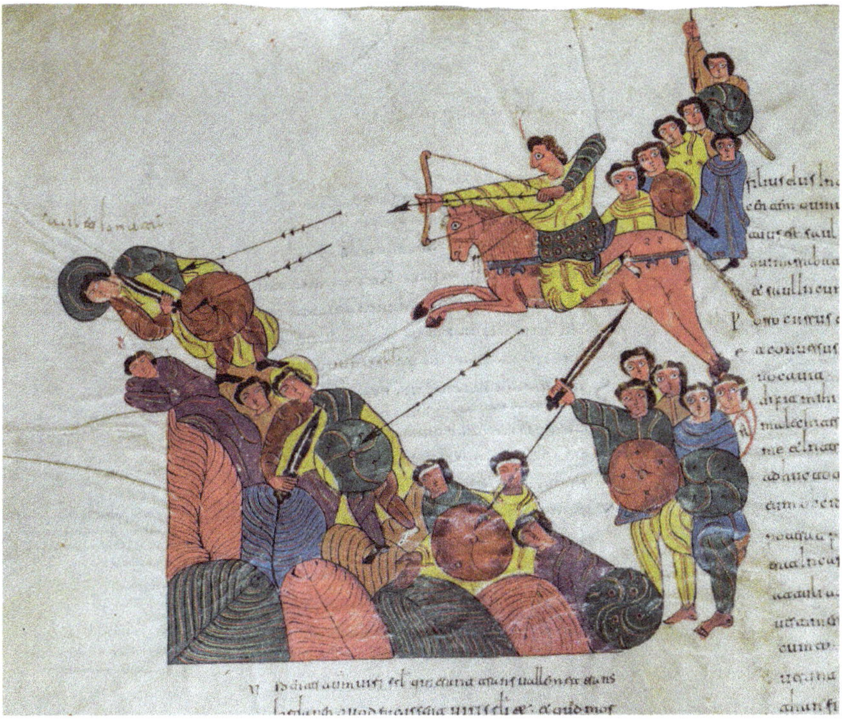

Image 8 Bible of León (960). The death of Saul and his sons at the battle of Mount Gelboe. The galloping horseman wields the bow, although he has no stirrups. The infantrymen carry long spears, centre-grooved swords and round shields. This may well have been the equipment of some of the caliphate's army corps.

number of tenth-century Beatus illustrations. In contrast, the saddles used by Berber horsemen, such as that which Caliph al-Ḥakam ordered to be burnt before he became an advocate of Berber equestrian skills, were characterised by a design that facilitated the rider's manoeuvres: the pommel and cantle were much lower, and the sides of the saddle thinner, as is described by Ibn Ḥayyān in meticulous detail. This new type of saddle is represented in images of riders in the León Bible.[49] In al-Andalus, the Leyre casket once more confirms that these changes had been incorporated at the start of the eleventh century.

[49] A North African-made saddle, 'the sides of the seat are very thin and its pommel and cantle very low, such as never had been seen before', Ibn Ḥayyān, *Muqtabis* VII, p. 190; trans. p. 229. A. Soler del Campo, 'Armas, arreos y banderas en las miniaturas del códice', in *Codex Biblicus Legionensis. Veinte Estudios*, León, 1999, 3.2.

Image 9 Bible of León (960). Elijah sleeping beside his mounts. The equipment of the horses includes stirrups and pendants.

The cavalry's importance in the caliphal army is also demonstrated by the variety and specialisation of its horsemen units, which are referred to with reference to the parades held as part of the caliphate's major celebrations. Although such parades were clearly intended to stage a certain scenic spectacle, which most probably was not transferred to the battlefield, nonetheless 'Īsā al-Rāzī's meticulous description of these events gives an idea of the variety of troops and equipment that made up the mounted troops who served the caliph.

The cavalry units in al-Ḥakam II's army included a corps of archer slaves. It goes without saying that the use of the bow (*qaws*) required an extraordinary and highly specialised skill.[50] Nowadays, with the tradition of using this weapon in combat being all but lost – those who practise archery do so standing still – it is hard to fully comprehend the high speed and deadly accuracy with which these cavalrymen unleashed their arrows, whether fighting on horseback or on foot.[51] Indeed, units of archers were always deployed on the North African campaigns. For example, Tangier was captured in the summer of 972 (361 AH) after a sortie of troops from the city was subjected to a shower of arrows from the Umayyad army; as a result, the forces of the besieged city were decimated. Mention is also made of archers with regard to the deployment of reinforcements from al-Andalus, which indicates that they were in particular demand by the *qā'id*s serving in Morocco, and this was very possibly due to their being highly effective against Berber horsemen.[52]

Horseback archers used flamboyant equipment, which was exhibited during the major celebrations held by the caliph at Madīnat al-Zahrā'. For example, a special group of them wore white cloaks, arrows slung over their shoulders, and quivers that it is said were from Zugar, a place in Syria renowned for making these items in the pre-Islamic period. It is very difficult to elucidate which type of bows they used. Our source mentions 'Arabic' and 'foreign' bows, but it is not possible to specify exactly what the difference was between them. 'Foreign' arrows were also highly valued.[53] The representations

50 If we are to believe the account of the battle fought by the governor of al-Andalus, Yūsuf al-Fihrī, in spring of 756 (38 AH) the founder of the Umayyad dynasty, 'Abd al-Raḥmān b. Mu'āwiya, fought that day on horseback armed with a bow, *Akhbār Majmū'a*, ed. and trans. pp. 87–8, 89; trans. James, p. 94.

51 Readers can consult online videos documenting the skills of contemporary archers such as Lajos Kassai and Lars Andersen which provide an idea of the enormous effectiveness that this type of soldiers could have.

52 The deployment of reinforcements in the summer of 973 (362 AH) included 100 free and slave (*'abīd*) archers under the command of vizier Yaḥyā b. Muḥammad b. Hāshim al-Tujībī, Ibn Ḥayyān, *Muqtabis VII*, ed. cit. pp. 89, 125, 129; trans. cit. pp. 112, 158–9, 163.

53 The description corresponds to the reception of Ja'far b. al-Andalusī and his family in September 971 (362 AH), Ibn Ḥayyān, *Muqtabis VII*, ed. cit. pp. 48–9; trans. pp. 67–8. A. Labarta has proposed that these foreign bows were Turkish. The text also refers to these archers as 'wearing a *maqārīf* over their hair (*mutaqalansī al-maqārīf*)'. I have not found any reference to any such *maqārīf*; perhaps the manuscript contains an error, whereby perhaps one should read *migfar*, which is effectively a piece of chain mail worn beneath the helmet, Lane Pool, *Arabic English Lexicon*, pp. 2,274–5. A. Labarta argued that it might have been some form of ceremonial military headgear, A. Labarta, 'Parada militar en la Córdoba omeya', p. 268. On the quivers made in Zugar, E. García Gómez cites a commentary by Ibn Rashīq al-Qayrawānī on some verses by Abū Du'ād al-Iyādī, a pre-Islamic poet, who was renowned for his poems about horses, in which he refers to

Image 10 Morgan Beatus (c. 940). A military expedition with infantrymen and knights. Note the presence of a flag tied to a lance, as was the case in the caliphal armies. The horsemen have no stirrups, use barrel saddles and are armed with bow, sword and shield. All the infantrymen are spearmen.

of horseback archers that appear in a number of tenth-century Beatuses seem to indicate the use of a composite bow, at least in some cases, with a design that is unlike anything seen in representations found in Carolingian psalters, while in contrast it is similar to the bows included in depictions of horseback archers in textiles with Persian origins.

Other horsemen from al-Ḥakam II's army carried lances and shields and wore coats of mail. The shields could either be round (*turs*) or comet-shaped (*daraqa*). In military parades both cavalry and infantrymen would also wear armour. While the armour could be made of leather, there is archaeological evidence that indicates the use of coats of mail.[54] Another class of horsemen

how in this Syrian city they made 'gilded red bandoliers', 'Armas, banderas, tiendas de campaña', pp. 165 and 167. The same verse in Yaqūt, *Mujam al-buldān*, ed. Beirut, 2007, III, pp. 142–3. I have not found any other references to these quivers from Zugar, which makes me think that this is a poetic reference by 'Īsā al-Rāzī. An-Nāṣir presented 20,000 'foreign' arrows (*'ajamiyya*) as a gift to a North African tribal leader, Ibn Ḥayyān, *Muqtabis V*, ed. and trans. p. 239.

[54] A small lead disc with an inscription that includes the name of 'Abd al-Raḥmān I also shows on its reverse the imprint of what seems to be a coat of mail which this disc would have been affixed to, T. Ibrahim, 'Nuevos documentos sobre la conquista omeya de Hispania: los precintos de plomo',

went into battle well-protected wearing a cuirass (*jawshan*), presumably made of overlapping metal plates sown onto a leather or cloth garment. In this case, a representation exists in a fragment of green and manganese ware found at the excavations of Madīnat al-Zahrā', which shows an armour-clad rider brandishing a lance and a decorated shield. The rider also wears a round helmet that provided protection for his ears.[55] Another group of horsemen in the caliphal army formed a unit of heavy cavalry (*al-fursān aṣḥāb al-tajāfīf*), with both rider and steed wearing heavy armour. Again, this type of equipment was of Eastern origin and was used by Arab armies at an earlier date. It was incorporated into the caliphal armies during the Umayyad and 'Abbāsid periods. In al-Andalus the use of this type of cavalry is recorded in a number of accounts of battles.[56]

In addition to these cavalry units, there were other types of mounted troops. The non-regular soldiers sent from the provinces who served in the capital are mentioned as being cavalrymen, as also were the slaves from the *khumsiyyūn*, who were probably captives belonging to the fifth part (*khums*) of the war booty. The *fursān al-riyāḍa* were a class of cavalry soldiers mentioned on a number of occasions, but they are hard to identify with any specific duty or appearance.[57]

Constant training was needed to maintain these cavalry units' military capacity. Having become an admirer of the skills of the Berber horsemen,

p. 159. The disc's inscription reads: 'Emir 'Abd al-Raṃān b. Mu'āwiya has an army that [defends] God's cause [and] which submits neither to conquest nor fear'.

55 For the differences between the shields and the coats of mail and plate armour I follow M. Gorelick, 'Oriental armour of the Near and Middle East', p. 33.

56 D. Nicolle, 'Horse Armour in the Medieval Islamic East'. During the rule of 'Abd al-Raḥmān III, the 'heavy cavalry' called *khayl thaqīla* was used on some of his campaigns, Ibn Ḥayyān, *Muqtabis V*, ed. cit. p. 67; trans. cit. p. 62. The Christians also used this type of cavalry, as is demonstrated by the incursion led by the Count of Castilla, García Fernández, against the territories of the Banū Timlīt in September 974 (363 AH), *Muqtabis VII*, ed. p. 188; trans. p. 227.

57 The troops called *wufūd* were non-regular soldiers sent by leaders of the territories which had submitted to the central power. They might be put on garrison duty in Córdoba, or else sent to fight on campaigns if needed, as occurred in April 975 (364 AH) when the *qā'id* Ghālib had to suddenly leave for Gormaz with a squadron consisting of stipendiary troops, *khumsiyyūn* slave soldiers, archers and members of the *wufūd*, Ibn Ḥayyān, *Muqtabis VII*, ed. cit. pp. 44, 223 and 227–8; trans. pp. 64, 263 and 269. *Akhbār Majmū'a* ed. and trans. p. 159; trans. James pp. 131–2, distinguishes between the emir's army that besieged Bobastro and the 'divisions of the various districts and tribes' (*ḥushūd al-kuwwār wa wufūd al-qabā'il*). The *fursān al-riyāḍa* served as guards for protocolary duties, but there was also a contingent of them that was incorporated into the Moroccan army in July 973 (*Shawwāl* 362 AH), Ibn Ḥayyān, *Muqtabis VII*. ed. cit. pp. 51, 125, 156, 199; trans. cit. pp. 70, 158–9, 197, 240.

Image 11 Detail of Leyre ivory casket (1004). Horsemen fighting. Note the use of stirrups and low saddles, making it easier to use the lance with both hands. The rider on the left wields a sword, while defending himself with a round shield.

al-Ḥakam II enjoyed watching them train at Madīnat al-Zahrā', which they did on the days they received their wages. The caliph admired the great skill they showed astride their horses. These training exercises turned into real competitions. In what is perhaps the first mention we have of a medieval tournament, in April 975 (364 AH) the caliph along with his son Hishām attended a joust of riders on the enclosure in front of the Bāb al-Sudda of the *alcázar* in Córdoba. The competitors were high-ranking soldiers and they attacked one another with their lances trying to unseat their opponents, while under strict orders to feint so as not to injure anybody. However, some competitors took the fun too seriously. One member of the regular army, a descendant of a well-established family that had originally hailed from the frontier, Walīd b. ʻAbd al-Malik b. Mūsā b. al-Ṭawīl, unseated and injured a member of the Banū Khazar, a member of the Berber troops that had only recently settled in Córdoba. The same competitive excess was displayed by another senior officer called Mundhir b. ʻAbd Allāh b. Hābil, who was also a descendant of a family that had once rebelled against the Umayyads but had ended up settling in Córdoba. Furious, the caliph ordered both soldiers to be imprisoned, while the injured were granted gifts.[58] There were perhaps many people that day who thought the injuries inflicted had not been merely the result of an excess of zeal.

Compared with the cavalry, infantry units played a lesser role in al-Ḥakam II's army. They undoubtedly took part in campaigns in higher numbers than the cavalry (remember the mortality figures for the battle of Faḥṣ Mahrān, where 1,000 infantry soldiers died compared with half the amount of cavalry), but their armed units were less varied and their potential for deployment on campaign much more limited. In contrast, their presence seems to have always been in demand for sieges, where the infantry could take up position for long periods, and they could also serve on garrison duty.[59]

During the parades held for the caliph's major receptions, and as will be seen in detail in Chapter 8, it was always the horsemen who played a prominent role, while the infantry played a less important part in the celebrations. One of the most revealing passages of the work of ʻĪsā al-Rāzī describes how the preparations for an impressive official reception involved temporarily recruiting young men from the neighbourhoods of Córdoba, who were supplied with spears and shields in order to make them look like infantry soldiers,

[58] Ibn Ḥayyān, *Muqtabis VII*. ed. pp. 193 and 223; trans. pp. 231 and 264. On the Banū al-Ṭawīl, whose indigenous lineage went back to the ninth century, and who had been lords of Huesca during the emirate before ending up settling in Córdoba, M. J. Viguera, *Aragón Musulmán*, p. 159. The case of the Banū Hābil was very similar: they were an indigenous family who controlled a range of castles in the Jaén region and had eventually been vanquished. They then settled in Córdoba and enlisted in the army. V. Salvatierra, *El alto Guadalquivir en época islámica*, pp. 110–12.

[59] For example, during the siege of Gormaz the *qāʼid* Ghālib used cavalry and 'compact infantry', Ibn Ḥayyān, Muqtabis VII, ed. p. 226; trans. p. 267. In the emirate era, the fortress of Calatrava lodged the cavalry, but also served as a fort for the infantry (*ribāṭ li-l-rijāl*), C. Barceló, 'Las inscripciones omeyas de la alcazaba de Mérida', p. 67, for which she draws on Ibn Ḥayyān's text. Also *Muqtabis V*, p. 309, with regard to the reconstruction and fortifying the fortress of Calatalifa, along the Middle Frontier, which is identified with the ruins found near what is today Villaviciosa de Odón (Madrid).

and were posted along the route taken by the festival cortège. It is unlikely that these men were actually deployed on the battlefield, which suggests that with regard to the army units stationed in the caliphate's capital, the size of the infantry was much lower than that of the cavalry.

An important group of infantry were the guardsmen (*maḥāris*), who were deployed in the city of Córdoba for grand receptions, and whose members also undertook police duties in the capital.[60] There were also two types of soldiers that made up the *alcázar*'s guard, those assigned pensions (*rijālat al-murtaziqīn*) and purchased infantrymen (*rijālat al-mushtarīn*); the latter were of slave origin, and had perhaps been manumitted.[61] In addition, there was also a unit of archer infantrymen, who were likewise divided into two groups, freemen and slaves. As was the case with the cavalry who used this weapon, these archers were distinguished by the uniforms they wore, made of coloured cloths of *firind*, which was a type of brocade that was made from silk, linen or wool.[62] Another infantry unit was the *Ja'farids*, whose spectacular equipment was commented on above.

The major difference between the different types of infantry soldiers was the weapons they used. It is highly significant that swords (*suyūf*) are not often described as part of the equipment used by the infantry. Instead the more frequently listed weapons are spears, shields, maces (*dammāghāt*) and a type of dagger known as *ṭabarzināt*, a weapon cited in Persian literature, which underwent a significant development during the early modern period.[63] In contrast, the majority of the references made to swords are to lavishly adorned

[60] Ibn Ḥayyān, *Muqtabis VII*. ed. pp. 45, 153 and 196; trans. pp. 65, 194 and 237.

[61] The 'purchased' infantry are recorded as early as the reign of 'Abd al-Raḥmān II, Ibn Ḥayyān, *Muqtabis II, 1*, ed. cit. P. 297; trans. cit. p. 185.

[62] The archers were dressed like this for their participation at the reception of Ja'far b. al-Andalusī and at the reception of *qā'id* Ghālib after his triumph in Morocco, Ibn Ḥayyān, *Muqtabis VII*. ed. pp. 49 and 196; trans. pp. 68 and 238. Both the edition and the translation of this text introduce the word *ifrind*, which should be corrected to *firind*, a word borrowed from the Persian *parand*, A. H. King, *Scent from the Garden of Paradise*. pp. 52–4.

[63] Ibn Ḥayyān, *Muqtabis VII*, ed. p. 198; trans. p. 239. García Gómez, 'Armas', pp. 165–6, with editing revisions. In particular, *dammāghāt*, which Dozy translates as 'portcullis', or in other words, the barred door that protects a castle, does not seem to make sense in this context, as reference is clearly made to a weapon carried by the infantry soldiers. It might be suggested that this was some type of mace, bearing in mind the significance of the root, which has the sense 'to break a head', F. Corriente, *A Dictionary of Andalusi Arabic*, Leiden, 1997, pp. 183–4. I have not managed to identify what the *ājwiza* were, which are translated as 'beams'. On *ṭabarzināt*, A. S. Melikian-Chirvani, 'The tabarzīns of Loṭf'alī', pp. 116–35.

ceremonial weapons that were worn by palace servants, and it may be assumed they underscored the status of whoever wore them: the presence in the major receptions of secretaries, eunuchs and other servants with swords adorned with precious stones and their handles likewise encrusted with jewels highlights the elaborate spectacle that was staged on occasions to display Umayyad power under al-Ḥakam II.[64]

According to Ibn Ḥayyān, the caliph's enthusiasm for the Berbers' skilful handling of their horses led him to recall some verses of the Eastern poet al-Mutannabī (915–65/303–54 AH): 'It might be said they were born beneath them [their horses]/and that they [their horses] were born beneath their [riders'] loins'. Although it is possible that this anecdote was fabricated by the author, it reflects the complete surrender of the caliphate's military capacity to these troops.[65] However, their arrival in al-Andalus was not accompanied by excessive approval from the local population, not even among sectors of the ruling class, who did not conceal their disdain for people who were unfamiliar with the refinements of the caliphate's capital. Yet, while the military parades were filled with figures wielding shields and spears, the military pressure on the caliphate was growing on two fronts: North Africa and the Christian North. In the following chapters, I will focus on an analysis of the events that took place in both regions.

[64] Ibn Ḥayyān, *Muqtabis VII*, ed. pp. 51 and 120; trans. pp. 69 and 153.

[65] Ibn Ḥayyān, *Muqtabis VII*, ed. p. 193; trans. p. 231. Instead, this must be a case of a degree of licence taken by the historian: although al-Mutannabī's poetry was well-known in al-Andalus thanks to intermediaries who had travelled to the East such as the Cordoban Ibn Qādim (d. 990/380 AH), the first commentary on his work was written somewhat later. Its author was the Cordoban philologist Ibn al-Iflīlī (963–1050/352–441 AH), who was well-known to Ibn Ḥayyān, who also wrote a biography of him, *Biblioteca de al-Andalus*, IV, no. 932 and III, no. 643, article by J. Mohedano Barceló.

5

The Struggle against the Fāṭimid Caliphate: (I) The Background

The Fāṭimid Revolution

One Thursday in early January in 910 (*Rabi' II*, 297 AH) an event took place that would mark the history of the Mediterranean region for more than two and a half centuries. On that day, Abū Muḥammad 'Abd Allāh, a man who was said to be a descendant of the Prophet Muḥammad, made his triumphal entry into the city of Qayrawān in Ifrīqiya (in modern Tunisia). Belonging to the Prophet's family was in its own right a badge of distinction, but for many Muslims a further degree of honour was bestowed on those who could trace their descent back to the marriage of the Prophet's daughter, Fāṭima, to one of the most significant and charismatic figures of early Islam: 'Alī b. Abī Ṭālib, the Prophet's cousin, who had been one of his first and most fervent followers. Hence, it comes as no surprise that the arrival in Qayrawān of someone who claimed to be a direct descendant of this renowned union was greeted by crowds of bystanders hoping to catch a glimpse of him. Observed by throngs of people and accompanied by his son and the troops that had won him a series of resounding military victories, Abū Muḥammad 'Abd Allāh entered the city, where he was met by the city elders, who gave him a courteous, yet tepid welcome. The following day, a Friday, he issued a lengthy edict in which he proclaimed himself caliph with the title of al-Mahdī, and promised harsh treatment for anyone who dared stand against him, and high hopes for those who placed their trust in the justice he would administer.[1] Thus began

[1] al-Qāḍī al-Nu'mān, *Iftitāḥ al-da'wa*, trans. H. Haji, pp. 204–13.

the long succession of Fāṭimid caliphs, who governed first in Ifrīqiya and then in Egypt, and went on to establish one of the most important medieval dynasties until its demise in 1171.

The proclamation of al-Mahdī as caliph in 297 of the Hijra, just three years prior to the end of the third century of the Islamic era, was an extraordinary event. All of a sudden much of what many Muslims considered to be certain was called into question, and for a time many became hopeful that major changes were about to take place. Since the death of the Prophet Muḥammad, a considerable number of Muslims had been debating whether the caliphate's political power and religious authority ought really to have been bestowed upon 'Alī b. Abī Ṭālib, the Prophet's cousin and son-in-law because he had married his daughter Fāṭima, and furthermore on the direct line of descendants from this marriage. The fact that this had not come to pass and that the caliphate had been usurped, first by the dynasty of the Umayyad caliphs and then by the 'Abbāsids, was for these Muslims a demonstration of the injustice that prevailed in the world. Nonetheless, this group remained firmly committed to the descendants of 'Alī b. Abī Ṭālib and his wife Fāṭima, and, what is still more surprising, they sustained this commitment over the course of many generations.

Increasingly known as *Shī'a* (from the Arabic *shī'at 'Alī* or 'followers of Alī'), this community was convinced that the role of guide to the Muslim community, or *imām*, had been transmitted down through the direct and single hereditary line of the descendants of 'Alī b. Abī Ṭālib and his wife Fāṭima. While the succession of Umayyad and 'Abbāsíd caliphs governed over the Muslim community in the name of what became known as 'Orthodox' or Sunni Islam, each of the series of Shī'ı *imāms* received their supporters' unshakeable fidelity, despite their being scattered across the Muslim world, and often forced to practise their beliefs in a clandestine manner, as they were subject to occasional persecutions. Furthermore, and to complicate matters still more, for the indefatigable Shī'ī followers, in 765 (148 AH) an important schism took place at the heart of this sect: following the death of the sixth *imām*, Ja'far al-Ṣādiq, a strong disagreement arose over which of his sons was to be his heir. The supporters of one of these sons, called Ismā'īl, claimed that he had gone into hiding. The members of this group formed the idea that the last days would be marked by the appearance of a figure calling himself the

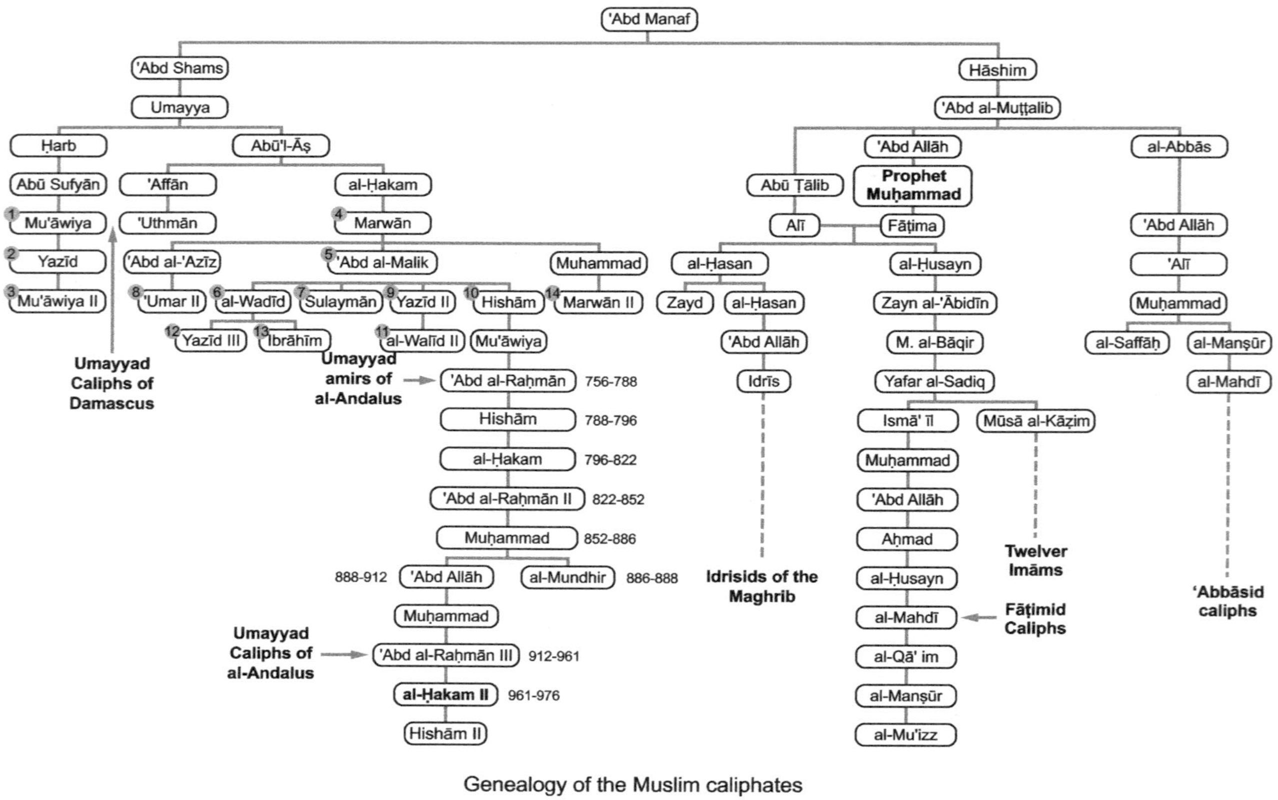

Figure 2 Genealogy of the Muslim caliphates

Mahdī, 'the well-guided', who would restore order and justice during the time prior to the Final Judgement. Others, in contrast, did not agree, and criticised Ismā'īl for lacking the signs and virtues that would have made him worthy of the imāmate. The greater part of the Shī'ī community tended to support the latter view, and accepted another of the sons of the deceased Ja'far, called Mūsā, as their *imām*. However, those who backed Ismā'īl held fast to their belief and began an effective campaign of proselytisation in various parts of Iraq, Syria and Iran over the course of the following decades.[2]

The activities undertaken by the supporters of Ismā'īl as the legitimate heir of the Shī'ī *imāms* gave rise to a complex doctrinal development. One of their most interesting ideas was that the message transmitted by each prophet, Muḥammad included, had an external aspect (*ẓāhir*) that was self-evident, normative and widely accessible to all. Yet it also had a hidden and esoteric (*bāṭin*) meaning known only by the *imāms* who had succeeded the Prophet and the initiates they had chosen. The past was thus conceived as a succession of explicit and implicit revelations over the course of which the prophets were succeeded by those who unveiled the concealed meaning of their revelations. Such was the case with the Prophet Muḥammad, whose mission could only be understood through the figure of 'Alī b. Abī Ṭālib, who had transmitted to his descendants the hidden significance of the divine revelation to the Prophet. However, as the revelation granted to the Prophet had been the last, this cycle was drawing to a close. As the end of time was approaching, the Ismā'īlī *imām* would appear as the *Mahdī* in order to establish for ever more the hidden meaning of the divine revelation, repeal unjust laws, and implement a government of justice that would be founded on the elements of the divine revelation, which had until then escaped human understanding.

The fascinating apocalyptic tones of the Ismā'ilí ideology were interwoven with a complex debate at the very heart of this community: the task of elucidating from which branch of the family the *Mahdī* would arise, as well as who he would be, and when the events prophesied by this doctrine would come to pass. At the end of the ninth century, an Ismā'īlī group that had been

[2] For the purpose of this chapter I follow: H. Halm, *The Empire of the Mahdi. The Rise of the Fāṭimids*, Leiden, 1996; M. Brett, *The Rise of the Fāṭimids. The World of the Mediterranean and the Middle East in the 10th Century C.E.*, Leiden, 2001, pp. 36–48.

based in the town of Salamiyya, in Syria, began to spread the idea that they had certain knowledge about these issues. A series of missionaries (*dāʿī*-s) firstly destined for Yemen and then for North Africa started to disseminate a message claiming to have sure proof that a descendant of the Ismāʿīlī *imāms*, who lived in Syria, was capable of fulfilling their doctrinal expectations: 'rejoice' – they said – 'as the day of the oppressors is drawing to their end'.[3]

The activity of these preachers, who progressively became known as 'Fāṭimids', was frenetic. One of them managed to communicate his message among a North African tribe, the Kutāma, which was a branch of the Ṣinhāja Berbers that had settled in the region between the Aurés Mountains (to the east of modern Algeria) and the sea. Their tribal support for the Fāṭimid programme or *daʿwa* is explained by the same pattern that had previously been demonstrated elsewhere: movements advocating profound religious reform often met with strong opposition in already Islamised urban zones, but they were well-received among tribes in marginal areas. Just as Caliph al-Ḥakam II left to Maghribid Berber tribes the task of fulfilling the strict Islamic regulations on taxation that he dared not apply in his own territories, elsewhere other Berber tribes provided social support for proselytising campaigns claiming to embody the true foundations of the Islamic message, support the Fāṭimid preachers could not win in urban contexts. A religious message offering grand aspirations such as the Fāṭimid *daʿwa* bestowed on these tribes an element of social cohesion and above all political stimulus. Thereby, these tribes went on to play an increasingly relevant role. The connection between this intense religious preaching and these tribes' military capacity forged an unbeatable alliance, capable of challenging the established social, political and ideological power. This is what happened in Ifrīqiya in the first decade of the tenth century (third AH), as it would with later socio-religious movements in the Maghreb, as was the case with the Almoravids and Almohads.

Fāṭimid preaching effectively galvanised the Kutāma into a military mobilisation that soon became a serious threat to the Aghlabids, the dynasty of emirs that had been ruling over Ifrīqiya until then. The Aghlabids were nominally subjects of the ʿAbbāsid caliph in Baghdad, but over the course of the ninth century (third AH) they had cut their ties with the metropolis, and had

[3] al-Qāḍī al-Nuʿmān, *Iftitāḥ al-daʿwa*, p. 21.

made their dynasty a hereditary one. Facing the Fāṭimid challenge, the dynasty suffered a series of disasters inflicted on its army by the Kutāma which led to its collapse and permitted the capture of Qayrawān at the start of spring 909 (296 AH). Months later, and after many vicissitudes, Abū Muḥammad 'Abd Allāh made his entry into the capital and, as a descendant of Fāṭima and 'Alī b. Abī Ṭālib, claimed the title of caliph, as has already been mentioned.

The reaction of the Islamic world to the proclamation of the Fāṭimid Caliphate oscillated between stupor and fear. It was the first time that a descendant of 'Alī b. Abī Ṭālib had managed to establish a caliphate, in which the aspirations of a messianic programme could feasibly become a reality. Many reacted by declaring al-Mahdī's claim to be a descendant of 'Alī and Fāṭima a grave act of deceit. His more benevolent opponents considered him to be a mere supporter of this line of *imāms*, and he had been wrongly identified as one of them; more hostile critics did not think twice about accusing him of being the great-grandson of a *mawlā*, or still worse an imposter of Jewish origin. Last but not least, his enemies insisted that belief in the Fāṭimid genealogy was nothing less than a leap of faith that lacked even the slightest basis in truth.[4] However, if the lineage claimed by the recently proclaimed caliph was accepted, the combination of his unexpected triumph and attractive doctrine, and the fact that finally a branch of Shī'ī *imāms* had been capable of implementing a caliphate at the start of the fourth century of the Hegira, prompted the thought that perhaps the world was in fact entering the antechamber that heralded the Last Days, in which the family of the Prophet would at last perform the role they deserved.

Furthermore, it was an especially propitious moment. With many Muslim populations tired of heavy taxation, the arbitrary use of power and the scant religious devotion shown by those who wielded that power, they were highly receptive to the Fāṭimids' message, which was ideally suited to the dawn of the tenth century (fourth AH). In Baghdad, the 'Abbāsíd caliphs were en route to becoming two-dimensional figureheads at the hands of the factions that governed their central bureaucracy and their army. A year before the Fāṭimid triumph in Ifrīqiya, al-Muqtadir had been chosen as caliph amid a growing political and social crisis that was summed up in the celebrated verdict of a

[4] F. Daftary, *The Ismā'īlīs. Their History and Doctrines*, 2nd ed., 2007, pp. 99–106.

contemporary author, who accused the caliph of having spent 7 million dinars on absurd expenses. The major decline of the caliphal institution in Baghdad heightened the Fāṭimid hopes, as it became increasingly clear that the conquest of Ifrīqiya was just the opening episode of a plan intended to establish absolute hegemony across the whole Islamic world (*dār al-Islām*): in 914 (301 AH) a Fāṭimid force attacked Egypt. The campaign failed, but it was the first of a series of military expeditions that eventually achieved their aim five decades later.

In al-Andalus, news of the establishment of the Fāṭimid caliphate in a region like Ifrīqiya, with which there were many commercial and scholarly ties, gave rise to considerable commotion. At the height of 910, the reign of the aged Umayyad emir ʿAbd Allāh (d. 912/300 AH) was coming to its end, and despite the fact that under his mandate the dynasty had managed to survive in Córdoba, the greater part of al-Andalus was in the hands of rebels who barely acknowledged his authority. The most powerful and conspicuous of these rebels was ʿUmar b. Hafṣūn, a descendant of an ancient aristocratic Visigoth family that had converted to Islam. Lord of the fortress of Bobastro, to the north of today's province of Málaga, ʿUmar b. Hafṣūn had sustained a harsh struggle against the Umayyad emir for several decades, and he made no secret of the fact that that his final goal was to eliminate the dynasty. Now, he made the most of his considerable gifts for political opportunism by hastily acknowledging the authority of the new Fāṭimid caliph, by which he intended to land a definitive blow against Umayyad legitimacy. An embassy sent by Caliph al-Mahdī arrived in al-Andalus and held an interview with the rebel at Bobastro; just as in Ifrīqiya the Berbers' support had ensured the triumph of the Shīʿa, so too it might prove to be that Muslim descendants of indigenous converts, the so-called *muwalladūn*, would help put an end to the Umayyad rule over al-Andalus.[5]

Yet it is very possible that ʿUmar b. Hafṣūn's audacious move had the opposite effect to the one he sought. In al-Andalus at that time, there was a solid network of *ʿulamāʾ* who made their allegiance to Sunni orthodoxy a

[5] É. Lévi-Provençal, *España musulmana*, p. 240. This is mentioned in the *K. al-Munāẓarāt*, a work by Abū ʿAbd Allāh b. al-Haytham, who formed part of the embassy that the Fāṭimid caliph sent to ʿUmar b. Ḥafṣūn, ed. and trans. W. Madelung and P. Walker, p. 2 of the ed.; pp. 63–4 in the trans.

rallying call, and their adherence to the Mālikite school of legal thought was their most treasured sign of identity. They maintained regular contacts with the orthodox *'ulamā'* of Qayrawān, as many Andalusis travelled to this city 'in search of knowledge', to study law and other religious disciplines under the respected scholars living there.[6] Undoubtedly, these people were well aware that the authority exerted by the new Fāṭimid dynasty created a challenging situation for the majority of the orthodox religious establishment in Ifrīqiya. Although no evidence has yet come to light, it seems plausible that in al-Andalus there was an orthodox reaction to the threat posed by this new Shī'a-inspired caliphate, one that was led by the considerable numbers of Mālikite *'ulamā'*, who opted to lend their support to the time-worn cause of the Umayyads in face of the possibility of a further expansion of Fāṭimid rule.

As a result, the accession in al-Andalus of the successor of the Umayyad emir, 'Abd Allāh, his grandson 'Abd al-Raḥmān III, in autumn 912 (300 AH) was accompanied by a surge of renewed support for the dynasty, which came from sectors of the regular army, but also from individuals such as 'Abd Allāh b. Muḥammad b. 'Abd al-Khāliq al-Ghassānī, who was *qāḍī* of Elvira. The new emir spent the first two decades of his reign fighting to stamp out the seditions that beset the country, and in particular the rebellion in Bobastro. It was only after subjugating this enclave that in January 929 (316 AH) 'Abd al-Raḥmān III decided to adopt the title of caliph, a decision that was the culmination of a campaign to defend Sunni Islam in al-Andalus in opposition to the Fāṭimid threat. The letter in which 'Abd al-Raḥmān III declared his decision to proclaim himself 'Commander of the Faithful' stated that 'anyone who uses it [the title of caliph], other than ourselves, do so inappropriately, in doing so he trespasses and assumes a title he is unworthy of'. The allusion could not be clearer, above all from someone who thought that 'to continue neglecting the use of this title, one which we deserve, is to allow a right that is ours to fall into decline'.[7]

At the time this letter was written, Caliph al-Mahdī had been governing Ifrīqiya for almost two decades. His authority had extended as far as Sicily, while military expeditions had been sent to the rest of the Maghreb in 917

[6] L. Molina, 'Lugares de destino de los viajeros andalusíes', pp. 585–610.
[7] *Crónica Anónima*, ed. and trans. pp. 79 and 153.

(305 AH) and 922–3 (308–9 AH). While these campaigns had only achieved ephemeral demonstrations of submission from the myriad Berber tribal leaders who occupied these regions, they nonetheless brought the Fāṭimid threat to the very borders of al-Andalus. The situation in North Africa thus became an absolute priority for the court in Córdoba, where fear set in that the Fāṭimids' authority would end up taking root among the Berber tribes of the Maghreb as had happened with the Kutāma in Ifrīqiya. All of a sudden, this region, which until then had scarcely merited the attention of the Umayyad chroniclers, became an object of growing interest and these authors began to include information about it in their works. This in turn allows us a reconstruction of the complex social and political situation that was unfolding there.

Society and Power in Tenth-century North Africa

The Berber Tribes

The geographical setting in which the rivalry between the Umayyad and Fāṭimid caliphates would be settled was an immense territory that extended from the edges of Ifrīqiya to the Atlantic coast of the Far Maghreb, which today is occupied by the countries of Algeria and Morocco. It is a territory that lacks accessible natural routes of communication running between east and west. In the Roman period, crossing the distance between Carthage and the city of Iol Caesarea (Cherchell in modern Algeria) took twenty-five days. To reach there from Ceuta or Tangier took the same time, as it was a more rugged and mountainous region. It was only by travelling by sea that these places could be reached more quickly: sailing from Carthage to Tangier took barely two weeks.[8]

Given that it was hardly practical to travel by land along the coast, in the Muslim period an east–west communications axis was developed that opened up an inland route. It left Qayrawān following the Hodna corridor, with the Aurés mountain range to the south, and headed towards the strategic city of Ṭubna, which had been founded by the ʻAbbāsids, and was located close to Barika in modern-day Algeria. It then continued on to al-Māsila,

[8] See the calculations in orbis.stanford.edu.

Tāhart, Tlemcen, Fez and, finally, Sijilmāsa. It was this route that permitted the Islamisation of North Africa from the time of the Arab conquest onwards, and, as a result, various dynasties arose along its axis: the Rustamids in the city of Tāhart, the Midrārids in Sijilmāsa, and the Idrīsids in Fez and Tlemcen. None of these dynasties managed to create a state comparable to those governed by the Umayyads or the Fāṭimids, and in fact all of them ended up adapting in one way or another to the Berber tribal milieu.

The second key line of communication in the region followed the coast and comprised a series of ports, of varying importance, such as Hippo Regius, Skikda, Jijel, Algiers, Cherchell, Ténès, Arshghūl, Melilla and Ceuta. At this time, none of them was an important political centre. However, the major development that began to take shape over the ninth, and above all the tenth, century (third–fourth AH) was the emergence or development of routes on a north–south axis that served to connect these ports with the sub-Saharan territories. This had a considerable impact on the Maghreb al-aqṣā and led to the expansion of cities such as Awdaghost, Tadhmakka and Sijilmāsa, as well as the ports of Tangier and Ceuta.[9] Thanks to the opening up of these routes to inland regions, African luxury products such as ivory, gold and slaves began to make their way north, which explains the Fāṭimids' and Umayyads' strategic interest in maintaining control over these territories.

The political fragmentation of North Africa was also a by-product of the region's social fabric, which was defined by the predominance of Berber tribes who had disparate control over the territories they had settled in. Andalusi authors highlighted their alien social structure, as part of their criticism of the Umayyad caliphs' committed foreign policy of seeking alliances with these tribes. One Andalusi chronicler called Ibn Mas'ūd reproached Caliph 'Abd al-Raḥmān III with having oppressed his subjects with 'an insupportable burden of unacceptable expenditure', caused by his dealings with 'ignorant Berbers, akin to the ostriches of the desert and lions of the bush, and who seemed barely akin to the peoples of al-Andalus, whose prosperity they envied'.[10] During the time of al-Ḥakam II, the poet Muḥammad b. Shujayṣ referred with disdain to the other side of the straits (*al-'idwa*) as a place where

[9] D. Valérian, 'Contrôle et domination politique de l'espace', pp. 135–43.
[10] Ibn Ḥayyān, *Muqtabis V*, ed. and trans. pp. 200–1.

there was no science or culture (*lā ʿilm wa lā adab*).[11] Ibn Ḥayyān included in his work deprecatory comments about the North African Berbers 'and their likely deceptions'.

Thus, there was in al-Andalus a clear sense that the inhabitants of the Maghreb lived in a social environment that was wholly distinct from that of the Umayyad caliphate. Berbers lived in a genuinely tribal society, that had nothing to do with that of al-Andalus, and their leaders operated in a complex social context in which alliances and enmities tended to be volatile, and therefore, in the eyes of an Andalusi, barely trustworthy. Obviously, things tended to be more complex. Trapped by the obligation to demonstrate loyalty either to the Fāṭimids or to the Umayyads, Berber tribal chieftains faced highly complex situations, given they had to explain their decisions to their kinsmen, as it is certain that supporting one caliph or other, one creed or another, gave rise to extensive internal controversies.

One of the North African tribes that played the most prominent role in the events of this period was the Maghrāwa, who were attached to the Zanāta branch of the Berber populations. They were a historic semi-nomadic confederation dominated by various powerful clans. One of them was the Banū Warzamār, from which the Banū Khazar family emerged. They had served as leaders of the tribe from the time of the Arab conquest, if not before. The founding member of this lineage was Khazar b. Ḥafṣ b. Ṣūlāt, whose father and grandfather had also been tribal leaders. By the mid-eighth century (second AH) Khazar had extended the Maghrāwa's hold over a significant part of the central Maghreb. His authority was recognised by other tribes and he took control of the enclaves that provided access to the principal communication routes. His descendants, the Banū Khazar, maintained this domination for a century and a half, but the proclamation of the Fāṭimid caliphate in Ifrīqiya upset the political balance that underpinned their tribe's control over the region. Muḥammad b. Khazar, a great-grandson of the family's legendary eponym, stood up to the new caliphs, who had won the support of the Ṣinhāja Berbers, arch-enemies of the Zanāta, the main branch to which the Maghrāwa belonged. Muḥammad b. Khazar staged a fierce resistance; his ambushes inflicted resounding defeats on the Fāṭimid forces, and he was capable of withdrawing to regions out of

[11] Ibn Ḥayyān, *Muqtabis VII*, ed. p. 160; trans. p. 200.

reach of the enemy's incursions if required.[12] It comes as no surprise that when 'Abd al-Raḥmān III decided to counter Fāṭimid influence in North Africa, Muḥammad b. Khazar became his natural ally. Recognised as head of the Zanāta Berbers (*'aẓīm 'umarā' Zanāta*), Muḥammad b. Khazar began to receive frequent embassies from Córdoba, as well as gifts that cemented the bonds between both rulers; the Berber leader responded by offering his submission.[13]

The result of these diplomatic contacts was an exchange of correspondence between the caliph and the tribal leader, which records detailed information about the latter's tribe and its movements. In one communication, for example, Muḥammad b. Khazar informed the Umayyad caliph of the war waged by the Maghrāwa against the Fāṭimids across an extensive region of what is today central Algeria. One of the 'fronts' of this war was in the region of the Zāb, an area around the city of Ṭubna. One hundred kilometres to the west, a brother of Muḥammad b. Khazar was also at war with supporters of the Fāṭimid caliph – who is discussed in more detail below – in the region around al-Masīla (today M'Sila). Finally, one of his sons followed suit in the coastal region, as he sought to take control of places such as Tenés or Chelif, some four hundred kilometres north of Ṭubna.

Such a wide range of operations confirm that the Maghrāwa tribe acted in a co-ordinated manner in distant locations across a very large expanse of land, which lacked a clear territorial structure but enabled the movements of this semi-nomadic tribe. In a letter sent to the Umayyad caliph in 931–2 (319 AH), Muḥammad b. Khazar recounts how the Maghrāwa had left the land (*balad*) of al-Ghūṭ and moved to a location called Madīnat al-'Alawiyyīn o T.sfā, one day away from Tlemcen.[14] Although we do not know exactly where the land of al-Ghūṭ was, it is clear that the journey had been long. Muḥammad b. Khazar stated that 'we used to be far from your lands', separated by long distances and

[12] T. Lewicki, *Encyclopaedia of Islam*, 2nd ed. s.v. *Maghrāwa*.

[13] One of the bonds invoked was the fact that one of the Berber leader's ancestors had been converted to Islam by the caliph 'Uthmān, who belonged to the Umayyad lineage, Ibn Ḥayyān, *Muqtabis V*, ed. and trans. pp. 169–70, also 177 and 221, where in a letter the caliph declared that 'we and our caliphal ancestors ... paid you a favour at the outset, whereby you were introduced to Islam and received grace, coming to adopt our obedience and loyalty in the broad way of truth'.

[14] Ibn Ḥayyān, *Muqtabis V*, ed. and trans. pp. 170–2 and 201–5.

deserts, but now they were close to 'the gates of al-Andalus'. The whole tribe had moved from an inland zone towards one close to the coast.

The same letter also explains that the decision regarding this movement had been made 'unanimously', which indicates a form of government in which the tribal leader, Muḥammad b. Khazar, listened to the opinions of his kinsmen. Once the decision had been taken, the move involved all the groups that made up the whole tribe, which included the 'family, sons, companions, mercenaries, servants, clients, loyalists and all classes of subjects, as we move with the whole tribe and our people, without leaving behind a single man of distinction among our supporters and the leading horsemen of our clan'. Therefore, the tribe combined an amalgam of people of various social and political ranks, ranging from the leader's close family members to slaves and clients, from the upper echelons of tribal society to the lowest strata, which demonstrates that it was not a homogeneous social group.[15] However, the Maghrāwa's move had not been as unanimous a decision as Muḥammad b. Khazar claimed. In the same letter, the leader acknowledges that his brother Fulful had separated from the others on the pretext of looking for 'fertile pasture for livestock', although in reality he had decided to join the ranks of the Fāṭimids 'with his sons and a throng of followers and supporters, who accompanied him in his error'. In other words, there had been a disagreement over Muḥammad b. Khazar's policy of maintaining an alliance with the Umayyads, which had led to a political division within the tribal ranks that had broken up under his brother's rival leadership. Such political division undermined the tribal leader's authority, as the tribe's 'segmentation' was considered to be the result of weak leadership. A strong leader would, in contrast, have been capable of ensuring unanimity for his decisions and maintaining the group's cohesion.

Social differences and the existence of tribal chiefdoms – although they were undermined by continual rivalries – provide an explanation for why

[15] Ibn Ḥayyān, *Muqtabis V*, pp. 202–3: 'family (*al-ahl*), children (*al-wuld*), companions (*al-aṣḥāb*), mercenaries (*al-ḥasham*), servants (*al-'abīd*), clients (*al-mawālī*), loyalists (*ahl wilāyati-nā*) and all types of subject (*ṣunūf ra'yyati-nā wa ḍurūb ahl ṭā'ti-nā*), nobility and people (*al-khāṣṣa wa l-'āmma*), as we travel with the whole tribe and our own [family] (*bi-qabīlati-nā wa jamā'ti min qibal-nā*), without leaving behind a single noteworthy man of our supporters (*ḥumā anṣāri-nā*) and cavalrymen (*jamā' fursāti-nā*), the principal ones of our clan (*wujūh 'ashīrati-nā*)'.

medieval Berber tribes were able to accommodate forms of centralised government with such ease. This process is clearly reflected in the case of the Ṣinhāja Berber tribe, the major rivals of the Zanāta in the central Maghreb during this period. In this case, we can also document the emergence of a dominant family within a clan, that of the Talkāta, whose best-known representative at this time was Zīrī b. Manād. Having become a distinguished tribal leader, Zīrī led a group that undertook frequent attacks on their enemies, the Zanāta, 'sacking, taking captives and booty, which he always shared out amongst his companions never keeping anything for himself'. When the Fāṭimids arrived in Ifrīqiya, Zīrī and the Ṣinhāja tribe became their allies, on the basis of claims of having supposedly maintained a long-term client relationship with the family of 'Alī b. Abī Ṭālib.[16] After receiving extensive favours from the new caliphs, Zīrī founded a city called Ashīr (in the commune of Kef Lakhdar, in modern-day Algeria), whose construction was assisted by an architect sent by the Fāṭimid caliph, who also supplied builders, carpenters, iron and other materials. The remains excavated in this site reveal a palace complex with a large number of rooms surrounding a central courtyard and a reception hall.[17] It is, therefore, clear that tribal leaders could easily adopt and imitate the forms used by the Fāṭimid and Umayyad caliphs at the palace complexes of Mahdiyya and Madīnat al-Zahrā' to display their power.

In this social milieu, marked by strong forms of hereditary leadership and complex hierarchies beset by rivalries and centrifugal tendencies, the strategy pursued by both Fāṭimids and Umayyads consisted of winning support from tribal chieftains, and from those who formed their kin and their political allies. To achieve this aim, a broad range of embassies had to be deployed in order to establish long-lasting ties that sought to gather the broadest possible support within the tribal group as a whole. Umayyad embassies always brought gifts that were not only for the tribe's leader, but also for members of his family and political supporters. These gifts consisted of luxury objects made in the caliphal workshops, which these people did not have easy access to, and consisted of caskets, swords, clothes, saddles, textiles, ivory pyxides, perfumes and even toothpicks. These presents provided a clear contrast with

[16] L. Golvin, *Le Magreb Central à l'époque des Zirides*, pp. 23–8.
[17] L. Golvin, 'Le palais de Zīrī ā Achîr (Dixième siècle J.C.)', pp. 47–76.

the camels, gazelles, ostriches and dromedaries that a Berber tribal leader might send as a reciprocal gift.[18]

As part of this diplomacy, in which presents served to strengthen ties and alliances, great care was devoted to ensuring that the quality and quantity of these gifts were chosen in proportion to the rank of the members of the tribe. Umayyad diplomacy was all too aware that conflicts could arise from overlooking tribal hierarchies, and such errors could cause offence and undermine the authority of the leader they were trying to forge an alliance with. In a list of gifts sent by al-Ḥakam II to eight senior figures of the Kutāma tribe established in the Rif, a clear difference was drawn between the sums of money, quality of textiles, horse breeds and type of weapons that were received by the leader (*shaykh*), Aḥmad b. ʿĪsā, his brother and his nephew, and those received by lower-ranking members of the tribe, who nonetheless played a relevant role.[19]

As they adapted to these circumstances, the political strategy pursued by the Fāṭimids and the Umayyads in the Maghreb never sought any form of effective territorial control over this extensive region, but rather an acknowledgement of their authority from the tribes and their leaders. In one of the letters sent to ʿAbd al-Raḥmān III, the leader of the Maghrāwa, Muḥammad b. Khazar, stated that he had rejected an offer from the Fāṭimid caliph to submit to him. In this offer the Fāṭimid caliph had stated 'that he did not want my gold, or silver, nor did he want to impose a sacrifice upon me, but rather that I add his name in the headings of my documents and in the invocation of the sermons given from the minbars, that I mint coins with his name, and send him one of my sons or brothers, so that people would spread the rumour that I submitted in obedience to him'.[20] In his dealings with another tribal leader, Mūsā b. Abī l-ʿĀfiya, head of the Miknāsa tribe that lived in the region around Tlemcen, ʿAbd al-Raḥmān III sought exactly the same as his rival, when he stated that he did 'not want from you, nor from your loyal allies, defenders of the dynasty (*anṣār al-dawla*), any tribute, nor advantage, nor cities'; rather, the caliph wanted 'wherever you extend [your territory] and whatever God bestows on you, to be yours, your sons' and descendants', in fief of the Emir

[18] Ibn Ḥayyān, *Muqtabis V*, ed. and trans. pp. 178, 179, 208, 216, 238, 289 and pp. 172, 174, 176 and 178.
[19] Ibn Ḥayyān, *Muqtabis VII*, ed. pp. 131–3; trans. pp. 166–8. On the content of this gift, see below.
[20] Ibn Ḥayyān, *Muqtabis V*, ed. and trans. p. 238.

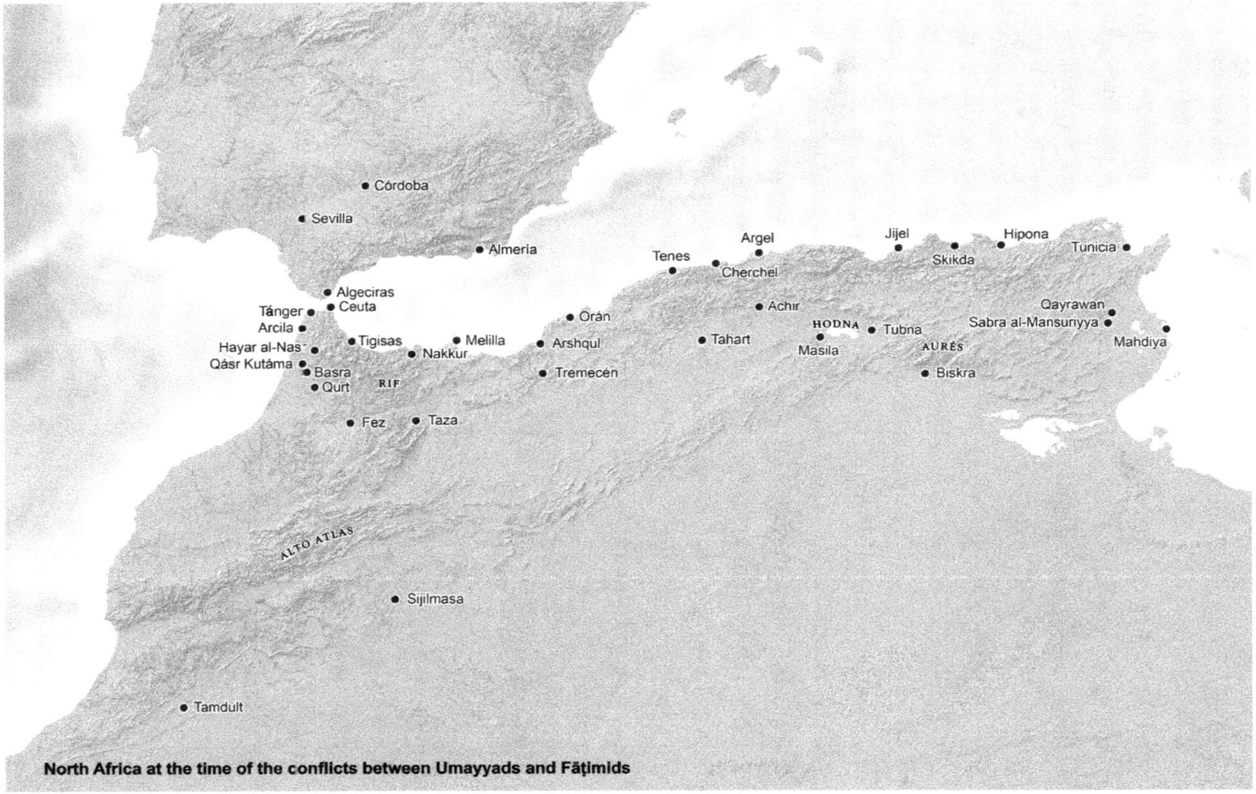

Figure 3 North Africa at the time of the conflicts between Umayyads and Fāṭimids

of the Believers (*iqṭāʿ min amīr al-Muʾminīn*), as a display of affection and recompense for your affection, a relationship that the caliph will not alter for you, nor your sons, nor your descendants, save to improve it and ennoble you still more'.[21]

It was thus a strategy that aimed to win the support of the tribal leaders by offering guarantees that their group was going to be neither subjugated nor taxed. What was sought was the recognition of caliphal sovereignty, through signs such as the invocation of the caliph's name in prayers or official documents, the recognition that a leader's rule over the tribe was a concession (*iqṭāʿ*) from the caliph, the hand-over of hostages or the issue of coins in the caliph's name.[22] All of this was intended to underscore the caliph's own authority and undermine that of their enemy. The compensation, reflected in the generous distribution of gifts, consisted of helping to reinforce the leadership of the tribal leader in question, so that support was given to ensure his authority became a hereditary form of power, as well as to neutralise possible enemies within or beyond the tribe. Such support for tribal leadership was especially important at a time in which the hostility declared between the two caliphates gave rise to internal fragmentation and stirred up pre-existing intertribal conflicts.

The Arab Families

A further element was added to this already complex panorama: the Maghreb was also home to a range of peoples who had arrived from the east and harboured a wide variety of ideological and political views. This was the case, for example, with the Rustamids in the city of Tāhart, a family of Persian origin and khārijite persuasion that had managed to found a dynasty immersed within the Berber tribal context. Despite the fact that their rule could not

[21] Ibn Ḥayyān, *Muqtabis V*, ed. and trans. p. 210.

[22] We have examples of coins issued on behalf of the Fāṭimids by al-Khayr b. Muḥammad b. Khazar around 330 H, T. Ibrahim, 'Consideraciones sobre el conflicto omeya-fatimí', pp. 295–302. Mention is also made of the minting of coins in the justification given by Mūsā b. Abī l-ʿĀfiya to the Umayyad caliph for having broken off all ties with the Fāṭimid caliph, Ibn Ḥayyān, *Muqtabis V*, ed. and trans. p. 209. Likewise, al-Ḥakam II's letter to the *kūras* after the victory against Ḥasan b. Qannūn in 974 (363 AH) mentions 'that now they cast [coins] in the mints with [the caliph's] name and in accordance to his pattern (*ʿiyār*)', Ibn Ḥayyān, *Muqtabis VII*, ed. p. 182; trans. p. 221.

resist the Fāṭimid tide, which overran their territory in 909 (296 AH), khārijite doctrines continued to exert a lasting presence in the region.

The most important Arab lineage to have become established in the Maghreb al-aqṣā was that of the descendants of Idrīs b. ʿAbd Allāh, another fugitive who had arrived in this region in 786 (170 AH) having failed to stage a rebellion against the ʿAbbāsíds. Just as the Fāṭimids did, the Idrīsids claimed to be descendants of Alī b. Abī Ṭālib, although through a different branch of the family. Idrīs b. ʿAbd Allāh's flight west took place prior to the development of the doctrine that shaped the Shīʿī community, whereby their descendants never became advocates of this sect, and in fact always maintained a very low profile when it came to their doctrines. Established in the most western part of the Islamic world, the descendants of this fugitive, known as Idrīsids, founded the city of Fez and their rule, which began at the end of the eighth and the start of the ninth century (second century AH), initially seemed capable of unifying the northern and southern territories of modern-day Morocco. However, as time went by they ended up succumbing to the region's dominant tribal milieu. Idrīs b. ʿAbd Allāh's descendants scattered across a mosaic of small domains. Although they upheld the importance of their lineage by stressing their common descent from the family of the Prophet, they were spread over a vast region and at times conflict broke out between them. In the words of one member of this family, their ancestor had set himself up among the Berbers in the role of 'arbitrator', a role that his descendants continued to play, while renouncing the creation of any form of state (*sulṭān*) over the Berbers, thus renouncing the ability 'to govern them or curb their aggression'.[23]

The arrival of the Fāṭimids was a salutary lesson for the Idrīsids of the Maghreb. Many of them embraced their cause out of family solidarity, given their shared lineage down from ʿAlī b. Abī Ṭālib. The support of these distant relatives permitted the Fāṭimid caliph to proclaim that his authority and that of the family of the Prophet was recognised across much of the region. In fact, one of the greatest difficulties faced by the Umayyad caliphs' North African policy was the Idrīsids' natural inclination to support the Fāṭimids,

[23] In the words of an Umayyad chronicler, the Idrīsids 'had settled in these remote parts, and invited the Berber inhabitants to take their side with flattery and intermarriage with them, thereby they had descendants and could reign ... until they faced internal dissent and the [dynasty] broke up', Ibn Ḥayyān, *Muqtabis V*, ed. and trans. pp. 194 and 173.

which greatly hindered forging alliances with them. However, on occasions this aim was achieved. For example, the Idrīsid ruler of the city of Arshghūl (today Rechgoun in Algeria), called Idrīs b. Ibrāhīm, was disposed to offer his loyalty to the Umayyads, despite the opposition of other members of his family, who reproached him for having ceased to be 'one of our own, given that he had deserted their cause (*da'wa*) for that of the opposition, turning from the family of 'Alī b. Abī Ṭālib to its enemies'. The argument used by the Umayyad caliph to counter this criticism consisted of invoking a shared lineage from Quraysh, as both families had distant Arab ancestors, whereby the Idrīsids and Umayyads were both descendants of 'Abd Manāf.[24] However, the Idrīsid's dependence on the complex tribal politics of the region, their continual internal quarrels and the family's widespread geographical dispersal across numerous enclaves of the Maghreb al-aqṣā greatly hindered these efforts and ended up forcing the Umayyad caliphs to invest a considerable quantity of resources to quell them, as will be seen below.

Despite not being able to lay claim to the Idrīsids' formidable lineage, another Arab family, known as the Banū al-Andalusī, also settled in the region, and went on to play a very important role in the events that unfolded in this period. Their ancestor was 'Abd al-Ḥamīd al-Judhāmī, an Arab who had arrived in al-Andalus in the mid-eighth century enrolled in the Syrian army. As a member of the *jund* of Damascus, he had originally settled in the circumscription of Elvira, in a village near Alcalá la Real (*Qal'at Yaḥṣub*), in what is today the province of Jaén. A century later, one of his great-grandsons, called Ḥamdūn, decided to leave al-Andalus and move to North Africa, perhaps prompted by a desire to escape the competitive environment he faced in the inner circle of his family. Having crossed the Straits of Gibraltar, he established a farmhouse near the city of Béjaïa (in modern Algeria), where his family came to be known as the Banū al-Andalusī.

One of his sons was called Tha'laba b. Ḥamdūn. He must have been a very pious man, as in 900 (287 AH) he decided to make the pilgrimage to Mecca. He began his journey from the region of Béjaïa, but as he made his way across the country of the Kutāma in Ifrīqiya he was caught up in the hubbub

[24] Ibn Ḥayyān, *Muqtabis V*, ed. and trans. pp. 174–5. On Arshqūl, al-Bakrī, ed. van Leuven and Farré, p. 747; trans. De Slane pp. 181–2.

stirred up by the Fāṭimid preaching. After having married there, he decided to embrace the cause. He changed his name of Tha'laba to 'Alī, and once the revolution had triumphed he became one of Caliph al-Mahdī's main supporters. Of particular note among the tasks he was commissioned to oversee was the building of the city of al-Masīla, where 'Alī b. Ḥamdūn went to live with his wife and children around the year 929 (317 AH). By founding this city, the Fāṭimid caliph sought to create a bastion against the Maghrāwa along the east–west route that traversed the region: indeed, in the letter Muḥammad b. Khazar wrote to the caliph of al-Andalus listing his conflicts with the Fāṭimids, he mentions this 'Alī b. Ḥamdūn, who had settled in al-Masīla, as one of his main enemies.[25]

'Alī b. Ḥamdūn was always a faithful servant of the Fāṭimid cause. Following the death of Caliph al-Mahdī in 934 (322 AH), his successor, al-Qā'im, had to face a formidable revolt supported by a number of Berber tribes, who were led by a khārijite leader called Abū Yazīd. Once the question of the leadership of the Muslim community had been opened up by the Fāṭimids, people like Abū Yazīd managed to gather widespread support among some Berbers by advocating the idea that the leader of the community should be the best Muslim, independent of his origin or family. This doctrine radically confronted the Fāṭimids' genealogical claims, which were based on the idea that leadership of the community was reserved for the descendants of 'Alī b. Abī Ṭālib. Although Abū Yazīd's rebellion nearly managed to put an end to the newly-founded Fāṭimid dynasty, it was eventually defeated in 947 (336 AH). During these difficult times, 'Alī b. Ḥamdūn al-Andalusī was one of the caliph's main supporters. After his death, in the midst of the revolt in 945 (334 AH), 'Alī was succeeded as governor of al-Masīla by his son Ja'far, born to a woman from the Berber Kutāma tribe called Maymūna bt. 'Alāham al-Jīlī. Half-Arab and half-Berber, Ja'far became one of the most influential individuals in the Fāṭimid caliphal court during this period. He and his brother Yaḥyā will crop up time and again over the pages that follow. Here, I want to underline the importance of this Arab family settled in the Maghreb, who had been

[25] Ibn Ḥayyān, *Muqtabis* VII, ed. pp. 32–4; trans. pp. 54–5. On this family see M. Canard, 'Une famille de partisans puis adversaires des Fāṭimides en Afrique du Nord', pp. 33–49, which offers a portrayal of this family, although he does not use the information provided by Ibn Ḥayyān that is drawn on here.

assimilated into the tribal and Berber milieu, yet they remained wholly aware of their genealogical origins and their position of pre-eminence thanks to their control over a strategic enclave, the city of al-Masīla.

In general terms, this was the complex social and political panorama that provided the setting for the confrontation between the Umayyads and Fāṭimids in North Africa. On the one hand, the Berber region was highly fragmented, dominated by powerful tribal leaders and immersed in frequent conflicts aimed at maintaining a grip on enclaves that permitted control over the routes traversed by semi-nomad groups. On the other hand, people from the East had been settling in the Maghreb since the eighth century (second AH) and their ideas had likewise taken root; these people maintained their distinctive identity, albeit subsumed in the overarching and predominant tribal society. It is against this background that the tenacious confrontation between the two caliphates arose. Some Andalusi authors, who wrote shortly after these events, thought that the chain of events that occurred during this time would prove to be of seminal importance for the destiny of the caliphate of Córdoba. And, given its results, there can be little doubt that they were right.

The Fāṭimids against the Umayyads

The Umayyads' direct engagement in North Africa began when ʿAbd al-Raḥmān III decided to occupy Ceuta in the spring of 931 (319 AH), barely two years after having proclaimed himself caliph. Apparently, the city was captured following an invitation from its population, who were dissatisfied with the way they were ruled by a branch of the Idrīsids.[26] The appointment of a governor and the deployment of troops to the city, whose fortifications also underwent a major overhaul, permitted the caliph to establish a North African outpost, which was vital for confronting the Fāṭimid expansion.

The strategy pursued by ʿAbd al-Raḥmān III was a cautious one. While the Fāṭimid caliph chose to send military expeditions to the Maghreb – such as that led by his general Maysūr in 934 (322 AH) – which managed to defeat and subjugate the Berber tribes who had declared themselves Umayyad allies, the Cordoban policy was focused on the use of diplomacy to attract tribes who

[26] Ibn Ḥayyān, *Muqtabis V*, ed. and trans. pp. 191–3.

could counter the Fāṭimid supporters in the region.[27] However, this strategy was hindered by the region's social and political complexity, which gave rise to major tensions between various tribes; the Fāṭimid military expeditions and the Umayyad embassies only served to exacerbate this. Thus, once Maysūr's lengthy campaign was over and the Fāṭimid troops had withdrawn, messages began to reach Córdoba in which various North African leaders exchanged mutual accusations of disloyalty, while also declaring they had always abominated the Shīʿī faction, something that was not always the case. The formal petitions for military support submitted to ʿAbd al-Raḥmān III by different groups at war over tribal disputes required the caliph and his ambassadors to weave especially intricate strategies to prevent their allies from tearing one another to pieces, as well as dissuading them from expressing their discontent by transferring their obedience to the Fāṭimid party.

ʿAbd al-Raḥmān III's North African policy found unexpected support amid the khārijite rebellion led by Abū Yāzid, which placed the Fāṭimid caliphs in check for four years and allowed the Umayyad caliph to consolidate his alliances in the region. However, the end of this revolt in 947 (336 AH) and the rise to power of the new caliph, al-Muʿizz, in 953 (341 AH) led to a revival of the Fāṭimid offensive in the Maghreb, which once more thwarted the many alliances created through Umayyad diplomacy. This was demonstrated in all its crudity when the new caliph managed to receive the allegiance of the leader of the Zanāta Berbers, the aforementioned Muḥammad b. Khazar, who, along with all his tribe, joined the Fāṭimid ranks and handed over his children as hostages.[28] The same leader that two decades earlier had sent letters swearing eternal loyalty to the Umayyads then became one of the main military supporters of a new Fāṭimid campaign, which was mobilised in 958–9 (347–8 AH) under the command of the general Jahwar. This new expedition subjugated all of central and far Maghreb, with the sole exception of Ceuta and Tangier, which were then under the direct control of the Umayyads. Cities such as Sijilmāsa and Fez, which had resisted before, ended up capitulating in the face of this campaign. The Fāṭimid poet Ibn Hānī did not pass up the opportunity to

[27] For the events of these years, É. Lévi-Provençal, *Historia de la España musulmana*, pp. 313–21, is still a good summary.

[28] Idrīs ʿImād al-Dīn, *ʿUyūn al-akhbār*, trans. S. Jiwa, pp. 77–9.

demonstrate his skills as a panegyrist when he proclaimed that the Umayyads had had its endeavours foiled, 'like a comb in search of hair on a bald man's head'.[29]

The North African disasters of the final years of 'Abd al-Raḥmān III's reign had consequences for the supply of gold to al-Andalus. From 929 (317 AH), the caliph had been minting dinars with gold from the inland region of Africa, specifically the upper course of the Niger Valley, which was transported along trade routes that were being opened around that time. Over various years, these gold coins were minted in Córdoba with a certain regularity, but there were very significant lapses. One of these lapses began in 934–5 (323 AH), which coincided with the campaign that had been launched the previous year by the Fāṭimid *qā'id* Maysūr. The hiatus lasted until 941–2 (330 AH), and during these seven years no gold dinars were minted in al-Andalus. It is tempting to identify the renewed issue of coins with the restored Umayyad presence in the Maghreb following the revolt of Abū Yazīd, which began in 943 (332 AH) and lasted four years. Following a period marked by the irregular issue of dinars between 340 and 348 AH (951–9), the major Fāṭimid campaign led by Jahwar in 347 AH coincided once more with a further interruption to the minting of dinars, which this time went on for a decade until the time of al-Ḥakam II in 357 AH (967).[30]

The Umayyad rule in North Africa had been greatly weakened when al-Ḥakam II became caliph in 961 (350 AH). However, the situation gradually began to favour Umayyad interests as Caliph al-Mu'izz steadily focused his military efforts on Egypt, which was then subject to a serious internal crisis. Following various failed attempts, the troops of the Fāṭimid general, Jahwar, finally achieved their aim of occupying the land of the Nile and they made their triumphal entry into its capital, Fusṭāṭ, in the summer of 969 (358 AH). Thereby, the self-proclaimed descendants of 'Alī b. Abī Ṭālib and Fāṭima managed to gain power over a country of immense wealth, a nexus for the long-distance trade routes and one of the principal centres of Islamic legal and doctrinal thought. While in Baghdad the 'Abbāsid caliphate languished, with its sovereigns stripped of any political relevance, the Fāṭimids had again

[29] Yalaoui, 'Les relations ...', p. 24.
[30] The series of mintings in A. Canto, 'El dinar en al-Andalus en el siglo X', pp. 327–38.

demonstrated their unstoppable momentum. Many people began to think that, although the apocalyptic prophecies announced by the dynasty had not been fulfilled immediately, such an extraordinary success confirmed that the major changes augured by the Fāṭimid message would soon come to pass.

In the summer of 971 (361 AH) – the moment at which ʿĪsā al-Rāzī's text-fragment begins – two years had already passed since the Fāṭimid armies had taken over Egypt. Caliph al-Muʿizz was still ruling in Ifrīqiya, but it was no secret that he intended to move to the land of the Nile, and the meticulous preparations for his departure were already well under way. In fact, he departed at the start of August the following year (972/362 AH). A long convoy took the caliph, his family members, his court and his administration to Cairo (*al-Qāhira*), the recently founded city which would soon become one of the major metropolises of the medieval world. The Fāṭimid caliph departed with all his belongings, which included the coffins of his ancestors, clear proof that his was a one-way journey. In North Africa, in al-Andalus, and in general, across all the *dār al-islam*, from Caliph al-Ḥakam down to the humblest Muslim, everyone was asking the same question: what is going to happen now?

6

The Struggle against the Fāṭimid Caliphate: (II) The Conflict

An Episode of Betrayal

In the summer of 971 (360 AH), while the Fāṭimid court in Ifrīqiya was immersed in preparations for its imminent transfer to Egypt, an event took place that had a series of unexpected consequences. ʿĪsā al-Rāzī offers a highly detailed account of this incident and its repercussions, which in conjunction with information provided by other sources reveals what happened with a degree of detail rarely encountered in this period. The description given of this episode offers a number of insights into the conflict between the Fāṭimids and Umayyads, and, furthermore, elucidates the strategic decisions taken in al-Andalus with regard to the political situation in North Africa, decisions that would eventually prove to have been mistaken.[1]

[1] Ibn Ḥayyān, *Muqtabis VII*, ed. pp. 32–8; trans. pp. 54–9. Our author departs here from merely transcribing the *Annals* of ʿĪsā al-Rāzī and includes information from two sources written contemporaneously with the events: the *Akhbār al-Magrib* by Muḥammad b. Yūsuf b. ʿAbd Allāh al-Warrāq and *al-Taʾrīkh fī akhbār Ifrīqiya* by Abū Jaʿfar b. al-Jazzār. The first was born in 904/5 (292 AH) and died in c. 973 (363 AH). Having moved from Qayrawān to the court of al-Ḥakam II, he served there as 'memorialist of the news from the Maghreb' thanks to his prodigious memory. None of the works attributed to him has survived; they were all concerned with the history of North Africa or the genealogies of the Berbers, but fragments of them have been preserved in the works of Ibn Ḥayyān and al-Bakrī, R. Pocklington, *Biblioteca de al-Andalus*, vol. 7, s.v. al-Warrāq. Abū Jaʿfar b. al-Jazzār (d. 1004/395 AH) was a celebrated author who came from Qayrawān and was known, above all, for a renowned work on medicine, but he also wrote on history, in particular one chronicle entitled *K. akhbār al-dawla*, which was devoted to the deeds of the Fāṭimids. It is this one which Ibn Ḥayyān most probably drew on for his information on these events, H. R. Idris in *Encyclopaedia of Islam*, 2 s.v. Ibn al-Djazzār.

Once the Fāṭimid armies had concluded their takeover of Egypt, and the decision had been taken to transfer the government there, Caliph al-Mu'izz decided to nominate a governor of Ifrīqiya. He chose Zīrī b. Manād, the leader of the Ṣinhāja tribe and founder of the city of Ashīr, who was mentioned in the previous chapter. The choice of Zīrī dealt a hammer blow to the aspirations harboured by his great rival, Ja'far b. al-Andalusī, who had settled in al-Masīla, and whose family had always been firm and loyal supporters of the Fāṭimid caliphs. Ja'far was milk brother to Caliph al-Mu'izz and had grown up with him, whereby if someone had been well-placed to be appointed as governor of Ifrīqiya following the caliph's departure it was him. Furthermore, Ja'far was an Arab who had converted the city of al-Masīla into a small court where there was no lack of secretaries or renowned poets, such as the Andalusi Ibn Hānī (d. 973/362 AH), who, undoubtedly due to an excess of enthusiasm, went so far as to compare his patron's court with that of Baghdad. Caliph al-Mu'izz himself had often praised Ja'far in the past by pointing out that he ruled over a population consisting of 'the most savage, stupidest, and simplest people to have ever existed, but God had made them humble thanks to his [Ja'far's] policy, worthy of all praise'.

An astute political calculation may well have influenced the caliph's decision; he probably considered that, as governor, Zīrī b. Manād was less likely to enter any form of alliance with the Sunni Arabs from Qayrawān, who, as a rule, had been fairly unyielding regarding the hopes and expectations promised by the Fāṭimid credo. It is also possible that al-Mu'izz's inclinations were influenced by allegations that Ja'far was failing to submit all the fiscal resources he collected in his district back to the central treasury. Nor should it be ruled out that the caliph had ceased to fully trust his governor in al-Masīla, as it was rumoured that an Umayyad agent was trying to persuade him to betray the Fāṭimid cause. Were this the case, Ja'far would have been aware of the risks; one person who knew him well, the poet Ibn Hānī, reminded him that the Fāṭimid dynasty was very capable of bestowing 'either its pardon and kindness, or else the iron [blade] that severs heads along with the leather mat for them to fall onto'.[2]

2 *Vie de l'ustadh Jaudhar*, trans. M. Canard, pp. 187–8, 197–8, 216–17. M. Canard, 'Une famille de partisans puis adversaires des Fatimides en Afrique du Nord', p. 35. L. Golvin, 'Buluggīn fils

Nonetheless, the decision to leave control of Ifrīqiya in the hands of Zīrī b. Manād was also a risky bet. It upset the difficult balance of power that had prevailed in the Zāb, the strategic zone that permitted movements along the Maghreb's major routes. This was the region where Zīrī had founded the city of Ashīr around a hundred kilometres to the north-east of al-Masīla. The proximity between Ja'far b. al-Andalusī and Zīrī b. Manād's domains had led to an ongoing series of disputes. Whenever Zīrī b. Manād pursued nomad groups for pillaging his territory, he often crossed over into his neighbour's district, but was obliged to retreat, as the nomads claimed they were under Ja'far's protection (*dhimma*).[3] Eventually, these disputes came to a head, and Caliph al-Mu'izz had to arrange a meeting between Ja'far and Buluggīn, Zīrī's son, so they could reach an agreement. However, this mediation proved fruitless.[4]

The Fāṭimid caliph's decision to offer the governorship of Ifrīqiya to the Ṣinhāja leader also displeased this tribe's traditional enemies, the Zanāta Berbers, and in particular the Maghrāwa. For various years, their leaders, the Banū Khazar, following their desertion of the Umayyad ranks, had fulfilled their role as allies of the Fāṭimids, but they now saw that the caliph was 'rewarding' their obedience by naming their arch-enemy, Zīrī, as governor of Ifrīqiya. The preference given to their rivals, the Ṣinhāja, was intolerable for the Maghrāwa: they broke with the Fāṭimids and returned once more to the side of the caliph of al-Andalus.

In these circumstances, it was just a matter of time until those who stood to lose out from Caliph al-Mu'izz's appointment came to some form of agreement. Ja'far b. al-Andalusī and the Banū Khazar were soon united by their shared animosity towards their common enemy, Zīrī b. Manād, and their rejection of the idea that the Ṣinhāja tribal leader should become the region's governor following the Fāṭimid caliph's relocation of his court to Egypt. Despite being undertaken with considerable secrecy, this alliance was brought to the attention of the Fāṭimid caliph in somewhat bizarre circumstances. During one of the recurring skirmishes between them, Zīrī b. Manād defeated

de Zīrī, prince berbère', pp. 95–6; Yalaoui, 'Les relations entre Fatimides d'Ifriqiya et Omeyyades d'Espagne', p. 22.

[3] Ibn Ḥayyān, *Muqtabis VII*, ed. p. 37; trans. p. 57.

[4] *Vie de l'ustadh Jaudhar*, pp. 152–4.

the emir of the Maghrāwa, Muḥammad b. al-Khayr b. Khazar. On realising he had been vanquished, Muḥammad took the decision to commit suicide rather than undergo the humiliation of falling into the hands of his rival. This allowed Zīrī to pillage the enemy camp unopposed and to make an unexpected find: among the Maghrāwa leader's belongings he found a horse with a brand identifying it as from the Fāṭimid stables, as it was one that had been given to Jaʿfar b. al-Andalusī by Caliph al-Muʿizz. The disdain shown for the caliph's generosity by passing on his gift to a rebel Berber chief was an incomparable insult. Zīrī lost no time in sending the undeniable proof of this betrayal along with correspondence he had also found, which demonstrated that Jaʿfar was collaborating with the emir of the Maghrāwa, who was now an open supporter of the Umayyad caliph of al-Andalus.[5]

Al-Muʿizz was furious. He dismissed Jaʿfar from the government of al-Masīla and ordered him, along 'with his wives, sons and riches', to make his way to the city palace of Ṣabra al-Manṣūriyya, near Qayrawān, where he was to present himself immediately before him. Jaʿfar sensed the gravity of the situation. He gathered all his family and left the city, but instead of going to meet the caliph he travelled in the opposite direction and sought refuge with the Banū Khazar. By spring 971 (360 AH), there was no need to continue hiding his allegiances, and before long Jaʿfar b. al-Andalusī openly declared his submission to the Umayyad caliph of al-Andalus, al-Ḥakam II.

Zīrī b. Manād then acted impulsively. Having unmasked his enemy, he thought that he could put an end to him and the Banū Khazar once and for all. When summer came, he led a campaign against them, by launching an attack alongside the Moulouya River. However, this time luck was not on his side: during the battle his horse fell and he died as a result. Just eight days later, on 15 July 971, this news reached Córdoba, where it caused great joy. Caliph al-Muʿizz's triumphal transfer to Egypt, which he had been planning for a considerable time, had been tarnished by a chain of dramatic and unexpected events: the man who was to be his governor in Ifrīqiya had been killed in an attack against a once-loyal servant of the dynasty, who in turn had become

[5] This detail is interesting as it reveals how Berber tribal leaders travelled with an archive of their correspondence. It will be recalled that the grandfather of this Muḥammad had exchanged letters with the caliph of al-Andalus. This reference supports the idea of an archival culture that was widespread at this period, M. Rustow, *The Lost Archive*, p. 12.

a traitor, switched sides, and taken his weapons and belongings over to the Umayyad side, accompanied by the leader of one of the main Berber tribes of central Maghreb, who had likewise renewed his obedience to the caliph of Córdoba. Things could not have gone worse for the Fāṭimids.[6]

Jaʿfar b. al-Andalusī was all too aware that there was no turning back; should a Fāṭimid agent lay hands on him, he and his family would be killed. However, it was not his intention to become a fugitive roving the territories of the Maghreb alongside his new allies, the Banū Khazar. Fearful 'of the evil and deceitful ways of the Zanāta', he decided to negotiate with the Caliph al-Ḥakam, and ask to be granted asylum in Córdoba. Therefore, he sent his secretary (*kātib*), ʿAlī al-Baghdādī, to the capital bearing a letter that formally declared his submission.[7] From this moment on, events gathered pace. Shortly afterwards his brother, Yaḥyā, reached al-Andalus accompanied by some members of the Banū Khazar family; he arrived bearing the head of Zīrī b. Manād under his arm, and swore an oath of loyalty (*bayʿa*) to the Umayyad caliph on 3 August 971 (7 *Shawwāl*). This convinced Jaʿfar b. al-Andalusī that the Umayyad caliphate's gates were wide open. On 30 August (5 *Dhū l-qaʿda*), with no prior warning, he disembarked at the port of Bezmiliana (Málaga), where he was welcomed and taken to Córdoba with all imaginable honours and pomp.[8]

The decision to stage a solemn and extravagant reception for Jaʿfar b. al-Andalusī, which will be discussed in more detail below, was taken on the basis that a resounding triumph had been achieved. Both al-Ḥakam and his court must have thought that the will of God had once more favoured them in North Africa: having barely lifted a finger, the Fāṭimids had lost the support of a prominent Arab family, the governor of the Maghreb was dead, and the Umayyad alliance with the Banū Khazar was functioning again as in the good old days. It looked as if everything was going to work out perfectly and the

[6] Ibn Ḥayyān, *Muqtabis VII*, ed. pp. 26–7; trans. p. 50. An abbreviated version of these events in Ibn-Khaldūn, *K. al-ʿIbār*, trans. II, pp. 7–9.

[7] It is possible that this secretary is the same one who was satirised by the poet Ibn Hānī, who called him Wahrānī and reproached him for 'having renounced two fidelities: that of the just caliph and the one of the immaculate faith', M. Yalaoui, 'Les relations entre Fatimides d'Ifriqiya et Omeyyades d'Espagne', p. 18.

[8] For his description of the details of the arrival of the Banū al-Andalusī in al-Andalus, Ibn Ḥayyān returns to the account given by ʿĪsā al-Rāzī, *Muqtabis VII*, ed. pp. 39ff; trans. pp. 59ff.

welcome given to Ja'far and his family provided an opportunity for a grand celebration of this major triumph.

Appearances were deceptive. Despite its sensational effect, the flight of the Banū al-Andalusī from the central Maghreb did not result in many practical outcomes that served the Umayyad's interests. The deceased Zīrī b. Manād was succeeded by his son, Buluggīn, whose appointment as governor of Ifrīqiya was confirmed by Caliph al-Mu'izz. The caliph's plans for moving to Egypt were not altered in the slightest, and he departed in August the following year (972/361 AH). His departure left Buluggīn ideally placed to govern: his principal rival in the Zāb region, Ja'far b. al-Andalusī, had gone, and if that was not enough, the caliph's withdrawal for Egypt allowed him to take up residence in his palace and strengthen his power over territories that the Fāṭimids progressively lost interest in. As for the Maghrāwa, they were defeated by Buluggīn, who expelled them from various enclaves that they controlled in central Maghreb. Thereby, they ceased to play a relevant role in the region for many years to come; they moved to regions of what is today Morocco, where the Banū Khazar family split into various branches. The end of the confrontation in Ifrīqiya and central Maghreb only had one winner, and this was none other than Buluggīn b. Zīrī, a sworn enemy of the Umayyads. Meanwhile, the problems faced by al-Ḥakam II in North Africa had barely begun.

Fāṭimid Infiltrators in al-Andalus

Ja'far b. al-Andalusī's desertion convinced al-Ḥakam II that it was possible to take advantage of the Fāṭimid caliph's relocation to Egypt to bring a large number of North African tribal chieftains under Umayyad influence. In this context, the Banū al-Andalusī family became a highly-esteemed trophy. Being able to show allies and strangers that one of the Fāṭimids' firmest supporters had deserted their ranks and embraced the sovereignty of the Umayyads was an opportunity that was too good to be missed. As a result, there was no skimping when it came to accommodating the Banū al-Andalusī in the best conditions possible. As has been discussed, Ja'far b. al-Andalusī and his brother, Yaḥyā, received astronomical monthly pensions and payments in kind, which must have prompted all sorts of comments in the Umayyad court.[9]

[9] On these figures and the way they were interpreted see above p. 91.

In accordance with this concern to promote Umayyad sovereignty, the pomp staged to welcome the Banū al-Andalusī in Córdoba was intended as a propagandistic spectacle addressed to a wide public. For al-Ḥakam II this was of great importance. One of the arguments used by the Fāṭimids was that Umayyad legitimacy was in decline, due to the high number of people who abandoned their country to join the side of the Shīʿites. This accusation was by no means far-fetched.[10] At the start of al-Ḥakam II's reign, in particular at some point between the years 961 and 964 (353 AH), an individual called Abū l-Khayr had openly declared across al-Andalus that the Umayyad caliphate was illegitimate; he advocated support for al-Muʿizz, whose military victories he had also boasted about. Abū l-Khayr was accused of having been preparing to raise an army of 5,000 horsemen in order to capture Madīnat al-Zahrā' in the name of the Fāṭimid caliph. No fewer than eighteen witnesses, some of them traders from the souk, were cross-examined during a celebrated trial that ended with Abū l-Khayr being found guilty of heresy (*zandaqa*) and sentenced to death by crucifixion.[11]

The episode of Abū l-Khayr reveals how fear that Fāṭimid agents might be operating in al-Andalus was wholly justified. In addition, a man called ʿAbd al-Malik b. Ṣamīt, very possibly a descendant of a prestigious Arab family, had also deserted the Umayyad ranks to join the Fāṭimids. He was located on the coast of Ifrīqiya by an Andalusi trader, called Muḥammad b. Sulaymān, who arranged for the admiral of the Umayyad navy, ʿAbd al-Raḥmān b. Rumāḥis, to send a boat with experienced sailors to capture the deserter and his son.[12] Both were transferred to Córdoba, and placed in the prison at Madīnat al-Zahrā', while his captors were splendidly recompensed by the caliph: the

[10] J. Aguadé, 'Some Remarks about Sectarian Movements in al-Andalus', p. 67, quoting the work by al-Qāḍi al-Nuʿmān.

[11] F. Dachraoui, 'Tentative d'infiltration šīʿite en Espagne musulmane sous le régne d'al-Ḥakam II', *al-Andalus*, 1958, XXIII, pp. 97–106; M. I. Fierro, *La heterodoxia en al-Andalus durante el período omeya*, Madrid, 1987, pp. 149–55, considers that Abū l-Khayr was a freethinker whose threat was exaggerated and who, once under arrest, was made to profess shīʿite doctrines.

[12] I suspect that he was one of the descendants of a man from Medina, ʿUbāda b. al-Ṣāmit, who had gained prominence at the time of the Prophet. The family had settled in Córdoba living alongside the Perfumer's Gate (*Bāb al-ʿAṭṭārīn*), where the family was known as the Banū Hārūn, Ibn Ḥazm, *Jambara*, ed. p. 354; trans. p. 338. In the environs of this gate in Córdoba, there was a mosque known as the 'mosque of Hārūn', see below Ch. 10. Abd al-Raḥmān b. Muḥammad b. Rumāḥis was the admiral of the navy, a post that his father, who had also been governor of Pechina, had filled before him, Ibn Ḥayyān, *Muqtabis V*, pp. 211, 313, 323.

trader received no fewer than 1,000 ja'farid dinars, as well as an apron made from valuable textiles, while the sailors were given 500 dinars each and garments made from *khazz*, which reveals the great importance attached to this capture.

Around that same time, in the summer of 972 (361 AH), a man named Qāsim was also placed under arrest. He was related to Caliph al-Mu'izz, but had fled the Fāṭimid court, allegedly following a disagreement with his relative. He then settled in al-Andalus, but had come under suspicion for circulating Shī'ī beliefs, for which the governor of Badajoz ordered his detention. Another individual called Muḥammad b. Sulaymān, but known as the Son of Master Ḥammuh (*Wallad Mu'allim Ḥammuh*), was imprisoned on the Upper Frontier for having also joined the Fāṭimid ranks. He had already been detained and pardoned once, but had slipped back into his old ways.[13]

The presence of Shī'ite agitators conspiring in the souks of Andalusi cities in conjunction with the uncertain situation in North Africa following the defection of Ja'far b. al-Andalusī gave rise to a complex and very fluid situation. At such a time of great uncertainty over what the future might hold in store, the balance of power could change quickly. The Umayyad's long-established legitimacy, which ever since the distant days of the early caliphs in Damascus had survived the most difficult circumstances, was now faced by the swift rise to power of a family who claimed to be descendants of 'Alī b. Abī Ṭālib, the arch-enemy of the Umayyad dynasty. The resounding Fāṭimid triumphs in Ifrīqiya and Egypt had begun to seriously alarm orthodox Muslims. The rivalry between both caliphates seemed to presage that whoever came out victor from this confrontation could aspire to become the dominant power across the Muslim world. It was in this context that al-Ḥakam II took the most significant decision of his caliphate.

The War in Northern Morocco

Troop Deployments and Defeat

On 27 June 972, in the middle of the month of *Ramaḍān* 361 AH, al-Ḥakam II gave an unexpected order: preparations should be made immediately to

[13] Ibn Ḥayyān, *Muqtabis* VII, ed. pp. 86–8; trans. pp. 110–12.

send the army to the region of what is today northern Morocco.[14] It was an unprecedented decision, as until then the Umayyad caliphs had maintained a policy of prudent diplomacy in the region. Troop deployments had been very limited and only carried out for specific aims, as was the case with the capture of Ceuta. The mobilisation now decreed by al-Ḥakam involved the transfer of the regular army (*jund*) to the other side of the Straits of Gibraltar, where they were to serve in a region whose various tribal groups were more often than not hostile. The decision seemingly aspired to effectively occupy the whole region, a plan that was undoubtedly fraught with risks.

The specific reasons that led the caliph to take such an important decision are not wholly clear. The official purpose of this military operation was to subjugate an Idrīsid leader called Ḥasan b. Qannūn, who ruled over a modestly-sized territory that had as its principal centres the city of al-Baṣra and a fortress (*ḥiṣn*) named Ḥajar al-Naṣr, which was located in the rugged terrain of the central zone of the Rif.[15] Ḥasan b. Qannūn, as well as his father and brother before him, were typical Idrīsid leaders, acknowledging the authority of the Fāṭimids or the Umayyads depending on the circumstances. In fact, for many years, Ḥasan had been a loyal supporter of ʿAbd al-Raḥmān III and al-Ḥakam II, but his loyalty seems to have run dry at some point prior to the summer of 972. Instead of trying to resolve the fractured relations through diplomacy, or by moving some of his many pawns in the region, the Umayyad caliph opted for an unprecedented strategy: deploy all his military power against a leader who was not overly relevant. Furthermore, he was by no means the first leader, and nor would he be the last, to shift his alliances on the complex chessboard of the Maghreb.

Al-Ḥakam II may perhaps have thought that it was wise to flex his muscle in the Maghreb in response to the Fāṭimid victories in Egypt; or perhaps he sought to gain definitive control over the route between Fez and Tangier, which had al-Baṣra as one of its intermediary points; or then again, perhaps this

[14] The whole account of this military operation in Ibn Ḥayyān, *Muqtabis VII*, ed. pp. 79–81; trans. pp. 102–4.

[15] N. Benco, 'Archaeological Investigation at al-Baṣra, Morocco', pp. 293–340. Ḥajar al-Naṣr is identified as a place thirty kilometres to the south-east of Jbel Sidi Habib close to the mausoleum of Sīdī Mazwār, P. Cressier, A. El Biudjay, H. El Figuigui and J. Vignet/Zunz, 'Ḥağar al-Naṣr, capitale idrisside du Maroc septentrional: archéologie et histoire (IVe H./Xe ap. J-C)', pp. 305–34.

excessive deployment of troops and the rounding up of Fāṭimid agitators in al-Andalus around the same period was intended to send a message of how the caliph was prepared to 'inflict the exemplary punishment that was deserved' upon whoever dared to reject the orthodox doctrines he upheld, a view he had also proclaimed in a document he had circulated. Nor should the timing of this decision be overlooked, as the Fāṭimid court in Ifrīqiya was in the midst of preparations for Caliph al-Muʿizz's definitive transfer to Egypt, which was planned to take place a few weeks later, at the start of August. Thereby, the Umayyad occupation of the North African territory may also have been intended to harass the Fāṭimid rearguard at a crucial moment. Finally, it is also possible that the caliph wanted to respond to Fāṭimid propaganda that accused the Umayyads of lacking military valour, as is exemplified by insulting poems, such as one that proclaimed that 'if their combat shields seem bloodstained, this is due to the menstruations of their concubines'.[16]

Any of these reasons, or perhaps all of them, or maybe another that went unrecorded, may have motivated the mobilisation of the caliphal army. The Umayyad *jund* was only deployed once a year on short campaigns that did not last longer than three months. The soldiers usually undertook rapid expeditions into the northern Christian territories, or else were assigned garrison duties in Córdoba. What was now decreed was the mobilisation of the army for an expedition that did not seem to have a clear end date. As a result, when news arrived that a Viking expedition had been detected on the western coasts at the same time, the only troops that could be sent to confront it were the stipendiary Tangerine soldiers (*ṭanjiyyūn*), who were not deemed to be exactly the finest units in the caliphal army.

The command of the expedition to northern Morocco was given to Muḥammad b. Qāsim b. Ṭumlus. He belonged to a family whose members had for generations, going back as far as the emirate, been appointed to various prominent posts, above all military ones. In previous years Muḥammad had served as vizier and commander of the stipendiary troops (*ṣāḥib al-ḥasham*). However, we do not know what military experience he had acquired prior to that, as he is only recorded undertaking ceremonial roles.[17] The caliph sum-

[16] Yalaoui, 'Les relations ...', p. 26.
[17] Ibn Ḥayyān, *Muqtabis VII*, ed. pp. 21, 25, 47.

moned him in late June 972 and they held a long discussion. The advice he gave to Muḥammad b. Qāsim b. Ṭumlus demonstrates that al-Ḥakam thought that the conquest of the hearts and minds of the Maghrebi population was the best strategy for the mission's success: 'put out the fire', 'use pardons', 'show a preference for leniency', seek 'peace, well-being and the best interests of the country and its subjects', 'assist those who start to demonstrate their obedience ... without taking into account their past behaviour' were the guidelines that the caliph offered to his *qā'id*. He accompanied his advice with the admonition that to re-establish 'the empire of the Book of God and the *sunna* of the Prophet', the *qā'id* would have to 'efface any vestiges of the Shī'ites and implement the traditions of the orthodox imām-s'. Prepared with all this advice and laden with the customary gifts the caliph gave when granting audiences, Muḥammad b. Qāsim b. Ṭumlus swiftly began preparations for the campaign.[18]

Little more than a month went by between the *qā'id* receiving his orders on 27 June (12 *Ramaḍān*) and the army's arrival in Ceuta on 2 August (18 of Shawwāl), which indicates the haste with which preparations were made and how well-oiled the Umayyad military machinery was. The standing army or *jund* was first mustered in Córdoba. It is possible that they were already there when the caliph's sudden order was issued to the *qā'id*, as the previous day they had been involved in a confrontation with the Tangerine troops, who were preparing to leave for the expedition against the Vikings (see above p. 153). Three days later, the army departed for Algeciras, from where a few weeks later the troops sailed for Ceuta. The crossing was overseen by the *qā'id* of the fleet and *ṣāḥib al-shurṭa*, 'Abd al-Raḥmān b. Rumāhis. Orders had been given for the deployment of two Umayyad squadrons: one from Almería, the other based in Seville, in which a group of soldiers embarked, whom the caliph had also called up for active service in North Africa, and whose ranks included a number of renowned individuals.[19]

[18] Ibn Ḥayyān, *Muqtabis VII*, ed. pp. 79–80; trans. pp. 102–4.

[19] Ibn Ḥayyān, *Muqtabis VII*, ed. p. 80; trans. pp. 104. Some of the soldiers who had been mustered were old clients (*mawālī*) of caliph 'Abd al-Raḥmān III, whose names (Qayṣar, Sa'd al-Jazarī and Rashīq al-Barghawaṭī) indicate an indigenous or Berber origin. Others were well-known aristocrats (*akābir al-aḥrār*): Ismā'īl b. 'Abd al-Raḥmān b. al-Shaykh was a descendant of a former rebel from the Levant region who had been subjugated by 'Abd al-Raḥmān III and had been obliged to reside in Córdoba, where he was given stipends and territorial concessions (*iqṭā*'s); his brother, Jahwar,

The start of the campaign was promising. In mid-August 972, the *qā'id* of the fleet, 'Abd al-Raḥmān b. Rumāhis, captured the city of Tangier and expelled Ḥasan b. Qannūn. Over the following days, the land army was deployed in the outlying areas of the city. Not long after, in early September, the other *qā'id*, Muḥammad b. Qāsim b. Ṭumlus, fought a battle against Ḥasan b. Qannūn, who was defeated and lost 200 men.[20] As a result of these operations, the Umayyad army was able to take the city of Zalul, an enclave forty kilometres to the south-east of Tangier 'filled with souks', that had been known as Zilil in the classical period, and is located in Dchar Jdid, not far from today's Had el-Garbia.[21] The city was razed to the ground and, making use of a peculiar rhetoric flourish, 'Īsā al-Rāzī declared that it had been left like 'the belly of an onager', in reference to a well-known Arab proverb.[22] On the following day, Muḥammad b. Qāsim b. Ṭumlus entered the coastal city of Aṣīla, around forty kilometres south of Tangier. The first thing he did was to go the mosque, where there was a *minbar* on which Caliph al-Mu'izz had had his name carved: the *minbar* was burnt, but the inscription containing the Fāṭimid's name was sent to al-Ḥakam back in Córdoba.

Despite these initial successes, things then began to go awry. Unfortunately, there is a lacuna in the manuscript of al-Rāzī's text copied by Ibn Ḥayyān, which coincides with the end of 361 AH and the start of the following year (i.e. from October 972 to March 973), whereby the Cordoban historian, and we also, have been denied any detailed knowledge of how the operations developed over the course of this period. However, Ibn Ḥayyān includes a brief account that records that Muḥammad b. Qāsim b. Ṭumlus suffered a devastating defeat at the hand of Ḥasan b. Qannūn on 30 December 972

was stationed in Córdoba and also served on defence duties on the frontier in Zaragoza; 'Abd al-Raḥmān b. Abī Jawshan was also descended from a Berber rebel from the same region, who had been subjugated by 'Abd al-Raḥmān III and seems to have resided in Córdoba. The last name on the list was 'Abd al-Raḥmān b. Yūsuf b. Armaṭil, about whom, by contrast, we know nothing, Ibn Ḥayyān, *Muqtabis VII*, ed cit. pp. 22, 106, 122, 127, 156, 164; al-'Udhrī, *Tarṣī*, pp. 13, 14, 15.

20 Ibn Ḥayyān, *Muqtabis VII*, ed. pp. 89–91; trans. pp. 112–14.

21 Ibn Ḥawqal, *Ṣūrat al-arḍ*, p. 79; E. Gozalbes Cravioto, 'Descubrimientos arqueológicos de Tingi (Tánger) en los siglos X al XVII', p. 840. Both the edition and the translation of the text of *Muqtabis VII* must be corrected, as they read 'Dhalūl'.

22 The reference comes from a proverb that states that 'all the hunt is in the belly of the onager' which is cited by Ibn 'Abd Rabbih as having been uttered by the Prophet. E. García Gómez, 'Hacia un refranero arabiogoandaluz. V', pp. 272–3.

(21 *rabīʿ I* 362) at a place called Faḥṣ Mahrān. The Umayyad *qāʾid* was killed along with 500 horsemen and 1,000 soldiers, while the rest of the troops had to seek refuge in Ceuta.[23]

It was a huge disaster, only comparable to the defeat suffered three decades earlier at the hands of the Christians by the troops of ʿAbd al-Raḥmān III at Alhándega, on the northern frontier. However, the defeat at Faḥṣ Mahrān, far from intimidating al-Ḥakam II, served only to reinforce his commitment to put an end to Ḥasan b. Qannūn, as well as occupy the Magreb al-aqsā. Yet things looked quite different to those on the ground. Neither the *qāʾid*s nor the troops deployed in the Maghreb were overly keen on extending a tough campaign in hostile territory, one they were not fully prepared for. The officials who remained in command of the army began to stall in fulfilling orders, such as the instructions to reinforce Tangier's fortifications, while opening negotiations with representatives from Ḥasan b. Qannūn with the intention of trying to obtain some type of agreement.[24]

Al-Ḥakam's response to these attempts at negotiations was an emphatic no. It is possible that around that time, it was already known in Córdoba that, after a long overland march from Qayrawān, al-Muʿizz had arrived in Egypt, where he had taken up residence in the new city of Cairo. Perhaps this new situation prompted al-Ḥakam's obstinate rejection of any arrangement being reached with Ḥasan b. Qannūn. In an elaborately rhetorical letter addressed to the army chiefs, the caliph refused any negotiation that did not result in the rebel's complete submission. Using long-winded arguments replete with Qur'anic quotations, the caliph explained that while an agreement with Ḥasan b. Qannūn would have been viable at one point, the rebel's persistent attitude, which was barely worthy of trust, had since made it impossible. In the past, al-Ḥakam had supported Ḥasan against his own family, following the Qur'anic precept that obliged establishing peace between two groups of believers in confrontation with one another. But the same Qur'anic passage also ordered

[23] Ibn Ḥayyān, *Muqtabis VII*, ed. pp. 95–6; trans. pp. 123–4. Ibn Abī Zarʿ, *Rawḍ al-Qirṭās*, ed. Benmansour, p. 112, trans. Beaumier, p. 124, identifies the site of the battle as Faḥṣ Banī Miṣra.

[24] Ibn Ḥayyān, *Muqtabis VII*, ed. pp. 105–6; trans. p. 135. These officials included the aforementioned *mawālī* Qayṣar, Rashīq al-Bargawaṭī and ʿAbd al-Raḥmān b. Yūsuf b. Armaṭil.

that combat be joined with whoever acted unjustly.[25] Ḥasan had undertaken to fortify Tangier and severed the family ties (*qurbā*) that bound him to the caliph, as both were members of the Qurashi lineage. He had decided to take sides with the Fāṭimids, while the rest of the Idrīsids had submitted to the Umayyads and, as a consequence, the caliph's patience had reached its limit, as the Eastern poet Abū Tammām (d. 845/231 AH) had also expressed: 'at times the fire even ignites the green sage (*salām*)'.[26] To crown his arguments, the letter mentioned a prophetic tradition, which was invoked to argue that, if Ḥasan had remained loyal, the caliph would have acted just as the Prophet Muḥammad had done when he entered Mecca, and declared he would never deny a post to any one from Quraysh if they asked for it.[27]

Al-Ḥakam II's flat refusal to engage in any type of negotiation meant that those who had tried to promote this strategy fell into disgrace.[28] In April 973 (*Jumāda II*), the caliph appointed a new *qā'id* in the Maghreb: the army's most famous commander, Ghālib b. 'Abd al-Raḥmān, who had cut his teeth in innumerable battles along the northern frontier of al-Andalus.[29] A fresh plan was set in motion, which consisted of an immense demonstration of military might, accompanied by an undercover strategy that involved spies infiltrating the Berber tribes supporting Ḥasan and persuading them to desert to the Umayyads; were they to agree to do this, their safety (*amān*) would be guaranteed in exchange for their recognition of the Umayyad caliph's authority. The design of this strategy was based on reports sent back by delegations that the caliph had dispatched to northern Morocco to study the situation on the ground. These delegations had

[25] 'If two groups of the believers fight, you [believers] should try to reconcile them; if one of them is [clearly] oppressing the other, fight the oppressors until they submit to God's command, then make a just and even-handed reconciliation between the two of them. God loves those who are even-handed.' Qur'an, 49, 9.

[26] Ibn Ḥayyān, *Muqtabis VII*, ed. p. 99; trans. p. 127. The verse in Abū Tammām, *Dīwān*, ed. Cairo, 1900, p. 269. The quotation of this verse in the caliph's letter confirms that the work of Abū Tammām was well-known in al-Andalus, as I proposed in E. Manzano, 'Oriental Topoi in Andalusian Historical Sources', pp. 42–58. I believe it is very probable that the letter was written by Ja'far al-Muṣḥāfī.

[27] The *ḥadīth* in question appears in the principal canonical collections. See, for example, al-Bukhārī, *Ṣaḥiḥ*.

[28] In August 973 (*Dhū l-qa'da* 362) the caliph ordered Rashīq al-Barghawāṭī, Ismā'īl b. 'Abd al-Raḥmān b. al-Shaykh and 'Abd al-Raḥmān b. Yūsuf b. Armaṭīl to rejoin the Maghreb army, and they were pardoned after having fallen into disgrace few months before, Ibn Ḥayyān, *Muqtabis VII*, ed. p. 129; trans. p. 163. On this episode see above, Ch. 3, n. 30.

[29] Ibn Ḥayyān, *Muqtabis VII*, ed. pp. 97–100 and 102; trans. pp. 124–8 and 130.

been composed of *qāḍīs* and *fuqahā'*, which reveals the increasing role being played by the Andalusi *'ulamā'* within the caliphal administration. The first, sent as early as September 972 (*Dhū l-qa'da* 361), had consisted of Qāsim b. Khalaf al-Jubayrī and Muḥammad b. Aḥmad b. Mufarraj, *qāḍī* of Rayyuh.[30] A few months later, following the disaster of Faḥṣ Mahrān, in May 973 (Sha'bān, 362 AH) another commission was sent. One of its members was Muḥammad b. Abī 'Āmir, who had by then added various posts to his service sheet. He was accompanied by another *'alīm*, as well as a treasurer.[31] This commission spent almost two months on the ground before returning to Córdoba to report back to the caliph. Shortly afterwards, Muḥammad b. Abī 'Amīr returned to Morocco, perhaps to supervise the situation in person.

The caliph's orders were effectively carried out to the letter. In his interview with Ghālib, al-Ḥakam had clearly stated to his *qā'id*, 'Follow the path of he who is not permitted to return unless victorious or excused by death. Extend your hand to spend, and if you so wish, I can pave the way that separates us with a bridge of money.'[32] In the months following the spring of 973 (362 AH), there was a frenetic deployment of troops. Men were recruited on the Upper Frontier of al-Andalus, and 100 archer slaves (*al-rumā al-mamālīk*) and a cavalry unit called the *fursān al-riyāḍa* were put under the command of members of the Tujībid family, who ruled over the Ebro valley. Now, they were sent across the Straits of Gibraltar and placed under Ghālib's command. Another contingent that was possibly destined for the Maghreb campaign consisted of 300 horsemen form Lérida, who happened to meet with the caliph by chance on the outskirts of Córdoba in March 974. Furthermore, 1,700 infantrymen equipped with white cloaks and Christian swords, who came from the frontier

[30] Qāsim b. Khalaf b. Fatḥ b. 'Abd Allāh b. Jubayra al-Jubayrī had been born in Tortosa and had travelled to Egypt and Iraq. After his mission to the Maghreb, he was named *qāḍī* of Seville. He was also at some point *qāḍī* in Tortosa. He died in 988 (378 AH), in the prison at Madīnat al-Zahrā', having been imprisoned by Muḥammad b. Abī 'Āmir on the charge of conspiring against Hishām II, Ibn al-Faraḍī, *Ta'rīkh*, n. 1.075. Iyāḍ, *Tartib*, VII, pp. 5–7. References in *Prosopografía de los ulemas de al-Andalus*, http://www.eea.csic.es/pua/, no. 7,579 (last accessed 12 November 2022). Muḥammad b. Aḥmad b. Muḥammad b. Yaḥyā b. Mufarraj had been born in Córdoba to a family of *mawālī*. He had spent eight years in the East and had served as *qāḍī* of Sidonia, following which he took up the same post in Rayyuh. He was also *qāḍī* of Écija, Ibn Ḥayyān, *Muqtabis VII*, ed. p. 86. Ibn al-Faraḍī, *Ta'rīkh*, n. 1,358.

[31] On this commission see Ch. 3, n. 30.

[32] X. Ballestí, 'Jil'a y monedas', p. 392, which includes the texts by *K. Mafākhir al-barbar*, of which I have provided the translation cited above.

near Toledo, were also incorporated into the North African campaign. The Banū Khazar, who were stationed in Fez, and Yaḥyā b. al-Andalusī himself, also received orders to join the North African expedition. With such numerous forces, Ghālib was able to send ahead expeditions of 500 horsemen and a similar amount of infantry, while leaving 1,500 men in rearguard positions, which considerably favoured the success of military operations.[33] The problem that arose was that, on the one hand, all these frenetic logistics involved an immense expenditure of resources in exchange for submissions that tended to be transient, and on the other, it gave rise to a series of decisions that disrupted the intricate balance of power at the heart of al-Andalus.

The Costly Task of Maintaining the Army

The military operation that the caliph decreed for North Africa was an immense undertaking. Ibn Ḥayyān states that the caliph deployed 'his best qā'ids' and 'all the cavalry of al-Andalus', covering the sea 'with fleets laden with riches, weapons, munitions and provisions'.[34] The provisions proceeded from the state grain reserves, while the weapons were manufactured in the caliphal workshop, the *dār al-ṣināʿa*, which produced not only luxury items but also military equipment. The workshop must have been working to maximum capacity. On a standard basis, every year it turned out 10,000 round shields (*turs/atrās*), and a similar amount of *adargas* or oval shields, coats of mail and bows; the latter were made with deer antlers, which were requisitioned in May each year. It also produced 8,000 swords and spears.[35] If these figures are taken as indicative of the size of the army, we can establish a possible range for the number of soldiers deployed to North Africa of between 5,000 and 10,000 troops. This estimate takes into account the fact that a part of the armaments manufactured were kept in the weapons' warehouses, or would have been reserved for the troops commissioned to man the garrisons.

[33] Ibn Ḥayyān, *Muqtabis* VII, ed. pp. 103, 117–18, 123–4, 125 and 129, 130, 134–5, 151–2; trans. pp. 130, 150, 157, 158 and 162–3, 164, 169–70, 192.

[34] Ibn Ḥayyān, *Muqtabis VII*, ed. p. 191; trans. pp. 229–30.

[35] *Dhikr bilād al-Andalus*, ed. and trans. pp. 172 and 183. These figures are consistent with others that record how al-Manṣūr's son and successor, al-Muẓaffar, went ahead with the delivery of 5,000 cuirasses and the same number of helmets and coats of mail shortly before departing on one of his campaigns in 1003 (393 AH) Ibn ʿIdhārī, *al-Bayān*, II, ed. p. 4; trans. p. 13. Also A. Labarta, 'Parada militar en la Córdoba omeya', p. 266.

The *dār al-ṣināʿa* also produced 8,000 tents (*khibāʾ*) for the army. They were used to build the encampments that were dominated by the pavilion assigned to the *qāʾid* who led the campaign. When, in July 973 (*Shawwāl* 362 AH), Ghālib crossed the Straits of Gibraltar to take control of the operations, he received from the caliph an impressive red pavilion (*qubba*), which was to be mounted in the middle of the camp and used to receive his subalterns. Pavilions of this type had leather reinforcements, posts, stakes, struts, guy ropes, vents, canopy, pegs and even a latrine. According to the notary documents, they could be hired – as could the double canvas tents – for a period of a few months by wealthy fighters in campaign, if they so wished.[36] It was fundamental that these tents were resistant and solid, in order to avoid embarrassing situations such as the one suffered by a doctor who served under ʿAbd al-Raḥmān III; while he was on a military expedition, his tent was blown away by a gust of wind, revealing to the whole army his amorous assault on a youth who accompanied him.[37]

Provisions, munitions and tents were not the only items that accompanied the army to northern Morocco. The troops also had to be paid. Al-Hakam's statement that he was ready to build a bridge of money across the Straits was not a mere boast. The leaders of the *jund* expected to receive 200 dinars per campaign, and their closest relatives ten dinars each; common soldiers were paid five dinars, which equates to forty dirhams per head.[38] The *jund* was usually mobilised for just three months per year, which was sufficient time for the *aceifas* against the northern territories or to tackle any rebel who might rise up within al-Andalus. However, the North African expedition was planned from the outset as a long campaign involving a permanent deployment of troops, whereby the first thing the unfortunate Muḥammad b. Qāsim b. Ṭumlus did when appointed commander was to meet with the viziers 'in order to definitively arrange the payment of the wages for the army that had to leave with him'.

[36] Ibn al-ʿAṭṭār *K. al-wathāʾiq*, ed. p. 194; trans. p. 348. Ibn Ḥayyān, *Muqtabis VII*, ed. p. 116; trans. p. 148. In June 972, the generals commissioned to undertake an expedition against a possible Viking attack also received a large tent (*miẓalla*) from the caliph so that they could use it for holding meetings there and addressing their men, ibid., pp. 79 and 102. Likewise, a grandiose tent with all kinds of tapestries was given to a Berber chief in *Ramaḍān* 362, ibid., pp. 115 and 146.

[37] The name of the Cordoban doctor was Ibn Umm al-Banīn, J. Vernet, 'Los médicos andaluces', p. 458.

[38] Payments were also made when the army departed for the *aceifa*, as happened in the spring of 975 (364 AH) during the campaign against the Christians in which an official was sent from Córdoba with sums of money to pay the troops, Ibn Ḥayyān, *Muqtabis VII*, ed. p. 223; trans. pp. 263–4.

A carefully planned system was set up to regularly send the soldiers' wages from Córdoba. Three months after the beginning of the campaign in the Maghreb, on 17 September 972 (5 *Dhū l-Ḥijja* 361 AH), twenty-five loads of dirhams were sent to pay the wages (*nafaqāt*). The delivery of these loads was assigned to a group of slaves, eunuch officials in charge of the postal service, as well as secretaries of the messengers. This was the first payment made in silver coinage; from them on, payments were made with considerable regularity.[39] At the end of April 973 (*Rajab* 362 AH) – perhaps with some delay – the *ṣāḥib al-makhzūn*, the person responsible for the treasury, Salama b. al-Ḥakam, left Córdoba for Morocco with further loads of money intended to pay the troops' stipends.[40] A few days later, and coinciding with the appointment of Ghālib as the new *qā'id*, 80,000 dinars in dirhams were sent to pay the wages for the following months. This was an advance payment and it would not have been by chance that it coincided with the arrival of the new *qā'id*: perhaps a sign that from then on the payments were going to be more regular.[41] Effectively three months later – in September/*Dhū l-Ḥijja* – another official in charge of the treasury left for Morocco with money to pay the wages and stipends (*nafaqāt wa l-a'ṭiya*). In January 974 (*Rabī' II* 363 AH) another shipment was sent and the same happened in March (*Rajab*), in June (*Shawwāl*) and in August (*Dhū l-Ḥijja*) that same year, with a regularity that indicates a concern to ensure the wages were paid on a quarterly basis. Once more, in March (*Rajab*) the following year, despite Ghālib's campaign being over, another shipment was sent to pay the troops who remained in Morocco.[42]

39 *Rijāl al-'abidiyyīn wa 'urafā' aṣḥābi al-rasā'il al-khiṣyāni wa kuttāb al-furāniqīn*. It is possible that a new shipment of money was sent at the end of the same year, which is to say three months later, but the aforementioned lacuna in the original manuscript means this cannot be confirmed.

40 Ibn Ḥayyān, *Muqtabis VII*, ed. pp. 91, 104; trans. pp. 114, 133. The mention of the *rijāl al-ṣayidiyyīn* that appears in the first shipment is very difficult to puzzle out, and therefore I follow, albeit with many doubts, the editor's suggestion that it should be read as 'al-'abidiyyīn'. The translation by García Gómez inclines to 'monteros [hunters]', which does not seem convincing to me.

41 Ibn Ḥayyān, *Muqtabis VII*, ed. p. 106; trans. p. 135. The Spanish translation by García Gómez mentions '80.000 dirhems destinados a los cuerpos de tropas *mushtarīn* de Tánger y Arcila [80,000 dirhams intended for the units of *mushtarīn* troops of Tangier and Asilah]'. It seems more correct to translate it as: '80,000 dinars in dirhams (*dīnār darāhim*) for the monthly wages of the armies of Tangier and Asilah'.

42 Ibn Ḥayyān, *Muqtabis VII*, ed. pp. 139, 149, 168, 177 (repeated on 183) and 210; trans. pp. 174, 189 (with an over-interpretation on [165] the same page, where the title refers to a 'nuevo envío de

Table 1 Shipments of money for soldiers' wages, with delivery dates and names and rank of those responsible

Islamic date	CE date	Person in charge	Position
5 *Dhū l-Ḥijja* 361	17 September 972		*'Urafā' aṣḥābi al-rasā'il al-khiṣyāni wa kuttāb al-furāniqīn*
23 *Rajab*, 362	29 April 973	Salama b. al-Ḥakam	*Ṣāḥib al-makhzūn*
29 *Dhū l-Ḥijja* 362	30 September 973	Tāyit b. Muḥammad	*Ṣāḥib al-makhzūn*
19 *Rabī' II*, 363	17 January 974	Abd al-Raḥmān b. Aḥmad b. Ilyās	*Khāzin*
3 *Rajab* 363	30 March 974	Durrī b. al-Ḥakam al-Hammāz	*Wakīl dār al-khayl*
1 *Shawwāl*, 363	25 June 974	Marwān b. Aḥmad b. Shuhayd	*Khāzin*
3 *Dhū l-Ḥijja* 363	25 August 974	Aḥmad b. Muḥammad b. Ḥafṣ b. Jābir	*Khāzin*
11 *Rajab*, 364	27 March 975	'Ubāda b. Khalaf b. Abī Jawshan Aḥmad b. Muḥammad b. Ḥudayr	*Khāzin bi l-'askar*

The quantities involved in these payments were astronomical: 80,000 dinars in dirhams alone were sent in May 973 (*Rajab* 362 AH), a sum which was worth around 640,000 dirhams. A crude calculation would mean that these 80,000 dinars in dirhams were shared out to the order of five dinars per soldier (the stipend received by each member of the *jund*), which would give a maximum of 16,000 men deployed in Morocco. This figure is obviously exaggerated, as there were many soldiers with much higher stipends, and besides not all the money was intended for the soldiers. Therefore, a figure of between five and ten thousand troops would match the figure discussed above with regard to the supply of equipment.[43]

Despite all the careful planning and lavish spending, the Moroccan campaign had become such a large-scale venture that Ghālib himself wrote to the caliph in August 973 (*Dhū l-qa'da* 362 AH) to express his concerns that it was

dinero a Marruecos [new shipment of money to Morocco]', but that does not appear in the text), 206–7, 216 (repeated on 222) and 250–1.

[43] Ibn Ḥayyān, *Muqtabis VII*, ed. pp. 102, 117–18; trans. pp. 130, 150.

becoming increasingly difficult to manage the operation. The caliph's response displays al-Ḥakam II's characteristic stubborn attitude: even the final grain of wheat and the very last coin was to be sent across the Straits in order to attain a victory. The caliph ordered one of his treasurers to go to Ceuta with one million dinars to facilitate payments. A network of horseback messengers established between Ghālib's encampment and the cities of Tangier and Aṣīla was ordered to ensure the money reached the army on a regular basis. Nothing was left to chance. The treasurer also received an order to release sums of money to pay for horse feed and the messengers' (*furāniqīn*') monthly salary. Along with all these measures, the caliph added a peculiar recommendation that was intended to assist the army's logistics: permit the field commanders to use teams of oxen to farm the land, although, given the caliph's concern to ensure 'the prosperity of the land and the security of its inhabitants', this was to be done without prejudicing the people of the region (*ahl al-bilād*).[44]

The absurd proposal that the army should provide for itself by farming the land could not hide the fact that the immense quantity of resources required for the campaign was draining the caliphal coffers. The Umayyad military system was designed for annual mobilisations of three months, not for a permanent campaign that gave rise to such high expenses. Maintaining an army on the ground was costly, as was demonstrated by the incredible sum of one million dinars released to ensure its supplies. This figure constituted a quarter of the caliphate's fiscal income for a single year. However, the caliph's order was also to obtain the support of the local population against the influence of Fāṭimid agents, whereby al-Hakam was keen to present the presence of the Umayyad army as a guarantor of the people's prosperity and security. He intended for his army to become an apparatus that redistributed the resources it received. The problem was that the cost was unaffordable.

Gifts and Political Alliances

The military frenzy that lasted throughout 973 (362 AH) was combined with a powerful diplomatic operation that was intended to win over to the Umayyad cause the Idrīsid and Berber tribal leaders who had until then been supporting Ḥasan b. Qannūn. An important part of these efforts consisted in sending

[44] Ibn Ḥayyān, *Muqtabis VII*, ed. pp. 135–6, 139; trans. pp. 170–1, 174.

gifts, whose formal presentation and acceptance gave visible form to the political bonds the caliph was trying to forge. This policy had been practised in the past, and now al-Ḥakam II decided to intensify it. As a result, shipments of dinars, precious textiles, horses and harnesses were sent across the Straits to be distributed among prominent social leaders.

A delivery sent to the *qā'id* Ghālib in the summer of 973 consisted of money, garments and weapons that had to be distributed among the tribes' notables (*wujūh al-qabā'il*) and leaders (*zu'amā'*). Ten thousand gold dinars were distributed; they had been minted in the name of the Emir of the Faithful, and this added a symbolic mark of legitimacy to their intrinsic monetary value. The fact they were presented to the tribal leaders and notables demonstrates the restricted social circulation of gold, which was reserved for individuals allied to the caliph. The shipment also included 350 items of precious textiles and ten ceremonial swords, clothes and special weapons. All of them had a widely acknowledged social value, and thanks to their quality, rarity, colour and appearance were especially eye-catching signifiers of rank. They were always distributed in accordance with their recipients' rank, as all these gifts were symbols of social status that were highly valued within the framework of tribal society.[45]

During the summer of 973 further gifts continued to be given to the Berber leaders at a steady rate. One of the most important was that received in June that year (*Ramaḍān* 362 AH) by Abū l-'Aysh b. Ayyūb b. Bilāl, who was the leader (*ra'īs*) of a branch of the Kutāma tribe that had settled in the Rif, and about whom it was said he was able to mobilise 3,500 horsemen and 6,400 infantry soldiers. Having arrived in Córdoba, this tribal leader and his son received loads of money, precious garments and an excellent horse with a saddle and harness at a ceremony that was celebrated in the House of Viziers at Madīnat al-Zahrā', during which other tribal leaders also received gifts.[46]

In return for these gifts, their recipients had to accept Umayyad sovereignty, which is why Abū l-'Aysh b. Ayyūb b. Bilāl not only received

[45] Ibn Ḥayyān, *Muqtabis VII*, ed. p. 108; trans. p. 138.

[46] Ibn Ḥayyān, *Muqtabis VII*, ed. p. 110; trans. p. 141. The saddle (*sarj*) is referred to as *mu'arraqa*. I think that this could possibly be linked to the word *'arrāqa*, which Lane Pool describes as 'a thing (app. a cloth for inhibiting sweat) that is put beneath the ... path of the sarj'. On the bridles, García Gómez, 'Armas, banderas', pp. 172–3.

Table 2 Precious items supplied to Ghālib for distribution among the leaders and notables of the Berber tribes

Number and class	Material	Description
10,000 dinars	Gold	
50 *jubbas*	Brocade	*al-dībāj al-muḍalla al-mulawwan*
50 *jubbas*	Silk	*al-khazz al-ʿubaydī al-mulawwan*
50 *jubbas*	Silk	*al-khazz al-ṭirāzī al-mulawwan*
100 *maṭārif*	Silk?	*al-maṭārif al-mufaṣṣala al-mulawwana*
100 *ʿamāʾim* (turbans)	*lāsa*?	*al-lāsiyya al-mulawwana*
10 *suyūf* (swords)	?	*al-suyūf al-ʿidwiyya al-ḥaliya*

substantial gifts, but also a diploma, which stated that the caliph conferred upon him authority over his tribe: the Aṭāna Mahrān, which belonged to the Kutāma. The content of this diploma offers an insightful explanation of how political ties based on loyalty were established between the caliph and the tribal leaders.[47] Its preamble explains that al-Hakam had decided to confer on Abū l-ʿAysh authority over his tribe, due to the caliph's predilection for and trust in him, and his desire to bestow welfare (*istiṣlāḥ*) upon him and his subjects. Abū l-ʿAysh was to fear and obey God, which implied obeying the caliph. On returning to his land, the Berber leader was to swear the oath of loyalty 'between the hands' (*bayna yaday*) of *qāʾid* Ghālib, as the caliph's representative in the Maghreb. This oath, which was intended to demonstrate the obedience and good counsel of Abū l-ʿAysh, also had to be sworn by the 'the notables of the tribe' (*wujūh al-qabāʾil*), a proviso that evidently sought to ensure there was no internal dissidence within the tribe. In exchange, the tribal leader had to wage war on, or make peace with, whoever the caliph waged war on, or made peace with, and inform the caliph of any news without distorting his reports, and in addition consult with the caliph about unexpected events, and undertake holy war against those who rebelled against the caliph.

Yet the diploma does not end there. Recognition of the Umayyad caliph's authority also meant commitment to a form of government in accordance with the religious guidelines issued by him, which was based on the principles of orthodox Islam. The diploma explicitly states that Abū l-ʿAysh's rulings

[47] Ibn Ḥayyān, *Muqtabis VII*, ed. pp. 111–14; trans. pp. 142–5.

(*aḥkām*) had to conform to the Qur'an and the *sunna* of the Prophet, both keys to Paradise and guarantors of the common good (*istiṣlāḥ*) of the subjects which was attained through the exercise of justice (*'adl*), which had to be applied equally to all. Thus the diploma also included very precise instructions as to the form in which prayers were to be offered, and how the canonical taxes were to be levied, as already discussed above (see above p. 65). Finally, the Caliph also stated that Abū l-'Aysh's obligations included the persecution of rebels, guaranteeing the security of the trade routes, which had to be freed of highwaymen, and the use of 'religious punishments'. In return for this, Abū l-'Aysh had the Caliph's backing that he should be listened to and obeyed by his subjects.

The style and content of this document reveals Umayyad caliphal authority at its zenith. The regulations for sound Muslim government that it sets out are based on mālikite legal manuals: a comparison of the rules on taxes stipulated by al-Ḥakam and the regulations compiled in the renowned *Risāla fī l-fiqh* by the Andalusi-born jurist Ibn Abī Zayd al-Qayrawānī (d. 996/386 AH) shows they accord almost to the letter.[48] The insistence placed upon Abū l-'Aysh's application of these rules among his subjects reveals how tribal society had been barely, if at all, Islamised. The caliph's proposal was to implement a new tier of government that emanated from his religious authority, and therefore special emphasis was placed on the application of the precepts of orthodox Islam. The application of these precepts was considered essential to ensure both the 'common good' of his subjects and the salvation of their souls. Thereby, political dominion operated as a vector of Islamisation, while also advocating an evocative concept of social justice.[49]

Gifts, the recognition of caliphal authority and the implementation of codes of behaviour that accorded with Islamic orthodoxy were combined in what was a complex mode of exercising sovereignty. A few days after Abū l-'Aysh received his diploma, another shipment of precious garments and hand-crafted swords was sent to Morocco, accompanied by the names of the

[48] Ibn Abī Zayd al-Qayrawānī, *Risāla*, ed. al-Ṭahṭawī, pp. 91–2, 95–7.

[49] That same day, another fifteen tribal leaders each received a diploma, perhaps similar to this one, which also granted them the right to rule over their tribes. Although our source cites the names of these tribes, it has only been possible to identify one of them, the Tarhūna, which belonged to a branch of the Hawwāra, who had settled near Fez, T. Lewicki, E.I. 2nd ed., s.v. Hawwāra.

tribal leaders to whom they were to be given. Over the course of this summer more deliveries of money – sixteen loads on just one occasion – and valuable items of clothing were sent over as gifts for tribal leaders.[50]

At the start of September 973, the caliph, having dispatched another unit of reinforcements, sent a long letter to Ghālib, to which he added a charter (*qindāq*) in which he listed the gifts to be given to eight Idrīsid and Berber tribal leaders.[51] This set of gift comprised a total of 15,500 dinars, around 58–60 precious textiles, eight Arab gilded and silvered swords and eight horses of different breeds equipped with valuable saddles and bridles. The eight recipients of each set of gifts were identified, and their status in the political hierarchy was also distinguished; their status was articulated by the gifts they received. It is also evident that a diplomatic effort was made to avoid any unnecessary offence being taken. They all received money, a sword, a harnessed horse and a number of textiles; however, it was the Idrīsids who received the most substantial gifts: Aḥmad b.ʿĪsā, who had been appointed *shaykh* of the Banū Muḥammad family (a branch of the Idrīsid line), was given 7,000 dinars, in addition to which his brother Ibrāhīm was given 5,000 and his son Ḥasan 1,000. The remaining beneficiaries – possibly the majority of whom were Berber tribal leaders – received 'just' 500 dinars each.[52] Similarly, the costliest pieces of cloth, the *ʿubaydis* imported from Iraq, were reserved for the *shaykh* and his brother. Undoubtedly the value of this latter cloth was much greater than that of the items made in the Cordoban *ṭirāz*, which were shared out among the less prominent individuals. An Arab sword with gold adornments and a coarse leather scabbard was also deemed more valuable than a silver and gold-plated sword, and the same can be said of the chestnut horses from the caliphal stables, which were reserved for the *shaykh* Aḥmad b. ʿĪsā and his brother, while the other steeds were of lesser quality.

The aim of all these diplomatic exchanges, undertaken in parallel to the military operations overseen by Ghālib against Ḥasan b. Qannūn, was to establish political ties that would enable the submission of the main Idrīsid

[50] For the other gifts, *Muqtabis VII*, ed. pp. 118, 126 and 129; trans. pp. 151, 159 and 163.

[51] Ibn Ḥayyān, *Muqtabis VII*, ed. pp. 131–3; 166–8. X. Ballestín, 'Jilʿa y monedas', pp. 398–410.

[52] I have only been able to identity one of the other beneficiaries, Ḥajjāj b. Khalūf, who was the brother of ʿAlī b. Khalūf, emir of the Ghumāra tribe and one of the main allies of Ḥasan b. Qannūn, Ibn Ḥayyān, *Muqtabis VII*, ed. pp. 134, 174, 176.

and Berber tribal leaders. This strategy seems to have had significant results. From spring 973 onwards, submissions to Umayyad authority occurred with increasing frequency. Around that time, ambassadors arrived in Córdoba to announce that the Idrīsid lord (*ṣāḥib*) of the city of al-Aqlām was willing to obey the Umayyad caliph. Shortly afterwards, the rulers of the two sectors of the city of Fez also offered their submission, in conjunction with two important Berber tribal leaders in the region.[53]

These submissions were accompanied by conditions similar to those imposed upon Abū l-ʿAysh with regard to the establishment of a government based on Islamic orthodoxy. In a letter sent to one of the rulers of Fez, al-Ḥakam II did not withhold offering his views on the distribution of resources derived from taxes, which were to be distributed among the people they corresponded to, or else spent on communal welfare projects (*maṣāliḥ*).[54] Were such admonitions listened to? It is hard to know. However, the letter's content confirms that subjugation to a specific authority, in this case the Umayyad caliph of Córdoba, also involved observance of the Islamic precepts which emanated from that authority. In other words, submission to the caliph's power also entailed the implementation of an Islamising component that was an implicit element of the exercise of Umayyad authority.

From a practical point of view, these submissions merely involved the caliph acknowledging a leadership that these tribal leaders already exercised; in other words, the caliph was granting, what in reality was already in the hands of the tribal leaders and rulers, while his admonitions regarding the regulations of

[53] Ibn Ḥayyān, *Muqtabis VII*, ed. pp. 103, 108, 117; trans. pp. 131, 138–9, 150. The city of Aqlām had been built by an Idrīsid not long before; it was fortified to defend itself against the rival Miknāsa tribe and it was one stade away from Baṣra, Ibn Ḥawqal, *Ṣūrat al-arḍ*, p. 80. Fez had always been divided into two distinct sectors, and this information confirms that in this period the city still had separate governments: the so-called sector of the Andalusis submitted in May 973 (*Shaʿbān* 326 AH), while the sector of the Qayrawānids did so in June (*Ramaḍān*). Our text presents here a number of errors about the name of the respective rulers of these two parts of the city: É. Lévi-Provençal, 'La fondation de Fès', pp. 23–53; M. García Arenal and E. Manzano Moreno, 'Légitimité et villes idrissides', in *Génese de la ville islamique*, pp. 257–84. The two Berber tribal leaders who also submitted to the Umayyad caliph at this time were Ismāʿīl b. Būrī and his brother Yaḥyā, from the Miknāsa tribe. Both were grandsons of the renowned tribal leader Mūsā b. Abī l-ʿAfiya, who for some years had been an ally of ʿAbd al-Raḥmān III.

[54] Ibn Ḥayyān, *Muqtabis VII*, ed. pp. 126–7; trans. p. 161. This text poses a problem, as the addressee of this letter is ʿAbd al-Karīm b. Yaḥyā, who was previously cited as the ruler of the bank of the Qayrawānids, while here he is referred to as the lord of the Andalusi section of the city.

good Muslim governance was something that, in the final instance, depended on the willing compliance of these leaders, as well as the internal pressure they might face from within their communities. Nonetheless, what few were able to question is that without the presence of the Umayyad army and without the prolonged shower of gifts and presents, it would have been far harder to ensure that these communities maintained their submission to the caliph.

The End of the Resistance

After having been appointed commander by the caliph, Ghālib b. ʿAbd al-Raḥmān took his time in crossing to the other side of the Straits. He received his appointment in April and shortly afterwards he travelled to Algeciras to oversee the arrival of reinforcements; nevertheless, he did not cross over to Tangier until July 973 (362 AH). The fact that he bided his time gives the impression that his first concern was to prepare the diplomatic terrain with gifts and alliances, and having been assured of the success of this strategy, he then undertook the military deployment, thereby it playing safe. These efforts soon began to bear fruit. Ḥasan b. Qannūn began to suffer major setbacks that undermined his scope for manoeuvre. His principal strength had been the support of Berber tribal leaders, who were able to operate on a terrain they knew well. As these tribal leaders began to transfer their loyalty to the Umayyad caliph, Ḥasan's military position became more vulnerable.

Yet the key to what subsequently happened was not only the advances gained through diplomacy and the reinforcements' contribution to the military operations. An idea began to take root that the Umayyad deployment of troops in northern Morocco was intended effectively to occupy the region, and that any North African resistance could only be crushed by severing its political leadership and effacing its military potential. Therefore, al-Ḥakam II decided to follow the precedent his father had set fifty years earlier when he had put an end to the internal rebellions that had blighted al-Andalus at that time: he made it a requirement that, following their defeat, the principal hostile leaders had to reside in Córdoba and their soldiers were to be incorporated into the Umayyad army.[55] The addition of these troops was also very welcome,

[55] M. Acién, *Entre el feudalismo y el islam*, pp. 55–70; E. Manzano Moreno, *Conquistadores, emires y califas*, pp. 354–59.

bearing in mind the limitations of the regular army, which were becoming apparent as the campaign went on.

Soon there was an exodus of members of the Idrīsid family, who moved to Córdoba, where they took up residence and were given life pensions, which meant they harboured few further aspirations to lead any form of resistance. This policy was extended to the Berber fighters, who could be accommodated as regularly paid professional soldiers. Thus, just a few months after the debâcle of Faḥṣ Mahrān, in March 973 (*Jumāda* II 362 AH), seventy Berbers from the Maṣmūda tribe (*qabīla*) arrived in Tangier with the intention of deserting the ranks of Ḥasan b. Qannūn's forces. Deemed 'valiant men', they were sent to Córdoba.[56] A few months later, a nephew of Ḥasan b. Qannūn also made his way to the capital and was given both accommodation within the medina of Córdoba and a pension (*jirāya*). Another group of seventy Berber horsemen led by their commander, some of whom were from the Ghumāra tribe, arrived soon after, and were received at court by the viziers, the palace officials and the army chiefs. They were also given pensions.[57]

As a consequence of all these developments, in the summer of 973 (362 AH) matters for Ḥasan b. Qannūn began to grow ostensibly worse. The most far-reaching military blow he suffered was the capture of the impregnable fortress of Jabal al-Karam, located to the north-east of Ksar el-Kebir, which took place in late August.[58] Ghālib was able to conquer this fortress thanks to the defection of the Kutāma Berber tribe who lived there; on seeing they were under attack, they betrayed the Idrīsid leader. The rebel fled as fast as he could, leaving behind munitions, weapons and provisions, as well as Andalusi prisoners and Berber tribesmen who had been taken hostage. The castle having been captured, the first measure Ghālib took was to add new fortifications in order to leave an Umayyad garrison there.[59]

[56] Ibn Ḥayyān, *Muqtabis VII*, ed. p. 96; trans. p. 124. They were initially installed in the so-called *Munyat Najda*, which perhaps had belonged to the individual with the same name who served as *qā'id* and head of the cavalry of al-Nāṣir, Ibn Ḥayyān, *Muqtabis V*, ed. and trans. pp. 230, 232, 298.

[57] Ibn Ḥayyān, *Muqtabis VII*, ed. pp. 109, 115; trans. pp. 139, 146–7.

[58] It was located in the Bni Gorfet massif, within the commune of Sebt Bni Gorfet, G. Lazarev, V. Martínez and J. Vignet Zunz, 'Proposition d'identification d'une forteresse idrissite', pp. 244–66.

[59] Ibn Ḥayyān, *Muqtabis VII*, ed. pp. 164–5; trans. pp. 169–71.

A month later, Ghālib inflicted another serious defeat on Ḥasan b. Qannūn, during which 400 of his men died, which forced the rebel to flee to his fortress of Ḥajar al-Naṣr. Then, on 8 October, it was the important city of al-Baṣra that surrendered to the Umayyad army after its inhabitants decided to betray and kill its Idrīsid ruler, a maternal uncle of Ḥasan b. Qannūn. His head was cut off and sent to Córdoba, where it was gleefully displayed at the entrance to the *alcázar*, while the messenger who had brought it was welcomed by the caliph and given 800 dirhams as a reward, a garment 'in accordance with his rank' (*rafīʿa*), a sabre and a horse with its saddle and bridle. The man responsible for killing him, one Thaʿbān b. Aḥmad al-Barbar, also went to Córdoba accompanied by his wives and children, where he remained and joined the army, in which he 'later proved his bravery ... and attained senior posts'. In contrast to this, the daughter of Ḥasan b. Qannūn, who had been found in the city, was at all times respected and sent to her father along with her servants in accordance with the caliph's express orders. The intention was to demonstrate to all the Idrīsids the caliph's willingness to respect the honour of the Quraysh family.[60]

As the military operations unfolded over the autumn of 973, the net closed ever tighter on Ḥasan b. Qannūn. Additional surrenders from other tribal leaders, such as that of the Rahūna, and the capture of enclaves, such as Jabal al-ʿUyūn, made his situation in Ḥajar al-Naṣr ever more desperate. During the final months of that year, delegations sent by Berber tribal leaders came thick and fast, as other members of the Idrīsid family also sought asylum in Córdoba. Meanwhile, in Ḥajar al-Naṣr, Ḥasan b. Qannūn's followers were abandoning him continually (up to 700 of them in just one day), including his own son and the prison warder who oversaw the hostages, who were all set free when their guardian decided to join the Umayyad ranks.[61]

[60] On the issues of the honour shown for the lineage and the codes of honour regarding women, P. Guichard, *al-Andalus. Estructura antropológica de una sociedad islámica en Occidente*, pp. 141–70. Once conquered, the city of Baṣra was left in command of ʿAbd al-Raḥmān b. Muḥammad b. al-Layth, who belonged to an old family of Berber origins whose ancestors had probably participated in the conquest, and later settled in the castle of Setefilla (Seville) as well as owning houses in Córdoba, E. Manzano Moreno, 'Quelques considérations', pp. 260–1.

[61] Ibn Ḥayyān, *Muqtabis VII*, ed. pp. 144, 145, 146–8; trans. pp. 182–3, 184 and 186–8. The Jabal al-ʿUyūn must be a reference to the large quantity of springs to be found in the environs of Ḥajar al-Naṣr, P. Cressier et al., 'Ḥağar al-Naṣr', pp. 329–30.

Nonetheless, the rebel continued to resist during the first few months of 974, confident in the impregnability of the fortress of Ḥajar al-Naṣr and the limitations of the Umayyad army. It is probable that Ḥasan b. Qannūn trusted that situation might change in his favour. The effort involved in the deployment of the Umayyad army and the purchase of the loyalty of the Berber tribal leaders could not be sustained for ever, and it is possible that the Idrīsid rebel considered that at some point the pressure being imposed on him would give way.

No such thing happened. At the end of winter, on 27 March 974 (29 *Jumāda* II 363 AH), after Friday prayers, in the mosque of Córdoba, the caliph announced to his viziers that Ḥasan b. Qannūn had surrendered. His submission had occurred at least a week before and it was most certainly the result of a negotiation. Neither Ḥasan b. Qannūn nor any of his followers suffered any form of punishment. Almost as soon as the news of his surrender had been received, orders were given to send jewels, cloths and horse bridles to the sons and cousins of Hasan, who were already in the Maghrebid coast on their way to Córdoba. On 4 April, they were in Algeciras.[62] Ḥasan b. Qannūn himself made his way to al-Andalus shortly afterwards. It is very possible that he was given a solemn public welcome at one of the spectacular receptions which al-Ḥakam II was so accustomed to hold. Regrettably, another lacuna in the manuscript of al-Rāzī used by Ibn Ḥayyān prevented him from recording the events that took place between the end of April 974 and the end of June the following year, which corresponded to the months of *Sha'bān* and *Ramaḍān* of 363 AH. It was during this period that Ḥasan b. Qannūn arrived, and he was granted a formal reception at the caliphal court.

Almost two years had gone by since the start of the campaign in Morocco, and one since al-Ḥakam had ordered his soldiers to fight for victory or death, in addition to his willingness to build a bridge of dirhams across the Straits of Gibraltar. A major triumph had been won and the caliph's court was exultant. This was the mood displayed at the celebration of the Breaking of the Fast (*'Īd al-fiṭr*) that year of 363 AH, 24 June 974, which took place in the eastern hall of the *alcázar* at Madīnat al-Zahrā'. The ceremony was presided over, as always, by Caliph al-Ḥakam, and it was attended by the defeated Ḥasan

[62] Ibn Ḥayyān, *Muqtabis VII*, ed. pp. 150–1; trans. pp. 190–2.

b. Qannūn, who was accompanied by his brother, sons and other Idrīsids.[63] Also present were Ja'far and Yaḥyā b. al-Andalusī, former allies of the Fāṭimid caliph, who had also taken up residence in al-Andalus. The occasion was a form of a celebration of the recent triumph won by al-Ḥakam II. He had good reasons to be proud, as he had in his presence people who had been his sworn enemies, but were now experiencing first-hand the grandiose display of caliphal magnificence.

Aside from the courtly pomp and grandeur, one thing Ḥasan b. Qannūn and his family members could not avoid was that this reception of the Breaking of the Fast would prove to be a very unpleasant occasion for them. Taking advantage of their presence, as well as the senior Umayyad dignitaries solemnly gathered at Madīnat al-Zahrā', al-Ḥakam II's court poets undertook to gleefully taunt the subjugated Idrīsid ruler in the poems it was customary to declaim at the reception. Muḥammad b. Shujayṣ was particularly cruel in his invectives. In front of Ḥasan b. Qannūn he dared to say:

> When the fool saw, having been abandoned by the hand of God,
> that the end, now clear before his eyes, was death;
> that the army of the prince (*amīr*) of God reaches
> whom is not reached by thoroughbred horses or camels,
> that the caliph's decision was irrevocable, and his wrath, death,
> and that wrath and death were also God's matter;
> and that, although he fled rapidly, he would arrive in China (*al-Ṣīn*),
> [...]
> he still hoped to escape, but the same hope informed him
> that destiny lay in wait for him everywhere.

This was just the beginning. During the subsequent round of verses, more insults were hurled. According to the poet, Ḥasan and his family claimed descent from the Quraysh family, but they did not merit any form of genealogy; they had been bred among the wild beasts of the desert, in a land without any learning, sipping miserable soups, and if Ḥasan was the head (*rā's*) of his lineage, the poet wished to know where its tail was. In contrast to the 'thinking always guided towards success' granted by God to the Umayyad caliph,

[63] Ibn Ḥayyān, *Muqtabis VII*, ed. pp. 155–68; trans. pp. 196–206.

someone like Ḥasan was the epitome of evil, who was only tolerated by the divinity in order to punish him all the better. When the defeated rebel had reached Córdoba, the troops had descended upon him like 'a cloud of locusts that jumped all around him', as they were governed 'by true intelligence and not by fraud and lies'. It was only the caliph's orders that had impeded a terrified Ḥasan from being received with hostility by the troops, and he could not be confident of being safe until he contemplated the 'splendour of the good omen', that is, the caliph 'guided by God'.

In the final part of his poem, Muḥammad b. Shujayṣ extolled the caliph to the same extent that he denigrated the defeated enemy. He could already delight in ruling over 'all the empire of the Maghreb', and the poet hoped that the army of victory would not delay its march on 'a route along which Egypt has become deaf and Aleppo cut off', which was by no means a veiled reference to the possibility that the Umayyad offensive would lead to the acquisition of Fāṭimid territories. Having accused Ḥasan of being a *rāfiḍí*, that is, someone who rejected the orthodox caliphs who had succeeded the Prophet Muḥammad, the poet concluded with the wish that the caliph's forehead should be crowned with the 'imperial crown' (*tajj al-mulk*), just as his ancestor Marwān's had been, and also his father, the 'well guided of the governors (*mahdī al-wulāt*)'.[64]

With open season now declared, the poet 'Abd al-'Azīz b. Ḥusayn al-Qarawī was not left far behind. Having branded the old rebel 'stupid' (*bā'is*), and celebrating the way in which death had hovered over him, his verses repeated the eulogy of the caliph's indulgence, without which 'the intestines and veins [of Ḥasan b. Qannūn] would have been wrenched from his body'. The same idea of his defeat being just the beginning of the major Umayyad expansion was repeated with references such as 'Syria will rise up to receive the Caliph because he has had rights over it for a long time', or 'it has already been too long that opinions immersed in error reign amongst the

[64] The poem also contains an especially subtle reference, as the whole *qaṣīda* takes the form of an imitation (*mu'āraḍa*) of the celebrated composition written by Abū Tammām in honour of the 'Abbāsid caliph al-Mu'taṣim following his conquest of the Byzantine town of Amorium in 838 (223 AH), S. T. Stetkevych, 'The *Qaṣīdah* and the Politics of Ceremony', pp. 32–41. It is worth nothing here that some elements of the account of this oriental episode imitated a report that had emir al-Ḥakam I as its protagonist, E. Manzano Moreno, 'Oriental Topoi', p. 46.

inhabitants of Iraq'. From there, the poet revealed a sensational rhetorical discovery: invoking Qur'anic references to the two orients, he announced that 'in the West the sun of a caliphate has risen', an idea I will analyse in detail below. Other poets, such as 'Abd al-Qadūs b. 'Abd al-Wahhāb and Abū l-Mujāhid al-Istijī, also contributed to the celebration, declaiming poems along similar lines; the latter in particular read out an *arjūza*, a type of poem that tended to take the form of lengthy compositions and was often used to recount facts of an epic nature.[65] It is barely probable that the literary evening was to the liking of Ḥasan b. Qannūn, who must have left the *'Īd al fiṭr* celebration without the slightest inclination to continue listening to the poetry. It is perhaps for this reason that there was no trace of his presence in the celebration held for the Feast of the Sacrifice in September that same year.

The poets' verses transmitted the certainty with which in mid-974 (363 AH) al-Ḥakam II and his administration considered that his policy had been a triumph and that his authority was unanimously recognised in the *Maghrib al-aqṣā*. A few weeks earlier, 'Abd al-Karīm b. Yaḥyā, ruler of the Andalusi sector of the city of Fez, had sworn an oath of loyalty (*bay'a*), and thereby acknowledged Umayyad sovereignty in that southern city. The document of submission included the obedience to the 'righteous imām al-Ḥakam al-Mustanṣīr bi-llāh, amīr al-mu'minīn'; war was to be waged against whomsoever he waged it, and alliances were not to be made with anybody else but him, to which was also added an express rejection of Shī'a doctrine. All of this was testified in front of God, the angels (*malā'ik*), prophets, envoys, all the creatures of Creation granted with knowledge, members of the Muslim community, and thirty-five people who acted as signatories, because 'on signing this obedience to the caliph they save both their faith and temporal existence, the other life and this perishing one'. Shortly afterwards, the hostages stipulated in this pact arrived from Fez in Córdoba; they were united with others sent by the Ghumāra tribe. Likewise, in August other members of the Idrīsid family arrived in Córdoba, and they were given residence in al-Andalus.[66]

[65] J. T. Monroe, 'The Historical arjūza of Ibn 'Abd Rabbihi, a Tenth-Century Hispano-Arabic Epic Poem', pp. 70–1.

[66] Ibn Ḥayyān, *Muqtabis VII*, ed. pp. 173–6; trans. pp. 212–15.

In the meantime, Ghālib was given orders to return to al-Andalus. The majority of his army continued to be deployed in the region. Yaḥyā b. Muḥammad b. Ḥasan al-Tujībī was left in command, possibly bearing in mind that the majority of the army was made up of frontier troops.[67] Shipments of money continued to be made, although it is very probable that soldiers were only stationed in strategic places: Tangier, Aṣīla, al-Baṣra, Jabal al-Karam, Ḥajar al-Naṣr and other enclaves that had been captured during the campaign. Many of the fortifications were strengthened to accommodate Umayyad garrisons, while in places such as Fez, and of course, in districts dominated by Berber tribes, all that mattered were the submission documents. The country was apparently pacified.

In an official letter addressed in June (*Dhū l-qa'da*) to the *qā'id*s and officers of all the provinces (*kūra*s) of al-Andalus and written by the vizier Ja'far al-Muṣḥafī, the caliph formally declared victory.[68] Amid praise to God, Qur'anic quotations and a long preamble that set out the dynasty's vision of itself, which will be analysed in more detail below, the letter proclaimed that the Umayyad caliphate had obtained obedience throughout the Maghreb, where prayers were now said in accordance with the orthodox canon. Buluggīn b. Zīrī had threatened to lead an expedition against the region, but this had been aborted, and the submission of the various tribal leaders and the rulers of Fez thus remained guaranteed. This letter was read out from all the pulpits of al-Andalus. Perhaps many people thought that this episode had been concluded, and that from then on the Maghreb would be integrated into the caliphate of al-Andalus as just another province.

The Consequences

The events that took place between 972 and 974 (361–3 AH) changed many things. The lives of many of its protagonists would never be the same again. Such was the case with the brothers Ja'far and Yaḥyā b. al-Andalusī, who had left the city of al-Masīla, where they had been landowners and rulers, and ended up settling in Córdoba with generous pensions, but as a lower rank of courtier, which meant they were obliged to fulfil the caliph's orders. Soon they

[67] X. Ballestí, *Al-Mansur y la dawla 'amiriyya*, pp. 101–2.

[68] Ibn Ḥayyān, *Muqtabis VII*, ed. pp. 178–81; trans. pp. 217–21.

would find out that this situation could bring in its wake consequences that were not always pleasant. At the crucial point of the campaign in Maghreb, in September 973 (*Dhū l-qa'da* de 362 AH) Yaḥyā received an order to join the caliphal army along with his men and a part of the *jund*. Although he did not have to serve for long, and in June the following year he was attending palace receptions once again, the military slaves (*'abīd*) who had accompanied him had come to the attention of the caliph. No sooner had the campaign ended when the caliph tried to buy them. To this effect he organised a meeting that was attended by Ziyād b. Aflaḥ, who was head of the cavalry and the person responsible for the stipendiary troops (*ḥasham*). There were also a number of jurists, legal consultants and arbitrators (*ḥukkām*), which demonstrates to what extent any issue linked to the property of slaves had an inevitable legal component. However, when the moment came to close the deal, Ja'far and his brother Yaḥyā refused to accept the sum that was offered to them. What is more, Ja'far went so far as to speak inconvenient phrases with regard to the caliph, 'displaying ... the firm Shī'ite convictions he still harboured in his inner heart'.

The caliph was informed, and his response was fulminating: both brothers and their sons were imprisoned. It was July 974 (*Shawwāl*, 363 AH), scarcely a few weeks after the reception held for the Feast of the Breaking of the Fast during which the poet's verses had humiliated Ḥasan b. Qannūn and his family. Ja'far and his brother Yaḥyā, who had up until then been provided for with extraordinary stipends, remained locked up in the prison of Madīnat al-Zahrā', whose grand ceremonial halls had hosted them just a few days before. There were probably suspicious-minded individuals – and I share this suspicion myself – who may have believed that it was no coincidence that they should fall from grace so soon after the victory won in Morocco; given the new situation, it evidently made little sense to maintain these Banū al-Andalusī in the sumptuous conditions that had been granted to them. Putting them in prison and saving their stipends was a form of acknowledging that there was less justification for continuing to use this family as part of the caliph's political strategy.

The Banū al-Andalusī spent nine months in prison. Then, all of a sudden, in early April 975 (*Rajab* 364 AH), the caliph gave the order to release Ja'far, his brother, Yaḥyā, and the rest of their family members. As if they had been freed from a Stalinist re-education camp, the two brothers were taken out of prison; they were cleaned up, had their hair cut, were dressed in precious clothes, and were placed on magnificent steeds to first go to their homes and then present themselves in the *alcázar* in Córdoba before the principal dignitaries of the administration. There, they were reminded of 'their failings and errors', which, they having passed through the re-education camp of the prison in al-Zahrā', both men acknowledged. They were then informed of the caliph's pardon and granted their freedom, as well as various sacks full of dinars, which prompted them both to bless and praise the caliph.[69]

Shortly afterwards the brothers renewed their attendance at the caliphal receptions, although we do not know if they received their previous salaries. In any case, their pardon was calculated. It is very probable that the caliph was already toying with the idea that the Banū al-Andalusī were the best candidates for commanding the army that remained in North Africa. The man in charge of the troops, Yaḥyā b. Muḥammad b. Ḥasan al-Tujībī, was a frontier landlord from Zaragoza, and he seemingly had no aspirations to remain permanently away from his lands. In late 975 (365 AH), Ja'far b. al-Andalusī and his brother Yaḥyā were sent to the other side of the Straits as the substitution for this *qā'id*. Ja'far's relations with the Maghrāwa and other Berber tribes were fundamental to recruiting troops on their own terrain, and the operations they carried out there seem to have always been undertaken with extreme loyalty to the Umayyad caliph.[70]

However, if there was any one winner in al-Ḥakam II's complex North African policy, with all its excesses, betrayals and occasional fireworks, it was the most unexpected individual in this whole saga: the obliging civil servant Muḥammad b. Abī 'Amīr, who during these years undertook a number of commissions to travel to the other side of the Straits to gain first-hand information about the situation there: his findings very possibly contributed to defining the strategies and policies that were implemented. Having been appointed to multiple and highly varied posts, in July 973 (*Shawwāl* 362 AH) he added a

[69] Ibn Ḥayyān, *Muqtabis VII*, ed. 128 and 171–4; trans. 164 and 209–12.

[70] Ibn 'Idhārī, *al-Bayān*, II, ed. cit. pp. 249 and 278–9. X. Ballestí, *Al Mansur y la dawla 'amiriyya*, pp. 102–9, who cites the testimony of the *Mafākhir* to indicate the interest shown by the principal members of the court in distancing the Banū al-Andalusī from Córdoba in the face of the imminent succession of al-Ḥakam II.

new one to his collection: supreme *qāḍī* of the North African side (*al-ʿidwa*), with responsibilities for the distribution and supervision of the funds and gifts that were sent there. His role was such that the army *qāʾid*s and officers received precise orders to do nothing without consulting him.[71]

Through this post Muḥammad b. Abī ʿAmīr was able to establish political relationships, which proved decisive for his later career. When al-Ḥakam II died in 976 (366 AH), he was already one of the caliphate's most powerful men thanks to his machinations and the networks of trust he had been gradually weaving in the Maghreb. The recruitment of the Berber troops, who ended up supplanting the regular army, paved the way for him to come to power or, as Ibn Ḥayyān wrote some years later, to 'sink into the darkness with them'. Once he was in power, Muḥammad b. Abī ʿAmīr took great care to continue maintaining the Umayyads' domination in northern Morocco in the same form as al-Ḥakam II had done, and in doing so he achieved resounding results. For example, in 986 (376 AH) the ruler of Sijilmāsa acknowledged Umayyad sovereignty, something which may well have increased Andalusi control over the sub-Saharan trade routes.

During those years, Jaʿfar b. al-Andalusī became the closest ally of Muḥammad b. Abī ʿAmīr. Jaʿfar assisted him with recruiting Berber troops and fought alongside him against those who opposed his rise to power. A grateful Muḥammad b. Abī ʿAmīr brought him back from North Africa and eventually appointed him vizier in 980 (378 AH). Shortly afterwards Muḥammad b. Abī ʿAmīr adopted the title of al-Manṣūr in 981–2 (371 AH), but for a reason that remains unknown, once he had gained control of power within the caliphate, he decided to dispose of those who had been faithful allies until then. One account tells of how Jaʿfar b. al-Andalusī was invited to a celebration in al-Manṣūr's house in January 982 (*Shaʿbān*, 372 AH). He drank and danced, and while returning home in the company of his retinue was killed without being able to defend himself due to being so drunk. His head and his right hand were sent to al-Manṣūr, who gave cynical demonstrations of his grief despite having given the order for the assassination.[72]

71 Ibn Ḥayyān, *Muqtabis VII*, ed. p. 123; trans. p. 156; Ibn ʿIdhārī, *al-Bayān*, II, ed. cit. p. 251.

72 Ibn ʿIdhārī, *al-Bayān*, II, ed. cit. pp. 279–281. The person responsible for his death was Maʿn b. Muḥammad al-Tujībī.

Ḥasan b. Qannūn, the former Idrīsid rebel, met an equally unfortunate fate. After a serious incident involving a large piece of amber that al-Ḥakam II had appropriated from him, Ḥasan and the rest of his family were invited to abandon al-Andalus: they do not seem to have found it easy to settle in a court that had welcomed them with insults. In 975 (365 AH), they were sent to Ifrīqiya, from where they travelled to Egypt. There they placed themselves under the protection of the Fāṭimid caliph, who felt himself obliged to shelter these distant relations. Some time later, Hasan returned to the Maghreb and challenged the Umayyad dominion in the region.[73] He managed to capture the city of al-Aqlām and even took the unusual decision of proclaiming himself caliph there, in a clear attempt to undermine Umayyad legitimacy in the region. The reaction from the all-powerful al-Manṣūr was to deploy a huge army that in a short time managed to defeat and capture the one-time rebel. Ḥasan b. Qannūn was once more sent to Córdoba, but this time considerably less attention was paid to him: he was executed before even reaching the capital in October 985 (*Jumāda I*, 385 AH).[74]

[73] Ibn Abī Zar', *Rawḍ al-Qirṭās*, ed. Benmansour, pp. 114–15; trans. Beaumier, pp. 127–8.
[74] X. Ballestí, *Al Mansur y la dawla 'amiriyya*, pp. 154–8.

7

Defending the Muslims

The Viking Danger

The massive military operation undertaken by the Umayyad caliphate in North Africa significantly weakened its capacity to respond to threats that arose on other fronts. One such threat was the Viking attacks, which had been taking place in al-Andalus for a considerable time and were inflicting major damage. Incursions by these Scandinavian pirates – which is what *vikingr* means in Old Norse, while its feminine form refers to their 'expedition' – had begun in the late eighth century using the impressive boats developed by this Norse people, with which they navigated across the Atlantic. Their boats could reach speeds that had never been achieved before, and their remarkable designs permitted them to sail up rivers, as well as transport a significant quantity of troops and provisions. Aside from the longships, which are undoubtedly their best-known vessel, they used other classes of ships, which played a support role and were used for loading and transporting the captives and booty obtained. They were also used to carry the cohorts of warriors that served under leaders – inspired by ideals of a 'good life' sailing the seas, fighting and plundering riches – who had invested huge sums in the construction of these ships. One of the places where such riches were to be found in abundance was in the south, in *Serkland*, the 'Land of the Saracens'.[1]

In the summer of 844 (229 AH), a Viking squadron formed of fifty-four ships along with a similar number of smaller ships attacked various locations

[1] P. Pentz, 'Ships and the Vikings', in G. Williams et al., *Vikings. Life and Legend*, London, 2014, p. 221.

along the north and west of Iberia, including Lisbon.[2] Having then headed south, the squadron sailed up the Guadalquivir River as far as Seville. This was a manoeuvre these Scandinavian pirates frequently used, and they did so at a later date against London and Paris: it consisted of sailing to the mouth of a river and from there navigating upstream to cities where they could pillage greater quantities of booty. This strategy had the further advantage of leaving their rearguard in a safer position as they were able to re-board their ships more swiftly. In Seville, the suddenness of the Viking attack and the delay with which Emir ʻAbd al-Raḥmān II mustered the army allowed the attackers to set up camp undisturbed for forty days. The city and its outlying region were pillaged and attacked; only the women and children were saved as captives. When the emir's troops finally arrived in Seville, the Vikings abandoned their camp. The Umayyad chroniclers state that the attackers suffered many losses as they retreated, although it is possible that it was in fact the end of summer that had prompted their decision to leave.

The sacking of Seville and the hardships suffered by its population left a harsh, bitter memory. The Viking attack had demonstrated the fragility of Umayyad power when faced by such an unexpected danger. Shortly afterwards, and despite the well-founded fears that it would facilitate a possible rebellion from the city, ʻAbd al-Raḥmān II ordered a defensive wall to be built around Seville to protect it from further attacks. Around the same date, the emir also commissioned the construction of a squadron to defend the coasts more effectively.[3] Thanks to these measures, the next Viking expedition inflicted less harm. In 859 (245 AH), more than seventy ships were sighted off the western coast of al-Andalus. These having been spotted before they reached the mouth of the Guadalquivir, the Umayyad squadron went to intercept them. Nonetheless, this new expedition also resulted in pillaging and the capture of prisoners, although the areas that suffered the worst were the regions beyond the Straits of Gibraltar, along the Maghribid coast.

For over a century, there is no further record of any other Viking incursions in Iberia. However, the memory of these strange northern people, who arrived in numerous ships with no other purpose than to sack towns and

[2] On this and the rest of Viking expeditions in al-Andalus, A. Christys, *Vikings in the South*, pp. 29ff.
[3] J. Lirola, *El poder naval de al-Andalus en la época del califato omeya*.

cities, and take captives, was etched into the memory of the chroniclers and those who had suffered at their hands. The Arab authors referred to them as *al-Majūs* or else as *al-Ardamāniyyūn*. The first name refers to their pagan character and linked them to the name with which Arab writers used to refer to the followers of the Zoroastrian religion; the second possibly reflects the term *Lordomanni* used by the author of the *Albeldense Chronicle* (881), which was adapted from the *Normanni* and *gens Nordomannorum*, 'peoples from the North', by which they are referred to in other contemporaneous Latin works.[4]

During the rule of al-Ḥakam II, in the summer of 966 (355 AH), these *Normanni* reappeared on the Andalusi coasts, and they were swiftly recognised as the same people who had sacked Seville over a hundred years before. This expeditionary force formed part of a series of Viking groups that were destroying monasteries and towns in Galicia. This time twenty-eight boats were also seen on the west coast near Alcacer do Sal, from where they rapidly launched an attack on Lisbon. The caliph's order to rapidly deploy military squadrons managed to halt the attackers in Silves and prevented them from making further progress on their voyage. Although their pillaging mission had failed, this expedition underscored how Viking attacks were once more being targeted on al-Andalus.

Five years later, at the end of June 971 (*Ramaḍān* 360 AH) reports arrived of sightings of Viking ships off the western coast of al-Andalus. On hearing the news, al-Ḥakam gave orders that preparations should be made immediately to tackle them. The order was carried out with astonishing speed. Scarcely, a few days later, on 3 July (6 *Ramaḍān*), the admiral (*qā'id al-baḥr*), 'Abd al-Raḥmān b. Rumāḥis, left Córdoba for Almería with orders to launch the squadron. Two of the caliph's servants (*fatās*), Mubārak and Mubashshir, were commissioned to requisition provisions in the provinces of Rayyuh (Málaga) and Sidonia, and establish supply posts along the coast, where the

[4] A. Christys, pp. 15ff. A. Benison, 'The Peoples of the North', pp. 169–71. I consider it highly probable that the *Lordomanni* referred to in the *Albeldense Chronicle* reflects an Arabised linguistic use by the Mozarabic author who wrote the work. In this regard, see the ideas set out by F. Corriente, who considers that, aside from *Normanni*, the word may also reflect the Arabic word *ardamūn* or 'mariners', *A Dictionary of Andalusi Arabic*, p. 10.

fleet could stock up on water and food. The task was completed so quickly that three weeks later, at the end of July (end of *Ramaḍān*), the squadron left Pechina (Almería) heading for Seville. So that nothing would be left to chance, land forces were also mobilised. The *qā'id* Ghālib was summoned by the caliph and given orders to leave with the army in order to prevent the Vikings from disembarking and extending their pillaging campaigns further inland along the western coast. Just two weeks after the sighting of the enemy, Ghālib departed Madīnat al-Zahrā' with an army unit.[5]

Fears of an imminent Viking attack increased following the arrival in Córdoba of a Christian ambassador who declared that the expedition had sailed up the River Duero. However, it should not be ruled out that these rumours were circulated intentionally to ensure that the Umayyad army was engaged with a bogus threat. In fact, neither the naval squadron nor the land troops encountered the supposed attackers. The fleet was mobilised all summer, and when it returned to Almería in September 971 (*Dhū l-qa'da* 360 AH) it had only engaged in one skirmish.[6] Ghālib, in turn, kept the land army on campaign for a further two months, until 24 November (2 *Ṣafar*), when he returned to Córdoba. The following day he made a triumphal entry into the *alcázar*, where he was welcomed by the caliph and presented with honorific garments (*khil'a*), despite not having taken part in any action worthy of being marked in this manner.[7]

On this occasion, the Viking threat had vanished, but the caliphate had once more demonstrated its capacity to govern by preventing a possible disaster that had loomed over the Muslim community. 'Īsā al-Rāzī attributed the failure of the Viking threat to the 'excellent defence that God delivered through the Muslims', or, in other words, to the military arrangements taken by the caliph. In his description of the troops, the chronicler included a quotation from the Qur'an: 'God spared the believers of fighting. He is strong and mighty.' This quotation offers the key to his narrative: the display of force deployed by the caliph, God's representative, had avoided the need for combat

[5] Ibn Ḥayyān, *Muqtabis VII*, ed. pp. 23–6, 27–8; trans. pp. 48–50, 51.
[6] Ibn Ḥayyān, *Muqtabis VII*, ed. p. 58; trans. pp. 76–7. In the edition of *Muqtabis VII*, the account of this episode is misplaced, and its placement in the translation is a preferable solution.
[7] Ibn Ḥayyān, *Muqtabis VII*, ed. pp. 66–7; trans. pp. 88–9.

and guaranteed the safety of the Muslims.[8] It had been a costly endeavour in terms of the supplies and wages required to keep a fleet on patrol for two months and an army on campaign for four months, but such displays, albeit somewhat disproportionate, were needed to underscore the caliphate's legitimacy and convince everyone of the credibility of the institution headed by al-Ḥakam II.

The following year, 972 (361 AH), news on Viking movements in the west of al-Andalus once more caused an exaggerated reaction. As soon as the news arrived, on 20 June (5 *Ramaḍān*), the caliph convened his private council (*majlisi-hi al-khaṣṣ*), which included the viziers. The news could not have arrived at a worse moment. Al-Ḥakam was on the brink of decreeing the mobilisation of the standing army in preparation for the campaign in northern Morocco, which meant he had to make recourse to the *Tangerins*, the poorly esteemed stipendiary troops. Their leader, Ziyād b. Aflaḥ, was also a vizier, and, as was discussed above, he had been also the recipient of a valuable ivory casket from the caliph. Ziyād was put in command of the expedition along with Hishām b. Muḥammad b. ʿUthmān, the *ṣāḥib al-shurṭa*, who had under his command the modest unit of troops used to maintain order in the capital, which probably joined the expedition as well.

As the standing army was being mobilised for the Moroccan campaign just as the *Tangerins* were called up, both military units were in Córdoba at the same time. Due to the antipathy between them, a confrontation flared up outside the *alcázar* on 26 June (11 *Ramaḍān*), and, as was discussed above, the city's population also took part and joined forces with the soldiers attacking the *Tangerins* (see p. 152). The incident perhaps prompted the caliph to hasten the departure of the expedition against the Vikings. That very same day, he convened Ziyād b. Aflaḥ and Hishām b. Muḥammad b. ʿUthmān once more and issued them with his final instructions. As was customary, they left the audience with the caliph bearing lavish gifts of honorific garments (*khilʿa*), turbans and swords. In addition, the caliph presented them with two flags, two standards and a magnificent pavilion, which was to be used for holding meetings while on campaign. The troops made their departure with

[8] The whole verse reads: 'God sent back the disbelievers along with their rage – they gained no benefit – and spared the believers from fighting. He is strong and mighty.' Qur'an 33, 25.

a degree of, perhaps intentional, martial pomp: the soldiers left Córdoba's *alcázar* watched by 'so many people, including the distinguished and the common people (*al-khāṣṣa wa-l 'āmma*), that no one, but their Creator could count them'.[9]

Again, the supposed Viking threat once more vanished into thin air. For just over two and a half months Ziyād b. Aflaḥ and Hishām b. Muḥammad b. 'Uthmān patrolled the western regions of al-Andalus without coming across a single Nordic warrior. They reached the town of Santarén, where they received news that the Vikings had left. Their spies, sent as far as Santiago de Compostela, 'in the most distant point of enemy country', confirmed that the Vikings had abandoned the region.[10] Following their return to Madīnat al-Zahrā', on 17 September (5 *Dhū l-Hijja*), they were received by the caliph, who they informed about their campaign. Once again, the danger – perhaps more imagined than real – had evaporated, but the caliph's legitimacy as protector of the Islamic community had been safeguarded. Furthermore, it is a fact that the Vikings did not return to the Andalusi coasts.

The Battle for the Duero Valley: the Beginning

Al-Ḥakam II always took his duty of guaranteeing the security of the Islamic community and the protection of their property very seriously. Ensuring the frontiers of al-Andalus were secure was part of that task and a key responsibility the caliph could not afford to ignore, especially if one takes into account that the Umayyad caliphate occupied the most westerly limit of the territory of Islam (*dār al-islām*).[11] The effective defence of this frontier (*thagr*), which separated al-Andalus from the Christian territories, was one of the arguments the dynasty used to convince all and sundry that the caliphate was a legitimate Muslim government which scrupulously fulfilled this obligation.

In contrast, Fāṭimid propaganda insisted that the Umayyads were not capable of effectively containing the Christian threat against Islam. The poet Ibn Hānī compared his patron's successes against the Byzantine empire with

[9] Ibn Ḥayyān, *Muqtabis VII*, ed. pp. 78–9; trans. pp. 101–2.

[10] Ibn Ḥayyān, *Muqtabis VII*, ed. pp. 92–3; trans. pp. 116–17. The edition of *Muqtabis VII* gives the date as 5 *Dhū l-qa'da*, which obviously must be corrected in line with the accurate date given in the translation.

[11] A. K. S. Lambton, *State and Government in Medieval Islam*, pp. 18–19 and 91.

the defeats the Umayyads were suffering in al-Andalus at the hands of the Christians.[12] In the mid-tenth century (fourth AH), there were reasons for optimism, but also for thinking along these pessimistic lines. On the one hand, it is true that the Christians had not managed to conquer any significant urban settlement in the peninsula since the troops of the Carolingian Louis the Pious had captured Barcelona in 800. However, during the last quarter of the ninth century and the beginning of the tenth highly significant changes had been taking place along the Middle Frontier (*al-thagr al-awsaṭ*), which extended from the region of the upper Ebro Valley, in the borderlands of La Rioja and Navarre, and formed an arc across the valleys of the Henares and Jalón Rivers, as far as the southern slopes of the Central System.

On the other side of the Middle Frontier were the territories of the Duero Valley, a region where intriguing events must have taken place during this period, although they are not always well-documented. Following the Arabic conquest in 711, the Duero Basin had become a marginal territory with scant recollection of the importance it had attained during the Roman period, when it had been studded with cities such as Astorga, Clunia, León or Segovia, as well as the elegant *villae* of the Roman aristocracy that were built between the third and fifth centuries. Although some of these cities were converted into bishoprics during the Visigothic period, they had all ceased to be significant before or after the Arab conquest, and in some cases they had even vanished. In the rural areas, some *villae* continued to exist for some time, but over the long term monasteries and noble estates administering both the land and people failed to emerge. All the evidence seems to indicate that there was a decline in the main urban and manufacturing centres along the Duero Valley, and although the end of the Roman Empire and the disappearance of the Visigoth kingdom seemingly contributed to this development, the truth is that we do not know the precise reasons of this decline.[13]

Some historians, above all C. Sánchez Albornoz, thought that this crisis was aggravated by the Duero Valley being abandoned after the Arab conquest, and that it became a no-man's land that was consciously created as a buffer

[12] Yalaoui, 'Les relations ...', p. 24.

[13] A. Chavarría, 'Romanos y visigodos en el valle de Duero (siglos V–VIII)', pp. 191–209. I. Martín Viso, 'Una frontera casi invisible', pp. 89–114.

zone by the northern Asturian kings in the mid-eighth century to safeguard them against any Andalusi incursions from the south. The problem with this explanation is that it is hard to imagine how these feeble kings managed to dismantle a network of cities and settlements in a territory extending over 90,000 square kilometres, however decayed its urban network may have been. Nor is it acceptable to think that the region was left as a strategic desert, because archaeological finds have clearly documented the presence of people in the enclaves at which it has been possible to undertake systematic excavations.[14]

Nonetheless, in the Duero Valley there is no evidence for the aspects of growth that can be documented in other regions of al-Andalus, as well as in other Christian territories during much of the ninth century. One proof of this is that the emirs of Córdoba could not, or did not want to, occupy these territories, and nor were the Christian kings and counts who ruled over the lands further north capable of implementing their control over them. As a result, the Andalusi chronicles tend to ignore this region, as do the Christian ones, whereby the Duero Basin vanishes from the textual register throughout the eighth century and for much of the ninth. It is likely that it became a marginal frontier zone; a no-man's land in the hands of communities, who lacked any administrative structure, and were clearly unwilling to accept any form of external sovereignty.[15]

This situation began to change during the last quarter of the ninth century. Conscious of the profound crisis faced by the Umayyad emirate at that time, and following the interruption of the regular military expeditions led against them, the Christian kingdoms and counties developed a political and social initiative that allowed them to occupy the Duero Valley. It is very probable that this was aided by internal dynamics within the region's communities, which enabled the consolidation and reinforcement of dominant local groups who formed pacts with those from the north. One of the results of this process was the creation of a new network of monastic establishments,

[14] See the studies published in I. Martín Viso, ed., *¿Tiempos oscuros? Territorio y sociedad en el centro de la Península Ibérica (siglos VII–XI)*, Madrid, 2009.

[15] The classic work on the Duero Valley continues to be C. Sánchez-Albornoz, *Despoblación y repoblación del valle del Duero*, Buenos Aires, 1966. While there are local archaeological studies, a global vision of the region is only gradually being pieced together, I. Martín Viso, 'Colapso político y sociedades locales: el noroeste en la península ibérica (siglos VIII–IX)'.

which functioned not only as centres for gathering material resources, but also as epicentres for cultural and religious transmission: the monasteries of San Pedro de Cardeña, San Pedro de Arlanza or Santos Cosme y Damián in Abellar are examples, among others, of a monastic network that, between the late ninth and early tenth centuries, began to exercise a powerful form of social as well as ideological control over the settlements that were being progressively incorporated into the new political and social frameworks.

As a consequence, over the course of these decades the Astur-Leonese monarchs and the kingdom's lay and ecclesiastical aristocracy were able to extend their domains and occupy enclaves as far as the River Duero itself.[16] Weakened by the internal rebellions that multiplied in al-Andalus, the Umayyad emirs could not, or did not know how to, contain this wave of expansion, which did not come at any cost to Muslim territories, but instead emerged across a region that had been politically and administratively abandoned for more than a century and a half.

Once he had managed to resolve the internal crisis within his own domains, ʿAbd al-Raḥmān III encountered an incipient urban network that had been formed against his northern frontier with cities such as Viseo, León, Zamora and Burgos, as well as a series of settlements and fortifications along the middle and upper course of the River Duero at places such as San Esteban de Gormaz, Osma, Clunia, Roa and Aza. It was now easier to harass Andalusi territories from these settlements, and this was taken advantage of by the Christians to launch attacks such as had rarely been seen before. An Umayyad expedition against the fortress of San Esteban de Gormaz (Soria) in 917 (305 AH) ended with the death of a *qāʾid* and a major defeat for the Muslim army. The following year, in June 918 (305 AH), King Ordoño II of León and King Sancho García of Pamplona joined forces to attack Nájera and Valtierra, while in the spring of 921 (307 AH) a Christian incursion sacked the region around the fortress of Alcolea del Pinar, which was in the territory of the governor of Guadalajara, and pillaged livestock and mules.[17] The wedge of fortresses and Christian settlements on the upper and mid-course of the River Duero enabled

[16] J. Escalona, 'Military Stress, Central Power and Local Response in the County of Castile in the Tenth Century', pp. 341–67. I. Martín Viso, 'Integración política y regeneración', pp. 207–39.

[17] Ibn Ḥayyān, *Muqtabis V*, ed. and trans. pp. 88–9, 94 and 105.

the Christians to attack territories between the so-called Upper Frontier, along the River Ebro, and those of the Middle Frontier, along the River Tagus basin. The situation became all the more dangerous as the Christian attackers could benefit from the unstable loyalty of various frontier leaders, who were known to ally with Christian kings and potentates when they sensed that the power exerted from Córdoba went against their interests.

'Abd al-Raḥmān III was very conscious of the serious danger that was entailed by this new situation along the northern frontiers. 'A long and famous epistle' drafted in autumn of 919 (307 AH) and read out in Córdoba's mosque incited the people 'to [wage] holy war and to take action against their enemies'. In the years that followed, of the four military campaigns the caliph personally led against Christian territories, three were targeted on the Duero Valley. During what was known as the Muez campaign, fought in summer 921 (308 AH), he attacked Osma, San Esteban de Gormaz and Clunia, from where the army headed towards Tudela, and then made its way into Navarrese territory. The Duero Valley was targeted by the caliph once more in the summer of 934 (322 AH), when he undertook the so called Osma campaign: aside from attacking Osma, which is today in the province of Soria, settlements like Huerta, Clunia, Gormaz and Caracena (*Qashtrub*) were also targeted. Finally, in the summer of 939 (327 AH), on the last major campaign commanded by the caliph, known as the 'Campaign of Great Power', the first target was Simancas, located at the confluence of the Rivers Pisuerga and Duero. Following a battle that took place there with the troops of the King Ramiro II of León, the caliph sought to reach San Esteban de Gormaz, possibly by following the River Duero. However, the people of Guadalajara convinced him that the army should take a different route through their region, as attacks were frequently being launched from settlements in the Riaza valley. It was while crossing this zone that the caliph and his army suffered the devastating ambush at Alhándega, which was the greatest military disaster suffered by the Umayyad caliphate, and from which 'Abd al-Raḥmān III barely escaped alive.[18]

This defeat had many consequences. One of them, as has been already discussed, was to show up the weaknesses of the Umayyad army, some of whose leaders were executed on the caliph's orders on their return to Córdoba.

[18] Ibn Ḥayyān, *Muqtabis V*, ed. and trans. pp. 102, 105–10, 224–32, 297–300.

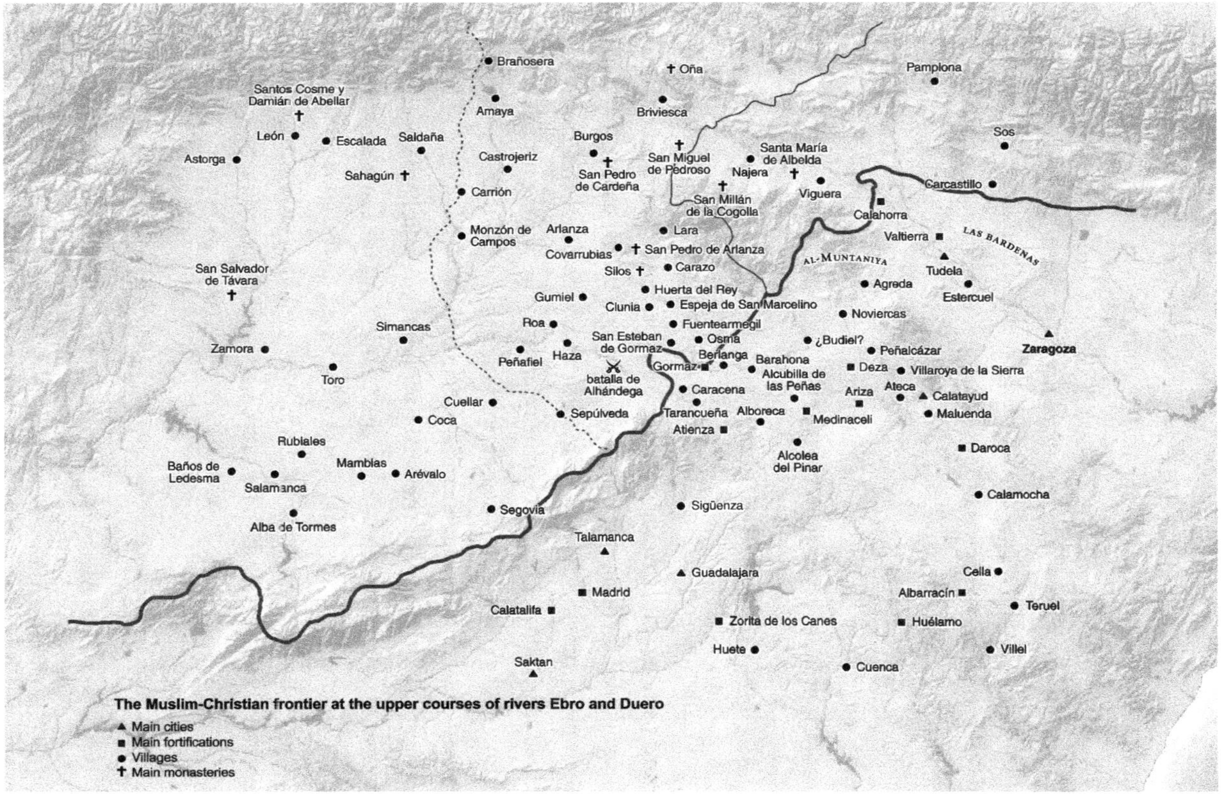

Figure 4 The Muslim–Christian frontier at the upper courses of the Rivers Ebro and Duero

Alhándega also demonstrated that the loss of control of the Duero Valley was beginning to place the caliphate in serious difficulties. The Christian kingdoms and territories were no longer the passive targets of summer campaigns (*aceifas*) undertaken by the Umayyad armies; instead they were beginning to demonstrate an unheard-of capacity to launch devastating attacks against Muslim territories. The humiliation suffered by the caliph had not been caused by any monarch or senior dignitary from Castile and León, but by an ambush launched by the people of the Duero region, people whose raids could reach as far as the region of Guadalajara or even inflict a crushing defeat on the Umayyad army at San Esteban de Gormaz.[19] Populated by settlements that were as varied as their political leaders, the Duero basin was becoming an intricate territory, in which the defence of the Andalusi frontier involved confrontations with increasingly determined enemies.

The Caliphate's Change of Strategy

The major disaster suffered at Alhándega marked a profound change in the caliphate's strategy. Its sovereigns never led expeditions against the Christian north again, and the long campaigns commanded by the caliph clad in chain mail became a thing of the past.[20] It is true that when they had been victorious, these campaigns had increased the ruler's prestige among his subjects, but they also entailed physical as well as political risks, given that a defeat would provide ammunition for the enemies of Umayyad sovereignty. Al-Ḥakam II was always very well aware of the need to preserve the caliphate's prestige, and he avoided exposing himself to such risks. Following the same policy that his father had launched in the final years of his reign, he too showed no interest in proving himself as a warrior caliph.[21] The new Umayyad strategy ceased to be based on the display of military supremacy under the military command of

[19] P. Chalmeta, 'Simancas y Alhándega', pp. 350–444.

[20] Ibn Ḥayyān, *Muqtabis V*, ed. and trans. pp. 296–7.

[21] Ibn Ḥazm states that 'Abd al-Raḥmān III was the last Umayyad caliph to personally lead an expedition, *Naqṭ al-ʿarūs*, ed. p. 177; trans. p. 14, which contradicts vague and somewhat generic data about al-Ḥakam II leading two expeditions. The first is mentioned following an account of the conclusion of the building work on the mosque of Córdoba, but no mention is made of where it was aimed; the second expedition led by al-Ḥakam was apparently targeted on Gormaz, but the scarcity of details suggests that the caliph only accompanied the troops as they set out on the expedition, Ibn 'Idhārī, *al-Bayān*, II, ed. cit. pp. 236 and 241.

the caliph. Instead, it was centred around three major tactical concerns, which were developed immediately after Alhándega and maintained throughout the reign of al-Ḥakam II; indeed, it was probably him who had defined them.

The first of these tactical decisions consisted of reinforcing the Andalusi frontiers by fortifying or rebuilding strategic enclaves, and stationing military garrisons in them. The soldiers that formed part of these garrisons were not members of the regular army (*jund*), whose military obligations were limited to undertaking one campaign per year; instead stipendiary troops (*ḥasham*) were used, who were regularly paid and could be established on a permanent basis. Aside from paying the wages of these troops, their provisions also had to be covered. Orders were given to store in these enclaves 'wheat, barley, food, salt, firewood and other items needed in case of a siege, all of which should be kept in abundant quantities in the upper part of the fortress in case of need'.[22] Naturally, the provisioning of all these products could only be guaranteed by the efficient functioning of the caliphate's administration, which remained in the hands of officials who served under the caliph's orders.

As a result of this policy, a range of places of singular strategic value on the frontier were fortified. Such was the case with Saktān and Calatalifa, two fortresses whose purpose was to control access to the mountain passes that crossed the Central System.[23] Shortly afterwards in 946 (335 AH), Medinaceli (today in the province of Soria) was rebuilt by frontier troops and carpenters overseen by the *qā'id*, Ghālib, who was assisted in this task by a *qāḍī*. The completion of this task meant that this strategic site overlooking the upper course of the River Duero had been reinforced, and it went on to play a key defensive role against the assaults launched by the Christians in the region.[24]

Al-Ḥakam II maintained the same policy of reinforcing enclaves along the frontier. In 965–6 (354 AH), Ghālib was commissioned to rebuild another fortress in the Duero Valley: Gormaz, built on an impressive hill overlooking

[22] Ibn Ḥayyān, *Muqtabis V*, ed. and trans. p. 309.

[23] The location of *Saktān* is not known. It must have been located between the passes of Arrebatacapas and Tornavacas, which allowed the Central System to be crossed. Calatalifa corresponds with the castle of la Mora, in the municipality of Villaviciosa de Odón (Madrid), E. Manzano, *La frontera de al-Andalus*, pp. 177–9.

[24] M. Bueno Sánchez, '¿Frontera en el Duero oriental?', pp. 165–90. The *qāḍī* who assisted Ghālib was Muḥammad b. Abī 'Īsā, M. Marín, 'Una familia de ulemas cordobeses: los Banū Abī 'Īsā', p. 309.

the course of the river, was located around eighty kilometres from Medinaceli. In the past it had changed hands on many occasions, but having come definitively under caliphal control it was rebuilt. The building work commissioned by Ghālib resulted in the enormous fortification that is still visible today: the elongated shape of this walled castle extends almost four hundred metres and is reinforced by twenty-seven square towers. The castle also has a monumental tower with a large horseshoe arch framed by an *alfiz*, which is similar in size and form to contemporary architectural projects undertaken by al-Ḥakam II in Córdoba. Undoubtedly what we see today is the work overseen by Ghālib, and this is confirmed by the foundation stone bearing the name Caliph al-Ḥakam II, which was found in a Christian church located at the base of the castle.[25]

Another fortification on the upper course of the Ebro, Calahorra (La Rioja), was also fortified by Ghālib in 968 (357 AH). In this case, it was an episcopal see from the Visigoth era that had become a castle (*ḥiṣn*), due to its location on the frontier between the territories of al-Andalus and the kingdom of Pamplona, and it had been the subject of continual military disputes between Muslims and Christians. The development of this fortification involved reinforcing the walls and building a tower, which ensured that it remained in Muslim hands until it was definitively conquered by the Christians in 1045. Another frontier enclave that was fortified during this period was Tortosa, where a dockyard was built.[26]

In addition to these major enclaves were many other smaller ones. In the section of the Middle and Upper Frontier between Guadalajara and Zaragoza 250 Andalusi fortifications and settlements have been identified.[27] Naturally, the caliph of Córdoba did not have the means to establish garrisons in each and every one of the fortresses along the Andalusi frontier from the Mediterranean to the Atlantic. It was for this reason that the second key tactical concern of the new caliphal policy was its dependence on the prominent families who had settled in the frontier regions and had long exerted control over these

[25] J. Zozaya, 'Evolución de un yacimiento: el castillo de Gormaz (Soria)', pp. 173–8. A. Almagro, 'La puerta califal del castillo de Gormaz', pp. 55–77; M. Ocaña, 'Lápida árabe en la ermita de San Miguel de Gormaz', pp. 450–2.

[26] Ibn 'Idhārī, *al-Bayān*, II, ed. p. 241; trans. p. 398. J. A. Souto, 'El noroeste de la Frontera Superior de al-Andalus en época omeya', pp. 253–67. T. Sáenz de Haro, 'Calahorra islámica', pp. 107–54. J. Negre Pérez and R. Martí Castelló, 'Urbanismo en la marca oriental de al-Andalus', pp. 187–201.

[27] V. Alejandre Alcalde, *El sistema defensivo musulmán*, p. 25.

border territories. Although, over the years, relationships between them and the central administration had often been strained, after Alhándega Caliph ʿAbd al-Raḥmān III chose to formally acknowledge the power they exerted over these territories, 'annually renewing their appointments with extensive powers, as well as those of their successors'.[28] In practice, this meant accepting that complete sectors of the frontier remained in the hands of these families, as they now obtained the caliph's express consent to make their dominions hereditary ones. In exchange, they committed themselves to supporting the caliph's policy for the defence of his frontiers, which involved controlling Christian incursions and endeavouring to make it unnecessary to launch further major expeditions against the north.

Although we do not how these families exercised their rule within their territories, their names are known, as well as their intricate family trees. This was the case with families such as the Tujībids, who ruled in Zaragoza and in other enclaves on the Upper Frontier; the Banū Razīn, who had taken control of the region of Albarracín; the Banū Dhī l-Nūn who held sway in the Santaver area – between what is today Guadalajara and Cuenca; and the Banū Zarwāl and the Banū Gazlūn, who had settled in areas of what is today the province of Teruel. While their origins were varied – the Tujībids were Arabs, the rest Berbers – their degree of Arabisation at that time was complete and they would all have fully identified with the caliphate's political programme, so long as they were suitably compensated. The control exerted by these families over their territories must have been pervasive, and it went unchallenged, as decades later their descendants naturally took on the Taifa kingdoms that arose in these same zones following the crisis and collapse of the Umayyad caliphate during the initial decades of the eleventh century (fifth AH).

During the caliphal era, the new strategy that took shape after Alhándega ensured that in the zones controlled by these families the defence of the frontiers was their responsibility. In contrast to the large and costly troop mobilisations of the past, a more limited form of frontier war was waged, which was considered more effective. The caliph had realised that an increased number of attacks launched in a range of zones produced better effects, as 'surprise cavalry raids and the deployment of squadrons did more harm to [the Christians]

[28] Ibn Ḥayyān, *Muqtabis V*, ed. and trans. pp. 296–7.

and it caused them more strife that attacking in just one place and finding them in complete [battle] formation'.[29] Attrition and containment was a more practical tactic than sending large expeditions which had only limited potential for deployment, and which the enemy could avoid by taking refuge in zones out of the army's reach, or retaliate against using guerrilla tactics. The bombastic victory communiqués, in which the caliph had always reported his campaigns when they ended, were replaced by letters sent by the frontier leaders or Umayyad *qā'id*s overseeing the garrisons that informed the caliph of the ongoing skirmishes they launched against the Christians.

Al-Ḥakam II maintained this policy, which he had probably devised himself during the final years of his elderly father's reign. In March 972 (*Jumāda I*, 361), for example, the four sons of the recently deceased Marwān b. Hudhayl b. Razīn, accompanied by their uncle, Yaḥyā, and their sons, arrived in Córdoba. The Banū Razīn were Berbers who had settled at an early date, probably at the time of the Arab conquest, in what is today Albarracín (present-day province of Teruel). This frontier territory, the *Sahlat Banī Razīn*, was named after them. The orphans of Marwān b. Hudhayl b. Razīn were welcomed by the caliph, who shared out the domains of their father among them by granting each of them a diploma testifying to the inheritance. The event took place in the House of Viziers in Madīnat al-Zahrā' and, as was customary, the Banū Razīn were presented with honorific garments (*khil'a*) and elaborately adorned swords. Two years later, in November 974 (*Rabī'* 364 AH), it was the nine sons of the aforementioned Yaḥyā b. Hudhayl b. Razīn who received diplomas for the castles their father had ruled.[30] Among those who received diplomas was Lubb b. Marwān, the grandfather of Hudhayl b. Jalaf b. Lubb, who would found the Taifa dynasty following the collapse of the Umayyad caliphate, which lasted up until 1104 (436 AH) when it was deposed by the Almoravids.

In May 972 (at the end of *Rajab* 361 AH), there were further arrivals in Córdoba: the four sons of the deceased al-'Āsī b. Ḥakam al-Tujībī, who besides being vizier and *qā'id* had been 'Lord of Calatayud' (*ṣāḥib Qal'at Ayyūb*) and a member of the powerful family of the Tujībids, who dominated a considerable

[29] Ibn Hayyan, *Muqtabis V*, pp. 305–6.
[30] Ibn Ḥayyān, *Muqtabis VII*, ed. pp. 72 and 203; trans. pp. 94 and 244.

part of the Upper Frontier. Again, in this case, the sons kept their positions, and shortly afterwards they were sent to northern Morocco. In addition, on this occasion the caliph took advantage of the succession to make changes to the appointments of the *qāḍī* in this region (*qāḍī al-balad*): the post-holder, Muḥammad b. Dāwūd, was removed and imprisoned – for reasons that 'Īsā al-Rāzī does not explain – and the same fate was suffered by the prayer leader (*ṣāḥib al-salā*): both positions were given to a well-known and respected legal scholar, al-Baṭarqūlī, who was renowned for his knowledge and religiosity.[31] Although the control exerted by members of the Tujībid family in Calatayud was not affected, these changes demonstrate that the caliph held onto the power to make the judiciary appointments in the region.

When it came to less prominent families, the diplomas were sent out from Córdoba. Thus, around the same date it was the sons of the deceased 'Amrīl b. Tīmalt who sought to succeed their father in a district (*'amal*) located in the north of the Jalón Valley, near Calatayud. This family, known as the Banū Maḍā, were originally Maṣmūda Berbers, who had settled in the area at least a hundred years earlier. Ghālib, who happened to be in the frontier as governor, wrote to Córdoba recommending that the inheritance be authorised. The petition was accepted and the district distributed between the deceased man's sons, who received gifts and honorific garments (*khil'a*) that confirmed the caliph's approval.[32] Likewise, in November 974 (*Rabī'* 364 AH) a dozen diplomas regarding castles (*ḥuṣūn*) and villages (*qurā*) were sent out to a series of individuals termed '*qā'ids* of the Middle March', who are all named in detail. They included, for example, three members of the Banū Gazlūn, who were of

[31] Ibn Ḥayyān, *Muqtabis VII*, ed. p. 75; trans. p. 97. M. J. Viguera, *Aragón Musulmán*, p. 159. A secretary of the deceased was also imprisoned. I have not been able to identify either the dismissed Muḥammad b. Dāwūd, or the prayer leader, Yūsuf b. Muḥammad. Their substitute is recorded in the biographical dictionaries: he was 'Abd Allāh b. Muḥammad b. Qāsim b. Ḥazm b. Khalaf al-Thagrī al-Qal'ī, al-Baṭarqūlī (d. 993/383 AH). He had been born in Calatayud and his descendants were a line of *'ulamā'* who were very prominent in the city until its conquest by the Christians, *Prosopografía de los Ulemas de al-Andalus*, id. 5.517.

[32] Ibn Ḥayyān, *Muqtabis VII*, ed. pp. 73 and 75–6; trans. pp. 95 and 98. The edition and translation differ on the *nisba* of 'Amrīl: the former calls him 'al-Magribī', the latter refers to him as 'al-Thagrī'. The distribution among the sons was as follows: 'Abd al-Raḥmān received the castle (*ḥiṣn*) of Budiel (perhaps Santa Bárbara, in Cardejón), Ghālib the castle (*ḥiṣn*) of Ateca, another son called Maḍā a place called Binna Ruyyah (Ribarroya), and Zarwāl took possession of another castle called al-Ṣukhayra (Peñalcázar). For the identifications of the place names, V. Alejandre Alcalde, *El sistema defensivo musulmán*, pp. 47-8.

Berber origin and were referred to as 'emirs of the frontier' (*umarā' al-thagr*) in the zone of Teruel and Villel; another family of Berber origin who also received diplomas were the Banū Abī l-Akhṭal, who had settled in Santaver, in what is today the provinces of Guadalajara and Cuenca.[33] With regard to the other families only a few can be identified.[34]

The policy of acknowledging the authority of these frontier families and their right to bequeath their territories was consolidated during this period. The caliphal authority gave its consent to the control exercised by these local lords over their territories, and they likewise had the approval of the representatives of the caliphal administration in the frontier. However, al-Ḥakam kept control over the judiciary and would most certainly have also received a share of the taxes levied in these regions; yet it is also evident that these frontier lords received part of the income generated by their territorial domains, which included castles and villages.[35] In exchange, these families fulfilled their obligation to defend the frontier against the Christians, and fully endorsed the terms stipulated, time and time again, on the diplomas issued during this period: to be at peace with whomsoever the caliph was at peace with while making war on his enemies. The political conflicts and rebellions against Umayyad power

[33] Ibn Ḥayyān, *Muqtabis VII*, ed. p. 203; trans. p. 243. H. de Felipe, *Identidad y onomástica*, pp. 98 and 128–31.

[34] Among those named was Ḍaygam b. Wahb b. Abī l-Adham, who belonged to the Banū Abī l-Adham family, who was also referred to as *umarā' al-thagr*; Khālid b. Zarwāl, member of the Banū Zarwāl, who was of Berber origin and was established in the zone of al-Muntāniya, in the mountainous region that separates the current provinces of Soria and Zaragoza; H. de Felipe, *Identidad y onomástica*, p. 92 and p. 253; E. Manzano Moreno, *La frontera de al-Andalus*, pp. 133–4. Diplomas were also received by 'Abd al-'Azīz and 'Ubayd Allāh, sons of 'Aqqāl b. Salama, who may have been ancestors of a series of legal scholars registered in geographical dictionaries from the eleventh/fifth AH centuries onwards and who used the *nisba* 'al-Fihrī' in Zaragoza and Valencia, *Prosopografía de los Ulemas de al-Andalus*, id. 6.763, 6.785, 9.905, 9.906, 9.408, 5.461, 11.659. I have not been able to identify other individuals who also received diplomas: the two sons of one Surūr b. Funnu called Muḥammad and 'Īsā; the two sons of an individual called Sulaymān b. 'Āmir; Muṭarrif b. Khalaf; Hudhayl and Khalaf, sons of Ghuṣn; 'Aṭiyya and Kulayb, sons of Fortūn; Yaḥya and Muḥammad, sons of 'Īsā. Another case of the confirmation of a family domain was that made in favour of Muṭarrif b. Ismā'īl b. Dhī l-Nūn for the castle of Huete (today's province of Cuenca), to which was added the majority of the castles and villages of the *kūra* of Santaver, Ibn Ḥayyān, *Muqtabis VII*, ed. p. 150; trans. p. 190.

[35] Ibn Ḥayyān, *Muqtabis V*, p. 276, includes the treaty drawn up to formalise the submission of Muḥammad b. Hāshim al-Tujībī in 937 (325 AH) following a lengthy rebellion in Zaragoza. In this document, among other things, his right to rule over the city is acknowledged, as is that of his descendants; the document also stipulates that fiscal contributions (*jibāya*) were to be sent to Córdoba.

that had taken place on the frontiers of al-Andalus decades before had been almost completely resolved in what seems to have been an arrangement that favoured the dominant social groups of the frontier regions, yet also integrated them into the caliphate's political structure.

The two tactical concerns, discussed thus far, that articulated the caliphate's strategy towards the Christian territories in the north of the peninsula involved a major rethinking of the relationships that the Umayyad dynasty had maintained in this region up until then. The frontier against the Christians was consolidated and its strategic importance was bolstered, firstly, through the policy of fortifying and defending frontier enclaves organised from Córdoba, and, secondly, through the territorial concessions made to the families who ruled over these regions 'with extensive powers', as well as the possibility of bequeathing them to their heirs. The arrangement seems to have worked well, as is demonstrated by the fact that, despite the tensions and quarrels that arose on occasions, al-Ḥakam II could rely on troops from the frontier for his campaign in northern Africa from the spring of 973 (362 AH) onwards. A member of the Tujībid family even served there as commander of the Umayyad troops. However, this well-functioning system, created following the disaster of Alhándega, needed a third tactical support to consolidate its efficacy: this third element consisted of an intense diplomatic campaign, such as had never been seen before in al-Andalus.

The Caliph's Diplomacy

After the battle of Alhándega the caliphate of Córdoba redoubled its diplomatic presence in the peninsula's northern territories, as well as the principal centres of power of the time. Emissaries and gifts began to be sent out and grand receptions were held at the caliphal court in numbers such as had never been seen before. It seems that orders were given to prioritise treaties over conflicts, to favour long-distance commercial exchange, and to exercise political influence over the Christian kingdoms and counties. They in turn exerted much less political and economic influence than the caliphate of Córdoba, and their internal quarrels could be manipulated in favour of Umayyad interests. For this purpose, the caliphate needed to be aware of what took place beyond the frontiers of al-Andalus, and to do so it first developed an efficient network of informers, and, secondly, established a nexus of shared interests and complicity with the major powers of the day, who the caliph of Córdoba in turn sought to emulate.

A priority focus for this diplomatic activity was the Carolingian counties in the north-eastern region of the peninsula and southern France.[36] Scarcely a year had passed since the disaster of Alhándega, when in May 940 (*Rajab* 328 AH) 'Abd al-Raḥmān III gave his approval for a treaty with Sunyer, count of Barcelona (911–47). The peace was negotiated by the caliph's doctor and advisor, Ḥasdāy b. Shabrūṭ, who was a leading Jewish cultural figure during this period, the founder of Talmudic studies in Córdoba and an active promoter of contacts between the Mediterranean Jewish communities that were emerging from the lengthy decline they had suffered over the past centuries. Shortly afterwards, the caliph also signed a peace treaty with Richilda of Narbonne, who was the niece of the count of Barcelona. Once again, the treaty was negotiated by a Jewish negotiator, this time called Bernat, who came to Córdoba to finalise the conditions for the treaty laden 'with strange and precious objects from his country'. Likewise, at that time truces were signed with the count of Arles, Hugo of Provence.[37]

What is significant about all these treaties is that besides resulting in the cessation of hostilities, they also made it possible for Frankish merchants to trade in Andalusi ports without the threat of their ships being attacked. For many years, the Western Mediterranean had been dominated by the seafaring activities of the so-called 'Saracen pirates', who had sacked settlements along the Christian coasts in search of booty and captives, and as a result there was little prospect for these communities to develop peaceful trading relationships. The new era begun by these treaties was marked by this violence being taken out of the equation when it came to trade. This coincided with an increasing influence being exerted by intermediary communities capable of operating on either side of the Straits of Gibraltar, which obtained copious profits as a result.

[36] P. Sénac, 'Note sur les relations diplomatiques', pp. 87–101.

[37] Ibn Ḥayyān, *Muqtabis V*, pp. 308–9. A consequence of the pact was to abort the attack that an Andalusi squadron was preparing to launch against Barcelona. The squadron had left from Almeria shortly before the treaty was formalised, which demonstrates that the decision to promote the peace negotiations was started suddenly, al-'Udhrī, *Tarṣī*, p. 81. Riquilda of Narbonne was the daughter of Wilfred II Borrel, the brother and predecessor of Sunyer. She had married Eudes, Viscount of Narbonne, who must have died between 924 and 931, T. Stasser, 'La maison vicomtale de Narbonne aux Xe et Xie siècles', pp. 489–91.

This change explains the role played by people such as Ḥasdāy b. Shabrūṭ as negotiators, as these treaties favoured the interests of Jewish communities, who were spread out among the Muslim and Christian communities, whereby they could take advantage of their role as intermediaries between both faiths.

It is also highly revealing that the caliphate's treaties were concluded with the counts of Barcelona, Arles and Narbonne, cities that were then emerging as trading emporiums on this side of the Mediterranean. In contrast, there is no record of any treaties with such a clear commercial outlook being established with other Christian territories in the northern regions of the peninsula; they were not able to offer, or act as intermediaries for the supply of, the goods and riches that were in great demand in caliphal Córdoba: slaves, furs and Frankish weapons.[38] During the second half of the tenth century, the flourishing trade in this 'merchandise' gave rise to fantastic earnings for whoever became involved. This was particularly true in the case of slaves. From 970 onwards there are numerous mentions in Catalan documents of gold coins, to such an extent that one can speak of an authentic gold rush in Barcelona during this period.[39] These golden coins, which are not referred to in any other peninsular Christian documentation, can only have been Andalusi dinars, which arrived as payment for the exchange of commodities brought in from afar that had been opened up following the treaties of 940, in which the trade in slaves and Frankish weapons predominated.

The Umayyad caliphate's diplomatic treaties were extended beyond the Iberian Peninsula. It is very possible that the embassies sent to the Germanic Emperor Otto I (d. 973) were initially motivated by an interest in obtaining access to the trade routes used to import slaves captured in pagan lands to al-Andalus: the celebrated embassy sent by Emperor Otto I to Córdoba in 953, and led by the monk John of Gorze, travelled aboard merchant ships from Verdún that traded with al-Andalus. The fascinating account of this embassy shows the capacity of 'Abd al-Raḥmān III to impose his own conditions on diplomatic exchanges, and likewise, the emperor's interest in ensuring the embassy's success.[40]

38 E. Manzano Moreno, 'Circulation de biens et richesses', pp. 160–70.
39 P. Bonnassie, *La Catalogne du milieu du Xe a la fin du XIe siècle*, p. 374.
40 *Vita Iohannis abbate Gorziensis*, ed. G. H. Pertz, pp. 370–1.

The caliphate's diplomatic missions also reached the Byzantine empire and from 946 onwards an ongoing exchange of embassies ensued.[41] Aside from their shared policy of hostility towards the Fāṭimids, the embassies between Córdoba and Constantinople contributed to defining a set of common signs within the language of power used by both the Umayyad caliphs and the Byzantine emperors. Proof of this was the 320 quintals of multicoloured, glazed and gilded tesserae that were sent from Constantinople, along with a mosaicist, which were to be used for the decoration of the *miḥrāb* that al-Ḥakam II commissioned for the mosque of Córdoba. The aforementioned interest in dying caliphal textiles with Tyrian purple, in the manner used at the imperial court, or the adoption of ceremonial elements derived from the Byzantine tradition in the caliph's receptions are demonstrations of how, despite their major political and ideological differences, both the caliph and emperor used common elements in their language of power.[42]

The exchange of gifts contributed to the creation of bonds of complicity and a shared language that was used to articulate forms of political power based on similar premises. One of the gifts Emperor Romanos I Lekapenos (d. 948) sent to Caliph ʿAbd al-Raḥmān III was a Greek illuminated manuscript that included a work entitled *De materia medica*, which had been written in the first century by a Greek physician called Dioscorides, whose work had sunk into oblivion in the West. For the Byzantine emperor and the Umayyad caliph, this work contained an important branch of knowledge: like all other human beings, these rulers suffered from colds, headaches, constipation, infections or lack of libido, and at such moments there was nothing they wished for more than a sound medical remedy. And this is what *De materia medica* consisted of; its catalogue of healing herbs and preparations prescribed for every sort of ailment was an authentic treasury for any doctor serving a powerful patron. An Arabic translation of this work had already been produced in Baghdad in the second half of the ninth century, but the translators had not always found the exact equivalents for the Greek plant names and therefore had chosen, prudently, to leave these names in the original language, hoping that someone

[41] J. Signes Codoñer, 'Bizancio y al-Andalus en los siglos IX y X', pp. 212–45.

[42] A. Cutler, 'Constantinople and Cordoba', p. 436. E. Manzano Moreno, 'Byzantium, al-Andalus and the Shaping of the Mediterranean'.

might one day make up for their lack of knowledge. Romanos I Lekapenos not only sent the Greek manuscript of Dioscorides' work to the caliph, but he also sent, at the caliph's request, a monk, called Nicholas, who knew Arabic; he arrived in Córdoba, where nobody knew Greek, around 951. He remained there for the rest of his life, helping to produce a translation of the *De materia medica* and collaborating with the splendid generation of doctors to be found in Córdoba, including their foremost representative Ḥasdāy b. Shabrūṭ, who cared for one of the most valued possessions of the powerful: their health.[43]

Thus, from 940 onwards, the reinforcement of the frontiers, the recognition of the military and social role of the families who held sway in the border regions, the pacts made with the ancient Carolingian counties that permitted access to the trading routes of slaves and weapons, and an intense campaign of diplomacy became the core concerns of the caliphate's foreign policy. For a long time, the results of this strategy were a resounding success. The caliphate's military, economic, cultural and political supremacy in the Iberian Peninsula allowed it to impose its own rules, whereby at various moments during the second half of the tenth century (fourth AH) the northern powers ended up becoming political satellites of Córdoba. When the kingdom of León, for example, suffered a major crisis from the 956 onwards, motivated by the dynastic dispute between Sancho I and his cousin Ordoño IV, both parties sought political and military support from the caliphate. The conflict, and the various alternatives that arose, resulted in episodes of such relevance as Sancho I's sojourn in Córdoba in 958: this man, known as *el Craso* (The Fat) was so obese he could not even ride a horse, and during his stay in the capital he was prescribed a herbal treatment that helped him swiftly lose weight.[44] If such a weight-loss treatment could be prescribed in the caliph's court, it was thanks to the enormous wealth of medical knowledge preserved there, that had been increased through the caliph's contact with the emperor in Constantinople. Everything was connected and acquired a greater significance through the diplomatic efforts of the Umayyad caliphate.

[43] Ibn Abī ʻUsayba, *ʻUyūn al-anbāʼ fī tabaqāt al-aṭṭibāʼ*, ed. and trans. H. Jehier and A. Noureddine, Argel, 1958/1377, pp. 36–40.

[44] *Crónica de Sampiro*: 'Sancius quidem rex cum esset crassu nimis, ipsi agareni herbam attulerunt et crassitudinem abstulerunt a ventre eius', ed. Pérez de Urbel and González Ruiz Zorrilla, *Historia Silense*, p. 170. Also *Primera Crónica General*, ed. Menéndez Pidal, p. 408.

With regard to the kingdom of León, al-Ḥakam II once more maintained the same diplomatic policy that his father had pursued during the latter period of his reign. As has already been mentioned, it is very probable that this was because he had designed this policy himself. In the dynastic dispute that continued in León, the caliph transferred his support to Ordoño IV, with whom he formed an alliance, as opposed to his cousin Sancho, but in essence the policy continued to be the same. Ordoño also went to Córdoba in the spring of 962 (351 AH) and the caliphate deployed all the pomp it was capable of offering in the form of a sumptuous reception held in Madīnat al-Zahrā', which culminated in the Christian declaring himself to be al-Ḥakam's 'slave'.[45] In addition to the dynastic disputes in the kingdom of León, which the caliph continued to engage in, numerous diplomatic contacts were maintained with Castilian, Leonese and Galician counts and magnates, who maintained highly complex relationships with their monarchs: they married their offspring to them, fought against them and betrayed them on a regular basis. The diplomatic skills of the Cordoban administration consisted in giving these counts a direct channel of communication with the caliph, which stirred up rivalries between them and undermined the authority of the Leonese kings.

The caliphate's relationships with the counts of Barcelona were conducted along somewhat different lines. As has been mentioned above, commercial interests must have dominated the content of their diplomatic exchanges, although there are also accounts of frontier skirmishes, which do not seem to have had much impact on diplomatic relations.[46] An insightful demonstration is provided by an embassy that was sent by the count of Barcelona, Borrell II, around this time, to request the renewal of the peace that had been established during his father's reign. The gift brought by the Catalan emissaries was highly significant; it included twenty eunuch slaves, twenty quintals of sable furs, five quintals of tin, ten Slavic cuirasses and 100 Frankish swords.[47]

[45] Al-Maqqarī, *Nafḥ*, I, pp. 388–94.

[46] Ibn al-Khaṭīb, *Iḥāta*, 1, pp. 378–9, records a concentration of troops in the summer of 964 (*Rajab* 353 AH), which it seems was defeated by the *qā'id* of Tortosa, Aḥmad b. Ya'lā, but he was on the point of calling for a support squadron to be sent. This was possibly the same skirmish as that referred to by al-Maqqarī, *Nafḥ*, I, p. 383.

[47] al-Maqqarī, *Nafḥ*, I, pp. 384–5. It is possible that at the start of al-Ḥakam II's caliphate there was an expedition into the count's territory, and in fact, the negotiation of the treaty implied the dismantling of frontier enclaves, P. Sénac, 'Note sur les relations diplomatiques', p. 92.

The fluidity of diplomatic and commercial relations between the caliphate and the count of Barcelona allowed for the transmission of knowledge and learning from al-Andalus, and this established the first direct and regular channel of Arabic culture to the Latin world of the Western Mediterranean. While al-Ḥakam II received a copy of a chronicle of the Frankish kings, the Bishop of Gerona, Miró Bonfill, had in his power in 984 a work that was entitled *De multiplicatione et divisione numerorum* by one Yoseph Hispanus. It was in Ripoll, during the time of Abbot Arnulf (948–70), that the monastery's celebrated manuscript no. 225 – a compilation of various treatises on astronomy and mathematics translated from Arabic – was composed. A young Occitanian called Gerbert of Aurillac, who was at that time studying in Vic, became aware of these sources, and years later, in 984, he requested them from his Hispanic interlocutors. Decades later, having become Pope Sylvester II, he never relinquished his interest in these matters, which he probably first came into contact with during his time in *Spania*.[48]

All the diplomatic fronts described here are reflected in the embassies that visited Córdoba between 971 and 975 (360–4 AH). For example, the embassy that arrived in the summer of 971 (360 AH) came, once more, from the count of Barcelona, Borrell II, and it was made up of twenty knights. It was led by Bonfill, an important figure at the count's court, a landowner and feudal lord of frontier castles such as Gelida, Cervelló, Miralles and Sacama. Another member of the embassy was the viscount of Barcelona, Guitard, who was also lord of territories on the county's southern frontier. The presence of these frontier lords in the Barcelona embassy bestowed a special significance on the gift they brought the caliph: thirty Muslim captives, men, women and children – who had almost certainly been captured during some uncontrolled skirmish – as well as weapons – it must be recalled how highly valued they were – and brocade (*dibāj*), possibly of Byzantine origin.[49]

[48] P. Sénac, 'Note sur les relations diplomatiques', p. 89, based on the testimony of al-Masʿūdī. On the Arabic treaties, Gerbert d'Aurillac, *Correspondance*, I, ed. P. Rice and J. P. Callu, I, pp. 48–51; on the Ripoll manuscripts, J. M. Millás Vallicrosa, *Estudios sobre historia de la ciencia española*, pp. 55–60. P. Riche, *Gerbert d'Aurillac*, pp. 80–3.

[49] Ibn Ḥayyān, *Muqtabis VII*, pp. 20–2; trans. pp. 44–6. The identification of Bonfill in A. Benet, 'L'origen de les familes Cervelló, Castellvell i Castellet', p. 79. On Guitard, J.-E. Ruiz Domènech, *Quan els vizcomtes de Barcelona eren*, pp. 24–5.

The special treatment granted to these ambassadors speaks volumes about the importance al-Ḥakam II attached to the peace treaty agreed with the count of Barcelona. On their arrival, the ambassadors and their entourage were given accommodation in one of the caliph's most luxurious estates or *almunias*, the *Munyat al-Nāʿūra*, on the banks of the Guadalquivir, not far from the city. Bonfill was summoned twice by the caliph to Madīnat al-Zahrā'. On the first occasion, just a few days after his arrival, on 1 July 971 (4 *Ramaḍān*), a fairly elaborate ceremony was held. The ambassador and knights, who were accompanied by the Umayyad governor of Tortosa, arrived in the city palace escorted by a squadron of the regular army and attended by five Christians from Córdoba, who acted as interpreters.[50] However, they were not led into the caliph's presence straight away; instead they were first taken to the 'House of the Army' (*Dār al-Jund*), where they awaited to be granted permission to proceed with the caliphal audience. When the caliph's permission was received, the ambassadors were led before al-Ḥakam, who was waiting for them in the reception hall surrounded by the principal members of his court: the emissaries knelt before him, kissed his hand, and standing, presented the letter that they brought. The caliph contemplated them – possibly amid a majestic silence – and then asked them questions about the situation in their homeland and expressed his satisfaction with them. Having finished the audience, the emissaries returned to the estate where they were lodged, while arrangements were made to ensure that the thirty Muslim captives who had arrived with them were given assistance to return to their homes.

The second reception held for the ambassadors took place a month later, in early August, and the ritual seems to have been identical, as they were escorted to Madīnat al-Zahrā' and were once more accompanied by the interpreters. When they were shown before the caliph, al-Ḥakam gave his reply to Count Borrell and he made it known to them 'how they should maintain themselves within the limits of obedience'.[51] Undoubtedly, the capture of Muslims was

[50] The governor of Tortosa was Hishām b. Muḥammad b.ʿUthmān, who was the nephew of the all-powerful vizier, Jaʿfar b. ʿUthmān al-Muṣḥafī. The squadron of the regular army that escorted the ambassadors was commanded by one of its principal commanders, Jahwar b. al-Shaykh, who was a descendant of a historic rebel from the region of Murcia who had been resettled in Córdoba by ʿAbd al-Raḥmān III, Ibn Ḥayyān, *Muqtabis V*, ed. and trans. p. 122, 127 and 156. Jahwar, as well as his brother Ismāʿīl, undertook military duties at al-Ḥakam II's court.

[51] Ibn Ḥayyān, *Muqtabis VII*, ed. p. 32; trans. pp. 46–7.

not deemed as being within those limits, and the previous presentation of these captives to the caliph was an implicit way of acknowledging this and of amending an error committed during some border skirmish. The caliph's reply implied that the incident was not going to put the existing peace at risk.

Castilian and Leonese embassies also arrived frequently during this period. Different embassies were often received by the caliph on the same day, without making any distinction as to whether they were sent by kings or counts. This is what occurred on 12 August 971 (16 *Shawwāl*, 360 AH), when al-Ḥakam received various Christian embassies in Madīnat al-Zahrā': the first to be brought into his presence were the envoys of the King Sancho Garcés II of Pamplona (94), who is given the title of 'emir of the Basques' (*amīr al-Bashkunis*). Then, it was the turn of those who came on behalf of Elvira, queen of León, who acted as regent to her nephew Ramiro III, the youngest son of Sancho I 'The Fat', who had succeeded him following his premature death in 966. The emissaries sent by the counts of Salamanca, Castile and Monzón were the next to be received.[52] The idea of meeting the envoys from Elvira and the magnates of her kingdom, whom experience had shown had at times schemed against the throne, on the same day, yet holding the audiences separately from one another was a way of stirring up mistrust between them, as well as mutual suspicions.

Embassies such as these arrived on a regular basis, which indicated the caliph's interest in maintaining fluid diplomatic contacts. In the middle of August 971 (*Shawwāl* 360 AH) the caliph received another envoy from Elvira, the queen regent in León, and then at the end of September (*Dhū l-ḥijja*) he gave a further audience to another envoy of hers. Again reflecting the regularity

[52] Ibn Ḥayyān, *Muqtabis VII*, ed. p. 241; trans. pp. 75–6. In the edition of *Muqtabis VII* this episode is not given in the right place, and the order in which it is included in the translation is preferable. The count of Castile who sent this embassy was, obviously, García Fernández, who had inherited the county the year before from his father, Fernán González. The count of Monzón, who also sent an emissary, was Fernando Ansúrez, who resided in the area along the River Cea. G. Martínez Díez, *El Condado de Castilla* II, pp. 541–3; A. Carvajal Castro, 'Superar la frontera', pp. 601–28. The identification of the count of Salamanca, referred to as Fernando Flaínez, who sent another emissary, is more problematic. Perhaps he was a member of the Flaínez family, who in this period had begun to rise to prominence around Tierra de Campos, but I have not found any other references to him, nor to their presence in Salamanca, P. Martínez Sopena, *La Tierra de Campos occidental*, pp. 341–6. The text cites two further ambassadors, and I interpret one of them as being a member of the Banū Gómez, but it has not been possible to identify the other one.

of these diplomatic exchanges, that same day he also received ambassadors from the count of Monzón, a Castilian magnate, and a brother of the king of Pamplona who was at that time a hostage in Córdoba.[53] In September 973 (*Dhū l-ḥijja* 362 AH), envoys were again received from the 'lord of Pamplona', the count of Monzón, the Banū Gómez, a family who dominated the region of Saldaña and Carrión (Palencia), and the Galician count, Rodrigo Velázquez.[54]

Interpreters were used for all these embassies. Arabic was the language used at the caliph's court, and in general, across all al-Andalus, and, for these diplomatic receptions, recourse was always made to interpreters, who had the obligation of transmitting in a very precise manner the words pronounced during the audience. This duty was usually performed by Arabised Christians – that is, Mozarabs – living in al-Andalus. The employment of such prominent individuals as the bishops of Seville, Toledo and Córdoba, as well as the judge and count of the Christians of Córdoba, who was in charge of the lawsuits and the administration of this community in the capital, demonstrates the care that was devoted to the selection of highly qualified people, who could realise the task of interpreting with guaranteed accuracy.[55]

[53] Ibn Ḥayyān, *Muqtabis VII*, ed. pp. 63–4; trans. p. 80. The Castilian magnate referred to is one Khamīs b. Abī Salīṭ, *ṣāḥib Qashtilīyya*, whom it has proved impossible to identify: what is most likely is that the word 'envoy' (*rasūl*) is missing, whereby this Khamīs would be a legate of the Castilian count.

[54] During that audience, which took place at a crucial moment of the military and diplomatic offensive in northern Morocco, envoys were also received from this latter region, and they were given precedence over the Christians, Ibn Ḥayyān, *Muqtabis VII*, ed. pp. 138–9; trans. pp. 173–4. The Christians present were ambassadors of the 'lord of Pamplona', or, in other words, Sancho Garcés II, and the count of Monzón, who at that time was Fernando Ansúrez, as well as those of the Banū Gómez and the Galician count Rodrigo Velázquez. The Banū Gómez were a lineage settled in the region of Saldaña and Carrión, thereby neighbours to the former, A. Carvajal, 'Superar la frontera', pp. 619–20. Rodrigo Velázquez was one of the major Galician counts from this period. In 972 (361 AH), it is possible that ambassadors also arrived in Córdoba during the summer, but a lacuna in the manuscript of 'Īsā al-Rāzī's work affects precisely those months.

[55] For the reception of the embassies celebrated in September 971 there were four interpreters: 'Ubayd Allāh b. Qāsim, Bishop of Seville, who had already served as an interpreter at a reception held for the dethroned king of León, Ordoño IV, who had arrived in Córdoba seeking help for his dispute against his cousin Sancho. On that occasion, 'Ubayd Allāh appeared as bishop of Toledo. The second interpreter, Aṣbagh b. 'Abd Allāh b. Nabīl, who is listed here as *qāḍī* of the Christians, who had also been present as an interpreter during the visit of Ordoño IV, although on that occasion with the title of Bishop of Córdoba, J. Zanón, 'Los intérpretes de la corte de al-Ḥakam II de Córdoba', pp. 323–47. With regard to the two individuals present at the interview analysed here, 'Īsā b. Manṣūr, Bishop of Córdoba, and Mu'āwiya b. Lubb, count (*qumis*) of the Christians of the same city, I can add nothing.

We scarcely know anything more than the names of the emissaries sent by Christian kings and magnates. It seems feasible to think they belonged to a group of people who moved between the peninsula's different centres of power bearing missives, gifts and information. As such, they undertook a highly important task. Visiting Córdoba during this period offered insights into, for example, the enormous sums of money and military effort that the caliph was deploying in the Maghreb, precious information of great interest for the kingdoms and counties of the north. Al-Ḥakam II himself had people who served him as emissaries for dealing with both the kings and counts of the north 'in order to obtain news about them, spy on developments and bring or take letters at every opportunity'. One of them was a jurist called Aḥmad b. 'Abd Allāh b. 'Arūs al-Ḥaḍramī al-Mawrūrī, who possibly spoke Latin.[56] It is also probable that, despite using interpreters, some Christian ambassadors spoke Arabic, or at least their names suggests this to have been the case: 'Abd al-Malik and al-Layth acted as emissaries for queen Elvira of León, and Ḥabīb b. Ṭawīla and Sa'āda did the same for Fernando Flaínez. In contrast, other emissaries were ecclesiastics.[57]

During the preparation of the audiences with the caliph, an effort was always made to avoid an ambassador bringing missives or complaints that might anger the sovereign. The celebrated account of the embassy of John of Gorze sent by Emperor Otto I described the laborious negotiations that had to be undertaken, prior to his being brought into the caliph's presence, in order to ensure that the terms of the missive brought by the cleric were acceptable

[56] Ibn Ḥayyān, *Muqtabis VII*, ed. p. 76; trans. p. 98. Although the translation reads Ibn Abī 'Amrūs, I agree with the editor that this individual is Aḥmad b. 'Arūs al-Mawrūrı, whom our source cites later as an envoy to the regent Elvira in November 973 (*Ṣafar* 363 AH), ed. p. 147; trans. p. 186. This individual, who died three years later, has been authoritatively identified in the biographical dictionaries, *Prosopografía de los ulemas de al-Andalus*, id. 1,261. A person called Sa'īd was appointed as his companion.

[57] It is possible that some of these emissaries came from the regions of the Duero Valley, where charters confirm that many men and women used Arabic names, perhaps as a result of frontier Arabisation, E. Manzano, *La frontera de al-*Andalus, p. 193, and also C. Aillet, 'Anthroponyme, migrations, frontières', pp. 23–4. One of those names that appears most frequently in the documentation is 'Habibe', which is also the name of one of the envoys of Fernando Faínez, V. Aguilar and F. Rodríguez Mediano, 'Antroponimia de origen árabe en la documentación leonesa (siglos VIII–XIII)', pp. 499–633. V. Aguilar, 'Onomástica de origen árabe en el reino de León (siglo X)', pp. 351–63. F. Rodríguez Mediano, 'Acerca de la población arabizada del reino de León (siglos X–XI)', pp. 465–72.

to ʿAbd al-Raḥmān III. Audiences with the caliph were not expected to raise problematic issues, which explains what happened in November 973 (*Ṣafar* 363 AH), when al-Ḥakam II received emissaries from Elvira, regent of León.[58] It is strange that an embassy should have arrived around that time (the customary practice was that they would be held in the summer), meaning it is possible that there was some urgent issue. The task of interpreter was given to the judge of the Christians of Córdoba, Aṣbagh b. ʿAbd Allāh b. Nabīl, who had performed this role on other occasions.[59] However, during the audience, the emissaries said something that greatly displeased the caliph. A furious al-Ḥakam ordered that the ambassadors retire from his presence and the interpreter was severely reprimanded for not having alerted them to the problematic nature of what was to be stated in his presence in such inappropriate terms. The ambassadors were given orders to return immediately to León accompanied by the aforementioned Aḥmad b. ʿAbd Allāh al-Mawrūrī, as well as the Bishop of Seville, who were instructed to clarify the disputed matter in the court of Queen Elvira.

As the harsh winter of 973 was under way, in northern Morocco the caliph's army was seeking to bring about the rendition of Ḥasan b. Qannūn, who was still refusing to surrender. Just as the caliph had first-hand knowledge of what was happening in the north of the Peninsula, the Christian ambassadors also knew of the problems faced during the North African campaign. Such was the price to be paid for maintaining such intense diplomatic relations: in Córdoba, just by asking one another, the Christian ambassadors had the possibility of obtaining vital information; for example, that the garrisons on the northern frontier had been dramatically reduced to sustain the military operation being undertaken by the caliphate on the other side of the Straits of Gibraltar.

The Enemy Offensive: the Christian Siege of Gormaz

What took place during the embassy sent by Queen Elvira in November in 973 seemed to be an isolated incident. At the end of June 974 (363 AH), as

[58] Ibn Ḥayyān, *Muqtabis VII*, ed. pp. 146–7; trans. pp. 185–6.

[59] He was a significant figure in the Mozarab community. His father had served the family of ʿUmar b. Ḥafṣūn and he had played a key role in the negotiations that led to the surrender of Bobastro to the caliphal army, Ibn Ḥayyān, *Muqtabis V*, pp. 74, 76, 91 and 92.

was customary, Christian emissaries once again arrived in Córdoba. However, a whole month went by until they were granted an audience by the caliph. Meanwhile, in Córdoba they would have witnessed the euphoric atmosphere that had overtaken the capital following the public announcement of the defeat and surrender of Ḥasan b. Qannūn in Morocco. They undoubtedly knew that the caliphal army had triumphed on its North African campaign, but they were also able to confirm that, in the meantime, the troops continued to be deployed there.[60]

On 1 August the caliph received the Christian ambassadors altogether in a solemn reception in Madīnat al-Zahrā'.[61] As was customary, the sovereign sat surrounded by the highest-ranking figures of his administration, while a number of army units flanked the ambassadors' route into the palace. The first to be received was Guitard, viscount of Barcelona. Three years before, Guitard had sent an emissary to the caliph and now he arrived himself in person as envoy of Count Borrell II. He was the first to be received as a demonstration of the consideration merited by his obedience. The next ambassador to appear before the caliph was another important figure, the envoy of Emperor Otto II, whose father had died the year before, although he was received along with emissaries sent by mere counts. The new emperor sought to 'renew the pact (*'ahd*) and strengthen the existing peace agreement (*'aqd*)', which indicates that after John of Gorze's embassy, diplomatic ties between the Umayyad and Ottonian dynasties had been maintained regularly.[62]

The next diplomat to be received by the caliph was the envoy of Nuño González, 'lord of Castile', along with that sent by Fernando Ansúrez, count of Monzón, and the emissary of a bishop, whom it has not been possible to identify. The missive they brought expressed their satisfaction with the existing situation of peace, and as a result they were well-received and given the

[60] Ibn Ḥayyān, *Muqtabis VII*, ed. pp. 168–9; trans. pp. 207.

[61] For everything that follows, Ibn Ḥayyān, *Muqtabis VII*, ed. pp. 182–3 and 188–9; trans. pp. 221–2 and 226–8.

[62] Unfortunately, the ambassador's name – Ashrāka b. 'Amm (?) Dāwūd – provides us with no clues, although the name Dāwūd perhaps suggests he was of Jewish origin. I think that we must rule out the editor's opinion (n. 6 in the edition), who considers that these were envoys of Hugh Capet: the form used in the manuscript is clearly '*Hutu*', Otto, and the fact that he is named '*malik al-Ifranj*' does not imply that this refers specifically to the king of the Franks; instead it is a generic name, which was very widely used in Arab sources.

customary gifts. Following the reception, the legates remained in Córdoba another month more, until the start of September, when they began to make their way back to their places of origin. However, what happened next was wholly unexpected. Around the same time that the ambassadors left for their homelands, on 12 September 974 (21 *Dhū l-hijja* 363 AH), news reached Córdoba that ten days earlier the count of Castile, García Fernández, had attacked an Andalusi enclave. His forces had entered the territory of the castle of Deza (in what is today Soria), which was governed by the sons of ʿAmrīl b. Tīmalt, who, as was commented on above, had recently had their authority over these territories confirmed by the caliph. Two of his sons, Maḍā and Zarwāl, had gone out to confront the attackers and try to prevent them from carrying off sheep and cows, but an ambush by the Christian cavalry had led to Zarwāl's death at a place known as *Faḥṣ al-Burayqa* (Alboreca, in Sigüenza, in the province of Guadalajara). As soon as the caliph learnt of this news, he gave the order that a messenger should be sent out to force the Castilian ambassadors to return to Córdoba. The ambassadors not only refused, but they even tried to kill the emissary, and a squadron of the standing army had to be dispatched to capture them near to Caracuel (today in the province of Ciudad Real).[63]

What in other circumstances would have been a simple frontier skirmish now took on the appearance of a provocation. While their ambassadors made all types of promises of peace in Córdoba, the count of Castile had attacked Andalusi territory and had killed a frontier lord, thereby showing up the caliph before his court.[64] However, for the present, and with the bulk of the Umayyad army still deployed in northern Morocco and the arrival of winter not far off, there was little that could be done. Furthermore, and to make matters worse, on 30 November 974 (*Rabīʿ I* 364 AH), Caliph al-Ḥakam suffered a stroke, which meant he could not take part in any decision-making. He did not recover until the spring of the following year, and even then his health was

[63] Ibn Ḥayyān, *Muqtabis VII*, ed. p. 188; trans. p. 227.

[64] There has been a great deal of speculation about the possibility that this episode could be related to a famous Castilian legend of the so-called seven infantes of Lara, a chanson de geste compiled in later chronicles. R. Menéndez Pidal advanced some rather forced arguments for this claim, J. Escalona, 'Épica, crónicas y genealogías', pp. 113–76; G. Martínez Díez, 'El cantar de los Siete Infantes de Lara', pp. 171–89.

still severely weakened. Once more, the news must have travelled fast, and it spurred on those on the Christian side who saw this as a unique opportunity to unleash a major blow against the caliphal frontier system.

It is very probable that during those months numerous messages were exchanged between Castilian, Leonese and Navarrese monarchs, counts and magnates in order to prepare an offensive. The army's deployment in northern Morocco provided an excellent opportunity to undertake this combined action. ʿĪsā al-Rāzī himself stated this to have been the case, when he noted that allies were moved by 'the greed to seek some advantage at the expense of the Muslims, knowing the grand army of the sovereign (*jund al-sulṭān*) was occupied with the war being waged against the Berber people, and aware of the great distance that this army, should it need to return, would have to cover in order to reach them'.[65]

Meanwhile, in Córdoba the Umayyad administration must have been aware of these preparations, and a response was mobilised. At the end of March 975 (*Rajab* 364 AH), the military commanders, known as the *aṣḥāb al-shurṭa*, received the order along with other civil servants to undertake the requisitioning of horses across al-Andalus as the sovereigns and magnates of the north 'were violating the treaty at that time'.[66] Two weeks later, and with the caliph having barely recovered from the stroke and having hardly renewed making public appearances, on 17 April 975 (2 *Shabān* 364 AH) news arrived in Córdoba that the aforementioned fortress of Gormaz on the River Duero, which scarcely ten years before had been fortified by Ghālib, was now under siege.[67]

The siege of the castle of Gormaz was an extraordinary event. In the previous decades, the Christians had led pillaging expeditions and numerous raids seeking booty and captives. Some of them, like the one the Christian troops led against Évora (Portugal) in 913 (301 AH), were aimed at very distant targets and had been a huge success. However, this was the first time that a frontier fortress was subjected to a formal siege, in which a coalition of Christian rulers took part: the king of Pamplona, Sancho II Garcés (970–94); García Fernández,

[65] Ibn Ḥayyān, *Muqtabis VII*, ed. p. 218; trans. p. 258.
[66] Ibn Ḥayyān, *Muqtabis VII*, ed. p. 216; trans. p. 256.
[67] Ibn Ḥayyān, *Muqtabis VII*, ed. p. 218; trans. p. 258.

Image 12 Castle of Gormaz (Soria). It was fortified by order of al-Ḥakam II, its impressive location allowing it to control access to the upper Duero. In the spring of 975 it was besieged by a Christian coalition, which led to the hasty dispatch of reinforcements from Córdoba.

count of Castile; Fernando Ansúrez, count of Monzón; the Banū Gómez; and the king of León, Ramiro III, who had only just gained his majority.[68] All of them had been sending embassies to Córdoba until the previous year, and all of them had now decided to form an alliance against the caliph, thus demonstrating that his diplomatic efforts had been to no avail. The attackers aspired to besiege and conquer the impregnable fortress which permitted control not only over the upper course of the River Duero, but also strategic mountain passes leading to the Ebro Basin.

Having received news of the Christian attack against Gormaz, on 22 April, al-Ḥakam II held a meeting with the vizier and *ṣāḥib al-madīna*, Jaʿfar b. ʿUthmān al-Muṣḥafī, and *qāʾid* Ghālib, who had recently returned from North Africa bathed in glory. Having scarcely recovered from his stroke and deeply concerned over the issue of who would succeed him, the caliph also made his son and heir, Hishām, attend the meeting, even though he was not

[68] A. Isla, *Ejército, sociedad y política*, p. 201.

even ten years old. At the meeting it was decided that Ghālib should leave immediately to assist the besieged fortress. And so he did. Two days later, a swiftly mobilised army left in haste for the north with what ʿĪsā al-Rāzī claims was a grandiose parade: the expeditionary force made its way past the *alcázar* of Córdoba, and the caliph and his son, Hishām, watched from the rooftop above the main gateway. They raised their arms beseeching divine aid and as a display of their concern for the fate of the Muslim garrison besieged on the frontier.[69]

The forces that Ghālib would have been able to mobilise at that time in April must have been very limited. The plan seems to have been that the renowned *qāʾid* was to set off as soon as possible, and while he headed to Gormaz the viziers and their subordinates would mobilise additional troops. A very heterogeneous reinforcement, including stipendiary soldiers, slaves and archers, left Córdoba a week later on 29 April (14 *Shaʿbān*). As had occurred during the mobilisation of the army in northern Morocco, the question of the soldiers' wages was a priority, whereby the treasurer, Muḥammad b. Aḥmad b. Shuhayd, also made his way north from Córdoba, carrying 'the huge sums of money that were sent to the *qāʾid* vizier Ghālib'.[70]

Ghālib took two weeks to cover the 550 kilometres that separate Córdoba from Barahona (today in the province of Soria), where he set up camp on 7 May (22 *Shaʿbān*). From there he headed to Berlanga, which was just thirty kilometres away. The castle of Gormaz was close by, only fifteen kilometres away. However, the Umayyad *qāʾid* had to cross the River Duero to join the besieged forces, and the only bridge was right in front of the castle and controlled by the besieging force. There were some feasible fording places, but the Christians had stationed cavalry and infantry forces that prevented Ghālib's army from crossing. With a limited number of troops at his disposal and a besieging army that threatened to cut him off, the situation faced by Ghālib was not promising. A skirmish at these fords along the River Duero, despite being narrated in terms of a major victory by ʿĪsā al-Rāzī, must have convinced

[69] Ibn Ḥayyān, *Muqtabis VII*, ed. pp. 219–21; trans. pp. 259–61.

[70] Ibn Ḥayyān, *Muqtabis VII*, ed. p. 223; trans. pp. 263–4. The slaves that were sent belonged to the contingent of the *ʿabīd khumsiyyūn*, which I interpret as slaves proceeding from the fifth of the booty.

the Umayyad *qā'id* that the best course of action was to retire a safe distance from Gormaz to Barahona, where he could await reinforcements.[71]

Meanwhile, in Córdoba emotions began to run high. The start of the month of *Ramaḍān* (mid-May) incited many people to join up as volunteers, and they were keen to head northwards and help those under siege. This attitude contrasted with that of some of the soldiers from the regular army, who, claiming to be ill, 'took their time before joining the army assisted by God'. They had to be reminded of their obligations 'under threat of incurring harsh punishments'. It is possible that these threats were successful, as on 26 May (12 *Ramaḍān*) new squadrons of the standing army (*jund*), slaves (*'abīd*), archers (*rumāt*) and soldiers who served in the capital (*wufūd*) left Córdoba with supplies and munitions taken from the *alcázar*. A week later, the *qā'id* Qāsim b. Muḥammad b. Qāsim b. Ṭumlus also left Córdoba accompanied again by stipendiary troops, archers, volunteers and soldiers serving in the capital.[72]

Nonetheless, it seems that a number of internal tensions were beginning to emerge. On 4 June, some military commanders were dismissed from their posts 'due to complaints made against them', although they were still ordered to join Ghālib's army. Aside from those who claimed to be sick and those who seemingly did not have the caliph's trust, the reinforcements that were so badly needed on the frontier were leaving in dribs and drabs. The siege had begun a month and a half before, and these are hints that the mobilisation of troops was not being carried out very efficiently. Another treasurer, 'Abd al-Raḥmān b. Aḥmad b. Muḥammad b. Ilyās, left to meet with Ghālib, again carrying huge sums of money.

Amid this tense atmosphere, in mosques and at social gatherings there were increasing displays of the fraught anxiety felt for the fate of the garrison of Gormaz. During a burial, a man who 'led a pious life' stood up to deliver an impassioned speech, in which he beseeched God 'to impede the spilling of the blood of your brothers, the believers, and your fellow Muslims, who defend the castle of Gormaz'. The effect among those present was instantaneous: tears from some, and a redoubling of prayers on behalf of the fate of those who were under siege, which underscores the extent of the commotion felt in

[71] Ibn Ḥayyān, *Muqtabis VII*, ed. p. 226; trans. p. 267.
[72] Ibn Ḥayyān, *Muqtabis VII*, ed. pp. 226 and 227, 228; trans. pp. 267 and 268, 269, 270.

Córdoba for what was taking place on the distant northern frontier. Suddenly, the Muslim community began to play a major role in terms of solidarity and public displays of feeling.[73]

The siege of Gormaz ended in a wholly unexpected and surprising manner.[74] Despite Ghālib's force having been joined by the various units of reinforcements, it was the castle's own garrison that finally defeated the Christian coalition. According to 'Īsā al-Rāzī's account, events came to a head in late June (mid *Shawwāl*). At that time the Christian camp consisted of the king of Pamplona, as well as the counts of Castile, Monzón and the Banū Gómez. Then King Ramiro III arrived, accompanied by his aunt, the regent Elvira. The young king, who was only just thirteen, nonetheless reprimanded those carrying out the siege for the lentitude of their operations and decided to lead the troops himself. The scene is so extraordinary that either the whole episode has been imagined by the Arab chronicler, or one has to conclude that Leonese royalty held such a degree of authority – according to 'Īsā, the members of the siege force renewed their oath of loyalty to Ramiro as soon as he arrived – that the child who embodied it could give orders to rough frontier counts and even the Navarrese monarch.

Either way, what is still more surprising is what happened next. Following sixty-two days of fruitless siege, on 28 June 975 Ramiro gave orders to launch a frontal attack against the fortress. For anyone who knows the topography of Gormaz, it is wholly evident that to attempt an attack of this type against 400 metres of castle wall was sheer folly: a steep slope has to be climbed and once outside the castle the soldiers would be confronted by a solid fortification built on an impregnable rocky spur and defended by the garrison. If this is what really happened, the result was the disaster that anyone could have predicted. The besieged garrison were not only able to repel the assault with ease, but they even sent out a sortie to pursue the attackers. The defeat was so resounding that the Christians had to relinquish the siege with all haste, leaving their camp free for the arrival of the auxiliary army. Barely a day after the battle, Ghālib could enter the fortress unopposed. During the following week, at the

[73] Ibn Ḥayyān, *Muqtabis VII*, ed. pp. 228–9; trans. pp. 270–1. The dismissed soldiers were Aḥmad b. Sa'd al-Ja'farī and Ya'la b. Aḥmad b. Ya'la, from the *shurṭa al-'ulya* and *al-wusṭa* respectively.

[74] Ibn Ḥayyān, *Muqtabis VII*, ed. pp. 234–7; trans. pp. 276–9.

beginning of July, the Umayyad *qā'id* undertook sacking and destruction missions in the territory of the count of Castile, and above all in the area around San Esteban de Gormaz.

Around that time, far from Gormaz, in a Castilian monastery, perhaps that of San Salvador de Távara (Zamora), a scribe called Senior completed a copy of the *Commentaries on the Apocalypse*. It was a work that had been written in the 786 by an Asturian monk known as Beatus of Liébana and had become an object of great interest in Castile and León in the decades leading up to the new millennium. The manuscript which Senior competed in July that year had been commissioned by the abbot, Dominico, and it included marvellous illustrations made by a woman called Ende, a painter and servant of God (*pintrix et Dei aiutrix*), and a monk called Emeterius the Presbyter. The colophon also indicates that the work had been completed on 6 July 975, while Fernando Flaínez was fighting in Mauritania: whereby, it may be asked whether that this seemingly confusing colophon is in fact making reference to the campaign fought at Gormaz. Or, even more intriguingly, was Flaínez serving with the Umayyad army in Morocco?[75]

After the Siege

The unexpected end of the siege of Gormaz allowed al-Ḥakam II to save this strategic enclave, whose loss would have been catastrophic for the defence of his frontiers. A number of important lessons were to be learnt from this the episode. First and foremost, the Umayyad diplomacy had been incapable of preventing the formation of a major coalition of Christian kings and counts: their emissaries maintained the fiction of their submission to Córdoba until just shortly before the attack was launched on the fortress on the River Duero. Given the ease with which the submissive Christians had become attackers committed to waging an offensive on the caliph's frontiers, the grandiose receptions had clearly not been of much use.

Secondly, the siege of Gormaz underscored the difficulty faced by the caliphate when it came to maintaining an army on two fronts. 'Īsā al-Rāzī's

[75] J. Marqués Casanovas, 'El Beato de Gerona', pp. 216–17. *Inveni portum volumine IIIa Feria Iia Nonas Iulias. In is diebus erat Fredenando Flaginiz a Villas toleta ciuitas addeuellando Mauritanie. Discurrente era millesima XIII.*

deferential courtly prose scarcely manages to dissimulate the major difficulties faced by the caliph when mobilising an auxiliary force capable of confronting the Christian siege force while the bulk of the army was still deployed on the other side of the Straits. After three years of long campaigns in the Maghreb, the Umayyad military machinery was exhausted and the problems it faced when it needed to mobilise this auxiliary expedition once more underscored the limitations involved in the mass deployment of the regular army in North Africa. It was again clear that the caliphate needed to have troops who were available at all times, especially given the growing threat raised by the Christian kingdoms of the north.

Despite the brilliance of the military parades in Madīnat al-Zahrā', in which the caliph's soldiers displayed their splendid weapons and luxurious uniforms, when it came to tackling real armed conflicts the caliph depended greatly on the frontier troops. Their mobilisation had been fundamental for the final victory in northern Morocco and in the war against the Christians they had proved to be indispensable. Just before news of the siege of Gormaz arrived, but when it was already evident that a Christian offensive was in the offing, al-Ḥakam had decreed that the Zaragoza frontier was to be reinforced. To undertake this, he had to have recourse to a member of the Tujībid family. Around that time other members of the family, who then resided in Córdoba, were given orders to take charge of other frontier fortresses like Daroca, Lérida and Monzón, an unequivocal sign that the defence of this frontier could not be achieved without the contribution of this family.[76]

A demonstration of the effectiveness of the frontier populations in the struggle against the Christians took place that same summer of 975 (364 AH).

[76] Ibn Ḥayyān, *Muqtabis VII*, ed. p. 222; trans. p. 263, Abd al-Raḥmān b. Yaḥyā al-Tujībī was ordered to make his way to this frontier area: he was the son of Yaḥyā, the *qā'id* of the forces deployed in Morocco. The order to leave for the Upper Frontier was given on 19 April (4 *Sha'bān*), that is, eleven days before news of the attack on Gormaz arrived. The order was delivered to the *qā'id* by the caliph's heir, Hishām, who was still a boy, which should be seen as an effort to heighten his role following the caliph's illness during the previous winter. M. J. Viguera, *Aragón Musulmán*, pp. 160–2. A person who belonged to a known family of legal scholars of Zaragoza, called Muḥammad b. Fūrtish, was also sent 'with the aim of inspecting the frontier and protecting its interests'. Although he belonged to the renowned family of the Banū Fūrtish, I have not been able to identify this particular individual, as none of the known members of this family coincides with the chronology of these events, L. Molina and M. L. Ávila, 'Sociedad y cultura en la Marca Superior', pp. 88–9.

On his return from the expedition that had liberated Gormaz, the *qā'id* of Zaragoza, 'Abd al-Raḥmān b. Yaḥyā al-Tujībī, encountered one of the brothers of the king of Pamplona, Sancho Garcés II, who, despite the recent defeat, was campaigning way beyond his lands located in the region of Sos and Carcastillo (*al-Qashtil*). The lookouts posted on the watchtowers in the area of Bardenas were given orders to follow the movements of this expedition made up of 500 horsemen. The vanguard of this expedition was located close to Estercuel (in what is today Ribaforada, Navarre) and it entered Andalusi territory to undertake the typical frontier raid consisting of taking livestock and captives: 'they were capturing the livestock they came across and took captive five men who were fishing nearby'. 'Abd al-Raḥmān b. Yaḥyā sent a detachment of cavalry, who intercepted the Christian vanguard in a skirmish that left five men dead. Later, he himself led an attack against the Christian expedition which also proved to be a victory: thirty-three Christian knights died and forty-seven horses were captured. What is more, the booty included a highly valuable flag and a silver horn for calling the troops. Both items of booty were sent to the caliph's chancery. The Muslims suffered only three casualties: a member of the army and two inhabitants of the city of Tudela.[77]

Although this skirmish had been a victory for the Muslims, the fact that a Navarrese magnate could mobilise 500 horsemen to undertake an expedition in territories that lay ninety kilometres from his dominions underscores how the war of attrition had been ratcheted up to dramatic proportions along the Andalusi frontiers. Without the co-operation of the Tujībids, retaliating against this offensive was becoming almost impossible.

The Battle for the River Duero: the Denouement

Al-Ḥakam II died the year after the Gormaz episode. He could barely have imagined that the strategy he had designed to confront the Christian danger would be shattered shortly afterwards. The person responsible for the change of policy was Muḥammad b Abī 'Āmir, who, having come to power in the years that followed, chose a radical change of policy consisting of continual aggression against the Christians as one of its most recognisable features. The future al-Manṣūr did not have any prior military experience of the northern

[77] Ibn Ḥayyān, Muqtabis VII, ed. pp. 237–9; trans. pp. 279–81.

frontier of al-Andalus, unlike what he had learnt during the time he had spent in Morocco. However, over the course of the years he spent confronting the internal enemies who sought to hinder his rise to power, in particular the *qāʾid* Ghālib, he also developed a first-hand knowledge of the situation on the Andalusi frontiers. It is possible that, by then, he had come to the conclusion that a different policy was needed.

The first change consisted of putting himself in command of the expeditionary forces. Campaigns became sustained military offensives against the Christian territories of the north. Naturally, this did not mean that al-Manṣūr renounced intervening in the internal affairs of the monarchs and counts, but his arguments ceased to be based on subtle diplomatic machinations and instead came down to one sole concern, the use of force. The radical reform of the army allowed the powerful *ḥājib* to have troops at his disposal at all times of the year, and their mobility enabled him to strike with unexpected attacks at any location, whether in winter or summer. The more than fifty expeditions attributed to al-Manṣūr during his twenty years of government gives an idea of the radical change of course the caliphate's strategy took during this period.

Where this new strategy gave rise to the most surprising result was in the case of the county of Barcelona. Up until then, the relationships between counts and caliphs had been excellent, and, what is more, they had been mutually beneficial. However, in July 985 (374 AH) Barcelona was attacked and brutally sacked in one of al-Manṣūr's most celebrated expeditions. The city was subjected to wilful destruction and, as multiple documentary testimonies record, the maximum damage possible was inflicted, including the burning of documents and attacks made against the Jewish community.[78] The conscious devastation of the dominions of count Borrell II, whose representatives had been the object of every possible attention in Madīnat al-Zahrāʾ scarcely ten years before, demonstrates al-Manṣūr's radical opposition to the previous policy of al-Ḥakam II. It is not easy to identify what this change was due to.[79] The most plausible explanation is that in contrast to the proliferation of a pacific culture of commerce, based on constant diplomatic activity, the

[78] M. Rovira i Solā, 'Notes documentals sobre alguns efectes de la presa de Barcelona per Al-Mansur', p. 35.

[79] P. Sénac, *Al-Mansur*, pp. 103–22.

powerful *ḥājib* backed securing a supply of slaves in the form of the many captives brought back from these military expeditions. Therefore, instead of allowing gold coins to leave al-Andalus to pay for slaves brought from distant latitudes, the Umayyad armies could justify their cost by capturing these slaves themselves during campaigns waged under the banner of the Holy War. Indeed, the sources discuss the immense quantities of prisoners captured during al-Manṣūr's expeditions, and although the figures they give are by no means reliable, they do demonstrate that the quantity of captives that arrived must have been very substantial and constant thanks to the continued campaigns. Following al-Manṣūr's death, the people of Córdoba criticised the lesser success of the military campaigns led by his son, al-Muẓaffar, and a saying repeated everywhere soon became famous: 'The importer of slaves has died'.[80]

The destruction inflicted by al-Manṣūr's expeditions against the Catalans was echoed in those led against León, Castile and Galicia. Once more, this was a modus operandi that was totally opposed to the sustained diplomatic action with which al-Ḥakam had sought to neutralise Christian aggressions. Many of the expeditions were led against the territories of the Duero Valley with attacks on places such as Sepúlveda, Simancas, Salamanca, Astorga, Osma or San Esteban de Gormaz: in other words, the main outposts of Christian expeditions against the Andalusi frontier. In some cases – such as, for example, Osma and San Esteban – these fortresses went on to be occupied by Andalusi garrisons.[81]

Despite his resounding triumphs and the terror that his expeditions caused in the Christian north, al-Manṣūr's idea that a state of perpetual 'holy war' would contain the Christians of the north, and even lead to the occupation of their territories, resulted in failure. His later campaigns did not live up to his expectations and following his death in 1002 (392 AH) his son al-Muẓaffar could barely replicate his successes. Then, the gradual disintegration of the caliphate that began in the year 1009 (399 AH) interrupted the series of campaigns that had been unleashed on the Christian lands during the previous decades. The same army that al-Manṣūr had deemed to be the solution to the problems

[80] F. Vidal Castro, 'Los cautivos en al-Andalus durante el Califato Omeya de Córdoba', pp. 370–6.
[81] L. Molina, 'Las campañas de Almanzor', pp. 209–63.

faced by the caliphate then became its greatest problem, due to the widespread rejection of the Berber troops, who were seen by the population as emblematic of a social and political order that was widely perceived as overtly oppressive and distant. The issue was, as has been discussed, that the demobilisation of the regular army left the caliphate with no military alternative to the reviled Berber troops. In the struggles that unfolded in Córdoba during the year of the *fitna*, some of the contenders needed to call on Castilian, Leonese or Catalan forces to fight alongside them against their enemies. Thereby, the magnates of Barcelona, who some years before had been captives in Córdoba following the destruction of their city, returned to the caliphate's capital as well-paid and better-treated soldiers. Likewise, in 1011 (401 AH) count Sancho García of Castile, whose father had taken part in the failed siege of Gormaz, demanded this same fortress in return for his support for one of the contenders in the struggle for the caliphate, and what is more he insisted on being given three other fortresses from the River Duero: Osma, Clunia and San Esteban.[82]

The handover of these four strategic enclaves was one of the milestones in the process of the Christian expansion southwards. The control of the area along the upper course of the River Duero played a key role in disrupting the Andalusi frontier system. Although it is true that, in the following decades, the fortifications along the upper course of the River Duero were the source of constant conflict and disputes, the definitive occupation of Gormaz, Barahona, Aguilera and the valley of the River Bordecorés by the Castilian King Fernando I in circa 1060 led to the definitive rupture of Andalusi control of this frontier. Just twenty-five years later, in 1085, the Christians conquered Toledo.

[82] P. Scales, 'The Handing Over of the Duero Fortresses: 1009–11 A.D. (399–401 A.H.)', *al-Qanṭara*, 5, 1, pp. 109–22.

8

The Authority of the Caliph

The Caliph as a Good Ruler

Al-Ḥakam II ruled over al-Andalus because, in addition to other factors, he belonged to the Umayyad dynasty, one of the oldest and most illustrious Arab families. In the aftermath of the Prophet Muḥammad's preaching, his ancestors were recognised as caliphs and the major Arab conquests were carried out during their reign. As caliph and a descendant of caliphs, al-Ḥakam was living proof of the impressive survival of a dynasty that had resisted the ravages of time and, despite having been on the point of annihilation on various occasions, had managed to restore itself amid great splendour on the far western edge of the Islamic world. For many, the Umayyads' endurance must have seemed a clear sign that their dynasty was under divine protection.

Not everyone could make the same claim. Around the time al-Ḥakam II was ruling in Córdoba, the ʿAbbāsid caliphs survived in Baghdad under the protection of the Buwayhids, a family of military leaders of humble Iranian origins, who had seized power in the caliphate's capital despite their well-known Shīʿī faith. When the Buwayhids took control of Baghdad in 946 (334 AH), they even considered killing the ʿAbbāsid caliph so they could replace him with a descendant of ʿAlī b. Abī Ṭālib and thereby fulfil the principal aim of Shīʿī doctrine. However, the sage advice they received from one of their supporters dissuaded them taking this step: 'While you have to deal with a caliph that neither you nor your followers consider a legitimate sovereign, you can order someone to kill him at any time, it being deemed licit to spill his blood. Yet, if you raise to the throne a descendant of ʿAlī, whom you and your followers consider as having the right to the caliphate, he could induce one of your followers to kill you.' This advice saved the ʿAbbāsids. Shut up in their palace with a pension assigned to them – one that tended to decrease as the years went by – the ʿAbbāsid caliphs gradually lost all trace of the power once wielded by their ancestors. What is more, they had to undergo humiliations such as having to leave the city to welcome the Buwayhid emir on his return from expeditions.[1] This situation was well-known in Córdoba, and it prompted the poet Muḥammad b. Shujayṣ to ridicule it. He referred to the contemporary ʿAbbāsid caliph, al-Muṭīʿ, as someone averse to everything except singing and drinking, who made Baghdad revive the days of Bilkīs, the name used to refer to the Queen of Sheba in Arabic literature.[2]

The alternative that arose in North Africa under the Fāṭimid rulers prompted an equally acerbic critique in Umayyad Córdoba. The poets at al-Ḥakam's court referred to these caliphs as *rāfiḍis*, a radical Shīʿī sect that rejected the authority of the early caliphs and went so far as to consider the Prophet's companions to be infidels for not having safeguarded the rights of ʿAlī b. Abī Ṭālib.[3] In the caliph's official correspondence, the Fāṭimids were accused of having altered what was established in the Qur'an and the tradition of the Prophet Muḥammad. It was even stated in some cases that they did not follow any religion, as their caliph 'is deified by the group that supports him, while others claim him to be a prophet'. All these reasons justified them being termed 'brothers of devils' (*ikhwān al-shayāṭīn*) or imams of heterodoxy (*a'immat al-ilḥād*).[4]

As the Islamic community was divided between the discredited ʿAbbāsid caliphate and the Fāṭimid discourse that distorted Islamic doctrine, the legitimacy of the Andalusi caliph sought to establish its authority in a visible form recognisable to all. This aspect of Umayyad ideology is highly important. There were no hidden components to it, neither esoteric messages nor apocalyptic

1 M. Kabir, *The Buwayhid Dynasty of Baghdad (334/946–447/1055)*, pp. 187 and 193. The episode is taken from Ibn al-Athīr.

2 Ibn Ḥayyān, *Muqtabis VII*, ed. p. 233; trans. p. 275. The poem was declaimed on the occasion of the Feast of the Breaking of the Fast of 975 (364 AH); the ʿAbbāsid caliph had died during the autumn of the previous year.

3 Ibn Ḥayyān, *Muqtabis VII*, ed. pp. 61, 162, 232, where the expression *dāʿī al-rawāfid* is used in reference to the Fāṭimid caliph; trans. pp. 83, 202, 274. EI, 2nd ed., s.v. al-Rāfiḍa.

4 Ibn Ḥayyān, *Muqtabis* V, ed. and trans. p. 221; Ibn Ḥayyān, *Muqtabis VII*, ed. p. 180; trans. p. 219. The accusation against the ismāʿīlis of *ilḥād*, or divergence from the correct religious path, was very common among Sunni authors, F. Daftary, *The Isma'ilis. Their History and Doctrines*, p. 517.

expectations: aside from anything else, the Umayyad caliphs of al-Andalus presented themselves as good Muslim rulers, whose principal achievement was to have preserved the principles of the Qur'an and the tradition (*sunna*) transmitted by God to his Prophet. Such principles not only ensured the salvation of their Muslim subjects, but also guaranteed a broader prosperity, which was a concern that was recognised as being of the utmost importance to ensure caliphal legitimacy.

The 'pragmatic' character of Umayyad ideology in al-Andalus is expressed in a multitude of texts.[5] For the Umayyad ideologues, God did not exert influence in the world in the form of messages with hidden meanings, but through revelations that clearly indicated the path to salvation, and adherence to this would guarantee the people's prosperity. It is this political discourse that was eloquently articulated in the Umayyad's official correspondence.[6] Written with a bombastic rhetoric and replete with Qur'anic quotations, the letters issued by the Andalusi caliphs place great emphasis on God's revelation to the Prophet Muḥammad as being the light that illuminates the way to paradise. The reception of the Qur'an, the establishment of Islamic law, and combating the enemies of the faith by waging *jihād* were all encompassed by this divine revelation. Following the death of Muḥammad, God had chosen the caliphs from among the same 'tribe' (*'itra*), and they were charged to be, among other things, the bearers of tradition (*sunna*) and the custodians of the law

[5] A poet called Ismā'īl b. Badr praised 'Abd al-Raḥmān III by stating that he had cast the 'Abbāsid caliphs into opprobrium by equalling the Umayyad caliph 'Abd al-Malik (685–705/65–86 AH), 'who was guided by the good path', This caliph had always been praised for his equanimity, organisational gifts and pragmatism, despite not having been a learned and wise caliph, which was due to the fact he had had to focus on political matters, *Akhbār Majmū'a*, ed. and trans. p. 165; trans. James, p. 142. Ismā'īl b. Badr was a secretary and poet who accompanied the caliph on a number of military campaigns. He was also the governor of Sidonia, witness to the *amán* of Zaragoza, and overseer of the souk: Ibn Ḥayyān, *Muqtabis V*, ed. and trans. pp. 39, 59, 227, 265, 277, 283; Ibn 'Idhārī, *al-Bayān*, II, ed. cit. p. 159; Ibn al-Faraḍī, n. 214. C. Robinson, *'Abd al-Malik*, London, 2005, pp. 142–4.

[6] The discussion that follows is based on two texts with different dates but containing an identical vision of Umayyad legitimacy. The first is a text written at the time of 'Abd al-Raḥmān III that condemns the teachings of Ibn Masarra, the renowned ascetic who died in 931 (319 AH) and whose doctrines were considered heretical following his death, Ibn Ḥayyān. *Muqtabis V*, ed. cit. pp. 22–4; trans. cit. pp. 27–30. The second text is part of the victory paean that the vizier and *ṣāḥib al-madīna*, Ja'far b. 'Uthmān al-Muṣḥāfī, wrote to mark the surrender of the Idrīsid leader Ḥasan b. Qannūn in June 974 (*Dhū l-qa'da* 363 AH); it was sent to the governors of all al-Andalus with instructions that it be read in the mosques under their jurisdiction, Ibn Ḥayyān, *Muqtabis VII*, ed. pp. 178–80; trans. pp. 217–19.

(*sharī'a*). The first *rāshidūn* caliphs, who succeeded the Prophet, fulfilled this mission, which is why they sought to destroy the schismatic sects, such as the *khārijites* – who thought that any Muslim could be caliph – and the *rāfiḍis* – who rejected the first caliphs for having supplanted 'Alī. One of the tenets that the first caliphs had fulfilled to the letter had been avoiding the doctrinal innovations that might distort the message of the divine revelation. However, the 'Abbāsid caliphs had neglected this obligation, whereby a 'diversity of sects' had arisen, which had led to an irreversible and lamentable situation. In contrast, nothing of this sort had happened in al-Andalus, where the Umayyad dynasty had upheld the Islamic faith and prevented the spread of such innovations (*bida'*).[7] With a zeal that had been transmitted from father to son down through the dynasty, 'Abd al-Raḥmān III had 'attended to the scripture and had proclaimed the sunna, showing his preference for it as well as fighting for it'; al-Ḥakam II had done the same, as he never allowed any 'innovation (*bida'*) introduced by heresy or criminal ambiguity' to go unchecked.

The central tenet of this discourse underscored how the Umayyad policy of preserving the Islamic creed brought prosperity. The justice (*'adl*) exercised by 'Abd al-Raḥmān III had ensured that the country remained at peace, whereby learning flourished and the people prospered; meanwhile the caliph himself 'devoted his zeal to caring for the interests of the community' (*maṣāliḥ al-umma*). The just reign of al-Ḥakam II had also made sure that 'the roads were safe, the frontier passes (*al-durūb*) of the Muslims fortified, their frontiers guarded, the enemies of Islam subjugated and the Muslim forces victorious over them'. The equation that combined divine revelation with its preservation by the caliphs, along with their eradication of innovation and the multiplying effect of the caliphs' just rule, resulted in the community's welfare (*maṣlaḥa*).[8]

[7] The 'innovations' (*bida'*) are the elements that men add to the Prophet's message and which distort the content of its revelation. In al-Andalus, a renowned scholar, Muḥammad b. Waḍḍāḥ (d. 900/287 AH), a descendant of a *mawlā* of the Umayyads, wrote a *K. al-bida'* (Treatise Against Innovations), ed. M. I. Fierro.

[8] The same idea was set out in a letter addressed to 'Abd al-Karīm b. Yaḥyā, ruler of the sector of the Andalusis in Fez: 'God permits the caliph to live at ease and to fulfil with delight all the roles and duties through which God protects the Community of Muslims, to defend their territories, to keep their enemies at bay and to fill the hands of the infidels with the entrails of these enemies', Ibn Ḥayyān, *Muqtabis VII*, ed. pp. 111–12; trans. p. 161.

The idea that the caliph's rule, based on his adherence to the tradition (*sunna*) of the Prophet, entailed benefits for the Muslim community (*umma*) recurs in numerous testimonies. In the preamble to the diploma issued in June 973 (*Ramaḍān* 362 AH) to ratify the submission of the Berber leader Abū l-ʿAysh b. Ayyūb b. Bilāl, an explanation is given for al-Ḥakam II's decision to confer on this chieftain authority over his Berber tribe: the caliph was motivated by his predilection for Abū l-ʿAysh b. Ayyūb b. Bilāl and his confidence in him, in conjunction with a concern to ensure the welfare (*istiṣlāḥ*) of both the leader and those he governed; thereby, they 'would have the means to live and resources to get by'. Abū l-ʿAysh was expected to fear and obey God, which implied obeying the caliph and acting in accordance with the rules for good Muslim governance, concerns that the same diploma discusses in detail.[9]

The same ideas appear in the letter that the caliph issued in January 975 (364 AH), which announced the reduction of the tax for exemption from military service or *maghārim al-ḥashd* by one sixth. This letter was also read out in all the mosques after the Friday prayers.[10] Its lengthy preamble describes the caliph as having been chosen by God to bear his trust (*amāna*) and protect his subjects (*raʿiyya*).[11] For this reason, al-Ḥakam keeps an unceasing vigil over them, attends to their affairs and seeks 'to lighten their burdens, improve their life, free them from worries, facilitate their union and ensure that justice (*al-ʿadl*) and safety (*al-amān*) reign amongst them'. The mission of helping, defending and attending to the interests (*maṣāliḥ*) of all Muslims, without making any distinction, is for the caliph above any material consideration. Al-Ḥakam conceives his rule as a combination of power (*mulk*), authority (*ʿamr*) and state (*sulṭān*), but neither the breadth of the former, nor the sublimity of the second, nor the majesty of the third are to distract him from his obligations, which are none other than the extirpation of error, the fostering

[9] Ibn Ḥayyān, *Muqtabis VII*, ed. pp. 111–14; trans. pp. 142–5. I have analysed this diploma above pp. 227.

[10] Ibn Ḥayyān, *Muqtabis VII*, ed. pp. 207–10; trans. pp. 247–9.

[11] A correction has been made to the critical edition of Ibn Ḥayyān's text to read *raʿiyya*. The use of the word *amāna* and the expression *wa irtaḍa-hu li-ḥaml amāniti-hi* – 'he gave his consent as custodian of [God's] trust' – refers to Qur'an 33:72, on which *tafsīr* writers highlighted that *amāna* involved the *khilāfa* that had been entrusted to man over the earth: 'We offered the trust (*inna ʿaraḍnā al-amānata*) to the heavens and the earth and the mountains, yet they refused to undertake it and were afraid of it; mankind undertook it (*ḥamala-hā*) – they have always been inept and foolish.'

of the knowledge of what is just, decreeing the implementation of equity and ordering the reduction of taxes. For that reason, since becoming caliph, al-Ḥakam had decreed various tax reductions, and when it came to ordering the aforementioned reduction in the tax on the exemption from military recruitment his aim was to alleviate his subjects (*ra'iyya*) and to bestow a benefit upon the 'people of the kingdom' (*ahl mamlakatihi*), without making any distinction between the 'close in relation to the distant, nor city dwellers over those who lived in the countryside'.

The idea of a caliphate arising from an amalgam of power, authority and state apparatus is undoubtedly highly innovative and demonstrates how the political understanding of Umayyad sovereignty had undergone an extraordinary development. But perhaps what is still more striking is the insistence placed upon the concept of the 'common good' or 'general interest' – *maṣlaḥa* (pl. *maṣāliḥ*) – which is cited in these texts to refer to the benefits obtained by the community as a result of the caliph's rule.[12] It is a concept that 'Īsā al-Rāzī also uses when he refers to the order given by the caliph to widen the main street running through Córdoba's souk, which was undertaken for the sake of obtaining the 'common good' or *maṣlaḥa* for his subjects. The same concept was used in Mālikite law as a foundation for the idea that the principal aim of Islamic law was to seek what benefited the community. In a later period, the Andalusi jurists also had recourse to this concept to legitimise the application of extra-canonical taxes levied on Muslims, arguing that, although illegal, they were a necessary source of income by which to guarantee the common good, for instance, by maintaining the army, which was essential to secure the frontiers and roads.[13] However, almost all legal discussions concerning this concept came much later, which makes its inclusion in official Umayyad texts at such an early date quite remarkable.[14]

The role of the caliph guided by orthodoxy, supported by an enduring dynasty and serving the common interest of the Muslims, sums up the

[12] See above, pp. 228 and below 415 below.

[13] Ibn Ḥayyān, *Muqtabis VII*, ed. p. 71; trans. p. 93. A. García Sanjuán, *Till God Inherits the Earth*, p. 395.

[14] M. Khadduri en EI, 2, sv. *maṣlaḥa*. The idea that prosperity was linked to good government was also elaborated by the Fātimids, see the fascinating discussion by M. Rustow, *The Lost Archive*, pp. 231–5.

principal elements of the Umayyads' claim to legitimacy. There were no hidden messages or esoteric claims. Al-Ḥakam II did not present himself as a charismatic figure, but instead as the continuation of a long line of caliphs who, like him, had preserved the legacy of God's revelation to the Prophet and had succeeded in increasing the prosperity of the *umma*. The issue of his subjects' prosperity was not a rhetorical topos. The Umayyad caliph was by no means the despot conjured up by superficial historiographical notions of medieval Muslim societies. His role as a Commander of the Faithful prevented him from behaving as a tyrant who turned his back on the interests and aspirations of the community he ruled over. This is something that is continually underscored in the discourse on Umayyad legitimacy: the 'tyrants' are the others, the illegitimate rulers such as the Christians of the north, or the Fāṭimid caliphs, who are presented as the counterpoint to an Umayyad authority, which is in contrast firmly committed to the defence of the interests of the Muslims.[15]

The defence of the common interests of the Muslim community explains why Umayyad ideology emphasised the 'protection' that the caliph provided for the *umma*. In the aforementioned letter announcing the tax reduction, al-Ḥakam II presented himself as someone who attended to the interests and affairs of the Muslims and also protected them (*muḥāmiyan 'an-hum'*). The idea of the 'protection' provided by the caliph is expressed here in the framework of the 'general interest' that was implied by the tax reduction. However, this idea could also be represented in a much starker manner. One of the most striking scenes in the caliphate of 'Abd al-Raḥmān III took place on a September day in 939 (327 AH), on which the feast of Minā was being celebrated in Córdoba. The atmosphere was very tense that day, as the people were highly agitated by the recent and terrible defeat that the caliph had suffered at Alhándega. To mark this feast day 'Abd al-Raḥmān III usually held a military parade. However, on this particular occasion, the caliph decided to decree the exemplary and public punishment of the officers responsible for the rout. They were singled out by the caliph and executed publicly in front of the horrified crowds attending the parade. In these dramatic circumstances, the furious caliph addressed the guilty officers with a short speech full of reproaches for having abandoned him on the day of the battle, which was

[15] Ibn Ḥayyān, *Muqtabis VII*, ed. pp. 146, 216; trans. pp. 185, 256.

heard by all those present. What he went on to add is the most explicit expression of the caliph's understanding of the power he wielded. 'Look at these poor people (*al-khalq al-ḍaʿīf*), he said, pointing to the populace who stared at them. Have they not given us power (*al-maqāda*) and made themselves our submissive servants, so that we defend and protect them (*li ḥimāyati-nā la-hum*)?'[16]

Clearly, there were two facets to the protection of the subjects. When 'Abd al-Raḥmān III confronted the army leaders that had betrayed him during that disastrous battle, the 'protection' referred to was the justification for the control he exerted and the necessary violence that accompanied it; when al-Ḥakam II wanted to demonstrate the benevolence of his policy, 'protection' shifted to the aspects of his rule that addressed the interests of the Muslims. In 'Abd al-Raḥmān III's address, he invoked the 'protection' that he and his soldiers provided to the common people as a reminder that the inability or refusal to exercise this form of *power* could result in death, while in al-Hakam's paternalistic missive, 'protection' formed part of the *authority* with which the caliph represented himself as the defender of the interests of the community. Neither reading of the notion was exclusive, as the Umayyad caliphs were convinced that the protection of the Muslims depended equally on their power and their authority.

This concept of Umayyad legitimacy demonstrates that the caliphs were highly conscious that the Muslim community was far from being a passive element in the political articulation of the state. Their acquiescence was as necessary as their submission. If anything was demonstrated by past rebellions, it was that mere violence was not sufficient to ensure the support of the *umma*; the caliph also needed their consent. In one of his letters 'Abd al-Raḥmān III insisted on the necessity that 'people were a single nation, obedient, calm, subjugated and not sovereign, ruled and not ruler'.[17] Implicit in this extraordinary declaration was the acknowledgement that at a certain point the community could, effectively, come to rule and become sovereign, which was an admission of the political weight of the *umma*. This political weight struck John of Gorze, the ambassador of the Emperor

16 Ibn Ḥayyān, *Muqtabis V*, pp. 302–3.
17 Ibn Ḥayyān, *Muqtabis V*, ed. and trans. pp. 142 and 155.

Otto I, who visited Córdoba in 954. One of the things that most surprised the German monk was seeing that in al-Andalus, once a regulation had come into force it could not be changed, as both the sovereign and the people had to obey this law, whose transgression was punished with the sword. If a crime was committed by the subjects, it was the sovereign who judged them, but were he to commit it, he would be judged by the people.[18] As M. Barceló eloquently demonstrated, this presupposed a sense of reciprocity between the *umma* and the caliph, 'which implied the caliphate's acceptance of certain forms of control, and an awareness of the possibility of this control being exercised by the *umma* and the religious groups who regulated civic life through the law'.[19]

To oppress the Muslims with abuses and arbitrariness, to escape from the battlefield when defending the frontiers of al-Andalus, or to avoid tax cuts when such a thing was possible were different forms of betraying the Muslim community's consent for the caliph's authority to exercise its power. Were it to prove necessary, the community had sufficient resources to stifle that authority by displaying its dissatisfaction in numerous ways: from promoting rumours and gossip against the caliph to stirring up moral censure through the *'ulamā'*, as well as staging protests, such as the tumults that broke out between soldiers of the caliphal army and the population of Córdoba. The presence of the people, exercised through the crowd's sense of 'moral awareness', was also recorded when an uncle of the Idrīsid, Ḥasan b. Qannūn, was killed by Umayyad troops in the autumn of 973 (363 AH) and his head was sent to Córdoba, where it was publicly displayed to the 'crowds of spectators, who launched every type of curse against the dead man and against all those of his sect'.[20]

Three decades after the death of Caliph al-Ḥakam, in February 1009 (399 AH), the same crowds unleashed the revolution that overran Córdoba at

[18] 'Lex enim tam inprovocabilis eos constringit, ut, quod semel antiquitus omni eiu genti prefixum est, nullo umquam liceat modo dissolvi; parique nodo rex populusque tenentur omnisque transgressio gladio feritur. Si quid ab inferioribus, rex, si quit rex ipse commiserit, cunctis in eum populis animadvertit.' Vita Iohannis Gorziensis, p. 371.

[19] M. Barceló, 'El califa patente', p. 155. Unfortunately, the rest of this study offers an explanation that runs contrary to what is brilliantly discerned in this interpretation of John of Gorze's text.

[20] Ibn Ḥayyān, *Muqtabis VII*, ed. pp. 78, 142–3; trans. pp. 101, 180 (I give an alternative translation of the expression *ahl al-tashrīq wa l-bid'a al-muḍilla*).

the start of the civil war. The population rose up against the regime that had been established by al-Manṣūr and his sons, and this led to the violent civil war known as the *fitna*. One episode that demonstrates how this *fitna* contained a powerful component of social protest was the ousting of one of the various members of the Umayyad family who had been appointed caliph during this turbulent period: having been called a 'tyrant', he accused the people of Córdoba of knowing no other language than that of the sword, which convinced them that he had to be deposed.[21]

During the caliphal period these social tensions, prompted by the high degree of fiscal pressure along with the serious inequalities encountered in al-Andalus, were contained, but this is not to say they did not exist. Al-Ḥakam II was perfectly aware of this and, above all, of the fact that the Muslim community had strong ideological alternatives to the legitimacy he embodied. This explains the disproportionate alarm generated by the slightest sign of Shīʿī activism in al-Andalus. The Umayyad concern was that Fāṭimid preaching on how the rule of the descendants of ʿAlī b. Abī Ṭālib would inaugurate a new era might nudge any latent social discontent towards the authority of the Shīʿī dynasty. At the height of the tenth century (fourth AH), one unequivocal lesson to be learned from the long history of the Muslim community was that no ruler should take for granted his legitimacy over that of the *umma*. Consequently, a major part of the efforts made by the Umayyad caliph was intended to avoid alternatives to his authority taking root among this community.

The Ideological Battle against the Fāṭimids

During the reign of al-Ḥakam II the complex ideological claims made on behalf of the Fāṭimid caliphate were widely known in the court circles of al-Andalus. The poems and letters written by al-Ḥakam II's poets and secretaries offer a clear demonstration of their familiarity with these ideas. These works also reveal that these writers were capable of turning them on their head to demonstrate that their meaning was very different from what was intended by Fāṭimid propagandists. Umayyad propaganda deployed an elaborate and

[21] The deposed caliph was al-Mustakfī, a descendant of ʿAbd al-Raḥmān III, *Dhikr bilād al-Andalus*, ed. and trans. p. 175.

complex set of arguments to counteract the possible influence of Fāṭimid claims. The tonic prescribed for this aim was very similar to that seen in the previous section: divine revelation and prophetic tradition have a clear, evident meaning; it had been preserved by the orthodox tradition, and put into practice by the Umayyad caliphs with excellent results for the Muslim community; meanwhile the Fāṭimids distorted both revelation and tradition into claims that were as vacuous as they were pernicious.

It is unlikely that Antonio Gramsci would have been thinking of the poets at the court of al-Ḥakam II when he devised his concept of 'organic intellectuals': conceived as 'the dominant group's "deputies" exercising the subaltern functions of social hegemony and political government', it nonetheless adapts perfectly to the role performed by the poets who served the caliph and received generous gifts in return.[22] During the grand caliphal receptions held to mark religious feasts, or during the audiences held to honour the arrival of important individuals in the main audience hall at Madīnat al-Zahrā', these organic intellectuals monopolised a part of these ceremonies and competed with compositions that invariably contained allusions to the caliph's political and military achievements as well as the major issues of the day, among which rivalry with the Fāṭimids was a dominant topic.

An especially appropriate moment for these poets to display their skills was the elaborate reception organised in Madīnat al-Zahrā' to celebrate the desertion of the Banū al-Andalusī from the Fāṭimid ranks to the Umayyads in September 971 (*Dhū l-qa'da* 360 AH). For the occasion, one of the most prolific court poets, Muḥammad b. Shujayṣ, composed a long poem, in which he took Fāṭimid ideological claims and reformulated them in an 'orthodox' context.[23] According to the poet, the defection of Ja'far b. 'Alī and his brother from the side of the Fāṭimid caliph, al-Mu'izz, was the result of a divine order, one that had been announced by astrologers in their horoscopes:

> With the most joyful arrival, accompanied by the most fortunate augury,
> news has come of an order derived from [divine] power
> [that] brings the fallen empire of Ma'add [i.e. Caliph al-Mu'izz]
> [over] to the empire that obeys the Mahdī of the Banū Marwān.

[22] A. Gramsci, *Selections from the Prison Notebooks*, p. 12.
[23] Ibn Ḥayyān, *Muqtabis VII*, ed. pp. 54–6; trans. pp. 72–4.

> Remarkable and glad tidings announcing
> the attainment of our wishes, dictated by our fortunate horoscopes![24]

The designation of al-Ḥakam II as *Mahdī* is a play on words: in the Shīʿite tradition the *Mahdī* is a figure that appears shortly before the end of time, to cleanse the world of evil in preparation for the Final Judgement; however, the poet does not use this term in the apocalyptic sense bestowed upon it by the Shīʿites, but instead with the word's original meaning of 'well-guided'.[25] By emphasising the original sense of this term, the poet's pun evidently seeks to erode a key concept of Fāṭimid propaganda. It is on this basis that al-Ḥakam is also spoken of as 'the well guided of the [Banū] Marwān' or the 'rightly guided of the nations' (*mahdī al-ummām*), who is deemed capable of providing 'continuity' for the Prophet's message. This message had been transmitted since the early days of the Umayyad caliph Marwān 'with the idea of bringing together all the aspirations of the community through a deliberative legacy (*wirāthat shurā*)', a concept that also goes against the idea of charisma being inherited through ancestry, as was upheld by the Fāṭimids.[26] At the Feast of the Breaking of the Fast in 363 AH (974) – which, as has been seen, turned into an ordeal for the Idrīsid Ḥasan b. Qannūn, who had recently arrived in Córdoba following his defeat by the Umayyad army – the same Muḥammad b. Shujayṣ accused him of having launched numerous disturbances against the 'dynasty of the Mahdī' (*dawlat al-Mahdī*), a malevolent play on words which could be interpreted in an ambivalent sense, and would have been gleefully received by the attendees.[27]

One of the central issues stirred up by the emergence of the Fāṭimid caliphate was the claim that these sovereigns were descended directly from the Prophet Muḥammad through his daughter's marriage to ʿAlī b. Abī Ṭālib. The Umayyads' ideologues counter-attacked by claiming their own ancestral relationship to the Prophet, as they were also descended from the lineage of the Quraysh, who was the distant common ancestor of the Umayyad, ʿAbbāsid

[24] Ibn Ḥayyān, *Muqtabis VII*, ed. p. 54; trans. p. 72.
[25] On this meaning see W. Madelung, *Encyclopaedia of Islam*, 2nd ed., s.v. *Mahdī*.
[26] The concept of inheritance and ancestral 'legacy' (*mīrāth*) is very important in the construction of the discourse of Umayyad legitimacy. M. García Arenal, *Messianism and Puritanical Reform*, p. 95.
[27] Ibn Ḥayyān, *Muqtabis* VII, ed. p. 161; trans. p. 201, which translates this as 'the orthodox caliph'.

and Fāṭimid caliphs. The Umayyad claim was based on the notion of *qarāba*, according to which the Prophet's lack of any male descendants meant that the clan of 'Abd Manāf, the Prophet's great-grandfather, as well as the Umayyads, were able to claim a common parentage. And given that the Umayyads had served as leaders in Mecca during the pre-Islamic era and had subsequently ruled as caliphs, their claim to be leaders of this clan was based on unquestionable historical evidence.[28]

Although, any attempt by the Umayyads to compete with the ancestry of the Fāṭimids concealed a somewhat forced argument, this did not hinder the poets of the Cordoban court from emphasising that their lords were members of the Prophet Muḥammad's family. Thus, during the Feast of the Breaking of the Fast in 975 (364 AH), Muḥammad b. Shujayṣ went on to refer to the caliph's son and heir, Hishām, as the best choice of heir from within the family of the Messenger of God (*āl rasūl Allāh*). Three years before, during the celebration of the Feast of the Sacrifice 972 (360 AH), the same poet had already praised the heir, stating nothing less than 'the Prophet is your uncle (*al-'amm*) and al-Ḥakam is your father'.[29]

In some of the verses declaimed to mark the Feast of the Breaking of the Fast in 972 (361 AH), another poet, Muḥammad b. Ḥusayn al-Ṭubnī, composed the following remarkable dithyramb on the heir Hishām:[30]

> The tree of Prophecy and that of the Caliphate are his trunk:
> the branch proceeds from these entwined roots.

The same botanical vision appears in a poem by Muḥammad b. Maḥāmis al-Istijī, which praises the caliph's government by highlighting its splendour, and support for the rule of law and the light of religion, so that the 'branch of power (*guṣn al-mulk*) flourishes and bears its fruit'.[31] In a fascinating poem,

[28] M. Sharon, 'The Development of the Debate around the Legitimacy of Authority in Early Islam', p. 30.

[29] Ibn Ḥayyān, *Muqtabis VII*, ed. pp. 83, 122, 46, 163, 206; trans. pp. 106, 155, 23, 203, 246. Also ed. p. 61; trans. p. 83.

[30] This poet had emigrated from North Africa to al-Andalus following the arrival of the Fāṭimids. He was the head of a prolific family of men of letters and died in old age in 1004 (394 AH), F. Navarro Ortiz, *Biblioteca de al-Andalus*, s.v. al-Ṭubnī Abū 'Umar.

[31] Ibn Ḥayyān, *Muqtabis VII*, ed. pp. 83 and 62; trans. pp. 107 and 83. al-Ṭubnī is an author who was originally from Ṭubna, in Zāb. He left this North African city for al-Andalus in 942–3 (331 AH), perhaps fleeing from the Fāṭimids. In Córdoba he became a court poet and was sent to North

that plays on a huge quantity of references, Ṭāhir b. Muḥammad al-Baghdādī, known as al-Muhannad, used the concept of 'quintessence' (*ṣafwa*) to refer to the Prophet himself – considered the 'quintessence of the creation of God' – but he also applies it to Caliph al-Ḥakam, whose ancestor had received the prophecy from the 'possessor of the throne' (*dhū l-'arsh*), whereas the posterity of the lineage had been awarded the caliphate.[32]

The poetic images of the double trunk upon which Umayyad sovereignty was established, along with those that portrayed the caliph as the quintessence and underscored how prosperity reigned in al-Andalus as a consequence, were also embodied in the iconography of the decorative panels that adorned the reception hall where these poems were declaimed. Throughout the palace of Madīnat al-Zahrā' there was a decorative programme consisting of 'a dense forest of trees formed of arabesque patterns', more specifically in what is known as the Salón Rico, where the celebrated receptions were held during which the poets declaimed their verses. Its walls were adorned with a series of panels, which to a large extent have survived to the present day. Their decoration was dominated by a stem or central trunk 'that established an axis of symmetry', around which was articulated a dense interweaving of vegetal ornamentation formed of an impressive combination of up to a thousand different floral motifs. A characteristic of this decoration is the interwoven decorative forms that recur throughout these panels.[33] The stems or central

Africa during the campaign led by Ghālib, who had sent for him. He survived al-Ḥakam, dying in 1004 (394 AH), E. Navarro Ortiz, *Biblioteca de al-Andalus*, s.v. al-Ṭubnī. Muḥammad b. Maḥāmis al-Istijī was not only a poet, but also a scholar specialising in Qur'anic exegesis. He had made the pilgrimage and died in April 987 (376 AH), ibid., s.v. Ibn Maḥāmis.

[32] Ibn Ḥayyān, *Muqtabis VII*, ed. pp. 232, 95, and 156–7; trans. pp. 274, 119, and 198. This poet had arrived in al-Andalus from Baghdad in 951 (340 AH). Although he survived al-Ḥakam and also composed panegyrics for al-Manṣūr, he spent the final years of his life in retirement devoted to ascetic practices, E. Saleh al-Khalifa, *Biblioteca de al-Andalus*, s.v. al-Muhannad al-Bagdādī. For the references to *ṣafwa*, Lane Pool, *Arabic English Lexicon*, s.v., which can be compared to the three opening verses of the poem of al-Baghdādī. The reference to the possessor of the 'throne' (*'arsh*) draws on Qur'an 40:15. However, I believe that these lines, which also refer to the creation (*khalq*), encompass an oblique *mu'tazili* reference, as this doctrine rejected the ascription of human attributes to the divinity, whereby the 'throne' of God is presented as an image of the creation (*khalq*), G. Vitestam, "Arsh and kursī. An Essay on the Throne Traditions in Islam', p. 372. To complicate matters still further, the whole composition seems to be an imitation (*mu'ārada*) of the panegyric composed by the 'Abbāsid court poet Abū al-Atāhiya in honour of the 'abbāsid caliph al-Mahdī, I. 'Abbās, *Ta'rīkh al-adab al-Andalusī*, p. 104, cit. by S. T. Stetkevych, 'The *Qaṣīdah* and the Politics of Ceremony', pp. 28–32, n. 30.

[33] C. Ewert, 'Elementos de decoración vegetal del Salón Rico de Madīnat al-Zahrā'', pp. 43–57.

Image 13 Madīnat al-Zahrā'. Parietal decoration in the reception *majlis* or Salón Rico. Courtly poets liked to use plants as images of the Umayyad dynasty: 'The tree of Prophecy and the tree of the Caliphate are its trunk/the branch comes from these intertwined roots'.

trunks always have a double root that recalls the double root that sustains the tree of prophecy and the caliphate, as referred to by the poet Muḥammad b. Ḥusayn al-Ṭubnī, while the profuse vegetal ornamentation growing from it evokes the abundance that Umayyad ideology proclaimed to be the result of its legitimacy.

The 'practical' nature of Umayyad ideology was thereby transposed to a highly visible medium. The decoration of the walls of the palace of Madīnat al-Zahrā' gave rise to a great profusion and variety of vegetal motifs, which may be read as representations of the caliphate's political programme, according to which the caliphs' custodianship of the Prophet's revelation and its tradition were deemed fundamental to ensuring general prosperity. Within the Salón Rico, these elements offered an abstract continuation of the plants in the gardens which the room opened onto, thereby establishing a symbiotic relationship between the natural world and the order imposed upon it by caliphal rule.[34] It was, to all intents and purposes, a rich and abundant earthly world, one that exalted the breadth of Umayyad ideology.[35] Or, in the words of Muḥammad b. Shujayṣ:

> May God conserve this land [...]:
> [its] soft earth, moist and gentle breeze
> pleasant appearance, comforting atmosphere,
> furthermore, [there are] as many gardens (*riyāḍ*) as you may wish for, their fruits
> are paradisiacal and their design splendid.[36]

The walls of the palace in Madīnat al-Zahrā' thereby became a forceful artistic expression of the celebration of an Umayyad legitimacy that was linked to the prosperity of al-Andalus. This was a recurring theme addressed in the caliph's official correspondence and extolled by the court poets. The stylised representation of nature incorporated an extraordinary variety of plant forms, amid which were recognisable symbolic elements linked to the dynasty, such as their genealogical roots, the multiplication of their fruit and the general well-being that accompanied Umayyad rule.

[34] J. Dodds, 'Relieve de Madīnat al-Zahrā'', in *al-Andalus. Las artes islámicas en España*, p. 242.

[35] This interpretation differs from that proposed by M. Acién in his brilliant reading of the Salón Rico, 'Materiales e hipótesis para una interpretación del Salón de 'Abd al-Raḥmān al-Nāṣir', pp. 179–95. In his study, Acién offers three possible responses to the question of how to interpret this decorative programme: the first consists in seeing its elements 'within strict Qur'anic correspondences to paradise'; the second considers the forms of vegetal decoration as emblematic representations of the lineages and groups present in the Umayyad state; and the third, which he is inclined to follow, is linked to an astrological interpretation of the hall's decoration, with references to esoteric writings such as the *Ghayāt al-ḥakīm*, a work whose date and authorship are subject to debate. This latter hypothesis does not strike me as convincing. Firstly, as I will set out below, the idea that Madīnat al-Zahrā' encompasses a symbolic representation of paradise is not possible, as it would have been unacceptable within orthodox Islamic belief; secondly, the texts cited by Acién are not from the official milieu of the caliphate but from what he considered to be the ideological Islamic matrix, which I do not believe can be applied in this particular circumstance and setting. In contrast, my interpretation seeks to frame the decorative programme within the available evidence, and it takes as its point of departure the view that it would have been impossible for the Salón Rico to include heterodox elements, as the Umayyad caliphal ideology set very specific limits on this issue. However, my interpretation has as its principal caveat the regrettable circumstance of it not having been possible to discuss it with this great historian and friend, who died far too early.

[36] Ibn Ḥayyān, *Muqtabis VII*, ed. pp. 85–6; trans. p. 108. I think that the translator, when speaking of 'paradisiacal fruit', is reading *bustanī*, which does not correspond with the editor's somewhat confused reading of this passage.

Umayyad legitimacy was also based on the caliph's virtues and good deeds. The poets praised al-Ḥakam II as possessing a superior eloquence to that of Saḥbān Wa'īl, a historic Arab poet about whom it was said he once spent half a day addressing an assembly without repeating the same word twice; his piety, his generosity or his knowledge of prophetic traditions (*ḥadīth*) and legal arguments (*ra'y*) allowed him to be compared with jurists of the calibre of Mālik b. Anas o al-Nakha'ī.[37] Consequently, epithets such as '*imām* of orthodoxy' (*imām al-hudā*) or 'sun of orthodoxy' (*shams li l-hudā*) were frequently bestowed on al-Ḥakam along with numerous references that even extended to the light that emanated from his person.[38]

Some poetic compositions went so far as to use expressions that, seemingly, linked the caliph with an apocalyptic outlook. This is the case with the poem that 'Abd al-'Azīz b. Ḥusayn al-Qarawī declaimed during the Feast of the Breaking of the Fast in 974 (363 AH):

> In the West the star of a caliphate has risen
> which is to shine bright with splendour in the two easts
> so that an *imām* zealous for the good of the pure religion (*al-dīn al-ḥanīf*)
> may dispel the darkness of unfaithfulness with the light of orthodoxy

The rising of the sun in the West is, in effect, one of the signs Muslim eschatology associates with the end of time; it is a portent of the coming of the Antichrist and other events foretelling the end of the world.[39] However, once more the poet seeks to underscore his knowledge of this idea, albeit without elaborating any apocalyptic interpretation: he uses it to emphasise how the Umayyads have proclaimed the caliphate in the most westerly point

[37] Ibn Ḥayyān, *Muqtabis VII*, ed. p. 85; trans. p. 108. *Encyclopaedia of Islam*, 2nd ed. T. Fahd, s.v. *Saḥbān Wa'īl*. Mālik b. Anas (d 795/179 AH) is the celebrated founder of the legal school that bears his name and was predominant in al-Andalus. More surprising is the mention of Ibrāhīm b. Yazīd al-Kūfī al-Nakha'ī (d. c. 717/96 AH), a jurist who transmitted the traditions of 'Ā'isha, the Prophet's wife, and who was one of the first to propose the use of *ra'y* or personal judgement as a source for the compilation of law, *Encyclopaedia of Islam*, 2nd ed. G. Lecomte, s.v. al-Nakha'ī. The reference to caliph al-Ḥakam uniting the knowledge of ḥadīth and *ra'y* alludes to the major conflict that a hundred years before had confronted the supporters of these two legal sources, M. I. Fierro, 'The Introduction of ḥadīth in al-Andalus', pp. 68–93.

[38] Ibn Ḥayyān, *Muqtabis VII*, ed. pp. 60, 120; trans. pp. 82, 153.

[39] J. P. Filiu, *L'Apocalypse dans l'Islam*, p. 45, drawing on the traditions with an Egyptian origin compiled in the work of Muḥammad b. Ḥibbān (d. 965).

of the Islamic world – 'In the West the star of a caliphate has risen' – but the poem then includes a very subtle Qur'anic reference. The expression 'the two easts' (*al-mashriqayn*) appears in the Qur'an, where it is stated that God is the Lord of the two easts and the two wests. Despite its strange formulation, Sunni Qur'anic commentaries insist that both expressions are perfectly intelligible and merely refer to the furthest points at which the sun rises and sets in the winter and summer. This image had already been used in a poem by Ismā'īl b. Badr, who served as secretary to Caliph 'Abd al-Raḥmān III, which stated:

> Thus, I seek to please the *imām* of the two wests
> He who does not wish to succumb to repose
> until he is caliph of the two easts.[40]

The pragmatic nature of Umayyad ideology and its adherence to orthodoxy is also demonstrated in what is recorded regarding the caliph's presence. The ceremonial created for the Fāṭimid caliphate enveloped the caliph's presence in a sense of mystery that permitted only sparing appearances of the *imām*; in contrast, the Umayyad caliph regularly took part in receptions, audiences and religious festivities, and he might also be encountered making his way along the streets of Córdoba, inspecting building work being completed on a bridge, visiting the workshops where the caliphate's textiles were made, and even accompanying a group of riders from Lérida that he had met by chance. Naturally, he was not a caliph who was easily accessible, as on other occasions access was governed by strict protocol, but nor was al-Ḥakam II a concealed caliph who made only fleeting public appearances.[41]

[40] Ibn Ḥayyān, *Muqtabis VII*, ed. p. 163; trans. p. 203. 'Lord of the Two Easts and Lord of the Two Wests', which Abdel Haleem interprets as 'Lord of the two risings and Lord of the two settings', Qur'an, 55: 16–17, p. 557. al-Ṭabarī, *Tafsīr*, vol. 22, p. 197. *Akhbār Majmū'a*, ed. and trans. p. 161; Spanish trans. p. 139. I do not follow, in this particular case, D. James's translation, p. 139, as he ignores both duals (al-magribayn, al-mashriqayn) when he translates 'seeking the approval of the imam of the Occident/he who can never rest until/he is caliph of the Orient'; cf. the same expression in another poem by Ismā'īl b. Badr: Ibn Ḥayyān, *Muqtabis V*, ed. cit. p. 91; trans. cit. p. 79.

[41] Ibn Ḥayyān, *Muqtabis VII*, ed. pp. 65, 92, 107, 151–2; trans. pp. 78, 115, 137, 192.

Nevertheless, this did not prevent poets from toying with the idea of the sovereign's absence in similar ways to those used by the Shīʿites. Thus, for example, regarding the heir Hishām:

> We love him with such excess that we see him when he is absent
> (*gha'ib*)
> and, in contrast, when he appears, his majesty makes him invisible
> (*mughayyab*).

The allusion to one of the most relevant Shīʿī concepts – that of the concealment (*ghayba*) of the *imām* and his reappearance at the end of time – could not be clearer. Yet, once more, this concept does not refer to the Shīʿīte idea of the 'hidden *imām*', whose reappearance would be the fulfilment of the expectations of the Fāṭimids; instead the sense of 'concealment' used by the Umayyad panegyrists underwent a subtle re-elaboration; it is the subjects' love that makes Hishām visible when he is absent, while it is his own majesty – and not any complex esoteric Shīʿīte idea – which makes him invisible when present.[42] Here, as in other cases studied in this chapter, the message is always the same: the concepts used in Shīʿī preaching to justify the rule of the Fāṭimid caliphs certainly derive from Muslim tradition, the very tradition that the Umayyads claim to be custodians of, but in their hands it has been distorted and its meaning clad in esoteric and hidden components that did not form part of the original prophetic message. For that same reason, 'Abd al-Raḥmān III defined himself in his correspondence as 'He who Maintains the Truth' (*al-Qā'im bi l-Ḥaqq*), using the same title that had been granted to his contemporary and rival, the Fāṭimid Caliph al-Qā'im.[43] The mechanism is again the same: to demonstrate how the concept to which the Fāṭimid caliphs want to give a concealed, eschatological meaning in fact has a clear and well-defined significance in the orthodox tradition that the Umayyads are the guardians of.

[42] Ibn Ḥayyān, *Muqtabis VII*, ed. p. 231; trans. p. 273.
[43] J. Safran, 'The Command of the Faithful in al-Andalus', p. 185, although I do not agree with this author's idea that the Umayyad caliph intended to represent himself as a 'Mahdi-like figure'.

The Caliph in the Mosque

A particularly important extension of the caliph's religious authority were the mosques, of which there was a dense network across al-Andalus due to the widespread Islamisation of society. In Córdoba alone, although the sources provide highly disproportionate figures, the number of mosques scattered across the city's neighbourhoods numbered well over a hundred. Following the extension of the main mosque that was undertaken by al-Ḥakam II between 962 and 965 (351–5 AH), more than seven thousand Muslims could congregate there.[44] It was in mosques that the name of al-Ḥakam was regularly invoked as Commander of the Faithful, inscriptions bearing his name adorned a range of locations, and the Muslim community gathered to partake in the religious foundations of his authority. Or as the poet Muḥammad b. Shujayṣ stated, 'the virtuous people fill every mosque and the libertines empty every place of amusement'.[45]

Five ritual prayers were held in all the mosques every day, with Friday prayers being of special importance; consequently, these temples were well-frequented places, which led to them fostering numerous forms of social contact. When the caliph wanted to make an important announcement, such as a tax reduction or news of a significant military victory, he sent a missive to his governors with the explicit order that it was to be read in the mosques of their district. Likewise, it was in the mosque that the caliph's subjects swore the oath of loyalty to the new sovereign, and oaths were also sworn there for important political treaties.[46]

The mosques were also places where the most reputed legal scholars and jurists taught. Yaḥyā b. Yaḥyā (d. 849/234 AH), who was responsible for the introduction of Mālikism in al-Andalus, held his gathering (*majlis*) in the central nave of the mosque of Córdoba, while his rival, 'Abd al-Malik b. Ḥabīb (d. 853/238 AH), met with his disciples beside the wall of its *qibla*.[47] These meetings could also become hotbeds of conspiracy, as the Umayyad sovereigns knew well from experience: the prolegomena to the famed revolt of the suburb

[44] M. Acién, 'Madīnat al-Zahrā'en el urbanismo musulmán', pp. 20 and 23.

[45] Ibn Ḥayyān, *Muqtabis VII*, ed. pp. 55–6; trans. p. 74.

[46] *Crónica Anónima*, ed. and trans. p. 30; Ibn Ḥayyān, *Muqtabis V*, ed. and trans. pp. 307–8.

[47] *Prosopografía de los ulemas de al-Andalus*, s.v. Yaḥyā b. Yaḥyā, id. 11.714.

of Córdoba in 818, which nearly brought down Emir al-Ḥakam I, was sparked off by people who were dissatisfied with the government's policies, 'whereby meetings and gatherings were held in the mosques to discuss the matter'. That was the reason why some of the *fuqahā'* in Córdoba insisted that these meetings could only be undertaken by pious, intellectual and morally trained people; in other words, they sought to exert control over the orthodoxy and intentions of those who took part in them.[48]

Other forms of socialising that took place in mosques were announcements made by individuals: when somebody found a bag of money, they were obliged to announce it 'at the doors of the mosque, the people's meeting places and the souks' prior to keeping it for themselves.[49] However, mosques were not just sites of pious practices. Ibn Ḥazm recounts in his *Ṭawq al-hamāma* the story of a young man from Córdoba who attended one of the city's mosques for the sole purpose of seeing a beautiful young man he had fallen in love with; he even scoured the oratory by night, and was nearly arrested on one occasion by the city guard (*al-ḥurs*) for loitering in the streets after hours.[50]

As emblematic buildings for the people to meet in, the mosques served to represent the idea of the Muslim community (*umma*) being gathered in order to practise their religion. A constant concern of the Umayyad ideology was to bestow a political significance on this religious congregation, which is why the caliph regularly attended these multitudinous prayer gatherings. However, the ruler does not appear to have played any role in the celebration of these rites, which were entrusted to the prayer leader and preacher. In fact, 'Abd al-Raḥmān III once made an attempt to have the Friday sermon shortened, as he was in a hurry for some reason – perhaps an early indication of the stress caused by the onset of the weekend – but his request met with a characteristic response from the preacher: he purposely lengthened his sermon.[51]

Despite not playing any role in the rites, the caliph's presence in the main mosques in Córdoba and Madīnat al-Zahrā' gave rise to a number of

[48] V. Lagardère, *Histoire et société en Occident musulman au Moyen Age*, p. 347; M. Marín, 'Learning at Mosques in al-Andalus', pp. 48–9.

[49] Ibn al-'Aṭṭār *K. al-Wathā'iq*, ed. pp. 127–8; trans. pp. 260–1.

[50] Ibn Ḥazm, *Ṭawq al-ḥamāma*, Arabic text and trans. pp. 138 and 139.

[51] M. Marín, 'Altos funcionarios', p. 93, with reference to Ibn Mashshāṭ al-Azdī. The anecdote ends with the caliph expressing his gratitude to the preacher for not having made concessions to his mundane whims.

arrangements in terms of protocol. Al-Ḥakam would enter both oratories directly from his palace or *alcázar*, and he did so using a special passageway called *sābāṭ*, which connected the palace with its neighbouring mosque, whereby the sovereign was saved from having to mix with the Muslims on the street. The first *sābāṭ* linking the *alcázar* of Córdoba with the mosque, which was located just in front of the palace, was built by Emir ʿAbd Allāh (d. 912/300 AH). The somewhat cynical reason given for the construction of this passageway was that whenever the emir entered via the main door, those attending the prayers stood up, which caused complaints from a number of pious men who argued that Muslims should only stand up before God. Emir ʿAbd Allāh tried to prevent people from standing up as he walked past, but having failed to do so, he chose to have a *sābāṭ* built; it allowed him to enter the mosque without being seen, and make his way to the *maqṣūra*, or special space reserved for him, all without disturbing those at prayer. When the prayers were over, ʿAbd Allāh would often remain in the mosque conversing with various senior dignitaries, which established a tradition his successors continued.

The extension of the Córdoba mosque undertaken by al-Ḥakam II involved moving the *qibla*, the wall which marked the direction faced by those at prayer. This also meant that the old *sābāṭ* had to be replaced with a new one linking the *alcázar* to the new *qibla*. Recent excavations have found on the adjacent street the remains of the two pillars that were used as the base for this second *sābāṭ*, which entered the mosque through a lintelled door that is still visible in the façade of Córdoba's mosque. The caliph left his apartments in the *alcázar* in a state of ritual purity and entered the mosque by crossing the *sābāṭ*, which was raised above the street.[52] Once within the temple, the door led to a corridor formed by the *qibla* and what is known as the *transqibla*, which served as the mosque's outer wall. Two doors opened onto this corridor and they are still visible today in the mosque's *miḥrāb*; it was through the first of these, known as the 'door of the *sābāṭ*' (*bāb al-sābāṭ*), that the caliph entered the temple. He made his entrance accompanied by various court dignitaries, and they took their places in the *maqṣūra* to recite the prayers. It seems highly

[52] A recent excavation in the patio of the Museo Diocesano de Córdoba has revealed the remains of a large latrine that was built in the *alcázar* to be used by a single person, and it was undoubtedly intended for the caliph to use prior to entering the *sābāṭ* that led to the mosque. I am grateful to Juan Murillo for having given me the opportunity to visit this fascinating excavation.

Image 14 Dome of the *miḥrāb* in the Mosque of Córdoba. The Umayyad caliphs and the emperors of Constantinople maintained excellent relations that allowed for exchanges of gifts and the presence of imperial specialists for the creation of the mosaics that adorned it.

probable that the caliph was separated from the rest of the Muslims by a carved wooden screen. Once the ritual was over, the caliph would take a seat in the mosque while he conversed with senior dignitaries of the caliphate, thereby continuing the custom established a century before by his great-great-grandfather, Emir ʿAbd Allāh. This is what happened on Friday, 27 March 974 (29 *Jumāda* II 363 AH) when al-Ḥakam II attended the prayers in the mosque of Córdoba; once the prayers were over, he sat in the *sābāṭ* of the *maqṣūra*, 'as he was accustomed to do', where he received the viziers, whom he informed of the news of Ḥasan b. Qannūn's surrender in Morocco.[53]

The ritual performed in the mosque at Madīnat al-Zahrā' was the same. Again, there was a *sābāṭ* connecting the *alcázar* with the city's mosque and inside the temple was a wooden screen, similar to that used in Córdoba, which

[53] Ibn Ḥayyān, *Muqtabis III*, ed. cit. pp. 57–9; trans. cit. pp. 93–5; G. Pizarro Berengena, 'Los pasadizos elevados entre la mezquita y el alcázar omeya de Córdoba', pp. 233–49. Ibn Ḥayyān, *Muqtabis VII*, ed. cit. p. 150; trans. cit. pp. 190–1.

separated the caliph, his son, Hishām, and some of his innermost circle of advisors from the other attendees; the mosque could hold around five hundred people. As in Córdoba, after the prayers, the caliph was accustomed to sit and converse with his closest advisors, as occurred on 26 March 975 (10 *Rajab* de 364 AH). On that occasion, al-Ḥakam, who was still recovering from the stroke he had suffered months before, attended Friday prayers in the mosque at Madīnat al-Zahrā', and once they were over he also sat down in the *sābāṭ*, where he welcomed *qā'id* Ghālib and the vizier Ja'far b. 'Uthmān al-Muṣḥafī, with whom he discussed the growing unrest which was then breaking out along the Christian frontier.[54]

The way in which the caliph attended prayers in the mosque like any other Muslim, and then took a seat to hold a meeting with the senior dignitaries of his administration, speaks volumes about the way in which Umayyad sovereignty was displayed. His presence in Córdoba's main mosque provided a vision of the caliph to the community who attended prayers. Despite being segregated from the caliph, Muslims were able to witness his presence in the company of his viziers. The visibility of government seems to have been the intended purpose of holding these meetings in the mosque, which the caliph could have held wherever and whenever he chose. Furthermore, it is also significant that al-Ḥakam II took advantage of these occasions to make important announcements to his viziers, like the victory over Ḥasan b. Qannūn in Morocco, or to demonstrate that, despite his recent illness, he was informed about the military events under way at the frontier. By choosing to hold these meetings in the mosque after the Friday prayers, the sovereign made it clear that he wished to be seen by the Muslim community after praying along with them.

The Rejection of Authority: Slander against al-Ḥakam

The physical description of al-Ḥakam indicates that he was clean-shaven and 'light skinned with a rosy complexion; [he had] large black pupils, an aquiline nose [and] a high-pitched voice; his legs were short, his body was strong and he had a long neck and forearms; his upper jaw protruded'.[55] He was forty-seven years old when he became caliph following his father's death in October 961

[54] Ibn Ḥayyān, *Muqtabis VII*, ed. cit. pp. 150 and 211 and trans. cit. pp. 190–1 and 251.

[55] M. Marín, 'Una galería de retratos reales', pp. 278 and 281.

(350 AH), which was a considerably advanced age for the era. However, what is most striking is that he had reached this age having neither taken a wife nor fathered any children. Among the sovereigns of a dynasty in which polygamy and concubines had always ensured an extensive progeny and a proliferation of candidates to exercise power, al-Ḥakam was a highly unusual case.

Contemporaries were well aware of this situation. ʿĪsā al-Rāzī refers to it and gives a rather surprising explanation: having named him as his heir, ʿAbd al-Raḥmān III obliged al-Ḥakam to live in the *alcázar* and to refrain from intercourse with women. Al-Ḥakam

> prudently accepted [this decision ...] although, as his father's reign went on, this became a burden and whittled away his best days. This deprived him of the intimate pleasures of life on account of the subsequent inheritance of the caliphate, which became his at an advanced aged and with few appetites ... having [had] to accept his obedience and deny himself man's greatest pleasure, the fulfilment of his sexual yearnings, which most people could not undergo, all to satisfy his father; it was due to this that stories began to circulate about him.[56]

Why ʿAbd al-Raḥmān III might have imposed this unusual celibacy on his son is discussed below, but first I want to address the principal outcome of this, which was none other than the fact that al-Ḥakam only conceived his heir once he had become caliph. His first son, who was named ʿAbd al-Raḥmān, died prematurely, while the one who would become his heir, Hishām, was born in June 965 (354 AH) to a slave (*jarīya*) of Basque origin called Ṣubḥ, who became *umm walad* and went on to play a prominent role in the *alcázar*. The father, al-Ḥakam, was fifty at the time. Suddenly, the issue of the caliphal succession began to be seen as a race against time, as for Hishām to become caliph he had to attain his majority before his father died.

In this context, the Umayyad court became rife with rumours. A palace chronicler such as ʿĪsā al-Rāzī, an unlikely candidate to stir up hearsay against the caliph, despite pondering the temperance and obedience with which al-Ḥakam had complied with the obligation of not taking a wife sooner, added in a somewhat mysterious manner that this was the reason for 'the stories

[56] Ibn Ḥayyān, *Muqtabis V*, ed. and trans. pp. 8 and 9.

(*ahkbār*) that circulate'. It is impossible to know exactly what the chronicler wanted to imply with this all too oblique reference. He was perhaps alluding to stories concerning al-Ḥakam's possible homosexuality, but it is clear that he was acknowledging that the caliph's private life was a subject of gossip. One source reveals, perhaps with malevolent intentions, that the caliph often called Ṣubḥ by the male name Ja'far, and that he especially liked to see her dressed as a young man.[57]

Gossip as a form of social activity played an important role in medieval societies. In rural communities, the emergence of gossip narratives could be taken up by groups of people and eventually lead them to embark on a variety of courses of action, yet in spaces as enclosed as a caliphal court rumours gained an extraordinary political dimension.[58] Gossip about the caliph, his concubine, the heir being a minor, and above all the circumstances surrounding the caliph's environment must have given rise to an endless stream of newsmongering, whereby the secrets shared led to affinities and loyalties being forged. Within a context in which various groups competed to gain power, the people closest to al-Ḥakam II thus became the subject of talk among those who sought to prop up or undermine the caliph's authority in accordance with their respective interests.

Aside from the stories that were told about al-Ḥakam, the rumours concerning Ṣubḥ, the mother of the caliph's heir, also began to multiply. All this tittle-tattle emerged in parallel to the rise of Muḥammad b. Abī 'Āmir, later known as al-Manṣūr, within the caliphal court. According to some sources, Ṣubḥ was responsible for the young scholar's meteoric and unexpected rise, which began in 967 when he was entrusted the management of Hishām's wealth. After this, an unprecedented succession of posts followed, each more influential than the last. The rapid elevation of someone who had until then been nothing more than a little-known aspirant to whatever post was available in the Andalusi judiciary sparked off rumours about his relationship with Ṣubḥ and gave rise to open insinuations that they were lovers.[59]

57 L. Bariani, *Almanzor*, p. 60.
58 C. Wickham, 'Gossip and Resistance', pp. 3–24.
59 L. Bariani, *Almanzor*, pp. 57–8.

The seriousness of this accusation must be understood in the context of the rigid patriarchal codes of Arab society, in which honour was measured by an individual's or group's capacity to retain their women and isolate them from the gaze of or dealings with strangers. Thus, it is striking to note the amazement which, according to one of our sources, was expressed by al-Ḥakam as he asked himself: 'What is it that Muḥammad b. Abī ʿĀmīr has used to win over my wives, and even gain control of their hearts? Why is it that, although they have all the pleasures of the world at their disposal, they do nothing but describe his gifts, and they are not satisfied with anything except what he gives them? Either I have a wizard full of wisdom, or else I have a diligent servant. I am fearful for what he holds in his hands.' Putting these words into the mouth of the caliph of al-Andalus was something that was unheard of. Implicitly, it was an acknowledgement that a free man aged about thirty had an astounding degree of intimacy with his wives. To have such access to the caliph's women and to be allowed, for example, to give Ṣubḥ a silver model of a palace seems difficult to believe. As discussed below, when the wives of the Banū al-Andalusī arrived in Córdoba they were brought into the city at night by eunuchs in order to avoid them being stared at and gossiped about. In contrast, Muḥammad b. Abī ʿĀmīr was a young Arab, who worked in the administration and was able to establish such an intimate relationship with no less than the women of the caliph: it is clear that, whether true or not, these rumours were intended to do as much harm as possible to the sovereign's honour.[60]

The defamations against al-Ḥakam II must have taken on an alarming dimension as his reign went on. In the spring of 972 (361 AH), under al-Ḥakam's express orders, Córdoba's *ṣāḥib al-madīna* imprisoned a group of individuals from the city who dedicated their time 'to derision, dissolution, speaking ill of the caliph, running down people's reputations and circulating their slander in poems, which they wrote in gatherings, in which they competed with one another'. Among the detainees – some managed to escape – were secretaries and renowned poets. One of them was ʿĪsā b. ʿAbd Allāh b. Qarlumān, a poet who belonged to a renowned line of *mawlā*s of the Umayyad family, whose

[60] P. Sénac, *Al-Mansūr*, pp. 15–23; M. Marín, 'Una vida de mujer: Ṣubḥ', pp. 426–33. X. Balestín Navarro, *al-Mansur*, pp. 63–4, whose translation is quoted. On the codes of honour, P. Guichard, *al-Andalus. Estructura antropológica de una sociedad islámica en Occidente*, pp. 64–85.

ancestors had played a crucial role in establishing the dynasty in al-Andalus.[61] Another was a *mawlā* of the caliph's half-brother, al-Mundhir, who was also known as Ibn al-Qurashiyya. The most prominent member of this group of slanderers was Yūsuf b. Hārūn al-Ramādī, a well-known figure within Umayyad palace circles and author of several panegyrics. Known for his liking for wine and his capacity for falling in love with people of either sex, al-Ramādī was involved in a celebrated case of love at first sight with a woman whom he had met in the middle of the street in Córdoba, and whose sight inflamed his passionate heart.[62] In one of his poems, al-Ramādī had satirised with keenly honed cynicism the extravagant number of people mobilised to stand at the reception held for Ja'far b. al-Andalusī, marvelling at the fact that the caliph had accumulated so many troops – it will be recalled that a great many of them were civilians mustered from the suburbs of Córdoba: 'well, if my beloved had let his face be seen/his gazes would have made up for so many troops'.[63]

As examples of al-Ramādī's satirical poetry, some verses written against the caliph are especially significant, as they harshly criticise his policy of granting appointments to positions in the administration:

> He appoints and dismisses [a person] all in one day
> neither in this nor in that does he get it right.[64]

Years later, in 978 (368 AH), once al-Manṣūr had come to power, al-Ramādī took part in a conspiracy to dethrone Hishām II in order to replace him with a grandson of 'Abd al-Raḥmān III. This conspiracy cost the life of 'Abd al-Malik b. Mundhir b. Sa'īd, the official whose investigation into the complaints made by the people of Guadalajara was discussed above. Although the poet once more managed to escape with his life, his collaboration in this risky attempt to bring about a dynastic change was possibly due to the same critical vision set out in his poetry.

[61] *Biblioteca de al-Andalus*, s.v. Ibn Qarlumān. One of his ancestors had been a poet from the court of 'Abd al-Raḥmān II.

[62] *Biblioteca de al-Andalus*, E. Navarro i Ortiz, s.v. al-Ramādī, n. 1.650. *Encyclopaedia of Islam*, H. Péres, s.v. al-Ramādī.

[63] Ibn Ḥayyān, *Muqtabis VII*, ed. p. 56; trans. p. 74.

[64] J. Vallve, 'El zalmedina de Córdoba', p. 309.

None of those detained for slander in spring 972 spent long in prison. They were released in mid-June that same year (*Sha'bān* 361 AH). However, the episode reveals the existence of a group of people close to the circles of power, who used poetry to launch a critique against the caliph. A year later a similar situation arose. Once more the *ṣāḥib al-madīna* of Madīnat al-Zahrā' ordered three people accused of having spread 'calumnies against the course of action of the Commander of the Faithful as well as indiscreet and troublesome gossip' to appear before him, which again highlights how there was deep concern over the caliph's public reputation and clear evidence of opposition to his policies.[65]

The Problem of the Succession

The matter that generated the most controversy during the final years of the reign of al-Ḥakam II, and that exerted a decisive influence on the destiny of the Umayyad caliphate of Córdoba, was the succession. As has been discussed, Hishām was born in June 965 (354 AH), so in the summer of 971, when the chronicle studied here begins, he was just six years old, while his father was fifty-six.

The possibility of Hishām succeeding his father was complicated by the fact that his minority meant he would be unable to act as caliph, or even to be designated as heir. The theory and practice of the Muslim caliphate stipulated that this position could only be held by an adult who had reached maturity (*bālig*) and therefore had a legal status that entitled him to act independently without any need for a guardian or representative. The age at which this could happen depended on the signs of puberty (the growth of body hair, height, sexual capacity, etc.) and intellectual maturity. In the east, for example, the 'Abbāsid Caliph al-Muqtadir had been designated heir when he was aged only thirteen, in 908 (296 AH), which might have been considered a precedent. So, in the best-case scenario, and at the time our chronicle begins, al-Ḥakam

[65] Ibn Ḥayyān, *Muqtabis VII*, ed. p. 104; trans. p. 133. The text provides us with the names of the three men who were arrested, but they are hard to identify: Aḥmad b. Hāshim b. Muḥammad b. Hāshim, who was placed under house arrest, was probably a member of the Tujībid family, as was Ibn al-'Āṣī, who was the son of the vizier al-'Āṣī b. al-Ḥakam. The other detainee was Ibn Muqīm, for whom I can find no additional information. A few months later, the two members of the Tujībid family had been pardoned and sent to join the army that was deployed in Morocco, ibid., ed., p. 125; trans. pp. 162–3.

still had to wait seven years for the appointment or the succession of his son to be considered legitimate. However, aside from the fact that the caliph's advanced age entailed the possibility that he might not live so long, the precedent of al-Muqtadir did not encourage optimism: his rule as caliph in Baghdad (908–32/295–320 AH) had been a disastrous period during which the ʿAbbāsid dynasty had undergone a profound crisis it never recovered from. Contemporaneous Eastern writers considered that al-Muqtadir had been appointed caliph far too young and with little experience, which had resulted in him devoting himself to a life of pleasure, while ignoring matters of government and allowing bureaucrats and military commanders to do and undo things at will.[66]

These facts were well-known at the Umayyad court. The caliph's age and the many years that remained before Hishām attained maturity thus became a serious concern. The earliest evidence of this anxiety are the verses that Muḥammad b. Shujayṣ declaimed at the Feast of the Sacrifice held in October 971 (360 AH). Hishām had just turned six; nonetheless, the poet launched an unheard-of defence of his virtues:

> The intelligence separated him from childhood before he even turned eight,
> and before he thrived, he merited being called mature.
> Why should he not be heir, as a child, if the one who has conveyed
> divine consent was appointed by his father when he was a child?
> Let us honour whoever has the imām as father!
> Let us praise whoever has the imām as son!

The tenor of the poets' defence of Hishām was heightened at the Feast of the Breaking of the Fast the following year, in July 972 (361 AH). Perhaps it is not by chance that it had been during the spring of that year that the aforementioned group of slanderers had been detained, all of whom, as has been seen, were close to the Umayyad court. Perhaps spurred on by this event, poets rivalled one another in making the staunchest and most forthright defence of Hishām's status as heir, despite the fact that they all knew it was illegal. Thus, Muḥammad b. Ḥusayn al-Ṭubnī proclaimed that, despite his being a minor, the order should be given for an oath of loyalty (*bayʿa*) to be sworn to him

[66] L. Osti, 'The Wisdom of Youth: Legitimising the Caliph al-Muqtadir', pp. 18 and 21–2.

straightaway, even by those who were reluctant to do so, and threats should be issued to anyone who refused:

> Everyone wishes to swear loyalty to him as heir; but, even though they did
> not want to,
> doing so would be one of the most obligatory matters.
> [...]
> The swearing of this oath to the heir is a satisfaction,
> which revives everyone who is pure,
> and a sword, which kills everyone who is not.

In that same ceremony, Muḥammad b. Shujayṣ went still further and did not hesitate to name Hishām as 'heir' (*walī l-'ahd*), despite the fact that he had never been proclaimed as such, and nor did he meet the relevant legal conditions. Despite this obstacle, the caliph and his supporters were committed to designating Hishām as heir, yet this gave rise to marked resistance from those who preferred to adhere to the letter of the law and opposed the project.[67]

Around this time, Hishām, who had just turned seven, began to receive a comprehensive education. A scholar called al-Qaṣtallī, who had travelled across the Near East and was an expert on prophetic traditions, law and Arab lexicography, was chosen as his first teacher. He had already assisted the caliph on other matters while working in his library, but with his appointment as preceptor to the heir, he was granted a salary, a horse, and the right to dine every day in the *alcázar* along with the heir and the other children who attended his classes.[68] These classes took place in a room in the *alcázar* of Madīnat al-Zahrā', known as the *dār al-Mulk*, which was suitably equipped, so that the heir could study there with the utmost comfort and convenience.

[67] A. García Sanjuán, 'Legalidad islámica y legitimidad política en el califato de Córdoba: la proclamación de Hišām II (360-366 H./971-976)', pp. 50-55. The references to the poems cited in Ibn Ḥayyān, *Muqtabis VII*, ed. pp. 61, 83–4, 95; trans. pp. 83, 107–8, 118–19.

[68] Ibn Ḥayyān, *Muqtabis VII*, ed. pp. 76–7; trans. p. 99. Al-Qaṣtallī's job at the court was criticised by Muḥammad b. Isḥāq b. al-Salīm, who reproached him for his assignment of a salary from the caliph: he therefore presented him with two stones so that he could hit himself with them. When Muḥammad b. Isḥāq b. al-Salīm was named *qāḍī* in 966 (356 AH), al-Qaṣtallī undertook a small act of revenge and left the stones in the house of the recently appointed judge. M. L. de Ávila and M. Penelas in *Biblioteca de al-Andalus*, V, n. 1.094.

The following year, from August 973 (*Dhū l-qaʿda* 362 AH), Hishām's education was given a more specific focus on Arabic language, which was taught to him by Muḥammad b. Ḥasan al-Zubaydī, one of the most brilliant grammarians of the day. As a member of an old Arabic family that had settled in Seville, al-Zubaydī had also played a role in the caliph's court for some time, and had dedicated to al-Ḥakam some of his most important works on Arabic grammar. However, his appointment as preceptor to the prince brought with it the opportunity to reside at Madīnat al-Zahrā' and receive a stipend, as well as an honorific garment (*khilʿa*).[69]

The fact that a few months later Hishām would fall ill with smallpox between February and March 974 (363 AH) seems to have hastened matters relating to the succession. At the Feast of the Sacrifice, held in September that year, for the first time the heir participated in a solemn reception of dignitaries and senior civil servants at Madīnat al-Zahrā' in a hall specially prepared for the event. Although on this occasion one of the poets once more referred to him as 'heir to the throne' (*walī al-ʿahd*), Hishām in fact went on to be given a rather elaborate official title: 'official candidate to the succession of the caliph' (*al-murashshaḥ li-wilāyat ʿahdi-hi*). It may be concluded that, despite the poets' praise, those who supported him as heir were treading on eggshells so as not to provoke those who, with the law to hand, were arguing that it was illegitimate to appoint as heir a child who had no legal status and could not even administer his own property.[70]

At the end of November 974 (*Rabīʿ I* 364 AH), al-Ḥakam II became seriously ill. He suffered a stroke, and for a month and a half the court's senior dignitaries ceased to have any contact with him. It was only in mid-January

[69] Ibn Ḥayyān, *Muqtabis VII*, ed. pp. 133–4; trans. p. 168. On al-Zubaydī, J. Haremska, *Biblioteca de al-Andalus*, VII, n. 1.887, containing a survey of this author's writings, most of which were on grammar, although he also wrote poetry. A particularly well-known poem of his is the one that he wrote to a slave of his, whom he could not visit in Seville due to the caliph having prohibited him from going there to see her: 'All proximity is ordered to distance and all bonds of union are called on to disappear', F. Pons Boigues, *Ensayo bio-bibliográfico de historiadores y geógrafos arábigo-españoles*, p. 91.

[70] A. García Sanjuán, 'Legalidad islámica y legitimidad política', pp. 56–7 and fn. 26. For the reception presided over by Hishām, ʿĪsā al-Rāzī indicates that there had been a precedent, at the time of ʿAbd al-Raḥmān III, when al-Ḥakam himself had undertaken a similar role during the Feast of the Sacrifice in 921 (308 AH) when he was just six years old. The title 'heir to the throne' was used in a poem declaimed that day by Aḥmad b. ʿAbd al-Malik, *Muqtabis VII*, ed. p. 187; trans. p. 226.

975 that the caliph seemed to have recovered and resumed his audiences with the viziers. His recovery caused great rejoicing among the poets. One of them, Yaḥyā b. Hudhayl, stated that during the caliph's illness their souls had felt 'like Jacob when he was given Joseph's tunic'. This was a somewhat elaborate allusion to the Bible story included in the Qur'an, which recounts how Joseph's brothers, envious of his virtues and their father's love for him, abandoned him in a well in the middle of the desert, and to demonstrate that Joseph had been killed by a wolf they showed their father his tunic stained with false blood. According to the poet, the Muslims seemed to have believed that, just like Joseph, the caliph had died, but Yaḥyā b. Hudhayl added that the caliph's restored health had returned joy to the dynasty (*dawla*), which in any case was to be entrusted to the 'heir' (*mutakhallif*), Hishām.[71]

Nonetheless, and despite the recovery, everyone knew that al-Ḥakam's health had been seriously weakened. In fact, in January 975, the sixty-year-old caliph had just over twenty months to live, and he must have been well aware that life was slipping through his fingers. It is perhaps for this reason that, following his return to public life, he took part in a series of ostentatious events. These were not only acts that any good Muslim who felt close to death might be expected to perform, but were also clearly intended to muster support for Hishām as successor to the caliphate, despite the legal impediments.

The first of these pious actions was spectacular, both in its content and as regards the subtle legal ploy that it involved. As soon as he had recovered, al-Ḥakam decided to free more than one hundred palace slaves and grant them the documents that testified to their manumission. The signing of these documents took place on 16 January 975 (*Rabīʿ II* 364 AH), in other words, the day after the doctors had allowed the caliph to resume his duties. To all appearances, this was a pious deed which complied in full with Islamic law, yet its implementation involved a subtle legal trick, which quite possibly everyone was aware of, and which can be reconstructed in detail.

[71] Ibn Ḥayyān, *Muqtabis VII*, ed. p. 205; trans. p. 245; Qur'an 12, 11–101. Yaḥyā b. Hudhayl was a jurist and traditionist who realised the major social influence that poetry could have, when he attended the tumultuous burial of the renowned literary figure Ibn ʿAbd Rabbihi, who died in 940. He composed various poems on Madīnat al-Zahrā' in which he describes its arches, pillars and gardens. He died in 999 (389 AH), T. Garulo in *Biblioteca de al-Andalus*, s.v. Ibn Hudayl al-Tamīmī.

The manumission of slaves was a practice highly recommended by Islamic dogma, as it allowed the freed individuals to become full members of the Muslim community. The act of freeing a slave had given rise to an extensive legal doctrine that established the terms and forms of the manumission, as well as the relationships to be maintained between the ex-slave and his or her owner. Without digressing on other issues, there were three types of manumission – definitive manumission (*ʿitq batl*), postponed manumission (*ʿitq muʾajjal*) and posthumous manumission (*ʿitq tadbīr*) – depending on whether the manumitter wanted to free their slaves immediately, at some prearranged future date, or else after the owner's death.[72]

These three forms of manumission were used by Caliph al-Ḥakam II to free the 100 male and female palace slaves on that January day in 975 (364 AH). He granted some of them immediate manumission, for others it was postponed, and for the rest it was to be posthumous, thus strictly adhering to the different forms of manumission set out in Mālikite doctrine.[73] To certify these 100 manumissions, the relevant documents were issued. It is reasonable to think that their contents had to be identical to the forms set out in the notarial formulas compiled by the contemporary jurist Ibn al-ʿAṭṭār for this type of legal act, whereby it is possible to take one of these legal models and adapt it to the circumstances taking place at this particular juncture. The content of one these manumission documents would therefore have read more or less as follows:[74]

> Document of definitive manumission granted by Abū l-ʿĀṣī al-Ḥakam b. ʿAbd al-Raḥmān in favour of his slave girl *So and So* and her young daughter. The slave girl's distinguishing features being *so and so*, and those of her daughter being *so and so*. Both are to become free Muslims, with their rights and obligations. From here onwards, nobody will have any right over them in terms of slavery, possession, nor servitude, other than as clients, which corresponds to the clientship of Abū l-ʿĀṣī al-Ḥakam b.

[72] The three models are listed by Ibn al-ʿAṭṭār, *K. al-wathāʾiq wa l-sijillāt*, ed. pp. 270, 275, 283; trans. pp. 467, 472, 480.

[73] Ibn Ḥayyān, *Muqtabis VII*, ed. p. 206; trans. p. 246.

[74] Ibn al-ʿAṭṭār *K. al-wathāʾiq*, ed. P. Chalmeta, p. 270; trans. M. Marugán, p. 467. I have taken model no. 104, but nos 106 (*tadbīr*) or 109 (*muʾajjal*) could also be adopted, as they were also used in the manumissions decreed by al-Ḥakam on that day.

> ʿAbd al-Raḥmān, the manumitter, and [subsequently] to his rightful successor, as stipulated in the Sunna of the Messenger of God – God bless Him and save Him. Through their manumission, made before God, Abū l-ʿĀṣī al-Ḥakam b. ʿAbd al-Raḥmān seeks his final dwelling place and recompense, so that for each limb of the manumitted slave girl and those of her daughter, God frees one of his kin from [eternal] fire, [when] the day [arrives], upon which neither wealth, nor children will be of any help, except for those whom God has granted a clean heart. Abū l-ʿĀṣī al-Ḥakam b. ʿAbd al-Raḥmān signs this document in the presence of the slave girl referred to as *So and So*, and her young daughter, after both have acknowledged [themselves] to be slaves of their owner until the aforementioned manumission is fully concluded.
>
> [The witnesses, whose signed declaration below endorses the validity of this document,] testify to the testimony required by Abū l-ʿĀṣī al-Ḥakam b. ʿAbd al-Raḥmān – following his admission to having understood it – They know him, have been informed and have confirmed that he is healthy and with the faculties to undertake what is set out in this document. Enacted 29 Rabīʿ II in the year 364.

The final part of the document, which required the witnesses' signatures, proved to be crucial. The caliph convened a series of prominent notables to act as witnesses for the documents of manumission, and each of them signed at the end of each document. The first signatory was Hishām himself, who acted as witness with the official title of 'candidate to be heir' (*al-murashshaḥ li wilāyat ʿahdi-hi*). Then, the caliph's three brothers, al-Mughīra, al-Aṣbagh and ʿAbd al-ʿAzīz, also signed. And then, the viziers and the *qāḍī* of Córdoba, Muḥammad b. Isḥāq b. al-Salīm. Finally, the documents were also signed by the arbitrators (*ḥukkām*), the *fuqahā'* who formed part of the consultative committee (*al-fuqahā' ahl al-shūrā*), and the legal consultants. In this way, different representatives of the state acted as witness to this legal deed. Up until here, everything was in order. The problem was that the heir, Hishām, had, in flagrant violation of Islamic law, acted as witness to these manumissions, despite being only nine years old; legally it was stipulated that any witness to a legal proceeding had to be an adult (*bālig*). It is absolutely certain that this issue was not overlooked by the *qāḍī*, the members of the judicial council or the legal consultants, but nobody seems to have dared to point out how unprecedented it was. Worse still, by stamping their signature next to Hishām's on these legal documents each of the witnesses – and especially the caliph's brothers – were implicitly recognising the validity of the proceedings and thereby endorsed his status as heir to the caliphate. This crafty manoeuvre was recounted in full detail by ʿĪsā b. Aḥmad al-Rāzī, whose chronicle provided an official image of what happened as if it were a snapshot of the event. In a subtle yet unappealable way, Hishām had come of age, as he had taken part in a legal proceeding without having his legal guardian present.[75]

The subtle legal coup orchestrated by the caliph allowed him to pave the way for his son to inherit the caliphate. It must also have changed the lives of the slaves who obtained their freedom thanks to these documents. It is in fact possible to provide epigraphic evidence of one of the caliph's female slaves who was granted manumission at that very time or not long after. Recent excavations undertaken in Córdoba have revealed an epitaph of 'a virgin (*ʿadrāʾ*) of the caliph and freedwoman (*mawlā*) of al-Ḥakam, Prince of the Faithful, may God have mercy upon him'. Although the epitaph lacks any date, it is possible to deduce that this woman must have died after the caliph's death in 976 (366 AH), as the eulogy 'may God have mercy upon him' is always included after the name of a deceased person. As M. A. Martínez has pointed out, 'on this basis it may be understood that the use of the expression *mawlat al-Ḥakam* on this epitaph to refer to this virgin, means she must have been a slave who acquired her freedom following her owner's death'. This confirms the use of the mechanism of posthumous manumission (*tadbīr*), which was one of those cited in the documents signed on that January day in 975 (364 AH).[76]

The day after the signing of these manumission documents, al-Ḥakam performed another good deed. On this occasion, it involved the creation of a pious legacy (*ḥabus*) to pay the salaries of the Qur'an teachers who undertook the education of the sons of the city's poor and whose income was to be raised

[75] Ibn Ḥayyān, *Muqtabis VII*, ed. p. 206; trans. p. 246. A. García Sanjuán, 'Legalidad islámica y legitimidad política en el califato de Córdoba', pp. 57–8.

[76] J. P. Monferrer Sala and E. Salinas Pleguezuelo, 'Epígrafe con epitafio de una virgen de al-Ḥakam II', *Anales de Arqueología Cordobesa*, 20, 2009, pp. 491–8; M. A. Martínez Núñez, 'Epigrafía funeraria de al-Andalus', *Melanges de la Casa de Velázquez*, 41, I, 2011, p. 188.

Image 15 Funerary inscription of a manumitted slave girl of Caliph al-Ḥakam.
[In the name of God, the compassionate, the merciful], [God] bless / Muḥammad. Praise be to God, Who reserves / eternity for Himself and compels His servants to extinction. This is / the tomb of the virgin of the caliph, freed by al-Ḥakam, e / mir of the believers, God have mercy on him. She / bore witness that there is no god but God, one / [without association] and that Muḥammad is [his] servant (trans. J. P. Monferrer Sala and M. A. Martínez).

from the saddlers' shops in Córdoba's souk. It was not the first time that a measure such as this had been taken. Eight years before, in 965 (356 AH), al-Ḥakam had founded three schools to teach the Qur'an near the main mosque and another twenty-four in the suburbs of Córdoba. On this occasion, it was the *qāḍī* of Córdoba who acted as witness, and apart from extending the teaching of the Qur'an to the most needy, this gesture was intended to win the support of the influential *'ulamā'* in the capital.[77]

[77] Ibn Ḥayyān, *Muqtabis VII*, ed. p. 207; trans. p. 247; Ibn Ḥayyān, *Muqtabis* II, I ed. p. 338 and trans. p. 218. A. García Sanjuán, *Till God Inherits the Earth*, p. 224. A. Carballeira Debasa, 'Caridad y poder político en época omeya', in A. Carballeira Debasa, ed., *Caridad y compasión en biografías islámicas*, Madrid, 2011, p. 104.

The following day, the caliph performed another extraordinary act, undoubtedly his most popular deed: the decision to reduce the tax for the exemption from military service (*naḍḍ li l-ḥashd*) by a sixth. The importance attached to this tax cut has already been discussed, along with the significant ideological contents of the letter announcing the decision (see above, p. 108). The fact that the order was sent out in mid-January, when the tax was meant to be collected in February, indicates how this measure had been decided upon under pressure. This can only be explained by the need to reinforce support for the caliph and the decisions he was taking at that especially delicate moment.

During the remainder of that year's harsh winter – it will be recalled that in January it even snowed in Córdoba – al-Ḥakam II did not make a single public appearance. It was only in March 975, once spring had arrived, that he allowed himself to be seen attending the Friday prayers in the main mosque at Madīnat al-Zahrā' accompanied by Hishām, the 'official candidate to the caliph's succession'. The next day (27 March/11 *Rajab*), al-Ḥakam followed the advice of the doctors and left the city palace, which was 'too exposed to the cold from the mountains', and took up residence in Córdoba. Although it was a journey of just under five kilometres it took his cortège two days, which was in part due to the caliph's precarious health, but was also because al-Ḥakam wished to appear before his subjects after having been absent for various months due to his illness.[78]

From them on, and after his father's fragile recovery, Hishām's political activities multiplied, despite him being barely ten years old: he accompanied the caliph during his meeting with the *qā'id* Ghālib to analyse the situaton after the Christian attack against Gormaz, and it was he who issued the order for 'Abd al-Raḥman b. Yaḥyā al-Tujībī to leave for Zaragoza to reinforce the frontier.[79] A child giving orders to career soldiers must have seemed to some the peak of extravagance, but the aim was to reinforce the idea that Hishām was quickly progressing through the phases that led to puberty, so that, despite his youth, when al-Ḥakam eventually died he would be ready to succeed him.

It was in this context that in the spring of 975 (364 AH) another preceptor for Hishām was appointed. The teacher arrived in the *alcázar* of Córdoba,

[78] Ibn Ḥayyān, *Muqtabis VII*, ed. pp. 211–12; trans. pp. 275–6.

[79] A. García Sanjuán, 'Legalidad islámica y legitimidad política', p. 58.

where father and son had taken up residence having left the city palace, and was welcomed by the vizier Ja'far b. 'Uthmān al-Muṣḥafī. During this third year of the heir apparent's education an effort was made to expand his legal training, after an initial general instruction in this subject had been followed by another devoted to language. On this occasion, the teacher was Yaḥyā b. 'Abd Allāh al-Laythī, a seventy-five-year-old legal scholar, who had been *qāḍī* in Pechina, Elvira, Jaén and Toledo. It was said he had taught 500 students. He was the member of a prestigious lineage of Berber origin, many of whom had been *qāḍī*s and *'ulamā'*, and whose ancestor, Yaḥyā b. Yaḥyā (d. 848/234 AH), had been one of the most influential scholars at the time when the Mālikite legal system was introduced into al-Andalus. One of the reasons for Yaḥyā b. 'Abd Allāh al-Laythī being commissioned to provide Hishām's legal education was the fact that his family possessed a recension by his ancestor, Yaḥyā b. Yaḥyā, of the principal work of the Mālikite legal school: Mālik b. Anas's *Muwaṭṭa*. Both 'Abd al-Raḥmān III and al-Ḥakam II had been taught Islamic law with this recension when they were children. It was the caliph's intention that the manuscript would now be used to teach his heir, who began to receive classes in the *alcázar* of Córdoba on Thursdays and Saturdays.[80]

In June 975 (364 AH), the Feast of the Breaking of the Fast was held in the *alcázar* of Córdoba, and it provided an opportunity for the ritual staging of the new political order, in which the figure of the heir now took front row. The caliph welcomed only his brothers, the viziers and the other senior dignitaries, while in a separate room Hishām presided over the reception of numerous attendees. Once more, the intention was to show how the child could behave as if he really were exercising caliphal authority, setting aside the issue of his being so young. Then, as the culminating moment of the celebration, the court poets again took turns to offer their praise. On this occasion, it was the enthusiasm expressed by Muḥammad b. Shujayṣ which stood out; he read a rare form of poem in praise of Hishām, which incorporated an acrostic, in which the first letters of each verse spelt out Abū al-Walīd Hishām.[81]

Still more striking, however, was what took place the day after the Feast of the Breaking of the Fast, on 15 June 975, which corresponded to 2 *Shawwāl*

[80] H. de Felipe, *Identidad y onomástica de los bereberes de al-Andalus*, pp. 156–7; M. Marín, 'Una familia de ulemas cordobeses: los Banū Abī 'Īsā', pp. 300 and 312–15.

[81] Ibn Ḥayyān, *Muqtabis VII*, ed. p. 231; trans. p. 273, n. 1.

364 AH. This was the day on which Caliph al-Ḥakam presented his son Hishām to the people of Córdoba from the terrace above the main gateway of the *alcázar*, the Bāb al-Sudda. Orders had been given that all the paupers, needy and underprivileged were to gather below in the main street (*al-Maḥajja*) leading from this gateway. Then, bags of money were brought from the treasury (*bayt al-māl*) and were distributed by the 'slave *fatā* servants' (*al-fityān al-khuddām al-ṣaqāliba*) among those present, who raised their voices offering blessings to the caliph.[82]

The episode reveals the characteristic careful staging of Umayyad Córdoba with the touch of extravagance typical of al-Ḥakam. Aside from the pious alms that were given out during *Ramaḍān*, there was an obligatory almsgiving that was held on the final day of the month in question, the day of the breaking of the fast, 1 *Shawwāl*. Charity during this day was deemed important, as the *Ramaḍān* fast was not considered valid if it was not accompanied by this almsgiving. The day before, the caliph and his son had been occupied presiding over the reception in the *alcázar*, wherefore it had to be on 2 *Shawwāl* that this ostentatious public display of almsgiving was held with both of them present.

It is clear that by the summer of 975 al-Hakam had become deeply concerned about the fate that awaited him in the life beyond, as well as what his heir would have to face in the years to come. Hence the instructions for the slaves' manumission – a typical testamentary deed that was considered very pleasing in the eyes of God; the reduction of an especially unpopular tax – a form of underscoring his authority and that of his heir; the establishment of a pious legacy in favour of the neediest inhabitants of Córdoba – a deed of great prestige among the *'ulamā'*; and, finally, the pious, as well as lavish, distribution of alms among the city's paupers. The fundamental beneficiary and spectator of these actions was the Muslim community; it was they who ultimately conferred authority upon the caliph.

The Caliph's Personal Circle

The only member of al-Ḥakam II's inner family circle mentioned by 'Īsā al-Rāzī is his son, Hishām. In contrast, not a single mention is made of Ṣubḥ throughout his work, although, as has been seen, this woman was referred to

[82] Ibn Ḥayyān, *Muqtabis VII*, ed. pp. 233–4; trans. pp. 275–6.

in other sources as a way of attacking the sovereign's reputation. It is possible that the caliph had other wives, and they may even have borne him other children, but the evidence is scant, and the palace chronicler does not make any mention of them.[83] The portrait of the *sulṭān*, described by al-Rāzī in an exhaustive manner throughout his work, makes no mention of a feminine presence, despite the fact that we know that a number of women worked as secretaries in al-Ḥakam II's *alcázar*. One of them, for instance, was an anonymous slave, who was a highly intelligent secretary (*kātiba*) and went on to become an expert astronomer; the caliph admired her for her excellent use of the astrolabe.[84] Another, called Lubnā (d. 984/374 AH), was an expert on grammar, a perspicacious mathematician and poet. One of her specialities was calligraphy, which was of particular importance for the writing of letters and diplomas, and she excelled above the other women of her day at this art.[85]

The absence of women in the narrative of the Umayyad caliphate does not mean that they did not play a role in the construction of the state. Aside from being an easy target for discrediting the caliph, Ṣubḥ must have been a very powerful figure in the court and have played an important role in the configuration of the caliph's environment. This is demonstrated by the title that was often given to her, the 'Grand Lady' or *al-Sayyida al-Kubrā*. Just as al-Ḥakam sought to create an administration and army to match his requirements, he also created a family circle unconstrained by political limitations. And just as had happened in the 'Abbāsid caliphate, this milieu became the means

[83] A. García Sanjuán, 'Legalidad islámica y legitimidad política', pp. 46–8. A gravestone has been found commemorating a woman called Shukra al-Balātiyya, who is referred to as 'mother of the son of al-Ḥakam, Prince of the Faithful'; she must have given birth to a son who died very young, before the year 976, É. Lévi-Provençal. *Inscriptions arabes*, n. 19; M. A. Martínez, 'Mujeres y elites sociales en al-Andalus', pp. 316–17.

[84] This slave had acquired a knowledge of astronomy from Abū l-Qāsim Sulaymān b. Aḥmad al-Anṣārī al-Ruṣāfī al-Qassām, an official who was given the order to hand out sacks of money among the poor in thanks for Hishām being cured from smallpox, Ibn Ḥayyān, *Muqtabis VII*, ed. p. 153; trans. cit. pp. 193–4; M. L. de Ávila, 'Las mujeres sabias en al-Andalus', p. 180.

[85] There many examples of Andalusi women who were renowned calligraphers. Examples of this, among many others, are Muzna, secretary to 'Abd al-Raḥmān III; Ā'isha bt. Aḥmad, who had a good script and made copies of the Qur'an; Fāṭima bt. Zakariyyā', who was a manumitted slave and an 'excellent secretary', died in 1036 (427 AH) at the age of ninety-four; Ṣafiyya bt. 'Abd Allāh al-Rayyī (d. 1027/417 AH) was also renowned for her fine calligraphy. She also wrote a beautiful poem to defend herself from another woman's criticism of her handwriting ('I approached my pens, pages and inkwell/and they wrote the three verses I composed'). M. J. Viguera, 'Dieciséis mujeres andalusíes', pp. 9–18.

through which a diverse and increasing group of people were able to obtain a considerable share in the exercise of power. In Baghdad there are examples of slave women who became the caliph's concubines and maintained their family ties; by introducing their relations into key posts in the administration, they were able to 'colonise' the caliph's family circle.[86]

Something similar happened in the Umayyad caliphate; the brothers of the caliphs' concubines who became mothers of the heir to the throne played an especially noteworthy role. It is possible that this reflected the wider Arab family structure, in which bonds of mutual support and defence were formed between a nephew and his maternal uncle (*khāl*). Such was the case with one Sa'īd b. Abī l-Qāsim, who was the brother of Muzna, the mother of Christian origin of Caliph 'Abd al-Raḥmān III. During his nephew's reign, this man undertook important roles in the administration and went on to become vizier. One of his sons was appointed governor of Seville.[87] However, in al-Ḥakam II's time, another of his sons was imprisoned in March 974 (*Rajāb* 363 AH) on the caliph's orders, for unknown reasons. Although he spent barely two weeks in prison, his arrest was very spectacular: the head of the *shurṭa* was commissioned to go to the *munya* owned by Muhammad b. Sa'īd b. Abī l-Qāsim along with a cohort of troops from different units. On not finding him there, they went to another large property of his where he was finally placed under arrest.

Similarly, during the reign of al-Ḥakam II, one Sa'īd b. al-Khāl was removed from his post as governor of Seville following complaints made about him in July 972 (*Shawwāl*, 361 AH). This Sa'īd was thus one of the caliph's maternal cousins, who it will be recalled was the son of a woman of Christian origin called Marjān. Consequently, it may be concluded that the brother of the concubine with whom 'Abd al-Raḥmān III conceived his heir, al-Ḥakam II, had likewise gained an important promotion within the state administration.

[86] J. Bray, 'Men, Women and Slaves in Abbasid Society', pp. 133–4.

[87] On Muzna, *Dhikr bilād al-Andalus*, p. 131. Sa'īd b. Abī l-Qāsim received many appointments: governor of the fortresses of Poley and Écija, *ṣāḥib al-madīna*, head of the cavalry, head of the *shurṭa*; he was eventually appointed vizier in 941 (329 AH), Ibn Ḥayyān, *Muqtabis V*, pp. 167, 213, 214, 304, 313, 318, 328; ibid., pp. 283 and 291. On his son 'Abd al-Raḥmān, governor of Seville, Ibn 'Idhārī, *al-Bayān*, II, ed. cit. p. 208.

The same prominent role of the maternal uncle seems to have been given to the brother of Ṣubḥ, Caliph al-Ḥakam II's concubine and the mother of his heir. In this case Rā'iq, a Basque, was promoted from the department responsible for army recruitment (*khuṭṭāt al-arḍ*) to the treasury and supplies department (*khuṭṭāt al-makhzūn*). His appointment was made on 20 June 972 (5 *Ramaḍān* 361 AH), exactly the same day on which his nephew Hishām began to take classes, something that probably did not happen by chance. Some months later, for some reason, Rā'iq fell from grace. However, in January 974 he was back in the caliph's favour, and was appointed *ṣāḥib al-shurṭa* and *qā'id* of Llano de los Pedroches (Faḥṣ al-Ballūṭ), as well as a number of enclaves in western al-Andalus which included Badajoz, Medellín and Mojáfar (near Villanueva de la Serena, Badajoz). This was an extensive region to govern over, and it put him in charge of a considerable quantity of resources. This appointment should very possibly be understood as a necessary precaution should the need arise to defend his nephew's interests. His role at court was also emphasised by his presence alongside Hishām at official receptions from that time onwards.[88]

In addition to this reduced family milieu – the caliph, his heir, the heir's mother and her brother – there would have been other concubines and, above all, a number of slaves and freedmen, who formed the nucleus of al-Ḥakam's domestic retinue. Beyond this core circle, there were other family members who do not seem to have played the slightest role in the apparatus of power. This was the case with al-Ḥakam's brothers, to whom their father, 'Abd al-Raḥmān III, had granted houses in Córdoba, states, properties, servants and substantial pensions, so that they could live comfortable lives, without entertaining ideas of disputing their brother's throne. When al-Nāṣir died, he left eight sons and five daughters, about whom little is known. During the period under discussion only three of al-Hakam's brothers are recorded as attending official ceremonies, al-Mughīra, al-Aṣbagh and 'Abd al-'Azīz, which suggests that the other male sons of 'Abd al-Raḥmān had possibly died by that time.

[88] Ibn Ḥayyān, *Muqtabis VII*, ed. pp. 77, 117, 149, 184 and 200; trans. pp. 100, 149, 189, 223 and 241. Two other places were under the jurisdiction of Rā'iq in the same region, al-'Arūsh (possibly the castle of Lares) and R.m.k.b, which is impossible to identify.

Nothing reveals what these three brothers of the caliph thought, or perhaps plotted. They appear in a silent and disciplined fashion playing their appointed role at all the receptions at Madīnat al-Zahrā'. However, it is clear that the issue of the caliphal succession put them under the spotlight, given the possibility that any of them could become a candidate to make a rival claim after their brother's death, especially given the all too evident minority of their nephew Hishām. Of these three brothers, the greatest attention was focused on the youngest, al-Mughīra, who at that time had recently turned twenty-five. It was said that he had been his father's favourite in his old age, and just before he died 'Abd al-Raḥmān III had charged al-Ḥakam to take care of him by sitting him on his lap. In his adulthood, there is no evidence that this young man did anything other than attend the official receptions chaired by his brother. He is also named in an inscription on a magnificent ivory pyxis made in 968 (357 AH), in which he is wished prosperity and happiness.[89]

Despite having not shown the slightest ambition, nor having hatched any known plot, al-Mughīra ended up suffering one of the cruellest fates in the history of the Umayyad caliphate. When his brother al-Ḥakam II died in October 976, as soon as news of the death was circulated those who thought it was folly to name an eleven-year-old child as caliph turned to him. In contrast, those who had assured the deceased caliph that they would support the proclamation of Hishām and had bound their fortunes to the child saw him as a potential rival to be taken down. Ja'far b. 'Uthmān al-Muṣḥafī led this group, which immediately took control of the reins of power and convinced the palace *ṣaqāliba* that their interests were also on the child's side. Given the circumstances, allowing al-Mughīra to remain alive gave the opposition a candidate with whom they could contest the proclamation of Hishām as caliph. That was why Ja'far sent a squad of soldiers to al-Mughīra's house with orders to kill him. Leading the soldiers was Muḥammad b. Abī 'Āmir, the individual whom numerous rumours had linked to the mother of the boy who was to be proclaimed caliph. Some initial uncertainty having been overcome, the execution order was fulfilled and the unfortunate al-Mughīra was strangled to death, despite having offered every kind of guarantee

89 Ibn Ḥayyān, *Muqtabis V*, ed. and trans. pp. 1 and 8. É. Lévi-Provençal, *Inscriptions arabes de l'Espagne*, p. 188.

Image 16 Al-Mughīra's pixys. The inscription on this ivory piece shows that it was dedicated to this unfortunate Umayyad prince: although he was the youngest and best-beloved son of his elderly father, ʿAbd al-Raḥmān III, he was killed on the death of his brother al-Ḥakam for fear that he might lead the opposition to his nephew Hishām II.

that he had no wish to make any claim on the caliphate and that it was his intention to acknowledge his nephew as ruler. His death, which marks the beginning of the end of the Umayyad caliphate, was claimed to have been suicide.

9

The Representation of Power

The Caliphate's Celebrations and Rituals

The early Muslim caliphs scorned the pomp staged by the infidel sovereigns. Although they had become the rulers of an immense empire, these caliphs liked to present themselves as simple people, who lived in modest houses with no other luxuries than the respect and veneration that emanated from their authority. Four centuries after the Hijra, in the mid-tenth century, the situation had changed significantly. The initial rejection of the ostentation of power had given way to a powerful court culture, which had evolved within the caliphal palaces and established complex protocols regulating access to the sovereign, as well as the occasions on which he made formal appearances. In the ʿAbbāsid court there was, for example, a head of protocol, the *ṣāḥib al-marātib*, who was responsible for ensuring that everyone was correctly placed when the caliph held audiences. In addition to residential quarters, the palaces built in newly-founded cities such as Baghdad, Samarra and Cairo had large audience halls that were used to represent the diverse aspects of caliphal sovereignty, which played a key role in the 'institutionalization of the court ceremonial'.[1]

In al-Andalus, the institutionalisation of court ceremonial was an especially characteristic feature of the caliphal period, yet it does not seem to have been a feature, or at least not such a prominent one, of the emirate era. During the reign of ʿAbd al-Raḥmān III, when the *alcázar* of Córdoba was still the

[1] D. Sourdel, 'Questions de ceremonial abbaside', pp. 121–48. N. M. El Cheikh, 'The Institutionalisation of ʿAbbāsid Ceremonial', p. 358. P. Sanders, *Rituals, Politics and the City in Fatimid Cairo*, p. 9. See also, Cardoso, 'The Scenography of Power in Al-Andalus and the ʿAbbasid and Byzantine Ceremonials', pp. 390–434, which was published after the first edition of this book had gone to press.

main caliphal residence, solemn receptions were held to mark the arrival of embassies or religious feasts.[2] However, following the transfer of the seat of the caliphate to Madīnat al-Zahrā', and especially during the reign of al-Ḥakam II, these ceremonial events became more numerous and complex. Archaeological evidence at Madīnat al-Zahrā' supports this claim. It has shown that over the course of the 950s, the new *alcázar* that had been built between 939 and 941 in the city was extensively remodelled, and these changes were in part intended to intensify the representation of power.[3]

The policy of honing the ways in which the caliphal institution was represented is evident as early as the proclamation of al-Ḥakam II as caliph. The ceremonial oath of loyalty that was sworn to the new sovereign was staged in two phases. On 4 October 961 (3 *Ramaḍān* 350 AH) the oath was sworn in the *alcázar* in Córdoba by the senior palace slaves (*ṣaqāliba*), led by Ja'far al-Ṣiqlabī, along with the main secretaries, officials, servants and courtiers. The following day, the second part of the ceremony was held in the new *alcázar* at Madīnat al-Zahrā'; al-Ḥakam's eight brothers had been brought there and had spent the night in what was referred to as the palace's *Dār al-Mulk*. On the morning of 5 October, the caliph's brothers, the viziers (along with their sons and brothers), the leaders of the *shurṭa* and other administrative personnel took up their places in the Western and Eastern Halls (*al-Majlisayn al-Sharqī wa l-Garbī*) and waited to approach the caliph, who was seated on his throne. The oath of fidelity (*bay'a*) was performed in accordance with a long-established formula. All those present sat on either side of the sovereign, except the vizier and secretary, 'Īsā b. Fuṭays, who remained standing and was responsible for receiving the oath sworn by each attendee. Adhering to an arrangement which, as will be seen, was repeated for other celebrations, the caliph's eunuchs and slaves formed two lines that ran all along both sides of the two halls and on throughout the *alcázar*.[4]

Following the impressive inauguration of his reign, al-Hakam's court became the setting for grand official receptions and triumphal processions. 'Īsā al-Rāzī

[2] For example, the reception of the ambassadors sent by the Byzantine emperor, which was attended by the caliph's sons and the viziers, Ibn 'Idhārī, *al-Bayān*, II, p. 213.

[3] A. Vallejo Triano, *La ciudad califal de Madīnat al-Zahrā'*, pp. 485–90.

[4] al-Maqqarī, *Nafḥ*, I, pp. 386–8. The text states that the rooms of the *Dār al-Mulk* in which the caliph's brothers were lodged were the 'porticoes' or *fuṣlān*. On the meaning of this term see, A. Labarta y C. Barceló, 'Las fuentes árabes sobre al-Zahrā'', pp. 98–9.

was present at these and devoted many pages of his chronicle to describing them. His meticulous account never fails to cite each and every one of those in attendance, and he always mentions their roles and the place that each person occupied during the reception or procession recounted. His detailed narrative functions as an official register of these ceremonies. He recorded where and in what order individuals were placed and their roles on each occasion, whereby his text could be consulted on future occasions, and if a new celebration was to be held if could be compared to previous events. ʿĪsā al-Rāzī's description makes clear that each event was meticulously prepared (every participant was assigned a specific place, the troops arranged with precision, and the order in which the attendees entered the caliph's presence was carefully planned), which required considerable effort and resources. As will be seen, literally whole nights were spent tirelessly working on the organisation of each detail.

The elaborate staging of celebrations and receptions at the Umayyad court owed a great deal to oriental models from the ʿAbbāsid caliphate. We know about elements of ʿAbbāsid court ceremonial thanks to, among other sources, the *Rusūm dār al-khilāfa* which was compiled by Hilāl al-Ṣābiʾ (d. 1056/498 AH); his grandfather had recounted a wealth of details regarding the ceremonial of the early caliphs, and to save this information from being forgotten Hilāl al-Ṣābiʾ decided to record it for posterity. For example, he recorded the reception held in Baghdad for a Byzantine embassy during which the administration's civil servants, along with the infantry and cavalry, who wore their smartest uniforms and carried their finest weapons, lined up in two rows flanking the path taken by the ambassadors to the vizier's residence, where the visitors awaited orders to present themselves before the caliph in his audience chamber. An identical arrangement was used in the ceremonial of the Umayyad caliphal court, where soldiers and civil servants also lined up either side of the path taken by the ambassadors and guests. The practice of waiting in a room prior to being given the order to appear before the caliph also appears in cases such as the embassy sent by the count of Barcelona at the end of June 971 (*Shaʿban* 360 AH), which had to wait in the 'House of the Army' (*Dār al-Jund*), where they received permission to make their way to the Eastern Hall where al-Ḥakam was waiting.[5]

[5] Al-Ṣābiʾ, *Rusūm dār al-khilāfa*, trans. cit. pp. 16–17. Ibn Ḥayyān, *Muqtabis VII*, ed. cit. pp. 20–2; trans. pp. 44–6. Exactly the same protocol was followed in March 962 (351 AH) during the visit of

It is possible that Umayyad court protocol was also influenced by elements of Byzantine ceremonial. From 946 onwards, there was a regular exchange of ambassadors between Córdoba and Constantinople, and during this period strict protocol was imposed by the Emperor Constantine VII (945–63). The *Book of Ceremonies* was composed at this time and provided an exhaustive description of imperial protocol, which was based on the 'tradition of our ancient customs' through which 'the imperial power obtains order and measure, thereby reflecting the harmony and movement of the Creator in relation to everything'. Some elements of Byzantine ceremonial were highly extravagant, such as the use of mechanical organs or devices to impress ambassadors, but other aspects were concerned with the display of flags and ensigns, which are very likely to have exerted an influence on the Andalusi caliphal ceremonial apparatus.[6]

In contrast, the Fāṭimid influence on the Umayyad court ceremonial would have been less important than tends to be supposed, and were there to have been any influence, its impact would have been primarily indirect, rather than any sort of literal imitation. During their North African period, prior to marching to Egypt, the Fāṭimid caliphs' taste for public displays of authority was restricted by the conventions of the North African social context, which imposed a sense of simplicity on the display of power. Proof of this is the accounts that record how Caliph al-Mu'izz would sit next to members of the Kutāma amid an atmosphere of tribal austerity. It is possible that the construction of the city palace of Ṣabra al-Manṣūriyya, near Qayrawān, from 946 (334 AH) onwards implied a development of the Fāṭimid ceremonial (and prompted, perhaps as a reaction, the remodelling of Madīnat al-Zahrā'), but it is clear that the grand processions and elaborate audiences of the Fāṭimid caliphs were only held once they had moved to Egypt in the summer of 973 (362 AH). The majority of the extant information on Fāṭimid ceremonial is, thus, much later in date and cannot be applied indiscriminately to the Andalusi court.[7]

the king of León, Ordoño IV, who also had to wait in the *Dār al-Jund* prior to being received by the caliph, al-Maqqarī, *Nafḥ*, I, p. 390.

6 Constantine Porphyrogennetos, *The Book of Ceremonies*, I, R4-5; II, R. pp. 570–83. C. Angelidi, 'Designing Receptions in the Palace', pp. 473–4. J. Signes Codoñer, 'Bizancio y al-Andalus en los siglos IX y X', pp. 177–246.

7 P. Walker, 'Social Elites at the Fatimid Court', pp. 105–22.

The 'institutionalization of ceremonial', the '*pompam regiam*' as it was denominated by the author of the account of the embassy of John of Gorze, not only sought to overwhelm ambassadors and visitors with a grand display of ostentation; it was also intended to visually represent the caliphate's internal hierarchy. It showed a highly detailed snapshot of the people and posts the Umayyad state consisted of, and how they were organised around the figure of the caliph. Arranged on a stage, members of the Umayyad family, senior dignitaries, bureaucrats, *'ulamā'*, military officers and notables from Córdoba and the provinces were congregated within a single space or setting and together formed an ensemble, which reflected the caliphate's structure with the utmost precision. Held within the walls of the *alcázar* of Madīnat al-Zahrā', those who attended these events were high-ranking people, who were participants and spectators of the power issued by the visible authority of the caliph of al-Andalus. In contrast, the celebrations of the caliphate's military victories, which also included palace audiences, were marked with solemn parades that made their way around Córdoba and its suburbs, thereby demonstrating the caliph's authority to the people, while the defeated witnessed the magnificence of his power.

The Appearances Made by the Caliph

The major emphasis that Umayyad legitimacy placed on the sovereign's role as Commander of the Faithful, who was deeply concerned with the welfare of the Muslim community, required him to maintain a visible presence. In previous chapters (see above p. 305), I have discussed various examples that record al-Ḥakam as being present on a range of different occasions. Therefore, he cannot be considered an 'evanescent caliph'. Even his contemporary and rival, the Fāṭimid caliph, could not afford to conceal himself, and was frequently seen surrounded by a crowd of people pestering him with petitions, or else attentively listening to him expound the profundities of the Shī'ī creed.[8] Obviously, this does not mean to say that caliphs were easily accessible to all.

[8] The expression 'evanescent caliph' in M. Barceló, 'El califa patente', pp. 155–6. The conduct of the Fāṭimid caliph in Idrīs 'Imād al-Dīn, '*Uyūn al-akhbār*, trans. cit. pp. 101–2. Al-Qāḍī al-Nu'mān advised the Fāṭimid caliph not to prolong his concealment from the public 'because this will render you suspect and cause you trouble, since people are human beings who do not know what is hidden from them', M. Rustow, *The Lost Archive*, p. 236.

The lords of frontier territories, who arrived in Córdoba to obtain diplomas acknowledging their rule, were not always received by the caliph, and at times they had to settle for receiving these from the viziers during ceremonies held in the House of the Viziers (*Bayt al-wuzarā'*) at Madīnat al-Zahrā'. When al-Ḥakam II went riding, he did so surrounded by menacing soldiers and *fatā*s, who controlled all access to him; at the forefront of these servants' minds were events such as the attempt by a madman to kill 'Abd al-Raḥmān III, as he was leaving the *alcázar* in Córdoba.[9] Despite the existence of these threats, the caliphs seem to have been seen crossing the main streets of their capital on a relatively frequent basis.

The caliph's public audiences were reserved for solemn occasions. During the years covered by the chronicle studied here, and without counting the meetings he held with viziers, *qā'id*s and emissaries, al-Ḥakam held twenty-seven audiences and receptions during which he appeared before ambassadors, guests, notables and members of the administration. Many of these audiences took place to mark the arrival of embassies, North African Berber leaders or senior provincial figures. Examples of the impressive pomp that was deployed on these occasions were the receptions held for King Ordoño IV in the spring of 962 (351 AH), or for Bonfill, the ambassador sent by the count of Barcelona in the summer of 971 (360 AH).[10]

The caliph's most elaborate audiences took place each year to mark the two main festivities in the Islamic calendar: the Feast of the Breaking of the Fast (*'Īd al-fiṭr*) and the Feast of the Sacrifice (*'Īd al-aḍḥā*). It is possible that the caliph attended the religious ceremonies associated with these celebrations, but, if that was the case, his presence at them was not accompanied by any special ritual. In contrast, the Fāṭimids' celebration of both religious festivities, as held once the dynasty was established in Egypt, began with a solemn procession during which the Shī'ī caliph rode towards the open-air oratory (*al-muṣallā*). There, he oversaw the rites while reciting various Qur'anic suras and then said

[9] When a group of riders from Lérida encountered the caliph making his way to Madīnat al-Zahrā', they were permitted to approach him once he had granted them permission to do so, Ibn Ḥayyān, *Muqtabis VII*, ed. cit. pp. 151–2; trans. p. 192. The issue of diplomas at the House of the Viziers in ibid., ed. pp. 72, 110–11 and trans. pp. 94, 141–2. The episode of the madman in M. I. Fierro, *'Abd al-Rahman III*, p. 108.

[10] Compare Ibn Ḥayyān, *Muqtabis VII*, ed. cit. pp. 20–2 and 115; trans. pp. 45–6 and 146.

prayers in the same form as ʿAlī b. Abī Ṭālib was reported to have done. The caliph then went on to give a sermon from the pulpit (*minbar*), while one of his servants held a parasol over him. Then, a procession, which often included exotic animals, made its way back to the palace, where a banquet was served.[11]

In accordance with their pragmatic ideology, the Umayyad caliphs never performed such a prominent religious role in these two festivities. At the Umayyad court these celebrations merely took the form of a court reception attended by members of the family, senior state officials and notables; they would firstly greet the caliph, and then, having taken their assigned positions, they listened to the court orators and poets, who declaimed a series of compositions written for the event, which frequently made political allusions. At least in the case of the Feast of the Sacrifice the reception was followed by a meal.[12]

The greater part of these receptions took place in what was known as the Eastern Hall (*al-Majlis al-Sharqī*) at Madīnat al-Zahrā'.ʿĪsā al-Rāzī mentions that this hall opened onto the Upper Terrace (*al-Saṭḥ al-ʿAlā*) above a garden, which permits it to be identified with the building constructed on a basilica-type plan with three naves separated by six arches that was discovered during the archaeological excavations undertaken at Madīnat al-Zahrā' in the first half of the last century. Although badly demolished in parts, sections of the original walls were still preserved up to a height of four metres. Given these finds, as well as the large quantity of decorative materials found in situ, during the 1950s and 1960s it was decided to rebuild the hall according to the plan that was revealed by the archaeological remains and the richly carved stone mural decorations that had been discovered.[13]

In front of this audience hall, excavations also identified the remains of three pools, and next to them the remains of another building, which was smaller, but also equipped with a portico and three naves. This latter building was clearly intended to function as mirror-like space opposite the Eastern Hall, and the reflections in the pools separating these two spaces would have

[11] P. Sanders, *Ritual, Politics and the City*, p. 47, which is based on the indications given by the *qāḍī* al-Nuʿmān and the account of a witness to the celebration held by al-Muʿizz. On the allegorical significance, p. 50.

[12] The meal was held in the '*Majlis al-Ajrā*', Ibn Ḥayyān, *Muqtabis VII*, ed. p. 137; trans. p. 171.

[13] A. Vallejo, 'El Salón de ʿAbd al-Raḥmān III: problemática de una restauración', in A. Vallejo, ed., *Madīnat al-Zahrā'. El Salón de ʿAbd al-Raḥmān III*, pp. 11–40.

enhanced this effect. Indeed, A. Vallejo's hypothesis that this building was the *al-Majlis al-Garbī*, or Western Hall (also known as the *Majlis al-Umarā'*), seems plausible. Textual sources describe various receptions and audiences being held there. Both halls' names – *al-Majlis al-Garbī* and *al-Majlis al-Sharqī* – would not have been intended to refer to their physical locations; instead they make a symbolic allusion to 'East' and 'West' as the epitome of the caliph's dominion over the world.[14]

The identification of the Eastern Hall (which is also known as the Salón Rico, the name used by the first archaeologists who studied it) and the Western Hall, as well as the restoration of many of their main decorative features, permits the detailed descriptions of the receptions held by Caliph al-Ḥakam given in the text by 'Īsā al-Rāzī to be located in a physical space, one visible today.[15] This offers a rare opportunity to bring together archaeological data with written evidence and allows the spectacle of Umayyad ceremonial to be discerned with great precision. Over the pages that follow, my aim is to describe this ceremonial with the aim of showing to what extent al-Ḥakam II's authority needed to be visualised and how a wealth of resources was deployed to achieve this.[16]

A Reconstruction of Umayyad Ceremonial at Madīnat al-Zahrā'

Al-Ḥakam II always presided over ceremonies held in the Eastern Hall sitting on a throne (*sarīr*) on a raised dais. It seems very possible that a carpet

[14] A. Vallejo Triano, *La ciudad califal de Madīnat al-Zahrā'*, pp. 497–8. See also 'El heredero designado y el califa. El Occidente y el Oriente en Madīnat al-Zahrā'', pp. 433–64. It is important to note that both halls were already in use by the time al-Ḥakam was proclaimed caliph and they were located above the terrace, as is made clear in the expression *al-Majlis al-Sharqī min majālis al-saṭḥi*, al-Maqqarī, *Nafḥ*, p. 389.

[15] Ibn Ḥayyān, *Muqtabis VII*, ed. pp. 28–31; trans. pp. 51–3 (*'īd al-fiṭr*, 360 AH); ed. pp. 59–62; trans. pp. 80–4 (*'īd al-aḍḥā*, 360 AH); ed. pp. 81–6; trans. pp. 105–9 (*'īd al-fiṭr*, 361 AH); ed. pp. 93–5; trans. pp. 117–19 (*'īd al-aḍḥā*, 361 AH); ed. pp. 119–23; trans. pp. 152–6 (*'īd al-fiṭr*, 362 AH); ed. pp. 136–8; trans. pp. 171–2 (*'īd al-aḍḥā*, 362 AH); ed. pp. 155–68; trans. pp. 196–206 (*'īd al-fiṭr*, 363 AH); ed. pp. 184–7; trans. pp. 222–6 (*'īd al-aḍḥā*, 363 AH).

[16] The texts devoted to these receptions were analysed by M. Barceló, 'El califa patente: el ceremonial omeya de Córdoba o la escenificación del poder', pp. 155–75. Despite presenting many interesting ideas, this study contains many errors (for example, it states that up to sixteen viziers attended the receptions), omissions (for example it does not refer to the *qāḍīs* and *'ulāmā'* who attended) and flawed interpretations (the *aṣḥāb al-shurṭa al-'ulyā* and *al-wustā* were not 'prefects who were responsible for handling crimes in the absence of the qāḍī', p, 161). Nor have I followed the diagrams he provides, which do not take into account the number of attendees who filled both halls.

ran across the length of the room reaching as far as the entrance.[17] There are no indications as to what the caliph wore, or the symbols of sovereignty he may have displayed. The 'Abbāsid caliphs would usually preside over their audiences wearing a tall black silk tiara, the Prophet's mantle and striking red shoes while carrying a sceptre; however, the Andalusi sovereign seems to have presented a considerably more austere image. He would undoubtedly have worn ceremonial garments, but the only element of sovereignty that the sources describe is the seal bearing an inscription that was always carried by the Umayyad rulers; in the case of al-Ḥakam his seal read, 'al-Ḥakam is satisfied with the decree of God'.[18]

The protocol for how foreign ambassadors should approach and greet the caliph included prostrating themselves before him, approaching to kiss his hand, and then withdrawing. However, it is unlikely that Muslim subjects had to prostrate themselves before the caliph during official events, as this practice was frowned on in religious circles and had also been adopted by the Fāṭimid caliphs; in contrast, most attendees would have most certainly have kissed al-Ḥakam's hand. However, kissing the caliph's hand was not applied to descendants of the Quraysh family, which means that the mode of greeting the caliph varied depending on the person's origin and rank.[19]

[17] Regarding the reference made to the *miḥrāb* in the Eastern Hall in the descriptions of the reception held for Bonfill's embassy from Barcelona and the Feast of the Breaking of the Fast held in 360 (July 971), I interpret this as feature as a 'dais', Ibn Ḥayyān, *Muqtabis VII*, ed. pp. 21 and 28; trans. pp. 45 and 51. I draw on the translation provided by a number of authors of 'an elevated place where people could be assured of the most eminent place', L. Golvin, 'Le miḥrab et sa éventuelle signification', pp. 53–4. The height of this dais, which was possibly made of wood, would have been the same as that of the socle that ran around the Salón Rico between the paved floor and the panels of vegetal decoration.

[18] F. Arnold, *Islamic Palatine Architecture*, p. 74. M. Marín, 'Una galería de retratos reales', p. 285.

[19] Ordoño IV prostrated himself various times before the caliph before touching his hand, and then withdrew without turning his back on the ruler, al-Maqqarī, *Nafḥ*, I, pp. 390–1. On Bonfill's embassy, Ibn Ḥayyān, *Muqtabis VII*, ed. p. 22; trans. p. 45. On the occasion when the caliph met with riders from Lérida, the caliph allowed them to kiss his foot; Ja'far b. al-Andalusī kissed the caliph's hand. In contrast, four years later, the Idrīsids who arrived at the Umayyad court only knelt before him and showed their reverence to him; when Muḥammad b. Abī 'Āmir took on the title of al-Manṣūr, the viziers began to kiss his hand and they addressed him with the invocation 'lord', Ibn Ḥayyān, *Muqtabis VII*, ed. pp. 52, 151, 199; trans. pp. 70, 192, 240; Ibn 'Idhārī, *al-Bayān*, II, p. 279. The kissing of the caliph's hand is compared to a religious sacrifice to God in the *arjūza* by Ibn 'Abd Rabbihi, J. T. 'The Historical arjūza of Ibn 'Abd Rabbihi, a Tenth-Century Hispano-Arabic Epic Poem', pp. 81, 29. On 'Abbāsid ceremonial, El Cheikh, 'The Institutionalization of 'Abbāsíd Ceremonial', pp. 362–4. Fāṭimid ceremonial required the subjects to kiss the floor before the caliph, Idrīs 'Imād al-Dīn, '*Uyūn al-akhbār*, trans. cit. p. 142. P. Sanders, *Ritual, Politics*, p. 17.

Before a reception began, the caliph would wait seated on his throne in the Eastern Hall. The Umayyad court did not use aspects of ʻAbbāsid ceremonial such as the curtain that would be pulled back to reveal the caliph once those participating in the event had assembled.[20] In Córdoba, in contrast, the caliph appeared before those attending a reception enthroned and fully visible to all. There was a side entrance located to the left of the hall that led to a building, which excavations have revealed contained a bath and three latrines. The only explanation for the presence of the bath next to the reception room is that the caliph appeared before his subjects in a state of ritual purity, whereby it is very possible that it was in this room that he washed and dressed prior to the reception. The ʻAbbāsid caliphate instructed that those attending an audience were to have washed, be well-dressed with their hair combed, and wear perfume, albeit not perfume that might displease the caliph. Washing one's teeth and using cotton underwear that prevented sweating were also rules that guests had to follow for any caliphal reception.[21]

At Madīnat al-Zahrā', while the caliph prepared in the rooms adjoining the reception hall, the attendees gathered either in the *Bayt al-wuzarā'* or the *Dār al-jund*. When they were given the order to proceed to the reception hall, they walked through the *alcázar*, making their way between troops and servants bearing ceremonial swords and elaborate garments. The first to enter were always the caliph's brothers, the sons of ʻAbd al-Raḥmān III, as symbols of dynastic continuity. The precedence that dictated their entrance and seats was in accordance with their age: ʻAbd al-ʻAzīz, the eldest, who shared the same mother as the caliph, entered first and took his seat on the right-hand side of al-Ḥakam; then another brother, al-Aṣbagh, sat on his left; and finally, the youngest, al-Mughīra, took up his place on the right, seated beneath his elder brother.

Then, the viziers entered. They came from the *Bayt al-wuzarā'* and, like the caliph's brothers, made their entrance through a door on the right side of the hall. Having greeted the caliph, they took their seats on either side of him next to his brothers, always leaving one space free. Four of them remained

On the day al-Ḥakam II left Madīnat al-Zahrā' for good, in March 975 (*Rajab* 364 AH), the senior civil servants and servants came outside to bid him farewell by kissing the ground, Ibn Ḥayyān, *Muqtabis VII*, ed. p. 212; trans. p. 252.

[20] N. M. El Cheikh, 'The Institutionalization of ʻAbbāsid Ceremonial', p. 362.

[21] Al-Ṣābi', *Rusūm dār al-khilāfa*, trans. cit. pp. 30–1.

Image 17 The central courtyard of the bath next to the reception hall of Madīnat al-Zahrā'. It is very likely that this is where the caliph prepared himself before entering the hall. The pavements and other elements have been reconstructed, and the cracks in them testify to the systematic destruction of the city during the civil war.

standing alongside the caliph, and they were responsible for ministering to him. Once more, a strict order was followed, and as a rule two viziers stood to the right of the caliph, with one vizier distinguished above the other, while the other two stood on the ruler's left arranged in a similar fashion.[22] The spectacle is thus easy to reconstruct and highly evocative: the caliph sat upon the throne, the Umayyad dynasty (*dawla*) was represented alongside him, and they were all flanked by the principal viziers.

The placement of the four standing viziers also highlights their internal hierarchy. Whenever the *qā'id* and vizier Ghālib was present, he occupied the privileged place to the right of the caliph. On these occasions, the vizier and *ṣāḥib al-madīna* of Córdoba, Ja'far b. 'Uthmān al-Muṣḥafī, was placed on the left.[23] However, when the *qā'id* was absent, it was Ja'far who was placed to the right of the caliph. Beneath them, and on either side of the caliph in varying positions, there might be the vizier and *ṣāḥib al-ḥasham*, Muḥammad b. Ṭumlus, or the vizier and *ṣāḥib al-madīna* of Madīnat al-Zahrā', Muḥammad b. Aflaḥ, or else his brother, the vizier and *ṣāḥib al-khayl*, Ziyād. It was less frequent to see other viziers or prominent members of the court in these privileged places close to the caliph.[24]

The rest of the caliphate's hierarchy then entered the hall. The principal heads of the administration would stand, and they formed two rows to the left and right of the caliph, continuing those marked by the standing viziers whose duty was to minister to the caliph. It is hard to determine in what direction these people faced, although I tend to think that they looked towards the caliph and were arranged along the length of the hall's naves. Beneath the reception hall's arcades, the following civil servants were arranged, always in the same order: the head of the upper police (*ṣāḥib al-shurṭa al-'ulyā*) and the middle police (*ṣāḥib al-shurṭa al-wusṭā*) of Córdoba and Madīnat al-Zahrā',

[22] However, the text is not always clear about this double arrangement on either side of the caliph, and on occasion it names people serving on the same side, which may be due to errors or lacunae. The verb used by al-Rāzī to refer to this function of 'ministering' is *ḥajaba* (literally 'to protect') The detail about the viziers who ministered to the caliph having to stand is given in Ibn Ḥayyān, *Muqtabis VII*, ed. p. 59; trans. p. 81.

[23] This is what happened at the reception of Bonfill, ambassador to the count of Barcelona, Ibn Ḥayyān, *Muqtabis VII*, ed. pp. 21–2; trans. 45.

[24] There were, however, some exceptions. At the Feast of Sacrifice in 361 Muḥammad b. 'Abd Allāh b. Abī 'Āmir (the future al-Manṣūr) was placed ministering to the caliph, possibly on his left in the second row, despite the fact he was only *ṣāḥib al-shurṭa al-wusta* and not a vizier.

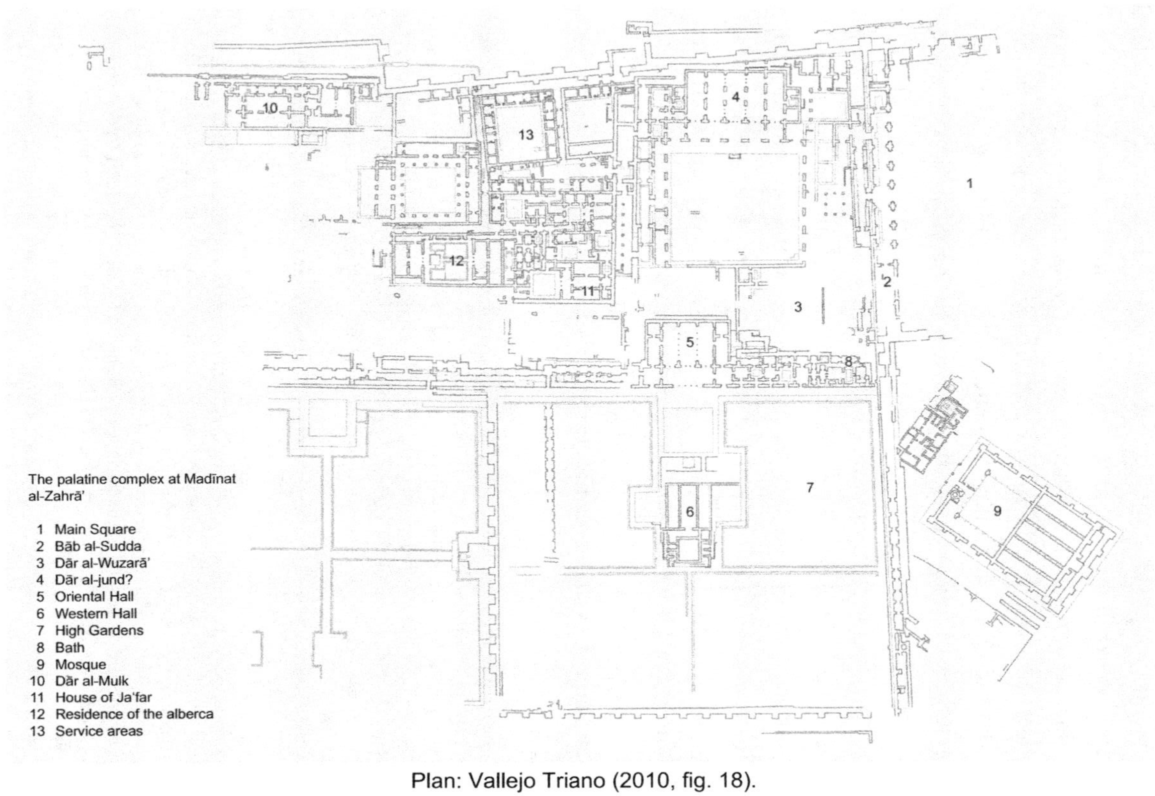

Figure 5 The palatine complex at Madīnat al-Zahrā’

those responsible for the caliphal warehouses, the four treasurers, those in charge of inspecting the troops (*'urrāḍ*), the secretaries and the caliph's *umanā'* or trusted men.[25]

A separate group was formed by the *qāḍī* of Córdoba and the city's legal arbitrators (*ḥukkām*), the head of the lower police (*ṣāḥib al-shurṭa al-ṣughrā*) and the officer responsible for judicial appeals (*ṣāḥib al-radd*). Another group of attendees were the descendants of the Umayyad emirs and the principal members of the Quraysh family, who entered the room through the central nave, greeted the caliph and took their places in the nave (*bahw*) to the left of the caliph, where the main Umayyad clients (*mawālī*) also took their places along with the leading representatives of the city of Córdoba.[26] There was also a place reserved for the provincial *qāḍī*s, the *fuqahā'* and legal consultants, and I think it probable that they sat in the nave to the right of the caliph alongside the *qāḍī* of Córdoba and the other members of the city's judiciary. The last group to enter the reception were the heads of the regular army and the military slaves (*'abīd*), and what seems most likely is that they stood on guard around the hall's walls, overseeing all the members of the caliphal state present and keeping watch over the entrance.[27]

[25] During the reign of al-Ḥakam I, the *'urrād* inspected the troops stationed in the *alcázar* twice a day, Ibn Ḥayyān, *Muqtabis*, II, 1, ed. cit. p. 147; trans. cit. pp. 60–1.

[26] The description of the Feast of the Sacrifice held in 360 (4 October 971) explicitly refers to how the Qurashis sat along the *bahw* located to the left of the caliph. I thus infer that the other groups also sat down and likewise took their places along this same *bahw*, Ibn Ḥayyān, *Muqtabis VII*, ed. p. 59; trans. p. 81. *Bahw* is a '*nef couverte [covered nave]*', Dozy, *Supplement aux dictionaires arabes*, I, pp. 123–4.

[27] This was the arrangement used for the celebration of the Feast of the Breaking of the Fast in 360 AH (28 July 971), Ibn Ḥayyān, *Muqtabis VII*, ed. pp. 29–30; trans. pp. 51–3. In some cases, the text provides details of the palace servants and members of the army spilling out of the room and being arranged along the route that led from the hall's entrance and as far as the Bāb al-Sudda, which was the grand entrance into the palace. The guests who came from Córdoba entered through this gate, and as they made their way to the Eastern Hall were always flanked by soldiers and members of the administration. This is what happened at the Feast of the Sacrifice in 361 (September 972) and also at the Feast of the Breaking of the Fast the following year (July 973). 'Īsā al-Rāzī's text shows how access from the Bāb al-Sudda to the Eastern Hall was channelled by two porticoes, one that the translator calls the 'pórtico delgado [narrow portico]' (*faṣīl murhaf*) and another the translator interprets as the 'pórtico dorado [golden portico]', which is more convincing than the text's edition, which presents many complications. I do not think that it is possible to offer a clear interpretation of the details of this topography Ibn Ḥayyān, *Muqtabis VII*, ed. pp. 94 and 120; trans. pp. 118 and 153. These same porticoes (*fuṣlān*) are also described in the account of the swearing of the oath of loyalty to al-Ḥakam, al-Maqqarī, *Nafḥ*, I. pp. 387–8, which contains a detailed description of the various types of servants and soldiers positioned in these rows.

On occasion, the order of the receptions could be changed due to the presence of individuals on whom the caliph wished to bestow special treatment. The most prominent member of the frontier family of the Tujībíds, Yaḥyā b. Muḥammad al-Tujībī, was a vizier and would usually take his place alongside his peers, but as sign of distinction to his family, on some occasions his brothers were placed among the civil servants.[28] The traditional order was also disregarded at the Feast of the Breaking of the Fast in 362 AH, July 973, when, for some reason, three eunuch *fatā*s were arranged around the caliph's throne, which seems to have been an exception.[29] The following year, in June 974, at the same festivity, the guest list for the celebration included the Idrīsids, who had just been defeated and transferred to Córdoba: Ḥasan b. Qannūn and his brother Yaḥyā were placed in a preferential group among the members of the Quraysh family, which gave them a 'front row seat' for the insults the poets competed to launch at them.

Months later, the Feast of the Sacrifice in 363 (1 September 974) marked one of the culminating moments of al-Ḥakam II's reign. Following the defeat of Ḥasan b. Qannūn a barely concealed atmosphere of euphoria permeated the Umayyad capital. This circumstance, combined with the efforts under way to ensure the caliph's succession, led al-Ḥakam to decree that his nine-year-old son, Hishām, would for the first time also preside over a celebration in the Western Hall, which was located on the other side of the terrace, opposite the Eastern Hall, thereby offering a mirror image of the reception staged by the caliph, the symbolism of which was apparent to all. It was ordered that servants were to form lines extending from the Eastern Hall across the terrace and its pools to the Western Hall occupied by al-Hakam's heir. Hishām was surrounded by a number of *fatā*s, who stood in attendance, while the main position was given to his maternal uncle, Rā'iq. Among those gathered in that room were the sons of past viziers, whose presence served to confirm the

[28] This arrangement was used for the Feast of the Breaking of the Fast in 360 AH, for which Ja'far b. al-Andalusī was present, and for whom, shortly beforehand, a triumphal welcome had also been held. He was given the order to enter with the Umayyad *mawālī* – a minor humiliation – but the caliph realised this and gave an order that he should join the central rows of civil servants. At the receptions held the following year, Yaḥyā al-Tujībī was seated with viziers, as was Ja'far.

[29] The *fatā*s who surrounded the caliph were Jawdhar, who was a falconer and in charge of the jewellers, Mursī, and Fā'iq, who was the head of the postal service and the *ṭirāz*. Jawdhar was responsible for the celebrated casket dedicated to Hishām that is today preserved in the Cathedral of Gerona.

notion of the dynasty's continuity, also following its recent victory over the Idrīsids. The latter family had to attend the ceremony once again, although on this occasion the poets were more restrained than the previous time.

The day after this moment of glory there was another major celebration of the triumph won in northern Morocco, which is discussed below, but in November 974 al-Ḥakam II fell seriously ill. When he made a significant recovery, in March 975, the doctors recommended that he leave Madīnat al-Zahrā' and take up residence in the *alcázar* in Córdoba. It was there on 14 June that the caliph held a reception for that year's (364 AH) Feast of the Breaking of the Fast. It was only attended by his brothers, the viziers and the senior civil servants, along with the *qāḍī* of Córdoba. Nobody else was invited to appear before the caliph. The location chosen within the complex of the Cordoban *alcázar* was the *Dār al-rawḍa*, a building that presumably stood near the *rawḍa*, the cemetery where the caliph's ancestors were buried, all the Umayyad emirs along with al-Ḥakam's father.[30]

There was thus something of a funerary air to this celebration, which doubled as a highly restricted audience granted by the sickly caliph. However, al-Ḥakam II, being obsessed by his son's succession, arranged for Hishām to preside over another reception in the same *alcázar*. Thereby, having greeted the caliph, the attendees made their way to a separate building in the *alcázar* complex (which had been given the significant name of *al-Zahrā'*), where the heir held an audience that sought to be exactly the same as those celebrated in the city palace: four viziers attended to the prince – who were joined by the omnipresent Muḥammad b. Abī 'Āmir – while the principal members of the administration took their places, along with the *fatā*s, guests invited to the ceremony, members of the Quraysh family, *mawālī*, *qāḍī*s and *'ulamā'*. The organisation of this event was intended to demonstrate how court life continued in accordance with custom. However, what is certain is that the old *alcázar* was not big enough to accommodate so many people, and this is why the attendees had to be distributed in various rooms and locations while they waited to be received by the heir.[31]

30 A. J. Montejo, 'La rauda del alcázar de Córdoba', pp. 237–56.
31 Ibn Ḥayyān, *Muqtabis VII*, ed. pp. 229–33; trans. pp. 271–5.

The following day, al-Ḥakam II made another public appearance, but this time before the people of Córdoba. It was, as has been seen in the previous chapter, an extraordinary appearance. From the main entrance to the *alcázar*, and once more accompanied by his son, he attended the distribution of alms by his slave *fatā*s among the city's poor. The fortunate beggars raised their voices, quite understandably, offering blessings to the caliph and his heir. Demonstrations such as this, and receptions like that held the previous day, at which Hishām had played a central role, made clear that it was the caliph's wish that his son was to inherit the caliphate. The static acquiescence of the members of state present at these receptions and the enthusiastic support given by the community, achieved through the prior distribution of dirhams, seemed to ensure that Hishām's path to the succession had been secured.

The Celebration of the Triumph

During the solemn receptions undertaken to mark the religious festivities described above primacy was given to the display of power to an audience, who, isolated within the walls of the palace, were both spectators of and participants in the spectacle. In contrast, the celebrations of military victories provided an opportunity to represent the caliph's power in a more dynamic fashion; these were above all public displays that took the form of a procession (*al-burūz*) that made its way through Córdoba, offering a triumphant spectacle for the caliph's subjects, and then went on to Madīnat al-Zahrā', where the senior military figures would be received by the caliph himself.

One public ostentation of a military triumph took place in October 973 (*Muḥarram* 363 AH) when, in the midst of the Morocco campaign, a letter arrived from *qā'id* Ghālib, announcing the capture of the city of al-Baṣra. The letter was accompanied by the head of the Idrīsid leader who had held control over the city, but whose inhabitants had decided to kill him and submit to the Umayyad army. The missive and the head were brought to Córdoba by a *fatā* called Qand, who was granted considerable honours and rewards. Firstly, he, along with the Idrīsid's head, was given accommodation in the *Munyat al-Nā'ūra*, from where the servant was escorted towards the Bāb al-Sudda of the *alcázar* in Córdoba by an army squadron with the severed head borne aloft on a lance. There they were received by a crowd who hurled insults and curses against the dead man and all those who followed heretical and innovative doctrines. On the orders of the representative of the *ṣāḥib al-madīna*, the head was raised on a post, where it remained on display above the road outside the gateway.[32]

The public exhibition of the heads of defeated enemies was a practice that extended back to the Late Roman Empire and was continued during the Byzantine Empire; in the event of a usurper seeking to take the throne being defeated, the triumphant emperor ordered for his head to be publicly displayed on a pike as irrefutable evidence that the revolt had been crushed.[33] In al-Andalus, a version of this practice that was particularly celebrated in the chronicles was the case of a rebel who launched an attack in the name of the 'Abbāsid caliph against Emir 'Abd al-Raḥmān I in 763 (146 AH): defeated and slain, his head and those of his followers were deposited in the market-place of Qayrawān, so that the news would reach the ears of the caliph of Baghdad, who on learning of what had happened gave thanks to heaven that there was such a large distance between him and a man capable of doing such a thing.[34] In later periods, the display of severed heads was also a common practice after victories won against rebels, and also following expeditions launched against the Christians.[35]

Another two major triumphal celebrations took place in Córdoba and Madīnat al-Zahrā' around this time. The first was held in the summer of 971 (360 AH), when, as has been discussed (see above p. 210), the defection of the family of Ja'far b. al-Andalusī from the ranks of the Fāṭimid caliphate and their transfer to Córdoba were claimed by al-Ḥakam II to be a resounding victory. The second, held three years later, was the subjugation of the Idrīsid rebel, Ḥassan b. Qannūn, following his defeat by the army led by *qā'id* Ghālib. Both events gave rise to grandiose public displays that involved the participation of a huge number of people and elaborate displays of caliphal power. Over the pages that follow, drawing on the extraordinarily meticulous data provided by 'Īsā b. Aḥmad al-Rāzī, I undertake an exhaustive description of these two celebrations. Using the details recorded by the chronicler, my intention is to transmit the incisiveness of his text, as it recounts the splendour of these

[32] Ibn Ḥayyān, *Muqtabis VII*, ed. pp. 141–3; trans. pp. 179–81.
[33] M. McCormick, *Eternal Victory*, pp. 60–1 and fig. 6, pp. 134–5.
[34] *Akhbār Majmū'a*, ed. and trans. pp. 103–4; trans. James, p. 102.
[35] M. Fierro, 'Violencia, política y religión en al-Andalus durante el s. IV/X', pp. 39–45.

triumphant victories, which undoubtedly seemed like glorious events to those present, although in history books nowadays they barely merit a passing reference. The punctilious account given of these events offers insights into a range of details related to the preparation and staging of such celebrations, as well as glimpses of daily life under the caliphate.[36]

All Roads Lead to Córdoba

The arrival in al-Andalus of the Arab leader Ja'far b. al-Andalusī and his brother Yaḥyā in September 971 (360 AH) took place, as has been discussed, in exceptional circumstances. After having been one of the major supporters of the Fāṭimid caliphs in Ifrīqiya, the family had broken with Caliph al-Mu'izz. The rupture was due to this caliph's decision to hand the governorship of Ifrīqiya over to the Ṣinhāja Berber leader, Zīrī b. Manād. This decision had a dramatic impact, coming just prior to the Fāṭimid caliph's move to Egypt. Ja'far, having defeated and killed Zīrī in combat in early July 971, had no alternative but to ask for asylum to the Umayyad caliph and move with his family to Córdoba. Following a series of brief negotiations, an agreement was reached on the conditions to be granted to the Banū al-Andalusīs and their allies, the Berber Banū Khazar. With scrupulous precision, 'Īsā al-Rāzī describes the arrival and journey to Córdoba made by these exiles and their entourage during the summer of 971 (360 AH).

Having agreed the terms on which they would be received in al-Andalus, Yaḥyā b. al-Andalusī landed in Pechina (Almería), on Wednesday, 3 August 971 (7 *Shawwāl* 360 AH). He was accompanied by his three sons and five daughters. He brought with him the heads of Zīrī b. Manād and one hundred of his supporters. Separately, three Berber leaders from the Banū Khazar tribe also disembarked in Almería, having also deserted the Fāṭimid side. They had all come to settle in al-Andalus and they brought their relatives and servants with them. As a result, their situation was highly precarious. They had been

[36] Ibn Ḥayyān, *Muqtabis VII*, ed. pp. 39–57 and 194–202; trans. pp. 60–75 and 235–42. We also have a very detailed description of King Ordoño IV's visit in 962 when he was received by the caliph in Madīnat al-Zahrā': it is recounted by al-Maqqarī, *Nafḥ*, I, pp. 388–94, who drew on Ibn Ḥayyān. It is also described with a great wealth of detail which coincides with the data on the triumphal celebrations that I discuss here, whereby I will make a number of references to this event in additional footnotes.

forced to flee their lands and had no previous ties to al-Andalus. They were thus dependent upon the magnanimity of Caliph al-Ḥakam and what he deigned to provide for them. On the one hand, they belonged to a distinguished family, while on the other, they were prisoners of the circumstances that had led them to al-Andalus.

Two weeks after Yaḥyā b. al-Andalusī and the Banū Khazar had landed in Almería, two officials of the caliphal storehouses accompanied by officials of the stables, riders and members of the army arrived from Córdoba. They brought the horses needed to transport the new arrivals back to the capital: 68 horses for the people and 150 mules to transport their baggage. In addition, they came with four leather pavilions (*abniya*), possibly reserved for Yaḥyā and his family, and three linen ones, presumably for the Banū Khazar. The other members of their party and servants were provided with sixty-four simpler tents, called *akhbiya*, of which forty-four were of linen, being those commonly used by slaves (*ʿabīd*), while the other twenty-four were of wool and were used by the *Ṭanjiyyūn*. The total number of pavilions and tents sent (71) is similar to that of the horses (68), which suggests that Yaḥyā and the three Banū Khazar had arrived with an entourage of around seventy people.

While these preparations were made on the coast of Almería, messages were sent out to the provinces (*kūra*s) summoning senior officials to attend the arrival in Córdoba of Yaḥyā b. al-Andalusī and the Banū Khazar, who were bearing the heads of Zīrī b. Manād and his followers. A decision had already been taken to stage a lavish entrance into the capital for these individuals, whose submission the caliph wanted to present as a major triumph, one that would celebrate the defeat and humiliation of the Fāṭimid enemy, while exalting the Banū al-Andalusī family, who had renounced their previous bonds of loyalty in favour of the Umayyads.

A few days later, on Wednesday, 30 August, the head of this family, Jaʿfar b. al-Andalusī, who had been waiting for the appropriate moment, disembarked in Bezmiliana (today Rincón de la Victoria, in Málaga) accompanied by his wives and three sons. Two of his sisters also arrived with him, one of whom was married and was accompanied by her husband and sons, while the other, a widow, brought one son with her. The family of the Banū al-Andalusī, who had disembarked in al-Andalus with Jaʿfar and his brother Yaḥyā, comprised a total of eighteen family members, aside from their wives and concubines.

They would all have brought other relatives with them, as well as clients and slaves.

Reports of Ja'far's arrival in Málaga reached Córdoba two days later, on Friday, 1 September. Four days later, Muḥammad Abī 'Āmir left the capital with all that was needed to welcome the new arrival and his entourage: four thoroughbred horses (*'itāq al-khayl*), a grey mule, fifty horses to transport the people and 200 mules for the baggage.[37] In addition, a similar number of tents and pavilions to those sent for Yaḥyā were brought, as well as tapestries, coverlets, glasses and other utensils to be used during the journey. There were also mules for carrying the litters and palanquins in which Ja'far b. al-Andalusī's wives and concubines would travel. Nothing was left to chance. The wives and concubines of a noble Arab leader could not travel amid riders and servants, exposed to the gazes of strangers. The rigid concept of patriarchal honour in Arab society meant that a family's capacity to conceal and safeguard its wives was viewed as a quality that bestowed esteem on their members, whereby it is evident that those who organised the arrival of the Banū al-Andalusī wished to show their respect to the recently arrived party.[38]

With his characteristic speed, Muḥammad b. Abī 'Āmir covered the 160 kilometres between Córdoba and Málaga in four days, at an average of 40 kilometres per day. He reached his destination on Sunday, 10 September. There, he met with Ja'far and the governors of the *kūra*, the brothers Basīl and 'Abd al-Ḥamīd b. Basīl, who had joined the new arrivals.[39] Barely pausing to rest, on Tuesday, 12 September, Muḥammad b. Abī 'Āmir began his journey back to Córdoba with the whole entourage. However, in the capital, someone seems to have realised that the four thoroughbred steeds that had been sent would

[37] None of the posts to which the future al-Manṣūr had been appointed at this time – *qāḍī* of Seville, head of the mint and overseer of vacant legacies – explains why he took on this role; but by the age of thirty-three he had won the caliph's trust and he seems to have been ready to perform missions of this type.

[38] P. Guichard, *al-Andalus. Estructura antropológica de una sociedad islámica en occidente*, p. 239. A century and a half before, when the celebrated musician from Baghdad, Ziryāb, arrived in Córdoba, the procedure used for his wives' travel was identical, Ibn Ḥayyān, *Muqtabis II, 1*, ed. cit. pp. 313–14; trans. cit. pp. 198–9.

[39] Both belonged to a family of senior civil servants. Their grandfather had served as a secretary and vizier during the reign of 'Abd al-Raḥmān III and their father, Aḥmad, had been *qā'id* of Tudela and Toledo, while in this period he is recorded as *ṣāḥib al-shurṭa*, Ibn Ḥayyān, *Muqtabis V*, ed. and trans. p. 72, 88, 121, etc. and 306; al-'Udhrī, *Tarṣī*, p. 69; *Muqtabis VII*, ed. p. 183, 185 and 228.

not suffice – Ja'far had two male sons and a brother-in-law – and it was decided to remedy this seeming display of parsimoniousness by sending one of the caliph's servants (*ghulām*) with six 'thoroughbred Arab' horses so that Ja'far could complete the journey in greater comfort.

On Saturday, 16 September, the group arrived in Cabra. There, they were joined by Yaḥyā and the Banū Khazar, who had made their way from Almería, accompanied by those who had gone to meet them with the supplies from the caliphal storehouses. They thus formed a large cortège. To the fifty to sixty people who came on horseback with Ja'far was now added the seventy individuals who travelled with his brother, whereby the entourage of the Banū al-Andalusī and Banū Khazar rose to over one hundred and twenty men. In addition, there were the women concealed in the palanquins and litters carried by the mules, as well as the Umayyad welcoming party who accompanied them, which was formed of the officials who had been sent to greet them, along with the governors of Rayyuh (Málaga) and a handful of troops.

The caravan, in which everyone rode on horseback, arrived on the outskirts of Córdoba on Monday, 18 September. A halt was made at Faḥṣ al-Surādiq, a place to the east of Córdoba, where embassies as well as troops on campaign would often camp.[40] Once more, the women received a special treatment. On the caliph's orders, they were taken in litters to the *Munyat al-Shamāmat*, a rural estate that was also on the eastern side of Córdoba. When night fell, a party of eunuchs from the postal service, along with instructors, led these women from this *munya* to the residences that had been assigned to the Banū al-Andalusī in the medina of Córdoba.[41] There could be no doubt that the Umayyad caliph was treating Ja'far b. al-Andalusī and his brother with the utmost esteem in deference to their status. On that September night in 971 (*Dhū l-qa'da*, 360 AH), both men broke their journey at Faḥṣ al-Surādiq, and the women, who now resided within the walls of the medina of Córdoba,

[40] We do not know where this place was. It has been suggested it was Turruñuelos, one kilometre west of Córdoba, where aerial photography reveals an extensive orthogonal site almost twelve hectares in size, a part of which was built on, M. Acién and A. Vallejo, 'Urbanismo y estado islámico', p. 126. However, this claim does not match with what is recorded in our source, which places Faḥṣ al-Surādiq to the east of Córdoba.

[41] The text refers mentions '*khiṣyān aṣḥāb al-rasā'il wa l-muqaddamīn*'. Among the renderings of the latter term is 'eunuch commissioned with a young woman's education', which is what I think should be used here, Dozy, *Supplement*, II, 317.

could sleep in peace. And there for the moment is where we will leave them to focus on the celebration of Ghalib's victory.

Exactly three years later, in September 974 (*Muḥarram* 364 AH), the political situation was very different. What had seemed to be a definitive blow for Fāṭimid sovereignty in North Africa had not proved to be the case: Caliph al-Mu'izz had transferred his court to Egypt, where he sought to establish his hegemony over the Near East, the government of Buluggin b. Zīrī had consolidated in Ifrīqiya, and the Umayyad caliph had decided to pursue a difficult and costly campaign in northern Morocco to obtain the support of the region's multitudinous tribal leaders, as well as the city of Fez. With regard to the brothers, Ja'far and Yaḥyā b. al-Andalusī, who had taken part in their triumphal arrival in Córdoba, they had seen their situation vary greatly. Having been fêted and honoured in every way possible, they had since been imprisoned following an untimely confrontation with Caliph al-Ḥakam, who had begun to realise these exiles were not as necessary as he had first thought.

It was amid this state of affairs and following the army's major triumph in Morocco – the capture of the rebel Idrīsid leader, Ḥasan b. Qannūn, who had been sent to Córdoba – that in August 974 *qā'id* Ghālib was given the order to return to al-Andalus. The Umayyad general left everything in order so the army could carry on its operations in his absence, and on 12 September he landed in Algeciras, from where he made his way to Córdoba. His entourage included soldiers, senior military officers and, above all, a group of members of the Idrīsid family who had decided to settle in Córdoba. They were led by Aḥmad b. 'Īsā, known as Qannūn, a distant relation of Ḥasan b. Qannūn, who had ruled over the city of al-Aqlām, which was located around a day's journey from Baṣra.[42] He was accompanied by a numerous group consisting of his brother, two cousins, and their wives and sons. Aḥmad alone had fifteen male sons, and his brother and cousins had a further ten. Once more, these people were in part prisoners and in part guests of the caliphate. It had been decided that they were all to be transferred to Córdoba, where they would join the uprooted North African community, who had no other means of subsistence than what al-Ḥakam chose to grant them.

[42] A. Ettahiri, 'La ville mediévale d'al- Basra et ses deux ports', p. 158.

Ghālib's arrival as victorious *qā'id* accompanied by the large Idrīsid party was converted into another triumphal celebration, one that was an almost exact replay of the ceremony held for the Banū al-Andalusī three years before. The initial elements were repeated down to the last detail. Firstly, the *qā'id* did not enter Córdoba straightaway. Instead, on 23 September 974 (3 *Muḥarram* 364 AH), he set up camp alongside the River Guadajoz, to the south of the city. Secondly, messengers were sent out to the provinces to request the attendance of the principal figures of the administration. And, thirdly, the wives of the Banū Idrīs were once more granted special treatment due to the family's noble ancestry and the importance of preserving their honour. For this reason, they were transferred to the houses assigned to them in the medina and suburbs of Córdoba, which had been decorated with carpets and rugs, and whose larders were stocked with cooking ingredients, such as sauces, oils and herbs, as well as firewood, utensils, cooking pots and tableware.[43]

Therefore, and despite being three years apart, the Banū al-Andalusī and the triumphal Ghālib accompanied by the Idrīsids all set up camp to the east and south of Córdoba respectively, where they had to await instructions to proceed from there. The wives that formed part of both cortèges were conveniently installed in the residences provided for these new arrivals in Córdoba and everything was arranged so that the caliph could celebrate what he considered to be one his great triumphs.

The Organisation of the Cortège

On 20 September 971 a sizeable group of soldiers on horseback were sent from Madīnat al-Zahrā' under the command of the city's *ṣāḥib al-shurṭa* to escort the Banū al-Andalusī to the *Munyat Ibn 'Abd al-'Azīz*, where they were to take up residence until they received the order to present themselves before the caliph. Three years later, the same procedure was followed for Ghālib: he was led to the *faḥṣ* of the *Munyat al-Nā'ūra*, where the *qā'id* set up his pavilion alongside those of the military leaders and the Idrīsids who accompanied him.[44]

[43] I have made a minor change to the translation: in the context of the 'cooking ingredients' with which the houses were provided, it makes more sense to render *al-aṣbāgh* as 'sauces' rather than 'dyes', while for *al-adhān* 'oils' is better than 'unguents'.

[44] Ordoño IV was also lodged at this *munya* before being received by the caliph in 962, al-Maqqarī,

Both estates were located to the west of Córdoba, whereby to arrive there the cortèges had to cross the capital. This was not done by chance. Everything was carefully planned so that the people of Córdoba could witness both processions, including the people subjugated by the caliph, as they made their way past. In the case of Jaʿfar b. al-Andalusī's procession, the heads of Zīrī b. Manād and his 100 soldiers played a central role: spiked on lances, the heads were carried by a member of the guard. This grisly sight formed the vanguard of the cortège, which was arranged in two columns, consisting of the Banū al-Andalusī and their entourage, along with their armed escort, leading worthies from Córdoba and members of the provincial delegations who had come to attend the celebration.

To reach the respective *munya*s they had been assigned to the west of the city, both cortèges had to pass in front of the Bāb al-Sudda of the *alcázar* of Córdoba. Ghālib's party arrives there having crossed the bridge over the Guadalquivir, where two lines of infantrymen stood with shields and lances. The premises of the *ṣāḥib al-madīna* of Córdoba were located at the entrance to the *alcázar*, and he had arranged the troops that served under him into a number of cohorts: officers (*ʿurāfa*), guards (*muḥāris*) and police units (*shurṭa*). Observed by large crowds, both cortèges made their way along the road that skirts the southern walls of the city before arriving at their respective *munya*s, which were located outside the medina, in the west of the city. They were instructed to wait in these *munya*s for the invitation to the caliph's reception. Meanwhile, the troops that had been sent to escort them had returned to Madīnat al-Zahrā' and their leaders reported to the caliph on the success of the welcome operation thus far.

In 971, the following day, 21 September, permission was granted to the Banū al-Andalusī to leave the *Munyat Ibn ʿAbd al-ʿAzīz*, where they were staying, and make their way to Madīnat al-Zahrā' to present themselves before the caliph. An order was given for armed men to flank the entire route taken by the party, an arrangement that seems to have been a constant element of caliphal protocol.[45] The heads of the stipendiary troops, the viziers Muḥammad b.

Nafḥ, I, p. 389. As was also the case with the cortèges described here, King Ordoño IV had reached this *munya* having passed in front of the *alcázar* of Córdoba.

45 This is made clear in the description of the embassy of John of Gorze, which states, 'Viam totam ab hospitio ipsorum usque ad civitatem et inde usque ad palatium varii hinc [inde] ordines consti-

Ṭumlus and Ziyād b. Aflaḥ, arranged for horsemen to undertake this task on the outskirts of the city palace. The rest of the armed men deployed along the route were infantry soldiers. And given that the army stationed in the capital did not have sufficient men to cover the whole road, recourse was made to an extraordinary solution: all the young men of Córdoba were called up, their names and place of residence noted down, and each given a shield and lance from the armoury storehouse. According to ʿĪsā al-Rāzī, this decision resulted in a flurry of secretaries and servants having to work through the night by candle and torchlight under the supervision of vizier Jaʿfar al-Muṣḥafī. As a result, the preparations continued until dawn on the reception day, and it is possible that they continued working throughout the morning, up until the very last moment.

On the day of the reception, both cortèges made their way to Madīnat al-Zahrā' escorted by the horsemen and led by a *qā'id*. It is highly probable that their route followed the so-called 'road of the *munya*s', which had been paved by Caliph ʿAbd al-Raḥmān III in 942. It was not the most direct route via which to reach the palace-city, but it was the most impressive one for a ceremonial procession; part of the way ran parallel to the Guadalquivir River and crossed some of the most exclusive zones of Córdoba's surroundings; a number of small streams had to be crossed by bridges, some of which have been preserved until today, which reveal that the road was seven metres wide.[46]

The whole route was flanked by armed men, arranged on either side of the road, and as the cortège approached Madīnat al-Zahrā' their uniforms became more elaborate and impressive. To begin with, when each cortège left its *munya* there were two rows of armed soldiers equipped with lances and helmets, who in the case of the cortège of the Banū al-Andalusī had been mustered in a hurry from among the suburbs of Córdoba, as I have just mentioned; they were more like extras than soldiers. According to ʿĪsā al-Rāzī there were 16,000 men, whose ranks, considering that they were arranged in two lines and a metre apart, would have extended for eight kilometres. Three years later,

pabant', ed. pp. 375–6. The text cites an order that is similar to the one set out here: infantrymen with lances, followed by others with javelins and pikes; then, men with light arms mounted on mules, followed by knights who would make their horses rear up and, to finish, some *mauri* who also performed a display with their horses, stirring up clouds of dust.

[46] A. Vallejo Triano, *La ciudad califal de Madīnat al-Zahrā'*, pp. 84–6.

Ghālib's cortège had to cover a shorter route, as he came from the *Munyat al-Nāʿūra*, but infantrymen with round wooden shields covered with leather and lances whose tips were shaped in laurel-leaf or rhomboid designs were also stationed along the route.[47]

When the cortèges reached the outskirts of Madīnat al-Zahrā', the infantry gave way to cavalry. Both cortèges were received by a deployment of cavalry guards organised in different units and regiments. They stood on parade on both sides of the route in accordance with their military rank. First, there were riders clad in armour, whose horses and equipment had been prepared by the palace slaves and servants. They were then followed by the Tangerine riders, who, as will be recalled, were the lowest-ranking unit in the army. Then, again on horseback, there were various units of military slaves: those who were originally captives and were drafted into the army (*khumsiyyūn*), and those equipped with swords and archers. The next squadron was formed of the specialised archers, who were recognised by their white tunics, a special sort of headgear and their Syrian bows and quivers.[48] The array of cavalry arranged on either side of the route as it approached Madīnat al-Zahrā' numbered at least five hundred men. As the parties drew closer to the city, they were met by trumpeters and drummers, performing some form of music, and next they reached the standard bearers, who carried an impressive array of flags adorned with figurative motifs. The final section of the route that led to the city's southern Statue Gate (*Bāb al-Ṣūra*) was flanked by cavalry from the caliph's stables with fifty riders on either side of the road, who stood on parade astride their horses adorned with elaborately crafted bridles. Once the party had made its way through the gate, a unit of slave cavalrymen clad in armour welcomed them.

The cortèges had reached the city, but there was still a final stretch of some five hundred metres before arrival at the caliphal palace or *alcázar*. Having crossed a broad avenue, which is clearly visible today in satellite images, they made their way through the Vaulted Gates (*Abwāb al-Aqbā'*), which separated the urban area of Madīnat al-Zahrā' from the palace.[49] The

[47] A. Soler del Campo, 'Armas, arreos y banderas en las minituras de códice', pp. 241 and 245.

[48] In the case of Ghālib's arrival, part of the route was occupied by Jaʿfarid riders with their characteristic cloaks, helmets, arches and quivers.

[49] These gates are referred to in the account of the triumphant procession held for Ghālib, *Muqtabis*

Image 18 Madīnat al-Zahrā'. Bāb al-Sudda. It was through this gate that the delegations that visited the caliph entered the palace, after dismounting in the large square that surrounded it.

whole route from there on was flanked by the city guard, which consisted of infantrymen and archers, as well as members of the caliphal workshops, who wore their distinctive garments, and carried Arab and Christian bows over their shoulders. The cortèges reached the stables (*Dār al-Khayl*), and from there they turned towards the triumphal Bāb al-Sudda (visible today after its reconstruction following its excavation), which provided access to the palace complex. In Madīnat al-Zahrā', as in Córdoba, the office of the *ṣāḥib al-madīna*, Muḥammad b. Aflaḥ, was alongside this gateway. In the arcades that ran alongside the Bāb al-Sudda, porters, slaves, pages (*ghilmān*)

VII, ed. p. 197; trans. p. 238, and that of the cortège of King Ordoño IV, al-Maqqarī, *Nafḥ*, I, ed. p. 390, in which they appear (in a singular form) as 'the first gate of the alcázar of al-Zahrā'. This gate is also referred to in the ceremony held for the swearing of the oath of loyalty to al-Ḥakam II with regard to how the ranks of troops and servants flanking the route extended from the Eastern Hall as far as this gate, which is exactly the same form as the triumphant celebrations studied here, al-Maqqarī, *Nafḥ*, I, ed. p. 388.

and officials waited, standing upon the stone benches, carrying ornate swords and brocade caps. They assisted the members of the cortège to dismount, as they had to enter the *alcázar* complex on foot.[50]

Once inside the palace, protocol dictated that the members of the cortège who had the rank of vizier, such as Ghālib, for example, had to make their way to the *Dār al-Wuzarā'*, while the others had to wait in the *Dār al-Jund*, where they were met by another squadron of archers wearing a variety of coloured uniforms and helmets. The principal guests were to take seats in the building's central nave upon brocade cushions while they awaited the order to make their way to the hall where the caliph was waiting for them.[51]

The Route towards the Caliph

The final part of this lengthy itinerary was the caliph's reception of the new arrivals in the Eastern Hall of Madīnat al-Zahrā'.[52] The protocol for access to the caliph established that once everything was ready, the *fatā*s who served as secretaries had to go the *Dār al-Jund* and inform the guests that they were to present themselves before the caliph. This was done with the Banū al-Andalusī, and exactly the same happened three years later with the Idrīsids. The route they took through the *alcázar* was also flanked by infantrymen and the *Ja'farid* troops, who wore armour, golden helmets and carried Frankish lances adorned with silver tubes. The cortège first marched from the *Dār al-Jund* to the *Dār al-Wuzarā'*, making their way through a number of porticoes where they were joined by senior figures from the *kūra*s who had also been invited to attend the celebration; they wore brocade bonnets (*qalansuwwas*) and carried exquisitely crafted swords.[53] At the *Dār al-Wuzarā'*, they reached the Portico of the Secretaries, where two lines of secretaries,

[50] During the reception of King Ordoño IV everyone dismounted at the Bāb al-Sudda, except the monarch and his companion Muḥammad b. Ṭumlus, p. 390.

[51] This division can be noted in the ruins of Madīnat al-Zahrā': just having passed through the Bāb al-Sudda there is a corridor, and a part of it leads towards what is known as the upper Basilical building, which must have been the House of the Viziers; in the other direction the corridor led towards the House of the Army, which was opposite in a part of the palace complex that has since been completely destroyed. As was noted above, Ordoño IV also had to wait in the *Dār al-Jund*.

[52] In this case the text refers to the 'South Hall' (*al-Majlis al-Qiblī*), but this must be an error, as there is no other mention of this hall and the reception was held in a similar form to that discussed here.

[53] The lines of soldiers stretched from the Portico of the Abī 'Urrāḍ outside the House of the Viziers up to the Portico of the Secretaries (*Faṣīl al-Kuttāb*).

instructors, senior servants and eunuchs joined the cortège, and took up their positions alternating with the provincial representatives. Once the viziers had joined the cortège, most likely at its head, they made their way to the Gate of the Porticoes, which opened onto the upper terrace. Two lines of ceremonial guards bearing ornate swords and wearing silver embossed helmets awaited them and lined their path up to the Eastern Hall, also known today as the Salón Rico.

The receptions held by the caliph in 971 and 974 reveal a number of small differences. During the first one, on reaching the door of the audience chamber, the Banū al-Andalusī family members approached the caliph and kissed his hand. As a show of deference, the caliph allowed them to sit down, although all the other attendees remained standing. A conversation began in which al-Ḥakam asked Jaʿfar b. al-Andalusī a number of questions about his situation, which he answered while standing up each time he gave a reply: a form of behaviour that was later widely commented on and considered to be a novelty, which reveals the high degree of scrutiny each detail of the protocol was subject to within Umayyad court culture.

At the reception held in 974, the arrangements were different. Al-Ḥakam had decided that on this occasion the prince, Hishām, should play a greater role. This meant that many more people attended the reception. Besides the usual attendees – the caliph's brothers, viziers, heads of the administration and *qāḍī*s – there were those responsible for the granaries, the senior *fatā*s (*khulafā'*, secretaries, servants) and the *ṣaqāliba* eunuchs. The latter two groups were provided with military equipment, such as ornate swords, armour and helmets, something which was rather unusual as they were members of the civil administration. They were arranged all along either side of the hall and the lines they formed continued across the terrace that surrounded the Western Hall. In this latter hall, there was a mirror-like arrangement: the caliph's heir, Hishām, sat there with his uncle Rā'iq and a vizier in attendance beside him, as well as palace servants of an equivalent rank to that of those who stood in attendance on his father in the Eastern Hall. The reception, thus, demonstrated al-Hakam's wish to create a spectacle that underscored the continuity of his dynasty.

Aside from this significant detail, the staging of the reception was similar to that of the previous one. Once Ghālib had made his victorious entrance, the eight Idrīsids who had arrived with him also presented themselves to the caliph. They greeted him, took their seats, and then al-Ḥakam addressed them to thank them for their submission and announced the pensions that had been assigned to them. He even gave them permission to present the eldest sons of the two senior members of the family, perhaps as a way of highlighting and underscoring the presence of the caliph's own son in the ceremony.

At the end of these two audiences, the guests left along the same route by which they had arrived. However, they did not return to the *munya*s where they had come from. They took up permanent residence in the houses that the caliph had assigned them in the medina of Córdoba (see below p. 376).[54] It was in these residences that they would begin their new life, supported by the generous pensions that the caliph had granted them, which in the case of the Banū al-Andalusī came to an astronomical sum (see above p. 91).

However, al-Hakam had not finished the audiences he had to grant. Provincial delegations had arrived in Córdoba, and they had to be given special attention. The reception in 971 where he did this occurred on Saturday, 22 September, following a protocol that, we are told, had been established by the first caliphs. The first to enter were the members of the *jund* of Damascus, which in al-Andalus corresponded to the *kūra* or province of Elvira; then came the *jund* of Ḥimṣ, which was settled in the *kūra* of Seville; then the *jund* of Qinnasrīn from the *kūra* of Jaén; they were followed by the *jund* of Palestine from the *kūra* of Sidonia, and finally came the *jund* of Jordan from the *kūra* of Rayyuh (Málaga). It was a form of underscoring how these *kūra*s, in which the regional cohorts of the Syrian *jund* had settled in the mid-eighth century following their arrival in al-Andalus, continued to form the backbone of the caliphate. It was only after these representatives had been received that senior figures from the *kūra*s of Cabra, Écija, Osuna, Tākurunnā and Niebla, among others, made their entrance. This audience was not merely a matter of protocol, as the caliph asked questions about the current situation of the provinces, as well as how their governors were behaving, something that sparked some criticisms.

[54] The same happened with Ordoño IV, who before the caliph's reception had slept at the *Munyat al-Nā'ūra*, and he then took up residence in the *Munyat al-Ruṣāfa*, *Nafḥ*, I, p. 393.

In the celebration held in September 974, this latter reception took place in the Eastern Hall, once the Idrīsids had left. It is clear in this case that the caliph's intention was that Hishām should be present at the audience granted to these notable provincial figures and that they should meet the intended heir to the caliphate. The protocol for access was the same as for the previous occasion, with the *junds* entering in accordance with the pre-established order.

When this final reception ended, Caliph al-Ḥakam must have felt a deep sense of satisfaction. He had commemorated Ghālib's major military triumph in northern Morocco, a series of important members of the Idrīsid had been uprooted and brought to Córdoba, and his son Hishām had appeared before them all in a highly visible and spectacular form as heir to the caliphate. It was the final days of September: two months later, al-Ḥakam II would suffer the stroke that started the rushing of things.

The Flags: Symbols and Rituals

Flags were one highly significant element in these receptions. As has been seen, when the cortèges approached the southern gate of Madīnat al-Zahrā', they were welcomed by riders and an explosion of drums and trumpets. The musicians were accompanied by standard-bearers displaying a number of ensigns. The descriptions of the symbols displayed by these flags are quite detailed and reveal the iconographic representations that the caliphal state makes of itself, which is fairly extraordinary for a medieval Muslim government and therefore merits being studied in detail.

In the pre-Islamic era, the Arab armies used ensigns (*rayā*) and flags (*liwā'*) to identify tribal contingents and military units respectively. Following the Arab expansion these ensigns and flags continued to be used. Their colours were highly varied. The Yemenites, for example, distinguished themselves with yellow turbans and flags, while some north Arab factions used red. Some ensigns were given names, such as the black flag of the Prophet known as *al-'Uqāb*, 'the Eagle'. Others had inscriptions, and some tribal ensigns might even contain figurative representations, such as lions.[55] On occasion, it has

[55] M. Hinds, 'The Banners and Battle Cries of the Arabs at Ṣiffīn', pp. 8–12. M. I. Fierro, 'al-Aṣfar Again', pp. 207–9, which also provides references to a prophecy that linked the future al-Manṣūr, of Yemeni origin, with the colour yellow.

been claimed that the ensign of the Umayyad caliphs of Damascus was white, but the evidence for this is not conclusive. On the other hand, the 'Abbāsids made black the colour of their dynasty, which was possibly a response to elaborations of Muslim traditions stating that the Prophet Muhammad had flown a black flag during his campaigns. The 'Abbāsids' use of black was not only applied to their flags, but also the caliph's garments and those of his closest circle, which had the effect that the rebel movements that rose against them adopted alternative colours.[56]

In al-Andalus, flags were also of great importance. As in the Orient, they were presented to mark the concession of a military command, and hoisting the standard of an Umayyad sovereign was synonymous with recognising his sovereignty. In contrast, receiving or accepting a black flag tied to a lance signified a proclamation of obedience to the 'Abbāsid caliphs.[57] Likewise, the Umayyad caliph could send flags as a gift to North African tribal leaders who accepted his rule.[58]

At the court of al-Ḥakam II, the use and design of flags were viewed as highly significant elements of the court culture, which underscores their importance. An especially elaborate ritual of the knotting of the standards was performed just before the army left on campaign, and this dated back to the emirate era. On this occasion, the three principal flags of the caliphate were brought out from their store in the *Bayt al-wuzarā'* at Madīnat al-Zahrā'. They were meticulously wrapped in a white quilt that had been made in the city palace.[59] They were then sewn onto lances by a tailor while an *imām* recited Sūra 48, Victory (*al-Fatḥ*):

56 K. Athamina, 'The Black Banners and the Socio-Political Significance of Flags and Slogans in Medieval Islam', pp. 307–26.

57 Ibn al-Khaṭīb, *Iḥāta*, ed. cit. pp. 110–11, on the appointment of *jund* leaders with flags; also *Akhbār Majmū'a*, ed. and trans. pp. 66; trans. James, p. 83. See also Ibn Ḥayyān, *Muqtabis* V, ed. and trans. p. 288, which refers to the appointment of the Muḥammad b. Hāshim al-Tujībī, a former rebel, as the caliph's governor of Zaragoza with 'flags, provisions, money and garments'. On the use of flags in the Orient during the Umayyad period see A. Marsham, *Rituals of Islamic Monarchy*, pp. 63, 65–6. With regard to the rebellion against the Umayyad ensign with the black ensign of the 'Abbāsids, *Akhbār Majmū'a*, ed. and trans. pp. 101–2; trans. James, p. 102.

58 'Abd al-Raḥmān III gave three decorated standards to Mūsa b. Abī l-'Āfiya in 326 AH, Ibn Ḥayyān, *Muqtabis V*, ed. and trans. pp. 289–90.

59 The text uses the expression *milḥafa bayḍā' zahriyya*, which the translator renders as 'a white *zahriyya almolafa*' In my view *almolafa* – which refers to a male garment – is not the most appropriate translation, whereby I propose the term 'quilt', for which I draw on Dozy, *Supplement*, II,

> Surely, We have given thee a manifest victory,
> that God may forgive thee thy former and thy latter sins, and complete
> His blessing upon thee, and guide thee on a straight path,
> and that God may help thee with mighty help.

The standard was fixed to the lance at the moment at which the recital of the twenty-nine verses that make up this *sūra* ended. Although the caliph did not participate in this ceremony, he did send a representative to take charge of its preparation, which was also attended by muezzins and commanders of the troops. Once the flags had been blessed in this way, they were carried by the expedition's *qā'id*, who received them at the Bāb al-Sudda, where the army would be on parade ready to leave on campaign. When Ghālib led the expedition against the Normans in July 971 (*Ramaḍān* 360 AH) this was the procedure that was used; he received the flags as soon as he had left the Córdoba's *alcázar* through the Bāb al-Sudda. It is highly likely that on other occasions a similar procedure was adhered to.[60]

There were three flags that were blessed and handed to Ghālib following this extraordinary ritual. They were called *al-'Uqda*, *al-Shaṭranj* and *al-'Alam*. The latter, 'the flag', must have been the Umayyad ensign *par excellence*, although regrettably we do not know what it looked like. With regard to *al-'Uqda*, it was 'the binding' or 'the knot', and it was almost certainly the ensign that had been carried by the founder of the Umayyad dynasty, 'Abd al-Raḥmān I, during his battles to win power in al-Andalus in the mid-eighth century (second AH). It is said that, not having a flag, he chose to bind his turban to a lance and that a renowned holy man called Farqad had prophesised he would adopt *al-'uqda*. The successive Umayyad emirs maintained

p. 519. *Zahriyya* evidently refers to the fact that this cover was made in Madīnat al-Zahrā'. The description of the celebrated gift that the vizier Aḥmad b. Shuhayd gave to 'Abd al-Raḥmān III also refers to quilts made in al-Zahrā', al-Maqqarī, *Nafḥ*, I, p. 358.

[60] Ibn Ḥayyān, *Muqtabis VII*, ed. and trans. pp. 25–6 and 48–50. The text contains a number of lacunae. The caliph's representative who was in charge of organising the ceremony was the treasurer Durrī. It was attended by the vizier and the head of the stipendiary troops (*ṣāḥib al-hasham*) Muḥammad b. Qāsim b. Ṭumlus and the head of the stables, who was also commander of the stipendiary troops, Ziyād b. Aflaḥ. The blessing was undertaken by Muḥammad b. Yūsuf b. Sulaymān al-Juhanī, the *qāḍī* of Cabra, who was serving as prayer leader and preacher at the mosque of Madīnat al-Zahrā', Ibn al-Faraḍī, *Ta'rīkh*, n. 1.335. *Prosopografía de los ulemas de al-Andalus*, no. 10.778. The knotting of the turban before a military expedition is also recorded in al-Nuwayrī, *Nihāyat al-arab fī funūn al-adab*, ed. and trans. pp. 71 and 64.

the custom of tying on new turbans over those that had grown old, but this practice had been lost by the time of ʿAbd al-Raḥmān II, when various civil servants decided to get rid of the old pieces. Nonetheless, *Al-ʿUqda* continued to be used (the turban of the current sovereign would be bound to the lance), most likely as an emblematic sign of identity that kept alive the memory of the founder of the dynasty. It is highly possible, therefore, that the practice of blessing it and the other standards was also intended to mark one of the foundational episodes of the dynasty (the moment when ʿAbd al-Raḥmān I confronted his enemies to win power), which offers a further insight into the conservation of traditions by the Umayyads, who associated the sovereign's turban bound to the lance with the dynasty's military success.[61]

With regard to the second flag handed to Ghālib, known as *al-Shaṭranj*, all that can be said is that it possibly, as its name indicates, was a flag with chequered pattern like a chessboard. A contemporaneous description in *De Cerimoniis* refers to a Byzantine ensign that had a pink chequerboard design, but it is impossible to know if there was any influence from this design. The chequerboard-patterned flag was an especially important one; it was referred to as 'the exalted chessboard' (*al-shaṭranj al-sāmī*), and it was displayed during the reception held for the Banū al-Andalusī.[62]

For the solemn audiences held at the court of al-Ḥakam II, other flags of the caliphate were flown, of which there were up to one hundred. Many of them contained figurative representations, such as 'lions with open jaws, terrifying leopards, eagles descending on their prey and horrendous dragons'. The flag 'of the great lion' was effectively one of the ensigns of ʿAbd al-Raḥmān III, who gave one of these flags to a North African tribal leader, in which the animal was represented with a silver head and blue eyes. This design may be related to a ceramic caliphal dish made in green and manganese ware, which was possibly produced in the workshops of Madīnat al-Zahrā'; it has an inscription reading *al-mulk* ('the power'). On its base it has a design with two lions facing one another with open jaws. The idea that the caliph's soldiers advanced against

[61] *Akhbār Majmūʿa*, ed. and trans. pp. 84–5; trans. James, pp. 92–3. An echo of this information, albeit in a rather different form in Ibn al-Qūṭiya, *Taʾrīkh*, ed. p. 26; trans. James p. 70.

[62] E. García Gómez, 'Armas, banderas, tiendas de campaña', pp. 168–9; A. Babuin, 'Standards and Insignia in Byzantium', p. 27.

their enemies 'as dragons that advance or dragons that devour' offers a parallel rhetorical trope to these representations.[63]

With regard to the theme of the eagle, it first appeared during a campaign against the Christian North commanded by 'Abd al-Raḥmān III in 934 (322 AH). It was then considered a great invention and gave rise to 'endless commentaries'.[64] A standard with this representation was also sent by Caliph 'Abd al-Raḥmān III to a North African tribal chieftain: the eagle was made with coloured thread, its head in embroidered silver and the outline in gold thread, whereas the eyes were made of red thread, and a green-coloured mount was displayed on the forehead.[65] Representations of eagles descending on their prey appear on caliphal marble basins from a later period: in particular one dated to just a few years after al-Ḥakam's death during the apogee of al-Manṣūr is preserved in the Museo Arqueológico Nacional. With regard to the dragon or serpent represented on the Umayyad standards, an illustration in the San Isidro Bible in León shows an ensign with this motif tied to a lance.

[63] Ibn 'Abd Rabbihi, *Arjūza*, trans. Monroe, p. 89, l. 276. Ibn Ḥayyān, *Muqtabis V*, ed. and trans. p. 207.

[64] Ibn Ḥayyān, *Muqtabis V*, ed. and trans. p. 224.

[65] Ibn Ḥayyān, *Muqtabis V*, ed. and trans. p. 239.

10

Córdoba and Madīnat al-Zahrā': Topography of Power and Urban Space

A History of Two Cities

Between 971 and 975 al-Ḥakam II divided his time between Madīnat al-Zahrā' and Córdoba. While the city palace was the caliph's main residence, he also spent lengthy periods at the *alcázar* in Córdoba, travelling frequently between the two places, which were just over five kilometres apart.[1] All the evidence indicates that the sovereign chose to maintain a dual capital, and this is confirmed by 'Īsā al-Rāzī, who refers to the existence of two capitals (*ḥaḍiratayn*), both of which had its own *ṣāḥib al-madīna* and Friday mosque with its prayer leader. However, no *qāḍī* seems to have been appointed to al-Zahrā', which demonstrates how the caliph's urban project in the new capital had still not attained its definitive form.[2]

1 The caliph's movements did not follow any discernible pattern. Having spent the summer of 971 in the palace-city, in autumn al-Ḥakam returned to Córdoba. He was there in June 972 when the expedition mounted against the Normans left, but a month later he would celebrate the Breaking of the Fast in al-Zahrā'. A visit made by the caliph to the Cordoban *dār al-tirāz* in September that same year was followed weeks later by the reception held for the Feast of the Sacrifice, which took place in the city palace, where the caliph spent April 973; this was the occasion on which he summoned *qā'id* Ghālib and instructed him to take charge of the Morocco campaign. In October the caliph was in the *alcázar* in Córdoba, but in November he was back at Madīnat al-Zahrā', where he received various Christian embassies. In March 974, in the mosque in Córdoba, he announced the news of the submission of Ḥasan b. Qannūn, but a few days later he returned to al-Zahrā', while his son Hishām remained in Córdoba recovering from smallpox. Then, in November that same year, the caliph was in the palace-city when he suffered a stroke.

2 M. Acién Almansa and A. Vallejo Triano, 'Urbanismo y estado islámico', pp. 193–4. Their views on the dual capital are confirmed by Ibn Ḥayyān, *Muqtabis VII*, ed. p. 93; trans. p. 117. On the prayer leader at Madīnat al-Zahrā', Ibn al-Faraḍī, *Ta'rīkh*, n. 1.357.

Al-Ḥakam II's continual comings and goings between the two cities came to a brusque end in late November 974 when he suffered a stroke while at Madīnat al-Zahrā', which meant he had to withdraw from court life and state affairs until mid-January. He remained at the palace-city throughout the winter, which brought snow and strong winds. Then, at the end of March 975, the doctors instructed that he should be transferred to Córdoba, 'due to his excessive exposure to the cold of the mountains, which they thought would disturb the balance of his humours'. Leaving Madīnat al-Zahrā', described by the chronicler 'Īsā al-Rāzī as the 'lady of palaces, mansion of pleasure and seat of joy', must have been a very difficult decision. The caliph consulted God and chose to follow the doctors' advice. According to our author, al-Ḥakam did this 'not out of hatred, but to take better care of his poor health ... so it is, at times, that beauty is disowned albeit not through any fault of her own'. Al-Rāzī's words offer an example of the 'symbolic feminization of place', a trope Andalusi authors repeatedly made recourse to when referring to topographical landmarks identified with caliphal power.[3]

Al-Ḥakam II had just a year and half to live, and he seemingly never returned to the city palace that had been the setting for some of the most brilliant moments of his caliphate. It is perhaps for this reason that 'Īsā al-Rāzī's description of his departure on the morning of Saturday, 27 March 975 (11 *Rajab* 364 AH) has a retrospective elegiac tone: accompanied by his son and heir, Hishām, the caliph left Madīnat al-Zahrā' through the southern gate, known as the Rose Gate (*Bāb al-Warda*); as they departed, they were seen off by the principal officials of the administration, clients (*mawālī*), troops and slaves (*'abīd*), who stood in attendance and bid the caliph farewell, effusively blessing him while some ran to kiss the floor in front of him: 'the sovereign, holding the reins of his horse, briefly paused to contemplate the admirable spectacle of his clients and slaves. He then set off on foot, followed by the prince, his son.'

The distance between the two cities could have been covered in just a few hours, but al-Ḥakam II took two days to complete the journey. The slow pace

[3] For example, al-Ḥijārī refers to Madīnat al-Zahrā' and al-Zāhira as two earrings that adorn Córdoba, which is described as a bride. Numerous other examples could be cited, J. M. Puerta Vílchez, 'La monumentalidad y el sentido artístico de Qurtuba', pp. 54 and 61–2.

must have been partly due to his delicate state of health. However, having been ill and out of the public eye for four months, the caliph also wanted to make an appearance before his subjects. Therefore, on leaving Madīnat al-Zahrā' the caliph travelled along the paved road that led to the *Munyat Arḥā' Nāṣiḥ* on the banks of the Guadalquivir, which can be identified with Cortijo del Alcaide, where significant archaeological remains from this period have been found.[4] Having spent the night there, the following day, a Sunday, the caliph went to the *Munyat al-Nā'ūra*, where the order was given for the viziers, the members of the *shurṭa*, the *ḥukkām*, the palace servants and senior dignitaries to join him there for the celebration of midday prayers. The prayers were held in the open air in the *munya*'s *faḥṣ*, very possibly amid a mood of solemn expectation and concern. Once the prayers were over, the caliph left the state via its main gate and, after crossing the *Muṣāra* – the large esplanade outside Córdoba – he entered the city from the west. Then, visible to all, he made his way through the souk before finally arriving at the *alcázar*.[5]

I will return to this particular journey below, because the caliph made his way through some of the major landmarks of the urban topography of Córdoba. Yet it is also important to underscore that this parade marked the end of an era, although those who witnessed it could not have imagined that this short journey heralded such change. After that March day, Madīnat al-Zahrā' never regained its past splendour, or at least the sources make no mention of it. The receptions celebrated for embassies or religious festivals were from then on held in the old *alcázar* in Córdoba, despite the fact that its rooms could scarcely host the numerous people who attended them. When al-Ḥakam II died in October 976 (*Ṣafar* 366 AH), his son Hishām was proclaimed caliph in the *alcázar*, and the most likely scenario is that the early period of his reign

[4] Ibn Ḥayyān, *Muqtabis VII*, ed. and trans. pp. 68, 171 and 212; 90, 210 and 252. C. Ewert, 'Die dekorelemente des spätumaiyadischen fund-komplexes aus dem Cortijo del Alcaide (prov. Córdoba)', pp. 356-491. The identification of Arḥā' Nāṣiḥ with Cortijo del Alcaide is based on the fact that the mills that its name refers to must have been found next to the river and the road linking the other *munya*s that led from Madīnat al-Zahrā' met the River Guadalquivir there, before then following its course in the direction of *Munyat al-Nā'ūra*. Once proclaimed caliph, Hishām II resided in Arḥā' Nāṣiḥ sometimes and it was the site of a number of important events of his caliphate, Ibn 'Idhārī, *al-Bayān*, III, ed. cit. pp. 16, 40–1; trans. cit. pp. 23, 46–7.

[5] Ibn Ḥayyān, *Muqtabis VII*, ed. cit. pp. 211–12; trans. pp. 251–2. A. Vallejo, *La ciudad califal*, pp. 84–6.

took place within its walls.[6] He being just an eleven-year-old child, it is unlikely that grand ceremonies of public display were staged to make a show of a caliph whose youth was a reminder of the irregularities that had marred his accession. Power was effectively exercised by the three main figures of the caliphal administration, Ja'far al-Muṣḥafī, Muḥammad b. Abī 'Āmir and Ghālib, which relegated the figure of the caliph to an increasingly testimonial position, one removed from any contact with his subjects.

The *coup de grâce*, both for the power wielded by the Umayyad caliph and Madīnat al-Zahrā', occurred in 980 (370 AH), when Muḥammad b. Abī 'Āmir gave orders for the palace precinct to remain closed to all visitors. By then, the powerful *ḥājib* had disposed of his other two partners, who had turned out to be his rivals, and also completed the construction of his own city palace, Madīnat al-Zāhira, located to the east of Córdoba, where he transferred the caliphate's treasury and administration. On the pretext that Hishām II, who was by then an adult, wished to dedicate his time to religious devotion, Muḥammad b. Abī 'Āmir ordered that walls and gates were to be built around Madīnat al-Zahrā', thereby isolating the caliph from any outside contact. Salaried gatekeepers and sentinels were instructed to keep watch on the caliph and prevent him from receiving any news that might alarm him. It is very likely that the changes made to the use of this palace-city led to architectural modifications, because numerous sealed-off gateways and passageways can be identified in the archaeological remains.[7] Having once been a grandiose residence and the setting of caliphal power, the city palace now became a prison within which was enclosed the shadow of the caliph's authority.

As a result, Madīnat al-Zahrā' only had four decades of significant use, which was by no means long enough for this urban project to become fully established. Its exclusive dependence on the caliphs' power led to a rapid decline as soon as the caliphate suffered its irreversible crisis. Córdoba, on the other hand, already had a thousand years of history behind it, and above all it was an urban environment embedded in a rich and deeply rooted social fabric.

[6] Ibn 'Idhārī, *al-Bayān*, II, ed. cit. p. 253.

[7] Ibn 'Idhārī, *al-Bayān*, II, ed. cit. p. 278. However, during the 'āmirid period Hishām II did not always reside at Madīnat al-Zahrā'. He also lived in the *Munyat Arḥā' Nāṣiḥ* and in Córdoba itself, ibid., III, ed. cit. pp. 16 and 41; trans. cit. pp. 23 and 46.

Although the civil war, which resulted in the demise of the Umayyad dynasty, had a considerable impact on Córdoba's urban structure, the city survived as one of the principal urban centres of al-Andalus up until the Christians' conquest of it in the summer of 1236.[8]

An explanation for the very different fates of these two cities, separated by just a few kilometres, is provided by the wholly distinctive urban evolution that shaped Córdoba and Madīnat al-Zahrā'. In the historic capital, some buildings and spaces were shaped following the topography of Umayyad power, yet its urban fabric was the product of diverse modes of social exchange and relations that had thrived independently of political power. Madīnat al-Zahrā', in contrast, was an urban project that had been planned from the top down, and it lacked its own social dynamics, as there was insufficient time for them to develop. As a matter of fact, it is possible to detect a latent tension between the exercise of power, which had a major impact on urban development, and the social fabric that typically shaped a city's growth, but whose inherent logic could both complement and cause conflict with the power wielded by the caliph. Over the course of this chapter, I will demonstrate how this tension provides an explanation for the physiognomy of both cities. While the foundation of Madīnat al-Zahrā' fulfilled the Umayyad caliphs' wish to create a 'disembedded capital', where it was possible to exercise a strict form of social and political domain, Córdoba's cityscape was instead the outcome of complex social processes, within which the mechanisms of political control could not always be applied. The destruction of Madīnat al-Zahrā' was caused by the turmoil of the period, but it also bears witness to the fact that it embodied a political and social project that had failed to materialise.

The Urban Space of the Medina of Córdoba

During the caliphal era, Córdoba was a large populous city. At times, implausible figures have been proposed for its population, in some cases similar to a sizeable modern metropolis. Nonetheless, the number of inhabitants must have been very high by tenth-century standards and probably oscillated between 50,000 and 100,000 inhabitants, although this latter figure must be

[8] A. León and R. Blanco, 'La *fitna* y sus consecuencias. La revitalización urbana de Córdoba en época almohade', pp. 699–726.

considered an overly-exaggerated maximum.[9] This population was distributed in two urban sectors: the 'medina', the walled city, where the main mosque and the *alcázar* of the Umayyads were located; and the suburbs that grew up outside the city walls, which were ill-defined urban districts surrounding the medina. These suburbs had already emerged like a nebula around the medina during the emirate period, but it was during the caliphate that they underwent considerable growth and planning. Archaeological finds testify to this, and they also confirm how Córdoba extended over a number of kilometres with a population density that varied considerably from zone to zone.

The medina was the nucleus of the Umayyad capital. During al-Ḥakam II's reign it was enclosed by a wall, which had seven gates, each guarded by gatekeepers and soldiers who sealed them off at night.[10] In general terms, the medina's perimeter was the same as that of the ancient Roman *urbs*, but its interior would have been unrecognisable to anyone who had lived in Córdoba during the classical period. The network of streets had changed significantly, and the city's centre of gravity had also been displaced from the north, where the ancient Roman forum had been, to the south, alongside the banks of the River Guadalquivir; this was the location for the Friday mosque, the Umayyad's palace or *alcázar*, and the city's main market or souk.

[9] L. Torres Balbas, *Ciudades hispanomusulmanas*, I, p. 104. A. Almagro, 'Planimetría de las ciudades hispanomusulmanas', p. 427. P. Chalmeta, *Historia socioeconómica de al-Andalus*, p. 184 estimates that Córdoba's population numbered half a million inhabitants, but aside from being based on the exaggerated data provided by the sources, these population figures are calculated on the city's size using a ratio of inhabitants per hectare. They do not take into account recent archaeological finds, which show that the urban fabric did not consist of a continual urban network, but also comprised empty spaces as well as areas used as cemeteries.

[10] These gates were: the Bridge Gate (*Bāb al-Qanṭara*), to the south of the city facing the old Roman bridge; the New Gate (*Bāb al-Jadīd*), to the east that led to the Axarquía (Ocaña refers to this as the Iron Gate or *Bāb al-Ḥadīd*, but this is clearly the Arab copyists' error, as the testimony provided by Ibn Ḥayyān in *Muqtabis II, 1* consistently refers to it with this name and indicates that it had been built by al-Ḥakam I, ed. pp. 162–3 and 171; trans. pp. 73 and 79); the Gate of 'Abd al-Jabbār (*Bāb 'Abd al-Jabbār*) in the north-eastern part of the city wall; the Jews' Gate (*Bāb al-Jahūd*), to the north of the city; the 'Āmir's Gate (*Bāb 'Āmir*) on the western side of the city, which led to the 'Āmir cemetery; the Walnut Tree Gate (*Bāb al-Jawz*), today the Almodóvar Gate with elements that clearly reveal craftsmanship from the caliphal era; and, finally, the Seville or Perfumers' Gate (*Bāb al-'Aṭṭārīn*), R. Ocaña, 'Las puertas de la medina de Córdoba', pp. 143–51; the closing of the city's gates is described in Ibn Ḥayyān, *Muqtabis VII*, ed. pp. 209–10; trans. pp. 249–50, confirmed by *Akhbār Majmū'a*, ed. and trans. p. 112; trans. James, p. 107, and Ibn al-Qūṭiya, *Ta'rīkh*, ed. p. 79; trans. James pp. 113–14. Soldiers and gatekeepers in Ibn Ḥayyān, *Muqtabis II, 1*, ed. p. 155; trans. p. 67.

Córdoba's celebrated main mosque was one of the city's principal landmarks. Al-Ḥakam II decreed that the building should be extended and the work was completed in 971, whereby the number of worshippers it could accommodate rose to 7,000. It was above all at Friday prayers, which were attended on occasions by the caliph and the principal figures of the court, that this huge number of people would gather. Once the prayers were over, and as the people left, the town crier would make announcements from the Alms House (*Dār al-Ṣadaqa*), located to the west of the mosque, and even ridicule the criminals who were publicly shamed and displayed in one of this building's upper galleries.[11]

Despite its impressive size, Córdoba's grand mosque was not the only mosque to be found in the city. Given its large population, the majority of whom had already been Islamised, both the 'medina' and the suburbs were studded with places of prayer. The scale of Córdoba's urban growth and the need to pray five times a day explains the multiplication of mosques close to residential areas and places of work, which could be considerable distances apart. Some sources claim there were over 3,800 mosques, which is a seemingly impossible figure. A more reasonable estimate is 491, as given by some eleventh-century (fifth AH) authors such as al-'Udhrī and al-Bakrī. This figure is still very high, but probably includes the oratories located in the countryside and mountains surrounding Córdoba. An exhaustive review of the extant sources allows over one hundred mosques to be identified both in the medina and the suburbs.[12]

[11] Ibn Ḥayyān, *Muqtabis VII*, ed. p. 19; trans. p. 43, which mentions that a certain Wāhib al-Ḥājib was publicly shamed for a crime he had committed. The gallery of the *Dār al-Ṣadaqa* was also used to ridicule Ibrāhīm b. Muḥammad al-Iflīlī and other individuals accused of impiety during the reign of caliph Hishām II, al-Marwānī, *'Uyūn al-imāma wa nawāẓīr al-siyāsa*, p. 47. The house had previously been the residence of the musician Ziryāb, when he moved to Córdoba during the rule of 'Abd al-Raḥmān II, who often took advantage of its proximity to the *alcázar* to request the musician to perform. The emir even had a door opened in the north wall of the palace so that the musician could arrive with greater ease; Ziryāb in turn had a bath house built behind his residence, which was in use until the caliphal era, Ibn Ḥayyān, *Muqtabis II, 1*, ed. pp. 313–14 and 315 (and n. 35); trans. p. 198 and 200. It was al-Ḥakam II who used this site to build the *Dār al-Ṣadaqa* in order to distribute the alms he shared out, al-Maqqarī, *Nafḥ*, I, pp. 555–6, based on Ibn Bashkuwāl.

[12] J. Zanón, *Topografía de Córdoba almohade*, pp. 91–107; M. A. Khallaf, *Qurṭuba al-islamiyya*, pp. 47–53 gives a total of 93 mosques. Some corrections and additions to this list based on a recently published source in M. J. Viguera, 'Referencias a mezquitas de Qurṭuba en la obra de al-Marwānī', pp. 11–29. The archaeological knowledge of these mosques has grown extensively in recent years, C. González Gutiérrez, *Las mezquitas de barrio de Madinat Qurtuba*, pp. 34–52.

Within the walls of the medina of Córdoba, I have been able to identify fifteen mosques, including the famous Friday mosque, built by the Umayyad rulers. Many of these mosques were founded by renowned figures, which indicates how a Muslim 'evergetism' was widely extended among ruling classes.[13] For example, the Ṭālūt b. 'Abd al- Jabbār mosque had been founded by this *faqīh* from the time of al-Ḥakam I. Another mosque was named after the Cordoban *qāḍī* Ibn Abī 'Īsā (d. 950/339 AH), who was an influential and affluent member of a family with Berber origins.[14] The Abū 'Uthmān mosque, to the north of the *alcázar*, had perhaps received this name from a renowned client who had helped the first Umayyad emir win power; it was used as a substitute for the main mosque when 'Abd al-Raḥmān II began a programme of extension works in this building. Other mosques within the medina were linked to members of the Umayyad administration; this was the case with the Surayj mosque, Surayj being one of al-Ḥakam I's eunuchs, while the al-Muṣḥafī mosque had probably been founded by Ja'far al-Muṣḥafī, the vizier of al-Ḥakam II. However, it is not so easy to identify Abū 'Allaqa, whose mosque was next to the New Gate, or Ṣawwāb, whose name is associated with a mosque located close to a synagogue in ruins.[15]

[13] Aside from the mosques that are cited in the footnotes that accompany this chapter, these mosques were as follows: Badr mosque; Abū 'Allaqa mosque (next to the New Gate); Sa'īd al-Khayr mosque; the Perfumists' or al-Saqqā' Mosque (next to the perfumists' souk, perhaps the same as the Abū Hārūn mosque); Ibn Khālid mosque; Ṭarafa mosque. References: Ibn Bashkuwāl, *Ṣila*, n. 812; M. J. Viguera, 'Referencias a mezquitas', pp. 19–21; Ibn al-Faraḍī, *Ta'rīkh*, n. 666 and J. Zanón, pp. 94–5; Ibn Ḥayyān, *Muqtabis 2.2*, ed. p. 132; Ibn Sahl, *Aḥkām*, ed. p. 425 and 599; trans. p. 173.

[14] On the Ṭālūt mosque, Ibn Ḥayyān, *Muqtabis II, 1*, ed. cit. p. 156; trans. cit. p. 68. On the *qāḍī* Ibn Abī 'Īsā, Ibn Bashkuwāl, *Ṣila*, n. 423. M. Marín, 'Una familia de ulemas cordobeses: los Banū Abī 'Īsā', pp. 291–320. This mosque was in the vicinity of the houses of the Banū 'Abd al-Jabbār.

[15] On the Abū 'Uthmān mosque, Ibn Ḥayyān, *Muqtabis II, 1*, ed. pp. 207 and 425; trans. pp. 110 and 289; al-Maqqarī, *Nafḥ*, I, p. 376. On the Surayj mosque, Ibn Ḥayyān, *Muqtabis II, 1*, ed. p. 233; trans. p. 132. Ibn Ḥazm, *Jamhara*, p. 96. On the al-Muṣḥafī mosque, J. Zanón, *Topografía de Córdoba almohade*, p. 99. On the Abū 'Allaqa mosque, *Prosopografía de los ulemas de al-Andalus*, no. 5.596 with the biography of the legal scholar who died in 927 and was muezzin there; J. Zanón, *Topografía*, pp. 94–5. On the Ṣawwāb mosque, M. J. Viguera, 'Referencias a mezquitas', p. 23; Ibn Sahl, *Aḥkām al-kubrā*, ed. p. 599; trans. p. 173. The 'Abd Allāh al-Balansī mosque was probably linked to a member of the Umayyad family; who was a a son of emir 'Abd al-Raḥmān I. This mosque was located in the neighbourhood (*ḥawma*) with the same name, in Abān Square (*raḥba*), near the 'Abd al-Jabbār's Gate, Ibn Sahl, *Aḥkām al-kubrā*, ed. p. 275; M. J. Viguera, 'Referencias a mezquitas', p. 20. This is the same mosque as that cited as *masjid raḥbat Abān*, J. Zanón, *Topografía*, pp. 96–7 and 101. Possibly, al-Khushanī, *Quḍāt Qurṭuba*, ed. and trans. pp. 47 and 57, although on this occasion the square is given the name 'Abd Allāh al-Balansī.

Mosques shaped their surrounding urban spaces, and urban districts were named after them. Each mosque was the centre of a *ḥawma* or neighbourhood, hence there was a *ḥawma* for the Friday mosque and one for the 'Abbād mosque. Notarial compilations confirm this, as they include models of documents stating that a particular house was located 'in the neighbourhood (*ḥawma*) of so-and-so mosque'.[16] These local mosques played an important role within the configuration of urban space, which was linked to mechanisms of social control. The religious authorities recommended prayers be performed as near as possible to wherever a person lived or worked, whereby a degree of control was exercised over those who were habitual attendees at prayers in a certain oratory and those who were not. Likewise, conducting Friday prayers in one's own house or in shops was frowned upon unless there was a good justification.[17]

It is difficult to know exactly who lived in the medina of Córdoba, but the sources give the impression that this walled precinct was a privileged residential zone populated by influential *'ulamā'*, senior civil servants and members of the Umayyad family.[18] Indeed, 'Abd al-Raḥmān III gave his sons houses in the medina, which, it will be recalled, formed part of his policy of distancing them from the *alcázar* when they reached majority. From then on, they had a residence in Córdoba (referred to as a *qaṣr*), a *munya* on the outskirts of the city and rural estates, whose revenues permitted them to live with sufficient ease without any need to become embroiled in political intrigues. However, to ensure that all his sons had houses in the city, 'Abd al-Raḥmān III had to buy a number of properties from distant relations; these were residences that had been bequeathed to other branches of the family in accordance with

[16] Ibn Sahl, *Al-Aḥkām al-kubrā*, ed. cit. p. 425. Ibn al-'Aṭṭār *K. al-Wathā'iq*, ed. pp. 117, 192, 357, 359, 371; trans. pp. 240, 346, 579, 581, 593. R. Pinilla, 'Jurisprudencia y ciudad', p. 564. I think the name invoked in the 'Abbād mosque must have been linked to the Banū 'Abādil, who are cited as the owners of a house inside the medina, see below, n. 19.

[17] Ibn 'Abd al-Ra'ūf, *Risāla fī adāb al-ḥisba wa l-muḥtasib*, ed. pp. 73 and 75; trans. pp. 19 and 22.

[18] The family of the renowned legal scholar 'Īsā b. Dīnār (d. 212 AH), which was of Arab origin, lived in the Main Street (*al-zuqāq al-kabīr*), L. Molina, 'Familias andalusíes', p. 48. Next to the *Bāb 'Āmir* there was a house built by 'Abd al-Raḥmān II, who gave it to his son Muḥammad, who lived there before inheriting the throne; he had as his neighbours a court astrologer and a scholar. The house, which had a bath, was later passed on to his son, emir 'Abd Allāh, and subsequently to the latter's grandson, caliph al-Nāṣir. Ibn Ḥayyān, *Muqtabis V*, p. 10; also, *Muqtabis II, 1*, ed. cit. pp. 398–9; trans. cit. pp. 264–5. Ibn al-Qūṭiya, ed. p. 79; trans. James pp. 113–14.

the inheritance regulations stipulated by Muslim law, which facilitated the dispersal of real estate.[19]

A further indication that Córdoba's medina was populated by the great and the good is the fact that during the time of al-Ḥakam II important visitors were provided with accommodation there. For example, following the arrival of Ja'far b. al-Andalusī and his brother Yaḥyā in Córdoba, they were given accommodation in the houses of a certain Qāsim b. Ya'ish and the Banū Hāshim family, the first of which had been left to the caliph in a will, while he had purchased the second. In addition, some of the embassies sent to the caliph were lodged in residences in the medina, such as the houses of the Banū Ghānim, which at some stage must have belonged to this family of high-ranking officials.[20]

The residences owned by senior statesmen in Córdoba's medina illustrate the power of attraction exercised by the Umayyad's *alcázar*, which had traditionally been the seat of power. The *alcázar* was located in the south-western

[19] Thus, the house received by Sulaymān b. 'Abd al-Raḥmān al-Nāṣir had been the property of the Banū 'Abādil family, from whose ownership it was passed on to 'Abd al-Raḥmān II. He reformed it for one of his sons, and it was inherited by his descendants until 'Abd al-Raḥmān III bought it and left it to this son Sulaymān. The one received by al-Mughīra had belonged to al-Ḥakam I, who transferred it to one of his sons, whereby it remained in his family: it must have been bought by 'Abd al-Raḥmān III, who also acquired another adjacent house from the heirs of a son of 'Abd al-Raḥmān II, Ibn Ḥayyān, *Muqtabis V*, ed. and trans. pp. 6–11. The same policy regarding the treatment of sons excluded from the inheritance of the throne had been followed by emir Muḥammad, M. Penelas and L. Molina, 'Dos fragmentos inéditos del volumen II del Muqtabis de Ibn Ḥayyān', pp. 238–41. The Arabic word *qaṣr* (pl. *quṣūr*) was used in the sense of a private residence akin to a palace. Ibn Ḥazm refers to how it was inappropriate to discuss in public those 'affairs conducted among [Muslims] and their families in the intimacy of the *quṣūr*, which have no place in any account', Ibn Ḥazm, *Ṭawq al-ḥamāma*, ed. and trans. pp. 20 and 21. For example, it was in the *quṣūr* that the wives kept by aristocratic families (*ahl al-buyūtāt*) lived, ibid., pp. 66 and 67.

[20] Ibn Ḥayyān, *Muqtabis VII*, ed. and trans. pp. 105 and 134, refers to the house owned by the Banū Ghānim in the medina, but in pp. 176 and 214 he mentions the house of Muḥammad b. Walīd b. Ghānim and the house of 'Umar b. Ghānim as being distinct. E. García Gómez, 'Notas sobre la topografía cordobesa', p. 368. Muḥammad b. Walīd b. Ghānim was a vizier, who was removed from office in 912 (300 AH), which is also when his son 'Umar was dismissed from his post as *ṣāḥib al-arḍ*, Ibn 'Idhārī, *al-Bayān*, II, ed. cit. pp. 159–60. This family descended from a *mawlā* of 'Abd al-Raḥmān I called Ghānim, M. Fierro, 'Mawālī', p. 82. Other houses used as residences for embassies were: the house of Yūsuf b. 'Alī b. Sulaymān, known as Ibn al-Bayyānī; the house of Ibn Umayya, in the medina; the house of Muḥammad b. Ṭarafa, close to the cemeteries of the Banū 'Āmir and the Banū Badr respectively; the house of Ziyād al-Waṣīf, close to al-Ghadīr; and the house of Sa'd in the suburb of the Mu'ta mosque, Ibn Ḥayyān, *Muqtabis VII*, ed. and trans. pp. 44, 52, 148, 109 and 200; trans. pp. 64, 71, 187–8, 139–40 and 241.

corner of the medina, where part of the episcopal palace stands today just in front of the main mosque. It stood on the site of a previous Visigothic palace or *Balāṭ*. This building went on to become the residence of the first Arab governors and was later made into the *alcázar* of emirs.[21] Under the Umayyads, the *alcázar* was developed into a complex range of lodgings and buildings, where the sovereigns resided and gave audiences, and which were also used by part of the caliphal administration.[22]

The relationship between the Umayyad *alcázar* and Córdoba's urban landscape is reflected in the location and use of the gates that gave access to the palace complex. Although data provided by the sources is not as coherent as one might wish, it is certain there were six entrances to the *alcázar*.[23] The most important of these was the Azuda Gate (*Bāb al-Sudda*), which was located within the southern wall of the palace precinct and had been renovated by 'Abd al-Raḥmān II. This gate was converted into a symbol of the Umayyads' authority; 'seek refuge at the Azuda Gate' or 'bring a rebel to the Azuda Gate' were commonly-used expressions by Umayyad writers to signify a chieftain's subjugation to Umayyad authority.[24]

The Azuda Gate was crowned by a large roof terrace (*saṭḥ*) which offered impressive views over the river and the *al-raṣīf* that ran past below. Many rebels or enemy Christians ended their days here, crucified with their bodies bristling with arrows 'like a hedgehog', or their heads stuck on pikes

21 M. Acién Almansa and A. Vallejo Triano, 'Urbanismo y estado islámico', pp. 110–11. C. Aillet, 'Islamisation et évolution du peuplement chrétien en al-Andalus (VIIIe-IXe siècle)', p. 168. The same happened with the *Balāṭ Mughīth*, which was the residence of the city's conqueror, Mughīth al-Rūmī, located not far from the Bridge Gate, *Akhbār Majmū'a*, ed. and trans. p. 21; trans. James, p. 53.

22 It is hard to get a sense of the interior of this palace complex due to the fact that subsequent building work has modified its appearance beyond recognition. It is only possible to trace remnants of it in the existing outer walls, through archaeological studies undertaken in the building, as well as the data provided by literary sources.

23 For the number of the *alcázar*'s gates the historians have tended to draw on the testimony given by al-Maqqarī, who in turn took his information from Ibn Bashquwāl, *Nafḥ al-Ṭīb* I, pp. 464–5. However, as was pointed out by García Gómez, this text is corrupt and of little use, *Notas de topografía*, p. 325, n. 9. More reliable and closer in date is the text by al-'Udhrī, which cites six gates listed in a clockwise direction: *bāb al-Sudda; bāb al-Jinān; bāb al-'Adl; bāb al-Ṣinā'; bāb al-Mulk* and *bāb al-Sābāṭ*, *Tarṣī al-akhbār*, ed. p. 123.

24 'But later he decided to take up residence in the Azuda Gate of the Prince of the Faithful with his wives and children to enjoy the peace and calm', Ibn Ḥayyān, *Muqtabis VII*, ed. p. 41 (also p. 176); trans. p. 62 (also p. 215). A use of this expression in official correspondence ibid., ed. p. 100; trans. p. 128.

as a symbol of victory.[25] It was not uncommon to see the Umayyad sovereign looking out from this terrace, for a variety of reasons. He would inspect the repair work being undertaken on the bridge over the Guadalquivir from there and pester the builders with a constant stream of instructions. Likewise, it was from this rooftop that he and his son, Hishām, supervised the distribution of alms in June 975 (364 AH), as well as the departure of the troops sent to reinforce the besieged fortress of Gormaz. On one occasion, in the street (*mahajja*) just beneath this terrace, a form of tourney was held between knights who fought one another while the caliph looked on. In addition, alongside this gate was the building that housed the office (*kursī*) of the *ṣāḥib al-madīna* of Córdoba. The grand ceremonial processions that arrived in Córdoba crossed the bridge over the Guadalquivir and then turned left on reaching the Bridge Gate. Finally, they made their way along the *alcazar*'s perimeter wall to parade past the Azuda Gate, where either the *ṣāḥib al-madīna* was visible in an upstairs room, or else one of his representatives.[26]

The Gardens Gate (*bāb al-Jinān*) was also located along the *alcazar*'s southern façade, again overlooking the road and the river; it too had a roof terrace where a representative of the *ṣāḥib al-madīna* would be stationed on public occasions. This gate was again built by Emir ʿAbd al-Raḥmān II, who equipped it with a fountain and a marble basin to provide the people with running water. It was through this gate that the troops departed en route to tackling the Norman threat in June 972 (*Ramaḍān* 361 AH). On leaving the gate, they turned to the right, continued along the *Muṣāra* or grand esplanade, from where they took the road that ran alongside the *Munyat al-Nāʿūra*. The same route had been taken a decade earlier by King Ordoño IV of León, when he had travelled to Córdoba to request al-Ḥakam II's support in his conflict

[25] Ibn Ḥayyān, *Muqtabis II, 1*, ed. cit. p. 280; trans. cit. p. 172; the reference to a body riddled with arrows by archers that 'was left tied to a post like a hedgehog for various days' in Ibn Ḥayyān, *Muqtabis* V, ed. and trans. pp. 130–1 and 138; Ibn Ḥayyān, *Muqtabis* VII, ed. cit. pp. 65, 143, 220, 223, 233; trans. cit. pp. 78, 180, 261, 264, 275; L. Torres Balbas, 'Bāb al-Sudda y las azudas de la España medieval', *al-Andalus*, 17, 1 (1952), pp. 165–75; M. Fierro, 'Violencia, política y religión en al-Andalus', pp. 41, 45, 53, 61–3, etc.

[26] Ibn Ḥayyān, *Muqtabis VII*, ed. cit. pp. 46, 194–5; trans. cit. pp. 65 and 236–7. It should be noted that the *ṣāḥib al-madīna* remained in charge of the *alcázar* while the caliph was absent, Ibn Ḥayyān, *Muqtabis V*, ed. and trans. pp. 40, 56, 128, 161, 187, 213.

against his cousin, Sancho I. His entourage passed along this side of the *alcázar* until it reached the Gardens Gate, where the king requested permission to visit the tomb of Caliph 'Abd al-Raḥmān III, which was located within the palace precinct in a cemetery called *rawḍa*, where all Umayyad sovereigns were buried.[27]

In contrast to the *alcazar*'s two principal southern entrances and their role in protocol, the opposite northern façade of the palace precinct had just one gate, which was referred to as the *bāb al-Ṣinā'*; it was usually kept shut and may well have led to the streets surrounding the medina.[28] An anecdote told about the renowned legal scholar Abū Ibrāhīm Isḥāq al-Tujībī recounts how he would often teach his pupils in the Abū 'Uthmān mosque, located close to the northern edge of the *alcázar*. On one occasion, the caliph ordered a eunuch to bring the scholar to him to address an urgent issue. Abū Ibrāhīm not only kept the messenger waiting until he had finished teaching his class, but also stated that he would not walk all the way round to the Azuda Gate. As the *bāb al-Ṣinā'* was closed, the messenger had to have it opened before the arrogant Abū Ibrāhīm would consent to visit the caliph.[29]

The eastern side of the *alcázar* precinct looked onto the main mosque and it had two gates, which provided the sovereign with access to the temple. One of them was known as the *bāb al-Mulk*, the other as the *bāb al-Sābāṭ*. The latter led to a passageway that ran directly from the *alcázar* to the oratory,

[27] Ibn Ḥayyān, *Muqtabis II, 1*, ed. p. 280; trans. pp. 171–2; Ibn Ḥayyān, *Muqtabis VII*, ed. pp. 78–9; trans. p. 102. al-Maqqarī, *Nafḥ*, I, p. 389. On the balustrade of the Gardens Gate stood the son of Ja'far al-Muṣḥafī on the day of the reception of the Banū al-Andalusī, Ibn Ḥayyān, *Muqtabis VII*, ed. p. 46; trans. p. 66.

[28] This gate would later be known as the Bath Gate (*Bāb al-Ḥammam*), after the bath house built in the later caliphal era, whose archaeological remains can be seen today in the Plaza de los Santos Mártires, A. Montejo, J. A. Garriguet and A. M. Zamorano, 'El alcázar andalusí de Córdoba y su entorno urbano', pp. 167-168.

[29] al-Maqqarī, *Nafḥ*, I, pp. 376–9. This gate is also mentioned in Ibn Ḥayyān, *Muqtabis II, 1*, ed. p. 281; trans. p. 172. Another mention of individuals moving around the medina of Córdoba in the direction to the *alcázar* is provided by the account of the rise to power of emir Muḥammad following his father's death, 'Abd al-Raḥmān II: various palace servants plotted to ensure he was transferred from his house to the *alcázar* at night, thereby evading any possible machinations by his brother and rival, 'Abd Allāh, whose residence was next to the Bridge Gate, and was unaware of the emir's death. Muḥammad lived next to the 'Āmir's Gate and had to leave his house disguised as a woman, and head for the Bridge Gate of the medina, which his acolytes opened for him, thereby evading the guards stationed at his brother's house; from there, he entered the *alcázar* through the Gardens Gate, but not without having first persuaded the gatekeeper on duty to let him pass, Ibn al-Qūṭiya, *Ta'rīkh*, ed. pp. 79-82; trans. James, pp. 113–15.

which allowed the sovereign to attend prayers without having to cross the street. When al-Ḥakam II undertook the extension of the mosque, this passageway had to be rebuilt to adapt it to the new location of the space reserved for the caliph within the mosque, known as the *maqṣūra*.[30] The western side of the *alcázar* looked onto another emblematic landmark of the Cordoban cityscape: the city's grand souk. However, there was no gateway to the Umayyads' palace on this side, and the market was located at the base of the western wall.

The proximity of the *alcázar* to the main market of the city is one of the features of the urban landscape of Umayyad Córdoba that deserves to be described in some detail. The *alcazar*'s sixth gate – the *bāb al-ʿAdl*, also known as the *bāb al-Jadīd*, or New Gate – was also on the far side of the southern wall, which thus had three points of access. This gate also had a fountain (*fawwāra*), built by ʿAbd al-Raḥmān III, which underscored the image of Umayyad power as a provider of abundance for those who wished to draw near.[31] It was through this New Gate, *bāb al-Jadīd*, that al-Ḥakam II entered the *alcázar* on Sunday, 28 March 975 (12 *Rajab* 364 AH), having definitively left Madīnat al-Zahrā'. As has already been discussed, having been absent from public life following his stroke, the caliph wished to show himself to his subjects by entering the *alcázar* where he could be seen by all. He came from the *Munyat al-Nāʿūra*, where he had performed the midday prayer in the company of a number of senior dignitaries, and he then entered the city through the Seville Gate, a very busy place and 'a meeting place for women'.[32] Having made his way from there, the caliph crossed the souk's main street, where he was welcomed by the *ṣāḥib al-sūq* along with the wealthiest people

[30] G. Pizarro Berengena, 'Los pasadizos elevados', pp. 239–46.

[31] The sources discuss the *alcázar*'s Garden Gate as being the central one on the southern side of the *alcázar*, which confirms the existence of three gates along this façade of the palace, Ibn Ḥayyān, *Muqtabis II, 2*, ed. cit. p. 117. Ibn Ḥayyān, *Muqtabis VII*, ed. cit. p. 45; trans. cit. pp. 64–5. The building of a fountain at this gate in *Crónica anónima*, ed. and trans. p. 57; trans. p. 126. C. Mazzoli Guintard, 'Du puits au cadi', pp. 110–12. Likewise, the same caliph ordered that the road leading from this gate to the so-called *Munyat al-Ramla*, in the eastern part of Córdoba, was to be laid with cobbles, Ibn Ḥayyān, *Muqtabis V*, ed. and trans. pp. 287–8.

[32] Ibn Ḥazm, *Ṭawq al-ḥamāma*, ed. and trans. pp. 72–3, highlights this aspect in relation to his celebrated account of the poet al-Ramādī, who fell in love with a woman he saw there. The Seville Gate was also known as the Perfumists Gate as it was close to their shops.

of Córdoba, who applauded the caliph's presence as he made his way to the *alcázar*, entering through the 'New Gate'.[33]

We should pause briefly to examine the souk's main street (*al-mahajja al-'uẓmā*), which al-Ḥakam II crossed on that March day. Despite its importance, the studies devoted to the city have, curiously enough, viewed this place, the true hub of social and material exchange, as being of little importance. Created shortly after the Arab conquest, Córdoba's grand souk (*al-sūq al-kubrā*) adhered to a model of urban development that was common in medieval Islamic cities and integrated the principal mosque and market into a space close to the residence of power. In the case of Córdoba, as we have just seen, the Umayyads' *alcázar* and the Friday mosque were located in front of one another; however, the market underwent a significant change of location. Its initial site had been in the Secunda suburb, across the bridge, on the left bank of the Guadalquivir, thereby forming a clearly recognisable triangle with the *alcázar* and the mosque of the Umayyads. Then, in 818 (202 AH), those living in this suburb rebelled against Emir al-Ḥakam I, and nearly brought his reign to an end. The emir responded by inflicting a harsh wave of repression; he executed the leaders of the uprising and banished the suburb's population. The suburb and its markets were razed to the ground, and al-Ḥakam I gave orders that nothing was ever to be built on their ruins. As a result of this order, the decision was taken to transfer the souk to the land alongside the western wall of the *alcázar*.[34]

Due to this change of location, the previous configuration of the mosque and *alcázar* linked to the market by the bridge was replaced by a contiguous arrangement of these three urban landmarks alongside the same bank of the Guadalquivir. The market was sited at the foot of the *alcazar*'s western wall, whereby to get to the mosque from the souk one had to follow the wall of the *alcázar* round. The seat of Umayyad power thus became an unavoidable urban landmark that conditioned the movement of people and goods through the

[33] A few years later, this gate was bricked up on the order of Ja'far b. 'Uthmān, in order to control the comings and goings of the palace staff, Ibn 'Idhārī, *al-Bayān*, II, ed. cit. p. 280. I identify this gate with the one that has been excavated on the ground floor of the Garaje Alcázar, Gerencia Municipal de Urbanismo de Córdoba, *Plan Especial Alcázar-Caballerizas Reales. Anexo I: Estudio Histórico Arqueológico*, fig. 38 (I am grateful to Juan Murillo for information about this and for having shown me this excavation).

[34] Ibn Ḥayyān, *Muqtabis II, 1*, ed. cit. pp. 164–5; trans. cit. p. 75.

south-western section of the city. Despite being far from ideal, the new location ensured the close and regular supply of goods and services for those who lived and worked in the *alcázar*. It is also highly possible that the souk was located on vacant plots of land owned by the Umayyad sovereigns, whereby the market traders and craftsmen who had shops in the souk had to pay rent to their rulers.[35]

In the caliphal era, the souk was crossed by a main street, the aforementioned *al-mahajja al-ʿuẓmā*, along which a range of shops were to be found. It stretched from the Seville Gate in the city wall and extended as far as the Post House (*Dār al-Burud*), which was at the end of the market beside the *alcázar*. This was an old building dating back to the time of ʿAbd al-Raḥmān I and it housed the administration's postal service. In July 936 (*Shāʿban* 324 AH), this building and the rest of the souk were engulfed by a serious fire. The fire started in the wool dealers' (*al-ṣawwāfīn*) and perfumists' (*al-ʿaṭṭārīn*) shops, which were located next to the Seville Gate and the neighbouring Abū Hārūn mosque, which was also destroyed. The fire extended through the silk merchants' (*al-ḥarrārīn*) and the bakers' (*al-shaqqaqīn*) shops, before reaching the Post House, which was likewise fodder for the flames. The disaster must have been immense, but a few months later Caliph ʿAbd al-Raḥmān III gave orders for work to begin rebuilding all the damaged buildings: the mosque, the shops and the Post House.

Some decades later, in November 971 (*Muḥarram* 361 AH), al-Ḥakam II issued a decree ordering a major extension of Córdoba's souk. The Post House lost its administrative role and was re-assigned as the silk merchants'

[35] The relationship between the western perimeter of Córdoba's city wall and the wall enclosing the Umayyad *alcázar* is a complex problem. Some authors consider that the Seville Gate opened directly onto the *alcázar* precinct, and it is shown like this on many maps, A. Montejo, J. A. Garriguet and A. M. Zamorano, 'El alcázar andalusí de Córdoba y su entorno urbano', p. 166. However, textual evidence makes it clear that there was a space between the *alcázar* and the Seville Gate, which was filled by the souk. Where this space was exactly located is not easy to determine. One possible solution is that the *alcazar*'s west wall crossed the square that is today known as Santo Campo de los Mártires, whereby the souk would have been located in the remainder of the plaza, so that the Seville Gate would have been located on the western side of the city wall. This is the most reasonable solution, and it explains how the souk was linked to the main mosque by a street that led from the northern edge of the square, as is the case today with Calle de Tomás Conde. However, a problem has been raised by the bath house that has been excavated in this square, which seems to have been part of the *alcázar* complex. Furthermore, an exterior wall has been excavated close to the bath house, and this undoubtedly formed part of the *alcázar*. Thereby one has to consider the solution set out in figure 7. Although this is not a fully satisfactory solution, it is the only possible one given the available data.

market, which provided additional space for the shops of the textile traders (*al-bazzāzīn*). The caliphate's postal services were moved to the building that had until then been used for the stables (*Dār al-Zawāmil*), located next to the *Muṣāra*, the large esplanade outside the city walls. The stables were in turn moved to the area surrounding the *Munyat al-Nāʿūra*. A few months later, in February 972, the caliph gave the order to widen the main street of the souk due to a number of shops spilling over into the road, which created bottlenecks as the crowds of shoppers tried to get past.[36]

The souk's main street, which led to the *alcázar*'s west wall, was taken up by a flourishing textiles market and perfumers' shops. One could find merchants selling cloth priced at twenty-four dinars – a very high price – as well as perfumes, spices and unguents made with herbs, some of which were brought from as far afield as India.[37] Another zone of the souk was the butchers' markets (*al-qaṣṣābīn*), located alongside the river, into which they would discard unwanted scraps of meat. This part of the market would be inundated in the event of the river flooding, as we saw happened in 974 (363 AH). During the reign of Emir ʿAbd al-Raḥmān II, a murder was committed in this part of the souk, and, as previously discussed, it was solved thanks to the detective skills of the then *ṣāḥib al-madīna*, Muḥammad b. Sālim. One of the decisions taken by this Muḥammad as part of his brilliant investigation was to display the cadaver on the road running by the river so that it could be seen by passers-by with the intention that someone might identify it.[38]

Not far from the butchers' shops were the dyers' workshops, which also suffered when the Guadalquivir flooded in December 1008 (399 AH). The shops of the leather workers must have been located close by. One of the devout deeds undertaken by Caliph al-Ḥakam II following his stroke was to establish a pious legacy with the income generated by these leather workers' (*al-sarrājīn*) shops. The caliph decreed that this income was to be used to pay the salaries of the teachers who taught religion to the children of the city's

36 Ibn Ḥayyān, *Muqtabis V*, ed. and trans. p. 259; *Muqtabis VII*, ed. and trans. pp. 66 and 70–1; pp. 87 and 93.

37 Some apothecaries defrauded their clients by mixing Indian spices with local ones, Ibn ʿAbd al-Raʾūf, *Risāla fī adāb al-ḥisba wa l-muḥtasib*, ed. É. Lévi-Provençal, p. 86; trans. R. Arié, pp. 36–7.

38 Ibn Ḥayyān, *Muqtabis VII*, ed. and trans. pp. 144–5; 183–4; Ibn al-Qūṭiya, *Taʾrīkh*, ed. pp. 69–70; trans. James p. 103; al-Khushanī, *Quḍāt Qurṭuba*, ed. and trans. pp. 164–5 and 203–4.

poor. However, this legacy would not last long: a few decades later the leather workers' shops were destroyed during the civil war.[39]

Another profession linked to the handling of animal skins was that of the parchmenters (*al-raqqaqīn*), and the neighbourhood surrounding these shops, just outside the Seville Gate, took its name from their trade. Their parchment was in great demand from the administrative departments in the *alcázar*, which explains why these craftsmen were located so close by. During this period, the church of Saint Acisclus was still located in this area. It housed the remains of a Cordoban martyr, who had died during the persecutions ordered by the Roman Emperor Diocletian.[40] Other groups of traders encountered in the souk were the barbers (*mashshāṭīn*) and lathers (*kharrāṭīn*), whose shops were destroyed by the fire in 918 (305 AH). It is probable that the timber merchants (*al-jashshābīn*) were to be found to the north of the main street; as will be discussed below, one of their products was the wooden ladders, which played a role in the downfall of the caliphate of Córdoba.[41]

Therefore, in Córdoba's main souk, there were a variety artisans and merchants selling a range of products (*aṣḥāb al-ṣināʿāt wa-tabaqāt al-tujjār*).[42] Remarkably, the spatial arrangement of the largest market of caliphal Córdoba can be mapped out with considerable precision. We also have a wealth of information about its bustling activity thanks to a text written around the time of al-Hakam II by Ibn ʿAbd al-Ra'ūf, a senior figure in the caliphal administration, who had served as *ṣāḥib al-madīna* and vizier in the time of ʿAbd al-Raḥmān III.[43] His work on the administration of the souk covers

[39] Ibn Ḥayyān, *Muqtabis VII*, ed. and trans. pp. 207 and 247; al-Nuwayrī, ed. and trans. pp. 77 and 71. One of the shops in the Shabulār suburb was given to a poet by emir ʿAbd al-Raḥmān II, and he rented it out for two dinars a month, Ibn Ḥayyān, *Muqtabis*, ed. cit. p. 338; trans. cit. p. 218.

[40] On the dyers' shops, Ibn ʿIdhārī, *al-Bayān*, III, ed. Lévi-Provençal, p. 105; trans. F. Maíllo, p. 97. They are referred to by al-ʿUdhrī, ed. p. 122. On Saint Acisclus, *Calendario de Córdoba*, ed. and trans. p. 167. *Akhbār*, ed. pp. 12–14; trans. James, pp. 52–3. In the emirate period, Saint Acisclus was the name of a neighbourhood (*ḥawma*), Ibn Ḥayyān, *Muqtabis II, 1*, ed. cit. p. 269; trans. cit. p. 165. It was also known as the 'Church of the Prisoners', due to a celebrated episode of the Arab conquest that took place there. The location of the parchmenters' suburb near to the Perfumers' or Seville Gate and a palm plantation in R. Pinilla, 'Jurisprudencia y ciudad', pp. 565–6. On the timber merchants, Ibn ʿIdhārī, *al-Bayān*, III, ed. cit. p. 57; trans. cit. p. 61.

[41] Ibn Ḥayyān, *Muqtabis V*, p. 94.

[42] Ibn Ḥayyān, *Muqtabis VII*, ed. p. 20; trans. p. 44.

[43] P. Chalmeta, *El zoco medieval*, p. 480. Further information can be added to that provided by this author. He was a descendant of a *mawlā* of caliph Marwān I, and one of his ancestors had been *qāḍī* under ʿUmar II. Having settled in al-Andalus, his family had undertaken a range of roles for

numerous subjects ranging from rules to avoid the stockpiling of products to methods of controlling prices, and also how to monitor the legitimate use of weights and measures. Ibn ʿAbd al-Raʾūf describes the tricks and malpractices of bakers, grain merchants, bakers, perfumers, milk sellers (they mixed milk with water), butchers (who sold goat's meat as lamb), fishermen, fruit sellers, cheese makers, mat makers, cobblers, furriers, oil merchants, honey traders and cooked and fried food sellers (the vendors of the latter would use poor-quality oil); he also indicates how they should be apprehended and punished. The insistence placed on the cleanliness of the shops (especially the fishmongers' and butchers'), the storage of products away from flies and the transparency of transactions confirms, once more, the Umayyad administration's concern to protect the interests (*ṣalāḥ*) of the Muslims.

The sound management of the souk also involved a set of by-laws, such as the prohibition on people sitting in circles in the street, unless they were trustworthy people, or the obligation to transport rubbish outside the city. The ceramics sellers had to avoid laying their wares out in the middle of the street so as not to bother passers-by, and likewise the fruit sellers and mat makers were required not to discard waste in the street. The streets swarmed with jugglers, conjurers, fake beggars, amulet sellers and storytellers (*quṣṣāṣ*), and a close eye had to be kept on all of them. The latter, the storytellers, were not allowed to tell stories about the Prophet Muḥammad due to their ignorance on this subject, but there was no problem if they told tales about the Israelites, presumably biblical stories. Likewise, the musicians were prohibited from singing on the streets, especially at times when sermons on Holy War were being preached, or when preparations were being made for the pilgrimage to Mecca.[44]

The souk's wealth of activity gave rise to a vibrant urban space right alongside the walls of the Umayyads' *alcázar*. In contrast to the solemnity that those in power sought to display at the Bāb al-Sudda, one had only to cross over to the other side of the *alcázar* to come face to face with a world

the emirs, including a number of provincial governorships, M. A. Makki, notes in the ed. of Ibn Ḥayyān, *Muqtabis II, 2*, pp. 401–2; also M. I. Fierro, 'Los mawālī de ʿAbd al-Raḥmān I', p. 81. Another two relatives undertook important roles during the caliphal era: Ibn Ḥayyān, *Muqtabis V*, ed. and trans. pp. 304 and 313; and pp. 318 and 328.

[44] Ibn ʿAbd al-Raʿūf, *Risāla fī adāb al-ḥisba wa l-muḥtasib*, ed. pp. 88 and 89; trans. p. 200. On the 'urban atmosphere' and the various prohibitions, ed. pp. 110–14; trans. pp. 360–3.

in which the merchants' shops invaded the public space, in which wandering poets recited compositions that might scandalise the pious, or where the slightest distraction meant an opportunity to steal a valuable item of merchandise.[45] The urban world that arose in the shadow of the *alcázar* of the Umayyads thus embraced a sensational paradox: on the one hand, it provided a social base for the dynasty, but on the other, it offered the greatest threat to the order it represented.

Almunias, Mosques, Cemeteries and Suburbs

The impact of caliphal power on the configuration of Córdoba's urban spaces and their social fabric is especially visible in the large urban zones that grew up outside the medina. While these areas had barely been urbanised prior to the Arab conquest, it was here that a number of suburbs emerged during the Umayyad period, whereby the city overflowed the medina's walled perimeter. The growth of these suburbs was by no means anarchic. Their genesis was underpinned by some form of intervention: the establishment of a *munya*, the foundation of a mosque, and even genuine urban planning. However, over time these suburbs formed their own dynamics that enriched the city's social fabric. Just as Córdoba's medina gravitated around the *alcázar*, the mosques and souk, the suburbs were structured around the residences of the powerful, the places of prayer and the spaces of exchange.[46] A distinctive factor that shaped the configuration of these suburbs, and that was absent within the medina, was the creation of cemeteries, which grew up outside the city at the same rate as the city itself. They were founded along the roads branching out from the urban walls and soon surrounded the whole city. The creation of the suburbs was thereby moulded by Muslim necropolises, which imposed insurmountable limits for new buildings and in turn configured a wholly discontinuous urban landscape.[47]

The peri-urban *almunias* played a seminal role in the initial formation of the suburbs of Córdoba, as they established centres of demand that fostered the

[45] See the history of the perfume seller who recounted how he was robbed of all the merchandise he had intended to sell at the fair that was held on the day before the Feast of the Sacrifice, Ibn Ḥayyān, *Muqtabis* V, ed. and trans. pp. 302–3.

[46] M. Acién Almansa and A. Vallejo Triano, 'Urbanismo y estado islámico', p. 127. F. J. Murillo, M. T. Casal and E. Castro, 'Madīnat Qurṭuba', pp. 257–81.

[47] J. F. Murillo et al. 'La transición de la *civitas* clásica cristianizada a la *madina* islámica', pp. 540–3.

production and distribution of products, goods and services. In the Umayyad period, an *almunia* was a walled property belonging to the ruling class. It had a residential area, the *qaṣr* or *alcázar*, and another area, known as *faḥṣ*, that was used for growing crops, grazing livestock or as gardens.[48] Depending on the relationship between the *faḥṣ* and the *qaṣr*, the *almunia* might combine productive and recreational roles. For example, the aforementioned *Munyat al-Rummāniyya* encompassed land farmed by slaves, and could also accommodate the caliph, his son and their entourage for a day in the countryside. The same must have happened with the *Munyat al-Buntīlī*, to the east of Córdoba. It would probably have had an area dedicated to growing crops, yet it was also used as accommodation for a hunting party led by Caliph ʿAbd al-Raḥmān III. Decades later the celebration held to mark the circumcision of the sons of the Idrīsid family took place at this *munya*. The use of *almunias* as sites of recreation for Córdoba's ruling class provided the basis for the accusations of profligacy levelled against one of al-Manṣūr's sons, of whom it was said that he did nothing else than go 'from almunia to almunia and from party to party'.[49]

In Umayyad Córdoba, the *almunias* had highly distinctive features that are not readily comparable to other types of rural residences found in other periods or regions. This specificity is noted in the word *munya* itself, which according to F. Corriente means 'wish', but in the sense of these walled peri-urban properties the term is scarcely documented elsewhere. The architectural sense of this word must have arisen in al-Andalus at an early date, as is demonstrated by the fact that the word was swiftly incorporated into Portuguese and Spanish: *almunia* appears in a Leonese document from 902, and then

[48] The existence of a boundary wall in the *almunias* in al-Khushanī, *Quḍāt Qurṭuba*, ed. and trans. p. 188 and 234, where the judge Aḥmad b. Muḥammad b. Ziyād personally undertakes to knock down the wall of the *almunia* built by his predecessor and enemy Aslam b. ʿAbd al-ʿAzīz in order to widen the road. The division between the *qaṣr* and *faḥṣ* is clearly demonstrated in the reference provided in *infra*, n. 53. Another reference to the *faḥṣ*, in this case the *Munyat Ibn ʿAbd al-ʿAzīz*, in *Muqtabis VII*, ed. p. 46; trans. p. 65.

[49] Ibn Ḥayyān, *Muqtabis* V, ed. and trans. p. 34; Ibn Ḥayyān, *Muqtabis VII*, ed. pp. 109–10; trans. p. 140, in which al-Muntalī must be corrected to al-Buntīlī. Ibn ʿIdhārī, *al-Bayān* III, ed. cit. p. 39; trans. cit. p. 45, referring to ʿAbd al-Raḥmān *Sanchuelo*. On 'al-Rummāniyya', see Chapter 2. A carved capital that contains a rare scene representing various musicians is conserved in the Museo Arqueológico de Córdoba; it has been interpreted by G. Anderson as a reflection of the type of entertainment that would take place in these *almunias*, *The Islamic Villa in Medieval Iberia*, pp. 80–3.

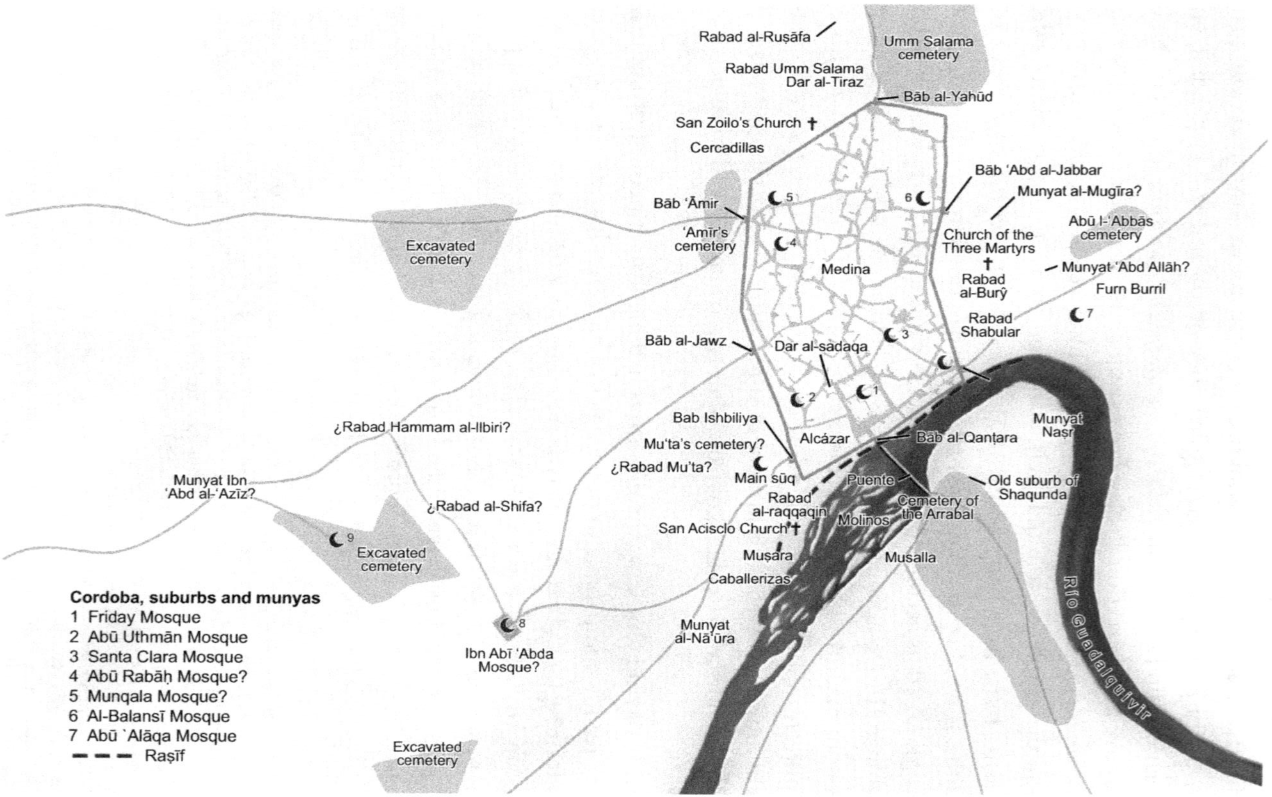

Figure 6 Córdoba, suburbs and *munyas*

recurs with relative frequency in Christian documents.[50] Furthermore, *munya* undoubtedly substituted the word *balāṭ*, which the conquerors used to refer to the Visigothic palace structures they found both in and outside Iberian cities. However, this latter word was never used for the buildings the Arabs built for themselves, which is a further indication that, despite the *almunias* also being owned by the ruling class, they were designed as a distinctive concept of residence.

The evidence for the Cordoban *almunia* of the Umayyad period reveals that they belonged to members of the ruling family or to individuals linked to the dynasty. It also demonstrates how the Umayyad sovereigns were able to amass a sizeable portfolio of real estate in the zones beyond the city walls and then identify it with their dynasty.[51] The layout of the only *almunia* whose remains have survived until today, the '*Munyat al-Rummāniyya*', was discussed above. It had belonged to the civil servant, Durrī al-Ṣaghīr, who subsequently gave it as a gift to al-Ḥakam II. Another of the caliph's *almunias* was al-Nā'ūra, a large property near the Guadalquivir, downstream from Córdoba. The estate had been bought by Emir Muḥammad and the building work undertaken by his successor, 'Abd Allāh. Caliph 'Abd al-Raḥmān III would often reside in this *almunia* on his return from military campaigns due to its proximity to Córdoba yet isolation from the city thanks to the *Muṣāra*, which was the large open esplanade that was devoted to recreational activities as well as equestrian training – it will be recalled that the state stables (*Dār al-Zawāmil*) were close by.[52] Like other *almunias*, al-Nā'ūra had a residential

[50] F. Corriente, *Diccionario de arabismos*, p. 203, which ruled out the Greek etymology proposed originally by García Gómez, 'Notas sobre la topografía', p. 334. M. Seco ed., *Léxico Hispánico Primitivo*, pp. 40–1. The references found in Christian documents are very interesting: from a Toledan text from 1088, which refers to *unam almuniam quam nos latine uocamus ortum*, to a document from Tamarite that refers to the *almunia de Yben Alfachi que uocatur Chamis*, in addition to others from San Juan de la Peña dated to 1076 and 1089 that mention *omnibus almuniis siue aldeis* o *illa almunia uel uilla*.

[51] F. López Cuevas, 'La almunia cordobesa, entre las fuentes historiográficas y arqueológicas', pp. 254–555. G. Anderson, *The Islamic Villa*, pp. 15–37.

[52] L. Torres Balbas, *Ciudades hispanomusulmanas*, I, p. 229. Ibn Ḥayyān, *Muqtabis III*, ed. cit. pp. 59–60. This location makes it very plausible to identify this *almunia* with archaeological remains that appeared in what was known as the Vado de Casillas, where excavations have revealed a series of walls and rooms built on a grand scale, G. Galeano Cuenca and R. Gil Fernández, 'Intervención arqueológica de urgencia en Casillas (término municipal de Córdoba)', pp. 285–90. F. Arnold, *Islamic Palatine Architecture*, pp. 110–11.

area (*qaṣr*) and an open space (*faḥṣ*), which is where the Idrīsids who arrived with Ghālib camped in their pavilions while waiting for the caliph to give them the order to make their way to Madīnat al-Zahrā' in September 974 (*Muḥarram* 364 AH).[53] In addition, al-Ḥakam II owned the *Munyat Arḥā' Nāṣiḥ* (Cortijo del Alcaide), where he resided on various occasions, which he bequeathed to his heir, Hishām. The caliph also eventually gained control of an *almunia* that his father had left to his brother, al-Mundhir, known as *Munyat Ibn al-Qurashiyya*. On the banks of the Guadalquivir, but to the east of the city, this *almunia* was used as accommodation for the wives of Ja'far and Yaḥyā b. al-Andalusī when they arrived in Córdoba at the end of the summer of 971 (360 AH). Four years later, its land was also used to pitch the tents of the troops that were sent as reinforcements to support the besieged fortress of Gormaz, which gives a good idea of the large size of this property.[54]

One of the earliest recorded Umayyad *almunias* was al-Ruṣāfa. It was built by Emir 'Abd al-Raḥmān I in the mid-eighth century to the north-east of Córdoba, in the foothills of the neighbouring mountain. The emir had bought this large property, consisting of a palace (*balāṭ*) and an olive grove, from the Berber leader Razīn al-Burnūsī, one of the tribal commanders of the army that had conquered a-Andalus.[55] The estate was transformed into an *almunia*, which the emir, moved by his yearning for his native land, named after a place in Syria to the south-east of what is today Raqqa, near ancient Sergiopolis, which had belonged to his grandfather, the caliph of Damascus, Hishām (724–43/105–24 AH). Caliph Hishām had built two palatial residences (*qaṣrayn*) surrounded by gardens and olive groves at this Syrian *Ruṣāfa*, which made use of a Roman water supply system. The Cordoban *almunia* of al-Ruṣāfa, located to the north of the city, was clearly inspired by

[53] Ibn Ḥayyān, *Muqtabis V*, ed. and trans. pp. 139, 165, 245, 322; *Muqtabis VII*, ed. cit. pp. 194–5, 212; trans. cit. pp. 237, 252–3. The expedition against the Normans sent in the summer of 972 (361 AH) left the *alcázar* of Córdoba, crossed the *Muṣāra* and then made its way to al-Nā'ūra, which is further proof that its *faḥṣ* could accommodate a large multitude of people, *Muqtabis VII*, pp. 79 and 102. This *almunia* was also used as a residence for King Ordoño IV during his visit to Córdoba in 962 (351 AH), al-Maqqarī, *Nafḥ*, I, p. 389.

[54] Ibn Ḥayyān, *Muqtabis VII*, ed. and trans. pp. 43–4 and 228; pp. 64 and 270.

[55] Ibn Ḥayyān, *Muqtabis II*, 2, ed. cit. p. 234 and n. 408, drawing on al-Rāzī, points out that this Razīn also left his mark on other places in Córdoba: a mosque was named after him in the western suburb, as was one of the gardens next to the Qubbash fountain in the same suburb. A historian, frequently cited by Ibn Ḥayyān and known as al-Qubbashī, took his name from this place.

this precedent. Roman water conduits were likewise revived here, which permitted the construction of a bath house and a residence (*qaṣr*). This *almunia* was frequented by the Umayyad emirs and later underwent major renovations in the time of emir Muḥammad.[56]

A suburb to cater for the needs of the living, as well as a cemetery to meet those of the dead, grew up around the *Munyat al-Ruṣāfa*, and this process of urban development soon came to define the growth of Córdoba's suburbs. We know that a number of *ʿulamāʾ* who died at the beginning of the tenth century (fourth AH) had lived in this suburb, which shows that it had emerged during the previous century.[57] However, it was during the caliphal era that this suburb underwent its major phase of growth, as has been shown by various archaeological excavations. It was then that a considerable number of houses were built using a highly homogeneous technique and adhering to a uniform plan structured around a patio with a well, which had a series of rooms, including latrines, distributed around it. Some of the latrines had advanced drainage systems consisting of ceramic channels, that took the residues down to a Roman water-pipe that had been broken open for use as a sewer.[58] These houses were designed according to a carefully arranged orthogonal urban plan, with streets that in some cases were as much as ten metres wide.

Muḥammad b. Abī ʿĀmir lived in this al-Ruṣāfa suburb, when he was merely a rising figure in the administration of al-Ḥakam II. A few years later, the renowned polygraph Ibn Ḥazm used to go to this suburb to attend lessons with one of his teachers.[59] At al-Ruṣāfa, lodging was also provided for soldiers from the caliph's stipendiary troops, which explains why this suburb in particular was ransacked during the *fitna* that broke out in the caliphate: the Cordoban population attacked the troops and sacked their residences. At that

[56] C. P. Haase and M. Marín, *Encyclopaedia of Islam*, 2nd ed., s.v. *al-Ruṣāfa*. J. F. Murillo, 'La almunia de al-Rusafa en Córdoba', p. 458. On the bath, which was overseen by a *ṣāḥib al-ḥammām*, *Akhbār Majmūʿa*, ed. and trans. p. 115; trans. James, p. 109.

[57] *Prosopografía de los ulemas de al-Andalus*, id. 10.593 (d. 906/294 AH); id. 2.827 (d. 923/311 AH); M. T. Casal, *Los cementerios musulmanes de Qurtuba*, pp. 54–6.

[58] B. Vázquez Navajas, 'Las condiciones higiénicas y de saneamiento en Madīnat Qurṭuba', pp. 304–5.

[59] J. F. Murillo et al., 'La almunia y el arrabal de al-Rusafa en el Yanib al-Garbi de Madinat Qurtuba', pp. 586–605. Ibn ʿIdhārī, *al-Bayān*, II, ed. cit. p. 258. Ibn Ḥazm, *Ṭawq al-ḥamāma*, ed. and trans. pp. 216–17: the itinerary taken by this author and his fellow students led from Balāṭ Mughīt and made its way through the cemetery to the ʿĀmir Gate, and from there took heading northwards.

time – 1009–10/400 AH – the residential section of the Umayyads' *almunia* in al-Ruṣāfa was also pillaged and destroyed.[60]

A similar extensive phase of urban development dated to the caliphal period has been identified in the nearby suburb of Cercadilla, to the north-west of Córdoba's medina, which grew out of a residential complex located outside the city walls dating back to late antiquity. A Christian community lived in this area, which had its own cemetery, where stelæ have been found commemorating Salvatus and Christophora, who died in 982 and 983 respectively. However, the Christian population was already in decline, as is demonstrated by the city's gradual encroachment on their burial grounds and the construction of a small mosque on the outskirts of this quarter.[61] The progressive Islamisation of this part of the city is confirmed by the analyses of animal remains, which reveal a drastic drop in the number of pig bones found in excavations. These social transformations were accompanied by changes to the cityscape, which in the caliphal era adopted a new design; squares were created at the intersection of streets and used for souks as well as housing; the latter adhered to the aforementioned pattern of patios surrounded by rooms and a latrine. As will be discussed, the crisis of the caliphate left this area in ruins and unpopulated.[62]

On the other northern side, to the north-east of the medina (the boundaries are not as precise as we might wish), the centre for urban development was the mosque of Umm Salama, which had been founded in the mid-ninth century by one of the wives of emir Muḥammad. She was a granddaughter of Emir al-Ḥakam I, which reveals the Umayyad dynasty's property ownership in this area. The suburb that grew up there along with the cemetery of Umm Salama reached as far as what was known as the Jews Gate or *Bāb al-Jahūd* of

[60] Ibn 'Idhārī, *al-Bayān*, III, ed. cit. pp. 75–6 and 101–2; trans. cit. pp. 75, 92. With regard to the aforementioned crime that was so astutely resolved by the *ṣāḥib al-madīna*, the murderer turned out to be a soldier from the city guard who lived in al-Ruṣāfa, Ibn al-Qūṭiya, *Ta'rīkh*, ed. pp. 69–70; trans. James p. 103.

[61] R. Hidalgo and C. Fuertes, 'Córdoba entre la Antigüedad clásica y el Islam: el caso de Cercadilla', pp. 223-64.

[62] C. Aillet, 'Islamisation', p. 173. M. García García, 'Some Remarks on the Provision of Animal Products to Urban Centres in Medieval Islamic Iberia', pp. 86–96. M. C. Fuertes Santos, 'Aproximación al urbanismo y la arquitectura doméstica de época califal del Yacimiento de Cercadilla', pp. 105–26; M. C. Fuertes Santos, 'El sector nororiental del arrabal califal del yacimiento de Cercadilla', pp. 49–68.

the Córdoba's medina. It was also a place where wine was sold.[63] On the outskirts of this suburb was a church, which preserved the remains of Saint Zoilus, a fourth-century martyr who had died in Córdoba. The caliphate's textile manufactory (*Dār al-ṭirāẓ*), which was visited by al-Ḥakam II in September 972 (*Dhū l-qa'da* 361 AH), was also located there. During that visit, the caliph saw how the cemetery of Umm Salama had grown dramatically, so he ordered the demolition of numerous houses in the suburb so the cemetery could be extended, which underscores again how caliphal rulings affected the urban configuration of Córdoba.[64]

A similar urban intervention by the Umayyad rulers is noted in a negative form on the other side of the city, in the southern area, on the far side of the bridge over the Guadalquivir, where urban expansion had been frustrated by the destruction of the Secunda suburb and market following the 818 uprising against Emir al-Ḥakam I. The archaeological excavations have demonstrated that, despite being just a stone's throw away from the *alcázar* and the mosque, the area ceased to have any urban physiognomy. Textual sources confirm that the area lacked major buildings. They only mention an orchard, which possibly belonged to Ṭarūb, a concubine of Emir 'Abd al-Raḥmān II, and a *Munyat Naṣr*, that belonged to this eunuch and high official in the administration of this emir. Following Nasr's execution for having masterminded a plot to put an end to 'Abd al-Raḥmān II, his *almunia* became an Umayyad property and was used for a range of purposes: it was the temporary residence of the celebrated musician Ziryāb before being remodelled during the time of Emir 'Abd Allāh, who would often spend time there escaping the pressures of court life. 'Abd al-Raḥmān III would also reside there on his return from military expeditions. By 949 (338 AH), the *Munyat Naṣr* had become the property of

[63] Ibn 'Abd al-Ra'ūf, *Risāla fī adāb al-ḥisba wa l-muḥtasib*, ed. p. 114; trans. p. 363.

[64] The findings on Umm Salama and its foundations in M. Penelas and L. Molina, 'Dos fragmentos inéditos del Muqtabis', p. 240. On the extension decreed by al-Ḥakam II, Ibn Ḥayyān, *Muqtabis VII*, ed. and trans. pp. 92 and 115–16. The archaeological data in J. F. Murillo, 'La almunia de al-Rusafa', p. 472 and S. Rodero Pérez and M. J. Asensi Llácer, 'Un sector de la expansión occidental de la Córdoba islámica', pp. 295–336. The reference to the Church of Saint Zoilus in *Calendario de Córdoba*, ed. and trans. pp. 73 and 163, which also mentions a *vico Tiraceorum* that should be linked to the *Dār al-ṭirāẓ*. Eulogius of Córdoba, one the leaders of the movement of voluntary martyrs of the ninth century, served as a priest of the 'basilica' of Saint Zoilus, which is where his body was interred, along with the other voluntary martyrs, Alvaro de Córdoba, *Vita Eulogi*, ed. I. Gil, *Corpus Scriptorum Muzarabicorum*, pp. 331, 338, 341.

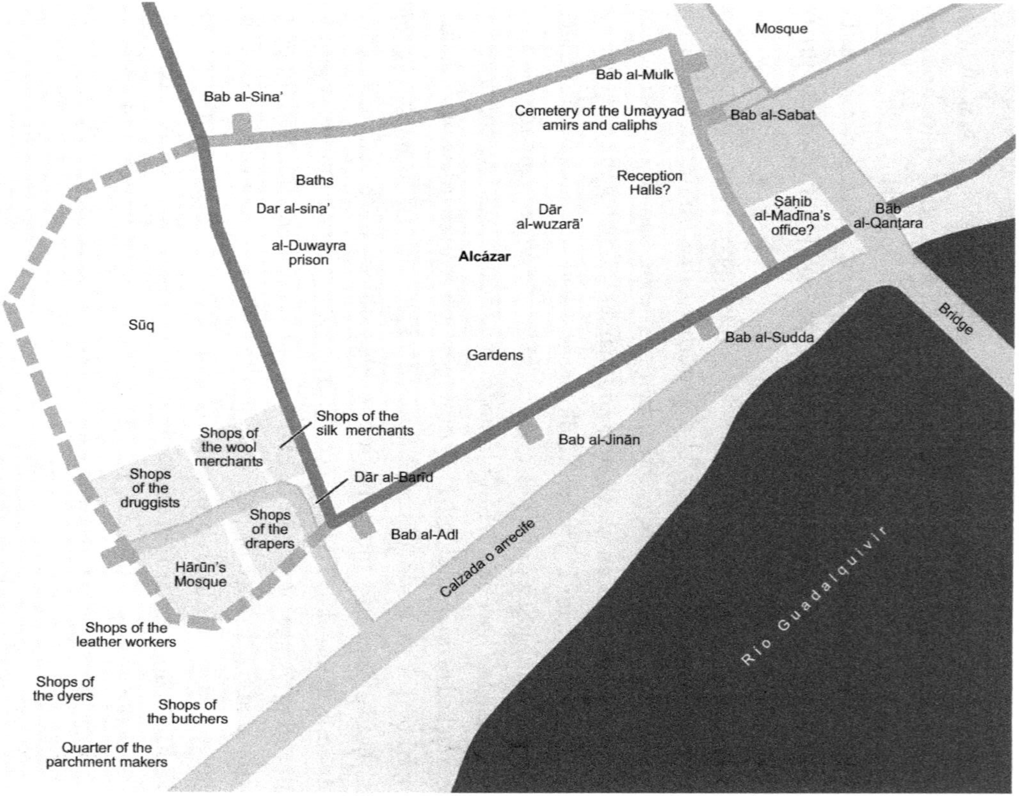

Figure 7 Córdoba: street plan

al-Ḥakam. It was used to host ambassadors, such as the Byzantine embassy which arrived that year, and the envoys sent by the count of Barcelona in the summer of 971 (360 AH).[65]

Again on the left bank of the river, opposite the *alcázar* and main mosque, was located the so-called 'al-Rabaḍ cemetery'. Excavations have identified it as having occupied both sides of the road that led from the ancient Roman bridge. A section of this necropolis was reserved as the Quraysh family cemetery. It also had an enclosed area, which was the *rawḍa* of the Banū Marwān, where members of the Umayyad family were buried, except for the emirs and caliphs, who were interred in the *alcázar* precinct. Some of these tombs were authentic funerary chambers or mausoleums, such as that which housed the remains of Marjān, the mother of Caliph al-Ḥakam, which consisted of a walled tomb entered via a doorway. Funerary stelæ commemorating members of the sovereigns' family circle have also been found in this area.[66] The suburb's *muṣallā* was close to this cemetery. This open-air oratory was used to hold popular celebrations for the Feast of the Breaking of the Fast, and prayers were also said there to beseech God for rain at times of drought, both of which attracted huge crowds.[67]

It is possible that in the pre-Islamic era the city had already begun to spread to the area east of the medina of Córdoba, but little is known for certain. It was the location of a *vico Turris*, hence the Arabs called the surrounding area the 'suburb of the tower' or *rabaḍ al-Burj*. It was the location of one of the city's main Christian churches, the Three Martyrs basilica, which in the caliphal era still preserved the tombs of three Cordobans who had died during

[65] Ibn Ḥayyān, *Muqtabis II, 2*, pp. 19–20. J. Vallve, 'Naṣr el valido de 'Abd al-Raḥmān II', p. 187; al-Maqqarī, *Nafḥ*, I, p. 367; Ibn Ḥayyān, *Muqtabis VII*, ed. cit. pp. 20–2; trans. 45–6.

[66] M. Acién Almansa and A. Vallejo Triano, 'Urbanismo y estado islámico', p. 116, n. 54. M. Ocaña, 'Nuevas inscripciones árabes de Córdoba', pp. 379–88; A. Labarta and C. Barceló, 'Dos nuevos fragmentos epigráficos cordobeses del cementerio del arrabal', pp. 549–57. Ibn Ḥazm, *Ṭawq al-ḥamāma*, ed. and trans. pp. 72–3, in the aforementioned story which recounts how the poet al-Ramādī fell in love with a woman he saw at the entrance to the souk, it is told that he followed her until he reached the mosque and bridge, which he then crossed towards Secunda and arrived at 'the gardens (*riyāḍ*) of the Banū Marwān ... which are planted over their tombs in the Arrabal cemetery'. On the mausoleums, C. Barceló, 'Epitaph of an 'Āmirī (Cordova 374/985 CE)', p. 126, which draws on the testimony of al-Nubāhī. Archaeology in M. T. Casal, *Los cementerios musulmanes de Qurtuba*, pp. 96–109.

[67] L. Torres Balbas, *Ciudades hispanomusulmanas*, I, pp. 221–2. Prayers for rain in Ibn Ḥayyān, *Muqtabis V*, ed. and trans. pp. 67, 132–3 and 321.

the persecutions of Diocletian.[68] The large eastern suburb of Shabulār grew up adjacent to the 'suburb of the tower'. It was linked to the medina by the New Gate (*bāb al-Jadīd*) that Emir al-Ḥakam had ordered to be built in the old city wall, which testifies to the growing importance of this suburb; from the interior of the medina, the gate was reached by what was called the 'Large Street' (*al-Zuqāq al-Kabīr*). One of the landmarks of this Islamic suburb was the mosque of emir Hishām, which has been identified with what is today the church of Santiago, which preserves the mosque's minaret as its bell tower.[69] The cemetery of Abū l-'Abbās was created close by in the late emirate period, and a section of it was known as *al-Burj*.[70] There is extensive archaeological evidence for this cemetery, which grew to a substantial size and possibly reached as far as the Furn Burrīl suburb, whose Latin name, 'Buriel's oven', suggests this area was inhabited prior to the Arab conquest. In January 971 (360 AH), Caliph al-Ḥakam visited this suburb and saw how the road running through it was too narrow and caused major agglomerations of passers-by, whereby he ordered for the shops that lined the road to be purchased and demolished in order to widen it.[71]

In this eastern area, the *almunias* established in the Umayyad period also formed nuclei fostering further urban development. The *Munyat al-Mughīra*

68 *Le Calendrier de Cordoue*, ed. cit. pp. 150–1. C. Aillet, 'Islamisation', p. 171.

69 M. Acién Almansa and A. Vallejo Triano, 'Urbanismo y estado islámico', p. 115. On the mosque, C. González Gutiérrez, *Las mezquitas de barrio*, pp. 151–7. On al-Ḥakam's construction of the New Gate, Ibn Ḥayyān *Muqtabis II, 1*, ed. pp. 162–3; trans. p. 73.

70 The name of this cemetery was linked to a vizier called Abū l-'Abbās. The only vizier I know of who used this *laqab* was Aḥmad b. Muḥammad b. 'Īsā b. Abī 'Abda, who had been appointed by emir 'Abd Allāh and continued in this role under 'Abd al-Raḥmān III until he died during the *aceifa* launched in the Christian territories in 917 (305 AH), Ibn Ḥayyān, *Muqtabis V*, ed. and trans. pp. 88–9. Two scholars had a house next to this cemetery and they prayed in the mosque of emir Hishām: 'Abd Allāh b. Sa'īd, known as Ibn al-Muḥtashim (d. in 1012/403 AH), who lived in the street (*zuqāq*) of Zur'a, and 'Abd Allāh b. Muḥammad al-Umawī, who lived in the street (*zuqāq*) of Duḥaym, *Prosopografía de los ulemas de al-Andalus*, id. 5.133, with information from Ibn Bashkuwāl.

71 Ibn Ḥayyān, *Muqtabis VII*, ed. cit pp. 67–8; trans. cit. pp. 89–90. The text states that the congestion meant the people were in danger of falling into the ditch (*khandaq*), which might allow this suburb to be located alongside one of the streams that ran from the north down to the Guadalquivir: the most plausible candidate would be that of Fuensanta or Las Piedras. On the cemeteries, M. Casal et al., 'Espacio y usos funerarios en la Qurtuba islámica', *Anales de Arqueología Cordobesa*, 17 (2006), pp. 264–5.

owed its name to a son of Emir al-Ḥakam I.[72] Its exact location is unknown, but a suburb with the same name was already thriving there by the caliphal era. Another *almunia* that gave rise to a suburb in this area was the '*Munyat ʿAbd Allāh*', which in the caliphal era belonged to Muḥammad b. Saʿīd b. Abī l-Qāsim, a son of ʿAbd al-Raḥmān III's maternal uncle.[73] In March 974 (363 AH), al-Ḥakam II fell out with this relative and sent a party of soldiers to arrest him at his *almunia*; they did not find him there, as he was at a property (*ḍayʿa*) he had in the countryside called *Manzīl Haytham*, where he was eventually found and transferred to prison. In that period, a sufficiently dense urban development had grown up around this *munya* for there to be a mosque nearby.[74] The immense wealth that could be contained in these eastern *almunias* and their outlying suburbs has been revealed by archaeologists, who have unearthed household ceramics of an exceptional quality.[75]

Córdoba's principal area of growth was concentrated to the west of the medina, in the direction of Madīnat al-Zahrā', which became a major centre of attraction following its foundation.[76] During the emirate period, cemeteries and mosques were founded in this western area, in particular by concubines of the emirs, which suggests they were built on land already owned by these women. For example, the mosque of Muʿta was founded by a concubine of

[72] Ibn Ḥazm, *Jamhara*, ed. cit. p. 98. Ibn Ḥayyān, *Muqtabis II, 1*, ed. cit. pp. 182–3; trans. cit. pp. 88–9. This data refutes the arguments for the location of this *munya* in the area of the church of San Lorenzo as proposed by M. Ocaña, 'Notas sobre la Córdoba de Ibn Hazm', pp. 55–62. Ibn Ḥazm had been born in the al-Mughīra suburb, whereby it is tempting to link this information with what we know about the location of his family house on the outskirts of Madīnat al-Zāhira, see below n. 110.

[73] Saʿīd b. Abī l-Qāsim was the brother of Muzna al-Rūmiyya, the mother of caliph ʿAbd al-Raḥmān III, and he was appointed to important posts during his reign, including *ṣāḥib al-madīna*, Ibn Ḥayyān, *Muqtabis V*, ed. and trans. pp. 167, 208, 213, 304, etc. *Dhikr bilād al-Andalus*, ed. p. 159; trans. p. 169.

[74] Ibn Ḥayyān, *Muqtabis VII*, ed. and trans. p. 153 and p. 194.

[75] V. Barea Pareja, 'Un sector de arrabal oriental en la Córdoba califal', pp. 167–81.

[76] This was where the conquerors' first architectural intervention was made a few years after 711: the creation of a cemetery by the Arab leader, ʿĀmir al-ʿAbdārī, who gave his name to the ʿĀmir Gate (bāb ʿĀmir) in the city wall. It was not far from a *munya* he owned called Qanāt ʿĀmir, alluding to the Roman conduits that brought water to the city reached this area, *Akhbār Majmūʿ*. ed. and trans. pp. 63; trans. James, p. 81. G. Pizarro Berengena, *El abastecimiento de agua a Córdoba*, pp. 44–8. ʿĀmir al-ʿAbdārī was an important figure, who belonged to an eminent family that had served in senior positions in pre-Islamic Mecca; he took part in a rebellion that broke out in Zaragoza and his successors established themselves in the village of Corbalán in the Teruel region, E. Manzano Moreno, *La frontera de al-Andalus*, pp. 208–14.

Emir al-Ḥakam I, who also gave her name to the adjacent cemetery and suburb. The mosque of al-Shifāʾ, named after one of ʿAbd al-Raḥmān II's concubines, was located in the suburb of the same name on the western side of the city alongside the Ḥammām al-Ilbīrī suburb, which had also emerged around an *almunia*.[77] Other concubines of the same emir, Ṭarūb, Fakhr and ʿAjab, each founded mosques in the western suburbs.[78]

A revealing case study for the foundation of these mosques by women of the ruler's harem is the one founded by Marjān, the concubine of ʿAbd al-Raḥmān III and mother of Caliph al-Ḥakam. The gossip that circulated about her in the harem portrays a very wealthy woman, one capable of spending the astronomical sum of 10,000 dinars to purchase the right to a night of pleasure with the caliph from Fāṭima, his Qurashi wife. Having successfully become ʿAbd al-Raḥmān III's favourite through this cunning ploy, Marjān devoted herself to undertaking pious deeds with the abundant resources at her disposal, which she may well have inherited from her Christian family. One outcome of this was the foundation of a mosque in the western suburb that was named after her and was considered to be one of the city's most spacious and finely-built mosques. It was well-equipped with guardians and washrooms, which were paid for thanks to a pious legacy (*waqf*) created by Marjān herself. The legacy was financed by an estate she owned, which was also to the west of Córdoba, whose income was used for the maintenance of this and other mosques in the capital.[79]

The suburban mosques that archaeologists have excavated in recent years have revealed small or medium-sized oratories, which were located in carefully planned streets and squares, whose uniformity is, once again, striking.

[77] During the elaborate welcome staged for the Banū al-Andalusī, the cortège, which made its way from the *alcázar*'s Azuda Gate, entered the *Muṣāra* and from there it turned northwards, climbing the hill to the Mosque of Ibn Abī ʿAbda, from where they reached the suburb of the Mosque of al-Shifāʾ and from there to the Ḥammām al-Ilbīrī suburb, and it was here they entered the *Munyat Ibn ʿAbd al-ʿAzīz*, where accommodation was provided for them, Ibn Ḥayyān, *Muqtabis VII*, ed. and trans. p. 46 and p. 65. On this *munya*, F. López Cuevas, 'La almunia cordobesa', p. 250. The Mosque of Ibn Abī ʿAbda must have been located where the Cruz Conde Park is today, A. Arjona, 'Las basílicas mozárabes', p. 37.

[78] Ibn Ḥayyān, *Muqtabis II, 1*, ed. cit. p. 288; trans. cit. p. 178. The house of Ibn Saʿd was located in the Muʿta suburb, which is where one of the Banū Idrīs, who arrived in Córdoba around this time, was accommodated, *Muqtabis VII*, ed. and trans. p. 200 and p. 241.

[79] Ibn Ḥayyān, *Muqtabis V*, ed. and trans. p. 6. A. García Sanjuán, *Till God Inherits the Earth*, p. 95.

One of these excavated oratories is the so-called mosque of El Fontanar, which can be unequivocally dated to the caliphal era. It is a substantial structure of three naves; just over two hundred people could gather in its prayer hall, and this number could be doubled if the courtyard was also used for prayers. Additional smaller mosques have also been excavated in other parts of this western area of the city, and they suggest this suburban sector was a compact and very well-defined urban development.[80]

Along with these mosques, and alternating with the landscape of the living, there were large cemeteries whose outer walls bordered the residential areas. The sources provide the names of these cemeteries (the *ʿĀmir*, *Muʿta* and *Balāṭ Mughīth* cemeteries), but it is the number of tombs uncovered by archaeologists which is more revealing: in some areas over five thousand graves have been found. Separated from the living by the boundary walls, these cemeteries were inserted into the urban network that took shape along the various roads running through these suburban areas.[81]

The major expansion of these residential western suburbs took place in the mid-tenth century. ʿAbd al-Raḥmān III's decision to open one of the western gates in the medina's city wall, the one known as *Bāb ʿĀmir*, which had until then been sealed off, indicates a significant increase in traffic between the city's centre and the outlying suburbs.[82] At the time of al-Ḥakam II, the urban development of the western suburbs exploded: various buildings from the emirate era were rebuilt, and vacant plots of land were used for new buildings, which led to this sector emulating the cityscape found in other suburban areas. Archaeological excavations have again identified traces of gravel-paved streets laid out according to an orthogonal plan, which on occasions formed genuine avenues over eight metres wide. The single, or perhaps two-storey, houses had, as in the other suburbs, a central patio and a well, which could be up to seven or eight metres deep. The layout of the patio could vary considerably: some

80 D. Luna and A. Zamorano, 'La mezquita de la antigua finca El Fontanar (Córdoba)', pp. 145–73. My calculation is based on the size of the building compared with the main mosque of Madīnat al-Zahrāʾ, for which M. Acién calculated its prayer hall could hold 564 people, 'Madinat al-Zahrāʾ en el urbanismo musulmán', p. 19. On the other mosques, C. González Gutiérrez, 'Las mezquitas de barrio de madīnat Qurṭuba 15 años después: espacios religiosos urbanos en la capital andalusí', pp. 267–92.

81 A. León and M. Casal, 'Los cementerios de Madinat Qurtuba', pp. 662–72.

82 Ibn Ḥayyān, *Muqtabis V*, ed. and trans. p. 67.

Image 19 The archaeology of the western suburbs of Córdoba. Aerial view of AAP P595-2006 Parcela 13c. The stone walls can be seen, as well as the different sewers coming from the buildings and draining into a main channel that meanders outside the walls of the houses.

had a sidewalk and occasionally a pond, but it was always surrounded by various bedrooms, hallways, living rooms, and, almost always, a latrine, and even in some cases a bath. These houses were also equipped with sewerage systems, which either flowed into drains running underneath the roads, or else led to cesspools. In some cases, it is even possible to follow the course of the sewer, which was covered with big slabs of calcarenite.[83] Larger buildings have also been excavated in this section of the city, and their layout suggests these were local souks containing shops and warehouses for storing merchandise.[84] These western suburbs were abandoned following the end of the caliphate of Córdoba.

The extraordinary growth that has been detected in the suburbs located to the north and west of Córdoba's medina in the mid-tenth century has been an unexpected archaeological discovery. The regular plan of the houses, the rectilinear streets and the spread of an urban development interwoven with the Islamic cemetery walls testify to a premeditated and carefully executed plan that was carried out at the same time as the creation of Madīnat al-Zahrā'.[85] Everything suggests that this urban plan was conceived to house the new staff for the complex centralised military, bureaucratic and diplomatic powerhouse the Umayyad caliphal state was creating for itself. Those who lived here were people such as Muḥammad b. Abī 'Āmir, who lived in the al-Ruṣāfa suburb, or the father of the polygraph Ibn Ḥazm, who also worked for the Umayyad administration and had a house in the western suburb of Balāṭ Mughīth.

The caliph's domestic staff were a further element that contributed to this urban growth. The sources state that 3,500 slaves worked in Madīnat al-Zahrā', a figure that is comparable to the eleven to twelve thousand servants employed by the 'Abbāsid and Fāṭimid caliphs.[86] Furthermore, there were the freedmen who formed part of the legion of employees working in the civic administration and the army. Where did all these people live? Undoubtedly,

[83] R. Clapés Salmoral, 'Un baño privado en el arrabal occidental de Madinat Qurtuba', p. 98. D. Ruiz Lara, 'El sector meridional del Yanib al-Garbi', pp. 636–9.

[84] R. Clapés Salmoral, 'La actividad comercial de Córdoba en época califal', pp. 225–54.

[85] It is possible that a similar phase of expansion took place on the eastern side of the city, but it is more difficult to document because this zone, the Axarquía, was the area that expanded during the medieval era, in contrast to the western and northern areas, which were not extensively urbanised until recently.

[86] A. Vallejo, *La ciudad califal*, p. 123, n. 20.

some of them lived in the city palace itself, but at present neither the excavations nor exploratory studies have identified neighbourhoods there with an urban density comparable to those of Córdoba's suburbs. It is thus evident that the exponential rise in the number of staff serving the caliphate effected the expansion of Córdoba's suburbs. In areas in which the dynasty appears to have exercised undisputed property rights, an urban environment was created that was intended for the personnel who were employed, in one way or another, by the caliph. The major urban project that formed part of the foundation of the city palace was thus not limited by its city walls: it also envisioned expansion across the old capital city.

The Caliph's Power and the Foundation of Madīnat al-Zahrā'

The first known reference to Madīnat al-Zahrā' is found in a poem composed in 938 (326 AH) by the then very young Ja'far al-Muṣḥafī, al-Ḥakam II's future vizier, when he could barely imagine his role in the rise and fall of this city palace: 'Your realm continues, O caliph' (al-Muṣḥafī proclaimed), 'the orchard of al-Zahrā' (*al-rawḍa al-Zahrā'*) is licitly yours.' Ten years later, the palace at the heart of the new city had already been built along with its main mosque.[87] In addition, in 336 AH (947–8) a mint issued dirhams cast in *City of al-Zahrā'*, or in other words, *Madīnat al-Zahrā'*.

The more we know about the remains of this city, the clearer what an impressive endeavour it was to build it becomes. It was located on a site where there had previously been a small village and an *almunia*, at the meeting point of the mountains and the lowland plain. The city's layout on a series of terraces meant major levelling work had to be undertaken.[88] Roman-era

[87] Ibn Hayyān, *Muqtabis V*, ed. and trans. p. 31. The poem was composed to mark the occasion of the caliph's departure from Zaragoza, where he had left his army besieging the rebel Muḥammad b. Hāshim al-Tujībī. This reference is important. This reference demonstrates that the city's name had already been decided on: until then, the site had been known by the Latin name, Qarqarīṭ, ibid., p. 322 and n. 13. On the dating of the city palace, see M. A. Martínez and M. Acién, 'La epigrafía de Madīnat al-Zahrā'", pp. 116–19. In the Spanish version of the book I incorrectly dated this poem to 935 (325 AH).

[88] Ibn Ḥayyān, *Muqtabis II, 2*, p. 190, cites a *munya B.w.qrīṭ* that had been owned by Hāshim b. 'Abd al-'Azīz, the powerful vizier of emir Muḥammad who later fell from favour and was executed by his successor. Makki identified it with *Qawqarīṭ* the place that, according to al-'Udhrī, served as the location for Madīnat al-Zahrā', ibid., n. 364, p. 551. This identification is confirmed by *Muqtabis V*, p. 322.

water-collecting works were incorporated into a complex hydraulic engineering project to build new subterranean pipes providing the city with running water. An army of overseers, stonemasons, carpenters, plasterers and tilers laboured to bring to fruition an urban plan based on 'an innovative modular architecture, which worked akin to a meccano'. Each stone ashlar was placed according to careful planning, and the different teams of craftsmen worked in parallel on distinctive parts of the building. The building work was complemented by the sculptors, who carved the vegetal decoration from the locally-mined soft limestone. Known as *ataurique*, this entwined leaf and flower decorative design adorned the exterior walls of the main buildings of the palace along with panels of Arabic epigraphy, columns and capitals. The interior decoration of many of the lodgings consisted of white and red-ochre plaster decoration. The enormous quantity of resources spent and the predominant use of locally or regionally sourced materials meant that the first buildings of Madīnat al-Zahrā' were completed at great speed, although some parts of this urban complex were subsequently and frequently remodelled, and some of its most emblematic buildings – such as the large audience hall – were only built in the 950s.[89]

The palace, *alcázar* or *qaṣr*, was intended to be the nucleus of the new urban project of Madīnat al-Zahrā'. It extended over four hectares, barely occupying 5 per cent of the 115 hectares comprised by the whole urban perimeter. It attracted civil servants, soldiers and servants, whose demand for products, goods and services must have in turn enticed merchants and artisans, whose activities were expected to encourage the new city to grow and expand. Ibn Ḥawqal succinctly summed up this idea when he mentioned that, on the one hand, the caliph had ordered for his treasury, administrative departments, prison, storehouses and supplies warehouses to be transferred to Madīnat al-Zahrā', and on the other that he planned for baths, palatial residences and sites for recreation to be built. The *sulṭān* thereby formed the heart of the city and around it arose the urban fabric that sustained it. It was for this reason that the first city wall was raised to surround the *alcázar* precinct, and only later,

[89] A. Vallejo, *La ciudad califal*, pp. 103–17, 139–40, 152–3, 320–1. The references made to the workers who built the city in A. Labarta and C. Barceló, 'Las fuentes árabes sobre al-Zahrā'', pp. 96–8.

during a second phase of building, was a wall constructed to enclose the rest of the urban perimeter.[90]

The Umayyad sovereigns clearly understood that the numerous people who gravitated around caliphal power in turn generated a high degree of demand, which incentivised urban growth. In 930 (318 AH), ʿAbd al-Raḥmān III had led a siege against the then rebel city of Toledo. His camp was located on the Chalencas Hills, not far from the renowned city on the banks of the River Tagus, and he gave orders for it to be converted into an 'urbanised camp' (*al-maḥalla al-muddana*). He ordered builders to come and build a city he called *Madīnat al-Fatḥ* (City of Victory). According to a contemporary source, the caliph 'actively attended to the prosperity of Madīnat al-Fatḥ ... endeavouring to supply it with food and markets, filling it with skilful builders, victuals and provisions, as well as various units of brave and battle-hardened troops'. A year later, the strategy bore fruit: the city of the siege force was replete with products and services, while the people of Toledo were beset by a lack of supplies, hence they agreed to submit to the caliph.[91]

The caliphs were clearly aware that the demand generated by its civil and military staff would attract craftsmen, traders and builders, who shaped the social fabric from which cities were built. In addition, they were inspired by a long-term concept of political sovereignty, which regarded the foundation of a well-guarded and wealth-generating urban environment as a distinctive accomplishment. In the Hellenistic period, for example, Alexander the Great and his Ptolemaic and Seleucid successors founded cities such as Alexandria, Ptolemaid and Antioch, which were all named after them.[92] The first Roman emperors did not found cities, although many were renamed after some of them. However, during the Late Roman Empire, in a context of widespread urban decline, the protection and expansion of cities were considered a clear

[90] Ibn Ḥawqal, *Ṣūrat al-arḍ*, ed. cit. pp. 111–12; trans. cit. pp. 110–11. A. Vallejo, *La ciudad califal*, pp. 121 and 176.

[91] Ibn Hayyān, *Muqtabis V*, ed. and trans. 188 and 214. Chalencas was probably located on the Cerro del Bu, to the south of Toledo on the other side of the river, where an excavation seeking prehistoric strata found evidence of the existence of a walled area from the Andalusi era, J. Jacobo del Cerro, *Aproximación al conocimiento de la Edad del Bronce en la Cuenca Media del Tajo*, pp. 78–81.

[92] P. M. Fraser, *Cities of Alexander the Great*; K. Mueller, *Settlements of the Ptolemies*, pp. 114–16; G. M. Cohen, *Hellenistic Settlements*, pp. 80–93.

sign of a ruler's deeds. When Emperor Constantine founded Constantinople in 330, he boasted of his efforts 'in building new cities, restoring old ones and repairing those which were about to disappear'. Two hundred years later, circa 530, the Emperor Justinian founded *Justiniana Prima* in Caričin Grad in what is today Serbia. This was emulated by the Visigothic King Leovigild, when he founded Recopolis, near to Zorita de los Canes (Guadalajara), which is said to have had suburbs of pleasing beauty, and which archaeological excavations have demonstrated continued to thrive after the Arab conquest.[93]

As they did with other cultural elements incorporated from the legacy of late antiquity, the Umayyad and 'Abbāsid caliphs sought to link their sovereignty to the existence of safe and well-supplied urban spaces. It is possible that Anjar, in what is today Lebanon, some fifty kilometres west of Damascus, was an unfinished attempt to found a city by the Umayyads during the eighth century. Its orthogonal plan, city wall flanked by towers and palace alongside the mosque testifies to a carefully designed urban project. In the case of Madīnat al-Salām, founded by the 'Abbāsid Caliph al-Manṣūr in 762 (145 AH) on the banks of the Tigris, there was an unequivocal link with the sovereignty of the new dynasty. Surrounded by a circular wall, the heart of the city consisted of the caliph's palace and the Friday mosque, while its four outlying suburbs were provided with markets, bath houses and residential areas. The success of the foundation of Baghdad contrasts with the building of Samarra, which proved to be a failure. It was founded by Caliph al-Mu'taṣim in 836 (221 AH) on the banks of the River Tigris, some 125 kilometres north of Baghdad. It was intended to become the new epicentre of the caliphal power and was extended on a number of occasions, in particular by Caliph al-Mutawakkil (d. 861/247 AH). However, Samarra was finally abandoned shortly before the death of Caliph al-Mu'tamid in 892 (279 AH). Although the city had barely existed for six decades, its archaeological remains show that Sāmarrā spread over at least forty kilometres from its southernmost point to the north, and in places it was as much as five kilometres wide.[94]

[93] J. Arce, 'La fundación de nuevas ciudades en el imperio romano tardío', pp. 31–62. L. Olmo Enciso, *Recópolis y la ciudad en época visigoda*.

[94] H. K. Chehab, 'On the Identification of 'Anjar (Ayn al-Jarr) as an Umayyad Foundation', pp. 42–8; A. Duri, *Encyclopaedia of Islam*, 2nd ed., s.v. 'Baghdad'; C. Robinson, ed., *A Medieval Islamic City Reconsidered*.

The rulers of the Islamic west also founded cities, but they were usually built in the vicinity of earlier settlements, perhaps due to the lower urban population density in this region. When Aḥmad b. Ṭūlūn (d. 884/270 AH) became the independent governor of Egypt he built a new city to the north of Fusṭāṭ, where he set up his administration and the renowned mosque that still bears his name today. Following his conquest of Egypt in 969 (357 AH), one of the first decisions of the Fāṭimid caliph, al-Mu'izz, was to found al-Qāhira, four kilometres north of Fusṭāṭ.

In Ifrīqiya, on the outskirts of Qayrawān, three new cities were built. The first, al-ʻAbbāsiyya, five kilometres south-east of Qayrawān, was established in 800 (184 AH) by the founder of the Aghlabid dynasty, Ibrāhīm b. al-Aghlab, while Raqqāda, a few kilometres further south, was built by his descendant, Ibrāhīm II, in 876 (263 AH). When the Fāṭimids ousted the Aghlabids, they also founded new cities: al-Mahdiyya, which still exists today, was built by ʻUbayd Allāh al-Mahdī (between 912 and 920/299 and 308 AH) on the east coast of Ifrīqiya, while Ṣabra al-Manṣūriyya, two kilometres south of Qayrawān, took its name from its founder, the Fāṭimid Caliph al-Manṣūr (945–8/334–6 AH). Even a tribal leader such as Zīrī b. Manād al-Ṣinhājī, the Fāṭimids' deputy in Ifrīqiya, built his own city, Ashīr, around the same time that work was begun on the foundation of Madīnat al-Zahrā' (935–6/324 AH). Located in the centre of what is today Algeria, this city adhered to the model of a palace surrounded by an urban space populated by artisans, traders and scholars.[95]

All these parallels demonstrate that when ʻAbd al-Raḥmān III decided to begin building Madīnat al-Zahrā' he was following precedents with a long historical tradition. We do not know if he was aware of the celebrated words that the ʻAbbāsid caliph, al-Mutawwakil, uttered having completed the enlargement of Sāmarrā – 'now I know that I am a king because I have built a city to live in'; but there is no doubt that he took into consideration urban models that other Muslim sovereigns had created in the Near East and North Africa.[96] The affirmation of the power of the Umayyad caliph was reflected in the act of founding a new city, but it was also given a material dimension

[95] A. Lézine, *Mahdiya*; S. Denoix, 'Founded Cities of the Arab World', pp. 115–39. P. Cressier and M. Rammah, 'Ṣabra al-Manṣūriyya. Une nouvelle approche archéologique', pp. 613–33.

[96] M. Acién, 'Madīnat al-Zahrā'en el urbanismo musulmán', pp. 11–26.

through the wealth and exuberance displayed in the palace precinct. A whole section of this precinct was intended as a grandiose stage for the representations of power during caliphal receptions; the scale of magnificence that was achieved at Madīnat al-Zahrā' would have been impossible within the walls of the historic and venerable *alcázar* of Córdoba.[97]

The need to stage power and the existence of precedents and parallels that linked sound government with the creation of urban centres are two fundamental reasons that underpinned the foundation of Madīnat al-Zahrā'. However, even when considered in conjunction with one another, these reasons do not provide a complete answer for why so many resources and such great effort was devoted to building entirely new cities just a few kilometres away from flourishing and well-established cities such as Córdoba or Qayrawān. Seemingly it would have sufficed to add new wings to existing palaces, or make improvements to the old city to ensure they met the caliph's needs; it is hard to fully grasp why it was necessary to found a whole new city so close to an existing one.

Less convincing, in my opinion, are attempts to explain the foundation of Madīnat al-Zahrā' as part of an ideological programme, in which this city is symbolically linked to the gardens of Paradise.[98] There is a well-known passage in the Qur'an which reads: 'Have you [Prophet] considered how your Lord dealt with [the people] of Ad, of Iram, [the city] of lofty pillars, whose like has never been made in any land ... your Lord let a scourge of punishment loose on them' (Qur'an, 89, 5–7 and 12). This fragment has usually been interpreted as a reference to the story of Shaddād b. 'Ad, who had created a garden he called Iram in pre-Islamic times. He intended it to rival that of Paradise, which led to its destruction, along with his demise by a huge roar from heaven.[99] No caliph would have dared to suggest the slightest parallel between his building projects

[97] A. Vallejo, *La ciudad califal*, pp. 120–6.

[98] M. I. Fierro, 'Madīnat al-Zahrā, el paraíso y los fatimíes', p. 326. A distinct matter is the use of motifs reflecting the splendour of temporal power in descriptions of Paradise by religious scholars. Also, the epigraphy from the mosque of Madīnat al-Zahrā' includes Qur'anic passages underscoring that those who did good deeds would be rewarded in the afterlife, M. A. Martínez and M. Acién, 'La epigrafía de Madīnat al-Zahrā'', pp. 124–6.

[99] P. Neuekirchen, 'Biblical Elements in Qur'an 89, 6–8 and its Exegeses', pp. 679–80, which shows how this story was reworked by Wahb b. Munabbih, although it does not appear in the early *tafsīr* treatises.

and the epitome of divine grandiosity embodied in Paradise, something which would have been interpreted as a blasphemous aspiration to be akin to God, whom Islamic dogma defined as being unique and lacking any form of association.

It is thus necessary to reconsider the motives that led the medieval Muslim sovereigns to undertake a building project on the scale of Madīnat al-Zahrā', as well as the other cities founded in this era. Over the pages that follow, I discuss how the creation of these urban enclaves needs to be considered in relation to the complex social and political balance which, as a rule, shaped these dynasties, and in particular that of the Umayyad caliphate of al-Andalus.

The Creation of a 'Disembedded Capital'

The overarching reason for the Umayyad caliphs' decision to build Madīnat al-Zahrā' is that they sought to establish a new capital that was disembedded from Córdoba. A 'disembedded capital' is an urban centre founded by a governing elite, who abandons its previous capital in order to exercise power more freely without the restrictions and hindrances that the original foisted on them. The process of disembedding a new capital from an existing one is underpinned by a concern to put into practice a new political programme which, for various reasons, is considered more easily achievable in the new urban environment. The foundation of disembedded capitals is encountered at a number of historical moments and in diverse political contexts, but always in centralised societies that take the city as their ideal frame of reference for the exercise of government.[100]

In such contexts, the foundation of a 'disembedded capital' always indicates the creation of a renewed political context, in which the group that seeks to monopolise power endeavours to centralise its rule in an exclusive and exclusionary manner. On this basis, for example, in a disembedded capital administrative roles are organised in a manner better suited to the interests of the ruling elite, and likewise the army is more closely monitored to ensure its political centralisation. The aim of disembedded capitals is not to replace the

[100] A. H. Jaffe, 'Disembedded Capitals in Western Asian Perspective', pp. 549–80. In the discussion that follows I develop some of the ideas proposed by this author. The concept was used for the first time by anthropologists in areas of Mesoamerica. A further interesting use of the concept in D. M. Deliyannis, *Ravenna in Late Antiquity*, pp. 2–3.

original ones, which would have been impossible, as they were always well-established urban centres, but instead to offer a political and social alternative to them and eventually absorb them. In addition, the foundation of disembedded capitals always gives rise to changes in the language of political legitimisation by using novel forms as its medium of expression. This is highlighted, for instance, by new iconographic programmes, which draw on a peculiar mix of historical and innovative motifs. Likewise, heretofore unknown materials are used to underscore the novelty of the political project embodied in the new 'disembedded capital'.

All the characteristic elements of disembedded capitals are encountered in the configuration of Madīnat al-Zahrā'. Its foundation and successive remodelling can only be understood in the new political context created by the Umayyad caliphate, which involved the implementation of a wholly renewed social and political model in contrast to that of the emirate period. At Madīnat al-Zahrā', therefore, not only did a new city palace emerge, but also a set of material, political and ideological elements, some of which were used for the first time, while other pre-existing elements acquired a new significance. The appearance of these diverse features was inspired by the innovative project of the caliphate, which was begun by 'Abd al-Raḥmān III and honed by al-Ḥakam II. The features that Madīnat al-Zahrā' incorporated as a disembedded capital must be viewed as profoundly novel and original, and despite there having been precedents for some of them, they can only be understood in the novel circumstances generated by the Umayyad caliphate.

A good example of this is the new shape of the administration. The caliphate did not pioneer the use of eunuch slaves or *ṣaqāliba* for bureaucratic roles (a number of emirs had already done so in sporadic form), but the caliphs used them on what was then an unknown scale. The massive use of this class of personnel formed part of a new policy, whose aim was to transfer the running of the caliphal administration to people who depended on the caliph. As has already been discussed, this was to the detriment of the senior families who had dominated the state apparatus up until then. The accommodation of at least a part of the administrative system within the walls of the palace-city sought to increase and make visible this centralisation, and thereby establish a form of control that could more effectively be exercised in Madīnat al-Zahrā' than in

Córdoba itself. The same happened with the army. The policy of recruiting slave and stipendiary soldiers was not new either, but the scale at which it was carried out during the second half of the tenth century (fourth AH) was intended to give the caliph total control over the military, and also tailor it to his own interests and needs. Al-Ḥakam II's obsession with preventing abuses being committed by his civil servants and having efficient troops on call at all times was the embodiment of a political idea that sought to keep tight control over the state apparatus; an idea that conceived authority and power as united in the figure of the caliph, who should be able to exercise both without any interference.

Another aspect of the new caliphal state project that became a prominent feature in Madīnat al-Zahrā' was the external projection of the caliphate, which contrasted with the more sporadic and dispersed diplomatic relationships that had taken place during the emirate. Under the emirs there was only one exchange of embassies between Constantinople and Córdoba (that between ambassador Teophilus and 'Abd al-Raḥmān II in 840), while between 946 and 972 at least thirteen diplomatic missions were exchanged between both courts.[101] As was discussed in Chapter 6, this major change in the caliphate's foreign policy led to regular contacts not only with the Byzantine Empire, but also with the Ottonian dynasty, and with the myriad political powers in the north of the Iberian Peninsula and North Africa. As a result, changes had to be made to the representation of caliphal power. In 947 (336 AH), the first embassy sent by the Byzantine emperor to Córdoba was received by 'Abd al-Raḥmān III in the old *alcázar*, as at that time the grand audience hall at Madīnat al-Zahrā' had not yet been built; it was not completed until some point between 953 and 957 (342–5 AH), and from then on it was used for major diplomatic receptions.[102]

Finally, the language of political legitimisation used at Madīnat al-Zahrā' always reveals unquestionable novelties: from figurative representations of animals and people that were depicted on objects made in a wide range of media (ivories, marbles, textiles and ceramics), for which there is no precedent

[101] J. Signes Codoñer, 'Bizancio y al-Andalus en los siglos IX y X', p. 241.

[102] On the embassy sent in 336 AH, al-Maqqarī, *Nafḥ*, I, pp. 364–5; on the dating of the audience chamber known as the Salón Rico, M. A. Martínez Núñez, 'La epigrafía del salón de 'Abd al-Raḥmān III', pp. 111–14.

whatsoever in the emirate era, to the new forms that characterise the epigraphic decoration that was used profusely in the city palace. Indeed, these Arabic inscriptions reflect the new image 'of an Umayyad caliphate, an Andalusi response to the 'Abbāsid and Fāṭimid caliphates who they competed with'.[103]

The young Ja'far al-Muṣḥafī had expressed this idea with forceful poetic clarity: 'licitly the orchard of al-Zahrā' is yours'. Over an immense area of land, which the caliph could legitimately consider to be his property, the palace and its residential setting (*qaṣr*) formed a massive reserve, which also accommodated a city, over which the caliphate could exercise a degree of control that was impossible (or at least much more difficult) to wield in Córdoba, where the Umayyad sovereigns could not claim property rights over the whole urban environment of the medina. In contrast, Madīnat al-Zahrā' had the potential to be converted into the caliphate's major material tangible asset; an asset that 'Abd al-Raḥmān III left exclusively to his son al-Ḥakam II, while he compensated the rest of his brothers with properties distributed across Córdoba and its outlying areas. His aim seems to have been to impede by any possible means the inheritance of Madīnat al-Zahrā' being broken up before the city had begun to flourish, whereby it is very likely that 'Abd al-Raḥmān III's prohibition against his son having any children before becoming caliph was linked to his concern to limit the number of heirs who could fragment the ownership of the immense urban environment he hoped would rise up around the palace complex. Al-Ḥakam II's insistence on being succeeded by his son Hishām, despite all the inconveniences that his minority brought with it, was also intended to link in a lasting form the rule of the caliphate and the ownership of this city to a progeny that the caliph hoped would be long and successful.

Despite the forthrightness with which it was established, 'Abd al-Raḥmān III and al-Ḥakam II's project failed to obtain unanimous support. The internal response to the decisions and policies taken by both caliphs led to the formation of a broad and influential political faction, who tried to prevent the whole state apparatus entirely depending on the caliph and a coterie of slaves tied to him, while excluding the families who had traditionally monopolised his administration. The support that this faction initially gave to Muḥammad b. Abī 'Āmir, an ambitious legal scholar who had thrived at the heart of the

103 M. A. Martínez Núñez, 'Epigrafía monumental y élites sociales en al-Andalus', p. 37.

caliphal administration, took advantage of the minority of Hishām II to strip him of his power and instead clothe him in a diffuse religious authority. One of the first things that Muḥammad b. Abī ʿĀmir – al-Manṣūr – did as soon as he felt sure of his power was to deprive al-Zahrā' of any function other than that of serving as a gilded cage for the caliph. Al-Manṣūr's new political project, based on the creation of his own dynasty, took as its point of departure the creation of a new 'disembedded capital', Madīnat al-Zāhira, and he sought to make the state's civil and military administration gravitate around his new city while severing any link between them and the caliph.

Caliphal Córdoba: an Assessment

The majority of the urban features discussed in the preceding pages were linked in one form or other to the Umayyad dynasty. The mosques, the *almunias* and the markets that structured the urban fabric of Córdoba and its suburbs were often foundations or properties belonging to the emirs and caliphs, their wives and sons, or else prominent figures linked to their administration. Taken together, therefore, these configured what I have termed a 'topography of power', which generated, articulated and incentivised urban growth. This topography was visible in the medina of Córdoba, which contained buildings of such prominence as the magnificent Umayyad mosque, the souk and the *alcázar*, but the elements that made up the topography of power were still more abundant in the suburbs with their numerous mosques, *almunias* and cemeteries linked in one form or other to the dynasty.

Let us take the case of the *almunias*. These were centres of production and demand located on the outskirts of the city, whereby it is difficult to imagine they were self-sufficient; hence the suburbs that flourished around them. On the one hand, these suburbs supplied the demand of the *almunias*' possessors, while, on the other, the suburban population benefited from the surplus generated by the *almunia* itself. However, over time, the suburb that arose alongside the *almunia* created its own social dynamics, which were stimulated by economic, social and intellectual exchanges that had sufficient vigour to become self-sustaining. The foundation of mosques served to accentuate this urban growth – oratories were not founded in places devoid of people – as they provided a form of social structure that enhanced the Islamic character of the new urban environment. Finally, the establishment of souks centralised, incentivised and facilitated increased commercial exchange, which was the sap of urban growth.

In recent years, archaeology has revealed an impressive growth and transformation of the urban space in Córdoba's northern and western suburbs during the caliphal period, which involved the orthogonal layout of large streets and the construction of hundreds of new buildings. Produced with a highly uniform construction technique, these buildings, which included houses, as well as baths, mosques and warehouses, must have been built in a very short period of time. The houses were spacious residences – in fact, some were subsequently divided into separate dwellings – and they were provided with especially advanced water supply and sewerage systems, which had until then only been seen in palace architecture.

The unprecedented growth of these suburbs emerged in relation to the creation of Madīnat al-Zahrā'. The people who lived in these areas were bureaucrats, *'ulamā'* and senior military commanders linked to the Umayyad dynasty, who gravitated around its power; in short, wealthy people whose resources depended completely on the smooth functioning of the caliphate's civil, military and religious apparatus. The traveller, and perhaps also spy, Ibn Ḥawqal, who visited Córdoba around 970, noted that the caliph had offered an incentive of 400 dirhams to whoever moved to the suburbs, and that as a result an almost unbroken line of buildings had grown up connecting Córdoba with Madīnat al-Zahrā', something that archaeological research is showing was not far from the truth.[104]

What was the true extent of the intervention and stimulus of caliphal power in this process? At what point can an independent urban dynamic be identified? It is very difficult to accurately separate these two questions. As a general rule, it may be stated that the areas where the urban fabric best resisted the fall of the Umayyad caliphate – in particular the medina and the Axarquía area – were those that had the most solid and consolidated social dynamics. In contrast, the northern and western suburbs, which archaeology has clearly confirmed were completely abandoned at the end of the Umayyad caliphate, reveal that their growth depended to a high degree on the existence of caliphal

[104] M. Acién Almansa and A. Vallejo Triano, 'Urbanismo y estado islámico', pp. 127–34; Ibn Ḥawqal, *Ṣūrat al-arḍ*, trans. cit. pp. 110–11.

power: they were deserted in as sudden a manner as they had been created, without there even being time for their ordered well-planned structure to succumb to change.

Where the urban structure had been transformed as an outcome of internal social dynamics, as occurred in the medina of Córdoba and very possibly also in the suburban area to the east of the city, the urban layout tended to be more sinuous in form, the outcome of increased economic, social and intellectual exchanges. There were some legal opinions that defended an individual's right to use public space, and this created the possibility for the private appropriation of small portions of avenues and streets, as long as it did not prejudice anyone or interfere with the needs of adjacent properties. The result was the expansion of houses, shops and warehouse along the public roads, which led to these thoroughfares becoming less regular and narrower.[105]

When al-Ḥakam II ordered that the roads crossing Córdoba's souk and the Furn Burrīl suburb be widened, he was endeavouring to revert to this trend: the regular, orthogonal and planned topography of power sought to regulate the pressure exerted by social forces that sought constant change in the urban planning. For this policy, the caliph had the support of legal scholars such as Saʿd b. Muʿād, who considered that 'everything that interrupts the roads of the Muslims should be destroyed, because if the people were to build an extension on one side of the road at their own cost, it would also have to be allowed for those on the other side of the road, whereby the roads of the Muslims would become narrower'. However, other jurists backed the point of view of the urban populace. They were more tolerant to the people's needs, arguing that if the street was sufficiently wide and a modest extension had to be made to the houses across the street there was no problem in doing so.[106] The historical and material evidence demonstrates that this latter option ended up prevailing, while that which defended caliphal power was quashed. The result was the loss of orthogonal planning and the emergence of the characteristic plan of alleys, passages and intricate streets that we have come to be associated with Islamic urbanism.

[105] M. Acién Almansa, 'La formación del tejido urbano en al-Andalus', pp. 11–32.

[106] A. M. Carballeira, *Legados píos*, pp. 134–5. Saʿd b. Muʿād (d. 920/308 AH) was a traditionalist from Jaén who had settled in Córdoba, ibid., p. 358.

Time, without a doubt, was a factor in this process of transformation which overlaid these complex urban grids on the previous topography of power. However, attributing such an important process to the mere passage of time would be too simplistic. The key factors were linked to the latent tension between caliphal power and the social environment it was founded upon. Indications of this tension can be detected in the divergent legal opinions concerning urban planning of the aforementioned jurists, as well as the continual reprimands issued by the souk administrators to ensure that strict urban regulations were adhered to. It is difficult to identify the day-to-day evolution of this tension, as the Umayyad chroniclers make scant reference to the urban social strata of Córdoba, which barely merits any mention in their texts. Out of the 500 individuals who feature in the annals written by 'Īsā al-Rāzī, the members of Córdoba's popular class (*'āmma*) are noteworthy for their absence from an account monopolised by the *khaṣṣa*, the elite associated with caliphal power.

Nonetheless, the popular urban class existed, and it clearly had considerable influence, as is frequently highlighted by the caliph's policy of improving their living conditions along with specific urban initiatives. Thus, the building work on Córdoba's bridge ordered by al-Ḥakam was done 'to attend to his subjects and protect their interests' (*maṣāliḥ*); the closure of the Post House to extend the souk addressed the traders' complaints, who on occupying this new space 'fulfilled a hope that went beyond their aspirations'; the extension of a street in the Furn Burrīl suburb was made by the caliph 'to look after his subjects and out of concern to do good deeds', while the extension of the souk was undertaken 'out of concern for the common good of the Muslims and to protect their interests (*maṣāliḥ*)'.[107]

The rhetoric of power, thereby, reiterated that the caliph undertook public works with the intention of improving the living conditions of the people who formed the urban community, despite the fact that Umayyad authors expressed a supreme disdain for these people by completely ignoring them. This is the reflection of a major latent paradox at the heart of the Umayyad caliphate. Al-Ḥakam II was wholly conscious that, without the authority

[107] Ibn Ḥayyān, *Muqtabis VII*, ed. and trans. pp. 65, 66, 67–8, 71 and 78, 85, 90, 93. On the composition of the 'āmma and the contempt shown by different Arab writers, P. Chalmeta, *Historia socioeconómica de al-Andalus*, pp. 149–54.

conferred upon him by the Muslim community, his claims to be Commander of the Faithful were unfounded, yet the power structure that permitted him to exercise his authority needed the routine deployment of elements of coercion over his subjects. Balancing both aspects required a good dose of political skill, but also a broad social and political consensus of support for his caliphate. In the wake of al-Ḥakam's death that consensus collapsed: the result was an outburst of the social resistance that had always been latent and only revealed itself at certain moments. Examples of these tensions were the brawls between the Cordobans and the Berber stipendiary troops, the *ṭanjiyyūn*, or still more serious events, such as that which took place at the time of al-Manṣūr, when the *qāḍī* of Córdoba had to seek refuge in the al-Rabaḍ cemetery; to escape the ire of the people of Córdoba, the *qāḍī* had to take sanctuary in nothing less than the mausoleum (*turba*) of the mother of Caliph al-Ḥakam II, Marjān, while the crowds reproached him for the repeated inefficiency of the prayers to end the drought afflicting them, and, above all, for his corrupt habits of accepting gifts 'worthy only of oppressors'.[108] Explosions of discontent such as these underscore the existence of highly critical attitudes towards caliphal power. These attitudes were potentially justified by and articulated in the impressive corpus of prophetic traditions, commentaries and complex casuistic arguments that provided a foundation for resistance to the outrages committed by caliphal power.

Various sources record an intense scene that succinctly summarises this situation while offering a powerful and suggestive insight into these social tensions. It took place on 15 February 1009 (16 *jumāda* II 399 AH), the day the revolt broke out in Córdoba against caliph Hishām II's plans to appoint a son of the renowned al-Manṣūr successor to the caliphate. The uprising was led by a descendant of ʿAbd al-Raḥmān III with the support of other members of the Umayyad family who loathed such an extravagant scheme. The plotters met in an emblematic location within the topography of power in Córdoba, the Bāb al-Sudda of the *alcázar*, where many triumphal parades had taken place in previous years. After having overpowered the guards protecting the entrance, the rebels then launched themselves on the lodgings of the *ṣāḥib al-madīna*,

[108] al-Nubāhī, *al-Marqaba al-ʿulyā*, ed. and trans. pp. 113–14 and 250–1. The event perhaps took place during the drought of 989 to which I refer in Chapter 1.

whom 'they found in the upper chamber, reeling in his drunkenness with two slave singers who sang for him'. They killed him and left his body 'in the middle of the road, so that the people's feet trod upon him until he was dismembered'. Targeting the official in charge of tax collection has always been a typical action of any social revolt. The death of the *ṣāḥib al-madīna* prompted the revolt to spread throughout the souk and the western suburbs among crowds composed of 'goatherds, slaughtermen, low people and other rabble from the souk'.

The episode that followed is still more revealing. All the people from the souks 'brought ladders from the timber merchants' market, and joining them together with ropes, the common people (*'āmma*) scaled the wall and climbed on to the roof of the alcázar'. The image of artisans and souk merchants climbing the walls of the palace of the Umayyads with ladders taken from the market-place illustrates the anger and frustration of the people of Córdoba. Over the next few weeks, the same people, who up until then had scarcely merited any mention from caliphal writers, became the protagonists of events that these same writers described with disdain tinted with marked indignation. They recounted how 'the common people' (*'āmma*) formed an army, which was in the hands of 'around ten men of the most vile amongst the *'āmma*: bloodletters, cobblers, poultry farmers and dustmen'. They were people who disdained the rudiments of social conventions 'through the ignorance that dominated them and the stupidity of their brains'.

It comes as no surprise, therefore, that during the events of the civil war (*fitna*) that led to the demise of the Umayyad caliphate, some of the landmarks that defined the topography of power in Córdoba and its suburbs were destroyed. The most evident case was Madīnat al-Zāhira, the city that al-Manṣūr had built to replace the city palace of the caliphs; it was demolished by a mass of the common people, who sacked 'the majority of its storerooms of clothes, tapestries and furniture, perfumes and ornaments, treasure, weapons and munitions'. The destruction reached Madīnat al-Zahrā' afterwards. The people of Córdoba entered 'in the Friday mosque and stole its tapestries, its lamps, its Qu'rans, the chains of its lamps and the doors of its entrances'. The looting took place in June 1010 (*Shawwāl* 400 AH) and was repeated scarcely two years later, when a group of people 'set fire to the mosque of al-Zahrā' and took what was left: its lamps, the panels of the doors, its minbar and its carpets'. Shortly beforehand, a similar fate befell the *almunia* of al-Ruṣāfa, which was destroyed and also burnt by the people of Córdoba.[109]

All these events brought down the most emblematic elements of the topography of Umayyad power, with the sole exception of the Umayyad mosque, which at this time was fully integrated into the social fabric of the city. Other zones and less symbolic locations, albeit equally linked to caliphal rule, suffered a similar fate. The father of the renowned polygraph Ibn Ḥazm, a senior figure of the caliphal administration, decided to abandon the residence he owned close to Madīnat al-Zāhira when this city was destroyed. The house he left behind must have been an imposing residence. Located in the suburb next to *Munyat al-Mughīra*, it was one of those aristocratic houses (*dūr al-rū'asā'*) where celebrations were attended by family members and protégés of the powerful. It had a garden (*bustān*) which surrounded an elevated residence (*qaṣaba*) with large windows offering views over Córdoba and its outlying environs. Ibn Ḥazm's family moved to another residence they owned in the western suburb of *Balāṭ Mughīth*, which was also left in ruins shortly afterwards.[110]

The ruins of Ibn Ḥazm's family sum up the destruction of the world which was at its peak during the years recorded in the annals of 'Īsā al-Rāzī. The collapse of the caliphal rule embodied by al-Ḥakam II meant the demise of the many people who had flourished under its shadow; it was a catastrophe of such dimensions that it was even transposed to the cityscape of Córdoba. Having visited this family home many years after the unrest, Ibn Ḥazm describes its destruction in *Balāṭ Mughīt* mentioning the 'sinister rocky ground', the 'scattered rubble' and the 'fearful gullies' that now surrounded it. The sudden ruin that befell it is what archaeologists find today when they uncover the remains

[109] Ibn 'Idhārī, *al-Bayān*, III, ed. cit. pp. 57, 63, 74–5, 95, 102, 107; trans. cit. pp. 61, 66, 74–5, 89, 94, 98.

[110] Ibn Ḥazm, *Ṭawq al-ḥamama*, ed. and trans. pp. 222–3 (with a correction made to the translation so it reads 'al-Zāhira'), 328 and 329. The house was near the Pedroche stream or *al-nahr al-ṣaghīr*, G. Pizarro Berengena, *El abastecimiento de agua a Córdoba*. pp. 34–6 and 41. An archaeological confirmation of the sumptuousness of the houses and *almunias* built in this period in the eastern suburb in the shadow of Madīnat al-Zāhira in V. Barea Pareja, 'Un sector de arrabal oriental en la Córdoba califal', pp. 159–82, in which a spectacular catalogue of late-caliphal ceramics is presented.

of the demolished or abandoned caliphal suburbs, which look very similar to Ibn Ḥazm's description. Such ruins also evoke the words of a poet, who, in the wake of the civil war that brought down the Umayyad caliphate, said of Córdoba:

> destiny made it a loan, but later reclaimed the whole debt.

Sources and Bibliography

Sources

Abū 'Abd Allāh b. al-Hayṯam, *K. al-Munāẓarāt*, ed. and trans. W. Madelung and P. Walker, *The Advent of the Fatimids. A Contemporary Shi'i Witness*, London (2000).

Abūlẖayr al 'Ishbīlī, *Kitābu 'undati ṭṭabīb fī ma 'rifati nnabāt likulli labīb*, ed. and trans. J. Bustamante, F. Corriente and M. Tilmatine, *Libro base del médico para para el conocimiento de la botánica por todo experto*, Madrid (2007).

Akhbār Majmū'a. ed. and trans. E. Lafuente Alcántara, *Colección de tradiciones*, Madrid (1867). English trans.: D. James, *A History of the Early al-Andalus. The Akhbār Majmū'a. A Study of the Unique Manuscript in the Bibliothèque Nationale, Paris, with a Translation, Notes and Comments*, London (2012).

Beati in Apolapsin libri duodecim. Beato de Liébana. *Comentario al Apocalipsis*, edición facsímil del Códice de Gerona, Madrid (1975).

Calendario de Córdoba, ed. and trans. C. Pellat, *Le Calendrier de Cordoue*, Leiden (1961).

Codex Biblicus Legionensis, *Biblia Visigótico mozárabe*, reproducción facsimil del ms. del año 960 conservado en el Archivo Capitular de la Real Colegiata de San Isidoro de León, León (1991).

Constantine Porphyrogennetos, *The Book of Ceremonies*, ed. and trans. A. Moffat and M. Tall, Canberra (2012).

Corpus Scriptorum Muzarabicorum, ed. I. Gil, Madrid (1973).

Crónica Anónima de 'Abd al-Raḥmān III al-Nāṣir, ed. and trans. E. Lévi Provençal and E. García Gómez, Madrid–Granada (1950).

Dhikr bilād al-Andalus, ed. and trans. L. Molina, *Una descripción anónima de al-Andalus*, Madrid (1983).

Fondo Asín Palacios–Jaime Oliver Asín. Biblioteca de la Universidad Nacional de Educación a Distancia (UNED).

Gerbert d'Aurillac, *Correspondance*, I, ed. P. Rice and J. P. Callu, Paris (1993).

Historia Silense, ed. Pérez de Urbel and González Ruiz Zorrilla, Madrid (1959).

Ibn 'Abd al-Ra'ūf, *Risāla fī adāb al-ḥisba wa l-muḥtasib*, ed. E. Lévi Provençal, *Documents arabes pour servir ā l'histoire sociale et économique de l'Occident musulman au Moyen Age. I Trois traités hispaniques de ḥisba*, El Cairo, 1955, p. 67–116; trans. R. Arié, 'Traduction annotée et commentée des traités de ḥisba de Ibn 'Abd al-Ra'ūf et de 'Umar al-Garsīfī', *Hespéris Tamuda*, I, II, and III (1960).

Ibn 'Abd Rabbihi, *Arjūza*, trans. J. Monroe, 'The Historical arjūza of Ibn 'Abd Rabbihi, a Tenth Century Hispano-Arabic Epic Poem', *Journal of the American Oriental Society*, 91, 1 (1971), pp. 67–95.

Ibn Abī 'Usayba, *'Uyūn al-anbā' fī Tabaqāt al-aṭṭibā'*, ed. and trans. H. Jehier and A. Noureddine, Argel (1958/1377).

Ibn Abī Zar', *al-Anīs al-muṭrib bi rawḍ al-qirṭās fī akhbār mulūk al-Magrib wa ta'rīkh madīnat Fās*, ed. A. W. Benmansour, Rabat (1973); trans. Beaumier, Paris (1860).

Ibn Abī Zayd al-Qayrawānī, *Risāla*, ed. A. M. Qāsim al-Ṭahṭawī, Cairo (2005).

Ibn al-'Aṭṭār, *Kitāb al-wathā'iq wa l-sijillāt*, ed. P. Chalmeta, Madrid (1983); estudio and traducción P. Chalmeta and M. Marugán, *Formulario notarial y judicial andalusí*, Madrid (2000).

al-Bakrī, *Kitāb al-masālik wa l-mamālik*, ed. A. P. van Leeuven and A. Farré, Túnez (1992); trans. de Slane, *Description de l'Afrique septentrionale*, Argel (1857).

Ibn Bashkuwāl, *al-Ṣila fī ta'rīkh imāma al-Andalus wa 'ulāma'him*, ed. B. Awwad Ma'ruf, Tunis (2010).

Ibn Bassām, *al-Dhakhīra fī maḥāsin ahl al-jazīra*, ed. I. 'Abbās, Beirut (1979).

Ibn al-Faraḍī, *Ta'rīkh 'ulāma al-Andalus*, ed. F. Codera, Madrid (1891–2).

Ibn Ghālib, *K. farḥat al-anfus fī ta'rīkh al-Andalus* ed. L. 'Abd al-Badī', *Revue de l'Institut de Manuscrits Arabes*, I/II (1955), pp. 272–310.

Ibn Ḥayyān, *Muqtabis, II, 1*: ed. M. A. Makki, *Al-sifr al-thānī min Kitāb al-Muqtabis*, Riad (2003); trans. M. A. Makki and F. Corriente, *Crónica de los emires Alḥakam I y 'Abdarraḥmān II entre los años 796 y 847*, Zaragoza (2001).

Ibn Ḥayyān, *Muqtabis, II, 2*: ed. M. A. Makki, *al-Muqtabis min anbā' ahl al-Andalus*, Cairo (1971).

Ibn Ḥayyān, *Muqtabis, III*: ed. I. al-Arabi, *Kitāb al-Muqtabis fī ta'rīkh al-Andalus*, Casablanca (1990); trans. G. Turienzo, A. del Río, M. A. al-Samarah al-Mazawda, *Kitāb al-muqtabis fī tārīj riŷāl al-Andalus', también conocido como 'Al-Muqtabis min al anbā' ahl al-Andalus' = ('El libro de la compilación noticiosa acerca de los varones andalusíes', o 'La compilación noticiosa acerca de los andalusíes'): traducción a la lengua española del fragmento de esta obra conocido como 'Al-Muqtabis III' (Crónica del emir 'Abd Allāh I entre los años 275 H.–888–889 d.C. y 299 H.–912–913 d.C.)*, Madrid (2017).

Ibn Ḥayyān, *Muqtabis V*: ed. P. Chalmeta, F. Corriente and M. Sobh, *al-Muqtabis V*, Madrid (1979); trans. F. Corriente and M. J. Viguera, *Crónica del califa Abderrahman III An-Nāṣir entre los años 912 y 942 (Muqtabis V)*, Madrid (1981).

Ibn Ḥayyān, *Muqtabis VII: al-Muqtabis fī akhbār balad al-Andalus*, ed. 'Abd al-Raḥmān 'Alī al-Ḥajjī, Beirut (1965); trans. *El califato de Córdoba en el Muqtabis de Ibn Ḥayyān. Anales Palatinos del califa de Córdoba al-Ḥakam II por 'Īsā ibn Aḥmad al-Rāzī (360–364=971–975 J.C.), traducción del ms. árabe de la Real Academia de la Historia* por Emilio García Gómez, Madrid (1967).

Ibn Ḥawqal, *Ṣūrat al-arḍ*, ed. J.-H. Kramers, Leiden (1967); trans. J.-H. Kramers and G. Wiet, *Configuration de la terre*, Paris (1964).

Ibn Ḥazm, *Jamharat ansāb al-'arab*, ed. A. S. M. Harun, Beirut (1982); trans. E. Terés, 'Linajes árabes en al-Andalus', *Al-Andalus* (1957), 22.1, 55–111; 22.2, 337–76.

Ibn Ḥazm, *Naqṭ al-'arūs*, ed. and trans. L. Seco de Lucena, Valencia (1974).

Ibn Ḥazm, *Ṭawq al-ḥamama*, Arabic text and trans. J. Sánchez Ratia, Madrid (2009).

Ibn 'Idhārī, *Kitāb al-Bayān al-Mughrib*, vols. I/II ed. G. S. Colin and E. Lévi Provençal, Leiden (1948–51); vol III, ed. E. Lévi Provençal, Paris (1930); trans. E. Fagnan, *Histoire de l'Afrique du Nord et de l'Espagne intitulée al-Bayano l-Mogrib*, Argel (1901–4); trans. vol. III, F. Maíllo, *La caída del califato de Córdoba y los reyes de Taifas*, Salamanca (1993).

Idrīs 'Imād al-Dīn, *'Uyūn al-ajbār*, trans. S. Jiwa, *The founder of Cairo. The Fatimid Imam al-Mu'izz and His Era*, London (2013).

Ibn Khaldūn, *Muqaddima*, ed. A. A. M. al-Darwish, Damascus (2004); trans. J. Feres, *Introducción a la Historia Universal (Al-Muqaddimah)*, Mexico (1977).

Ibn-Khaldūn, *K. al-'Ibār*, ed. Beirut (1981); trans. De Slane, *Histoire des Berberes et des dynasties musulmanes de l'Afrique Septentrionale*, Paris (1978).

Ibn Khaqan, *Matmaḥ al-anfus wa masraḥ al-tānnus fī mulḥ ahl al-Andalus*, ed. Constantina (1884/1302).

Ibn al-Khaṭīb, *al-Iḥāta fī akhbār Gharnaṭa*, ed. M. A. 'Inān, Cairo (1973/7).

Muḥammad b. Waḍḍāḥ, *Kitāb al-bidā' (Tratado contra las innovaciones)* ed. M. I. Fierro, Madrid (1988).

al-Nuwayrī, *Nihāyat al-arab fī funūn al-adab*, ed. and trans. parciales G. Remiro, *Historia de los musulmanes de España y África por En-Nuguairí*, Granada, 1917.

Ibn al-Qūṭiya, *Ta'rīkh ifitītāḥ al-Andalus*, ed. P. de Gayangos, E. Saavedra and F. Codera; trans. J. Ribera, *Historia de la conquista de España de Abenalcotía el Cordobés: seguida de fragmentos históricos de Abencotaiba*, Madrid (1926); trans. D. James, *Early Islamic Spain. The History of Ibn al-Qūṭiya*, Abingdon (2009).

Ibn Sahl, *al-I'lām bi nawāzil al-aḥkām al-ma'rūf bi l-Aḥkām al-kubrā*, ed. N. M. al-Tuwayjirī (1995); trans. R. Daga Portillo, *Organización jurídica y social en la España Musulmana. Traducción y Estudio de al-Aḥkām al-Kubrā de Ibn Sahl*, unpub. doctoral thesis, University of Granada (1990).

al-Khushanī, *Kitāb al-quḍāt bi Qurṭuba*, ed. and trans. J. Ribera, *Historia de los jueces de Córdoba por Aljoxani*, Madrid (1914).

al-Khushanī, *Akhbār al-fuqahā'wa l muḥaddithīn*, ed. M. L. Ávila and L. Molina, Madrid (1992).

Kitāb fī tartīb awqāt al-ghirāsa wa l-maghrūsāt, ed. and trans. and with notes by Á. C. López López, Un tratado agrícola andalusí, anónimo, Madrid (1990).

Liutprando de Cremona, *Legatio*, ed. Becker, *Liudprandi Opera*, *Monumenta Germaniae Historica, SRG in usum scholarum* (1915).

al-Maqqarī, *Nafḥ al-ṭīb min guṣn al-Andalus al-raṭīb*, ed. I. 'Abbās, Beirut (1968).

al-Marwānī, *'Uyūn al-imāma wa nawāẓīr al-siyāsa*, ed. B. Awwād Ma'rūf and Ṣ. Muḥammad Jarrar, Tunis (2010).

al-Nubāhī, *Kitāb al-Marqaba al-'ulyā fī man yastaḥiqq al-qaḍā'wa l -futyā*, ed. and trans. A. Cuellas Marqués, Granada (2005).

al-Qāḍī 'Iyāḍ, *Tartīb al-madārik wa taqrīb al-masālik li ma'rifat a'lām madhhab Mālik*, ed. Rabat (–1983).

al-Qāḍī al-Nu'mān, *Iftitāḥ al-Da'wa*, trans. Haji, H. *Founding the Fatimid State: The Rise of an Early Islamic Empire: An Annotated English Translation from al-Qadi al-Nu'man's Iftitah al-Da'wa*, London, New York (2006).

al-Ṣābi', *Rusūm dār al-khilāfa. The Rules and Regulations of the 'Abbāsid Court*, trans. E. A. Salem, Beirut (1977).

The Taktika of Leo VI, ed. and trans. G. T. Dennis, Washington (2010).

al-'Udhrī, *Tarṣī' al-akhbār wa tanwī al-āṭār wa l-bustān fī garā'ib al-buldān*, ed. al-Ahwānī, Madrid (1965).

Vie de l'ustadh Jaudhar (contenant sermons, lettres et rescrits des premiers califes fatimides) écrite par Mansûr le secrétaire a á l'epoque du caliphe al-'Aziz billâh 365–386/975–996), trans. M. Canard, Argelia (1958).

Vita Ihoannis abbate Gorziensis, G. H. Pertz (ed.), *Monumenta Germaniae Historica, Scriptores*, IV, Hanover (1841).

al-Zuhrī, K., *al-Jaʿrāfiyya*, ed. M. Hadj Sadok, *Bulletin d'Etudes Orientales*, XXI (1968), pp. 7–312; trans. D. Bramon, *El mundo en el siglo XII. El tratado de al-Zuhrī*, Barcelona (1991).

Bibliography

Abdelhamid, A. (2006). *Manuscrits et bibliotèques musulmanes en Algérie*, Arles.

Acién Almansa, M. (1987). 'Madīnat al-Zahrā'en el urbanismo musulmán', *Cuadernos de Madīnat al-Zahrā'*, I, pp. 11–26.

Acién Almansa, M. (1995). 'Materiales e hipótesis para una interpretación del Salón de 'Abd al-Raḥmān al-Nāṣir', in A. Vallejo (ed.), *Madīnat al-Zahrā' El Salón Rico de 'Abd al-Raḥmān III*, pp. 179–95.

Acién Almansa, M. (1997). *Entre el feudalismo y el islam. 'Umar b. Ḥafṣūn en los hstoriadores, en las fuentes y en la historia'*, 2nd ed., Jaén.

Acién Almansa, M. (2020). 'On the Role of Ideology in the Characterization of Social Formations. The Islamic Social Formation', in *Obras Escogidas*, vol. I, pp. 171–222.

Acién Almansa, M. (2001). 'La formación del tejido urbano in al-Andalus' in J. Pasini (ed.), *La ciudad medieval: de la casa al tejido urbano: Actas del primer curso de Historia y Urbanismo Medieval organizado por la Universidad de Castilla-La Mancha*, Toledo, pp. 11–32.

Acién Almansa, M. and A. Vallejo Triano (1998). 'Urbanismo y Estado Islámico: De "Corduba a Qurtuba-Madīnat al-Zahrā"', in P. Cressier, and M. García Bernal (eds), *Genèse de la villa islamique en Al-Andalus et au Maghreb Occidental*, Madrid, pp. 107–36.

Aguadé, J. (1986). 'Some Remarks about Sectarian Movements in Al-Andalus', *Studia Islamica*, 64, pp. 53–77.

Aguilar Sebastián, V. (1994). 'Onomástica de origen árabe en el reino de León (siglo X)', *Al-Qanṭara*, 15, 2, pp. 351–64.

Aguilar Sebastián, V. and F. Rodríguez Mediano (1994). 'Antroponimia árabe en la documentación leonesa (siglos VIII–XIII)', in *El Reino de León en la alta Edad Media, IV*, León, pp. 499–633.

Aguirre Sádaba, J. and C. Jiménez Mata (1979), *Introducción al Jaén islámico*, Jaén.

Aillet, C. (2008). 'Anthroponyme, migrations, frontières: notes sur la 'situation mozarabe' dans le nord-ouest ibérique (IXe–Xie siècle)', *Annales du Midi* 120/261, pp. 5–32.

Aillet, C. (2010). *Les Mozarabes. Christianisme, islamisation et arabisation en péninsule Ibérique (IXe–XIIe siècle)*, Madrid.

Aillet, C. (2015). 'Islamisation et évolution du peuplement chrétien en al-Andalus (VIIIe–IXe siècle)' in D. Valérian (ed.), *Islamisation et arabisation de l'Occident musulman medieval (VIIe–XIIe siècle)*, Paris, pp. 151–92.

Alejandre Alcalde, V. (2014). *El sistema defensivo musulmán entre las Marcas Media y Superior de al-Andalus (siglos X–XII)*, Zaragoza.

Algora Weber, M. D. (2015). 'Emilio García Gómez: de catedrático a embajador. La experiencia de una década (1958–1969)', in M. Hernando Larramendi, I. González González and B. López García (eds), *El Instituto Hispano-Árabe de Cultura. Orígenes y evolución de la diplomacia pública española hacia el mundo árabe*, Madrid, pp. 47–58.

Almagro, A. (1987). 'Planimetría de las ciudades hispanomusulmanas', *al-Qanṭara*, VIII, 1 and 2, pp. 421–48.

Almagro, A. (2008). 'La puerta califal del castillo de Gormaz', *Arqueología de la Arquitectura*, 5, pp. 55–77.

Alonso, N., F. Antolín and H. Kirchner (2014). 'Novelties and Legacies in Crops in the Islamic Period in the Northeast Iberian Peninsula: The Archaeobotanical Evidence in Madīna Balagī, Madīna Lārida and Madīna Turṭūša', *Quaternary International*, 346, pp. 149–61.

Al-Andalus. Las artes islámicas en España. Catálogo de la exposición (1992). Madrid.

Anderson, G. (2013). *The Islamic Villa in Early Medieval Iberia: Architecture and Court in Umayyad Córdoba*, Surrey.

Angelidi, C. (2013). 'Designing Receptions in the Palace (*De Cerimoniis*, 2.15)', in A. Beihammer, S. Constantinou and M. Parani (eds), *Court Ceremonies and Rituals of Power in Byzantium and the Medieval Mediterranean: Comparative Perspectives*, Leiden–Boston, pp. 465–85.

Aparicio Sánchez, L. and Cano Montoro, E. (2010), 'Fragmento cerámico con decoración antropomorfa en verde y manganeso hallado en el arrabal de El Fontanar (Córdoba)', *Antiquitas*, 22, pp. 183–96.

Arce, J. (2000). 'La fundación de nuevas ciudades en el imperio romano tardío: de Diocleciano a Justiniano (s IV–VI)' in G. Ripoll López and F. Gurt Esparraguera (eds), *Sedes Regiae (ann. 400–800)*, Barcelona, pp. 31–62.

Arjona, A. (2008). 'Las basílicas mozárabes', *al-Mulk*, 8, pp. 34–52.

Arnold, F. (2017). *Islamic Palatine Architecture in the Western Mediterranean*, Oxford.

Arnold, F., A. Canto García and A. Vallejo Triano (2006). 'La almunia de Rummaniyya. Resultados de una documentación arquitectónica', *Cuadernos de Madīnat al-Zahrā*, 6, pp. 181–204.

Athamina, K. (1989). 'The Black Banners and the Socio-Political Significance of Flags and Slogans in Medieval Islam', *Arabica*, 36, pp. 307–326.

Ávila, M. L. (1984). 'La fecha de redacción del Muqtabis', *al-Qanṭara*, V, pp. 93–108.

Ávila, M. L. (1989). 'Las mujeres sabias en al-Andalus', in M. J. Viguera, *La mujer en al-Andalus: reflejos históricos de su actividad y categorías sociales*, Seville, pp. 139/184.

Ávila, M. L. (dir.) (2018) *Prosopografía de los ulemas de al-Andalus*, http://www.eea.csic.es/pua/

Ávila, M. L. and L. Molina (1984). 'Sociedad y cultura en la Marca Superior de al-Andalus', in *Historia de Aragón*, III, Zaragoza, pp. 83–108.

Babuin, A. (2001). 'Standards and Insignia in Byzantium', *Byzantion*, 71, 1, pp. 5–59.

Balaña Abadía, P. (1982). 'Indices de los Anales palatinos de al-Ḥakam II', *al-Qanṭara*, III, pp. 227–48.

Ballestín Navarro, X. (2004). *Al-Mansūr y la dawla 'amiriya. Una dinámica de poder y legitimidad en el Occidente muslmán medieval*, Barcelona.

Ballestín Navarro, X. (2006). 'Jil'a y Monedas. El poder de los Banu Marwan en el Magrib al-Aqsā', *al-Qanṭara*, XXVI, 2, pp. 391–415.

Balog P., Yvon J. (1958). 'Monnaies à legends arabes de l'Orient latin', *Revue numismatique*, 6, 1, pp. 133–68.

Balog, P. (1961), 'History of the Dirhem in Egypt from the Fāṭimid Conquest until the Collapse of the Mamlūk Empire', *Revue Numismatique*, 3, pp. 109–46.

Barceló, C. (2004). 'Epitaph of an 'Āmirī (Cordova 374/985 CE)', *Journal of Islamic Archaeology*, 1.2, pp. 121–42.

Barceló, C. (2004) 'Las inscripciones omeyas de la alcazaba de Mérida', *Arqueología y Territorio Medieval*, II, I.

Barceló, C. and Labarta, A. (1988). 'Ocho relojes de sol hispanomusulmanes', *al-Qanṭara*, IX, 2, pp. 231–47.

Barceló, C. and Labarta, A. (1991). 'Acerca de dos cuadrantes solares de Medina Azahara', *al-Qanṭara*, XII, 1, pp. 281–3.

Barceló, M. (1995). 'El califa patente: el ceremonial omeya de Córdoba o la escenificación del poder', in A. Vallejo Triano (ed.), *Madīnat al-Zahrā'. El Salón de 'Abd al-Raḥmān III*, Córdoba, pp. 155–6.

Barea Pareja, V. (2010). 'Un sector de arrabal oriental en la Córdoba califal. Propuesta de tipología cerámica', *Antiquitas*, 22, pp. 159–82.

Barrera, M. Gómez, C. and Burón, M. (2014) 'Estudios previos y metodologia aplicada a la conservación de ajuares funerarios textiles en Castilla y León', in L. Rodríguez Peinado and A. Cabrera Lafuente, *La investigación textil y los nuevos métodos de estudio*, Madrid, pp. 89–98.

Barrucand, M. (1995). 'Observaciones sobre las iluminaciones de Coranes hispano-magrebíes', in *Arte islámico en Granada: Propuesta para un museo de la Alhambra: 1 de abril–30 de septiembre de 1995, Palacio de Carlos V, La Alhambra*, Granada, pp. 166–7.

Bazzana A. (2005). 'Subsistances et réserves de securité au villages: greniers, jarres et silos dans les habitats musulmans d'al-Andalus', in *Cinquante années d'études médiévales*, pp. 575–608.

Beckwith, J. (1960). *Caskets from Cordoba*, London.

Benco, N. (2002). 'Archaeological Investigations at Al-Basra, Morocco', *Bulletin d'Archéologie Maroccaine*, 19, pp. 293–340.

Benet, A. (1983). 'L'origen de les families Cervelló, Castellvell i Castellet', *Acta Historia et Archaeologica Mediaevalia*, 4, pp. 79.

Bennison, A. K. (2007). 'The Peoples of the North in the Eyes of the Muslims of Umayyad al-Andalus (711–1031)', *Journal of Global History*, 2, pp. 157–74.

Bernis, C. (1954). 'Tapicería hispano-musulmana (siglos IX–XI)', *Archivo Español de Arte*, 27, 107, pp. 197–8.

Biblioteca de al-Andalus (2012–13), Almería, 7 vols. Apéndice y Balance de resultados e índices.

Blair, S. (2005) 'What the Inscriptions Tell Us: Texts and Message on the Ivories from al-Andalus', *Journal of the David Collection*, 2, pp. 75–100.

Bonnassie, P. (1957). *La Catalogne du milieu du Xe ā la fin du XIe siècle: Croissance et mutations d'une société*, Toulouse.

Bosworth, C. E. (1969). "Abdallāh al-Khwārazmī on the Technical Terms of the Secretary's Art', *Journal of the Economic and Social History of the Orient*, 12, pp. 113–64.

Bray, J. (2004). 'Men, Women and Slaves in Abbasid Society', in L. Brubaker and J. M. H. Smith, *Gender in the Early Medieval World*, Cambridge, pp. 121–46.

Brett, M. (2001). *The Rise of the Fatimids. The World of the Mediterranean and the Middle East in the Fourth Century of the Hijra, Tenth Century CE*, Leiden.

Bueno Sánchez, M. (2012) '¿Frontera en el Duero oriental? Construcción y mutación de funciones en el *tagr Banū Sālim* (siglos VIII–XI)', in Martos, J. and M. Bueno Sánchez (eds) *Fronteras en discusión: la Península Ibérica en el siglo XII*, Madrid, pp. 165–90.

Büntgen, U., et al. (2006). 'Summer Temperature Variations in the European Alps, A. D. 755–2004', *Journal of Climate*, 19, pp. 5,606–23.

Büntgen, U. et al. (2011). '2500 years of European Climate Variability and Human Susceptibility', *Science*, 331, pp. 578–82.

Buresi, P. (2008). 'Une relique almohade: l'utilisation du Coran de la Grand Mosquée de Cordoue (attribué ā Utman b. 'Affan 644–656)', in *Lieux du cultes: aires votives, temples, églises, mosquées*, Paris, pp. 273–80.

Camarero Castellano, I. (2003). 'Acerca de las calamidades agrícolas: el concepto de *ŷā'iḥa* en los tratados malikíes de al-Andalus', *Miscelánea de Estudios Árabes y Hebraicos*, 52, pp. 63–78.

Camarero Castellano, I (2015). *Sobre el 'Estado de Ŷā'iḥa'. Teoría y práctica jurídica de la calamidad rural y urbana en al-Andalus (ss. VII–XV)*, Seville.

Canard, M. (1957). 'Une famille de partisans, puis adversaires des Fatimides en Afrique du Nord', in *Mélanges d'histoire et d'archéologie de l'Occident musulman*, II, Hommage ā Georges Marçais, pp. 33–49.

Cano Piedra, C. (1996) *La cerámica verde-manganeso de Madínat al-Zahrā*, Granada.

Canto Garcia, A. (1994). 'De contenidos metálicos en la moneda Hispano-Arabe de Epoca Omeya', *Anaquel de Estudios Arabes*, 5, pp. 129–37.

Canto Garcia, A. (1995). 'Las monedas del período 361–362 de la ceca de Madinat al-Zaḥra', *Boletín del Museo Arqueológico Nacional*, III, 2, pp. 205–10.

Canto García, A. (2004). 'El dinar en al-Andalus en el siglo X', *Cuadernos de Madīnat al-Zahrā'*, 5, pp. 327–38.

Canto García, A. (2007). *Maskukat. Tesoros de monedas andalusíes en el Museo Arqueológico de Córdoba*, Cordova.

Canto García, C. and P. Cressier (eds) (2008). *Minas y metalurgia en al-Andalus y Magreb occidental. Explotación y poblamiento*, Madrid.

Carballeira Debasa, A. (2002). *Legados píos y fundaciones familiares en al-Andalus (siglos IV/X–VI–XII)*, Madrid.

Carballeira Debasa, A. (2011). 'Caridad y poder político en época omeya', in *Caridad y compasión en biografías islámicas*, Madrid, pp. 98–104.

Carballeira Debasa, A. (2017). 'The Use of Charity as a Means of Political Legitimation in Umayyad al-Andalus', *Journal of the Economic and Social History of the Orient*, 60, pp. 250–1.

Cardoso, E. (2018), 'The Scenography of Power in Al-Andalus and the 'Abbasid and Byzantine Ceremonials', *Medieval Encounters*, 24, pp. 390–434.

Carvajal Castro, A. (2012). 'Superar la frontera: mecanismos de integración territorial entre el Cea y el Pisuerga', *Anuario de Estudios Medievales*, 42, 2, pp. 601–28.

Casal, M. T. and León, A. (2003). *Los cementerios musulmanes de Qurtuba*, Cordova.

Casal, M. T. et al. (2006). 'Espacio y usos funerarios en la Qurtuba islámica', *Anales de Arqueología Cordobesa*, 17, pp. 257–90.

Casamar, M. and Zozaya, J. (1991). 'Apuntes sobre la ŷuba funeraria de la colegiata de Oña (Burgos)', *Boletín de Arqueología Medieval*, 5, pp. 39–60.

Casulleras, J. (1998). 'The Contents of Qāsim b. Muṭarrif al-Qaṭṭān's *Kitāb al-Hay'a*', in M. I. Fierro and J. Samsó (eds), *The Formation of al-Andalus*, II, *Language, Religion, Culture and the Sciences*, pp. 339–58.

Chalmeta, P. (1976). 'Simancas y Alhándega', *Hispania*, 36, pp. 350–444.

Chalmeta, P. (1982), 'Deux précisions d'historiographie hispano-arabe', *Arabica*, XXIX, 3 (1982), pp. 330–5.

Chalmeta, P. (1987). 'Acerca del 'amal en al-Andalus. Algunos casos concretos', *Anuario de Historia del Derecho Español*, 57, pp. 339–64.

Chalmeta, P. (2001) 'Fiscalité musulmane: au sujet du ṭabl', in F. Sanagustin (dir.), *L'Orient au cœur: en l'honneur d'André Miquel*, Paris, pp. 217–22.

Chalmeta, P. (2010), *El zoco medieval. Contribución al estudio de la historia del mercado*, Almería.

Chalmeta, P. (2013) 'Derecho y práctica fiscal musulmana: el primer siglo y medio', in X. Ballestín (ed.), *Lo que vino de Oriente: Horizontes, praxis y dimensión material de los sistemas de dominación fiscal en al-Andalus*, Oxford.

Chalmeta, P. (2021) *Historia socioeconómica de al-Andalus*, Almería.

Chavarría, A. (2004–5). 'Romanos y visigodos en el valle del Duero (siglos V–VIII)', *Lancia*, 6, pp. 187–204.

Chehab, H. K. (1993). 'On the Identification of 'Anjar (Ayn al-Jarr) as an Umayyad Foundation', *Muqarnas*, 10, pp. 42–8.

Christys, A. (2015). *Vikings in the South. Voyages to Iberia and the Mediterranean*, London.

Clapés Salmoral, R. (2013). 'Un baño privado en el arrabal occidental de Madinat Qurtuba', *Arqueología y Territorio Medieval*, 20, pp. 97–128.

Clapés Salmoral, R. (2014–15). 'La actividad comercial de Córdoba en época califal a través de un edificio hallado en el arrabal de poniente', *Anales de Arqueología Cordobesa*, 25–6, pp. 225–54.

Codera, F. (1892), *Misión histórica en la Argelia y Túnez*, Madrid.

Cohen, G. M. (2006). *The Hellenistic Settlements in Syria, the Red Sea Basin, and North Africa*, Berkeley.

Córdoba de la Llave, R. et al. (2008), *Los molinos hidráulicos del Gudalquivir en la ciudad de Córdoba. Estudio histórico y arquitectónico*, Madrid.

Corella, J. P. et al. (2011). 'Climate and Human Impact on a Meromictic Lake during the Last 6,000 Years (Montcortés Lake, Central Pyrenees, Spain)', *Journal of Paleolimnology*, 46, pp. 351–67.

Corriente, F. (1997). *A Dictionary of Andalusi Arabic*, New York.

Cressier, P., A. El Boudjay and H. El Figuigui (1998). 'Ḥağar al-Naṣr, "capitale" idrisside du Maroc septentrional: archéologie et histoire (IVeH./Xe ap. J-C.)', in P. Cressier and M. García Arenal (eds), *Genèse de la ville islamique en al-Andalus et au Maghreb occidental*, Madrid.

Cressier, P. and M. Rammah (2006). 'Ṣabra al-Manṣūriyya. Une nouvelle approche archéologique', *Comptes rendus des seánces de l'Académie des Inscriptions et Beellers Lettres*, pp. 613–33.

Cutler, A. (1997). 'Constantinople and Cordoba: Cultural Exchange and Cultural Difference in Ninth and Tenth Centuries', in M. Morfakidis and A. Roldán (eds), *La religión en el mundo griego de la Antigüedad a la Grecia moderna*, Granada, pp. 417–38.

Cutler, A. (2005). 'Ivory Working in Umayyad Córdoba: Techniques and Implications', *Journal of the David Collection*, 2, 1, pp. 37–47.

Dachraoui, F. (1958). 'Tentative d'infiltration šī'īte en Espagne musulmane sous le régne d'al-Ḥakam II', *al-Andalus: revista de las Escuelas Árabes de Madrid y Granada*, 23, pp. 97–106.

Daftary, F. (1990). *The Isma'ilis: Their History and Doctrines*, 2nd ed., Cambridge.

De Felipe Rodríguez, H. (1997). *Identidad y onomástica de los beréberes en al-Andalus*. Madrid.

Deliyannis, D. M. (2010). *Ravenna in Late Antiquity*. Cambridge.

Denoix, S. (2008). 'Founded Cities of the Arab World from the Seventh to the Eleventh Centuries', in S. K. Jayyusi et al. (eds), *The City in the Islamic World*, 2, I, Leiden–Boston, pp. 115–39.

De Prémare, A. L. and P. Guichard (1981). 'Croissance urbaine et société rurale à Valence au début de l'époque des royaumes de Taifas (XIe siècle)', *Revue de l'Occident musulman et de la Méditerranée*, 31, pp. 15–30.

Devries, K. and R. D. Smith (2007). *Medieval Weapons. An Illustrated History of their Impact*, Santa Barbara.

Domínguez Castro, F. et al. (2014). 'Climatic Potential of Islamic Chronicles in Iberia: extreme droughts (711–1010)', *The Holocene*, 24, 3, pp. 370–4.

Ehrenkreutz, A. (1964). 'The taṣrīf and tas'īr Calculations in Mediaeval Mesopotamian Fiscal Operations', *Journal of the Economic and Social History of the Orient*, 7, pp. 46–56.

El Cheikh, N. (2013). 'An Abbasid Caliphal Family', in L. Brubaker, L. and S. Tougher (eds), *Approaches to the Byzantine family*, Farnham, pp. 335–6.

El Cheikh, N. (2014). 'The Institutionalization of 'Abbāsíd Ceremonial', in J. Hudson and A. Rodríguez López (eds), *Divergent Paths? The Shapes of Power and Institutions in Medieval Islam and Christendom*, Leiden, pp. 358–64.

Encyclopaedia of Islam (1960–2007) 2nd ed., ed. P. Berman et al. Leiden.

Escalona, J. (2000). 'Épica, crónicas y genealogías. En torno a la historicidad de la leyenda de los infantes de Lara', *Cahiers de Linguistique Hispanique Médiévale*, 23, pp. 113–76.

Escalona, J. (2013). 'Military Stress, Central Power and Local Response in the County of Castile in the Tenth Century', in J. Baker, S. Brookes and A. Reynolds (eds), *Landscapes of Defence in Early Medieval Europe*, Turnhout, pp. 341–67.

Ettahiri, A. (2004). 'La ville mediévale d'al-Basra et ses deux ports', in L. de Maria and R. Turchetti (eds), *Rotte e porti del Mediterraneo dopo la caduta dell'Impero Romano d'Occidente. Continuità e innovazioni tecnologiche e funzionali*, Genoa, pp. 157–70.

Ewert, C. (1995). 'Elementos de decoración vegetal del Salón Rico de Madīnat al-Zahrā': los tableros parietales', in A. Vallejo (ed.), *Madīnat al-Zahrā' El Salón Rico de 'Abd al-Raḥmān III*, Cordova, pp. 43–57.

Ewert, C. (1998). 'Die dekorelemente des soätumaiyadischen fund-komplexes aus dem Cortijo del Alcaide (prov. Cordoba)', *Madrider Mitteilungen*, 39, pp. 356–491.

Fierro, M. I. (1985), 'Los mālikíes de al-Andalus y los dos árbitros (al-ḥakāman)', *al-Qanṭara*, XII, 1, p. 89–95.

Fierro, M. I. (1987). 'Bazī', mawlā de 'Abd al-Raḥmān I y sus descendientes', *Al-Qanṭara*, VIII, I, pp. 99–118.

Fierro, M. I. (1987). *La Heterodoxia en al-Andalus durante el period omeya*, Madrid.

Fierro, M. I. (1988). 'The Introduction of ḥadīṯ in al-Andalus', *Der Islam*, LXVI, pp. 68–93.

Fierro, M. I. (1996). 'Caliphal Legitimacy and Expiation in al-Andalus', in M. Khalid Masud, B. Messick and D. S. Powers (eds), *Islamic Legal Interpretation. Muftis and their Fatwas*, Harvard, pp. 55–62.

Fierro, M. I. (1997). 'El alfaquí bereber Yaḥya b. Yaḥya al-Laythi (m. 234–848). "El inteligente de al-Andalus"', in M. Marín, M. and M. L. Avila (eds), *Biografías y género biográfico en el occidente islámico*, Madrid, pp. 269–344.

Fierro, M. I. (1998). 'al-Aṣfar again', *Jerusalem Studies in Arabic and Islam*, 22, pp. 198–213.

Fierro, M. I. (1999). 'Los mawālī de 'Abd al-Raḥmān I', *al-Qanṭara*, XX, pp. 65–97.

Fierro, M. I. (2004). 'Madīnat al-Zahrā, el paraíso y los fatimíes', *al-Qanṭara*, XXV, 2, pp. 299–327.

Fierro, M. I. (2004). 'Violencia, política y religión en al-Andalus durante el S. IV/X: el reinado de 'Abd al-Raḥmān III', in M. I. Fierro (ed.), *De muerte violenta. Política, religión y violencia en al-Andalus*, Madrid, pp. 39–45.

Fierro, M. I. (2005). *'Abd al-Rahman III. The First Cordoban Caliph*, Oxford.

Fierro, M. I. (2007) 'The Mobile Minbar in Cordoba', *Jerusalem Studies in Arabic and Islam*, 33, pp. 149–68.

Filiu, J. P. (2008). *L'apocalypse dans l'Islam*. Paris.

Fraser, P. M. (1976). *Cities of Alexander the Great*, Oxford.

Fuertes Santos, M. C. (2002). 'Aproximación al urbanismo y la arquitectura doméstica de época califal del Yacimiento de Cercadilla', *Arqueología y Territorio Medieval*, 9, pp. 105–26.

Fuertes Santos, M. C. (2007). 'El sector nororiental del arrabal califal del yacimiento de Cercadilla. Análisis urbanístico y arquitectónico', *Arqueología y Territorio Medieval*, 14, pp. 49–68.

Galeano Cuenca, G. and R. Gil Fernández (2004). 'Intervención arqueológica de urgencia en Casillas (término municipal de Córdoba)', *Anuario Arqueológico de Andalucía 2001*, Seville: Junta de Andalucía Consejería de Cultura, pp. 285–90.

García Arenal, M. (2006). *Messianism and Puritanical Reform. Mahdis of the Muslim West*, Leiden.

García Arenal, M. and E. Manzano Moreno (1998). 'Légitimité et villes idrissides', in P. Cressier and M. García Arenal (eds), *Génese de la ville islamique*, Madrid, pp. 257–84.

García Blánquez, L. (2015). 'Las aceñas de acequia (islámicas) del sistema hidráulico andalusí de Murcia (Senda de Granada) Antecedentes tecnológicos y propuesta funcional', *Arqueología y Territorio Medieval*, 22, pp. 23–61.

García García, M. (2017). 'Some Remarks on the Provision of Animal Products to Urban Centres in Medieval Islamic Iberia: The Cases of Madinat Ilbira (Granada) and Cercadilla (Cordova)', *Quaternary International*, 460, pp. 86–96.

García Gómez, E. (1947). 'Algunas precisiones sobre la ruina de la Córdoba omeya', *al-Andalus: revista de las Escuelas Árabes de Madrid y Granada*, XII, 2, pp. 267–94.

García Gómez, E. (1948). 'Al-Ḥakam II y los beréberes según un texto de Ibn Ḥayyān', *al-Andalus: revista de las Escuelas Árabes de Madrid y Granada*, XIII, 1, pp. 209–26.

García Gómez, E. (1965). 'Notas sobre la topografía cordobesa en los anales de Al-Hakam II por Isa Razi', *Al-Andalus: revista de las Escuelas Árabes de Madrid y Granada*, 30, pp. 319–79.

García Gómez, E. (1967). 'Armas, banderas, tiendas de campaña, monturas y correos en los "Anales de al Hakam II" por Isā Razi', *Al-Andalus: Revista de las Escuelas de Estudios Árabes de Madrid y Granada*, 32, 1, pp. 163–80.

García Gómez, E. (1970). 'Tejidos, ropas y tapicería en los Anales de al-Hakam II por Isa al-Razi', *Boletín de la Real Academia de la Historia*, 156, pp. 43–53.

García Gómez, E. (1972). 'Hacia un "refranero" arábigo-andaluz. V: Versión del libro sobre refranes de 'al-'Iqd al-Farīd (siglo X). A) Preliminares y Refranero de Akṯam y Buzurŷmihr', *al-Andalus: revista de las Escuelas Árabes de Madrid y Granada*, 37, 2, pp. 249–323.

García Lobo, V. (1999). 'Génesis del Códice', in *Codex Biblicus Legionensis: Veinte Estudios*. León.

García Sanjuán, A. (2007). *Till God Inherits the Earth. Islamic Pious Endowments in al-Andalus (9–15th centuries)*, Leyden.

García Sánchez, E. (1989). 'El azúcar en la alimentación de los andalusíes', *Actas del Primer Seminarios Internacional, La Caña de azúcar en tiempos de los grandes descubrimientos (1450–1550)*, Motril, pp. 212–13.

García Sánchez, E. (2011). 'La producción frutícola de al-Andalus: un ejemplo de biodiversidad', *Estudios Avanzados*, 16, pp 51–70.

García Sanjuán, A. (2008). 'Legalidad islámica y legitimidad política en el califato de Córdoba: la proclamación de Hišām II (360–366/971–976)', *al-Qanṭara*, 29, 1, pp. 26–58.

Gerencia Municpal de Urbanismo de Córdoba (2009). *Plan Especial Alcázar-Caballerizas Reales. Anexo I: Estudio Histórico Arqueológico*, August.

Golvin, L. (1957). *Le Maghreb central ā l'époque des Zirides: Recherches d'archéologie et d'histoire*, Paris.

Golvin, L. (1966). 'Le palais de Zīrī ā Achîr (Dixième siècle J.C.)', *Ars Orientalis*, 6, pp. 47–76.

Golvin, L. (1983). 'Buluggīn fils de Zīrī, prince berbère', *Revue de l'Occident musulmane et de la Mediterranée*, 35, 1, pp. 93–113.

Golvin, L. (1988). 'Le miḥrab et sa éventuelle signification', in A. Papadopoulo (ed.), *Le miḥrāb dans l'architecture et la religion musulmanes*, Leiden, pp. 53–5.

González Gutiérrez, G. (2012). *Las mezquitas de barrio de Madinat Qurtuba: Una aproximación arqueológica*, Cordova, 2012.

González Gutiérrez, G. (2016). 'Las mezquitas de barrio de madīnat Qurṭuba 15 años después: espacios religiosos urbanos en la capital andalusí', *Anales de Arqueología Cordobesa*, 27, pp. 267–92.

Gorelick, M. (1979). 'Oriental Armour of the Near and Middle East from the Eighth to the Fifteenth Centuries as Shown in Works of Art', in R. Elgood, R., *Islamic Arms and Armour*, London, pp. 30–63.

Gozalbes Cravioto, E. (2000). 'Descubrimientos arqueológicos de Tingi (Tánger) en los siglos X al XVII', in M. Khanoussi, P. Ruggeri and C. Vismara (eds), *L'África Romana. Geografi, viaggiatori, militari nel Maghreb: alle origini dell'archeologia nel Nord África*, Rome, pp. 844–52.

Gramsci, A. (1967). *La formación de los Intelectuales*. Mexico.

de la Granja, F. (1969). 'Fiestas cristianas en al-Andalus (Materiales para su estudio) I', *al-Andalus: revista de las Escuelas Árabes de Madrid y Granada*, 34, 1, pp. 1–53.

de la Granja, F. (1970). 'Fiestas cristianas en al-Andalus (Materiales para su estudio) II', *al-Andalus: revista de las Escuelas Árabes de Madrid y Granada*, 35, 1, pp. 119–42.

Guerin, S. M. (2013). 'Forgotten Routes? Italy, Ifrīqiya and the Trans-Saharan Ivory Trade', al-Masaq, 25, 1, p. 70–91.

Guichard, P. (1976). *Al-Andalus. Estructura antropológica de una sociedad islámica en occidente*, Barcelona.

Guichard, P (2001). *al-Andalus frente a la conquista cristiana. Los musulmanes de Valencia (siglos XI–XIII)*, Valencia.

Haldon, J. (1993). *The State and the Tributary Mode of Production*, London.

Haldon, J. (2015). 'Mode of Production, Social Action, and Historical Change: Some Questions and Issues', in L. da Graca and A. Zingarelli (eds), *Studies in Precapitalist Modes of Production*, Leiden–Boston, pp. 204–36.

Halm, H. (1989). 'Al-Andalus und Gothica sors', *Der Islam*, 66, pp. 252–63.

Heinz, H. (1996). *The Empire of the Mahdi: The Rise of the Fatimids*, Leiden.

Hernández, Jiménez F. (1959). 'El almimbar móvil del siglo X en la mezquita de Córdoba', *al-Andalus: revista de las Escuelas Árabes de Madrid y Granada*, XXIV, pp. 381–99.

Hernández Bermejo, J. E. and E. García Sánchez (2008). 'Las gramíneas en al-Andalus', in E. García Sánchez and C. Álvarez Morales, *Ciencias de la naturaleza en Al-Andalus. Textos y estudios*, VIII, Granada, pp. 235–87.

Herrero Soto, O. (2016). *El perdón del gobernante al-Andalus (siglos II–V/VIII–XI)*, Helsinki.

Hidalgo, R. and C. Fuertes (2001). 'Córdoba entre la Antigüedad clásica y el Islam: el caso de Cercadilla', in F. Valdés and A.Velázquez (eds), *La islamización de la Extremadura romana (Cuadernos Emeritenses, 17)*, Mérida, pp. 223–64.

Hinds, M. (1971). 'The Banners and Battle Cries of the Arabs at Ṣiffīn', *al-Abhath: The Quarterly Journal of the American University of Beirut*, 24, pp. 3–42.

Ibrahim, T. (1990). 'Consideraciones sobre el conflicto omeya-fatimí y las dos acuñaciones de al-Jayr ibn Muhammad ibn Jazar al-Magrewi', *Boletín de la Asociación Española de Orientalistas*, XXVI, pp. 295–302.

Ibrahim, T. (2011). 'Nuevos documentos sobre la conquista omeya de Hispania: los precintos de plomo disco', *Zona Arqueológica*, 15, pp. 145–61.

Idris, H. R. (1965). 'Les Birzalides de Carmona', *al-Andalus: revista de las Escuelas Árabes de Madrid y Granada*, XXX, 1, pp. 49–62.

Isla, A. (2010). *Ejército, sociedad y política en la península ibérica entre los siglos VII y XI*, Madrid.

Jacobo del Cerro, J. (2014). *Aproximación al conocimiento de la Edad del Bronce en la Cuenca Media del Tajo: El Cerro del Bu (Toledo)*, Madrid.

Jacoby, D. (2004). 'Silk Economics and Cross-Cultural Artistic Interaction: Byzantium, the Muslim World, and the Christian West', *Dumbarton Oaks Papers*, 58, pp. 197–240.

Jaffe, A. H. (1998). 'Disembedded Capitals in Western Asian Perspective', *Comparative Studies in Society and History*, 40, 3, pp. 549–80.

Jallaf, M. A. (1978) *Qurṭuba al-islamiyya fī l-qarn al-jāmis al-hijrī*, El Cairo.

Jankowiak, M. (2017) 'What Does the Slave Trade in the Saqaliba Tell Us About Early Islamic Slavery?', *International Journal of Middle Eastern Studies*, 49, 1, pp. 169–72.

Jiwa, S. (2013), *The Founder of Cairo: The Fatimid Imam Caliph al-Mu'izz and His Era*, London: I. B. Tauris, pp. 77–9.

Kabir, M. (1964). *The Buwayhid Dynasty of Baghdad (334/946–447/1055)*, Calcutta.

Keech Macintosh, S. (1981). 'A Reconsideration of Wangara/Palolus Island of Gold', *Journal of African History*, 22, pp. 145–58.

Kennedy, H. (2005). *The Armies of the Caliphs. Military and Society in the Early Islamic State*, London and New York.

King, A. H. (2017), *Scent from the Garden of Paradise. Musk and the Medieval World*, Leiden.

Kühnel, E. (1957). 'Abbassid Silks of the Ninth Century', *A. Orient*, 2, pp. 367–71.

Kühnel, E. (1971). *Die Islamischen Elfenbeinskulpturen VIII–XIII Jahrhundert*, Berlin.

Labarta, A. (1990). 'Las lápidas árabes de la provincia de Jaén', *Homenaje a Manuel Ocaña Jiménez*, Cordova, pp. 123–37.
Labarta, A. (2015). 'La arqueta de Hišām: su epigrafía', *Summa*, 6, pp. 1–24.
Labarta, A. and Barceló, C. (1987). 'Las fuentes árabes sobre al-Zahrā'. Estado de la cuestión', *Cuadernos de Madīnat al-Zahrā'*, I, pp. 93–106.
Labarta, A. and C. Barceló (1992). 'Dos nuevos fragmentos epigráficos cordobeses del cementerio del arrabal', *al-Qanṭara*, XIII, pp. 549–57.
Labarta A. and C. Barceló (1995). 'Un nuevo fragmento de reloj de sol andalusí', *al-Qanṭara*, XVI, 1, pp. 147–50.
Lagardère, V. (1995). *Histoire et société en occident musulman au Moyen Âge: analyse du Mi'Yār d'al-Wansarisi*, Madrid.
Lambton, A. K. S. (1962). 'Justice in the Medieval Persian Theory of Kingship', *Studia Islamica*, 17, pp. 91–119.
Lambton, A. K. S. (1981). *State and Government in Medieval Islam, An Introduction to the Study of Islamic Political Theory: The Jurists*, Oxford.
Lapesa, R. (2003). *Léxico hispánico primitivo. Sglos VIII al XII*, Madrid.
Lazarev, G., V. Martínez and J. Vignet Zunz (2012). 'Proposition d'identification d'une forteresse idrissite. Les ruines de Koudiet Demna/Hisn al-Karam ā Bni Gorfet', *Bulletin d'Archéologie Marocaine*, XXII, pp. 244–66.
Lazaris, S. (2005). 'Considérations sur l'apparition de l'étrier: contribution à l'histoire du cheval dans l'Antiquité tardive', in A. Gardeisen (ed.), *Les équidés dans le monde méditerranéen antique*, pp. 275–88.
León, A. and R. Blanco (2010). 'La fitna y sus consecuencias. La revitalización urbana de Córdoba en época almohade', in D. Vaquerizo Gil and F. J. Murillo Redondo (eds), *El anfiteatro romano de Córdoba y su entorno urbano*, Cordova, pp. 699–726.
León, A and M. Casal (2010). 'Los cementerios de Madinat Qurtuba', in D. Vaquerizo Gil and F. J. Murillo Redondo (eds), *El anfiteatro romano de Córdoba y su entorno urbano*, Cordova, pp. 662–72.
Lev, Y. (1992). *State and Society in Fatimid Egypt*, Leiden.
Lev, Y. (1997). 'Regime, Army and Society in Medieval Egypt, 9th–12th Centuries', in Y. Lev, *War and Society in the Eastern Mediterranean, 7th–15th Centuries*, Leiden, pp. 115–52.
Lévi-Provençal, E. (1931). *Inscriptions árabes d'Espagne*, Paris.
Lévi-Provençal, E. (1938). 'La fondation de Fès', *Annales de l'Institut d'Etudes Orientales d'Alger* IV, pp. 23–53.
Levi-Provençal, E. (1950). *Historia de España*, IV, *España musulmana hasta la caída del califato de Córdoba (711–1031 de J. C.)*, Madrid.

Levi-Provençal, E. and L. Torres Balbas (1957). *Historia de España*, V, *España musulmana hasta la caída del califato de Córdoba (711–1031 de J. C.). Instituciones y vida social e intelectual. Arte califal*, Madrid.

Lézine, A. (1965). *Mahdîya, recherches d'archéologie islamique*, Paris.

Levtzion, N. (1968), 'Ibn Hawqal, the Cheque, and Awdaghost', *The Journal of African History*, 9, 2, pp. 223–33.

Lirola Delgado, J. (1993). *El poder naval de al-Andalus en la época del califato omeya (siglo IV hegira/X era Cristiana)*, Granada.

Lirola Delgado, J. (2006). *Biblioteca de Al-Andalus*, 4, Almería: Fundación Ibn Tufayl de Estudios Árabes, pp. 167–8.

López Cuevas, F. (2013). 'La almunia cordobesa, entre las fuentes historiográficas y arqueológicas', *Onoba*, 1, pp. 243–60.

López Martínez de Marigorta, E. (2020), *Mercaderes, artesanos y ulemas. Las ciudades de Elvira y Pechina en época omeya*, Jaén.

Luna, D. and A. Zamorano (1999). 'La mezquita de la antigua finca El Fontanar (Córdoba)', *Cuadernos de Madīnat al-Zahrā'*, 4, pp. 145–73.

Manzano Moreno, E. (1991). *La Frontera de al-Andalus en época de los Omeyas*, Madrid, pp. 177–9.

Manzano Moreno, E. (1992). 'Oriental "Topoi" in Andalusian Historical Sources', *Arabica*, 39, 1, pp. 42–58.

Manzano Moreno, E. (1993). 'El asentamiento y la organización de los *yund-s* sirios en Al-Ándalus', *al-Qanṭara*, XIV, pp. 327–59.

Manzano Moreno, E. (1997). 'El medio cordobés y la elaboración cronística en al-Andalus bajo la dinastía de los Omeyas', in M. I. Loring (ed.), *Historia social, pensamiento historiográfico y Edad Media. Homenaje al Prof. Abilio Barbero de Aguilera*, Madrid, pp. 59–85.

Manzano Moreno, E. (1999). 'Relaciones sociales en sociedades precpitalistas: una crítica al concepto de modo de producción tributario', *Hispania*, 58, 200, pp. 881–914.

Manzano Moreno, E. (2004). 'El círculo de poder de los califas omeyas', *Cuadernos de Madīnat al-Zahrā'*, 5, pp. 9–29.

Manzano Moreno, E. (2004). '¿El fin de la historia? La historiografía árabe en torno al año 1000', in P. Bonnassie et P. Toubert (eds), *Hommes et sociétés dans l'Europe de l'An Mil*, Toulouse, pp. 407–19.

Manzano Moreno, E. (2006). *Conquistadores, emires y califas*, Barcelona.

Manzano Moreno, E. (2011). 'Quelques considérations sur les toponymes en *banū* comme reflet des structures sociales d'al-Andalus', in D. Valérian (ed.),

Islamisation et Arabisation de l'Occident Musulman Médiéval (VIIe–XIIe siècle), Paris, pp. 247–64.

Manzano Moreno, E. (2013). 'Circulation de biens et richesses entre al-Andalus et l'Occident européen aux VIIIe–Xe siècles', in L. Feller and A.Rodríguez López (dir.), *Objets sous Contraintes. Circulation des richesses et valeur des choses au Moyen Âge*, Paris, pp. 147–80.

Manzano Moreno, E. (2015). 'Moneda y articulación social en al-Andalus en época omeya' in P. Sénac and S. Gasc, *Monnaies du Haut Moyen Age: Histoire et Archéologie. Peninsule Ibérique-Maghreb*, Villa 5, Madrid.

Manzano Moreno, E. (2015). 'Why Did Islamic Medieval Institutions Become So Different from Western Medieval Institutions?', *Medieval Worlds*, I, pp. 118–37.

Manzano Moreno, E. (2018). 'Entre faits et artefacts: interprétations historiques et données archéologiques en al-Andalus', in L. Borgeois et al. (eds), *La culture materielle un objet en question. Anthropologie, archeologie et histoire*, Caen.

Manzano Moreno, E. (e.p.). 'Byzantium, al-Andalus and the Shaping of the Mediterranean in the Early Middle Ages' in L. Brubaker (ed.), *Global Byzantium*.

Manzano Moreno, E. and A. Canto García (2020). 'The Value of Wealth: Coins and Coinage in Iberian Early Medieval Documents' in S. Burton and R. Portass (eds), *Beyond the Reconquista*, Leiden, pp. 169–97.

Marín, M. (1985). 'Una familia de ulemas cordobeses: los Banū Abī ʿĪsā', *Al-Qanṭara*, 6, pp. 309.

Marín, M. (1994). 'Inqibāḍ ʿan al-sulṭān: ʿulamāʾ and political power in al-Andalus', in *Saber religioso y poder político en el islam*, Madrid, pp. 127–39.

Marín, M. (1996). 'Learning at Mosques in al-Andalus', in M. Khalid Masud, B. Messick and D. S. Powers (eds), *Islamic Legal Interpretation. Muftis and their Fatwas*, Harvard, pp. 47–54.

Marín, M. (1997). 'Una vida de mujer: Ṣubḥ', in M. L. Ávila and M. Marín (eds), *Biografías y género biográfico en el Occidente islámico*, Madrid, pp. 426–33.

Marín, M. (2001). 'Signos visuales de la identidad andalusí', in M. Marín (ed.), *Tejer y vestir: de la Antigüedad al Islam*, Madrid, pp. 137–80.

Marín, M. (2004). 'Altos funcionarios para el califa: jueces y otros cargos de la administración de ʿAbd al-Raḥmān III', *Cuadernos de Madīnat al-Zahrā*, 5, pp. 91–105.

Marín, M. (2011). 'Una galería de retratos reales: los soberanos omeyas de al-Andalus (siglos II/VIII–IV/X) en la cronística árabe', *Anuario de Estudios Medievales*, 4, 1, pp. 273–90.

Marqués Casanovas, J. (1975). 'El Beato de Gerona', in *Beati in Apolapsin libri duodecim. Beato de Liébana. Comentario al Apocalipsis*, Madrid, pp. 216–17.

Marsham, A. (2009). *Rituals of Islamic Monarchy: Accession and Succession in the First Muslim Empire*, Edinburgh, pp. 63, 65 and 66.

Martín Puertas, C. et al. (2008). 'Arid and Humid Phases in Southern Spain during the Last 4000 Years: The Zoñar Lake Record, Córdoba', *The Holocene*, 18, 6, pp. 907–21.

Martín Viso, I. (2005). 'Una frontera casi invisible: los territorios al norte del Sistema Central en la Alta Edad Media (siglos VIII–XI)', *Studia Historica*, 23, pp. 89–114.

Martín Viso, I. (ed.) (2009). *¿Tiempos oscuros? Territorio y sociedad en el centro de la Península Ibérica (siglos VII–XI)*, Madrid.

Martín Viso, I. (2016). 'Colapso político y sociedades locales: el noroeste en la península ibérica (siglos VIII–IX)', *Reti Medievali Rivista*, 17, 2.

Martín Viso, I. (2017). 'Integración política y regeneración: el sur del Duero en el reino asturleonés', *Edad Media*, 18, pp. 207–39.

Martínez Díez, G. (2005). *El Condado de Castilla (711–1038) La historia frente a la* leyenda, Valladolid.

Martínez Díez, G. (2014). 'El cantar de los Siete Infantes de Lara: la historia y la leyenda', *Cahiers de Linguistique Hispanique Médiévale*, 37, pp. 171–89.

Martínez Núñez, M. A. (1995). 'La epigrafía del salón de 'Abd al-Raḥmān III', in A. Vallejo (ed.), *Madīnat al-Zahrā'. El Salón de 'Abd al-Raḥmān III*, Córdoba, pp. 106–52.

Martínez Núñez, M. A. (1999). 'Epígrafes a nombre de al-Ḥakam en Madīnat al-Zahrā'', *Cuadernos de Madīnat al-Zahrā'*, 4, pp. 83–103.

Martínez Núñez, M. A. (2006). 'Mujeres y élites sociales en al-Andalus a través de la documentación epigráfica', in M. I. Calero (ed.), *Mujeres y sociedad islámica: una visión plural*, Málaga, pp. 289–328.

Martínez Núñez, M. A. (2007). *Epigrafía árabe*, Madrid.

Martínez Núñez, M. A. (2011), 'Epigrafía funeraria de al-Andalus', *Melanges de la Casa de Velázquez*, 41, I, pp. 188.

Martínez Núñez, M. A. (2015). 'Epigrafía monumental y élites sociales en al-Andalus', in A. Malpica Cuello and B. Sarr Marroco (eds), *Epigrafía árabe y Arqueología medieval*, Granada, pp. 19–60.

Martínez Núñez, M. A. (2015). 'Recientes hallazgos epigráficos en Madīnat al-Zahrā' y nueva onomástica relacionada con la dār al-sinā'a califal', *Anejos de Arqueología y Territorio Medieval*, 1, pp. 1–74.

Martínez Núñez, M. A. (2020). 'Al-Andalus durante el período almorávide a través de la documentación epigráfica', in R. Azuar Ruiz (ed.), *Arqueología del al-Andalus almorávide*, Alicante, pp. 59–78.

Martínez Núñez, M. A. and M. Acién (2004). 'La epigrafía de Madīnat al-Zahrā', *Cuadernos de Madīnat al-Zahrā*, 5, pp. 107–58.

Martínez Solares, J. M., and J. Mezcua Rodríguez (2002). *Catálogo Sísmico de la Península Ibérica (880 a.C.–1900)*, Madrid.

Martínez Sopena, P. (1985). *La Tierra de Campos occidental. Poblamiento, poder y comunidad del siglo X al XIII*, Valladolid.

Mazzoli Guintard, C. (2014). 'Du puits au cadi. Gestion et conflits de l'alimentation en eau ā Cordoue (ss. VIII–XIII)', *Anaquel de Estudios Árabes*, 25, pp. 99–128.

McCormick, M. (1986). *Eternal Victory. Triumphal Rulership in Late Antiquity, Byzantium and the Early Medieval West*, Cambridge.

McCormick, M. (2002). 'New Light on the "Dark Ages": How the Slave Trade Fuelled the Carolingian Economy', *Past and Present*, 177, pp. 17–54.

Melikian-Chirvani, A. S. (1979). 'The tabarzīns of Loṭf'alī', in R. Elgood (ed.), *Islamic Arms and Armour*, London, pp. 116–35.

Meouak, M. (1999). *Pouvoir souverain, administration centrale et élites politiques dans l'Espagne Umayyade (IIe–IVe/VIIIe–Xe siècles)*, Helsinki.

Meouak, M. (2000). 'Las instituciones políticas del islam temprano. Notas sobre siyāda, sulṭān y dawla', *al-Andalus*–Magreb, 8–9, pp. 37–41.

Meouak, M. (2004). *Ṣaqāliba: eunuques et esclaves ā la conquête du pouvoir*, Helsinki.

Mesa Fernández, E. (2008). *El Lenguaje de la Indumentaria: Tejidos y Vestiduras en el Kitab al-Agani de Abu L-Faray al-Isfahani*, Madrid.

Miguel Rodríguez, J. C. de. (1988). 'Precipitaciones y sequías en el valle del Guadalquivir', *Anuario de Estudios Medievales*, 18, pp. 55–76.

Millás Vallicrosa, J. M. (1991) *Estudios sobre historia de la ciencia española*, Madrid.

Mintz, S. W. (1996). *Dulzura y poder: el lugar del azúcar en la historia moderna*, Mexico.

Molina, L. (1981). 'Las campañas de Almanzor a la luz de un nuevo texto', *al-Qantara: Revista de Estudios Árabes*, 2 (1, 2), pp. 209–63.

Molina, L. (1988). 'Lugares de destino de los viajeros andalusíes en el Ta'rīj de Ibn al-Faraḍī', in M. Marín (ed.), *Estudios onomástico-biográficos de al-Andalus*, Madrid, pp. 585–610.

Molina, L. (1994). 'El estudio de las familias de ulemas como fuente para la historia social del Islam', in M. García Arenal and M. Marín (eds), *Saber religioso y poder político en el Islam*, Madrid, pp. 160–73.

Molina, L. (2006) 'Técnicas de *amplificatio* en el *Muqtabis* de Ibn Ḥayyān', *Talia Dixit*, I, pp. 55–79.

Molina, L. and M. L. Ávila (1984). 'Sociedad y cultura en la Marca Superior de al-Andalus', *Historia de Aragón*, Zaragoza, III, pp. 83–104.

Molina Lopez, E. (1999–2000). 'El Mustajlas Andalusí (I). S. VIII–XI', *Revista del Centro de Estudios Históricos de Granada y su Reino, 2ª época*, 13–14, pp. 99–189.

Monroe, J. T. (1971), 'The Historical arjūza of Ibn 'Abd Rabbihi, a Tenth-Century Hispano-Arabic Epic Poem', *Journal of the American Oriental Society*, pp. 67–95.

Montejo, A. J. (2006). 'La rauda del alcázar de Córdoba', *Anales de Arqueología Cordobesa*, 17, 2, pp. 237–56.

Montejo, A., J. A. Garriguet and A. M. Zamorano (1999). 'El alcázar andalusí de Córdoba y su entorno urbano', *Córdoba en su historia. La construcción de la urbe: Actas del Congreso, Córdoba 20–23 de mayo 1997*, Cordova, pp. 163–72.

Morelló, M. et al. (2011). 'Climate Changes and Human Activities Recorded in the Sediments of Lake Estanya (NE Spain) during the Medieval Warm Period and Little Ice Age', *Journal of Paleolimnology*, 46, pp. 423–52.

Moreno, A. et al. (2012). 'The Medieval Climate Anomaly in the Iberian Peninsula Reconstructed from Marine and Lake Records', *Quaternary Science Reviews*, 43, pp. 16–32.

Morín, J. P. et al. (2014). 'Evidencias arqueosísmológicas en la Colonia Patricia Romana de Córdoba (Valle del Guadalquivir, España)', *Resúmenes de la 2ª Reunión Ibérica sobre Fallas Activas y Paleosismología*, Lorca, pp. 158–62. Instituto Geográfico Nacional, 'Terremotos más significativos por provincias en España', http://www.ign.es/web/ign/portal/terremotos-importantes

Mottahedeh, R. (1980). *Loyalty and Leadership in an Early Islamic Society*, Princeton.

Mueller, K. (2006). *Settlements of the Ptolemies: City Foundations and New Settlement in the Hellenistic World*, Leuven.

Müller, C. (2011). 'Redressing Injustice. Maẓālim Jurisdictions at the Umayyad Court of Cordoba (Eighth–Eleventh Centuries CE)', in A. Fuess and J. P. Hartung (eds), *Court Cultures in the Muslim World. Seventh to Nineteenth Centuries*, London–New York, pp. 93–104.

Murillo, J. F. (2009). 'La almunia de al-Rusafa en Córdoba', *Madrider Mitteilungen*, 50, pp. 449–90.

Murillo, J. F., M. T. Casal and E. Castro (2004). 'Madīnat Qurṭuba. Aproximación al proceso de formación de la ciudad emiral y califal a partir de la información arqueológica', *Cuadernos de Madīnat al-Zahrā'*, 4, pp. 257–81.

Murillo, J. F. et al. (2010). 'Investigaciones arqueológicas en la muralla de la Huerta del Alcázar', *Anejos de Anales de Arqueología Cordobesa*, 2, pp. 183–230.

Murillo, J. F. et al. (2010). 'La transición de la *civitas* clásica cristianizada a la *madina* islámica a través de las transformaciones operadas en las áreas suburbiales', in D. Vaquerizo and F. J. Murillo (eds), *El anfiteatro romano de Córdoba y su entorno urbano*, Cordova, pp. 503–47.

Murillo, J. F. et al. (2010). 'La almunia y el arrabal de al-Rusafa en el Yanib al-Garbi de Madinat Qurtuba', in D. Vaquerizo and F. J. Murillo (eds), *El anfiteatro romano de Córdoba y su entorno urbano*. Cordova, pp. 586–605.

Mussa Rashid, A. (1983). 'The Role of the Shurṭa in Early Islam', unpub. Ph.D. dissertation, University of Edinburgh.

Negre Pérez J. and R. Martí Castelló (2015) 'Urbanismo en la marca oriental de al-Andalus durante el califato (940–974): el ejemplo de Madīna Ṭurṭūša a través de las fuentes arqueológicas y escritas', *Saguntum*, 47.

Neuekirchen, P. (2013). 'Biblical Elements in Koran 89, 6–8 and Its Exegeses: A New Interpretation of Iram of the Pillars', *Arabica*, 60, pp. 651–700.

Nicolle, D. (2017). 'Horse Armour in the Medieval Islamic East', *Arabian Humanities. Revue Internationale d'archéologie et des sciences sociales sur la péninsule Arabique*, 8, http://cy.revues.org/3293; DOI: 10.4000/cy.3293.

Nixon, S., T. Rehren and M. F. Guerra (2011), 'New Light on the Early Islamic West African Gold Trade. Coin Moulds from Tadmekka, Mali', *Antiquity*, 85, pp. 1,353–68.

Ocaña Jiménez, M. (1935). 'Las puertas de la medina de Córdoba', *al-Andalus: revista de las Escuelas Árabes de Madrid y Granada*, 3, 1, pp. 143–51.

Ocaña Jiménez, M. (1943). 'Lápida árabe en la ermita de San Miguel de Gormaz', *al-Andalus: revista de las Escuelas Árabes de Madrid y Granada*, 8, pp. 450–2.

Ocaña Jiménez, M. (1952). 'Nuevas inscripciones árabes de Córdoba', *al-Andalus: revista de las Escuelas Árabes de Madrid y Granada*, 17, pp. 379–88.

Ocaña Jiménez, M. (1963). 'Notas sobre la Córdoba de Ibn Hazm', *al-Mulk*, 3, pp. 55–62.

Ocaña Jiménez, M. (1970). *El cúfico hispánico y su evolución*, Madrid.

Ocaña Jiménez, M. (1976). 'Ya'far el eslavo', *Cuadernos de la Alhambra*, 12, pp. 217–23.

Ocaña Jimenez, M. (1984). 'Las ruinas de "Alamiria", un yacimiento arqueológico erróneamente denominado'. *al-Qanṭara*, V, 1–2, pp. 367–82.

Ocaña Jiménez, M. (1988–90). 'Inscripciones árabes fundacionales de la mezquita-catedral de Córdoba', *Cuadernos de Madīnat al-Zahrā'*, 2, pp. 9–28.

Olmo Enciso, L. (2008). *Recópolis y la ciudad en época visigoda*, Madrid.

Osti, L. (2007). 'The Wisdom of Youth: Legitimising the Caliph al-Muqtadir', *al-Masaq*, 19, 1, pp. 17–27.

Ouerfelli, M. (2008). *Le sucre. Production, commercialisation et usage dans la Méditerranée médiévale*, Leiden–Boston.

Partearroyo, C. (2001). 'Almaizar de San Pedro de Montes', *El esplendor de los omeyas cordobeses. La civilización musulmana de Europa occidental. Legado*, Córdoba, II, p. 264.

Partearroyo, C. (2007). 'Tejidos andalusíes', *Artigrama*, 22, pp. 371–419.

Penelas, M. and L. Molina (2011). 'Dos fragmentos inéditos del volumen II del Muqtabis de Ibn Ḥayyān', *al-Qanṭara*, 32, pp. 229–41.

Peña Chocarro, L. et al. (2017). 'Roman and Medieval Crops in the Iberian Peninsula: A First Overview of Seeds and Fruits from Archaeological Sites', *Quaternary International*, https://doi.org/10.1016/j.quaint.2017.09.037

Pentz, P. (2014). 'Ships and the Vikings', in G. Williams et. al., *Vikings. Life and Legend*, London, pp. 202–27.

Peres, H. (1983). *Esplendor de al-Andalus. La poesía andaluza en árabe clásico en el siglo XI: sus aspectos generales, sus principales temas y su valos documental*, Madrid.

Pinilla, R. (2000). 'Jurisprudencia y ciudad. Notas sobre toponimia y urbanismo en la Córdoba altomedieval extraídas de al-Aḥkām al-Kubrā de Ibn Sahl en el siglo XI', in J. C. Martín de la Cruz and R. Román Alcalá, *Las ciudades históricas. Patrimonio y sociabilidad. Actas del 1er Congreso Internacional*, Cordova, pp. 559–74.

Pizarro Berengena, G. (2013). 'Los pasadizos elevados entre la mezquita y el alcázar omeya de Córdoba. Estudio arqueológico de los sābāṭāt', *Archivo Español de Arqueología*, 86, pp. 233–49.

Pizarro Berengena, G. (2014). *El abastecimiento de agua a Córdoba. Arqueología e Historia*, Cordova.

Pons Boigues, F. (1898). *Ensayo bio-bibliográfico de historiadores y geógrafos arábigo-españoles*, Madrid.

Pons Boigues, F. (1952). *Estudios breves*, Tetuán.

Prado-Vilar, F. (1997). 'Circular Visions of Fertility and Punishment: Caliphal Ivory Caskets from an-Andalus', *Muqarnas*, 14, pp. 19–41.

Premare, A. L. and P. Guichard (1981). 'Croisssance urbaine et société rural à Valence au début de l'époque des royaumes de Taifas (Xie siècle)', *Revue des mondes musulmans et de la Mediterranée*, 31, pp. 15–30.

Puerta Vílchez, J. M. (2003), 'La monumentalidad y el sentido artístico de Qurtuba', *Awraq*, 7, pp. 43–80.

Quesada, F. (2005). 'El gobierno del caballo montado en la Antigüedad clásica con especial referencia al caso de Iberia. Bocados, espuelas, y la cuestión de la silla de montar, estribos y herraduras', *Gladius*, XXV, pp. 97–150.

Riche, P. (1987) *Gerbert d'Aurillac. Le pape de l'an Mil*, Paris.

Robinson, C. (2002). *A Medieval Islamic City Reconsidered: An Interdisciplinary Approach to Samarra*, Oxford.

Robinson, C. (2005). *'Abd al-Malik*, London.

Rodero Pérez S. and M. J. Asensi Llácer (2006). 'Un sector de la expansión occidental de la Córdoa islámica: el arrabal de la carretera de Trassiera (II). El sector central', *Romula*, 5, pp. 295–336.

Rodríguez, A. 'À propos des objets nécessaires. Dotations monastiques et circulation d'objets au royaume de León dans le haut Moyen Âge', in L. Feller and A. Rodríguez (eds), *Objets sous contrainte. Circulation des objets et valeur des choses au Moyen Âge*, pp. 63–90.

Rodríguez, M. (1988). 'Precipitaciones y sequías en el valle del Guadalquivir', *Anuario de Estudios Medievales*, 18, pp. 55–76.

Rodríguez Mediano, F. (1994). 'Acerca de la población arabizada del reino de León (siglos X–XI)', *Al-Qanṭara*, 15, 2, pp. 465–72.

Rodríguez Peinado, L. (2014). 'Púrpura. Materialidad y simbolismo en la Edad Media', *Anales de Historia del Arte*, 24, pp. 471–95.

Rosser-Owen, M. (1999). 'A Córdoban Ivory Pyxis Lid in the Ashmolean Museum', *Muqarnas*, 16, pp. 19.

Rosser-Owen, M. (2004). 'Questions of Authenticity: The Imitation Ivories of Don Francisco Pallás y Puig (1859–1926)', *Journal of the David Collection*, 2, pp. 249–67.

Rosser-Owen, M. (2012), 'The Metal Mounts of Andalusi Ivories: Initial Observations', in V. Porter and M. Rosser-Owen (eds), *Metalwork and Material Culture in the Islamic World: Art, Craft and Text. Essays Presented to James W. Allan*, pp. 301–16.

Rovira i Sola, M. (1980). 'Notes documentals sobre alguns effectes de la presa de Barcelona per Al-Mansur', *Acta Historica et Archaeologica Mediaevalia*, 1, pp. 31–54.

Ruiz Bueno, M. D. (2017). 'Actividad sísmica en el mediodía ibérico durante el siglo III d.C. La incidencia arqueológica en Corduba (Córdoba)', *Pyrenae*, 48, 2, pp. 29–51.

Ruiz Domènech, J.-E. (2006). *Quan els vescomtes de Barcelona eren. Història, crònica i documents d'una família catalana dels segles X, XI i XII*, Barcelona.

Ruiz Lara, D., E. Castro, A. León Muñoz and S. Sánchez (2010). 'El sector meridional del Yanib al-Garbi', in D. Vaquerizo and F. J. Murillo (eds), *El anfiteatro romano de Córdoba y su entorno urbano*. Cordova, pp. 636–9.

Rustow, M. (2020), *The Lost Archive. Traces of a Caliphate in a Cairo Synagogue*, Princeton.

Sáenz de Haro, T. (2007) 'Calahorra islámica (siglos VIII–XI). Notas sobre la organización de los espacios urbano y rural', *Brocar*, pp. 107–54.

Safran, J. (1998), 'The Command of the Faithful in al-Andalus: A Study in the Articulation of Calipha Legitimacy', *International Journal of Middle Eastern Studies*, 30, 2, pp. 183–98.

Safran, J. (2013), *Defining Boundaries in al-Andalus. Muslims, Christians and Jews in Islamic Iberia*, Cornell.

Said, S. S. and F. R. Stephenson (1996). 'Solar and Lunar Eclipse Measurements by Medieval Muslim Astronomers', *Journal of the History of Astronomy*, 27, pp. 259–73; 28 (1997), pp. 29–48.

Salvatierra, V. (2006), *El Alto Guadalquivir en época islámica*, Jaén.

Samsó, J. (1994). 'La primitiva versión árabe del Libro de las Cruces', in J. Vernet (ed.), *Nuevos Estudios de Astronomía Española en el siglo de Alfonso X*, Barcelona.

Sanchez Albornoz, C. (1966). *Despoblación y repoblación del valle del Duero*, Buenos Aires.

Sánchez Lopez, G. et al. (2016). 'Climate Reconstruction for the Last Two Millennia in Central Iberia: The Role of East Atlantic (EA), North Atlantic Oscillation (NAO) and their Interplay over the Iberian Peninsula', *Quaternary Science Reviews*, 149, pp. 135–50.

Sanders, P. (1994). *Ritual, Politics and the City in Fatimid Cairo*, New York.

Scales, P. (1984). 'The Handing Over of the Duero Fortresses: 1009–1011 A.D. (399–401 A.H.)', *al-Qanṭara*, V, 1, pp. 109–22.

Schlumberger, D. (1986). *Qasr el-Heir el-Gharbi*, París.

Sénac, P. (1996). 'Note sur les relations diplomatiques entre los comtes de Barcelone et le califat de Cordoue au Xe siècle', *Histoire et archèologie des terres catalanes au Moyen Age*, Perpignan, pp. 87–101.

Sénac, P. (2006). *Al-Mansūr: Le fléau de l'an mil*, Paris.

Serjeant, R. B. (1972). *Islamic Textiles. Material for a History of Islamic Textiles up to the Mongol Conquest*, Beirut.

Shalem, A. (2005). 'Trade in the Availability of Ivory: The Picture Given by the Medieval Sources'. *Journal of the David Collection*, 2, 1, pp. 29.

Sharon, M. (2012). 'The Development of the Debate Around the Legitimacy of

Authority in Early Islam', in F. M. Donner (ed.), *The Articulation of Early Islamic State Structures*, London, pp. 15–36.

Signes Codoñer, J. (2004). '"Bizancio y al-Andalus" en los siglos IX y X', in I. Martín and P. Bádenas (eds), *Bizancio y la Península Ibérica. De la Antigüedad Tardía a la Edad Moderna*, Madrid, pp. 177–246.

Silva Santa Cruz, N. (2014). 'Dádivas preciosas en marfil: la política del regalo en la corte omeya andalusí', *Anales de Historia del Arte*, 24, pp. 527–41.

Soler del Campo, A. (1999). 'Armas, arreos y banderas en las miniaturas del códice', in *Codex biblicus legionensis. Veinte estudios*, León, pp. 239–52.

Soravia, B. (1999), 'Ibn Ḥayyān, historien du siècle des taifas. Une relecture de Dahira, I/2, 573–602', *al-Qanṭara*, XX, I, pp. 99–118.

Sourdel, D. (1960). 'Questions de ceremonial abbaside', *Revue des Edtudes Islamiques*, XXVIII, pp. 121–48.

Sourdel, D. (2001). 'Robes of Honour in 'Abbasid Baghdad during the Eighth to Eleventh Centuries', in S. Gordon (ed.), *Robes and Honour. The Medieval World of Investiture*, pp. 137–46.

Souto, J. A. (2005). 'El noroeste de la Frontera Superior de al-Andalus en época omeya: población y organización territorial', *García Sánchez III 'el de Nájera'. Un rey y un reino en la Europa del siglo XI. XV Semana de Estudios Medievales de Nájera*, Logroño, pp. 253–67.

Stasser, T. (1993) 'La maison vicomtale de Narbonne aux Xe et Xie siècles', *Annales du Midi*, 105/204, pp. 489–91.

Stetkevych, S. T. (1997). 'The *Qaṣīdah* and the Politics of Ceremony. Three 'Īd Panegyrics to the Cordoban Caliphate', in R. Bran (ed.), *Languages of Power in Islamic Spain*, Cornell, pp. 1–48.

Stillman, Y. K. (2000). *Arab Dress from the Dawn of Islam to Modern Times. A Short History*, Leiden.

Suárez González, A. I. (1999). 'Arqueología del códice' in *Codex Biblicus Legionensis: Veinte Estudios*, León, pp. 88.

Terés Sádaba, E. (1986), *Materiales para el estudio de la toponimia hispanoárabe: nómina fluvial*, Madrid.

Torres Balbas, L. (1952). 'Bāb al-Sudda y las azudas de la España medieval', *al-Andalus: revista de las Escuelas Árabes de Madrid y Granada*, 1, pp. 165–75.

Torres Balbas, L. (1970). *Ciudades Hispanomusulmanas*, 2 vols., Madrid.

Trouet, V. et al. (2009). 'Persistent Positive North Atlantic Oscillation Mode Dominated the Medieval Climate Anomaly', *Science*, 324, pp. 78–80.

Uphoff, N. (1989). 'Distinguishing Power, Authority and Legitimacy: Taking Max Weber at his Word by Using Resources-Exchange Analysis', *Polity*, 22, 2, pp. 295–322.

Uribelarrea, D. and G. Benito (2008). 'Fluvial Changes of the Guadalquivir River during the Holocene in Cordoba (Southern Spain)', *Geomorphology*, 100, pp. 14–31.

Vallejo Triano, A. (1990). 'La vivienda servicios y la llamada casa de Ya'far', in J. Bermúdez López and A. Bazzana (eds), *La casa hispano-musulmana. Aportaciones de la arqueología*, Granada, pp. 129–45.

Vallejo Triano, A. (ed.) (1995), *Madīnat al-Zahrā'. El Salón de 'Abd al-Raḥmān III*, Cordova.

Vallejo Triano, A. (2010). *La ciudad califal de Madinat al-Zahra': arqueología de su excavación*, Cordova.

Vallejo Triano, A. (2016). 'El heredero designado y el califa. El Occidente y el Oriente en Madīnat al-Zahrā'', *Mainake*, XXXVI, pp. 433–64.

Vallejo Triano, A. and J. Escudero Aranda (1999) 'Aportaciones para una tipología de la cerámica común califal de Madinat al-Zahra', *Arquelogía y Territorio Medieval*, 6, pp. 133–76.

Valérian, D. (2011). 'Contrôle et domination politique de l'espace dans le Maghreb central (VIIe–XIe siècle)', in A. Nef and É. Voguet (eds), *La légitimation du pouvoir au Maghreb médiéval*, Madrid, pp. 135–43.

Vallve, J. (1985). 'Naṣr el valido de 'Abd al-Raḥmān II', *Al-Qantara*, 6, pp. 179–98.

Vallve, J. (1999). 'El zalmedina de Córdoba', *al-Qantara*, II (1, 2), pp. p. 277–318.

Vaquerizo D. and Murillo, F. J. (eds) (2010). *El anfiteatro romano de Córdoba y su entorno urbano*, Cordova.

Vaquero J. M. and M. C. Gallego (2001), 'Two Early Observations of Aurora at Low Latitudes', *Annales Geophysicae*, 19, pp. 809–11.

Vázquez Navajas, B. (2016). 'Las condiciones higiénicas y de saneamiento en Madīnat Qurṭuba durante el siglo X', *Anales de Arqueología Cordobesa*, 27, pp. 293–324.

Vernet, J. (1981–2). 'Algunos fenómenos astronómicos observados bajo los omeyas españoles', *Revista del Instituto Egipcio de Estudios Islámicos en Madrid*, XXI, pp. 23–30.

Vidal Castro, F. (2008). 'Los cautivos en al-Andalus durante el Califato Omeya de Córdoba. Aspectos jurídicos, sociales y económicos', *Miscelánea de Estudios Árabes y Hebraicos*, 57, pp. 359–98.

Viguera Molins, M. J. (1981). *Aragón Musulmán*, Zaragoza.

Viguera Molins, M. J. (1983). 'Referencia a una fecha en que escribe Ibn Ḥayyān', *al-Qanṭara*, IV, 1, pp. 429–32.

Viguera Molins, M. J. (2012). 'Voyager et chercher en Afrique du Nord: les livres comme objectif', *Comptes Rendus de l'Académie des Inscriptions*, I, pp. 695–710.

Viguera Molins, M. J. (2015). 'Referencias a mezquitas de Qurṭuba en la obra de al-Marwānī sobre "Biografías cordobesas"', *al-Mulk*, 13, pp. 11–29.

Viguera Molins, M. J. (2016). 'Dieciséis mujeres andalusíes biografiadas por el cordobés Ibn Baskuwal (494/1101–578/1183)', *al-Mulk*, 14, pp. 9–18.

Villanueva Etcheverría, R. (1996). 'Perfil y andanzas diplomáticas del embajador Emilio García Gómez', *Awraq*, XVII, pp. 135–58.

Viso, M. (2005). 'Una frontera casi invisible: los territorios al norte del Sistema Central en la Alta Edad Media (siglos VIII–XI)', *Studia Historica*, 23, pp. 89–114.

Viso, M. (2016). 'Colapso político y sociedades locales: el noroeste en la península ibérica (siglos VIII–IX)', *Reti Medievali Rivista*, 17, 2, pp. 335–69.

Vitestam, G. (1990). "Arsh and kursī. An Essay on the Throne Traditions in Islam', *Living Waters. Scandinavian Orientalistic Studies Presented to F. Lokkegaard*, Copenhagen, pp. 369–78.

Walker, P. (2014) 'Social Elites at the Fatimid court', in A. Fuess and J. P. Hartung (eds), *Court Cultures in the Muslim World*, London, pp. 105–22.

Wassenburg, J. A. et al. (2013). 'Moroccan Speleothem and Tree Ring Records Suggest a Variable Positive State of the North Atlantic Oscillation During the Medieval Warm Period', *Earth and Planetary Science Letters*.

White, L. (1962). *Medieval Technology and Social Change*, Oxford.

Wickham, C. (1998). 'Gossip and Resistance Among the Medieval Peasantry', *Past and Present*, 160, pp. 3–24.

Wickham, C. (2009). *Framing the Early Middle Ages. Europe and the Mediterranean* 400–800; Spanish trans.: *Una historia nueva de la Alta Edad Media. Europa y el mundo mediterráneo, 400–800*, Barcelona.

Yalaoui, M. (1973). 'Les relations entre Fatimides d'Ifriqiya et Omeyyades d'Espagne ā travers le *Dīwān* d'Ibn Hāni', *Actas del II Coloquio Hispano-Tunecino (1972)*, Madrid, pp. 13–30.

Zanón, J. (1989). *Topografía de Córdoba almohade a través de las fuentes árabes*. Madrid.

Zanón, J. (2013). 'Los intérpretes de la corte de al-Ḥakam II de Córdoba', *Hermeneus*, 15, pp. 323–47.

Zozaya, J. (1988). 'Evolución de un yacimiento: el castillo de Gormaz (Soria)', in A. Bazzana (ed.), *Castrum 3. Guerre, fortification et hábitat au Moyen* Age, Madrid, pp. 173–8.

Zubkova, E. S. et al. (2009). 'Studies of the Textiles from the Excavation of Pskov in 2006', in E. B. Andersson Strand et al. (eds), *North European Symposium for Archaeological Textiles X*, Ancient Textiles Series 5, pp. 291–8.

Index of Persons

'Abd Allāh, *Umayyad emir*, 6, 188–9, 307–8, 375n18, 379n29, 389, 393, 396n70
'Abd Allāh b. Muḥammad b. 'Abd al-Khāliq al-Ghassānī, 189
'Abd Allāh b. Muḥammad b. Qāsim al-Qal'ī, al-Baṭarqūlī, 259
'Abd Allāh b. Muḥammad al-Umawī, 396n70
'Abd Allāh b. Sa'īd Ibn al-Muḥtashim, 396n70
'Abd al-'Azīz b. 'Abd al-Raḥmān III, 320, 328, 340
'Abd al-'Azīz b. 'Aqqāl b. Salama, 260n34
'Abd al-'Azīz b. Ḥakam al-Tujībī, 140n84
'Abd al-'Azīz b. Ḥusayn al-Qarawī, 236
'Abd al-Ḥamīd b. Aḥmad b. Basīl, 137n77, 351
'Abd al-Ḥamīd al-Judhāmī, 200
'Abd al-Karīm b. Yaḥyā, 230n54, 237, 289n8
'Abd al-Malik, *Umayyad caliph*, 288n5
'Abd al-Malik b. Ḥabīb, 35n8, 41n19, 305
'Abd al-Malik b. Mundhīr b. Sa'īd al-Ballūṭī, 116–18, 313
'Abd al-Malik b. Ṣamīt, 212
'Abd al-Qadūs b. 'Abd al-Wahhāb, 237
'Abd al-Raḥmān I, *Umayyad emir*, 4, 47, 62, 139n81, 149, 154, 176n54, 348, 374n15, 382
'Abd al-Raḥmān II, *Umayyad emir*, 37, 41n19, 54, 56, 92n59, 133, 135, 154, 180n61, 244, 373n11, 374, 375n18, 376–9, 383, 393, 398, 410
'Abd al-Raḥmān III al-Nāṣir, *Umayyad emir and caliph*, 1–3, 6–8, 44, 51, 57, 62–3, 73, 77–8, 87, 109–10, 112n20, 115, 120n34, 122–5, 128, 131, 132n59, 134nn67–9, 140–1, 151–8, 160, 162, 164, 176–7, 189, 191, 193, 196, 202–4, 212–18, 222, 230n53, 249, 251–4, 257, 262–4, 268n50, 272, 288nn5–6, 289, 292–3, 303–6, 310, 313, 317n70, 324, 326n85, 327–31, 336, 340, 351n39, 356, 363n58, 364n59, 365–6, 375–6, 379–82, 384, 387, 389, 393, 396n70, 397–9, 404, 406, 409–11, 416,
'Abd al-Raḥmān b. Abī Jawshan, 217n19
Abd al-Raḥmān b. Aḥmad b. Ilyās, 224, 278
'Abd al-Raḥmān b. al-Ḥakam al-Mustanṣir, 87, 310
'Abd al-Raḥmān b. al-Manṣūr, *Sanjūl*, 8, 367n49
'Abd al-Raḥmān b. Muḥammad b. al-Layth, 233n60
'Abd al-Raḥmān b. Muḥammad b. Rumāḥis, 134n67, 141n88, 212, 216–17, 245
'Abd al-Raḥmān b. Mūsā b. Ḥudayr, 115–16, 120
'Abd al-Raḥmān b. Nu'aym, 139n81
'Abd al-Raḥmān b. Yaḥyā al-Tujībī, 141n88, 159, 281n76, 282, 323
'Abd al-Raḥmān b. Yūsuf b. Armaṭil, 216n19, 219n28
'Abd al-Wāḥid b. Isḥāq al-Ḍabbī, 38
'Abda b. Muḥammad b. Abī 'Abda, 108n12

Abū l-ʿAysh b. Ayyūb b. Bilāl, 65, 67–8, 226–30, 290
Abū Bakr, *caliph*, 93
Abū Ibrāhīm Isḥāq al-Tujībī, 53, 114, 379
Abū Ikrima Jaʿfar b. Yazīd, 118n31
Abū l-Khayr, 212
Abū Jaʿfar b. al-Khazzār, 206n1
Abū Muḥammad ʿUbayd Allāh al-Mahdī, 182–3, 187–8, 201, 406
Abū l-Mujāhid al-Istijī, 237
Abū Tammām, 219, 236n64
Abū Yazīd, 201, 203–4
Aflaḥ b. ʿAbd al-Raḥmān, 128n50, 134n69
Aghlabids, 186–7
Aḥmad b. ʿAbd Allāh b. ʿArūs al-Ḥaḍramī al-Mawrūrī, 271–2
Aḥmad b. ʿAbd al-Ḥamīd b. Basīl, 141n88
Aḥmad b. ʿAbd al-Malik b. Shuhayd, 136n76, 364n59
Aḥmad b. Fāris, *astrologer*, 142n89
Aḥmad b. Hāshim b. Muḥammad b. Hāshim al-Tujībī, 314n65
Aḥmad b. Ibrāhīm, *treasurer*, 135n73
Aḥmad b. ʿĪsā, *Idrīsid shaykh*, 196, 229, 353
Aḥmad b. Muḥammad al-Kalbī, 117n30
Aḥmad b. Muḥammad al-Qasṭalī, 84n48, 316
Aḥmad b. Muḥammad al-Rāzī, 40
Aḥmad b. Muḥammad b. ʿAbbās, 137n77, 141n88
Aḥmad b. Muḥammad b. Ḥafṣ b. Saʿīd b. Jābir, 136n74, 224
Aḥmad b. Muḥammad b. ʿĪsā b. Abī ʿAbda, 396n70
Aḥmad b. Muḥammad b. Ziyād, 387n48
Aḥmad b. Naṣr b. Khālid, 54, 116, 123–5
Aḥmad b. Qulzum, 47
Aḥmad b. Saʿd al-Jaʿfarī, 279n73
Aḥmad b. Shuhayd, 44, 115n25
Aḥmad b. Ṭūlūn, 406
Aḥmad b. Yaʿlā, 134n68, 266n46
Āʾisha bt. Aḥmad, 326n85
ʿAjab, 398
Alexander the Great, 404
ʿAlī b. Abī Ṭālib, 182–3, 185, 187, 195, 199, 200–1, 204, 213, 287, 295, 297, 337
ʿAlī (Thaʿlaba) b. Ḥamdūn, 200–1
ʿAlī b. Ḥammūd, 34n6
ʿAlī b. Khalūf, *emir of the Ghumāra*, 229n52
ʿĀmir al-ʿAbdārī, 397n76
ʿAmrīl b. Tīmalt, 259, 274
ʿArīb b. Saʿīd, 39
Arnulf, *abbot of Ripoll*, 267
Aṣbagh b. ʿAbd Allāh b. Nabīl, 270n55, 272
Aṣbagh b. ʿAbd al-Raḥmān al-Nāṣir, 320, 328, 340
Aṣbagh b. Muḥammad b. Fuṭays, 108
al-ʿĀṣī b. Ḥakam al-Tujībī, 120, 258, 314n65
Aslam b. ʿAbd al-ʿAzīz, 387n48
Aṭāna Mahrān, *Kutāma tribe*, 227
ʿAṭiyya b. Fortūn, 260n34

Badr, *ḥājib*, 134n69
Al-Bakrī, 373
Banū Abī ʿAbda or Jahwar, 110, 120, 140
Banū Abī l-Adham, 260n34
Banū Abī l-Akhṭal, 260
Banū Basīl, 110
Banū Bassām, 47
Banū Birzāl, 163
Banū Dhī l-Nūn, 257
Banū Fuṭays, 110, 120
Banū Gazlūn, 257, 259
Banū Gómez, 269n52, 270, 276
Banū Hābil, 179n58
Banū Ḥudayr, 110–11, 120, 141n86
Banū Khazar, 179, 192, 208–11, 221, 349–52
Banū Maḍā, 259
Banū Razīn, 257–8
Banū Shuhayd, 120, 140
Banū al-Ṭawīl, 156n19, 179n58
Banū Timlīt, 177
Banū l-Zajjālī, 120
Banū Zarwāl, 257, 260n34
Basīl b. ʿAbd al-Ḥamīd b. Aḥmad b. Basīl, 137n77, 351

Bilkīs, 287
Bonfill, 267–8, 336
Borrell, Count of Barcelona, 266–8, 273, 283
Buluggīn b. Zīrī b. Manād, 208, 211, 238, 352
Buwayhids, 286–7

Constantine VII, *Byzantine emperor*, 334

Ḍaygam b. Wahb b. Abī l-Adham, 260
Diocletian, *Roman emperor*, 384, 396
Dioscorides, 264–5
Dominico, *abbot of San Salvador de Tavara*, 280
Durrī al-Ṣaghīr, 87, 92, 96–7, 126–7, 133
Durrī b. al-Ḥakam al-Hammāz, 135n70, 224

Elvira, regent of León, 269, 271–2, 279
Emeterius, *Presbyter*, 280
Ende, *pintrix*, 280

Fā'iq, *fatā*, 124, 126n44, 345n29
Fakhr, 398
Fāṭima al-Qurashiyya, 1–2, 398
Fāṭima bt. Muḥammad al-Zahrā' 183, 187, 204
Fāṭima bt. Zakariyyā', 326n85
Fernán González, *Count of Castile*, 269n52
Fernando Ansúrez, 269n52, 270n54, 273, 276
Fernando Flaínez, 269n52, 271, 280

García Fernández, *Count of Castile*, 177n56, 269n52, 274–6
Gerbert of Aurillac, 267
Ghālib b. 'Abd al-Raḥmān, 90, 120n35, 128–9, 132–3, 140n84, 156n18, 157, 165, 170, 177n57, 159n59, 180n62, 219–27, 229, 231–3, 238, 246, 255–9, 275–9, 283, 299, 323, 342, 347–8, 353–9, 361–70, 390
Ghumāra, *Berber tribe*, 229n52, 232, 237
Guitard, viscount of Barcelona, 267

Ḥabīb al-Ṣiqlabī, 127
Ḥabīb b. Ṭawīla, 271
Al-Ḥakam I, 46n30, 48n35, 99, 110, 115, 120n34, 138–9, 154, 236n64, 306, 343n25, 372n10, 374, 376n19, 381, 392–3, 395–8
Al-Ḥakam II al-Mustanṣir, 2–3, 7–10, 12–13, 22–4, 26, 32, 34, 41, 49–51, 53–4, 61–5, 67, 69–70, 74, 77, 82, 84, 87–9, 91, 93–4, 96, 99, 101–2, 105, 107–11, 114–45, 147, 153–69, 173–4, 176, 178–9, 181, 186, 191, 196, 204–6, 209–23, 225–8, 230–1, 234–7, 240–2, 245, 247–8, 254–6, 258, 260–1, 264, 266–76, 280–99, 302–3, 305–42, 344–9, 353, 357, 360–9, 372–4, 376, 378, 380–4, 389–93, 395–9, 402, 409–11, 414, 416
Ḥajjāj b. Khalūf, 229n52
Ḥalīl b. Aḥmad, 117n30
Ḥarīth b. Abī Sa'd, 139n81
Ḥasan b. Muḥammad b. 'Alī b. al-Ḥasan b. Abī l-Ḥusayn, 141n87
Ḥasan b. Qannūn, 198n22, 214, 217–18, 225–39, 242, 272–3, 288n6, 294, 296–7, 308–9, 345, 348, 353, 367n1
Ḥasdāy b. Shabrūṭ, 262–3, 265
Ibn Ḥazm, 306, 376n19, 391, 401, 418
Hilāl al-Ṣābi', 333–4
Hishām caliph of Damascus, 390
Hishām I, *Umayyad emir*, 48n35, 110n18, 396
Hishām II, *Umayyad heir and Caliph*, 7, 54, 61, 84n48, 87, 96, 117n30, 119, 125n43, 127, 128n49, 131n54, 143, 156n18, 164, 178, 276–7, 298, 304, 310–11, 313–26, 345, 360, 367n1, 369, 416
Hishām b. Ja'far b. 'Uthmān al-Muṣḥafī, 130
Hishām b. Muḥammad b. 'Uthmān al-Muṣḥafī, 130n52, 137n77, 139, 141n88, 247–8, 268n50
Hudhayl b. Ghuṣn, 260n34
Hudhayl b. Jalaf b. Lubb b. Razīn, 258

Ibn 'Abd Rabbihi, 318n71
Ibn 'Abd al-Ra'ūf, 384
Ibn Abī 'Īsā, 374
Ibn Abī Zamanīn, 35n8
Ibn Abī Zayd al-Qayrawānī, 35n8, 228
Ibn al-'Aṭṭār, 35n8, 94
Ibn Faḍlān, 100
Ibn Hānī, 93n60, 203, 207, 210n7, 248
Ibn Ḥawqal, 51, 69–70, 76, 109, 160, 170–1, 403, 413
Ibn Ḥayyān, 19–24, 161–8, 173, 189, 192, 217, 221, 234, 241
Ibn Masarra, 288n6
Ibn Mas'ūd, 166, 191
Ibn Muqīm, 314n65
Ibn Qādim 181n65
Ibn al-Qūṭiyya, 110
Ibn Umm al-Banīn, 222n37
Ibrāhīm b. al-Aghlab, 406
Ibrāhīm II, 406
Ibrāhīm b. Ja'far b. al-Andalusī, 92
Ibrāhīm b. Muḥammad al-Iflīlī, 181n65, 373n11
Ibrāhīm b. Ya'qūb al-Turtūshī, 100
Ibrāhīm b.Yazīd al-Kūfī al-Nakha'ī, 302
Idrīs b. 'Abd Allāh, 199
Idrīsids, 105, 156n18, 191, 199–200, 202, 214, 219, 225, 229–30, 232–5, 242, 294, 339, 345, 347–8, 353–4, 359, 361–2, 367, 390
Ilduara, 91n55
'Īsā al-Rāzī, 19–26, 33, 36, 39–40, 42, 43n26, 50, 56, 61, 76, 92, 106, 161, 164, 168, 174, 176n53, 205, 206, 217, 234, 246, 259, 275, 277, 279–80, 291, 310, 317n70, 321, 325, 332–3, 337–8, 341n22, 344n27, 348, 349, 355–6, 367–8, 390n55, 415, 418
'Īsā b. 'Abd Allāh b. Qarlumān, 312
'Īsā b. Fuṭays, 332
'Īsā b. Manṣūr, Bishop of Córdoba, 270n55
'Īsā b. Surūr b. Funnu, 260n34
Ismā'īl b. 'Abd al-Raḥmān b. al-Shaykh, 216n19, 219n28
Ismā'īl b. Badr, 288n5, 303
Ismā'īl b. Būrī al-Miknāsī, 230n53
Ismā'īl b. Ja'far, *Sixth Imām*, 183, 185

Ja'far al-Ṣādiq, *Fifth Imām*, 183
Ja'far al-Ṣiqlabī, 122–6, 128n49, 131, 135, 155, 332
Ja'far b. al-Andalusī, 91–2, 144, 163n31, 170, 180n62, 201, 207–11, 213, 235, 238–41, 348–52, 376, 390
Ja'far b. 'Uthmān al-Muṣḥafī, 74, 105, 122, 129–33, 139, 141n86, 142, 268n50, 276, 288n6, 309, 324, 329, 342, 356, 370, 374, 381n33, 402, 411
al-Jāhiz, 76–7
Jahwar b. al-Shaykh, 268n50
Jahwar b. 'Ubayd Allāh b. Abī 'Abda, 134n68
Jahwar, *Fāṭimid qā'id*, 203–4
Jawdhar, *fatā*, 124, 126n44, 345n29
John the Baptist, 57
John of Gorze, 263, 271, 273, 293, 335, 355n45
Justinian, 405

Khalaf b. Ghuṣn, 260n34
Khalaf b. Yaḥyā al-Farrash, 62
Khālid b. Hāshim b. 'Umar, 123–5
Khālid b. Zarwāl, 260
Khazar b. Ḥafṣ b. Ṣūlāt, 192
Kulayb b. Fortūn, 260n34
Kutāma tribe, 65, 68, 105n6, 166, 186–7, 190, 200–1, 226–7, 232, 334

Leo VI, Byzantine emperor, 148n1
Leovigild, Visigothic king, 405
Louis the Pious, 249
Liutprand of Cremona, 72–3
Lubb b. Marwān b. Hudhayl b. Razīn, 258
Lubnā, 326

Maḍā b. ʿAmrīl b. Tīmalt, 274
Maghrāwa, *Berber tribe*, 192, 194, 201, 208–9, 211, 240
Magyars, 160
Mālik b. Anas, 302, 324
Maʿn b. Muḥammad al-Tujībī, 241n72
Maʿqil, *fatā*, 126n45
al-Manṣūr, ʿAbbāsid caliph, 405
al-Manṣūr, Fāṭimid caliph, 405
Marjān, *mother of al-Ḥakam II*, 2–3, 328, 395, 398, 416
Marwān b. Aḥmad b. ʿAbd al-Malik b. Shuhayd, 136n76, 224
Marwān b. Hudhayl b. Razīn, 258
Maṣmūda, *Berber tribe*, 232, 259
Al-Masʿūdī, 79
Maymūna bt. ʿAlāham al-Jīlī, 201
Maysūr, *Fāṭimid qāʾid*, 202–4
Maysūr al-Jaʿfarī, 156n18
Miknāsa, *Berber tribe*, 196, 230n33
Miró Bonfill, 267
Muʿāwiya b. Hishām al-Shabīnisī, 63
Muʿāwiya b. Lubb, 270n55
Mubārak al-Jaʿfarī, 156n18, 245
Mubashshir al-Jaʿfarī, 156n18, 245
al-Mughīra b. ʿAbd al-Raḥmān III, 89, 320, 328–30, 340, 376n19
al-Muqtadir, *ʿabbāsid caliph*, 187, 314–15
Mursī, 345n29
Muḥammad b. ʿAbd Allāh, Umayyad emir 375n18, 379n29, 389, 391–2, 402n88
Muḥammad b. ʿAbd Allāh b. Ḥudayr, 134n68
Muḥammad b. Aflaḥ, 127–8, 133, 142, 342, 358
Muḥammad b. ʿAlī, *descendant of caliph Abū Bakr*, 92
Muḥammad b. Abī ʿĀmir al-Manṣūr, 7–8, 41, 63, 80n41, 92, 115–17, 125n44, 130, 136n74, 115–17, 125n43, 130–1, 136n74, 142–6, 156n18, 164–6, 170, 220, 240–1, 282–4, 311–12, 330, 339n19, 342n26, 346, 350–1, 370, 391, 401, 411–12
Muḥammad b. Abī ʿĪsā, 112n20
Muḥammad b. Abī Qādim, 47
Muḥammad b. Aḥmad b. Mufarraj, 220
Muḥammad b. Aḥmad b. Shuhayd, 277
Muḥammad b. ʿAlī b. al-Ḥasan b. Abī l-Ḥusayn, 117n30, 141n87
Muḥammad b. Dāwūd, 259
Muḥammad b. Fūrtish, 281n76
Muḥammad b. Furtūn b. al-Ṭawīl, 156n19
Muḥammad b. Fuṭays, 108n13, 120
Muḥammad b. Ḥasan al-Zubaydī, 128n49, 317
Muḥammad b. Hāshim al-Tujībī, 260n35, 363n57, 402n87
Muḥammad b. Hishām b. ʿAbd al-Jabbār b. ʿAbd al-Raḥmān an-Nāṣir, 164
Muḥammad b. Ḥusayn al-Ṭubnī, 298, 300, 315
Muḥammad b. Isḥāq b. al-Salīm, 118–19, 143, 316n68, 320, 383
Muḥammad b. Jaʿfar b. ʿUthmān al-Muṣḥafī, 130n52, 153n9
Muḥammad b. al-Khayr b. Khazar, 192–6, 201, 203, 209
Muḥammad b. Maḥāmis al-Istijī, 298
Muḥammad b. Muḥammad b. Abī Zayd, 141n87
Muḥammad b. Nuʿmān, 108n13
Muḥammad b. Qāsim b. Ṭumlus, 89, 120, 134n66, 153n9, 215–17, 222, 278, 342, 355, 359n50, 364n60
Muḥammad b. Rizq b. al-Ḥakam al-Jaʿfarī, 141n88, 156n18
Muḥammad b. Sālim, 383
Muhammad b. Saʿīd b. Abī l-Qāsim Ibn al-Khāl, 115n26, 140n83, 327, 397
Muḥammad b. Shujayṣ, 87, 191, 235–6, 287, 296–8, 301, 305, 315–16, 325
Muḥammad b. Sulaymān, 212
Muḥammad b. Sulaymān Wallad Muʿallim Ḥammuh, 213
Muḥammad b. Surūr b. Funnu, 260n34
Muḥammad b. Tamlīkh, 123–4

Muḥammad b. Ṭumlus, 115n25
Muḥammad b. Walīd b. Ghānim, 376n20
Muḥammad b. Yūsuf b. ʿAbd Allāh al-Warrāq, 206
Muḥammad b. Yūsuf b. Sulaymān al-Juhanī, 364n60
Muḥammad b. Waḍḍāḥ, 57, 289n7
al-Muʿizz, *Fāṭimid caliph*, 203–5, 208–11, 212, 215, 217–18, 296, 334, 349, 352, 406
Mu'min b. Saʿīd, 74n29
Mundhir b. ʿAbd Allāh b. Hābil, 179
al-Mundhir b. ʿAbd al-Raḥmān al-Nāṣir Ibn al-Qurashiyya, 313, 390
Mundhir b. Saʿīd al-Ballūṭī, 117, 122–3
al-Muqaddasī, 76
Murtāḥ, *fatā*, 126n45
Mūsā b. Abī l-ʿĀfiya, 196, 198n22, 230n53, 363n58
Al-Mustakfī, *ʿabbāsid caliph*, 295n21
al-Mu'tamid, 405
Al-Mutannabī, 181
Muṭarrif b. ʿAbd al-Raḥmān, 123–5
Muṭarrif b. Ismāʿīl b. Dhī l-Nūn, 260n34
al-Muʿtaṣim, *ʿabbāsid caliph*, 236n64, 405
al-Mutawakkil, *ʿabbāsid caliph*, 405–6
al-Muṭī, *ʿabbāsid caliph*, 287
Al-Muẓaffar b. al-Manṣūr, 8, 221n35, 284
Muzna al-Rūmiyya, 327, 397n73

Najda, 110, 135
Naṣr, *fatā*, 393
Nicholas, *Greek monk*, 265
Nikephoros II Phokas, *Byzantine emperor*, 92
Al-Nuʿmān, al-Qāḍī, 335n8, 337n11
Nuño González, 273

Ordoño II, *King of León*, 251
Ordoño IV, *King of León*, 255, 266, 270n55, 334, 336, 339n19, 348n36, 354n44, 357n49, 359n50, 361n56, 378, 390n53
Otto I, *German emperor*, 72, 263, 271, 293
Otto II, *German emperor*, 273

al-Qā'im, *Fāṭimid caliph*, 201, 304
Qand, *fatā*, 90, 347
Qāsim b. Aḥmad b. Muḥammad al-Kalbī, 117n30
Qāsim b. Khalaf al-Jubayrī, 220
Qāsim b. Muḥammad b. Qāsim b. Ṭumlus, 134n66, 278
Qāsim b. Muṭarrif al-Qaṭṭān, 38, 58
Qāsim b. Walīd al-Kalbī, 117n30
Qāsim b. Ya'ish, 376
Qayṣar, 216n19
Quraysh, 200, 219, 233, 235, 297, 339, 342, 345–6, 395

Rabīʿ b. Muḥammad, 47
Rabīʿ b. Zayd, 39
Rahūna, *Berber tribe*, 233
Rā'iq b. al-Ḥakam, 136n76, 137n77, 141n88, 328, 345, 360
Ramiro II, King of León, 252
Ramiro III, King of León, 269, 276, 279
Rashīq b. ʿAbd al-Raḥmān al-Barghawāṭī, 117n30, 216n19, 219n28
Razīn al-Burnūsī, 390
Richilda of Narbonne, 262
Rodrigo Velázquez, 270
Romanos I Lekapenos, *Byzantine emperor*, 264–5
Rustamids, 198
Rosendo, *bishop of Dumio*, 91n55

Saʿāda, 271
Saʿd al-Jazarī, 216n19
Saʿd b. al-Ḥakam al-Jaʿfarī, 128, 134n68, 156
Saʿd b. Muʿād, 414
Ṣādiq, *fatā*, 124, 126n44
Ṣafiyya bt. ʿAbd Allāh al-Rayyī, 325n85
Saḥbān Wa'īl, 302
Saʿīd b. Abī l-Qāsim al-Khāl, 115n26, 134n69, 327–8
Saʿīd b. Jassās, 107
Saʿīd b. Saʿīd b. Ḥudayr, 140n84

Salama b. al-Ḥakam al-Ja'farī, 136n76, 156n18, 223–4
Sancho I, *El Craso*, *King of León*, 265–6, 269, 270n55, 379
Sancho I Garces, *King of Pamplona*, 251, 265–6
Sancho II Garces, *King of Pamplona*, 8, 269, 270n54, 275, 282
Sancho García, *Count of Castile*, 285
Shāṭir al-Ja'farī, 156n18
Ṣinhāja, *Berber tribe*, 186, 192, 195, 207–8
Ṣubḥ, 87, 136n76, 141n86, 143, 310–11, 325–8
Sukkar, *fatā*, 126n45
Sulaymān, *Umayyad caliph*, 118n31
Sulaymān b. 'Abd al-Raḥmān al-Nāṣir, 376n19
Sulaymān b. Aḥmad al-Anṣārī al-Ruṣāfī al-Qassām, 326n84
Sulaymān b. 'Āmir, 260
Sunyer, *Count of Barcelona*, 262
Sylvester II, *Pope* see *Gerbert of Aurillac*

Ṭāhir b. Muḥammad al-Baghdādī al-Muhannad, 299
Ṭalā
Tarhūna *Hawwāra tribe*, 228n49
Ṭarūb, 393, 398
Tāyit b. Muḥammad, 224
Teophilus Byzantine emperor, 410
Tha'bān b. Aḥmad al-Barbar, 233

'Ubāda b. Khalaf b. Abī Jawshan Aḥmad b. Muḥammad b. Ḥudayr, 224
'Ubayd Allāh b. 'Aqqāl b.Salama, 260n34
'Ubayd Allāh b. Qāsim, Bishop of Seville, 270n55
Al-'Udhrī, 373
'Umar b. Ḥafṣūn, 6, 151, 188
'Umar b. Muḥammad b. Walīd b. Ghānim, 376n20
'Uthmān, *caliph*, 193

Vikings, 152, 160, 216, 244, 246–8

Walīd b. 'Abd al-Malik b. Mūsā b. al-Ṭawīl, 179
Wallāda bt. 'Abd al-Raḥmān III, 88
Witiza *Visigothic King*, 110

Yaḥyā b.'Abd Allāh al-Laythī, 324
Yaḥyā b. al-Andalusī, 91, 163n31, 201, 211, 221, 235, 238–40, 349–51, 353, 376, 390
Yaḥyā b. Būrī al-Miknāsī, 230n53
Yaḥyā b. Hudhayl, 318
Yaḥyā b. Hudhayl b. Razīn, 258
Yaḥyā b. Isḥāq, 134n68
Yaḥyā b. Muḥammad b. Hāshim al-Tujībī, 120, 175n52, 238, 240, 281n76, 345
Yaḥyā b. Qannūn, 345
Yaḥyā b. 'Ubayd Allāh b. Yaḥyā b. Idrīs, 136n77, 141n88
Yaḥyā b. Yaḥyā, 57, 305, 324
Yaḥyā b. Yūnus al-Qabrī, 141n87
Ya'lā b. Aḥmad b. Ya'lā, 141n88, 279n73
Yūsuf b. Muḥammad, 259
Yūsuf b. Hārūn al-Ramādī, 313, 380n32, 395n66

Zakarīyā' b. Yaḥyā al-Shabulārī, 135n73
Zanāta, *Berber tribe*, 192–3, 195, 203, 208, 210–11
Zarwāl b. 'Amrīl b. Tīmalt, 274
Zīrī b. 'Aṭiyya, 80n41
Ziyād b. Aflaḥ, 87, 128, 134, 153n9, 239, 247–8, 342, 356, 364n60
Zīrī b. Manād al-Ṣinhājī, 207–11, 349, 354, 406
Ziryāb, 56–7n51, 74, 92, 351n38, 373n11, 393

Index of Places

Al-ʿAbbāsiyya, 406
Alcacer do Sal, 245
Alcalá la Real, 200
Alcolea del Pinar, 251
Aleppo, 236
Alexandria, 111, 404
Algeciras, 51–2, 92, 142, 216, 231, 234, 353
Algeria, 11–12, 19, 186, 190, 193, 195, 200, 406
Algiers, 191
Alhándega, *battle of*, 110, 158–61, 166, 218, 252, 254–5, 257, 261–2, 292
Almería, 52, 106–7, 134, 152n67, 216, 245–6, 262n37, 349–50, 369
Almuñécar, 44
Amalfi, 72–3
Anjar, 405
Aqlām, 230n53, 353
Arabia, 111
Arles, 100, 262–3
Armenia, 76
Arshghūl, 191
Ashīr, 195, 207, 406
Aṣīla, 225, 238
Astorga, 249, 284
Ateca, 259
Aures, 186, 190
Awdaghost, 69, 191
Aza, 251

Badajoz, 137, 141n88, 213, 328
Baghdad, 3, 4, 14, 74, 92, 153, 186–8, 204, 207, 264, 286–7, 299, 315, 327, 331, 333, 348, 351n38, 405
Balearic Islands, 129, 170
Barcelona, 100, 249, 262–3, 266–8, 273, 283, 285, 333, 336, 339n17, 342n23, 395
Barahona, 170, 278, 285
Barika, 190
Baṣra, *city in Morocco*, 214, 230n53, 233n60, 238, 347, 353
Baṣra, *city in Iraq*, 79
Beja, 149
Béjaïa, 200
Berlanga, 277
Bezmiliana, 144, 210, 350
Binna Ruyyah, 259
Bobastro, 6, 177n57, 188–9, 272n59
Budiel, 259
Burgos, 251

Cabra, 352, 361, 364
Cairo, 205, 218, 331, 406
Calahorra, 128n49, 157, 256
Calatalifa, 179n59, 255
Calatayud, 120, 134n68, 140n84, 258–9
Caracena, 252
Caracuel, 274
Carcastillo, 282
Carmona, 117, 163n32
Carrión, 270
Carthage, 190
Castile, 157, 254, 269, 273, 274, 276, 279, 280, 284–5

Celanova, *monastery*, 91n55
Cervelló, 267
Ceuta, 23, 149, 161–2, 190–1, 202–3, 214, 216, 218, 225
Chelif, 193
Cherchell, 190–1
China, 76, 79, 235
Clunia, 249, 251–2, 303
Constantinople, 72, 78, 263, 265, 405, 410
Córdoba, 1, 31, 33n3, 34, 36, 39, 40, 41, 43, 46n30, 51, 53, 64, 79, 84, 89, 93–5, 97, 110–44, 150–70, 175–81, 188, 190, 193, 202–26, 230–85, 367–419
  Alcázar, 1, 37, 47, 55, 58, 78, 131, 133, 153, 178, 233, 247, 278, 316, 323–5, 331, 336, 345–8, 355, 367, 369, 372, 377–82, 416
  Bāb 'Abd al-Jabbār, 372n10
  Bāb 'Āmir, 372n10, 390n59, 397n76, 399
  Bāb al-'Aṭṭārīn or *Bāb Ishbīliyya*, 212n12, 372n10, 380, 384
  Bāb al-Jadīd, 38, 372n10, 396
  Bāb al-Jahūd, 372n10, 392
  Bāb al-Jawz, 372n10
  Bāb al-Qanṭara, 38, 372n10, 378
  Cemetery of Balāṭ Mugīth, 399
  Cemetery of Banū 'Abbās, 48, 396
  Cemetery of Banū 'Āmir, 376n20, 399
  Cemetery of Banū Badr, 376n20
  Cemetery of Mu'ta, 399
  Cemetery of al-Rabaḍ, 395, 416
  Cemetery of Umm Salama, 393
  Church of St Acisclus, 384
  Church of the Three Martyrs, 395
  Church of St Zoilus, 393
  Dār al-Burud, 382
  Dār Ibn al-Bayyānī, 376n20
  Dār Ibn Umayya, 376n20
  Dār Muḥammad b. Ṭarafa, 376n20
  Dār al-Ṣadaqa, 373
  Dār al-Ṭirāz, 71, 77, 367n1, 393
  Dār al-Zawāmil, 383, 389
  Dār Ziyād al-Waṣīf, 376n20
  Dūr Banī 'Abd al-Jabbār, 374n14
  Dūr Banī Ghānim, 376
  Faḥṣ al-Surādiq, 352
  Friday Mosque, 82, 123–4, 139, 304–9, 379
  Al-Ghadīr, 376n20
  Al-Maḥajja, 325, 378
  Mosque of 'Abbād, 375
  Mosque of 'Abd Allāh al-Balansī, 374n15
  Mosque of Abū 'Allaqa, 374
  Mosque of Abū 'Uthmān, 114n23, 374, 379
  Mosque of 'Ajab, 398
  Mosque of Badr, 374n13
  Mosque of Fakhr, 398
  Mosque of Hārūn, 212,n12
  Mosque of Hishām, 396
  Mosque of Ibn Abī 'Abda, 398n77
  Mosque of Ibn Khālid, 374n13
  Mosque of Marjān, 398
  Mosque of al-Muṣḥafī, 374
  Mosque of Mu'ta, 376n20, 397
  Mosque of Ṣawwāb, 374
  Mosque of al-Shifā', 398
  Mosque of Surayj, 374
  Mosque of Ṭālūt, 374n14
  Mosque of Ṭarafa, 374n13
  Mosque of Ṭarūb, 398
  Mosque of Umm Salama, 392
  Muṣallā, 40, 43, 55, 395
  Muṣāra, 41n19, 369, 378, 383, 389, 390n53, 398n77
  Rabaḍ Balāṭ Mugīth, 401, 405
  Rabaḍ al-Burj, 395
  Rabaḍ Furn Burrīl, 396, 415
  Rabaḍ Ḥammām al-Ilbīrī, 398n77
  Rabaḍ al-Mughīra, 397n72
  Rabaḍ Mu'ta, 376n20, 398n78
  Rabaḍ al-Ruṣāfa, 391–2, 401
  Rabaḍ Shabulār, 384n39
  Rabaḍ Shaqunda, 37, 40, 110, 393, 395
  Raṣīf al-Qaṣṣābīn, 37
  Rawḍa Banī Marwān, 395

Shabulār (suburb), 37–8, 62
Sūq, 62, 125n43, 321–2, 372, 381–6, 415
Al-Zuqāq al-Kabīr, 375n18, 396
Zuqāq Duḥaym, 396n70
Zuqāq Zur'a, 396n70
Coria, 40
Cuenca, 257, 260

Damascus, 149, 161, 361, 363, 390, 405
Daroca, 120, 281
Deza, 274
Duero river, 147, 158, 246, 248–55, 271n57, 275–85

Ebro river, 157, 159, 220, 249, 252, 256, 276
Ecija, 31n1, 117, 220n30, 327n87, 361
Egypt, 62n2, 76, 93, 111,117n30, 148–9, 166, 183, 188, 204–15, 218, 220n30, 236, 242, 334, 336, 349, 352,406
Elvira, *kūra*, 39, 73, 107–8, 129, 149, 151, 173, 189, 200, 324, 361
Estanya, 32
Estercuel (Ribafora, Navarre), 159, 282
Evora, 275

Faḥṣ al-Ballūṭ, 43, 117, 137, 328
Faḥṣ al-Burayqa (Alboreca), 274
Faḥṣ Mahrān, *battle of*, 120n35, 134n66, 161, 178, 218, 220, 232
Fars, 77
Fez, 93n60, 106, 191, 199, 203, 214, 221, 228n49, 230, 237–8, 289n8, 352
Fusṭāṭ, 204, 406

Galicia, 245, 266, 284
Gelida, 267
Gerona, 267
Ghana, 69
al-Ghūṭ, 193
Gormaz, 129, 140n84, 153n11, 156n18, 170, 177n57, 179n59, 252, 254n21, 255, 272–82, 285, 323, 378, 390

Greenland, 32
Guadajoz river, 353
Guadalajara, 117n30, 128n49, 137, 158, 251–4, 256–7, 260, 274, 313, 405
Guadalimar river, 52n42
Guadalquivir river, 31, 37–8, 40, 41n19, 47, 50–2, 118, 244, 268, 355–6, 369, 372, 378, 381, 383, 389–90, 393, 396n71
Guadiana river, 5

Ḥajar al-Naṣr, 214, 233–4, 238
Henares river, 249
Ḥimṣ, 149, 361
Hippo Regius, 191
Huerta del Rey, 252
Huesca, 32, 156n19, 179n58

Iceland, 36
Ifrīqiya, 6, 105n6, 111, 182–3, 186–92, 195, 200, 205, 206–15, 242, 349, 352, 406
India, 79, 155n15, 383
Iraq, 15, 24, 76–9, 90, 185, 220n30, 229, 237

Jabal al-Karam, 232, 238
Jabal al-'Uyūn, 233
Jaén, 34,n6, 137, 141n88, 149, 179n58, 200, 324, 361, 414n106
Jalón river, 249, 259
Al-Jawf, 128n49, 141n88
Jazīrat Qabṭīl, 50
Jijel, 191
Jordan, 149, 351
Justiniana Prima, 405

Kūfa, 76
Khurāsān, 76

Llano de los Pedroches *see Faḥṣ al-Ballūṭ*
León, 74n28, 172–3, 249, 251–2, 254, 265–6, 269, 270n55, 271–2, 275–6, 279–80, 284–5, 334, 366, 378, 387
Lérida, 137, 141n88, 336n9, 339n19

Lisbon, 244–5
London, 244
Lower Saxony, 36

Madīnat al-ʻAlawiyyīn, 193
Madīnat al-Fatḥ, 404
Madīnat al-Zahrā', 9, 43, 50, 52–3, 55, 58, 68, 78, 81–2, 84, 88, 95–7, 123, 126, 128–9, 133, 135, 141, 175, 177, 178, 195, 212, 235, 246, 248, 266, 268–9, 273, 281, 299, 314, 362, 367–419
  Dār al-Jund, 268, 333, 340, 359
  Dār al-Khayl, 157, 357
  Dār al-Mulk, 316, 332
  Bāb al-Sudda, 344n27, 357–9
  Bāb al-Ṣūra, 357
  Bāb al-Warda, 368
  Bayt al-wuzarā', 226, 258, 336, 340, 359–60, 363
  Faṣīl al-Kuttāb, 360n53
  Friday Mosque, 306, 308–9, 323
  Majlis al-Ajrā', 337n12
  Al-Majlis al-Gharbī, 332, 338
  Al-Majlis al-Sharqī, 299–302, 332–3, 337–8, 359
  Al-Qaṣr, 234, 403
  Prison, 239–40
Madīnat al-Zāhira, 369n3, 370, 412
Mahdiyya, 195, 406
Málaga, 43, 351
Al-Māsila, 190, 193, 201–2, 207–9, 238
Mecca, 42, 55n47, 93, 200, 219, 298
Medellín, 328
Medina, 42, 55n47, 111, 212n12
Medinaceli, 157, 255–6
Melilla, 191
Mérida, 152n7
Miralles, 267
Mojáfar, 328
Montcortes, 32
Monzón, 269–70, 273, 276, 279
Morocco, 32, 65, 68, 144, 156–7, 160–1, 165, 175, 180n62, 190, 199, 211, 213–24, 228, 231, 234, 239, 241, 247, 259, 270n54, 272, 274–5, 277, 280–3, 308–9, 314n65, 345, 347, 352–3, 362, 367n1
Morón, 117
Moulouya River, 209
Munyat ʻAbd Allāh, 397
Munyat ʻAjab, 99
Munyat Arḥā' Nāṣiḥ, 369, 390
Munyat al-Buntīlī, 387
Munyat Ibn ʻAbd al-ʻAzīz, 354–5, 398
Munyat Ibn al-Qurashiyya, 390
Munyat al-Mughīra, 396, 418, 418
Munyat Naṣr, 393
Munyat al-Nāʻūra, 268, 347, 354, 356, 369, 378, 380, 389, 390n53
Munyat al-Ramla, 380n31
Munyat al-Rummāniyya, 96–9, 126, 387, 389
Munyat al-Ruṣāfa, 390–1, 418
Munyat al-Shamāmat, 352
Murcia, 44, 268

Nájera, 251
Narbonne, 110n38, 262–3
Niebla, 50, 117, 134, 361

Oman, 79
Osma, 251–2, 269, 284–5

Palestine, 149, 351
Pamplona, 8, 251, 256, 269–70, 275, 279, 282
Paris, 244
Pechina, 73, 106–7, 129, 134n67, 135, 166n36, 212n12, 246, 324, 349
Poley, 327n87

Qalʻat Yaḥṣub *see* Alcalá la Real
Qayrawān, 105n6, 111, 182, 187, 189, 190, 206n1, 207, 209, 218, 334, 348, 406–7
Qinnasrīn, 149, 351

Raqqa, 390
Raqqāda, 406
Rayyuh, *kūra*, 62, 108, 120, 125n43, 137, 144, 149,220, 245, 352, 361
Recopolis, 405
Riaza river, 158, 252
Rif, 65, 67, 196, 214
Ripoll, 267
Roa, 251
Ruṣāfa, Syria, 390
Russia, 100

Ṣabra al-Manṣūriyya, 209, 334, 406
Sacama, 267
Sahlat Banī Razīn (Albarracín), 257–8
Saktān, 255
Salamanca, 269, 284
Salamiyya,186
Saldaña, 270
Salobreña, 44
Samarra, 331, 405–6
San Esteban de Gormaz, 251–2, 254, 284–5
San Pedro de Arlanza, *monastery*, 251
San Pedro de Cardeña, *monastery*, 251
San Pedro de Montes, *monastery*, 74–5
San Salvador de Távara, *monastery*, 280
Santarén, 248
Santaver, 257
Santiago de Compostela, 248
Santos Cosme y Damián de Abellar, *monastery*, 251
Scandinavia, 100
Secunda, 37, 40
Segovia, 249
Senés, 51
Sepúlveda, 284
Setefilla, 233n60
Seville, 31n1, 44, 50–1, 112, 115, 117, 134, 143–4, 145, 164n32, 216, 220n30, 244–6, 270, 272, 317, 327–8, 350n37, 361, 372n10, 380, 382, 384
Sicily, 189
Sidonia, 43, 118, 125n43, 149, 220n30, 245, 288n5, 361
Sijilmāsa, 69, 191, 241
Simancas, 284
Skikda, 191
Straits of Gibraltar, 89, 147–8, 160, 162, 165, 200, 214, 220, 222, 234, 244, 262, 272
Sos, 159, 282
Al-Ṣukhayra, 259
Sūs, 76
Syria, 93

Tādhmakka, 69, 191
Tagus river, 5, 252, 404
Tāhart, 163n32, 191
Tangier, 152, 170, 175, 190–1, 203, 214, 217–19, 223n41, 225, 231–2, 238
Tenés, 191, 193
Teruel, 257, 260
Tlemcen, 190–1, 193, 196
Toledo, 114, 118n31, 125n43, 128n49, 134, 141n88, 221, 270, 285, 324, 351n39, 404
Torrox (*qarya* in Algeciras), 142
Tortosa, 100, 130n52, 137, 141n88, 220n30, 256, 266n46, 268
Ṭubna, 190, 193, 298n31
Tudela, 252, 282, 351n39
Trujillo, 43
Tudmīr, 149

Valencia, 44, 130n52
Valtierra, 251
Venice, 72
Verdun, 100, 263
Villel, 260
Viseo, 251

Yemen, 93, 186

Zāb, 208–9, 211, 298n31
Zalul (Dchar Jdid), 217

Zamora, 251
Zaragoza, 112, 120, 134, 141n88, 217n19, 240, 256–7, 260n34, 281–2, 288n5, 323, 363n57, 397n76, 402n87
Zoñar, 32
Zugar, 175–6

EU representative:
Easy Access System Europe
Mustamäe tee 50, 10621 Tallinn, Estonia
Gpsr.requests@easproject.com

www.ingramcontent.com/pod-product-compliance
Lightning Source LLC
Chambersburg PA
CBHW061340300426
44116CB00011B/1932
* 9 7 8 1 3 9 9 5 1 6 1 3 6 *